Lecture Notes in Computer Science 3140

Commenced Publication in 1973
Founding and Former Series Editors:
Gerhard Goos, Juris Hartmanis, and Jan van Leeuwen

T0181462

Nora Koch
Piero Fraternali
Martin Wirsing (Eds.)

Web Engineering

4th International Conference, ICWE 2004
Munich, Germany, July 26-30, 2004
Proceedings

 Springer

Volume Editors

Nora Koch
Martin Wirsing
Ludwig-Maximilians-Universität München
Institut für Informatik
Oettingenstr. 67, 80538 München, Germany
E-mail: {nora.koch,martin.wirsing}@ifi.lmu.de

Piero Fraternali
Politecnico di Milano
Dipartimento di Elettronica e Informazione
Piazza Leonardo Da Vinci 32, 20133 Milan, Italy
E-mail: piero.fraternali@polimi.it

Library of Congress Control Number: 2004109140

CR Subject Classification (1998): D.2, C.2, I.2.11, H.4, H.2, H.3, H.5, K.4, K.6

ISSN 0302-9743
ISBN 3-540-22511-0 Springer Berlin Heidelberg New York

Springer is a part of Springer Science+Business Media

springeronline.com

© Springer-Verlag Berlin Heidelberg 2004
Printed in Germany

Typesetting: Camera-ready by author, data conversion by PTP-Berlin, Protago-TeX-Production GmbH
Printed on acid-free paper   SPIN: 11303220   06/3142   5 4 3 2 1 0

Preface

Web engineering is a new discipline that addresses the pressing need for systematic and tool-supported approaches for the development, maintenance and testing of Web applications. Web engineering builds upon well-known and successful software engineering principles and practices, adapting them to the special characteristics of Web applications. Even more relevant is the enrichment with methods and techniques stemming from related areas like hypertext authoring, human-computer interaction, content management, and usability engineering. The goal of the 4th International Conference on Web Engineering (ICWE 2004), in line with the previous ICWE conferences, was to work towards a better understanding of the issues related to Web application development. Special attention was paid to emerging trends, technologies and future visions, to help the academic and industrial communities identify the most challenging tasks for their research and projects.

Following a number of successful workshops on Web engineering since 1997 at well-known conferences, such as ICSE and WWW, the first conference on Web engineering was held in Cáceres, Spain in 2001. It was followed by ICWE 2002 in Santa Fe, Argentina and ICWE 2003 in Oviedo, Spain. In 2004 ICWE moved to the center of Europe and was held in Munich, Germany from July 26 to 30. ICWE 2004 was organized by the Institute for Informatics of the Ludwig-Maximilians-Universität (LMU) Munich.

The ICWE 2004 edition received a total of 204 submissions, out of which 25 papers were selected by the Program Committee as full papers (12% acceptance). Additionally, 60 papers describing ongoing research results were included, as either short papers or posters. The selected papers cover a wide spectrum of topics, including Web development processes, design methods, Web usability, security and performance, Web metrics, personalized and adaptive Web applications, the Semantic Web, and more.

ICWE 2004 attracted people from five continents, with a wide and uniform geographical distribution of the papers' authors. ICWE 2004 also hosted for the first time a tool demonstration track, and featured a two-day tutorial and workshop program, consisting of five tutorials and four workshops. Workshops and tutorials gave to the conference attendees the opportunity to enjoy a more informal forum for discussing the newest Web engineering topics, from Web quality, to the development of secure Web applications, to MDA applied to the construction of Web applications. Links to the workshops and tutorials can be found at the conference Web site: www.icwe2004.org

We wish to express our gratitude to all the individuals and institutions who made this conference possible. We are very grateful to Lutz Heuser, Gerti Kappel and Roel Wieringa for presenting their keynotes at the conference. We would like to acknowledge all workshop organizers and tutorial presenters and the local organizing committee. Our thank goes also to the workshop and tutorial co-chairs as well as to the demo and poster chair for their engagement. In particular, Maristella Matera did an excellent job managing the workshops organization. Our special thanks go to the program committee members and additional referees for the very professional work done during the review process. The Online Conference System (OCS) was used during the review process for bidding and gathering submitted papers and reviews. We would like to thank the technical support team (Martin Karusseit and Markus Bajohr) at the University of Dortmund, which provided invaluable assistance on the use of the Online Conference Service of METAFrame Technologies. We are also grateful to Springer-Verlag for their helpful collaboration and quick publication schedule. Our deep recognition is due to Florian Hacklinger for his contribution in setting up and updating the conference Web site.

Last but not least, we want to thank the more than 450 authors from over 35 countries who contributed to this book and the conference. We thank them for their submissions and presentations and for providing us with the material in time. We count on them for the next conference edition, ICWE 2005, to be held in Sydney, Australia.

Munich and Milan, May 2004   Nora Koch
                                                              Piero Fraternali
                                                              Martin Wirsing

Organization

Executive Committee

Conference Chair	Nora Koch	LMU Munich and FAST GmbH, Germany
Program Chair	Piero Fraternali	Politecnico di Milano, Italy
Organizing Chair	Martin Wirsing	LMU Munich, Germany

Organizing Committee

Workshop Co-chairs	Maristella Matera	Politecnico di Milano, Italy
	Sara Comai	Politecnico di Milano, Italy
Tutorial Co-chairs	Klaus Turowski	Universität Augsburg, Germany
	Jose Emilio Labra	Universidad de Oviedo, Spain
Demo and Poster Chair	Alexander Knapp	LMU Munich, Germany
Local Organization	Michael Barth	LMU Munich, Germany
	Hubert Baumeister	
	Anton Fasching	
	Florian Hacklinger	
	Axel Rauschmayer	
	Gefei Zhang	

Steering Committee

Juan Manuel Cueva Lovelle	Universidad de Oviedo, Spain
Martin Gaedke	Universität Karlsruhe, Germany
Luis Joyanes Aguilar	Universidad Pontificia de Salamanca, Spain
San Murugesan	Southern Cross University, Australia
Luis Olsina	Universidad Nacional de La Pampa, Argentina
Oscar Pastor	Universidad Politécnica de Valencia, Spain
Gustavo Rossi	Universidad Nacional de La Plata, Argentina
Daniel Schwabe	PUC Rio de Janeiro, Brazil
Bebo White	Stanford Linear Accelerator Center, USA

International Endorsement

 IW^{3}C^2

Program Committee

Paolo Atzeni (Italy)
Luciano Baresi (Italy)
Philip A. Bernstein (USA)
Michael Bieber (USA)
Alex Buchmann (Germany)
Christoph Bussler (USA)
Leslie Carr (UK)
Fabio Casati (USA)
Vassilis Christophides (Greece)
Ernesto Damiani (Italy)
Paul Dantzig (USA)
Olga De Troyer (Belgium)
Yogesh Deshpande (Australia)
Klaus R. Dittrich (Switzerland)
Asuman Dogac (Turkey)
Juliana Freire (USA)
Athula Ginige (Australia)
Jaime Gómez (Spain)
Martin B. Gonzalez Rodriguez (Spain)
Manfred Hauswirth (Switzerland)
Geert-Jan Houben (The Netherlands)
Martti Jeenicke (Germany)
Gerti Kappel (Austria)
Nick Kushmerick (Ireland)
Frank Leymann (Germany)
Xiaoming Li (China)

Stephen W. Liddle (USA)
Tok Wang Ling (Singapore)
David Lowe (Australia)
Luis Mandel (Germany)
Massimo Marchiori (USA)
Heinrich Mayr (Austria)
Giansalvatore Mecca (Italy)
Emilia Mendes (New Zealand)
Sandro Morasca (Italy)
Moira Norrie (Switzerland)
Vicente Pelechano (Spain)
Mario Piattini (Spain)
Arthur Ryman (Canada)
Arno Scharl (Australia)
Klaus-Dieter Schewe (New Zealand)
Michel Scholl (France)
Wieland Schwinger (Austria)
David Stotts (USA)
Jianwen Su (USA)
Bernhard Thalheim (Germany)
Antonio Vallecillo (Spain)
Jean Vanderdonckt (Belgium)
James Whitehead (USA)
Carlo Zaniolo (USA)
Yanchun Zhang (Australia)

Additional Referees

Bugrahan Akcay
Claudio Ardagna
Simi Bajaj
Hubert Baumeister
Per Bendsen

Alejandro Bia
A. Binemann-Zdanowicz
Daniele Braga
Marco Brambilla
Timo Bretschneider

Cristina Cachero
Coral Calero
Alessandro Campi
Sven Casteleyn
Paolo Ceravolo

Sara Comai
Graham Cooper
Marco Cremonini
Valter Crescenzi
S. De C. di Vimercati
A. De la Puente Salán
Lois Delcambre
Astrid Dickinger
Cedric Du Mouza
Mehmet Erkanar
M.J. Escalona Cuaresma
E. Fernandez-Medina
Gunar Fiedler
Joan Fons
Flavius Frasincar
Chris Freyberg
Xiang Fu
Cristiano Fugazza
Irene Garrigós
Guozheng Ge
Cagdas Gerede
Marcela Genero
Gabriele Gianini
J. Anupama Ginige
J.A. Gómez Rodríguez
M. González Gallego
Sabine Graf
Thomas Grill
Ozgur Gulduren
Yavuz Gurcan

Florian Hacklinger
Yildiray Kabak
Roland Kaschek
Sunghun Kim
Markus Klemen
Alexander Knapp
Reinhard Kronsteiner
Alexander Kuckelberg
Gokce Banu Laleci
Pier Luca Lanzi
Changqing Li
Beate List
Sergio Luján Mora
Mauro Madravio
Ioakim Marmaridis
M. de los Angeles Martín
Andrea Maurino
Lorraine McGinty
Johannes Meinecke
Paolo Merialdo
Elke Michlmayr
T. Daniel Midgley
Eva Millan
Peter Mork
Gaston Mousques
Martin Nussbaumer
S. Ocio Barriales
J. Angel Olivas
Kai Pan
Janaka Pitadeniya

Pierluigi Plebani
Rachel Pottinger
Giuseppe Pozzi
Maya Purushotaman
Axel Rauschmayer
Werner Retschitzegger
Daniel Riesco
Alessandro Rizzi
Francesca Rizzo
Francisco Ruiz
Petra Schubert
Imen Sebei
Aida Seifi
R. Sembacuttiaratchy
Siyamed Seyhmus Sinir
Mark Slater
Giovanni Toffetti
Horst Treiblmaier
Seda Unal
Bhuvan Unhelkar
Richard Vdovjak
Aurora Vizcaino
Dan Vodislav
Albert Weichselbraun
Gao Xiangzhu
Qingqing Yuan
Ali Yildiz
Murat Yukselen
Gefei Zhang

Sponsoring Institutions

Workshops and Tutorials

Workshops

IWWOST 2004
4th International Workshop on Web-Oriented Software Technologies
Gustavo Rossi
Universidad Nacional de La Plata, Argentina
Oscar Pastor
Universidad Politécnica de Valencia, Spain
Daniel Schwabe
PUC Rio de Janeiro, Brazil
Luis Olsina
Universidad Nacional de La Pampa, Argentina

AHCW 2004
Adaptive Hypermedia and Collaborative Web-Based Systems
Rosa Carro
Universidad Autonoma de Madrid, Spain
Johann Schlichter
Technical University of Munich, Germany

WQ 2004
Web Quality
Luciano Baresi
Politecnico di Milano, Italy
Sandro Morasca
Università degli Studi dell'Insubria, Italy

DIWE 2004
Device Independent Web Engineering
Markus Lauff
SAP AG, Germany

Tutorials

Developing Secure Web-Based Applications with UML: Methods and Tools
Jan Jürjens
Technical University of Munich, Germany

MDA Standards for Ontology Development

Dragan Gašević, Vladan Devedžić, Dragan Djurić
FON – School of Business Administration, Belgrade, Serbia and Montenegro

An Introduction to Web Quality

Luciano Baresi
Politecnico di Milano, Italy
Sandro Morasca
Università degli Studi dell'Insubria, Italy

Using MDA for Designing and Implementing Web-Based Applications

Antonio Vallecillo
Universidad de Málaga, Spain

Providing Interoperability of Information Systems Through Semantically Enriched Web Services

Asuman Dogac
University of Ankara, Turkey
Chris Bussler
National University of Ireland, Galway, Ireland

Table of Contents

Web Services and Distributed Processes and Systems

Web Metrics, Cost Estimation, and Measurement

Personalization and Adaptation of Web Applications

Code Generation and Tools

Development Process and Process Improvement of Web Applications

Semantic Web and Applications

Performance

Web Data Models, Query and Representation Languages

Web Interface Engineering

Security, Safety, and Reliability

Web Mining, User Models, and Data Analysis

Posters

Tool Demonstrations

The Real World or Web Engineering?

Lutz Heuser

Vice President Global Research & Innovation
SAP AG

A couple of years ago practitioners and researchers began to realize that the traditional issues covered in software engineering do not fulfil all of the requirements raised by the proliferation and growth of web-based information and application systems.

> "Fundamental differences [between hypermedia and other disciplines] however, make a pure transposition of techniques both difficult and inadequate. An important part of hypertext design concerns aesthetic and cognitive aspects that software engineering environments do not support,"
>
> [Nanard and Nanard, 1995]

As a result, researchers currently make significant and ongoing contributions to a discipline that is called Web Engineering (WebE). Web Engineering aims to address and resolve the multifaceted problems of Web-based systems development. Even there are quite some different definitions for Web Engineering, the main focus of is usually on the establishment and use of sound scientific, engineering, and management principles and systematic approaches to the successful development, deployment and maintenance of high-quality Web-based systems and applications [San Murugesan, Yogesh Deshpande: Workshop Web Engineering ICSE2000].

> Web Engineering is the application of systematic, disciplined and quantifiable approaches to the cost-effective development and evolution of high-quality applications in the World Wide Web.
>
> [www.webengineering.org, March 2004]

> "Web Engineering is a discipline among disciplines, cutting across computer science, information systems, and software engineering, as well as benefiting from several non-IT specializations"
> "While Web Engineering adopts and encompasses many software engineering principles, it incorporates many new approaches, methodologies, tools, techniques, and guidelines to meet the unique requirements of Web-based systems. Developing Web-based systems is significantly different from traditional software development and poses many additional challenges"
>
> [IEEE Multimedia]

After taking a closer look at the Web Engineering principles and approaches that have already been developed, we recognise that most of these concepts assume that

N. Koch, P. Fraternali, and M. Wirsing (Eds.): ICWE 2004, LNCS 3140, pp. 1–5, 2004.

systems and applications are developed from scratch and that the target environment is the smaller/mid-size business environment.

Both of these assumptions do not apply to many of the established software companies and especially not to SAP. Founded in 1972, SAP is the recognized leader in providing collaborative business solutions for all types of industries and for every major market. SAP solutions are installed at more than 60,000 customer locations in 120 countries. Comprehensive solutions are currently available for 23 distinct industries and each solution is tailored to the specific standards, processes, and challenges of the respective industry. And they're developed, implemented, and supported by 28,700 professionals operating out of a global network of offices.

Thanks to SAP's unified technology platform, all solutions share common values, including:
- **Seamless integration:** Removes the barriers that stand between people, systems, and information
- **Scalability:** Accommodates virtually unlimited growth
- **Adaptability:** Allows easy customization of features and functions – and helps to cope with constant change
- **Ease of implementation:** Helps the customer to get up and running sooner
- **Lower total cost of ownership:** Helps minimize long-term costs
- **Industry expertise:** Supports the real-world processes employed every day

As SAP has always been committed to the development of technology-independent business solutions, the evolution from the mainframe-based R/2 system to R/3 for Client/Server and Distributed Open Systems was just as natural as the progression towards web-based systems.

Now SAP has announced that the future product portfolio will be based on an enterprise service architecture utilising web services on common business objects and business processes. This requires a "real world" definition of what a Web Service could be.

SAP's software engineering process is based on the Product Innovation Lifecycle (PIL), which describes how SAP invents, produces, and manages products throughout their entire lifetime from invention to transition and across multiple releases. The PIL is primarily driven by Portfolio & Solution Management and involves virtually all of SAP's line of business functions (e.g. development, production, support).

Fig. 1. SAP's Product Innovation Lifecycle

The SAP Product Innovation Lifecycle (PIL) is based on a waterfall model that can be complemented by spiral/parallel approaches within PIL phases as needed.

The deliverable-oriented phases of the PIL transform ideas into software releases, which in turn are deployed to create successful implementations.

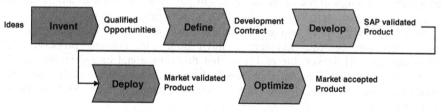

Fig. 2. Information flow in the PIL

Having said this, the following sections will sketch some of the key challenges in the discipline of Web Engineering where SAP would like to evaluate how the concepts of numerous ambitious and skilful researchers could be implemented in the real world. The examples also outline how the scientific Web Engineering phases could be mapped to SAP's PIL.

1   Example: WebE: Requirement Engineering / PIL: Invent, Define

Successfully defining the stakeholders' requirements is critical to the development of an application that delivers quality and meets expectations. Difficulties during the development process or creation of an unsuccessful application usually result from mistakes such as missing or not well-defined requirements as well as inclusion of superfluous requirements.

In the real world, application development is often not carried out for a single customer but for a market segment. Standard applications have to fulfil the needs for a superset of customers of a specific business area (e.g. Enterprise Resource Planning, Human Resources) or coming from a specific industry (e.g. Automotive, Retail).

Another real-world aspect that has to be addressed is the prioritisation of requirements according to the context of use with respect to the user as well as the application. Additionally, changes and advances in technology (e.g. user agents, standards, protocols) dynamically influence the set and prioritisation of requirements.

Starting with a wide array of concepts and tools for the selection of relevant requirements, the Requirement Engineering phase is arguably lacking in well-defined and systematic support for the each of its components, which include the formal description, validation, management, and risk assessment of requirements as well as the cost forecasting/estimation analysis.

Within SAP, it is agreed that any development to be initiated requires a so-called business case. It clearly defines why the development should be done in terms of customer demands or market opportunities. It is also necessary to justify required investments and to position the possible solution in relation to the competition.

2 Example: WebE: Analysis, Design / PIL: Define, Develop

For the analysis and design aspects of Web Engineering, the initial steps in the PIL Development phase are the detailed planning and the detailed design. Keeping in mind that SAP products are used at 60,000 customer locations in more than 120 countries, the design of the applications has to pay close attention to unique cultural aspects, localisation, and configuration of the local IT infrastructures.

Web Engineering often arranges the analysis and design activities into orthogonal dimensions for content, interaction, navigation, presentation, processes, and communication. However, the reality is that this orthogonal categorization doesn't necessarily map well to existing systems and earlier development, as they are often stored in legacy systems, follow earlier process models, or have been set by the customer.

In addition, current scientific approaches often do not fully take changing technologies and even changing development and architectural paradigms (e.g. client/server towards enterprise service architectures) into consideration when establishing analysis and design concepts for broad use.

With respect to these aspects, the implementation of the Analysis and Design concepts developed in Web Engineering, have not been previously implemented very often because they do not take into account pre-existing legacy systems and development and sometimes neglect the reality that technology is constantly evolving.

3 Example: WebE: Implementation / PIL: Develop

In 1992, Derek Patridge stated, "Conventional software-system development is the process of designing a correct HOW for a well-defined WHAT." Whereas the "WHAT" has already been defined in the previous phases of the Web Engineering process, the "HOW" should now clarify details about the implementation.

As a result, emerging Web Engineering concepts often try to answer this by answering the question regarding "HOW the latest Web-technologies (e.g. SMIL, XForms, XSL-FO) could be applied." Whenever a new version of a particular Web-technology appears, the answer it provides is usually a new and of course improved solution for the "HOW" compared to the previous version.

In the real world, Partridge's question about the "HOW" could meanwhile be rephrased as, "HOW all of these technologies should be combined and HOW to keep pace with the technological evolution?" Neither concepts that have been previously developed nor the tools that are currently being used allow developers and researchers to use the latest technology and to use them in conjunction with legacy technologies.

4 Conclusion

Beginning with the provoking question, "The real world or Web Engineering?" this brief overview has provided on one hand a short review of the roots of the discipline of Web Engineering and on the other hand introduced SAP's background and Product Innovation Lifecycle. Three examples also demonstrated where a mismatch between SAP's real world requirements and scientific Web Engineering results could be seen.

The conclusion however is that Web Engineering is a scientific discipline with a solid theoretical basis that delivers valuable and important pieces in solving the puzzle of how to build large, complex web-based systems.

Research opportunities have been identified to answer questions such as, "How should these pieces be put together?" and "What is the best way to deal with the rapid evolution of technology and the resulting heterogeneity of these systems?"

Web Engineering – Old Wine in New Bottles?

Gerti Kappel[1], Elke Michlmayr[2], Birgit Pröll[3],
Siegfried Reich[4], and Werner Retschitzegger[5]

[1] Business Informatics Group (BIG), Vienna University of Technology
Favoritenstr. 9, A-1040 Vienna, Austria
gerti@big.tuwien.ac.at
[2] Women's Postgraduate College on Internet Technologies (WIT)
Vienna University of Technology
Favoritenstr. 9, A-1040 Vienna, Austria
michlmayr@wit.tuwien.ac.at
[3] Institute for Applied Knowledge Processing (FAW)
Softwarepark Hagenberg, Hauptstraße 119, A-4232 Hagenberg, Austria
birgit@faw.uni-linz.ac.at
[4] Salzburg Research
Jakob Haringer Straße 5/III, A-5020 Salzburg, Austria
siegfried.reich@salzburgresearch.at
[5] Department of Information Systems (IFS), Johannes Kepler University Linz
Altenbergerstr. 69, A-4040 Linz, Austria
werner@ifs.uni-linz.ac.at

Abstract. Modern Web applications are full-fledged, complex software systems. Therefore, the development of Web applications requires a methodologically sound engineering approach called Web Engineering. It is not clear, however, to which extent existing solutions from relevant areas, most notably software engineering can be reused as such for the development of Web applications and consequently, if Web Engineering is really a discipline on its own. This paper highlights the characteristics of Web application development as found in existing literature thus providing a prerequisite for analyzing the appropriateness of existing engineering solutions. The characteristics are categorized according to four dimensions, comprising the software product itself, its development, its use and evolution as a cross-cutting concern.

1 Introduction

The World Wide Web has a massive and permanent influence on our lives. Economy, industry, education, healthcare, public administration, entertainment – there is hardly a part in our daily life that has not been pervaded by the World Wide Web. The reason for this omnipresence lies especially in the very nature of the Web, which is shaped by the global and permanent availability and comfortable and uniform access to often widely distributed information producible by anyone in the form of Web pages

N. Koch, P. Fraternali, and M. Wirsing (Eds.): ICWE 2004, LNCS 3140, pp. 6–12, 2004.

[2, 25]. Web applications today are full-fledged, complex software systems providing interactive, data intensive and customisable services accessible through different devices, working state-based for the realization of user transactions and usually storing the used data in an underlying database. Despite the fundamental changes in the orientation of the Web, from an informational to an application medium, the development of Web applications is still seen as a one-time event, spontaneous, usually based on the knowledge, experiences and development practices of individual developers, limited to be reused in the sense of the "Copy&Paste paradigm", and ultimately characterized by inadequate documentation of design decisions. A survey of the practice of Web application development reported that there is only limited use of design techniques, documentations are produced seldom and testing procedures are most often not formalized [31]. Keeping this practice in mind, it is no surprise that a survey done by the Cutter Consortium [7] found out that the top problem areas of large-scale Web application projects were the failure to meet business needs (84%), project schedule delays (79%), budget overrun (63%), lack of required functionality (53%), and poor quality of deliverables (52%). The current situation of ad hoc[1] development of Web applications reminds us of the software development practices of the 1960s, before it was realized that the development of applications required more than programming expertise [8, 9, 28].

Now, the problems seem to be the same, so are the solutions the same, too? Is the notion of Web Engineering just a new application domain of software engineering reusing and slightly adapting already existing approaches in terms of methodologies, principles, standards and best practice guides, or is it really a discipline in its own calling for new solutions (cf., e.g., [13, 15, 16])? One of the prerequisites to answer this question is to clarify, how far Web application development is different to traditional software development. Answering this question would allow to reason about the applicability and appropriateness of approaches already existing in relevant computing fields.

2 Characteristics of Web Application Development

Web applications are software systems based on technologies and standards of the World Wide Web Consortium (W3C). They provide Web-specific resources such as content and services through a user interface, the Web browser. With this definition of Web applications in mind, we try to explore the characteristics of Web application development, heavily relying on existing literature [1, 5, 11, 15, 16, 20-29, 32]. We structure our discussion into four different dimensions, comprising the *software product* itself, its *development*, its *use* and *evolution* as a cross-cutting concern [14, 19]. It has to be emphasized that we don't claim that each of these characteristics is unique to Web application development never occurring when developing traditional, i.e., non-Web applications. Characteristics mentioned in existing literature to be

---

[1] Note that the term "ad hoc" is interpreted as "doing something in an unstructured way", and not in its original sense of "focused at the problem at hand" (cf. [12]).

unique for Web development seem to be not that outstanding compared to certain traditional software development domains [15, 16]. This is not least due to the fact that for each characteristic the degree of difference depends on the category of Web application considered (examples for such categorizations can be found in [19, 26, 29]).

2.1 Application-Related Characteristics

When developing Web applications one has to consider not only functionality but equally address *content*, *hypertext*, and *presentation* aspects.

Content. The origin of the Web is its role as information medium. Beyond the required functionality, Web applications are thus heavily content-driven. Content comprises not only structured data residing in database systems but also unstructured and semi-structured data such as textual descriptions or multi-media information. Complexity arises especially from the fact that content is often highly *dynamic* and continuously updated. Also, users typically demand high *content quality* in terms of topicality, accurateness, consistency, and reliability [30]. Consequently, the development of Web applications is not only a complex engineering task but relies heavily on *authors* responsible for the content.

Hypertext. Web applications advocate the hypertext paradigm [6] as the fundamental paradigm for structuring information. The basic elements of the Web's notion of hypertext are nodes, links and anchors. Typical examples of accessing hypertextual information include browsing (like in online stores' catalogues), querying (like in e-learning applications), or guided tours (like in virtual exhibitions). The essential feature of the hypertext paradigm is its *non-linearity* requiring from both authors and users to address the potential issues of *disorientation* and *cognitive overload*. This can be achieved for example through specific navigation design (site maps, keyword searches, traversed paths, etc.) and is essential to preserve *quality of access* [10].

Presentation. In conventional software systems the "look and feel" is often to a large extent determined by standardized user interface elements and style guides. Presentation is a central quality factor for Web applications not least to the high competitive pressure on the Web where *visual appearance* is subject to (ever-changing) fashion, trends, and new technical features [29]. In addition, as application designers cannot expect Web users to consult a user's manual Web applications need to be *self-explanatory* requiring particular attention to visual design and the consistency of the interaction style behaviour.

2.2 Usage-Related Characteristics

Unlike in more traditional settings, the users of Web applications often vary in numbers and cultural background, use heterogeneous devices and can freely choose the time and location of accessing the Web application [18]. Developers frequently cannot predict all these potential settings.

Natural context. This includes aspects of the *location* and *time of access*, offering the opportunity of new kinds of context-based services, not least due to the advent of mobile computing. In addition, the possibility of *immediate* and *permanent availability* of Web applications requires special quality considerations such as 24/7 availability.

Unpredictable technical infrastructure. Available end-user devices vary in hardware and software capabilities such as display size, computational power, or browser version. Also network connections differ with respect to bandwidth, reliability, stability and availability, all affecting the *quality of service* [29]. Complexity is increased even further due to the fact that the actual representation of the Web application on the client device is to a large extent outside the control of the developers. For example, users configure their browsers individually and may even disallow certain essential features (e.g., cookies or JavaScript).

Diversity and magnitude of user base. Web application users differ in age, social and cultural backgrounds, goals, intentions, skills, and capabilities [17]. These heterogeneity has to be considered by application developers since the Web entails no obligation and Web applications will only be used if they bring immediate advantage. The way users interact with the Web application can be hardly predicted and users may leave the Web application at any time [15]. Also, the number of users accessing the Web application may vary considerably making *scalability* another crucial quality aspect.

2.3 Development-Related Characteristics

Web application developers need to deal with conditions, risks, and uncertainties not always present in traditional software projects.

Development team. Web application development is a *multi-disciplinary* effort comprising a mixture of print publishers, authors, software developers, marketing experts, and art designers [26]. Such teams are also dominated by significantly *younger team members* which are less willing to adhere to conventions and more inclined towards applying new (and often still immature) technologies [24]. Another important characteristic is the involvement of *open source communities*.

Development environment. The technical infrastructure used for developing a Web application is characterized by a high degree of *volatility and heterogeneity*. Web application development relies on a broad spectrum of different COTS components (e.g., Web server, application server, database system, publishing framework etc.). Because of the increased time-to-market pressure these components are often immature and fall short in stability, reliability, and desired functionality.

Legacy integration. Web applications often need to integrate legacy systems [21]. The external services provided by these systems are, however, rarely documented and often change without notice, thus negatively affecting the quality of the overall Web application.

Process. Web application development processes are characterized by frequent changes and adjustments, which are necessary due to rapid technological developments, fast changing trends, volatile requirements, and rigid schedules. This calls for highly iterative, flexible, and prototype-oriented development methods [3, 24].

2.4 Evolution-Related Characteristics

Web applications are subject to frequent changes and permanent evolution. Their development is driven by rapidly changing technology and the volatility of Web users leads to a highly competitive situation where immediate Web presence and short time to market are considered crucial: "Unlike conventional application software that evolves over a series of planned, chronologically spaced releases, Web applications evolve continuously." [28]. In the course of evolution, negotiability of quality often sacrifices maintainability [14, 20].

3 Conclusion

To say it with the words of Robert Glass [13], "… there have always been important differences between software projects, diversity is the key part of software development. Information systems have always been developed differently from scientific systems, and critical projects have been treated differently from more mundane ones. Why should we be surprised that the same condition holds for Web and non-Web projects?" There are, however, important differences between the two, urgently requiring to systematically re-think the applicability and appropriateness of existing solutions in the whole area of software engineering, eventually based on the knowledge areas defined by the SWEBOK [4]. The clarification of this issue would be a major step towards establishing Web Engineering as a discipline on its own.

References

[1]   Balasubramaniam, R., Pries-Heje, J., Baskerville, R., *Internet Software Engineering: A Different Class of Processes*, Annals of Software Engineering, 14 (1-4), Dec., 2002, pp. 169-195.

[2]   Berners-Lee, T., *WWW: Past, Present, and Future*, IEEE Computer, 29 (10), Oct., 1996, pp. 69-77.

[3]   Boehm, B., Turner, R., *Balancing Agility and Discipline, A Guide for the Perplexed*, Pearson Education, 2004.

[4]   Bourque, P., Dupuis, R., Abran, A., Moore, J. W., Tripp, L. L. *The Guide to the Software Engineering Body of Knowledge*, IEEE Software, vol. 16, pp. 35-44, Nov/Dec. 1999.

[5]   Botterweck, G. and Swatman, P. A., *Towards a Contingency Based Approach to Web Engineering*. 7th Australian Workshop on Requirements Engineering (AWRE), Melbourne, 2002.

[6]   Conklin, J., *Hypertext: An Introduction and Survey,* IEEE Computer, 20 (9), Sept., 1987, pp. 17-41.

[7]   Cutter Consortium, *Poor Project Management Number-one Problem of Outsourced E-projects,* Cutter Research Briefs, November, 2000, http://www.cutter.com/research/2000/crb001107.html.

[8]   Deshpande, Y., Hansen, S., *Web Engineering: Creating a Discipline among Disciplines,* Special Issue on Web Engineering, IEEE Multimedia, 8 (2), April-June, 2001, pp. 82-87.

[9]   Deshpande, Y., Hansen, S., Murugesan, S., *Web Engineering: Beyond CS, IS and SE – An Evolutionary and Non-Engineering View,* Proc. of the 1st ICSE Workshop on Web Engineering (held in conjunction with the Int. Conference on Software Engineering (ICSE), Los Angeles, May, 1999.

[10] German, D., Cowan, D., *Towards a Unified Catalogue of Hypermedia Design Patterns,* Proc. of the 33rd Hawaii International Conference on System Sciences (HICSS), Maui, Hawaii, January, 2000.

[11] Ginige, A., *Web Engineering in Action,* Proc. of the 2nd ICSE Workshop on Web Engineering (held in conjunction with the Int. Conf. on Software Engineering (ICSE), Limerick, Ireland, June, 2000.

[12] Glass, R.L., *Searching for the holy grail of software engineering,* Communications of the ACM 45(5), 2002.

[13] Glass, R.L., *A mugwump's-eye view of Web work.* Communication of the ACM 46(8), 2003.

[14] Grünbacher, P., Ramler, R., Retschitzegger, W., Schwinger, W., *Making Quality a First-Class Citizen in Web Engineering,* Proc. of the 2nd Workshop on Software Quality (SQW), held in conjunction with the 26th Int. Conf. on Software Engineering (ICSE), Edinburgh, Scotland, May, 2004.

[15] Holck, J., Clemmensen, T., *What Makes Web Development Different?,* Presented at the 24th Information Systems Research Seminar in Scandinavia (IRIS) Ulvik, Norway, August 2001.

[16] Kautz, K. & J. Nørbjerg: *Persistent Problems in Information Systems Development: The Case of the World Wide Web,* in Ciborra et. al. (eds.): Proc. of the European Conf. on Information Systems, Naples, Italy, June, 2003

[17] Kobsa, A., *Generic User Modeling Systems,* User Modeling and User-Adapted Interaction, 11 (1-2), Ten Year Anniversary Issue, 2001, pp. 49-63.

[18] Kappel, G., Pröll, B., Retschitzegger, W., Schwinger, W., *Customisation for Ubiquitous Web Applications – A Comparison of Approaches,* International Journal of Web Engineering and Technology (IJWET), Inderscience Publishers, January, 2003.

[19] Kappel, G., Pröll, B., Reich, S., Retschitzegger, W., (eds.), *Web Engineering – Systematic Development of Web Applications,* dpunkt.verlag, 2004.

[20] Levine, L., Baskerville, R., Loveland Link, J.L., Pries-Heje, J., Ramesh, B., & Slaughter, S.. Discovery colloquium: Quality software development @ Internet speed. (SEI Technical Report CMU/SEI-2002-TR-020) Pittsburgh, Software Engineering Institute, 2002.

[21] Lowe, D., Hall, W., *Hypermedia and Web: An Engineering Approach,* Wiley & Sons, 1999.

[22] Lowe, D., *Engineering the Web - Web Engineering or Web Gardening?* WebNet Journal, 1 (1), January-March, 1999.

[23] Lowe, D., *Web System Requirements: An Overview,* Requirements Engineering Journal, Vol. 8, No. 2, 2003

[24] McDonald, A., Welland, R., *Web Engineering in Practice*, Proc. of the 4th Workshop on Web Engineering (in conjunction with 10th Int. Conf. on WWW), Hong Kong, Mai, 2001.

[25] Murugesan, S., Deshpande, Y., Hansen, S., Ginige, A., *Web Engineering: A New Discipline for Web-Based System Development*, Proc. of the 1st ICSE Workshop on Web Engineering (held in conjunction with the Int. Conference on Software Engineering, ICSE), Los Angeles, USA, May, 1999.

[26] Powell, T., Jones, D., Cutts, D., *Web Site Engineering: Beyond Web Page Design*, Prentice Hall, 1998.

[27] Pressman, R. S., *Can Internet-Based Applications Be Engineered?*, IEEE Software, 15 (5), September-October, 1998, pp. 104-110.

[28] Pressman, R. S., *What a Tangled Web We Weave*, IEEE Software, 17 (1), Jan/Feb., 2000, pp. 18-21.

[29] Pressman, R. S., *Chapter 29: Web Engineering.* In: Software Engineering: A Practitioner's Approach, 5. Edition, McGraw-Hill, 2000.

[30] Strong, D.M., Lee, Y.W., Wang, R.Y., *Data Quality in Context,* Communications of the ACM, 1997. 40(5): pp. 103-110.

[31] Taylor, M.J., McWilliam, J., Forsyth, H., Wade, S., *Methodologies and website development: a survey of practice*, Information and Software Technology, 44, 2002.

[32] Vidgen, R., *What's so different about developing web-based information systems?* Proc. of 10th European Conference on Information Systems, Gdansk, Poland, June 2002.

Requirements Engineering: Problem Analysis and Solution Specification (Extended Abstract)

R.J. Wieringa

University of Twente, the Netherlands
roelw@cs.utwente.nl

1   Introduction

Taken literally, the term "requirements engineering" (RE) is a misnomer. A requirement is something that is wanted; engineering, according to *Webster's*, is calculated manipulation. If our wants would arise by calculated manipulation, then something would be wrong. Our wants should not be engineered. What should be engineered, are solutions that meet our wants.

So what is requirements engineering? In this talk I discuss two views of RE, as problem analysis and as solution specification, and show that these two views meet in the discipline of IT systems architecting.

Architecture is central to web engineering because the web is an infrastructure for distributed coordination. Requirements engineering for web aplications therefore must deal with a distributed and sometimes fuzy set of stakeholders and with evolving requirements that will change once people use the application and explore new coordination mechanisms. In this context, requirements engineering is a distributed and concurrent process of problem analysis and solution specification.

2   Requirements Engineering and Problem Solving

The frequently heard mantra of software engineers is that requirements specify *what* a system should do, whereas a design says *how* it should do it. But the distinction between "what" and "how" is meaningless. We can ask *how* a system behaves externally and *what* its internal structure is, just as we can ask *what* its external behavior is and *how* it is structured internally. A better distinction is that between problem and solution. A *problem* is a difference between what is perceived to be the case and what is desired, that we want to reduce; a *solution* is an action that reduces this difference [1, 2]. One view of requirements is that they specify a problem; another view is that they specify a solution. I discuss both views in this talk.

Note that problem analysis and solution specification need not be sequentially related. In general, problem analysis and solution specification proceed jointly, with the engineer spending most, but not all of her time on problem analysis at

N. Koch, P. Fraternali, and M. Wirsing (Eds.): ICWE 2004, LNCS 3140, pp. 13–16, 2004.

the start of the process, and spending most, but not all of her time on solution specificatioon towards the end of the process [3, 4].

3   Requirements Engineering as Problem Analysis

If requirements specify a problem, then a requirements specification should describe

- what the problematic phenomena are,
- what the cause relationships between these phenomena are,
- by which norms these phenomena are problematic, and
- which stakeholders have these norms.

An example of this approach to RE is *goal-oriented RE*, which starts from a top-down analysis of user goals and refines these until desired properties of solutions are found [5–8]. Another example is the *problem frame* approach of Michael Jackson, in which frequently occurring problem structures are identified and are related to a frame concern, which relates the solution specification to a goal in the problem domain. A third approach sees problem-oriented RE as *theory-building*, in which a theory of the problematic phenomena is built, that will help us to specify a solution that takes away the causes of the problems [9]. All these approaches take a rather top-down approach in which the assumption is that users can specify their goals (even if these may be mutually inconsistent). In cases where users cannot specify their goals, yet other approaches are suitable, such as the task-support style of requirements specification proposed by Lauesen [10] or an evolutionary approach in which users are observed in their work, from which conclusions about their requirements are drawn [11, 12].

4   Requirements Engineering as Solution Specification

The view RE as solution specification is taken by the IEEE 830 standard [13] and by other authors on requirements [14, 15]. In this view, a requirements specification consists of

- a specification of the context in which the system will operate,
- a list of desired system functions of the system,
- a definition of the semantics of these functions,
- and a list of of quality attributes of those functions.

Classical techniques for software solution specification are structured analysis and, to some extent, object-oriented techniques [16, 17]. Note however that object-oriented techniques such as the UML are primarily oriented towards specifying the internal structure of software solutions, not towards specifying their requirements.

5   IT Systems Architecture

The two views of requirements come together in the concept of system architecture. I define an *architecture* as the set of relationships between the components of a system, that jointly ensure emergent properties of the system as a whole. The architecture of a building is the set of relationships between parts of the building that cause the building to have desired properties, such as room, shelter, functionality and appearance. In the same way, the architecture of a software system is the set of relationships between its components that cause the system to have desired properties, such as a desired functionality, behavior, semantics, and quality of service.

Architecture links requirements as problem characteristics to requirements as solution properties. Consider a set of problem-oriented requirements, that characterize a business problem, and a set of solution-oriented requirements, that specify desired solution properties. If part of this solution is a software system, then other parts may be novel work procedures and a new physical layout of an office. Thus, the solution has an architecture that is expected to solve the business problem and the desired software system plays a role in this architecture. And it is the architecture that links the software solution to the business problem. The same holds, *mutatis mutandis*, at lower levels of the aggregation hierarchy. For example, the component architecture of a software system links the component specifications to the software problem that they are intended to solve.

Architecture is the central problem in web applications because these applications should enable distributed coordination between people, and the architecture of these coordination mechanisms evolves by itself as well as is designed by people. As far as it evolves by itself, it may link unforeseen solution properties to unforeseen problems. If left to its own, evolutionary processes tend to deteriorate the architecture of a system. The challenge of requirements engineering for web applications is therefore to design architectures that enable this process.

References

1. Dewey, J.: How We Think: A Restatement of the Relation of Reflective Thinking to the Educative Process. D.C. Heath and Company (1933)
2. Gause, D., Weinberg, G.: Exploring Requirements: Quality Before Design. Dorset House Publishing (1989)
3. Cross, N.: Design cognition: results from protocol and other empirical studies of design activity. In Eastman, C., McCracken, W., Newstetter, W., eds.: Design Knowing and Learning: Cognition in Design Education. Elsevier (2001) 79–103
4. Wieringa, R.: Requirements Engineering: Frameworks for Understanding. Wiley (1996)
5. Antón, A., Potts, C.: The use of goals to surface requirements for evolving systems. In: International Conference on Software Engineering (ICSE'98), IEEE Computer Society (1998) 157–166
6. Dardenne, A., Lamsweerde, A.v., Fickas, S.: Goal-directed requirements acquisition. Science of Computer Programming **20** (1993) 3–50

7. Mylopoulos, J., Chung, L., Yu, E.: From object-oriented to goal-oriented requirements analysis. Communications of the ACM **42** (1999) 31–37
8. Yu, E.: An organization modelling framework for information systems requirements engineering. In: Proceedings of the Third Workshop on Information Technologies and Systems (WITS'93). (1993)
9. Wieringa, R., Heerkens, H.: Requirements engineering as problem analysis: Methodology and guidelines. Technical report, University of Twente (2003)
10. Lauesen, S.: Software Requirements: Styles and Techniques. Addison-Wesley (2002)
11. Beyer, H., Holtzblatt, K.: Contextual Design: Defining Customer-Centered Systems. Morgan kaufmann (1998)
12. Bondarouk, T., Sikkel, N.: Implementation of collaborative technologies as a learning process. In Cano, J., ed.: Critical Reflections on Information Systems–A Systemic Approach. Idea Group Publishing (2003) 227–245
13. IEEE: IEEE Guide to Software Requirements Specifications. In: Software Engineering Standards. IEEE Computer Science Press (1993) IEEE Std 830-1993.
14. Davis, A.M.: Software Requirements: Objects, Functions, States. Prentice-Hall (1993)
15. Robertson, S., Robertson, J.: Mastering the Requirements Process. Addison-Wesley (1999)
16. Wieringa, R.: A survey of structured and object-oriented software specification methods and techniques. ACM Computing Surveys **30** (1998) 459–527
17. Wieringa, R.: Design Methods for Reactive Systems: Yourdon, Statemate and the UML. Morgan Kaufmann (2003)

Automated Evaluation of Web Usability and Accessibility by Guideline Review

Jean Vanderdonckt[1], Abdo Beirekdar[1,2], and Monique Noirhomme-Fraiture[2]

[1] Université catholique de Louvain, Information Systems Unit, Place des Doyens, 1
1348 Louvain-la-Neuve, Belgium
{vanderdonckt,Beirekdar}@isys.ucl.ac.be
http://www.isys.ucl.ac.be/bchi

[2] Fac. Univ. Notre-Dame de la Paix, Institut d'Informatique, rue Grandgagnage, 5
5000 Namur, Belgium
{abe,mno}@info.fundp.ac.be

Abstract. A novel approach is presented for automatically evaluating of the usability and accessibility (U&A) of web sites by performing a static analysis of their HTML code against U&A guidelines. The approach relies on separating guidelines evaluation logic from the evaluation engine. Due to this separation, the whole evaluation process can be divided into two main phases: specifying formal guidelines and web page evaluation. In the first phase, the formal structure of a guideline is expressed in terms of Guideline Definition Language (GDL). In the second phase, the web page is parsed to identify its contents and structure and link them to relevant guidelines to be evaluated on the page parsed. This approach enables the simultaneous evaluation of multiple guidelines selected on demand from different sources. It also optimises evaluation by automatically identifying common sub-structures among structured guidelines. It also supports the expression, by evaluators with different usability practises, of alternative evaluation strategies.

1 Introduction

The World Wide Web has become a predominant mean for communicating and presenting information on a broad scale and to a wide audience. Unfortunately, web site usability and accessibility continue to be a pressing problem [1]. An estimated 90% of sites provide inadequate usability [2], and an estimated 66% of sites are inaccessible to users with disabilities [3]. Although numerous assistive devices, such as screen readers and special keyboards, facilitate use of web sites, these devices may not improve a user's ability to find information, purchase products and complete other tasks on sites. For example, sites may not have links to help blind users skip over navigation bars, or sites may not enable users to increase the text font size, so that they can read it. A wide range of Usability and Accessibility (U&A) evaluation techniques have been proposed and a subset of these techniques is currently in common use. Automation of these techniques became much desired [4,5] because they required

N. Koch, P. Fraternali, and M. Wirsing (Eds.): ICWE 2004, LNCS 3140, pp. 17–30, 2004.
© Springer-Verlag Berlin Heidelberg 2004

U&A specialists to conduct them or to analyse evaluation results, which is very re-source consuming especially for very large, continuously growing web sites. In addi-tion, there is a lack of experts due to an increased demand. A possible solution to that problem consists in relying on U&A guidelines and recommendations to be reviewed and applied by designers and developers. Some studies show that applying guidelines by designers is subject to interpretation, basically because of the inappropriate struc-turing or formulation [6]. For this reason and others, automation has been predomi-nately used to objectively check guideline conformance or review [5]. Several auto-matic evaluation tools were developed to assist evaluators with guidelines review by automatically detecting and reporting ergonomic deviations from these guidelines and making suggestions for repairing them. In this paper, a novel approach is presented that automate the evaluation of a web site against U&A guidelines by checking a formal representation of these guidelines on the web pages of interest. The aim of the approach is to overcome the major shortcomings of existing tools. The main charac-teristic of this approach is the separation between the evaluation logic and the evalua-tion engine. In this way, the U&A guidelines can be expressed in terms of conditions to be satisfied on HTML elements (i.e., tags, attributes). A formal specification lan-guage supporting this approach implements a framework [7] that enables the trans-formation of such U&A guidelines from their initial expression in natural language into testable conditions on the HTML code. Once expressed, the guidelines can be evaluated at evaluation-time by configuring their formal expression in an improved way depending on the guidelines to be evaluated and the HTML elements contained in the page. This process consequently considers guidelines relevant to the targeted evaluation context, and factors out sub-structures that are common across these guidelines, even if they come from different sets of guidelines.

This paper is structured as follows: Section 2 briefly describes some automatic U&A evaluation tools. Section 3 presents a global view of the evaluation process and the fundamental concepts of our evaluation approach. Section 4 exemplifies the ap-proach on guidelines which is not found in existing tools. Section 5 underlines the possibilities of evaluation improvement, the most original part of our approach. Sec-tion 6 concludes the paper by stressing major advantages of the proposed approach.

2   Related Work

Depending on the evaluation method, U&A may involve several activities such as:
1. **Capture**: it consists of collecting U&A data, such as task completion time, errors, guideline violations, and subjective ratings.
2. **Analysis**: it is the phase where U&A data are interpreted to identify U&A prob-lems in the web site.
3. **Critique**: it consists of suggesting solutions or improvements to mitigate the pre-viously identified problems.

Many evaluation tools were developed to provide automation of some of the above activities. In this section we would like to report on some tools used for Web evalua-tion by guideline review, a particular evaluation method that has been selected for its simplicity, its capability to be conducted with or without users, and its wide applicability. Some of the tools are dedicated only to usability, some others to accessibility, but none of them to both U&A:

- A-Prompt [9] is an off-line tool designed to improve the usability of HTML documents by evaluating web pages for accessibility barriers and then providing developers with a fast and easy way to make the necessary repairs. The tool's evaluation and repair checklist is based on accessibility guidelines created and maintained by the Web Accessibility Initiative (http://www.w3.org/WAI).
- Bobby [10] is a comprehensive web accessibility tool designed to help evaluate and repair accessibility errors. It tests for compliance with WCAG1.0 and Section 508 guidelines. It offers prioritised suggestions based on the WCAG1.0. It also allows developers to test web pages and generate summary reports highlighting critical accessibility issues sorted by rank on priority.
- LIFT OnLine (http://www.usablenet.com) tests web pages against a subset of all usability and accessibility guidelines (rules), and then sends an e-mail with the link to a usability report on line. As soon as the analysis is completed, LIFT On-line shows a list of the pages in the web site containing potential usability problems. Each problem is ranked by severity and is described in details.
- WebSAT (http://zing.ncsl.nist.gov/WebTools/WebSAT/overview.html) inspects the HTML composition of web pages for potential usability problems. It can perform inspections using either its own set of usability rules or those of the IEEE Std 2001-1999.
- WebCriteria (http://www.webcriteria.com) is a tool for comparative evaluation of a web site with respect to a benchmark derived from similar well-established web sites that are considered as reference.

The common major shortcoming of the above existing U&A evaluation tools is that the evaluation logic is hard coded and hard wired in the evaluation engine, which makes them very inflexible for any modification of the evaluation logic. Introducing a new guideline, possibly a custom one, or modifying an existing guideline remains impossible. In addition, many of them do not offer many possibilities of controlling the evaluation process like choosing which guideline to evaluate, the level of evaluation at evaluation time, or the level of priority. For example, Bobby only provides the choice of the guidelines set to evaluate: W3C or Section508.

3   The Evaluation Approach

To address the above shortcomings, the evaluation process is structured in our approach by decomposing the whole evaluation process into two distinct but related phases: specifying formal guidelines which is achieved only once before any evaluation and evaluating a web site, which is conducted at any time. The two main phases remain totally autonomous, thus giving many possibilities to improve each of them. The different steps of these phases are now further described.

Structuring. The first step in our approach consists of structuring U&A guidelines in terms of evaluation conditions so as to obtain a formal guideline, expressed in a format that can be processed by an automaton as opposed to the natural language format of the initial guideline found in the literature. Guidelines structuring requires a thorough understanding of both the U&A knowledge and the HTML language to bridge the gap between them. It is also influenced by the understanding of the original guideline semantics that may lead to several interpretations of the same guideline. The formal guideline is expressed according to Guideline Definition Language (GDL), a XML-compliant language supporting the approach by formalising the structuring of U&A guidelines toward automatic evaluation. The most original characteristic of the GDL is its naturalness, i.e. the possibility offered by the language to straightforwardly map the informal statement of initial guidelines onto formal statement expressed in the GDL language. GDL is aimed at modelling HTML evaluable aspects only (e.g., colour contrast, alternative text for visual content). Other frameworks have to be used to cope with other direct usability aspects such as user satisfaction, consistency, and information organisation. Meta-information is then added to each GDL-compliant guideline according to taxonomy on indexes [?].

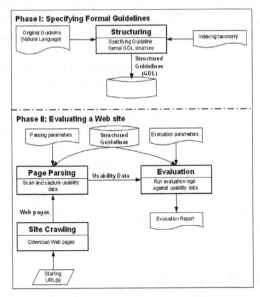

Fig. 1. The two main phases of evaluation process based on the proposed approach

Site crawling. The web pages of interest, whether they are static or dynamically generated, are simply specified by their URL, automatically downloaded from the web and stored in a dedicated directory where the rest of the process will take place.

Page parsing. This step is done by a single scan for each web page to be evaluated. During this scan, the parser captures the instances of the evaluation sets specified in the formal guidelines to be checked. Parsing parameters can be specified to control this process: which guidelines to evaluate, number of desired instances (e.g., a given maximum, all instances), whether incomplete set instances could be kept, etc.

Evaluation. After parsing the web page, the evaluation conditions that have been defined during guidelines structuring in GDL are processed to check their satisfaction by performing a property checking. Every condition is applied on the captured instances of its corresponding set to determine its respect or violation. In this way, a detailed evaluation report can be generated on respected/violated sets, number of detected instances, and percentage of respect/violation.

4   Fundamental Concepts

To facilitate the different phases of the evaluation process, several new concepts had to be identified and defined. Fig. 2 depicts a global view of the fundamental concepts of our approach and their interactions. These concepts form the building blocks of GDL. To exemplify how GDL can be exploited to transform a natural language guideline into a formal counterpart, let us select a first guideline: "Use a limited number of fonts in a single web page".

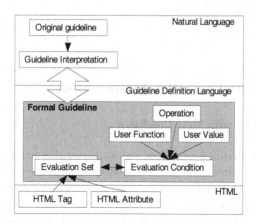

Fig. 2. Fundamental Concepts

As guidelines are generally expressed at a high level of abstraction, the original guideline expressed in natural language should be transformed into a concrete form that can be understood by designers and manipulated by the system. This re-expression is called an *interpretation* of the guideline. In general, interpretation is used to limit the focus of the original guideline to some extent that can be considered satisfactory in the targeted evaluation context. Of course, even with interpretation, evaluation of some guidelines cannot be totally automated. For this reason, every interpretation is assigned to a factor indicating the level of abstraction reflected. In our example, the guideline needs to be interpreted because "limited number" is very abstract. If we have an evaluation logic that can be applied on many evaluation sets with some difference, we can define a *meta evaluation condition* for all these sets, then we defined a *mapped evaluation condition* for every evaluation set. Otherwise, we specify a *direct evaluation condition*. In a meta evaluation condition, we use meta variables to specify the evaluation logic. The instantiation of the condition for a given evaluation set is done by mapping between the Meta variables and the corresponding concrete set elements. Global conditions (Meta or direct) are formed of operations. These operations provide a mechanism for identifying potential common parts among evaluation conditions. They are assigned a priority indicator to avoid ambiguity and to facilitate the execution of global conditions. A direct condition that can be associated to the evaluation set of our example could be NBR_INSTANCES(S1)<4, where NBR_INSTANCES is a predefined GDL function. In the GDL expression below corresponding to the condition, we start by finding the number of set instances captured from the parsed web page, then we test if it is smaller than 4.

```
<Direct_Condition set="S1">
    <Operation id="O1"
        Symbol="NBR_INSTANCES"
        return="number" Order="1">
    <Arg type="Set" value="S1"/>
    </Operation>
    <Operation id="O2"
        Symbol="<" return="Bool" Order="2">
        <Arg type="Operation" value="O1"/>
        <Arg type="number" value="4"/>
    </Operation>
</Direct_Condition>
```

5 Examples with Evaluation Improvement

5.1 Basic Examples with Meta Condition

The evaluation approach is now applied on two reasonably complex guidelines. The first one is: GDL1="Select colors that will make your page easy to read by people with color blindness"[10]. As such, GDL1 cannot be automated in a straightforward manner as there is no calculable way to assess to what extent a page is easy to read or not, depending on the users. However, if we refer to the research conducted by Murch [11], an interpretation Inter_GDL1 of this guideline can be produced: "The combination between background color and foreground color should belong to the best color combinations or should not belong to the worst color combinations proposed by Murch". This interpretation will not cover all colors because Murch dealt with basic color only, but we will use it for simplification. For Inter_GDL1, we have the following evaluation sets:

- S1controls text color over the whole page. S1={Body.bgcolor^{Page}, Body.text ^{Page}}.
```
<SET id="S1" name="Global color control" priority="AAA">
    <Element id="E1" tag="Body" Attribute="text" scope="Page"/>
    <Element id="E2" tag="Body" Attribute="bgcolor" scope="Page"/>
</SET>
```
- S2 controls color by Body and Font. S2={Body.bgcolor^{Page}, Font.color$^{Body. bgcolor}$}.
```
<SET id="S2" name="Body Font color control" priority="AAA">
    <Element id="E2" tag="Body" Attribute="bgcolor" scope="Page"/>
```

```
<Element id="E3" tag="Font" Attribute="color" scope="E2"/>
</SET>
```

The remaining evaluation sets can be obtained by analogy:

•• S3 controls color in Font and Table. S3={Table.bgcolor^{Page}, Font.color$^{Table.bgcolor}$}.

• ••S4: controls color in Font and TH. S4={TH.bgcolor^{Page}, Font.color$^{TH.bgcolor}$}.

••• S5: controls color in Font and TR. S5={TR.bgcolor^{Page}, Font.color$^{TR.bgcolor}$}.

••• S6: controls color in Font and TD. S6={TD.bgcolor^{Page}, Font.colorTD.^{bgcolor}}.

••• S7: controls color in Body and TH. S7={TH.bgcolor$^{Body.text}$, Body.text^{Page}}.

•• S8: controls color in Body and TR. S8={TR.bgcolor$^{Body.text}$, Body.text^{Page}}.

•• S9: controls color in Body and TD. S9={TD.bgcolor$^{Body.text}$, Body.text^{Page}}.

•• S10: controls color in Body and Table. S10={Table.bgcolor$^{Body.text}$, Body.text^{Page}}.

According to our experience with HTML 4.0, these sets cover all the possibilities provided by HTML to manipulate color of normal text (not links). So, we can consider that the evaluation of Inter_GDL1 (and thus GDL1) can be totally automated. The evaluation conditions associated with the above sets are very similar. Thus, we can define a Meta evaluation condition that can instantiated for every evaluation set by mapping the Meta variables to corresponding concrete set elements. The Meta evaluation condition corresponds to the next pseudo specification (PS):

```
(BackgroundColor IN ListOfMurchColors) AND
(ForegroundColor IN ListOfGoodColors(BackgroundColor)) OR
(ForegroundColor NOT IN ListOfBadColors(BackgroundColor))
```

where ListOfGoodColors and ListOfBadColors are two lists of predefined values (colors). As mentioned earlier in this section, we will use Murch color combinations. For this purpose, basic colors are defined as user values:

```
<User_V id="Black"    type="Color" val="#000000"/>
<User_V id="White"    type="Color" val="#ffffff"/>
<User_V id="Red"      type="Color" val="#ff0000"/>
<User_V id="Geen"     type="Color" val="#00ff00"/>
<User_V id="Blue"     type="Color" val="#0000ff"/>
<User_V id="Cyan"     type="Color" val="#00ffff"/>
<User_V id="Magenta"  type="Color" val="#ff00ff"/>
<User_V id="Yellow"   type="Color" val="#ffff00"/>
```

Then, we specify lists of values corresponding to Murch colors, good and bad foreground colors for a given background color:

```
<User_V id="MurchColors" type="Sequence"
        val="Black White Red Green Blue Cyan Magenta Yellow"/>
<User_V id="GoodFgBlackBg" type="Seq" val="White Yellow"/>
<User_V id="BadFgBlackBg"
        type="Sequence" val="Blue Red Magenta"/>
<User_V id="GoodFgWhiteBg"
        type="Sequence" val="Blue BlackRed"/>
<User_V id="BadFgWhiteBg"
        type="Sequence" val="Yellow Cyan"/>
<User_V id=?GoodFgRedBg?
        type="Sequence" val="White Yellow"/>
<User_V id="BadFgRedBg"
        type="Sequence" val=?Magenta Blue"/>
```

```
<User_V id="GoodFgGreenBg"
        type="Sequence" val="Black Blue Red"/>
<User_V id="BadFgGreenBg"
        type="Sequence" val="Magenta Cyan"/>
<User_V id="GoodFgBlueBg"
        type="Sequence" val="Green Red"/>
<User_V id="BadFgBlueBg"
        type="Sequence" val="Red Magenta"/>
<User_V id="GoodFgCyanBg"
        type="Sequence" val="White Yellow"/>
<User_V id="BadFgCyanBg"
        type="Sequence" val="Yellow White"/>
<User_V id="GoodFgMagentaBg"
        type="Sequence" val="White Black"/>
<User_V id="BadFgMagentaBg"
        type="Sequence" val="Green Red"/>
<User_V id="GoodFgYellowBg"
        type="Sequence" val="Black Blue"/>
<User_V id="BadFgYellowBg"
        type="Sequence" val="White Cyan"/>
```

Then, a meta condition can be defined corresponding to the above pseudo specification (PS). One will easily notice that specification of conditions is relatively long. This is due to our desire to provide a GDL specification language that is as flexible and rich as possible.

```
<Meta_Condition MC_ID="MurchModel">
    <Meta_Vars>
        <Meta_Var Name="BgColor" Type="Color"/>
        <Meta_Var Name="FgColor" Type="Color"/>
    </Meta_Vars>
    <Model Expression="">
        <Operation id="O1" Symbol="IN" return="Bool" Order="1"
                Stop_Val="False" Stop_Msg="Unrecognized Background color.">
            <Arg type="Var" value="BgColor" Pos="1">
            <Arg type="value" value="MurchColors" Pos="2">
        </Operation>
        <Operation id="O2" Symbol="IN" return="Bool" Order="2"
                Stop_Val="True" Stop_Msg="Good color combination.">
            <Arg type="Var" value="FgColor" Pos="1">
            <Arg type="value" value="GoodFg(BgColor)" Pos="2">
        </Operation>
        <Operation id="O3" Symbol="NOT IN" return="Bool" Order="3"
                Stop_Val="True" Stop_Msg="Not bad color combination.">
            <Arg type="Var" value="FgColor" Pos="1">
            <Arg type="value" value="BadFg(BgColor)" Pos="2">
        </Operation>
        <Operation id="O4" Symbol="OR" return="Bool" Order="3"
                Stop_Val="True" Stop_Msg="Good color combination." Stop_Val="False">
            <Arg type="Op" value="O2" Pos="1">
            <Arg type="Op" value="O3" Pos="2">
        </Operation>
        <Operation id="O5" Symbol="AND" return="Bool" priority="3">
            <Arg type="Op" value="O1">
            <Arg type="Op" value="O4">
        <Operation>
    </Model>
</Meta_Condition>
```

Notice that the above specification is long because we wanted to have complete control over the execution by using the concept of Stop Value that allows stopping the execution after any operation if its result corresponds to a given value. In this way, we can generate highly customised output messages via the Stop_Msg. The evaluation expression can also be specified as a single piece of text (the Expression attribute of the Model element) to be interpreted by the evaluation engine at execution time. This way is clearer and shorter than the above way, but the specified expression must respect a predefined syntax to be correctly interpreted. After defining the meta condition we instantiate it on every evaluation set via the mapping rules.

```
<Mapped_Condition Set_ID="S1" Meta_ID="MurchModel">
    <Meta_Mapping Meta="BgColor" Instance="E1"/>
    <Meta_Mapping Meta="FgColor" Instance="E2"/>
</Mapped_Condition>
<Mapped_Condition Set_ID="S2" Meta_ID="MurchModel">
    <Meta_Mapping Meta="BgColor" Instance="E1"/>
    <Meta_Mapping Meta="FgColor" Instance="E3"/>
</Mapped_Condition>
```

Other mappings can be defined similarly for the remaining sets. Let us know consider another guideline oriented toward accessibility: "Web pages shall be designed so that all information conveyed with color is also available without color" (Section 508). GDL2 needs to be interpreted as well. As the guideline suggests, information conveyed by color can be conveyed using markup. We will consider the following markup tags: Bold <b>, Italic <i>, text size <Font.size> and text font <Font.face>. Thus, the interpretation of GDL2 could become Inter_GDL2: "Web pages shall be designed so that all information conveyed with color is also available using any combination of the above markup elements". This means that, in our evaluation context, Inter_GDL2 is considered violated even if colored information was conveyed using other means than the above markup tags. For Inter_GDL2, we have the following evaluation sets:

- S1A: conveying colored information using bold tag.
```
<SET id="S1A" name="bold conveyance" Priority="AAA">
        <Element id="E1" tag="Body" Attribute="bgcolor" scope="Page"/>
        <Element id="E2" tag="Font" Attribute="color" scope="E1"/>
        <Element id="E3" tag="b" Attribute="" scope="E2"/>
</SET>
```
- S1B: conveying colored information using bold tag.
```
<SET id="S1B" name="bold conveyance" Priority="AAA">
        <Element id="E1" tag="Body" Attribute="bgcolor" scope="Page"/>
        <Element id="E3" tag="b" Attribute="" scope="E1"/>
        <Element id="E2" tag="Font" Attribute="color" scope="E3"/>
</SET>
```
- S2A: conveying colored information using italic tag.
```
<SET id="S2A" name="italic conveyance" Priority="AAA">
        <Element id="E1" tag="Body" Attribute="bgcolor" scope="Page"/>
        <Element id="E2" tag="Font" Attribute="color" scope="E1"/>
        <Element id="E4" tag="i" Attribute="" scope="E2"/>
</SET>
```
- S2B: conveying colored information using italic tag.
```
<SET id="S2B" name="italic conveyance" Priority="AAA">
        <Element id="E1" tag="Body" Attribute="bgcolor" scope="Page"/>
        <Element id="E4" tag="i" Attribute="" scope="E1"/>
```

```
            <Element id="E2" tag="Font" Attribute="color" scope="E4"/>
</SET>
```

- S3: conveying colored information using font face.

```
<SET id="S3" name="font face conveyance" Priority="AAA">
            <Element id="E1" tag="Body" Attribute="bgcolor" scope="Page"/>
            <Element id="E2" tag="Font" Attribute="color" scope="E1"/>
            <Element id="E5" tag="Font" Attribute="face" scope="E2"/>
</SET>
```

- S4: conveying colored information using font size.

```
<SET id="S4" name="font size conveyance" Priority="AAA">
            <Element id="E1" tag="Body" Attribute="bgcolor" scope="Page"/>
            <Element id="E2" tag="Font" Attribute="color" scope="E1"/>
            <Element id="E6" tag="Font" Attribute="size" scope="E2"/>
</SET>
```

Notice that we defined S1A and S1B to cover the case of bold tag. We needed to do so because the two expressions <Font color="...">Colored bold text</Font> and <Font color="...">Colored bold text</Font> give the same visual result. We did the same thing for italic tag. To specify the evaluation conditions, we can see that the evaluation logic is similar in all the above sets and it corresponds to the following pseudo condition: EXIST(FgColor, bgColor, Alternative) where alternative can be one of the HTML tags: b, I, Font.face, and Font.size. The XML form of this condition would be:

```
<Meta_Condition MC_ID="ColoredInfoModel">
    <Meta_Vars>
        <Meta_Var Name="BgColor" Type="Color"/>
        <Meta_Var Name="FgColor" Type="Color"/>
        <Meta_Var Name="Alternative" Type="HTML_Elem"/>
    </Meta_Vars>
    <Model Expression="Exist(FgColor, BgColor, Alternative) AND IN(Alternative, AltList)"/>
</Meta_Condition>
```

where EXIST is a predefined GDL function. AltList is the user value given as follows:

```
<User_V id="AltList" type="Sequence" val="b I Font.face Font.size"/>
```

Notice that the evaluation expression is provided a non structured text. As mentioned earlier, this is very simple but requires that the specified text respects the GDL syntax for text evaluation expression. After defining the Meta condition we instantiate it on every evaluation set via the mapping rules. We specify similar mappings for the remaining sets.

```
<Mapped_Condition Set_ID="S1A" Meta_ID="ColoredInfoModel">
    <Meta_Mapping Meta="BgColor" Instance="E1"/>
    <Meta_Mapping Meta="FgColor" Instance="E2"/>
    <Meta_Mapping Meta="Alternative" Instance="E3"/>
</Mapped_Condition>
<Mapped_Condition Set_ID="S1B" Meta_ID=" ColoredInfoModel ">
    <Meta_Mapping Meta="BgColor" Instance="E1"/>
    <Meta_Mapping Meta="FgColor" Instance="E2"/>
    <Meta_Mapping Meta="Alternative" Instance="E3"/>
</Mapped_Condition>
```

5.2   Evaluation Optimization

Decomposing the evaluation process into independent steps in the phases as described above offers the possibility for optimising evaluation at each of them.

Structuring step. As parsing web pages is based on evaluation sets and evaluation conditions defined in this step, we can optimise the evaluation at two levels: for a single guideline, there are two ways: identifying the minimum ensemble of sets needed to evaluate the targeted guideline, and expressing conditions in the most forward way to minimise the number of operations that evaluation engine would need to execute them. At the level of many guidelines, we can optimise evaluation by identifying common structures or sub-structures. This optimisation cannot be neglected since guidelines are expressed at a high abstraction level, and as they come from different sources, it is very possible to have guidelines that are totally or partially semantically identical.

Parsing step. The first significant optimization at this step is the use of the concept of *exclusion* among evaluation sets. By definition, one evaluation set *Excludes* one (many) other evaluation set(s) if its presence excludes its evaluation. This concept is based on the *Scope* concept related to HTML elements (tags and attributes). Generally, the excluding set has an element whose scope is within the scope of an element of the excluded set. Of course, these two elements must have the same rendering effect. For example (Fig. 3), in the context of text color evaluation, a set containing the attribute Table.bgcolor (like S1={Body.text, Table.bgcolor}) excludes a set containing the attribute Body.bgcolor (like S2={Body.bgcolor, Body.text}), because the scope of Table.bgcolor is within the scope of Body.bgcolor. The second optimisation is to combine parsing and evaluation in one step. This means that an evaluation condition is triggered as soon as an instance of the associated evaluation set is completely detected in the evaluated web page. This combination would be optional because, in some situations like the need for a detailed evaluation report, it is desired to capture all instances of evaluation sets (even non completed or negative ones).

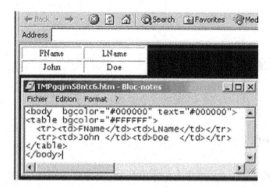

Fig. 3. Scope of Table.bgcolor is within the scope of Body.bgcolor

Evaluation step. The optimisation that can be done at this step relies mainly on optimising the execution of evaluation conditions. We introduced the concept of *basic*

condition to identify similar or identical parts of evaluation conditions. For example, in Inter_GDL 1 of our example, the evaluation conditions for S1 (Cond1) and S2 (Cond2) are very similar (same Body.bgcolor). As Cond1 will be executed before Cond2, the results of executing Cond1 can be kept if another instance of Cond2 is met with Font.color having the same value of Body.text. Fig. 4 shows how multiple instances of foreground and background colors can be evaluated positively (the color combination is one of the recommended ones), negatively (the color combination is not recommended at all), or unknown (the color combination does not belong to any recognised color pattern). In Fig. 4, we can observe that

- In instance !1, Table.bgcolor has no effect because TD.bgcolor overcomes it, but we captured Instance1 of Set3 because we did not considered TD in our evaluation sets. This is very easy to repair by modifying the formal structure.
- In instance !2, it useless in this example, because this combination has no effect.
- In instance !3, Set2 excludes Set1 and Set3, thus the instance of Font.color did not cause the creation of instances of Set1 or Set3.

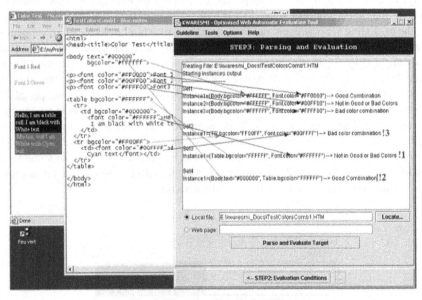

Fig. 4. Example of evaluation report

6   Conclusion

This paper presented an approach for optimizing automated evaluation of Web U&A guidelines based on the concepts of evaluation sets and conditions. This approach would present some advantages over approaches adopted by existing U&A evaluation tools:

- **Targeted guidelines**: traditional evaluation tools cannot evaluate any guideline outside the precompiled set of guidelines hard coded in the evaluation engine of the tool. As for a tool adopting our evaluation approach, its main distinctive feature is its capability to enable the evaluation of any evaluable guideline. A guideline is said to be *evaluable* if we can find HTML elements that reflect its semantics (e.g., the foreground and background colours) and if we can specify the needed evaluation conditions using the vocabularies provided by the evaluation tool. Thus, such a tool should at least be capable of evaluating guidelines that are evaluable by existing tools.

- **Improvement of the evaluation process**: using the same methodological framework to structure all guidelines enables us to obtain non conflicting structures: the structuring would show common evaluation sets and common evaluation conditions if some exist. Partially similar or conflicting guidelines can be identified as well. In this way, no guideline is evaluated twice and no evaluation condition will be checked more than once. We can also combine parsing and evaluation steps to stop evaluating a guideline if one of its evaluation conditions is not verified. This is useful for guideline checking, where there is only a need to know whether the guideline is verified, as opposed to guideline checking, where we want to know to what extent a guideline is respected.

- **Flexibility of the evaluation process**: separating evaluation logic from evaluation engine in independent phases gives many new evaluation possibilities like choosing to evaluate a part of a guideline by using a sub-set of its evaluation sets, choosing to evaluate particular HTML elements (e.g., images, tables) by selecting guidelines that have these elements in one of their evaluation sets, etc.

- **Customisation of evaluation reports**: the flexibility of our approach should allow us to generate a custom evaluation report (e.g., a possible simple format is given in Fig. 4). In addition to traditional guideline-based evaluation reports generated by existing evaluation tools, we should be able to generate reports based on objects (images, fonts), customised error messages, etc.

- **Identification of conflicts and similarities among guidelines**: expressing guidelines in a logical and structured form allows us to identify potential conflicts and/or common elements among guidelines.

- **Guidelines Management**: at anytime, a guideline can be added, removed or modified without consequence on the evaluation engine. This independence allows the evaluation system to import new sets of guidelines from outside into the tool repository.

References

1. ATRC, A-Prompt: Web Accessibility Verifier. Adaptive Technology Resource Center (University of Toronto) and Trace Center (University of Wisconsin), Canada & USA. Online at http://www.snow.utoronto.ca.

2. Beirekdar, A., Vanderdonckt, J., Noirhomme-Fraiture, M.: A Framework and a Language for Usability Automatic Evaluation of Web Sites by Static Analysis of HTML Source Code. In: Proceedings of 4th Int. Conf. on Computer-Aided Design of User Interfaces CA-DUI'2002 (Valenciennes, 15-17 May 2002). Kluwer Academics Pub., Dordrecht, 2002, pp. 337-348

3. Brajnik, G.: Automatic Web Usability Evaluation: Where is the Limit? In: Kortum, Ph., Kudzinger, E. (eds.): Proceedings of the 6th Conference on Human Factors & the Web (Austin, 19 June 2000). University of Texas, Austin, 2000. On-line at http://www.tri.sbc.com/hfweb/brajnik/hfweb-brajnik.html

4. Cooper, M.: Evaluating Accessibility and Usability of Web Sites. In: Proc. of 3rd Int. Conf. on Computer-Aided Design of User Interfaces CADUI'99 (Louvain-la-Neuve, 21-23 October 1999), Kluwer Academics Publisher, Dordrecht, pp. 33-42.

5. Forrester Research: Why most web sites fail. 1999. On-line at http://www.forrester.com/Research/ReportExcerpt/0,1082,1285,00.html

6. Ivory, M.Y., Hearst, M.A., State Of The Art In Automating Usability Evaluation Of User Interfaces. ACM Computing Surveys, 2001

7. Ivory, M.Y., Mankoff, J., Le, A.: Using Automated Tools to Improve Web Site Usage by Users With Diverse Abilities. IT&Society (Special Issue on Web Navigation Skills) 1,3 (Winter 2003) 195–236. On-line at http://www.stanford.edu/ group/siqss/itandsociety/v01i03/v01i03a11.pdf

8. Jackson-Sanborn, E., Odess-Harnish, K., Warren, N.: Website Accessibility: A Study of ADA Compliance. Technical Report TR-2001-05. School of Information and Library Science, University of North Carolina at Chapel Hill, 2001. On-line at http://ils.unc.edu/ils/research/reports/accessibility.pdf

9. Murch, G.M.: Colour Graphics - Blessing or Ballyhoo? The Visual Channel. In: Baecker, R.M., Buxton, W.A.S. (eds.): Readings in Human-Computer Interaction - A Multidisciplinary Approach. Morgan Kaufmann Publishers, Los Altos, 1987, pp. 333–341

10. Scapin, D., Leulier, C., Vanderdonckt, J., Mariage, C., Bastien, C., Farenc, C., Palanque, P., Bastide, R.: A Framework for Organizing Web Usability Guidelines. In: Kortum, Ph., Kudzinger, E. (eds.): Proceedings of the 6th Conference on Human Factors & the Web (Austin, 19 June 2000). University of Texas, Austin, 2000. On-line at http://www.tri.sbc.com/hfWeb/scapin/Scapin.html

11. Vanderheiden, G.C., Chisholm, W.A., Ewers, N., Dunphy, S. M., Unified Web Site Accessibility Guidelines, Version 7.2, Trace Center, University of Wisconsin-Madison, 1997. Online at http://trace.wisc.edu/text/guidelns/htmlgide/ htmlgide.htm

"I Need It Now": Improving Website Usability by Contextualizing Privacy Policies

Davide Bolchini[1], Qingfeng He[2], Annie I. Antón[2], and William Stufflebeam[2]

[1] TEC lab - Faculty of Communication Sciences - University of Lugano, Switzerland
davide.bolchini@lu.unisi.ch
[2] Requirements Engineering Research Group, NC State University, North Carolina, USA
{qhe2, aianton, whstuffl}@ncsu.edu

Abstract. Internet privacy policies are complex and difficult to use. In the eyes of end-users, website policies appear to be monolithic blocks of poorly structured texts that are difficult to parse when attempting to retrieve specific information. In an increasingly privacy-aware society, end-users must be able to easily access privacy policies while navigating a website's pages and readily understand the relevant parts of the policy. We propose a structured methodology to improve web design and increase user's privacy awareness. This systematic approach allows policy makers to effectively and efficiently reshape their current policies by structuring policies according to the subject that is relevant to specific user interaction contexts, making them more user-centered and user-friendly. The methodology is built upon prior work in privacy policy analysis and navigation context design.

1   Introduction

Privacy has become a more and more important issue and has recently received a lot of attention from consumers, government officials, legislators, and software developers due to concerns about increasing personal information collection from customers, information disclosure to third parties without user consent, and information transfer within and across organizations [5, 7, 8, 9].

Nowadays, most companies and organizations have posted one or more privacy policy documents on their websites. A privacy policy is a comprehensive description of a website's practices on collecting, using and protecting customer information. A privacy policy should define what information is collected and for what purpose, how this information will be handled, stored and used, whether customers are allowed to access their information collected by the website, how to resolve privacy-related disputes with this website, etc [6].

Unfortunately, current privacy policies published on websites are usually long and increasingly complex and difficult for users to understand. Research has found that many online privacy policies lack clarity and most requires a reading skill considerably higher than the Internet population's average literacy level [1]. There is a need to improve the current web design to help Internet users better navigate and understand website privacy policies and increase users' privacy awareness.

N. Koch, P. Fraternali, and M. Wirsing (Eds.): ICWE 2004, LNCS 3140, pp. 31–44, 2004.
© Springer-Verlag Berlin Heidelberg 2004

We further elaborate this problem from the following four aspects of privacy policies: (1) content, (2) structure, (3) navigation, and (4) accessibility.

1. *Content*. The language used in privacy policies is often difficult for users to understand (e.g. either too technical or too legal), thus preventing them from easily understanding the benefits and potential threats entailed by the submission of their personal data. As recent studies have demonstrated [1], website privacy policies are often ambiguous and conflicting, and therefore preventing users from understanding how their personal information will actually be treated.

2. *Structure*. Different websites use different ways to present their privacy practices to users. For example, some policies (see www.bn.com) firstly explain *what* information they collect, and then *how* the organization will use and share this information. Other policies (see www.buy.com) tell *where* on the site they will collect user information and then focus on the strategy and technology used to *protect* that information. Other sites (see www.amazon.com) organize their policy's content with a list of frequently asked questions (FAQs), abruptly varying from very general issues (such as the kind of information collected) to technical details (e.g. the use of cookies) in the attempt to promptly answer the recurrent issues raised by the website's customers. In most of the cases, whichever strategy is chosen to organize the content of the privacy policy, the structure presented to users takes the shape of a long document with several sections (sometimes split into different physical web pages). Putting all of a privacy policy's information into one document may be useful to get a general overview of the site's privacy practices, however, having such a structure, policy texts are generally difficult to be contextualized into usage scenarios (e.g. inserting credit card information while buying a product) in which users may be concerned about the treatment of specific data (e.g. protection and storage of credit card number).

3. *Navigation*. With a monolithic structure such as this, privacy policy *navigation* is context-independent: wherever a user is navigating on the site, she can only access the entire privacy policy document as it is. No matter what the user is doing on the site, the policy always tells the same story in the same order. The question is, is that really what the user needs? For example, if a user connects to a site and realizes that she is promptly recognized personally by the site as a returning customer (e.g. "Hi <user's name>, here are our recommendations for you), she may wonder how (and for how long) her session data and shopping habits are stored and used by the organization. To reach such information, the user must go to another page and read a long, and possibly confusing document explaining in very general terms the importance of privacy, the effort spent by the organization to protect personal data, the technology used, and the conditions of use of her personal data (any of which may or may not be relevant for the described context of use), etc. Because of this, it is clear that users in a situation like this are presented with significant hurdles to retrieve the information they are interested in, and thus will more likely make the decision to blindly proceed with their site visit, being uninformed as to how their personal information will be used.

4. *Accessibility. The accessibility* of privacy policies is also usually very poor. The link to the privacy document is often difficult to spot, many times being designed as a recurrent pattern, in small font at the very bottom of the page. Even if it is accessible from every page of the site, it is not relevant to specific website pages. Once accessed, the privacy policy is still difficult to parse when attempting to retrieve specific information, as discussed in the previous bullets.

Taking these four dimensions of the problem into account, we can now formulate more clearly the specific problem we wish to address in this work.

In general, concerning the requirements for a "usable" online privacy policy, we argue that *users should be assisted while browsing or shopping on the site by understanding the privacy issues relevant to the current context of interaction.* More specifically, we should *provide users with **direct** access to **relevant** portions of the privacy policy concerning the information exchanged within the current context.* We propose that instead of "tell me the whole story about this organization's privacy practices", websites policies should "tell me *now* how the site treats my data that I'm *now* concerned with".

This paper proposes a systematic approach, which is built upon an existing goal-based policy analysis method, to address the aforementioned issues. Our approach allows policy makers and web designers to reshape their current privacy policies according to subject matters, thus meeting the specific needs relevant to the contexts of users' interactions. The expected benefits of applying this structured methodology for policy design are in two aspects. On one hand, users can have a better understanding of websites' privacy practices by accessing the relevant information quickly and increase their privacy-awareness. On the other hand, websites can build the trust from end-users by specifying privacy policies in an easy to access, easy to understand way to satisfy users' specific privacy needs.

The remainder of the paper is structured as follows: Section 2 discusses relevant previous work on goal mining, a powerful technique to examine and analyze privacy policy content. Section 3 details the proposed methodology and the expected results of the approach. Examples of application and concrete results are presented in section 4. Finally, section 5 summarizes the method, discusses some limitations of this approach and outlines our plans for future work.

2 Related Work

Privacy policy analysis has not been paid enough attention until recently. Studies following a structured approach to privacy policy analysis led to the development of specific analysis techniques based on goal-oriented requirements engineering practices [1, 2, 3, 4]. These conceptual methods and tools, which are based on goal-mining, turned out to be particularly effective for examining website privacy policies.

Goals are objectives and targets of achievement for a system in requirements engineering. In the case of privacy policies, a goal describes a statement expressing a privacy practice having a coherent and unitary meaning. Goal mining refers to extracting goals from data sources (in this case, privacy policies) by applying goal-based requirements analysis methods. The extracted goals are expressed in structured natural language in the form of "VERB object" such as "COLLECT site usage information", "PREVENT storing credit card information using cookies", etc.

To identify goals, each statement in a privacy policy is analyzed by asking, *"What goal(s) does this statement or fragment exemplify?"* and/or *"What goal(s) does this statement obstruct or thwart?"*

All action words are possible candidates for goals. Goals in privacy policies are thus also identified by looking for useful keywords (verbs). The identified goals are worded to express a state that is true, or the condition that holds true, when the goal is realized. Consider *Privacy Policy #1* from the "Bank of America" Privacy Policy (www.bankofamerica.com):

Privacy Policy #1: Employees are authorized to access customer information only when they need it, to provide you with accounts and services or to maintain your accounts.

By asking the goal identification questions, we identify the goal **G144**: *PROVIDE access to CI (Customer Information) to authorized personnel with authorized roles* from Privacy Policy #1.

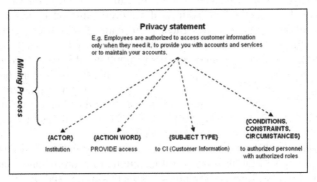

Fig. 1. Goal mining.

Figure 1 shows how a privacy statement is decomposed into four basic components of a privacy goal during the goal-mining process: *actor, action word, subject type,* and *conditions-constraints-circumstances.* The actor represents the stakeholder responsible for the goal to be achieved; the action word represents the type of activity described by the statement; the subject type describes the kind of user information at issue; finally, a goal usually recounts the conditions under which the goal actually takes place, the constraints to be respected, or other circumstances that provide the context to establish the scope of the goal.

The goal-mining process and the subject classification serve as the basis of the method proposed in this paper. This process of discovery, decomposition and representation cannot be entirely automated because it requires significant semantic content analysis. Goal-based analysis is best carried out by a team of analysts who do not simply chop each statement in a policy into pieces, but who carefully extract each statement's meaning, thus specifying goals that truly reflect the meaning of the original document. However, tool support can greatly enhance the efficiency of the goal mining process[1].

3 Crafting Usable Policies

Based on previous discussion, we believe that users may benefit from directly accessing the corresponding parts of the privacy policy that are relevant to the web page a user is currently on. In this section, we propose a method to structure website privacy policies according to the subject matters and make them easily accessible to users. The goal of the proposed methodology is to make the transition from monolithic, poorly structured privacy documents to agile units of privacy policy content relevant to the current usage scenarios.

3.1 A Process Overview

We have identified five steps that will help designers create context-dependent policies (see Figure 2 for an overview):

1. Analyze existing privacy policy and identify privacy goals (goal mining)
Goal mining is the first step of this process and it enables analysts to gather a repository of privacy goals that represents the organization's privacy policies. This process is shown as step 1 in Figure 2. The process, techniques and heuristics to extract privacy goals from policy statements were detailed in [2, 3, 4].

2. Organize goals by subject type
These goals may be organized according to different criteria. For example, goals may be clustered by actor, action word and subject type. Organizing goals by subject type, which describes the kind of user information that a goal concerns, appears to be a very promising strategy for our purposes. Examples of subject types are, for example, *PII (Personal Identifiable Information), credit card information, session data, purchase history, shipping data, account data, user preferences, usage habits* and *shopping habits, authentication information (e.g. user name and password),* etc. Other more domain-dependent subject types may be explored by analyzing policies from different application domains and business. For banking websites, for example, "bank account information" is particularly relevant, whereas it would not be relevant for B2C (business-to-consumer) type of e-commerce websites. In this step, we structure the collection of goals produced in step 1 according to the subject type. Each subject type is associated with a set of goals. It is noted that a goal could belong to more than one subject type. This process is shown as step 2 in Figure 2.

---

[1] In our approach, extracted goals are then documented in our Privacy Goal Management Tool (PGMT), a web-based tool developed at North Carolina State University. PGMT maintains a goal repository for analyses of policies and other documents from which goals can be derived. Each goal is associated with a unique ID, a description, a responsible actor, its sources and a privacy taxonomy classification.

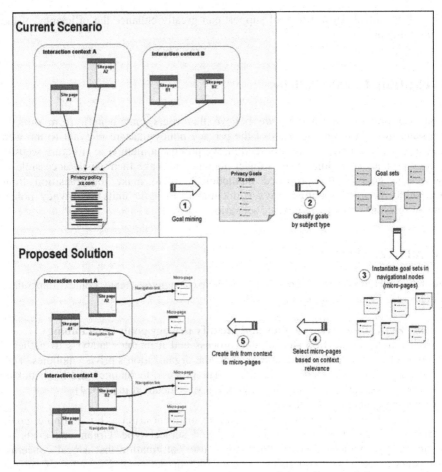

Fig. 2. A process overview for contextualizing privacy policies

3. Create a node for each goal set

Each set of goals (having the same subject type) may be compiled into a navigational node, a micro policy web page recounting the privacy goals in natural language.

4. Identify one or more contexts of user interaction that are relevant to a subject classification and associate them with the navigational node concerning that subject matter.

This is a crucial step, in which designers and policy makers must put themselves in user's shoes and envision the usage scenarios in which a user may need information about the organization's privacy policies (e.g., opening an account, purchasing a product, accessing personal information, modifying personal profile, etc.). Two lines of inquiry that may lead this task are:

    a)   *"For which task will a user need privacy policy information?"* The scenarios identified by answering this question usually take place in a given context of interaction, i.e., while a user is browsing a certain set of web pages. Therefore, the second line of inquiry becomes relevant.

b) *"Where in the site will a user need privacy policy information to accomplish his/her task"?* For example, on the page where a user is entering credit card information or on the set of pages concerning the selection of shipping and payment preferences.

Thus, the result of this step is the identification of contexts of interaction where users may need privacy information (the *when* and the *where*).

Of course, each context of interaction should be associated with the privacy policy content relevant for users to accomplish the task in a given context, and since we have created a navigational node for each potentially relevant subject type (see step 3), we can associate one or more goal sets with each navigational context identified.

5. Create a link from each page of a navigational context to the associated goal set(s).

Once an interaction context has its goal sets associated with it, it is necessary to create links from the pages of the interaction context to the pages of the associated goal sets. Once this is done, a user may easily and directly navigate from a given page to the policy information relevant to the task she is doing. The relationship between goal sets and context of interaction is bidirectional. On one hand, an interaction context (e.g. shopping cart) may be associated with multiple goal sets (e.g.- the privacy goals concerning "buying history" and the goals concerning "user buying preferences"). On the other hand, the same goal set (e.g. goals concerning "buying history") may concern several interaction contexts, such as "access to homepage" (where recommendations are provided on the basis of user's buying habits), "shopping cart" (where related items are provided), "wish list", "customized pages", etc.

Links to privacy policy micro-pages should be clearly visible and easily accessible to users while they are performing a task (i.e., not at the very bottom of the page in small font).

3.2 Modeling Expected Results

We now discuss the expected outcomes of this process. Consider a navigation context such as the "Purchase process" in a generic e-commerce website. After having selected one or more products to buy, user is typically guided through a number of steps to complete the transaction. Each step is usually setup in a navigational node (an individual web page in this case). In some of these nodes, the user is asked to enter, confirm or modify the information concerning the transaction: in one page, the user has to enter payment information (credit card number, expiration date, type of card, name of the cardholder); in the subsequent page the user has to enter shipping information such as full address for delivery, delivery methods, and so on.

Currently, if the user wants to know more about the collection, storage and the security of payment information when he is on the "payment information" page, he has to scroll down to the bottom of the page, spot the small "privacy notice" link and start reading the long policy document while trying to find some clues and keywords to reveal the content of interest.

To overcome this problem, in our approach, a clearly visible link (for example with a text anchor like "privacy of payment information") is placed on the "payment information" page and leads the user directly to the relevant privacy micro-page (e.g. a side page unit or a pop-up) telling the user how payment information is handled and stored (see Figure 3).

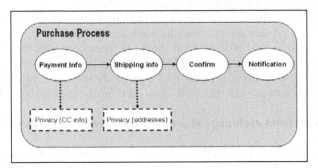

Fig. 3. Contextualized policy for the "Purchase process".

Additionally, in our approach policy may not only be made more accessible to the user, but the site might also raise awareness in the user about less-evident privacy practices, such as organization's privacy practices on session data. It is the case, as mentioned before, that the data about the user sessions (such as session time, IP, type of browser, information stored in cookies) are often associated to PII (Personal Identifiable Information) such as name, email, address, etc. Providing direct access to privacy information about these kinds of data helps raise user's privacy awareness on protecting their PII.

Likewise, on the homepage (which is often personalized through the use of session data) it may be relevant to have links to policy micro-pages concerning the treatment of session data. This may help users understand the reasons why the site gets increasingly customized as users access and provide information on various pages of the site, and for what other purposes this information is used by the organization.

The previously presented scenarios are intentionally generic to highlight the wide scope of applicability of the proposed methodology. The next section will focus on application examples taken from a well-known e-commerce website, thus defining more specific solutions and emphasizing the benefits for the user experience.

4 Application Examples

To demonstrate our approach, we now present some examples taken from an analysis of Amazon.com [10]. We have chosen this application because Amazon.com is a successful and typical e-commerce website familiar to most Internet users, which has a quite complex privacy policy and which may really benefit from adopting a contextualized perspective on its privacy communication. Although this is a specific case, most of the situations presented are likely common to many websites that gather user data for online transactions and better communication with their customers.

For each relevant interaction context, we will present contextualization solutions by detailing the following aspects:

- **Interaction context:** *web pages where the user may need specific and relevant policy information*
- **User issues:** *possible concerns of the user while navigating in the interaction context*
- **Link to relevant policy:** *a link available to the user pointing to relevant privacy policy micro-pages*
- **Policy micro-page content:** *the specific privacy information contained in the linked micro-pages (in terms of relevant privacy goals)*

The discussion of the examples is based on the assumption that web designers have applied our methodology described in Section 3 and produced sets of privacy goals according to the subject matters.

Scenario 1:

Let us consider the scenario in which a first time user of Amazon (a non-customer) connects to the site and declares her interest in a product by putting it in the shopping cart and then proceeds to check out. At this point, Amazon asks the user whether she is already an Amazon customer or not. The registration page for a new customer is shown in Figure 4.

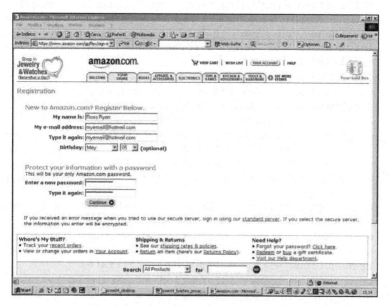

Fig. 4. Registration page for a new customer.

On this web page, a privacy-aware user might ask this question: how will Amazon use my name, email, date of birth and password? Currently, to clarify her issues the user has to know that at the very bottom of the page there is a link "Privacy Notice" that opens a page starting with the following section "What Personal Information About Customers Does Amazon.com Gather?" and then goes on with "What About

Cookies?" First, it is unlikely that a first time user (especially a non-frequent web surfer) knows a priori that by scrolling to the bottom of the page she will find the privacy policy link. Secondly, the privacy policy, as it is, presents the user with information that is completely irrelevant to her current context of use: the user already knows what kind of information Amazon is collecting from her; moreover, details on cookie use are not of interest to the user here. In the other two scenarios described in this section, there exists similar situation where the user has to scroll down to the very bottom of this page, find the small "Privacy Notice" link, and then read a long privacy policy statement to find the relevant information she needs to know.

Now let us examine this situation using our approach.

Interaction context (Figure 4): within the registration process, the user is on the new customer registration page.

User issues: "How will Amazon use my name, email, date of birth and password?"

Link to relevant policy: a link called "see how we treat your registration information" or "privacy for data exchanged in this form," positioned right beside or below the form.

Policy micro-page content: all privacy goals with subject matter {registration data}. Amazon's privacy policy contains the following privacy goals about this subject:

- G_{1349}: ALLOW customer to access personally identifiable information (including name, email, password, etc.)
- G_{1338}: AVOID companies and individuals who perform functions on our behalf using customer personal information for other purpose other than performing the specified functions
- G_{72}: AVOID selling customer information to others
- G_{748}: COLLECT information (e.g. personally identifiable information, assets, income, investment objectives, etc.) from forms submitted by customer (e.g. applications)
- G_{1339}: EMPLOY other companies and individuals to perform functions (such as processing credit card payments) on our behalf using customer information
- G_{88}: GUARD data during transmission using SSL encryption technology
- G_{1350}: SEND customer offers on behalf of other business without giving them name and address
- G_{639}: SHARE customer information among subsidiaries
- G_{168}: SHARE customer information related to your transactions with corresponding affiliates
- G_{492}: SHARE customer information as permitted by law
- G_{1132}: SHARE customer information with other organizations with customer consent
- G_{1351}: TRANSFER customer information as assets in case of buying/acquiring other companies or being acquired

Scenario 2:

In a different scenario, an existing customer may put products in the "Shopping Cart" while browsing the product catalog.

As soon as a product is put in the Shopping Cart, the user is presented with a page displaying suggestions of other potentially interesting products to put in the cart (Figure 5). Let us examine this situation.

Interaction context (Figure 5): Shopping cart suggestions.

User issues: "Amazon suggests several additional items for me to consider according to the purchase habits of other customers. For what other purposes will Amazon use information about my purchase habits?"

Link to relevant policy: a link called "privacy of your purchase history", positioned right below the page title "Customers who shopped for...also shopped for..."

Fig. 5. Amazon Shopping Cart suggestion page.

Policy micro-page content: all privacy goals having as subject matter: {user history or previous purchases, etc}.

Amazon's privacy policy contains five goals about this subject:

- G$_{1348}$: ALLOW customer to access recent product view history
- G$_{1347}$: ALLOW customer to access recent purchase history
- G$_{1344}$: ANALYZE purchase history
- G$_{487}$: COLLECT information about customer online account (e.g. balances, transactions, email, bills, payment history)
- G$_{1346}$: USE cookies to store items in your shopping cart between visits

Scenario 3:

Finally, let us consider one of the most debated issues in the treatment of consumer privacy: the handling and use of credit card information. Figure 6 shows the page where the user has to enter payment information such as credit card details.

Interaction context (Figure 6): "Shipping & Payment" page of the purchase process.

User issue: "How will Amazon use and protect my credit card information?"

Link to relevant policy: a link called "Privacy of credit card information" positioned right beside the question "Paying with a credit card?" (see Figure 8).

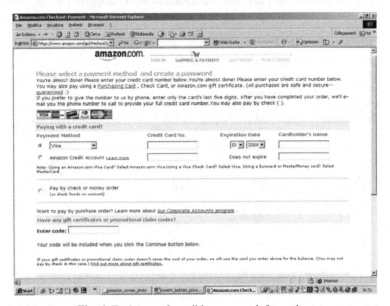

Fig. 6. Exchange of sensible payment information.

Policy micro-page content: all privacy goals having as subject matter: {credit card or user payment information}

Amazon's privacy policy contains the following privacy goals about this subject:

- G_{1337}: ALLOW customer to access payment settings (including credit card information, etc.)
- G_{1338}: AVOID companies and individuals who perform functions on our behalf using customer personal information for other purpose other than performing the specified functions
- G_{37}: COLLECT credit card information for billing
- G_{1339}: EMPLOY other companies and individuals to perform functions (such as processing credit card payments) on our behalf using customer information
- G_{88}: GUARD data during transmission using SSL encryption technology

- G₁₃₄₁: REVEAL only the last five digits of your credit card numbers when confirming an order
- G₁₃₄₂: USE credit history information from credit bureaus to help prevent and detect fraud
- G₁₃₄₃: USE credit history information from credit bureaus to offer credit or financial services to customers

Once selected, goals may be properly rephrased from their formal structure to a fluent narrative to make them more understandable for the user.

5 Summary and Future Work

Most online privacy policies are poorly structured, hard to understand, long documents that do not satisfy end-user's need for a concise policy statement for specific context. In this paper, we present a new method to analyze privacy policies to produce privacy goals, and then structure these goals according to the subject matters. By doing this, web designers can associate the context of web page to appropriate privacy goal sets that concerns the current subject.

This method is based on a structured and validated policy analysis process. This ensures the completeness and consistency of the goal sets displayed in policy micro-pages.

Both users and organizations can benefit from applying the proposed methodology in web design.

For users, they quickly get direct access to the relevant policy information at the right time (i.e. when they need it). This enhanced accessibility makes policies more and more visible to the users, thus raising overall awareness of Internet users to many privacy concerns. It also helps users evaluate the privacy practices declared by the organization in a much more straightforward manner.

Applying the proposed methodology (or even simply adopting the general idea), organizations can more easily evaluate the coverage of their privacy policy. By analyzing the different interaction contexts, site stakeholders have the opportunity to verify whether or not their policy contains information relevant for the user in that given context, not just generic and essentially useless information about privacy. A contextualized policy also builds trust of users to websites, since it communicates more clearly with site privacy practices, showing attention to the concrete needs of the user. Finally, contextualizing policies means enhancing the user experience on the site, providing more (or less) reasons for visitors to become customers.

The methodology we proposed and results gathered so far are even more useful for multi-channel applications, which are increasingly available on a variety of smaller devices, such as PDAs, handhelds, and smart phones. The visualization and interaction requirements of such devices pose more strict constraints to user's capability of interacting with and reading long documents such as privacy policy. In these cases, the contextualization and design of agile mini-policies are very important to make privacy policy really usable to end-users.

The method has yet to be empirically validated on large scale and across different domains through the validation of prototypes and usability testing. Moreover, return-of-investment (ROI) for this change in policy communication still needs to be evaluated.

For future work, we are looking for other relevant interaction contexts where contextualized privacy policies can play a key role in improving user experiences. We are going to apply this methodology to other domains, such as banking and financial institutions websites, which we have already conducted goal-mining and privacy policy analysis studies.

One further extension of the approach that may be explored is that semantic associations between goal sets may further enhance privacy policy usability. For example, the "session data privacy" micro-page may be linked to the "recommendation system" privacy micro-page used by the organization, which exploits session data. Similarly, the "Recommendation system privacy" micro-page may be linked to the "shopping habits privacy" micro-page, since recommendations are built on previous shopping habits of the user, and so on. Such design solutions may lead to a privacy policy whose agile navigation highlights even more the semantics underlying the privacy practices.

References

[1]   A.I. Antón, J.B. Earp, D. Bolchini, Q. He, C. Jensen and W. Stufflebeam. The Lack of Clarity in Financial Privacy Policies and the Need for Standardization, Accepted, to appear in: *IEEE Security & Privacy*, 2004.

[2]   A.I. Antón and J.B. Earp. A Requirements Taxonomy to Reduce Website Privacy Vulnerabilities. To Appear: Requirements Engineering Journal, Springer Verlag, 2003.

[3]   A.I. Antón, Q. He, and D. Bolchini. The Use of Goals to Extract Privacy and Security Requirements from Policy Statements, Submitted to: *the 12th IEEE International Requirements Engineering Conference (RE'04)*, January 2004.

[4]   A.I. Antón, J.B. Earp and A. Reese. Analyzing Web Site Privacy Requirements Using a Privacy Goal Taxonomy. 10th Anniversary IEEE Joint Requirements Engineering Conference, Essen, Germany, 9-13 September 2002.

[5]   J.B. Earp and D. Baumer. Innovative Web Use to Learn about Consumer Behavior and Online Privacy. *Communications of the ACM*, 46(4), April 2003.

[6]   The Code of Fair Information Practices, U.S. Department of Health, Education and Welfare, Secretary's Advisory Committee on Automated Personal Data Systems, Records, Computers, and the Rights of Citizens, viii, http://www.epic.org/privacy/consumer/ code_fair_info.html, 1973.

[7]   Privacy Online: A Report to Congress, http://www.ftc.gov/ reports/privacy3/, Federal Trade Commission, June 1998.

[8]   National Telecommunications and Information Administration. A Nation Online: How Americans Are Expanding Their Use of the Internet, http://www.ntia.doc.gov/ntiahome/dn/ Washington, D.C. February 2002.

[9]   W.F. Adkinson, J.A. Eisenach and T.M. Lenard. Privacy online: A Report on the Information Practices and Policies of Commercial Web Sites. Washington, DC: Progress & Freedom Foundation, 2002. Downloaded July 18, 2003: http://www.pff.org/publications/privacyonlinefinalael.pdf.

[10]   Amazon.com, Inc., http://www.amazon.com, Last visit: February 17th 2004.

A Linear Regression Model for Assessing the Ranking of Web Sites Based on Number of Visits

Dowming Yeh, Pei-Chen Sun, and Jia-Wen Lee

National Kaoshiung Normal University
Kaoshiung, Taiwan 802, Republic of China
{dmyeh, sun}@nknucc.nknu.edu.tw

Abstract. Many web sites are designed and established without sufficient professional skills and resources. The quality of these websites is often dubious. Therefore, how to evaluate the quality of a web site has become an important issue. In this work, the stepwise regression method is applied to assess the ranking of web sites for two different categories. The ranking is based on the average number of visits per day. A total of fourteen factors frequently found in the literature are considered as independent variables in developing the model. The regression analysis result shows that the regression models differ for two different categories of web sites, but there are three variables common to the two resulting models, Latest update, Broken links, and Help features. The average prediction accuracies of both models exceed 75%.

1 Introduction

Constructing a web site are nowadays straightforward, demanding few technological efforts. Besides professional developers, there are more and more amateurs engaged in the production of many web sites [1]. Although the number of sites flourishes extensively, the content and the quality of some sites do not improve simultaneously. Therefore, how to evaluate the quality of a web site has become an important issue [4].

A web site should be evaluated from both the content and the design of the site [5]. The content covers the content of an entire site as well as an individual web page. The characteristics of the content for the entire site include not only the information content, but also support for transaction and elements of entertainment [1]. The content of a web page comprises of elements of text, color, graphics, mages, audio, animation, and so on. The criteria for assessing the content include correctness, periodical update, completeness, organization and clearness, attractiveness, value [3].

The design of a web site consists of the interface or the layout design of web pages and the navigational design of web sites. It could be evaluated in four aspects [6]: usability, functionality, reliability, and efficiency. Usability concerns how to assist users in using the site effectively. Functionality includes search and navigational mechanisms. Reliability addresses the correctness of the link and the errors incurred

N. Koch, P. Fraternali, and M. Wirsing (Eds.): ICWE 2004, LNCS 3140, pp. 45–49, 2004.

by different configurations. Efficiency tackles factors that might affect the download speed of web pages and the accessibility of the information on a page. Ivory and Hearst evaluate web pages with 11 measures covering both the content and the design aspects [2]. In this work, the stepwise regression method is applied to assess the ranking of web sites for two different categories in Taiwan. The ranking is based on the average number of visits per day. Such ranking represents somehow the ranking of user satisfaction, and therefore the quality of a web site.

2 Research Variables

An indicator of the ranking of web site may be based on how often the site is utilized, which reflects true opinions of real users somewhat. Therefore, we base the dependent variable on the average number of visits per day to a web site during a span of three months. Because the number of visits varies enormously for top sites and poor sites, we map these numbers into their ranking positions instead of the using the actual numbers. The definition of the variable follows:

$$Y_i = 100 - \frac{100}{(n-1)} \times (i-1)$$

Y_i is the score of the i-th ranked in the set of sites, and n is the number of web sites in the set under study.

The possible values for independent values are all scaled to the range from 0 to 100 for easier manipulation and exploration of the model. There are a total of fourteen independent variables under consideration as follows:

1. Site map: A numerical function X_1 is defined to be 100, if the site provides a site map or a TOC; 50, if the site provides a navigational menu; 0, if none is provided.
2. Help feature: The corresponding function X_2 is given as 100, if providing organized help feature such as FAQ; 80, providing interactive help feature such as bulletin board; 60, providing email and responding within a week; 40, providing email and responding more than a week; 0, providing none.
3. Latest update: We define its function X_3 to be 100, updated within 3 days; 75, updated within a month; 50, updated within 3 months; 25, updated within a year; 0, otherwise (including no update indication).
4. Font count: Function X_4 is defined as $100 - 20 \times |n - 3|$, where n is the number of fonts and $1 \leq n \leq 7$; 0, otherwise.
5. Color count: Function X_5 is defined to be $100 - 20 \times |n - 7|$, where n is the number of colors and $3 \leq n \leq 11$; 0, otherwise.
6. Foreign Language Support: The corresponding function X_6 is defined to be 100, if providing both English and Simplified Chinese versions; 80, if providing English or Simplified Chinese version, plus another version for other language; 60, if providing English or Simplified Chinese version; 0, otherwise.
7. Search mechanisms: Function X_7 is given as 100, if providing search mechanism covering the entire site; 50, if providing search mechanism covering part of the site (bulletin board, for example); 0, if providing none.

8. Link count: The corresponding function X_8 is defined as in [6].
9. Scrolling: Let n be the ratio of the length of the page divided by the length of the screen. The function X_9 is 100, if $n \leq 3$; $100 - 15 \times (n - 3)$, if $4 \leq n \leq 6$; $55 - 10 \times (n - 6)$, if $7 \leq n \leq 8$; $35 - 5 \times (n - 8)$, if $9 \leq n \leq 10$; 0, otherwise.
10. Word count: We define the variable X_{10} as (n is the total word count) 100, if $651 \leq n \leq 1300$; $100 - 20 \times \text{ceiling}((n - 1300) / 650)$, if $1301 \leq n \leq 3900$; 80, if $326 \leq n \leq 650$; 60, if $160 \leq n \leq 325$; 40, if $n < 160$; 0, otherwise.
11. Broken link: We adopt the function proposed by Olsina et al. in [6] as X_{11}.
12. Static page size: Function X_{12} is defined as (let the size be n) 100, if $n \leq$ 80 KB; 90, if 80 KB $< n \leq$ 100 KB; $100 - 10 \times \text{truncate}(n / 50 \text{ KB})$, if 100 KB $< n \leq$ 500 KB; 0, otherwise.
13. Image label: The function proposed by [6] is used as X_{13}.
14. Number of panes regarding frames: Function X_{14} is the same as that Olsina et al. propose [6].

Our initial regression model therefore takes the following from:

$$Y = b_0 + b_1 X_1 + b_2 X_2 + b_3 X_3 + b_4 X_4 + b_5 X_5 + b_6 X_6 + b_7 X_7 + b_8 X_8 + b_9 X_9 + b_{10} X_{10} + b_{11} X_{11} + b_{12} X_{12} + b_{13} X_{13} + b_{14} X_{14}$$

3 Data Analysis

The source data of this research comes from a web site called HotRank (http://www.hotrank.com.tw). HotRank maintains visit information for several thousand web sites. Theses web sites are further classified into different categories from which two categories, *academy and literature* and *shopping* are chosen. The sites that appear in the seasonal ranking list from January to March 2003 are chosen as sample data.

To ensure the uniformity of the visit data, we further requires that the chosen sites are operational since January 1st 2003. The number of sites in the academy and literature category conforming to the condition stated above is 305. However, all sites ranked after the 90th position are eliminated because their average number of visits per day falls to zero and other sites failing to provide the average number of visits per day are also taken out. After reduction, there are a total of 60 sites from the academy and literature category. Similarly for the shopping category, the number of sites reduces to 198. We randomly select 30 sites respectively from two categories to conduct regression analysis. Some of the data for the independent variables result from average values of the homepage and other nine pages randomly selected from the site.

Before the stepwise regression analysis, the Pearson analysis is performed and the results indicate that all the interdependency values between any two independent variables are less than 0.55, so there is no collinear relationship between any two of the fourteen independent variables. Therefore, it is appropriate to consider all these variables in the stepwise regression analysis. The Durbin-Watson (DW) test is employed to examine that the error e_i of independent variables should not be self-related. From our analysis, the DW values of the models for the academy and literature category and shopping category are 1.476 and 1.589, respectively. This reveals that there is no significant self-relation in the two models and the prediction of the models can be trustworthy. Results of the stepwise regression analysis are described in the following paragraphs.

F test examines the overall regression model, also called as Analysis of Variance (ANOVA). The F values of the analysis result are 20.324 and 20.637 respectively for the academy and the shopping categories. Both of the P-Values are less than 0.005. Therefore, the linear relationships of our models are well established.

The coefficient of multiple determinations measures the proportion that independent variables are able to explicate the dependent variable. Another related measure is the adjusted coefficient of determination, which is considered more representative than the coefficient of determination. Applying these measures, the coefficient of multiple determination and adjusted coefficient of determination for the model of the academy and literature category are 0.765 and 0.727, respectively. As for the shopping category, the coefficient of multiple determinations and adjusted coefficient of determination are 0.768 and 0.730, respectively. This indicates that the independent variables in the models can account for around 73 % of the dependent variable.

Finally, the t test is to examine whether there is a significant linear relationship between every independent variable and the dependent variable. If there is no significant linear relationship between an independent variable Xi and the dependent variable Y, the coefficient of the variable b_i should be set to zero. Applying the t test to all the fourteen independent variables, the result shows that the final regression model of the academy and literature category is

$Y = - 58.308 + 0.493 \times Last\_update + 0.472 \times Broken\_links + 0.219 \times Site\_map + 0.475 \times Help\_feature$

And the model for the shooping category is

$Y = - 46.345 + 0.494 \times Help\_feature + 0.371 \times Static\_page\_Size + 0.378 \times Last\_update + 0.259 \times Broken\_links$

The adjusted coefficients of determination of the two models are 0.727 and 0.730, respectively. Considering the diversities of web sites, such degree of accounting precision is well acceptable.

In order to check the applicability of our model, another 15 sample sites are randomly selected for each category from the set of sites that is not selected previously in establishing the models. We apply the model to predict the rankings of these sites and compare them with the actual rankings. The result shows that the average prediction accuracy of the model for the academy and literature category is 76.0 %, and that of the model for the shopping category is 79.2 %.

4   Discussions and Conclusions

The difference of the independent variables in the two models suggests that there are indeed different indicators for different categories of web sites and the effects of these indicators are also different. There are three variables common to the two resulting models, Latest update, Broken links, and Help features. These three variables address different aspects of a site, information, reliability and usability, respectively. This implies a good web site must excel in various aspects. Latest update involves the content of the web site and more specifically how often the content of the site is updated. In a fast changing world, this is certainly a great concern to the site users. Broken links address the reliability issue as well as the correctness of the content in a web site. It is always frustrating for users to chase after a link only to find it leads to nowhere. Help features, on the other hand, tackle the usability of a web site. As the a web site evolve in functionality and complexity, usability issues commonly found in software applications surface inevitably and online help plays an important part in usability of a software system.

The Site map variable address yet another important aspect of a web site, i.e., navigation issues. The reason that it is not present in the model of the shopping category is that the content of sites in this category map directly to a hierarchical structure reflecting the structure of product catalogue. However, the static page size is a significant factor for these online shopping sites. A page with an immense number of bytes would take time to download, which is not contradictory to the efficiency that most online shopper expects. While we may imagine users in the sites of the academy and literature category to be more leisurely when they surf these sites, thus efficiency is not a great concern.

We apply linear regression method for assessing the ranking of a web site based on the number of visits per day. A total of fourteen factors frequently found in the literature are considered as independent variables in developing the model. The regression analysis result shows that the regression models differ for two different categories of web sites. The average prediction accuracy of the model for the academy and literature category is 76.0%, and that of the model for the shopping category is 79.2%.

References

1. Huizingh, E. K. R. E., "The content and design of web sitesan empirical study," *Information & Management* 37, 2000, pp.123-134.
2. M.Y. Ivory, R.R. Sinha, and M.A. Hearst, "Empirically Validated Web Page Design Metrics," *Proc. Conf. Human Factors in Computing Systems*, vol. 1, ACM Press, New York, Mar. 2001, pp. 53-60.
3. Katerattanakul, P. and Siau, S., "Measuring information quality of web sites: development of an instrument, " Proceeding of the 20th international conference on Information Systems, January 1999, pp.279-285.
4. Lin, J. C., and Lu, H., "Towards an understanding of the behavioral intention to use a web site," *International Journal of Information and management* 20, 2000, pp.197-208.
5. McMurdo, G., "Evaluation web information and design," *Journal of Information Science*, 24(3), 1998, pp.192-204.
6. Olsina, L., Godoy, D., Lafuente, G. J., and Rossi, G., "Quality Characteristics and Attributes for Academic Web Sites," *Proc. Of Web Engineering Workshop at WWW8*, Toronto, Canada, 1999.

A Framework for Exploiting Conceptual Modeling in the Evaluation of Web Application Quality

Pier Luca Lanzi, Maristella Matera, and Andrea Maurino

Dipartimento di Elettronica e Informazione, Politecnico di Milano
P. zza L. da Vinci 32, 20133 - Milano - Italy
{lanzi,matera,maurino}@elet.polimi.it

Abstract. This paper illustrates a method and a toolset for quality evaluation of Web applications that exploits conceptual specifications, deriving from the adoption of model-based development methods, for the evaluation in pre- and post- delivery phases.

Keywords: Conceptual Modeling, Web Application Quality, Web Usage Mining.

1 Introduction

The ever-increasing spread of the Web asks for new methods for improving the quality of Web applications. Conceptual modeling improves the quality of final applications by fostering regularity and the definition and reuse of effective solutions. However, little attention has been put on using conceptual specifications for enhancing the evaluation activities occurring throughout the whole development process.

Wa have defined a model-based framework that exploits conceptual schemas for evaluating Web applications both at design time and after the application deployment [6, 7]. This paper illustrates some recently introduced components that assist evaluation activities performed after application deployment. More specifically, such components elaborates Web usage logs enriched through meta-data deriving from the application conceptual schema.

Our evaluation framework has been defined for a specific conceptual model, WebML [2], and has been implemented extending a commercial CASE tool [8]. WebML offers a set of visual primitives for defining conceptual schemas that represent the organization of the application contents and of the hypertext interface. The organization of data is expressed though the Entity-Relationship model (E-R). The hypertext is then specified by composing elementary pieces of contents retrieved from the database, called *content units*, to form *pages*. WebML primitives are also provided with an XML representation that specifies additional properties, not conveniently expressible in the visual notation.

This paper introduces the Web log analysis covered by our evaluation framework, and shortly describes the architecture of an accompanying tool-set supporting the automatic execution of the proposed evaluation method. A deeper description, as well as results of applying the quality evaluation method to real-life Web applications can be found in [5].

N. Koch, P. Fraternali, and M. Wirsing (Eds.): ICWE 2004, LNCS 3140, pp. 50–54, 2004.

2   The Evaluation Framework

Our evaluation framework supports three kinds of analysis, based on the knowledge of the application conceptual schema.

In the pre-delivery phase, the *Design Schema Analysis* (DSA) verifies the correctness and the internal coherence of specifications [3,6]. It operates directly on conceptual schemas by looking for design errors and inconsistency.

In the post-delivery phase, evaluation still exploits the schema knowledge. Thanks to an advanced logging mechanism extending the runtime engine of WebML applications, Web logs are enriched with meta-data related to the application conceptual schema, thus obtaining the so-called *conceptual logs* [7]. The evaluation then focuses on such enriched logs, according to two techniques:

- *Web Usage Analysis* (WUA) produces reports on content access and navigation paths followed by users.
- *Web Usage Mining* (WUM) applies mining techniques for discovering interesting (sometimes unexpected) associations between accessed data. The aim is to identify possible amendments for accommodating newly discovered user needs.

The peculiarity of the post-delivery evaluation is the exploitation of *conceptual logs*, defined as XML-based "enriched" Web logs that integrate the conventional HTTP log data, generated by Web servers in ECLF (Extended Common Log Format) format, and meta-data about the computation of page contents. As can be seen in Figure 1, for each requested page such meta-data include: *i)* identifiers of the page and of its content units, as resulting from the application conceptual schema, that provide references to detailed properties defined in the conceptual schema but not traced by the logging mechanism; *ii)* primary keys of database instances used at runtime to populate content units.

DSA has been illustrated in [3,6]. Therefore, in the next subsections we concentrate on the two analysis approaches operating over *conceptual logs*.

2.1   Web Usage Analysis

WUA analyzes conceptual logs for computing access reports on user content access and user navigation paths. The main objective is identifying the contents most requested by users and evaluating if the hypertext design accommodates such user needs.

WUA comes in two flavors: *Access Analysis*, and *Navigation Analysis*.

Access Analysis computes traffic statistics, with the aim of verifying if the communication goals the Web application has been designed for are supported by the hypertext interface. The model-based approach, which distinguishes between data modeling and hypertext modeling, allows performing:

- *Data Access Analysis*: it computes statistics for the access to data schema entities and their specific instances.
- *Hypertext Access Analysis*: it focuses on the usage of the hypertext elements (content units, pages, areas) publishing specific data elements.

```
1  <Logs>
2    <Request id_P="3178">
3      <Page SchemaRef="page33"/>
4      <LocalTime>
5        ... ...
6      </LocalTime>
7      <User>
8        ... ...
9      </User>
10     <PageUnits>
11       <Unit>
12         <Unit_Id SchemaRef="data_unit84"/>
13         <DataInstance>17</DataInstance>
14       </Unit>
15       <Unit>
16         <Unit_Id SchemaRef ="index_unit9"/>
17         <DataInstance>10</DataInstance>
18         <DataInstance>5</DataInstance>
19         <DataInstance>9</DataInstance>
20       </Unit>
21     </PageUnits>
22   </Request>
23   ... ...
24 </Logs>
```

Fig. 1. Extract from the conceptual logs.

It therefore results that our Access Analysis extends the statistics normally offered by state-of-the-practice traffic analyzers, which mostly address page visits, and do not log database instances populating dynamic pages.

Navigation Analysis then verifies if the hypertext topology supports content accessibility. It reconstructs navigation paths adopted by users for reaching core application contents, with the aim of identifying if end users exploit navigation paths embodied within the designed hypertext, or else adopt alternative access mechanisms. The reconstruction of the user interaction results to be precise and detailed, as it exploits the conceptual schema of the application hypertext. Also, reconstructed user paths, as well as the identified problems, are represented on top of the visual specification of the conceptual schema; this facilitates the comparison between the designed hypertext and its actual use by users.

2.2 Web Usage Mining

WUM operates on conceptual logs, and applies XML mining techniques [1] for discovering interesting (sometimes unexpected) associations among visited hypertext elements and accessed data. The execution of mining tasks produces:

– *XML association rules* of the form $X \Rightarrow Y$, stating that when the log element X (called the *rule body*) is found, it is likely that the log element Y (called the *rule head*) will be also found. Depending on the adopted mining statement, the retrieved association can be related to database entities or instances, hypertext components (areas, pages, content units), or also hypertext components coupled with their populating data instances.

- *XML sequential patterns*, whose rule body and head are also bounded to their position in the log sequence, thus representing temporal relations.

Based on such rules, so far we have focused on two mining tasks:

- Finding data that are often accessed together, considering as transaction a user request, implemented through the mining of association rules between data entities and instances accessed within the same user session. It is worth noting that such associations are not easily discovered in traditional logs that do not record data instances used to populate dynamic Web pages, and generally require several post-processing efforts.
- Analyzing user navigation sequences for accessing some core information contents, by mining sequential patterns related to sequences of pages and content units within the same user session. The WebML characterization of information concepts and content units allows filtering sequences, concentrating the analysis on relevant navigation paths leading to some selected core concepts.

3   The Framework Architecture

The software architecture of our evaluation framework is organized in three distinct layers:

- The *Data Extraction Layer* gathers inputs needed for evaluation (Web server access, logged execution data, the application conceptual schema and the application data source), and transforms them into the format required by the three analysis techniques. It also generates conceptual logs.
- The *Analysis Layer* includes software components for the execution of DSA, WUA and WUM over data gathered through the Data Extraction Layer.
- The *Result Visualization Layer* allows evaluators to invoke the different analysis tasks and shows graphically the analysis results, through a graphical user interface.

Some XML repositories enable the interaction between layers:

- The *Analysis Data Warehouse* stores inputs gathered and elaborated by the Data Extraction Layer, represented in XML format.
- The *Result Warehouse* stores the results produced by the Analysis Layer in XML format. Such data are then used by the graphical user interface for generating and visualizing the analysis reports.
- The *Analysis Tasks Repository* stores the analysis procedures that can be expressed both in XSL and XQuery.

The ubiquitous use of XML technologies improves the number of strategies the evaluator can adopt in order to manipulate and query data. Also, the quality evaluation framework results to be very flexible and extensible: new analysis tasks can be easily specified and added to the framework. Therefore, each design team can define its own quality criteria, code their measures in XSL or XQuery, two extensively used W3C standards, and adding them within the the *Analysis Tasks* repository. Additionally, the use of warehouses between layers improves the framework extensibility, since it is possible to add new software modules, for example for performing new kinds of analysis, without affecting other components.

4   Conclusion

During last years, several methods and tools have been proposed for the analysis of Web logs [4]. The majority of them are however traffic analyzers. In addition to calculating traffic statistics, our Web Usage Analysis is able to compute advanced statistics, related to database entities and instances, and to hypertext components of any granularity.

Thanks to the intensive use of the application conceptual schema, our framework introduces a number of advantages also with respect to Web usage mining. Several data mining projects have demonstrated the usefulness of a representation of the structure and content organization of a Web application [4].

Our future work will concentrate on the incremental enrichment of the statistics and mining tasks for analyzing Web usage data. We are also working on the improvement of the graphical user interface, for allowing designers to define new analysis tasks though a visual paradigm, without the need of manual XSL and XQuery programming.

References

1. D. Braga, A. Campi, S. Ceri, M. Klemettinen, and P. Lanzi. A Tool for Extracting XML Association Rules. In *Proc. of ICTAI'02, November'02, Crystal City, USA*. IEEE Computer Society, 2002.
2. S. Ceri, P. Fraternali, A. Bongio, M. Brambilla, S. Comai, and M. Matera. *Designing Data-Intensive Web Applications*. Morgan Kauffmann, 2002.
3. S. Comai, M. Matera, and A. Maurino. A Model and an XSL Framework for Analyzing the Quality of WebML Conceptual Schemas. In *Proc. of the ER'02-IWCMQ'02 Workshop, Tampere, Finland, October'02*, LNCS. Springer, 2002.
4. R. Cooley. The Use of Web Structures and Content to Identify Subjectively Interesting Web Usage Patterns. *ACM TOIT*, 3(2), May 2003.
5. P. Fraternali, P. Lanzi, M. Matera, and A. Maurino. Model-Driven Web Usage Analysis for the Evaluation of Web Application Quality. Technical Report, Polytechnic of Milan, April 2004.
6. P. Fraternali, M. Matera, and A. Maurino. WQA: an XSL Framework for Analyzing the Quality of Web Applications. In *Proc. of ECOOP'02-IWWOST'02 Workshop, Malaga, Spain, June'02*, 2002.
7. P. Fraternali, M. Matera, and A. Maurino. Conceptual-level Log Analysis for the Evaluation of Web Application Quality. In *Proc. of LA-Web'03, Santiago, Chile, November'03*. IEEE Computer Society, 2003.
8. WebRatio. http://www.webratio.com.

Using Adaptive Techniques to Validate and Correct an Audience Driven Design of Web Sites

Sven Casteleyn[1], Irene Garrigós[2], and Olga De Troyer[1]

[1] Vrije Universiteit Brussel, Department of Computer Science, WISE, Pleinlaan 2,
1050 Brussel, Belgium
{Sven.Casteleyn, Olga.DeTroyer}@vub.ac.be
[2] Universidad de Alicante, IWAD, Campus de San Vicente del Raspeig, Apartado 99 03080
Alicante, Spain
igarrigos@dlsi.ua.es

Abstract. An audience driven philosophy for web site design takes the different target audiences as an explicit starting point, and organizes the basic navigation structure accordingly. However, for the designer it is not always easy, or sometimes even impossible, to assess the different requirements of the different target audiences correctly. In this paper, we show how to correct for such possible flaws using adaptive behavior. A mechanism for detecting both missing and superfluous information in a certain user's navigation path, by observing user's browsing behavior, is provided. The designer specifies possible adaptive changes based upon this detection at design time, using a language (Adaptation Specification Language) designed specifically to express changes in the navigation structure of a website.

1 Introduction

One approach described in the literature to improve usability [10] of web sites is the Audience Driven design philosophy [5][6]. For a web site design, it takes as a starting point the identification of the different target audiences, and arranges them in a hierarchy according to their requirements. From this hierarchy, the main structure of the web site is derived. Concretely, for the visitors this results in links on the homepage, each representing a different navigation path for a different kind of visitor (called *audience track*) containing all information/functionality relevant for that kind of visitor.

Although this design philosophy significantly reduces the amount of information the visitor needs to plough through, it can also be a cause of annoyance if the user cannot find the information he is looking for in the chosen audience track, or if his track contains information of no interest to him. As it is more difficult for web designers[1] to

---

[1] Target audiences for web sites are often more difficult to access and perform standard requirements engineering techniques (e.g. questionnaires) upon, compared to classical prospectus users of a standard application.

N. Koch, P. Fraternali, and M. Wirsing (Eds.): ICWE 2004, LNCS 3140, pp. 55–59, 2004.
© Springer-Verlag Berlin Heidelberg 2004

assess the exact requirements relevant or irrelevant for a certain user, it is well possible that some information fulfilling a requirement is missing in the audience track for a certain visitor (but present in another), or other information is put wrongly in that track. In this paper, we will tackle this problem by describing how to identify such missing or superfluous information for a certain target audience, and how to correct for it, by adapting the structure and navigation in the website. The framework for this work is the Web Site Design Method (WSDM) [6], an audience driven design method.

Web design methods that have support for adaptation include WebML[3], Hera[7], UWE[9] and OOH[8]. However, these methods focus either on personalization (e.g. towards different devices, content personalization), or handle a bottom-up approach to constructing pages from basic concepts. As far as the authors are aware of, there is no other research combining design support for altering an existing structure based upon user access, to improve the structure of the site towards all users.

2   Identifying Missing or Superfluous Information

Three steps are involved in detecting superfluous or missing information in a certain audience track:

1. **Determine to which audience class the current user belongs**

    Due to audience driven design, the user has to choose an audience track with his first click, thus choosing to which audience class he belongs.

2. **Determine if and which information the user visits, both within and outside his audience track.**

    As we want to keep track of which information is visited outside a particular audience track, and relate this information to the frequency of visits inside the track, we cannot just store the (total) number of accesses to every piece of information (modeled as a *chunk* in WSDM). Instead, we need to store the number of visits to each piece of information relative to each audience class. This data can be conveniently stored in a matrix, which we will call the *information access matrix*. Rows of the matrix represent the information (chunks) that represents the different elementary requirements, while the columns represent the different audience classes. Over time, the matrix contains a good summary of the amount of accesses to the different chunks for each audience class.

3. **Analyze the accumulated data to determine if superfluous or missing information for a certain audience track is detected.**

    We fall back on known statistical techniques: we consider the problem of detecting missing information as the problem of deciding whether a certain value (i.e. the amount of accesses to *foreign information,* information outside an audience track) *fits well* in a given sample data set (i.e. the set of amounts of accesses to *native* information, information within the audience track). Although different statistical techniques can be used, we have chosen in this paper to use median (which is robust) as a measure of central tendency combined with median absolute deviation as a measure of spread. As most values (see [4] for a more exact estimate) of a dataset probably lie within the distance of the spread from the middle value, we can use (median – MAD), calculated over the set of accesses to native information as a threshold value above which accesses to foreign information is considered relevant.

We consider the problem of detecting superfluous information as the problem of detecting outliers [1] (i.e. the amount of accesses of possible superfluous information) within a given dataset (i.e. the set of amount of accesses to *native* information). Although different statistical techniques can be used, we have chosen in this paper to use a double strategy to find *low* values: find values that lay both *far* below the middle value of the given dataset and *far* from their bigger neighbor. To determine which point lies *far* from the middle value, we again calculate the median and MAD for the given dataset, and test which values of the dataset lay below the threshold (median – MAD). To determine which values are far from their neighbor, we take the ordered dataset, and calculate the distances between each 2 consecutive values. These distances give us a new dataset, for which we calculate mean and standard deviation (= std). Calculating the interval [(mean–std) (mean+std)] gives us the range in which most of the distances (i.e. 50% for normally distributed data) lay. Distances above the (mean+std) are thus relatively big, compared to the other distances, and we have identified two points that are relatively far from each other.

3 Clarifying Example

To clarify this method, let's consider a real life example of a website (partly) built according to an audience driven design philosophy: the NASA web site (http://www.nasa.gov/). The information access matrix for these tracks is shown in figure 1. For simplicity, we consider only the audience classes "Media & Press" (with *native* information *inf1* to *inf6*) and "Educators" (with native information *inf7* to *inf12*). As explained, each cell in the matrix denotes the number of visits to some information by a certain audience class. As we were unable to obtain the *real* access information for the NASA website, we have used for this example fictitious data.

Let's now analyze the accesses to the native information of the Educators audience track (inf7 ... inf12), and determine if accesses to foreign information (inf1 ... inf6) were significant compared to these accesses:

Data set (ordered): 10 15 20 30 50 56
Median: 25 ; MAD: 12.5 ; Threshold: 25 – 12.5 = 12.5
Detected foreign requirements: Press Release Archive (40 accesses)

We can thus conclude that this information should somehow be included in the Educator track (how and where this information is added is the subject of the next section). Let's now consider the calculations to identify possible superfluous information in the "Media & Press" audience track.

Data set (ordered): **16** 31 38 40 49 52   Data set of distances: **15** 7 2 9 3
Median: 39; MAD: 9   Mean: 7.2 ; Standard deviation: 4.7
Lower limit: 39 – 9 = 30   Upper limit: 7.2 + 4.7 = 11.9

As the first element ('Fact Sheets', 16 accesses) of the original dataset lies below the corresponding lower limit (30), and the distance between the first and the second element (15) lies above the corresponding threshold (11.9), we can conclude that 'Fact Sheets' is detected as (possibly) superfluous for Media & Press audience class.

		Media & Press	Educators
Inf.1	Press Release Archive	52	40
Inf.2	Press Contacts	49	4
Inf.3	Press Kits	31	10
Inf.4	Fact Sheets	16	5
Inf.5	Speeches	40	5
Inf.6	Images	38	12
Inf.7	Contacts for educators	0	56
Inf.8	Professional development	5	50
Inf.9	Student opportunities	1	30
Inf.10	Fellowships and grants	0	10
Inf.11	Teaching Internet Resources	3	20
Inf.12	Teaching Multimedia Resources	2	15

Fig. 1. Information Access Matrix

4   Correcting Missing or Superfluous Information

Having identified missing or superfluous information in a certain audience track, the structure of the web site can be adapted (automatically) to correct the detected deficiencies. To specify this possible adaptation at design time, we use the Adaptation Specification Language (ASL) [2] defined over the navigation model of WSDM.

Possible actions taken upon detection of missing information within an audience track varies from duplicating the information in the place it is missing, provide a link to the existing information, or totally re-arrange the structure of the site. The approach shown in this paper consists of duplicating the detected nodes, and offering a link to the information at the root of the audience track:

Foreach *AudienceClass* **in** Website
 Foreach *node* **not in** NodesOfAudienceTrack(*AudienceClass*):
   if *node* **in** *MissingInformation(AudienceClass)*
   then addLink(root(Audience*Track(AudienceClass)*, duplicate(*node*))

Information identified as superfluous in a certain audience track does not necessarily need to be removed. Although visited only few times, it might still be valuable for (a small amount of) visitors. Automatic adaptation is possible (for example, apply link sorting), but more tricky and lengthy to describe; due to space restrictions we cannot describe it here. For now, we consider the detection of superfluous information rather as an alert to the web master, than something that requires (automatic) adaptation.

5 Conclusions and Further Work

In this paper, in the context of an audience driven design method for web sites, WSDM, we provide a mechanism for adaptively correcting the structure of the web site. By observing the user browsing behavior and the use of statistical techniques, missing or superfluous information in a particular audience track are automatically detected. At design time, the designer can specify (using the Adaptive Specification Language) the adaptive actions that should be taken in case such situations are detected at run time. By doing so, the structure of the web site will be better tailored to the needs of the different audience classes.

Future work includes accommodating the Adaptation Specification Language to make it possible to acquire all necessary information (e.g. creating and updating the information access matrix). Further research in analyzing the data from the matrix is being performed. In particular, detecting correlations between (the same) missing or superfluous information in different audience classes, and a cleverer way to adapt the structure of the site accordingly. Different adaptation strategies upon detection of missing/superfluous information are also a way to continue the research.

References

1.   Barnett, V. Lewis, T.: Outliers in Statistical Data. Wiley 3rd Edition (1995)
2.   Casteleyn, S., De Troyer, O., Brockmans, S.: "Design Time Support for Adaptive Behaviour in Web Sites", In Proceedings of the 18th ACM Symposium on Applied Computing, Melbourne, USA (2003)
3.   Ceri S., Fraternali P., and Bongio A: "Web Modeling Language (WebML): a modeling language for designing Web sites", In WWW9 Conference, First ICSE Workshop on Web Engineering, International Conference on Software Engineering (2000)
4.   DeGroot, M..H.: Probability and Statistics. Addison-Wesley, Reading, Massachusetts (1989)
5.   De Troyer, O.: "Audience-driven web design", In Information modelling in the new millennium, Eds. Matt Rossi & Keng Siau, IDEA GroupPublishing, ISBN 1-878289-77-2 (2001)
6.   De Troyer, O. ,Leune, C.: "WSDM: A User-Centered Design Method for Web Sites", In Computer Networks and ISDN systems, Proceedings of the 7th International World Wide Web Conference, Elsevier, pp. 85 – 94 (1998)
7.   Frasincar, F., Houben G., and Vdovjak R.: Specification Framework for Engineering Adaptive Web Applications, In Proceedings of the World Wide Web Conference, Honolulu, Hawaii, USA (2002)
8.   Garrigós, I., Gómez, J. and Cachero, C.: "Modelling Dynamic Personalization in Web Applications", Third International Conference on Web Engineering (ICWE'03), LNCS 2722, pages 472-475. Springer-Verlag Berlin Heidelberg (2003)
9.   Koch, N.: "Software Engineering for Adaptive Hypermedia Systems, Reference Model, Modeling Techniques and Development Process", PhD Thesis, Verlag UNI-DRUCK, ISBN 3-87821-318-2 (2001)
10. Nielsen, J.: Finding usability problems through heuristic evaluation. Proceedings of the SIGCHI conference on Human Factors and Computer Systems. Monterey, California, United States Pages: 373 – 380. ISBN:0-89791-513-5 (1992)

Modeling User Input and Hypermedia Dynamics in Hera

Geert-Jan Houben, Flavius Frasincar, Peter Barna, and Richard Vdovjak

Technische Universiteit Eindhoven
PO Box 513, NL-5600 MB Eindhoven, The Netherlands
{houben, flaviusf, pbarna, rvdovjak}@win.tue.nl

Abstract. Methodologies for the engineering of Web applications typically provide models that drive the generation of the hypermedia navigation structure in the application. Most of these methodologies and their models consider link following as the only materialization of the navigation structure. In this paper we see how extended user input can dynamically influence the navigation structure. By means of Hera it is shown how one can define this extended user input and capture the functional aspects related to the hypermedia dynamics in the RDF(S)-based design models. For this purpose we discuss the definition of input controls, the representation of state information, and the embedding of both in the application model. We also present the XML/RDF-based architecture implementing this.

1 Introduction

Under the influence of the World Wide Web we have seen the development of a new type of (data-intensive) information systems. These so-called Web Information Systems (WIS) [1] are characterized by the use of hypermedia navigation through the content of the system, in combination with the traditional functions of an information system allowing to update and query the content. As examples of WIS applications we mention online services like real-estate sales, employee information, museum information, or mail order catalogs.

The engineering of WIS requires different methodologies than the ones than we have been using for information system development over the last decades. In the traditional approach, used for example in more database-oriented applications, we see that most of the engineering activity is related to structuring the data so that the structure matches the standard software component, i.e. relational database. The subsequent design of presenting the content to the user is considered in the query facility associated with the software. On the other hand, with the original hypermedia approaches we see a different pattern, since they typically assume a process of manually linking documents. The design process centers on the design of the navigation in the presentation of the content in terms of a hyperdocument.

In the engineering of a WIS the designer has a challenging task. On the one hand, the designer has to provide the users with all benefits from using the hypermedia paradigm and particularly the notion of navigation through the information offered by the system. On the other hand, the designer has to support the users in their maintenance of the content by allowing updates and queries to the data. Many of today's data-intensive Web applications show the designer's attention for the maintenance of the data, but at the

N. Koch, P. Fraternali, and M. Wirsing (Eds.): ICWE 2004, LNCS 3140, pp. 60–73, 2004.

same time they show the risk of losing those benefits of hypermedia that have been the foundation for the success of the Web.

In the research field of WIS engineering we have seen proposals for methodologies that extend and improve the methodologies for manual hypermedia design for application in data-intensive information systems: we mention as representatives RMM [2], WebML [3], OOHDM[4], OOWS [5], UWE [6], OO-H [7], and Hera [8]. Typically these methodologies distinguish themselves from standard information system development methodologies by their explicit attention for the navigation design. Since however the WIS applications contain content that is highly dynamic, the design has to support the dynamics involved with the content. This support includes not just updating the content stored in the system, but also allowing the user to affect the hypermedia presentation of the data. Illustrative examples of this influence of the user on the hypermedia presentation are the history facility that allows the user to go back outside of the presented hyperlinks, or the shopping basket concept that allows the user to store some information temporarily during a browsing session. Such influence implies that a certain "state" is stored by the system to allow the user to interact with the hypermedia presentation and particularly with its navigational structure.

As we indicated earlier the available WIS engineering methodologies have a strong focus on the generation of navigation over the content. The user's actions consisted of following links, and as a consequence all the system could do was based on that. The history facility is a straightforward example. Giving the user more possibilities to interact with the generated hypermedia presentation can help to define or limit the hyperspace and thus to realize personalization and adaptivity. In a museum application asking the user to define what is interesting for him can help the system to create a more suitable navigation structure with specific information about those items on display that interest the user/visitor. Another example of user influence would be the role of a shopping basket in the sales communication based on a product catalog; not so much for the registration of the sales order, but certainly for the adjustment of the presentation in accordance with the user input, for example by showing a page with the complete contents of the shopping basket (order). As one of the consequences of this extended user influence there is a need to deal with navigation data, i.e. data primarily there to support the user in influencing (e. g. restricting, selecting) the navigation view over the application domain data. In this paper we show how to model this dynamic navigation through Hera models that allow the specification of the extended user input, the management of navigation information, and the effect of both of them on the hypermedia presentation. For this specification Hera uses semantic web languages that are very suitable for modeling of semi-structured data and describing their semantics.

In Section 2 we discuss how related work supports this kind of extended user input in relation to hypermedia dynamics. Section 3 highlights the main principles of the Hera approach, before we discuss in Section 4 the details of extended user input and dynamics in Hera: first we present the input controls, then the navigation data model, its effect on the application dynamics, and finally the architecture of the implementation. In the conclusion we name the main advantages of this approach compared to other approaches.

2   Related Work

In this section we take a closer look at two well-known representative methodologies WebML and OOHDM to see how they support modeling of user input and hypermedia (navigation) dynamics.

In WebML [3] the page content and navigation structure is captured in the (advanced) hypertext model using a predefined set of modeling primitives. The infrastructure for user input consists of data entry units that have associated with them operation units. A data entry unit contains a set of input fields that can be filled by users or can have default values. Data entry units have one or more outgoing links that are activated when the user fills input fields and submits the information. With a link can be associated parameters that transfer the input values to the destination unit(s), for example for further processing by an operation unit. There are several predefined operation units, for instance for activating external web services or content management operations like creation, deletion, and update of entities and relations. The whole library of units is open (new units can be defined in XML) and contains a number of data entry units for different kinds of user inputs. All contextual information passed between the units by link parameters is described in separate XML files.

The user input is in OOHDM [4] specified by means of interface objects that are defined on top of the navigation structure specification. The navigation is described using navigation classes derived from concept classes, navigation contexts representing collections of navigation objects, and access structures like links, indices, or guided tours. The interface objects are instances of interface classes expressed by Abstract Data Views (ADV). Every ADV defines a set of events (triggered by users) it can handle via methods of navigational classes, and a set of attributes that can be perceived by users. The processing of user-triggered events is specified in ADV charts, where the events are mapped to messages that are sent to navigation objects and can change their state.

3   Hera Methodology

The Hera methodology [8,9] is a model-driven methodology for designing WIS. Before we concentrate on user input and hypermedia dynamics in the next section, we will briefly describe the main aspects of Hera. In response to a user query a WIS will gather (multimedia) data possibly coming from heterogeneous sources and will produce a meaningful hypermedia (Web) presentation for the retrieved data. The Hera methodology automates such a process by providing high level abstractions (in terms of models) that will drive the (semi-)automatic presentation generation. Moreover, Hera enables the presentation adaptation based on user preferences and device capabilities, which means that the presentation generation takes into account issues like the platform being used (e. g. PC, PDA, WAP phone) [10].

Based on the principle of separation of concerns and for the sake of interoperability several models have been distinguished. Because these models are considered Web metadata descriptions that specify different aspects of a WIS, we chose to use the Web metadata language, i.e. RDF(S) [11,12], to represent all models and their instances. Our choice is also justified by the RDF(S) extensibility and flexibility properties that enabled us to extend the language with model specific primitives to achieve the desired power of expression. As RDF(S) doesn't impose a strict data typing mechanism it proved to be very useful in dealing with semistructured (Web) data.

The Hera toolset implements this methodology by offering software for the automatic generation of hypermedia based on the different Hera models. In order to facilitate the building (and visualizing) of these models, several Visio solutions were implemented. Such solution is composed of a stencil that will display all the model shapes, a drawing template, and a load/export feature providing the RDF(S) serialization of Hera models. Throughout the paper we use a running example based on the metadata associated to about 1000 objects from the Rijksmuseum. Figure 1 depicts (in the CM Builder) a part of the CM for our example, while Figure 2 illustrates the corresponding AM.

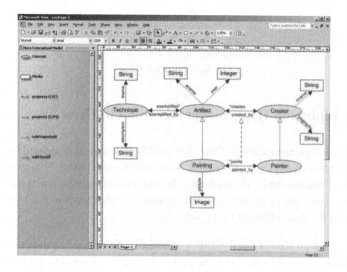

Fig. 1. Conceptual model

The conceptual model (CM) describes the structure (schema) of the application domain data. This structure is described using RDFS in terms of concepts and concept relationships. A concept has attributes, i.e. properties that refer to some media instances. For concept relationships we define their cardinalities and their inverse relationships.

The application model (AM) specifies the structure of navigational view over the application domain data. This structure is also defined using RDFS, where the hypermedia presentation is described in terms of slices and slice relationships (inspired by RMM). A slice is a meaningful presentation unit that groups concept attributes (from CM) that need to be presented together on the user display. There are two types of slice relationships: compositional relationships (for embedding a slice into another slice) and navigational relationships (as hyperlink abstractions).

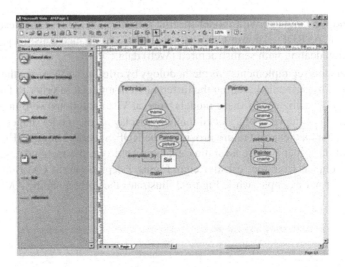

Fig. 2. Application model

4   User Input and Hypermedia Dynamics in Hera

In most WIS design methodologies, the only kind of interaction considered is link following: the use of the navigation structure is equivalent to wandering through the structure
by clicking on anchors and following links. In our extended approach we go a step further
and consider other forms of user input and dynamics with respect to this hyperstructure.
Therefore, in the next subsections we describe:

- information for navigation dynamics, defined in the navigation data model
- user input controls with associated processing of navigation information
- application model extended with the user input
- architecture of a Hera system

We illustrate this by an example from our museum application that allows the visitor
to buy posters of the paintings in the museum.

4.1   Navigation Data Model

In addition to the data in the aforementioned models CM and AM, interaction requires
a support for creating, storing, and accessing data that emerges while the user interacts
with the system. This support is provided by means of a so-called navigation data model
(NDM). The purpose of this model is to complement the CM with a number of auxiliary
concepts that do not necessarily exist in the CM (although this is the decision of the
designer in concrete applications) and which can be used in the AM when defining the
behavior of the application and its navigation structure.

The NDM of our example is depicted in Figure 3; it consists of the following concepts:

- The *SelectedPainting* concept is a subclass of the *Painting* concept from the CM. It represents those paintings which the user selected from the multi-selection form.
- The *Order* concept models a single ordered item consisting of a selected painting (the property *includes*) and the *quantity* represented by an Integer.
- The *Trolley* concept represents a shopping cart containing a set of orders linked by the property *contains*.

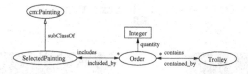

Fig. 3. Navigation data model

We remark that from the system perspective the concepts in the NDM can be divided into two groups. The first group essentially represents views over the concepts from the CM, the second group corresponds to a locally maintained repository. A concept from the first group can be instantiated only with a subset of instances of a concept existing in the CM, without the possibility to change the actual content of the data. A concept from the second group is populated with instances based on the user's interaction, i.e. the data is created, updated, and potentially deleted on-the-fly.

The instantiation of both groups of concepts is triggered by a certain action (an acknowledgement such as pressing the submit button) specified in the AM. Each such action can have an associated query which either defines the view (the first group) or specifies what instances should be inserted in the concept's extent (instantiation). The data resulting from the query execution is represented in the NDM instance (NDMI) and stored as state information till the next change (query) occurs[1]. The AM can refer to the concepts from NDM as if they were representing real data concepts.

In the example the *SelectedPainting* concept belongs to the group of view concepts whereas both the *Order* and the *Trolley* are updatable concepts with the values determined at runtime. This is reflected also in the NDMI depicted in Figure 4 that results from the user's desire to buy 3 posters of the selected painting. The instance *Painting*1 comes from the CM, i.e. it is not (re)created: what is created however, is the *type* property associating it with the *SelectedPainting* concept. Both instances *Order*1 and *Trolley*1 are created during the user's interaction; they, as well as their properties, are depicted in bold in Figure 4. Note that for presentation purposes (backwards link generation) we also generate for every property its inverse.

---

[1] We can see an entire spectrum, going from updating the content to just using state data to help change the hypermedia structure. In this paper we focus on the state data that helps specifying the interaction with the navigation structure (since updating the content is possible but outside presentation generation).

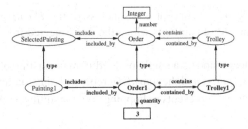

Fig. 4. Navigation data model instance

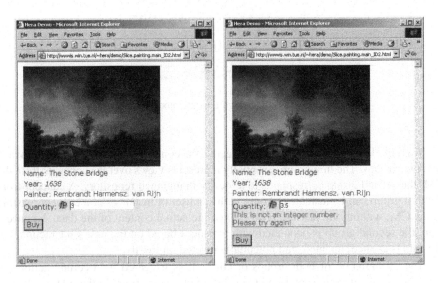

(a) Good input   (b) Bad input

Fig. 5. Form with input in browser

4.2 Input Controls

In Figure 5(a) we see from the implementation a slice of a painting selected by the user. It shows that in this slice the user is provided with a form to enter a quantity that represents the number of posters of this painting that the user considers to buy. In Figure 5(b) we see another example where the form is instructed to respond to the user's attempt to enter a non-integer value.

In the Hera software we implemented the user input forms using the XForms [13] standard. As an XForm processor we used formsPlayer [14], a plug-in for Internet Explorer[2]. In defining application forms we were inspired by XForms' clean separation of data from controls.

For these forms we need primitives in the AM that specify the functional embedding of the controls in the navigation structure. Figure 6 shows three examples of how we specify the embedding of controls in AM. In the leftmost example, the *SelectForm*

---

[2] The small logo labelled "fP" in Figure 5(a) is the $f$orms$P$layer signature in the implementation.

allows to make a choice for multiple items out of a list of paintings. The AM primitive shows the concept that "owns" the form, in this case *Painting*; it shows the items that are displayed in the form, in this case names; finally, it shows the items that are handed over by the form to the subsequent navigation: the name of the selected painting. In the middle example the form is similar but allows a choice of exactly one out of multiple options. The rightmost example shows a form called *BuyForm* that allows user input, in this case to enter the quantity of posters considering to buy. The form hands over the tuple consisting of the entered quantity and the painting name (the painting information is taken from the form's context).

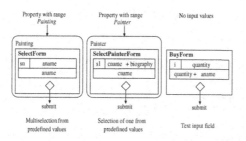

Fig. 6. Forms in AM

So we see that for the user input controls we specify in the diagram for the AM the relevant parameters that make up the form. Thus we describe the relevant functional aspects of the form, and are able to abstract in the diagram from the actual form code. Similar to XForms we distinguish between the input controls and their state information stored in separate models.

Figure 7 presents the models for the forms *SelectForm* and *BuyForm*. It consists of two form types, *Form1* defines the type of the *SelectForm* and *Form2* defines the type of the *BuyForm*. A Hera form model instance represented in RDF/XML corresponds to the associated XForms model instance. The *Integer* type matches the XML Schema [15,16] type *xsd:integer* and the *String* type matches the XML Schema type *xsd:string*. In case that the user enters a value of a different type than the one specified in the form model, an XForms implementation (see Figure 5(b)) will immediately react with an error message (due to its strong type enforcement capabilities).

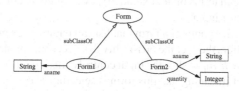

Fig. 7. Form models

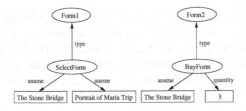

Fig. 8. Form model instances

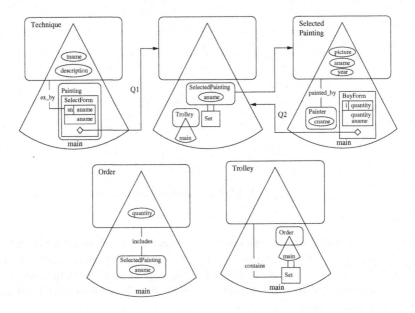

Fig. 9. Extended application model

Figure 8 describes two possible model instances for the form models given in Figure 7. In the *SelectForm* the user selected two paintings and in the *BuyForm* the user decided to buy one of these paintings.

4.3 Application Model

With the aid of the aforementioned primitives we are able to express the user input in our museum example in terms of an (extended) AM. Figure 9 depicts the part of the AM which captures the user input.

The *Technique* slice contains a form that lists all paintings exemplifying that particular technique and offers the user the possibility to select some of these paintings. For the latter we see in the *Technique* slice the input control called *SelectForm* with *Painting* as its owning concept (meaning that this form is selecting *Painting* concepts). We also see that the form lists the paintings by their *aname* property and produces for each selected painting the *aname* property to identify the selected paintings.

After selecting a painting, the outgoing slice navigational relationship denotes that the form in the *Technique* slice results in navigation to a slice that represents the set of selected slices, each represented by their *aname*, and also in a *Trolley* that, while initially empty, will contain the paintings that actually are going to be bought. A *Trolley* contains a set of *Order*s, while an *Order* represents the request to buy a poster of a (selected) painting in a certain quantity.

The navigation can go further to the *SelectedPainting* slice. That slice includes not only all the properties that represent the painting, but also a form called *BuyForm* with a user input control. That control allows the user to specify the quantity (of posters of this painting to buy). After filling this form the user can navigate via the outgoing slice relationship to the next slice where the trolley is maintained (and where the user can decide to select another painting for considering in more detail).

With these slices and slice navigational relationships in the AM we have specified the entire navigation structure. In the AM diagram we exploit the fact that the functionality of the controls is standard, e. g. the selection of n items from a list; therefore the diagram only indicates which standard control is used. What we also do indicate is the signature: we give the properties displayed in the form, and the identification of the concepts forwarded via the slice navigational relationship. Note that both slice navigational relationships that emerge from the forms ($Q1$ and $Q2$) are in fact queries. In the query definition we will use the prefix cm: for concepts/properties coming from the conceptual model, the prefix ndm: for concepts/properties specified in the navigation data model, and $form$: for concepts/properties introduced in the form model.

The RDF model instance of *SelectForm* is given in Figure 10. The query $Q1$ creates a view over painting instances from the CM instance (CMI) which were selected by the user in *SelectForm*. This view defines the instances of the *ndm:SelectedPainting* class from the NDM.

```
<Form1 rdf:ID="SelectForm">
    <aname>The Stone Bridge</aname>
    <aname>Portrait of Maria Trip</aname>
</Form1>
```

Fig. 10. Model instance for SelectForm

Figure 11 describes this query in the SeRQL [17] notation. The actual form is modelled as an RDF resource with multiple *form:aname* properties containing the names (values) of those paintings which were selected by the user.

The RDF model instance of *BuyForm* is given in Figure 12. The query $Q2$ associated with the *BuyForm* creates a new instance of the NDM concept *ndm:Order* each time the user decides to buy a poster of a selected painting.

The SeRQL translation of this query is presented in Figure 13. The form is modeled similarly as before by an RDF resource with two properties *form:quantity* and *form:aname*. Note that the (old) instance of the *ndm:Trolley* exists outside this form and is created beforehand during the initialization of the session.

```
CONSTRUCT
    {P}<rdf:type>{<ndm:SelectedPainting>}
FROM
    {P}<rdf:type>{<cm:Painting>};
        <cm:aname>{Paname}
WHERE
    Paname IN SELECT Faname
              FROM    {SF}<form:aname>{Faname},
                      {SF}<rdf:type>{<form:Form1>},
                      {SF}<rdf:ID>{Fname}
              WHERE Fname = "SelectForm"
```

Fig. 11. User query Q1

```
<Form2 rdf:ID="BuyForm">
    <aname>The Stone Bridge</aname>
    <quantity>3</quantity>
</Form2>
```

Fig. 12. Model instance for BuyForm

```
CONSTRUCT
    {O}<rdf:type>{<ndm:Order>};
        <ndm:quantity>{Fquantity};
        <ndm:includes>{Fpainting},
    {T}<ndm:contains>{O}
FROM
    {T}<rdf:type>{<ndm:Trolley>},
    {Fpainting}<cm:aname>{Paname};
                <rdf:type>{<ndm:SelectedPainting>},
    {BF}<form:quantity>{Fquantity};
        <form:aname>{Faname},
    {BF}<rdf:type>{<form:Form2>},
    {BF}<rdf:ID>{Fname}
WHERE
    Paname = Faname AND
    Fname = "BuyForm"
```

Fig. 13. User query Q2

4.4 Architecture

While in the previous subsections we have paid attention to the specification of user input and hypermedia dynamics and the way in which the AM can support this extended interaction specification, we now turn to the implementation. As we have indicated earlier the software of the Hera toolset can generate the hypermedia structure from the given models. In other work [8] we have sketched the (software) architecture for the case of normal link following. In Figure 14 we see how we extended the architecture such that it supports the handling of user input, e. g. via the forms[3].

We see that the *presentation engine* is responsible for serving the generated presentation to the user. As soon as the engine discovers user input it hands this over to the *form processor* that is going to interpret the actual user input (and possibly the contextual information that explains with what the user input is associated). So, the *form processor* can get the quantity of posters to buy and the context that explains

---

[3] We have focussed here on the part of the architecture for extended user interaction, and left out the architecture description for the rest of the software.

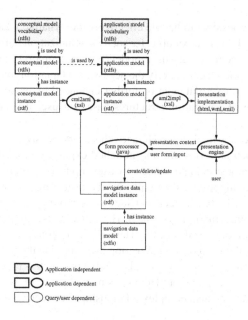

Fig. 14. Presentation generation

what the painting is for which the user wants to buy this quantity. The *form processor* can produce data that is added to the NDMI. The information from NDMI and CMI is used together in order to generate/update the AM instance.

As we have indicated in Figure 14 the implementation fits nicely in the RDF-based approach that we already had for the link following. By adding the additional model information in RDF(S) we can perfectly manage the additional functionality of explicit user input resulting in a different hypermedia presentation. We implemented data transformations (see *cmi2ami* and *ami2impl* in the figure) by means of XSLT stylesheets [18]. This was made possible due to the XML serialization of RDF model instances and the fact that XForms [13] is XML-based. Besides its XML interoperability XForms offers also device independence, which enables to use the same form on multiple platforms. X-Smiles [19] provides a good view on how the same XForms will look like on desktop, PDA, WAP phone etc. As an XSLT processor we used Saxon [20] which implements XSLT 2.0 and XPath 2.0. In the form processor we employed the Java-based Sesame [21] implementation of the SeRQL query language [17].

5   Conclusion

By providing new primitives in Hera, e. g. for capturing the user input, it is possible to considerably extend the class of applications that can be specified. As an example we mention the use of primitives like the "shopping basket" or "list selection" that are so typical for applications in the context of services provided via the Web. Another extension is the increased support of dynamics. With the new primitives and the navigation data model it has become possible to handle effectively the dynamic adaptivity known from adaptive hypermedia [22]. For example, for such personalization purposes the navigation data model can store the necessary user model (both its temporary and persistent parts), while the application model can specify the necessary adaptation rules. The construction of the navigation view over data can be further enhanced by existing generic methods for the development of navigation structures based on user interaction modeling, for instance [23].

Comparing these new facilities in Hera to other work, we see that the explicit support of input controls such as forms are not modelled explicitly in OOHDM for example. It does distinguish mouse-related aspects of user input, but compared to Hera it does have a more limited support of data-entry by the user. This aspect of user input is a strong point of WebML, but in fact that facility is more concerned with the content management of the information system. In Hera this is also supported, at the level of the conceptual model, but besides of this Hera allows to combine the stored data in the conceptual model with the auxiliary navigation data stored in the navigation data model. WebML has, next to the link parameters, also global parameters that can model a "state" in terms of attribute-value pairs, but Hera goes much further in the specification of this state information allowing also complex relationships between concepts (represented in graphs).

The fact that Hera uses RDF(S) representations of the models gives a number of advantages over other approaches. To start with, it supports the semistructured data that is so typical for the Web. With RDF(S) Hera offers increased interoperability, e. g. for the exchange and sharing of user models. It also allows to express complex queries (e. g. in the design of the dynamics) that make use of the subclassing mechanism. Moreover, the modeling in Hera of the extended user input inherits good principles from existing standard like XForms. It chooses to separate in the user input the controls (the presentation aspects) from their models (the data aspects). Opposed to other approaches, Hera has a concrete implementation based on these standards.

In future we plan to incorporate the possibility of web service invocation within applications designed using Hera on different levels: on the conceptual (data) level (web services will act as virtual instances of data concepts), and on the application level (web services will provide building blocks of slices). Furthermore, we investigate general properties, mutual relationships, and constraints of Hera models that would help us to build tools for the automated checking of correctness of the models.

References

1. Isakowitz, T., Bieber, M., Vitali, F.: Web information systems. Communications of the ACM **41** (1998) 78–80
2. Balasubramanian, V., Bieber, M., Isakowitz, T.: A case study in systematic hypermedia design. Information Systems **26** (2001) 295–320
3. Ceri, S., Fraternali, P., Bongio, A., Brambilla, M., Comai, S., Matera, M.: Designing Data-Intensive Web Applications. Morgan Kaufmann (2003)
4. Schwabe, D., Rossi, G.: An object oriented approach to web-based application design. Theory and Practice of Object Systems **4** (1998) 207–225

5. Pastor, O., Fons, J., Pelechano, V.: Oows: A method to develop web applications from web-oriented conceptual models. In: International Workshop on Web Oriented Software Technology (IWWOST). (2003) 65–70

6. Koch, N., Kraus, A., Hennicker, R.: The authoring process of the uml-based web engineering approach. In: First International Workshop on Web-Oriented Software Technology. (2001)

7. Gomez, J., Cachero, C. In: OO-H Method: extending UML to model web interfaces. Idea Group Publishing (2003) 144–173

8. Vdovjak, R., Frasincar, F., Houben, G.J., Barna, P.: Engineering semantic web information systems in hera. Journal of Web Engineering **2** (2003) 3–26

9. Frasincar, F., Houben, G.J., Vdovjak, R.: Specification framework for engineering adaptive web applications. In: The Eleventh International World Wide Web Conference, Web Engineering Track. (2002) `http://www2002.org/CDROM/alternate/682/`.

10. Frasincar, F., Houben, G.J.: Hypermedia presentation adaptation on the semantic web. In: Adaptive Hypermedia and Adaptive Web-Based Systems, Second International Conference, AH 2002. Volume 2347 of Lecture Notes in Computer Science., Springer (2002) 133–142

11. Brickley, D., Guha, R.V.: Rdf vocabulary description language 1.0: Rdf schema. (W3C Working Draft 10 October 2003)

12. Lassila, O., Swick, R.R.: Resource description framework (rdf) model and syntax specification. (W3C Recommendation 22 February 1999)

13. Dubinko, M., Klotz, L.L., Merrick, R., Raman, T.V.: Xforms 1.0. (W3C Recommendation 14 October 2003)

14. x-port.net Ltd.: (formsPlayer) `http://www.formsplayer.com`.

15. Biron, P.V., Malhotra, A.: Xml schema part 2: Datatypes. (W3C Recommendation 02 May 2001)

16. Thompson, H.S., Beech, D., Maloney, M., Mendelsohn, N.: Xml schema part 1: Structures. (W3C Recommendation 02 May 2001)

17. Aidministrator Nederland b.v.: (The serql query language) `http://sesame.aidministrator.nl/publications/users/ch05.html`.

18. Kay, M.: Xsl transformations (xslt) version 2.0. (W3C Working Draft 12 November 2003)

19. X-Smiles.org et.al.: (X-Smiles) `http://www.x-smiles.org`.

20. Kay, M.: (Saxon) `http://saxon.sourceforge.net`.

21. Aidministrator Nederland b.v.: (Sesame) `http://sesame.aidministrator.nl`.

22. Bra, P.D., Houben, G.J., Wu, H.: Aham: A dexter-based reference model for adaptive hypermedia. In: The 10th ACM Conference on Hypertext and Hypermedia, ACM (1999) 147–156

23. Schewe, K.D., Thalheim, B.: Modeling interaction and media objects. In: Natural Language Processing and Information Systems. Volume 1959 of Lecture Notes in Computer Science, Springer (2001) 313–324

A Behavioral Semantics of OOHDM Core Features and of Its Business Process Extension

Hans Albrecht Schmid and Oliver Herfort

University of Applied Sciences,
Brauneggerstr. 55
D - 78462 Konstanz
xx49-07531-206-631 or -500
schmidha@fh-konstanz.de

Abstract. OOHDM models hypermedia-based Web applications by an object model on three layers. Recently, an OOHDM extension by business processes has been proposed. In all cases, the definition includes a formal description of the syntactical aspects and a verbal description of the semantics. In this paper, we give a behavioral definition of the semantics of the OOHDM core features: navigation and advanced navigation; and of the proposed extension by business processes. We derive application-specific model classes from predefined behavioral model classes that have operations with a well-defined semantics. The behavioral model classes collaborate with a Web Application virtual Machine (WAM). The WAM models basic Web-browser characteristics, i.e. HTTP-HTML characteristics. Thus, the semantics of an OOHDM Web application model is precisely defined in an executable way.

1 Introduction

The Object-Oriented Hypermedia Design Method OOHDM by Schwabe and Rossi [SR98] is a modeling and design method for Web applications, which describes hypermedia-based navigation by an object model on three levels, the conceptual level, the navigational level and the interface level. Recently, Schmid and Rossi proposed an extension of OOHDM by business processes [SR02] [SR04]. The definition of OOHDM includes a formal description of syntactical aspects and a verbal description of the semantics.

However, verbal descriptions like that are not always precise, but often vague and open to misunderstandings and doubts. A formal definition of the semantics is required to cope with this problem. Since OOHDM uses object models, it lends itself to a behavioral definition of the semantics in form of the object behavior.

We focus in this paper on a behavioral definition of the semantics of the OOHDM core features, which are navigation and advanced navigation; and of the proposed OOHDM business process extension. OOHDM models a Web application by application-specific classes with a semantics that is given verbally. Our approach is to

N. Koch, P. Fraternali, and M. Wirsing (Eds.): ICWE 2004, LNCS 3140, pp. 74–87, 2004.

derive these classes from predefined behavioral model classes that have operations with an executable semantics definition. The behavioral model classes, called shortly model classes, collaborate with a Web Application virtual Machine (WAM). The WAM models basic Web-browser characteristics, i.e. HTTP-HTML characteristics. Thus, the semantics of an OOHDM model of a Web application is precisely defined in an executable way.

We present and explain an OOHDM model of a Web shop that includes navigation, advanced navigation and a business process in section 2. Section 3 introduces the Web Application virtual Machine WAM and related classes and services. Section 4, 5 and 6 define the semantics of the OOHDM navigation, advanced navigation and business process constructs by a behavioral model. Section 7 surveys shortly related work.

2   The Web Shop as an Example for an OOHDM Model

We use the Web shop presented in [SR04] as an example for an OOHDM model that includes navigation, advanced navigation and a business process. OOHDM (for details see [SR98]) models the objects forming the application domain in a conceptual schema (see Figure 1); it models abstracted Web pages and the navigation possibilities among them in a navigational schema (see Figure 2); and the presentation aspects of Web pages (which we disregard) in an interface schema.

The conceptual schema is partitioned in entities (bottom) and in processes with classes and activities (top), and the navigational schema in entity nodes, among which you may navigate (left), and in activity nodes that belong to processes (right). UML stereotypes, which OOHDM considers just as a classification, indicate the category to which each object class belongs. But for the behavioral model definition, each stereotype indicates the model class an application-specific class is derived from. Note that the classes shown in Figure 1 and 2 do not give a complete application model of the example Web shop, to avoid an overloading with details. The required details will be given in sections 4-6.

The relationship between objects in the conceptual and navigational schema, like that between an entity node CDNode and an entity CD, is given explicitly in the OOHDM node definition syntax [SR98], but represented in the schemas only by the correspondence of the names.

Pure Navigation

Consider, for example, the navigation possibilities in the CD store. On the left of the navigational schema (see Figure 2), you find entity nodes (which are an abstraction of Web pages) like CDNode or ShoppingCartNode. Links among nodes are represented as directed edges which may be labeled with the link name. There are links representing the navigation possibilities from the customer HomePageNode to the CDNode or to the ShoppingCartNode, from the CDNode to the ShoppingCartNode and back, and from one CD to other related CDs by using the "related" link between CDNode's.

Advanced Navigation

More advanced hypermedia applications are not composed of read-only pages; they use Web pages as the interface for triggering different kind of actions that may change the internal state of the application. An atomic action, like adding a product to a shopping cart, calls an operation of an entity like ShoppingCart. When the user presses the "add to shopping cart" button on the Web page that displays the CDNode, called CDNode interface on the OOHDM interface layer, that button invokes, as described on the OOHDM interface layer, the *addToCart* operation of the selected CDNode. The CDNode sends the message *add*(CD) to the ShoppingCart object, which changes its state.

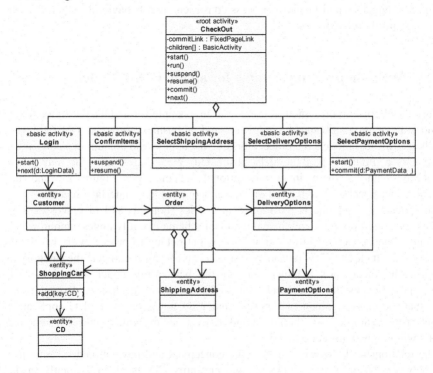

Fig. 1. OOHDM conceptual schema of a Web shop including entities and a business process

Business Processes

An entity object like CD or Customer has a permanent lifetime and state; a process object like CheckOut has a temporary state and no permanent lifetime (see [S99] [SR04]). Processes and activities are modeled in the OOHDM conceptual schema (see Figure 1 top), and activity nodes in the OOHDM navigational schema (see Figure 2 right).

Typically, a business process like CheckOut (see Figure 1 top) is composed of several activities like Login, ConfirmItems, SelectShippingAddress, etc. This is represented by an aggregation relationship in the conceptual schema. We consider a business process as a root activity that may consist itself of a set of activities. An activity is either basic, like Login etc., or composed from other activities, like CheckOut, following the composite pattern [GHJV95]. An activity collaborates with application entities, like Login with Customer. An activity provides operations like *start*, *next*, *commit*, *suspend* and *resume*, that allow to execute a business process.

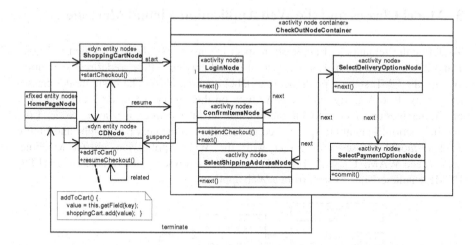

Fig. 2. OOHDM navigational schema of a Web shop including navigation, advanced navigation and a business process

An activity node like LoginNode models abstractly a Web page, presenting the output of an activity and accepting its input. The OOHDM interface layer (not shown) describes which buttons, like commit or next, a node contains. Pressing a button triggers a matching method of the activity node, like *next* of LoginNode, which calls the matching method of the activity, like *next*(d:LoginData) of Login, passing the user input. An activity node is shown in the context that is created by its process. This context is represented as an ActivityNodeContainer, like CheckOutNodeContainer (Figure 2 right).

An edge labeled with a reserved label *start*, *terminate*, *suspend*, *resume* or *next* does not represent a navigational link, but the possibility to go from or to get to an activity node by process execution. Informally, the edge semantics is as follows (see [SR04]). The *start* edge from the ShoppingCartNode to the CheckOutNodeContainer represents starting the CheckOut process from navigation, the *terminate* edge terminating it and taking navigation up again. A *next* edge among activity nodes, e.g. from LoginNode to ConfirmItemsNode, represents the transition from one to the next activity, including the completion of the first and the starting of the next activity. An activity diagram (not shown) that forms part of the conceptual schema shows the possible flow of control among the activities.

A Web application may allow that a business process is suspended to do temporarily some navigation. E.g., a user may suspend checking out at the ConfirmItemsNode and navigate to the CDNode to get more information about CDs he is buying. This is represented by a *suspend* edge. A *resume* edge from an entity node to an activity node container, like the one leading from CDNode to CheckoutNodeContainer, represents returning from the temporary navigation and resuming the business process at the state it was suspended.

3 Model Classes and the Web Application Virtual Machine

To define the semantics of application-specific classes like those presented in Figure 1 and 2, we derive them from behavioral model classes with a predefined semantics. We use the UML stereotype "model" to label a model class. The basic model classes are: Entity, RootActivity, and BasicActivity on the conceptual layer; Node and Link on the navigation layer; and InteractionElement on the interface layer. Node, Link and InteractionElement are specialized as described in the next paragraphs and Figure 3. The model classes collaborate with the Web Application virtual Machine, abbreviated WAM. The WAM models basic Web-browser characteristics, i.e. HTTP-HTML characteristics as seen from a Web application.

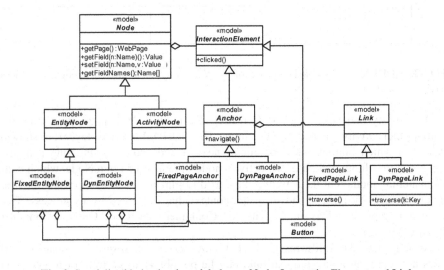

Fig. 3. Specialized behavioral model classes Node, InteractionElement and Link

The model class Node models a Web page abstracting from many of its concrete characteristics, and the model class InteractionElement models interaction elements like anchors and buttons.

The class InteractionElement defines the operation *clicked()* which is called when an end user clicks at the interaction element. We refine the class InteractionElement in Anchor and Button, and Anchor in FixedPageAnchor and DynPageAnchor. Their detailed characteristics are presented in section 4 and 5.

The class Node defines the (abstract) operations *getPage()*: WebPage, *getField(* n:Name): Value, *setField(*n: Name, v: Value), *getFieldNames()*: Name []. It contains an array of InteractionElements. We refine a Node into EntityNode and

ActivityNode: an EntityNode may contain Anchor's and Button's, an ActivityNode only Button's as InteractionElements. The class Link is refined into FixedPageLink with a method *traverse*(), and DynPageLink with a method *traverse*(k: Key).

The WAM has the attribute currentNode, a reference to the currently displayed Node, and an operation *display*(n:Node) {currentNode=n; showPage(n.*getPage*());}. When a user enters or edits data on the currently displayed page, the WAM calls the *setField*-method of the currentNode to change the state of the Node. When a user clicks at an interaction element, the WAM calls the operation *clicked* of the corresponding Anchor or Button of the currentNode.

In the following sections, the behavioral model gives the executable definition of the operations in the form of UML notes in Java. As an alternative to Java, we might use the action semantics of UML 1.5/2.0. Operations defined by the behavioral model are printed in bold fonts to distinguish them from application-specific operations. For lack of space, the behavioral model presented does not include items like error cases.

4   The Behavioral Semantics of Navigation

Navigation allows a user to navigate from a given node to a linked node by clicking at the link. Its main characteristic is that the state of navigation is determined only by the page displayed by the browser and its content [SR04]. The behavioral model of navigation mirrors this characteristic: it shows that navigation does not cause any state changes but that of the current node of the WAM.

We distinguish two kinds of navigation, navigation among Web pages with a fixed content and navigation among Web pages with a dynamic content.

Navigation Among Web Pages with a Fixed Content
Fixed page navigation follows a link to a node without dynamically generated content, like the link from CDNode to HomePageNode in the navigational schema Figure 2. The behavioral model shown in Figure 4 contains, besides the user-defined classes for the source and target node of the link, only the model classes: Anchor, FixedPageAnchor, and FixedPageLink; which are instantiated and configured to work together. These model classes have executable definitions of the methods *clicked*, *navigate* and *traverse*.

A node like the CDNode contains a FixedPageAnchor instance, which references a FixedPageLink instance, which, in turn, references the target node of the link. Each reference is set by a constructor parameter. When the WAM displays a Web page, i.e. a Node, and a user clicks at the Anchor of a fixed page link, the WAM calls the *clicked*-operation. This forwards the call to the *navigate* operation of the FixedPageAnchor, which calls the *traverse*-operation of the FixedPageLink. The *traverse*-operation calls the *display*-operation of the WAM with the target node as a parameter. The WAM sets, as described in section 3, that node as the current node and calls its *getPage*-operation in order to display the page.

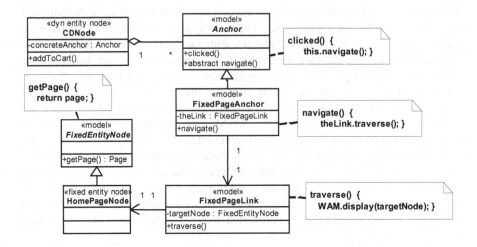

Fig. 4. Static navigation from CDNode to HomePageNode

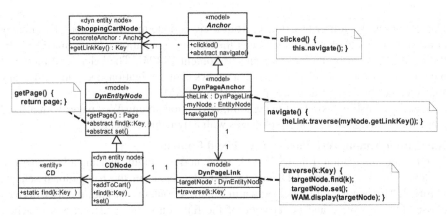

Fig. 5. Dynamic navigation from ShoppingCart Node to CDNode

Navigation to Web Pages with a Dynamically Generated Content

Navigation to a dynamic page is similar to fixed page navigation, except for the key required to identify the dynamic content (see Figure 5). The differences are:

- A source node of a dynamic link has an operation *getLinkKey* that returns a key identifying the dynamic content of the target node.

- A DynEntityNode defines an operation *find*(k: Key) that fetches the dynamic node content from the associated entity (calling its static *find*(k:Key)-operation), and a *set*-operation to set the (found) dynamic content into the attribute fields.

- The class DynPageAnchor has a *navigate*-operation that fetches the key of the dynamic content from the source node, called myNode, and passes it as a parameter with the call of the *traverse*-operation. The *traverse*-method of the DynPageLink class calls the *find*-operation of its target node of type DynEntityNode with the key as a parameter, and then its *set*-operation so that the target node sets its dynamically generated content. Last, it calls the *display*-operation of the WAM with the target node as a parameter.

5 The Behavioral Semantics of Advanced Navigation

Advanced navigation allows a user to trigger an atomic action by pressing a button on a Web page. An atomic action enters or edits information in a Web application, modifying the state of application objects that are modeled in the conceptual schema. Consequently, the Web application state is composed by the state of the current node displayed by the browser, and by the state of the application objects. The behavioral model of advanced navigation shows that not only the current node of the WAM, but also application domain objects may change their state.

For example, consider the *addToCart* operation of the CDNode in Figure 2, which is triggered by the AddToCartButton. The behavioral model for advanced navigation (see Figure 6) shows the model class Button with the operations *clicked* and *action*. A derived application-specific class, like AddToCartButton, implements the *action*-method, which calls an operation of the source node, like *addToCart* of CDNode.

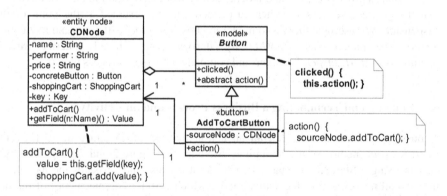

Fig. 6. Triggering the execution of the atomic *addToCart*-action by a button

When the WAM displays a Web page, i.e. a node, and a user clicks at a button on this page, the WAM calls the operation *clicked* of this button. The *clicked*-method forwards the call to the *action*-method, which forwards the call to the *addToCart*-method of the CDNode. This method fetches the value from the key-field of the (currently presented) CD and sends the message *add*(value) to the ShoppingCart object, which changes the state of the shopping cart.

Note that the execution of an atomic action does not imply the navigation to another node. This would have to be modeled by adding a Link to CDNode and *addToCart* calling additionally the *traverse*-method of the link.

6   The Behavioral Semantics of Business Processes

The main characteristics of a business process (see [SR04]) are that it:
- drives the user through its activities. This means it defines the set of activities to be executed, and the possible control flow among them.
- keeps its state internally. The state can be changed only by the process itself on a user interaction, but not by the user pressing a browser button.

The behavioral semantics of a business process mirrors these characteristics. The behavioral model defines the semantics of process state transitions, which are represented by process-related edges like *start* and *next* in the navigational schema (see Figure 2): it shows that a business process changes its state only when a process state transition is triggered by the user, and that, in general, the process, and not the user, selects the next activity for execution.

To make the behavioral model not unnecessarily difficult to understand, we make the restriction (not made by [SR04]) that there are only two levels of process execution, i.e. a process consists of a root activity with basic activities as children. The behavioral model defines the classes RootActivity and BasicActivity, with operations like *start, run, next, commit, suspend,* and *resume* with a predefined semantics, given by final methods or inherited from class Thread. Application-specific activity classes are derived from them.

A business process is executed independently from navigation in an own thread, so that it can preserve its state when suspended, and be resumed at the point of the suspension. We use Java threads to model the business process threads and navigation thread. The model class RootActivity, derived from Thread, inherits Thread-operations to *start, suspend, resume* and complete a business process thread.

6.1   Starting and Terminating a Business Process and an Activity

A business process is started from an action method of an entity node. E.g., the *startCheckout*-method of the ShoppingCartNode (see Figure 2 and 7), triggered by a user pressing a StartButton, starts the Checkout process and suspends the navigation thread, calling *suspend* of the Thread under which it runs. The mechanics of buttons and invocation of the action-method is exactly the same as described in section 5; so we do not present it again here and in the following examples and figures.

The behavioral model for starting and terminating a business process is shown in Figure 7. The *start*-method that Checkout inherits from Thread calls the predefined *run*-operation of the business process thread. The final *run*-method of the model class RootActivity, which realizes that operation, is a template method [GHJV95] that is inherited by the application-specific Checkout root activity. It calls the application-specific methods *startHook* for initialization and *getNextActivity* to select the basic activity to be executed, sets this activity, like Login, as current (-ly executed) activity, and starts it.

Starting a Basic Activity

The predefined *start*-operation of the model class BasicActivity initializes the content data of the associated activity node and displays it as Web page. It is a template method that is inherited by an application-specific activity like Login. The *start*-method calls the application-specific *startHook*-method. This method usually gets the data to be presented to the user from the application domain objects and puts them into the attribute fields of the associated ActivityNode; but the Login activity presents no data in the LoginNode. Then the *start*-method calls the *display*-method of the WAM passing the activity node like LoginNode as a parameter, so that the WAM displays it as a Web page.

Completing a Basic Activity

All activity nodes of the Checkout process have a next-button to complete the activity and go to the next one, except for the SelectPaymentOptionsNode which has a commit-button, since it completes the SelectPaymentOptions activity and then the Checkout process.

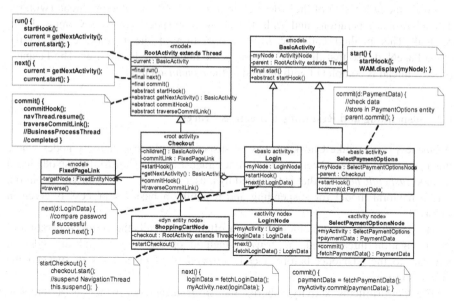

Fig. 7. Starting the CheckOut process from the ShoppingCartNode and completing it from the SelectPaymentOptionsNode.

For example, the LoginNode has a next button which triggers its *next*-method. This method fetches the data from the LoginNode which the user has entered during the Login activity, and passes them as parameters with the call of the method *next(d:LoginData)* of the Login activity. This method compares the entered user name and password with the associated Customer object, and calls, if the check is successful, the *next*-method of Checkout. This method is a template method inherited from the model class RootActivity; it selects the activity to be executed next by calling the application-specific hook method *getNextActivity*, sets this activity as current (-ly executed) activity and starts it.

Terminating the Checkout Business Process
A business process like Checkout is terminated when it has completed its work, that is when the last of its child activities, SelectPaymentOptions, has completed its work and Checkout has completed the customer order and sent it off.

The SelectPaymentOptions activity completes its work when the commit-button triggers the *commit*-method of the SelectPaymentOptionsNode (see Figure 7 bottom right). This method fetches the payment options data, which the user has entered during the SelectPaymentOptions activity, and passes them as parameters with the call of the *commit*(d: PaymentData) method of the SelectPaymentOptions activity. This method checks the entered data and stores them in the PaymentOptions object. Then it calls the *commit*-method of its parent activity Checkout.

The Checkout activity inherits the template method *commit* from the model class RootActivity. The *commit*-method calls the application-specific *commitHook* to complete the processing of the order before it resumes the navigation thread (with the Thread *resume*-operation) and calls the application-specific traverseCommit Link-method. This method calls the *traverse*-operation of the FixedPageLink to the HomePageNode, so that the WAM presents the home page to the user. The business process thread is completed with the end of the *commit*-method.

6.2   Suspending and Resuming a Business Process

A business process like Checkout may be suspended only from activity nodes where this is provided for by a Web application designer. E.g., the ConfirmItemsNode has a method *suspendCheckout* that is triggered by a user pressing a NavigateToCD-button. The behavioral model for suspending and resuming a business process is given in Figure 8.

The *suspendCheckout*-method of ConfirmItemsNode calls the *resume*-operation of the navigation thread, and the *traverse*-method of the suspendLink in order to navigate to the CDNode, before it calls *suspend* of ConfirmItems to suspend the business process.

The ConfirmItems activity inherits the *suspend*-method, which is a template method, from the model class BasicActivity. This method calls the *suspendHook*, which saves the activity state if required, as e.g. after user inputs during the activity, and stores it temporarily in the activity state, and then the *suspendBP*-method of the Checkout activity. The *suspendBP*-method, which the Checkout activity inherits from the model class RootActivity, calls the application-specific *suspendHook* that performs application-specific actions before the suspension, and then the Thread *suspend*-operation to suspend the business process thread.

Resuming the Checkout Business Process
A business process like Checkout may be resumed only from entity nodes where this is provided for by a Web application designer. E.g., CDNode has a *resumeCheckout*-

method that is triggered by a user pressing a ResumeCheckout-Button during the temporary navigation. Figure 8 gives the behavioral model for resuming a business process, which suspends the navigation thread.

The *resumeCheckout*-method of CDNode calls *resume* of the Checkout process (if Checkout is not suspended, an exception is returned) and then the *suspend*-method that the navigation thread inherits from Thread. The *resume*-method, which Checkout has inherited via the model class RootActivity from Thread, resumes the business process thread which has been suspended in the *suspendBP*-method. When this method is resumed, it calls the application-specific *resumeHook*, which may e.g. restore some state if required. Finally, it calls the *resume*-method of the basic activity like ConfirmItems that was active when the business process was suspended.

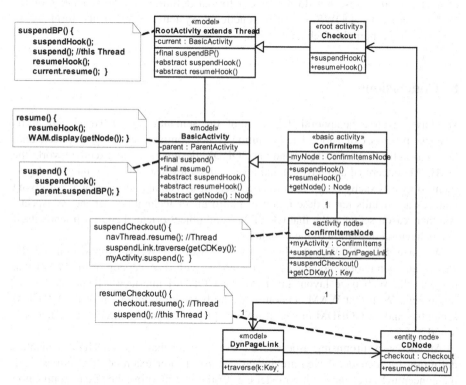

Fig. 8. Suspending the CheckOut process from ConfirmItemsNode and resuming it from CDNode

ConfirmItems has inherited the *resume*-method from the BasicActivity class. The *resume*-method calls first the application-specific *resumeHook*. This method restores the data, which were presented to the user and saved when the activity was suspended, from the application state or temporary objects, and puts them into the attribute fields of the associated ActivityNode, like ConfirmItemsNode. The *resume*-method calls then the *display*-method of the WAM passing the ConfirmItemsNode as a parameter so that the WAM displays the ConfirmItemsNode as a Web page, and the user can go on with the execution of the Checkout process.

7 Related Work

Many Web application design methods proposed in the last years, like WebML by Ceri, Fraternali, and Paraboschi [C00] and W2000 by Baresi, Garzotto, and Paolini [B00], do not have special constructs to model business processes. Recent proposals like UWE by Koch and Kraus [KKCM03], OO-H by Cachero and Melia [KKCM03], and OOWS by Pastor, Fons and Pelechano [PFP03] have constructs for the modeling of business processes., but do not give a formal definition of the semantics of the model constructs. OOWS captures functional system requirements formally to construct from them the Web application.

8 Conclusions

We have given a behavioral definition of the semantics of OOHDM and of its business process extension. The definition is not complex and easy to understand. One reason for that seems to be that the OOHDM designers did an excellent work: the OOHDM conceptual and navigational layers, and a few aspects of the interface layer, seem to focus exactly on all important aspects of a Web applications, without giving unnecessary details nor a description of platform- or technology dependent aspects. Another reason seems to be that OOHDM as an object-oriented approach lends itself to a behavioral definition of the semantics.

We have defined a Web Application virtual Machine WAM. Application-specific classes and behavioral model classes collaborate with it. A version of the WAM that neglects the Web page layout given by the OOHDM interface schema, is easy to implement. With that WAM version, both the behavioral definition of the OOHDM semantics and an OOHDM model of a Web application can be directly executed and tested.

Another very promising aspect is the use of the behavioral OOHDM semantics definition for a model driven architecture approach. For example, the entities from the conceptual layer may either model e.g. Corba or Enterprise JavaBean application objects from an existing back-end application, or they may conceptualize non-existing lightweight entities that provide just an interface to a database management system. In the first case, a generator just generates code to invoke the existing application objects from the servlets that realize the OOHDM nodes, whereas in the second case, a generator generates servlets that realize the OOHDM nodes and embody the database access provided by the lightweight entities.

Acknowledgements. Our thanks for a partial support of the project are due to the International Bureau of the BMBF, Germany, Bilateral Cooperation with Argentina, and SeCTIP, Argentina; and to the Ministerium fuer Wissenschaft, Forschung und Kunst, Baden-Württemberg.

References

[B00]   L. Baresi, F. Garzotto, and P. Paolini. "From Web Sites to Web Applications: New issues for Conceptual Modeling". In Procs. Workshop on The World Wide Web and Conceptual Modeling, Salt Lake City (USA), October 2000.

[C00]   S. Ceri, P. Fraternali, S. Paraboschi: "Web Modeling Language (WebML): a modeling language for designing Web sites". Procs 9th. International World Wide Web Conference, Elsevier 2000, pp 137-157

[GHJV95]   E. Gamma, R. Helm, R. Johnson, J. Vlissides: "Design Patterns: Elements of Reusable Object-Oriented Software". Addison-Wesley, 1995

[KKCM03]   N.Koch, A.Kraus, C.Cachero, S.Melia: "Modeling Web Business Processes with OO-H and UWE". IWWOST 03, Proceedings 3rd International Workshop on Web-Oriented Software Technology, Oviedo, Spain, 2003

[PFP03]   O. Pastor, J. Fons, V. Pelechano: "OOWS: A Method to Develop Web Applications from Web-Oriented conceptual Models". IWWOST 03, Proceedings 3rd International Workshop on Web-Oriented Software Technology, Oviedo, Spain, 2003

[S99]   H.A. Schmid: "Business Entity Components and Business Process Components"; Journal of Object Oriented Programming, Vol.12, No.6, Oct. 99

[SR02]   H.A. Schmid, G. Rossi: "Designing Business Processes in E-Commerce Applications". In E-Commerce and Web Technologies, Springer LNCS 2455, 2002

[SR04]   H. A. Schmid, G. Rossi " Modeling and Designing Processes in E-Commerce Applications". IEEE Internet Computing, January 2004

[SR98]   D. Schwabe, G. Rossi: "An object-oriented approach to web-based application design". Theory and Practice of Object Systems (TAPOS), Special Issue on the Internet, v. 4#4, pp. 207-225, October, 1998

XGuide – Concurrent Web Engineering with Contracts

Clemens Kerer and Engin Kirda

Vienna University of Technology, Distributed Systems Group
Argentinierstrasse 8/184-1, A-1040 Vienna, Austria
{C.Kerer,E.Kirda}@infosys.tuwien.ac.at

Abstract. XGuide introduces the concept of contracts to the Web engineering domain. Contracts define the characteristics of Web components and pages. They serve as specifications for pages, enforce strict separation of concerns, are composable and enable concurrent implementation. As a result, time-to-market is shortened and support for maintenance and evolution scenarios is provided. The XGuide development process iteratively extends and refines conceptual models towards concrete implementations and thus bridges the gap between the conceptual and implementation space.

1 Introduction

Various methods were proposed to support Web engineering [1] processes—often influenced by and building on results from other fields of computer science. Existing approaches include database-centric, graph-based, logic-based, object-oriented and component-based methods. Most approaches share several key requirements and concepts. The ability to model a Web-based system on a conceptual level that is subsequently transformed into a concrete implementation is one. Dividing the system into smaller modules and components that can be reused and composed to form larger components is another. Additionally, the principle of *separation-of-concerns* is identified as being crucial and is supported to various degrees.

The goal of the XGuide approach is to propose precise specifications and design-by-contract [2] for Web pages and Web components (page fragments). We call these specifications *Web contracts*. Web contracts serve as the basis for the composition and integration of Web components into Web pages. Furthermore, they support the separation of design concerns by clearly specifying the concerns (and their dependencies) involved in the creation of a page or component. Such concerns include the content management, layout design and application logic programming. After the contract design, XGuide includes a step-wise refinement of these design artifacts towards a concrete implementation. Based on the concern and dependency specifications in the contracts, XGuide strives to reduce the overall time-to-market by supporting a concurrent implementation phase. A prototype development environment called *XSuite* supports and automates the XGuide method.

2 Contract-Based Development with XGuide

The XGuide development process is structured into seven phases: requirements analysis, feasibility decision, conceptual modeling and design, implementation, testing, deploy-

N. Koch, P. Fraternali, and M. Wirsing (Eds.): ICWE 2004, LNCS 3140, pp. 88–92, 2004.

ment, and evolution and maintenance. For space reasons, we focus on the design phase in this paper. A complete discussion of the XGuide method can be found in [3].

In the design phase, a conceptual model of the Web site is created. This model consists of pages, components, component references and application logic processes. To illustrate the approach, we use a snippet from the Vienna International Festival (VIF, http://www.festwochen.at) 2003 case study. The VIF is an annual cultural festival in Vienna featuring operas, theatre performances, concerts, exhibition and other cultural events. The VIF Web site not only offers information about the programme, venues, press releases, etc. but also provides a shopping cart application for ordering tickets online. Figure 1 displays a simplified version of the conceptual model for the shopping cart of the VIF Web site.

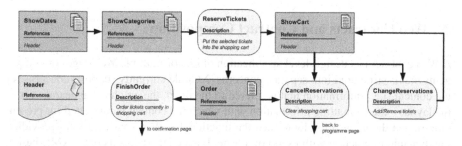

Fig. 1. A snippet from the component web for the VIF shopping cart application.

A *page* (depicted as a rectangle in the model) denotes a unit that will be presented to the user in her browser. From the user's point of view, all interactions are with pages; the internal structure of pages (i.e., its decomposition in components) is not visible. *Components* (depicted as rectangles with curved lower borders) represent page fragments that are reused on several pages. Typical examples for components are page headers, footers and global access structures such as hierarchical navigation menus. A component can be included in another component or page by referencing it in the *References* section of the component or page. For the purpose of this discussion, we only defined a single component *Header* in Figure 1 that is included in all pages. Finally, *application logic processes* (rectangles with rounded corners) represent the back-end processing (if any) that takes place on a server round-trip (e.g., when moving from one page to another by following a link or submitting a form).

So far, we did not distinguish between static and dynamically-generated pages or any information flow between them. The content of dynamic pages usually depends on some input values provided by the framework or the user. Customized navigation bars, for example, take a page identifier as input and render the currently viewed entry in the menu differently than the others. In our example, the *ShowDates* page requires an event identifier as input to determine which event's dates it should present. In XGuide, we denote the set of arguments a page requires to be created at the server side as the page's *input interface*.

After the input interfaces for all components and pages, we can define the corresponding *output interfaces*. An output interface is the opposite concept and describes what values a page, a component or an application logic process provides. Pages and components can provide values using embedded forms where the user can enter information and submit it. Since a page can contain multiple independent forms, a page can have multiple output interfaces as opposed to a single input interface. Similarly, application logic processes can offer multiple output interfaces based on values created, calculated or retrieved at runtime.

With the interfaces for all components and pages, the conceptual model (called *XGuide sitemap*) is complete. It serves as a basis for the detailed page and component specifications. The next section discusses Web contracts, their internal structuring into concerns, and how they can be composed.

3   Web Contracts and Contract Composition

A Web contract is a design-level specification of one or multiple Web pages or components that is structured into separate concerns. XGuide currently supports concerns for the content (i.e., information that is offered to the user), the graphical appearance (i.e., the layout – the formatting information with which the content is formatted for presentation), and the application logic (i.e., the functionality that is necessary for providing the dynamic interaction with users) of a page. Each concern has its own (XML-based) specification vocabulary; the contract itself acts as a container for the concerns.

```
1   <xcontract version="1.0">
2     <concern docElement="webpage" type="Content"> <!-- XML schema --> </concern>
3     <concern type="AppLogic"> <!-- XML interface definition --> </concern>
4
5     <compositionreferences>
6       <reference version="1.0" to="header.contract">
7         <composition type="Content">
8           <operator elementName="webpage" position="beginning" />
9         </composition>
10        <composition type="AppLogic">
11          <in>
12            <param-ref name="page_id">
13              <operator type="omit" value="/webpage/@id" />
14            </param-ref>
15          </in>
16        </composition>
17      </reference>
18    </compositionreferences>
19  </xcontract>
```

Fig. 2. The contract for the programme page of the VIF Web site.

The *content* concern specifies the structure and type of the page's content using an XML schema. This concern is used by the content manager to prepare the content for the page and by the layout designer to apply style information to the content elements. The *application logic* concern, on the other hand, captures the input and output interface requirements of the page and is used by the programmer. The contract shown in Figure 2 defines the two concerns in lines 2 and 3 and would include an XML schema and an XML-based interface definition in the respective `<concern>` elements.

Contracts also form the foundation of XGuide's concurrent implementation phase. They capture all information necessary to implement the various aspects of the page independently of each other, i.e., the content manager, layout designer and programmer can work in parallel based on the information provided in the contract.

In the example in Figure 1, all pages reference the header component and thus their contracts need to be composed with the header component's contract. In Figure 2 the composition information is represented by the `<compositionreferences>` element (lines 5-18). Contract composition works on a per concern basis. Consequently, each concern defines its own composition operator.

3.1   Content Composition

Since the content concern uses an XML schema to define the structure and the data types used for content modeling, composing content concerns can rely on schema composition. To keep the operation simple, we currently restrict content composition to extending an existing element definition either by inserting a new element at the beginning or appending it at the end of an existing element's content model.

Figure 2 shows the programme page's contract that references the header component's contract. The content composition operator (lines 7-9) defines that the `webpage` element should be extended at the beginning with the referenced header.

3.2   Application Logic Composition

The composition of application logic concerns requires a more sophisticated composition operation. We distinguish between composition of input interfaces and composition of output interfaces. Since output interfaces represent Web forms that are embedded in a page, composition of forms is cumulative. This means that if we reference a component that contains a form, i.e., has an output interface, we add a new output interface to the referencing component.

For input interfaces, the situation is more complex. Since Web components do not exist on the client-side (because they are represented as HTML), the task is to create an input interface for the whole page (for page creation at the server side) that subsumes the input requirements of all components on the page. As a consequence, the composition operation does not deal with the whole input interface but defines a composition operator for every parameter in the input interface of a referenced component. We distinguish three cases when composing a component input value c_i of a component C with the input interface of a page P. If c_i is not related to any value in P's input interface, it is added to the new input interface (*composition-by-addition*). If the input value c_i happens to be already represented in P's input interface (because the page also needs this value as input), the composition operation does not need to modify the input interface but merely adds a mapping from the existing value to c_i (*composition-by-unification*).

Finally, c_i can be directly provided by the content of the embedding page P. In this case, c_i is mapped to an XPath expression identifying the value for c_i in the content of P (*composition-by-omission*). Figure 2 gives an example for this case (see lines 10-16). The value for the *page_id* input parameter of the header component is provided by evaluating the */webpage/@id* XPath expression on the embedding page. Thus though the header component requires a *page_id* input parameter, it does not appear in the page's input interface. For more information on the XGuide contract calculus see [3].

In addition to the currently supported content and application logic concerns, we are working on two additional concern plug-ins capturing the specification information for meta-data and access control to page content based on user identity. Each concern plug-in again consists of an XML language to express the specification information and the corresponding composition operators. Given the contracts for all pages, developers can start implementing the specified concerns. Because of the strict separation of concerns in the contracts, they can even do so in parallel and assemble the concern implementations at the end.

To support the development process, we provide a prototype tool called *XSuite* that supports the XGuide method. XSuite is an Eclipse plug-in and supports visual modeling via Microsoft Visio. It provides dialogs and wizards to create contracts for all artifacts in the XGuide sitemap, to define pages based on the created contracts, to implement these pages in the MyXML [4] implementation technology (other implementation technologies are supported via a plug-in mechanism), and to test and deploy the implemented pages.

4   Conclusion

This paper describes how we apply the concept of design-by-contract to the field of Web engineering and proposes the use of specifications (Web contracts). It demonstrates the use of contracts in the XGuide approach and shows how they influence the composition of Web components and facilitate a parallel implementation. A simple example from deploying XGuide in the VIF 2003 case study is shown. The strict separation of concerns adds additional benefits through an increased reuse potential and eased maintenance.

References

1. Ginige, A., Murugesan, S.: Web Engineering: An Introduction. IEEE Multimedia, Special Issue on Web Engineering **8** (March 2001) 14–18
2. Meyer, B.: Applying "Design By Contract". IEEE Computer **25** (1992) 40–51
3. Kerer, C.: XGuide - Concurrent Web Development with Contracts. PhD thesis, Technical University of Vienna (2003)
   http://www.infosys.tuwien.ac.at/Staff/ck/downloads/xguide.pdf.
4. Kerer, C., Kirda, E.: Layout, Content and Logic Separation in Web Engineering. In: 9th International World Wide Web Conference, 3rd Web Engineering Workshop, Amsterdam, Netherlands, May 2000. Number 2016 in Lecture Notes in Computer Science, Springer Verlag (2001) 135–147

A Proposal for Petri Net Based Web Service Application Modeling

Daniel Moldt, Sven Offermann, and Jan Ortmann

University of Hamburg, Computer Science Department
Vogt-Kölln-Str. 30, D-22527 Hamburg
{moldt,4offerma,ortmann}@informatik.uni-hamburg.de

Abstract. Web engineering can be seen as the application of software engineering in a particular environment – the Web. Its most important aspect is the orientation towards distributed systems and their current technology. Current specification techniques like UML do not cover concurrency, distribution and deployment in a sufficient way.
We propose a modeling technique based on high-level Petri nets, called reference nets. They naturally allow for the modeling of processes. Additionally we introduce a framework that covers the other aspects of Web application modeling. Finally we introduce a tool set based on RENEW, a tool for reference nets, to support these modeling approach.

Keywords: High-level Petri nets, nets within nets, reference nets, RE-NEW, Web service, modeling, specification, MULAN

1 Introduction

Web Engineering as it is seen here is the attempt to perform high-quality software engineering in distributed systems for autonomous (often independent) participants. These systems are characterized by distribution, concurrency and often autonomy; the term Web indicates the current embedding of this process in the Internet as the underlying execution platform.

One important area in Web engineering is the area of Web services which are easier to handle than agents in general but which still contain the aspects of distribution and adaptability. Web services are self-describing, self-contained encapsulated applications. The modeling approaches currently often applied in practice are structured analysis and object-oriented analysis. The first one is generally not considered to be sufficient for future applications, while there is a large amount of research effort going into the development of the second and its main representatives the set of modeling techniques: UML [7] (Unified Modeling Language).

Especially the open problems of Web engineering, however, can not be solved by using a relatively simple concept like e.g. State charts for concurrency, autonomy and distribution. When building distributed and concurrent applications a true concurrency semantics has to be used to cover the problems which can be encountered at any time and level of the implementation. Here, an interleaving semantics is no longer sufficient.

N. Koch, P. Fraternali, and M. Wirsing (Eds.): ICWE 2004, LNCS 3140, pp. 93–97, 2004.

Distributed applications might no longer behave like an object, but might show an autonomous behavior. This leads to a modeling approach that is closely related to the agent concepts. Another aspect is the execution of distributed tasks. Here the support of workflow-like concepts is crucial. The UML does not offer a clear intuitive modeling technique for these concepts and so a lot of the specification is often implicitly done by the code.

One of the techniques that should be taken into closer consideration for modeling Web service applications are higher-level Petri nets naturally allowing to model distribution and concurrency. With MULAN [5] a proposal for the integration of agents and Petri nets has been made.

By adapting MULAN for the Web service context, we present a modeling technique that is designed to solve the central problems of Web engineering on a conceptual level. The MULAN-framework allows to build specifications that cover the above mentioned aspects of distributed applications. Our proposal extends the usual set of techniques which is available for Web engineers and provides a powerful architectural basis and structuring mechanism for web applications.

In the following section the underlying concepts and tools used in our approach are introduced. Section 3 explains the use of our approach for Web service orchestration whereas section 4 shows its application to Web service system design and adapts the existing MULAN agent framework for Web services. Section 5 summarizes the paper and gives a short outlook.

2   Reference Nets

The modeling approach described in the sequel is strongly supported by a tool called RENEW[9]. RENEW is a Petri net simulator implemented in Java which allows for the construction and the execution of reference nets.

Reference nets enrich the Coloured Petri net (CPN) formalism [4] by adding concept of nets-within-nets introduced by [10]. Nets-within-nets represent a concept of having tokens within a Petri net as net instances. This way nets can have multiple object nets within a single system net as tokens. The communication between these nets is done through synchronous channels. They allow for the exchange of parameters between the net instances and within a single net instance. This way they offer a way to communicate between net instances. Those object nets can be dynamically instantiated from a template. Multiple net instances can be generated at runtime having different parameters. By having transitions inscribed with arbitrary Java code, RENEW additionally offers an easy integration of Java and can therefore as well execute Web services.

3   Composition of Web Services

A common approach to build new software applications is to identify the needed functionalities that must be provided by modular units of the application and than implement and/or reuse components matching certain requirements. In the context of distributed systems a growing trend is to build such software components platform-independent and make them available in a distributed environment. On this basis new Web applications can be largely composed/assembled from a set of appropriate distributed components, called Web services.

A natural approach to model the order of the interactions needed to fulfill a complex business collaboration is the use of some kind of business process model. This can be described by a variety of different process markup languages. They specify the control and data flow of a business process or the interaction protocols describing the message exchange between the parties involved. A proposal for a model to specify dynamic composition of Web services based on Java, reference nets and current web languages is presented in [8], where the tasks for the realization of a new business service, like interactions or message transformations, are modeled by inscriptions of transitions in a reference net and a platform for the model based composition of Web services is implemented by the use of the Petri net simulator RENEW.

Petri nets offer a single formalism and a visual modeling technique for control flows as well as for the data flow. As a modeling technique for workflows, Petri nets have been thoroughly investigated [1]. Apart from their graphical visualization, they offer for some net variants means to verify properties of workflows like liveness or the absence of deadlocks [2].

Within the component oriented view we provide a conceptual framework and a tool set to dynamically compose Web services. Allowing for the execution of Petri nets, RENEW offers a tight integration of the specification of the control flow and its implementation. This is further supported by the formal semantics of Petri nets. As shown in [1] and demonstrated by the implementation in [3] Petri nets are powerful enough to represent all workflow concepts, which is equally true for the control flow concepts used in Web service description.

4   Requirements for Web Service Architectures

Besides the control flow of Web services we consider the physical or logical location of Web services to be another important area of modeling. Web services are hosted on some kind of Web server which is again located on a platform.

The access to Web services might fail or Web services might not be able to handle certain requests. In these cases the caller has to be able to dynamically switch to another service offering similar functionality. This is closely related to agents with respect to their autonomy and adaptation, what justifies a modeling approach for Web services that was adopted from the agent research area. MULAN [5] is a Petri net based modeling approach for multi-agent systems. Figure 1 depicts the basic architecture adopted for Web services. Here we see that Web services are located on some kind of physical host that they are deployed upon and that they have a logical platform (which might range over multiple hosts). The protocols specifying their behavior are again modeled as Petri nets. The *ZOOM* lines show a refinement from one layer to the succeeding layer. Web services might fail or might no longer be available. In these cases the caller can

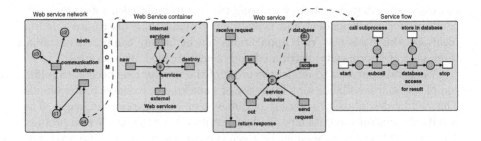

Fig. 1. Web service architecture

ask directory services on the (logical) platform for another similar service. The four layers distinguish different aspects of Web service applications.

The first layer consists of the hosts where one or more Web service containers might be deployed. These hosts offer the basic communication infrastructure.

On top of this layer we have the Web service container offering more specific communication based on SOAP and WSDL as well as access to internal services on the one hand and means to deploy and remove Web services on the other hand. A Web service implementation makes use of this layer to communicate to the outside world (e.g. to other Web services) and to internal services (e.g. databases and repositories).

The actual Web service implementation is located on top of this layer. Calls on the container are forwarded to the appropriate Web service. The Web service might then call other Web services or access internal services to handle the request.

The control flow to handle the request represents the fourth layer. An incoming request triggers a certain control flow and then passes back the results.

The architecture in figure 1 reflects the different aspects of Web services. Each of these layers can be further refined if necessary. This allows for arbitrary granularity in the modeling process. The internal and external behavior of the Web services is modeled by protocol nets. These can also be generated out of OWL-S and BPEL4WS descriptions[6].

5   Summary and Outlook

UML can be seen as the lingua franca. Its different modeling techniques support different views on a system. During the last years considerable effort has been put into the development of the techniques, tools and methods that are necessary for software development. A formal semantics, however, has often been neglected. and key features of current Web applications are not supported: concurrency, autonomy and adaptivity.

Even Petri nets equipped with a precise semantics do not provide sufficient means to cover these features in their models. What is missing is a software architecture. Here the MULAN-framework provides a conceptual and practical solution. The very high-level Petri nets are combined with agent concepts to integrate the advantages of both areas.

In this paper, a formal modeling technique has been adopted to fit the needs when modeling complex web applications. In practical work the suitability of the facets of the approach have been demonstrated. The tool set covers important aspects of web engineering. Due to the complex domain, the facets have been developed in isolation, demonstrating their respective strength. During student projects with 20 to 50 participants the approach has been applied successfully for the last three years in the area of agent-oriented software development.

We will continue to extend RENEW as the basic tool and we will focus on the Petri net aspects in combination with agents and their Web technological embedding. On the other hand we take care to use web and software engineering experience wherever it is possible. As demonstrated in [8] non-agent based structuring is investigated. In and [6] the same is shown for the Semantic web.

References

1. Wil M.P. van der Aalst and Arthur H.M. ter Hofstede. Workflow pattern homepage. Technical report, URL: http://tmitwww.tm.tue.nl/research/patterns/, 2003.
2. C. Girault and R. Valk. *Petri Nets for Systems Engineering - A Guide to Modeling, Verification, and Applications.* Springer-Verlag, 2003.
3. Thomas Jacob. Implementierung einer sicheren und rollenbasierten Workflow-Management-Komponente für ein Petrinetzwerkzeug. Diplomarbeit, Universität Hamburg, Fachbereich Informatik, 2002.
4. K. Jensen. High Level Petri Nets. In A. Pagoni and G. Rozenberg, editors, *Applications and Theory of Petri Nets*, number 66 in Informatik Fachberichte, pages 166–180, Berlin, 1983. Springer-Verlag.
5. Michael Köhler, Daniel Moldt, and Heiko Rölke. Modelling the structure and behaviour of Petri net agents. In *Proc. of 22nd International Conf. on Applications and Theory of Petri Nets 2001 (ICATPN 2001) / J.-M. Colom, M. Koutny (Eds.), Newcastle upon Tyne, UK*, pages 224–242. Lecture Notes in Computer Science 2075, edited by G. Goos, J. Hartmanis and J. van Leuwen, Springer, June 2001.
6. Daniel Moldt and Jan Ortmann. DaGen: A Tool for Automatic Translation from DAML-S to High-level Petri Nets, 2004. to appear, excepted as tool paper to FASE 2004.
7. Object Management Group. UML resource page. Technical report, 2004.
8. Sven Offermann. Ein Referenz-Netz-basiertes Modell zur dynamischen Komposition von Web Services. Master's thesis, Universität Hamburg, Fachbereich Informatik, 2003.
9. Renew – the reference net workshop. URL http://www.renew.de/. Reference to the program, the source code and the documentation of the Renew simulator.
10. R. Valk. Petri nets as token objects - An introduction to elementary object nets. In J. Desel and M. Silva, editors, *Proc. Application and Theory of Petri Nets, Lisbon, Portugal*, number 1420 in LNCS, pages 1–25, Berlin, 1998. Springer-Verlag.

Extending Navigation Modelling to Support Content Aggregation in Web Sites[*]

Pedro Valderas, Joan Fons, and Vicente Pelechano

Department of Information Systems and Computation
Polytechnic University of Valencia
Camí de Vera s/n
46022 Valencia, Spain
{pvalderas, jjfons, pele}@dsic.upv.es

Abstract. Currently, web sites are integrators of heterogeneous information and services that are oriented to providing content aggregation. From a Model-Driven perspective, web applications need conceptual mechanisms that make it easy to describe, manage and reuse contents and services in order to deal with content aggregation at a higher level of abstraction. Our work presents conceptual modelling techniques that extend the OOWS navigational modelling by refining the navigational context definition and introducing the concept of information abstraction unit to specify the contents of web applications of this kind. These new abstractions provide powerful reuse mechanisms that produce considerable benefits because both development time and effort can be reduced. Finally, the paper presents some ideas to implement content aggregation taking these enhanced navigational models as input.

1 Introduction

Web sites are assuming a greater leading role in Internet. Web sites like Yahoo (www.yahoo.com), MSN (www.msn.com), Lycos (www.lycos.com) or Terra (www.terra.es) are ranked among the web applications that receive the most visits. The main characteristic of applications of this type consists of providing the users with web pages that are built from aggregation of contents. These pages provide a lot of information and services on issues of a diverse nature. Figure 1 shows the home page of the Terra web site that is build from the aggregation of diverse contents or information blocks.

From a methodological point of view, the most outstanding approaches (OOHDM [2], WebML [5], WSDM [1], etc.) focus their efforts on defining web applications from conceptual models that allow them to specify hypermedial and functional requirements. The mechanisms for hypermedia modelling allow the analyst (1) to define web pages as conceptual schema views and (2) to interconnect these views to define the navigational structure of the web application. However, considering a web

---

[*] This work has been partially supported by the MCYT Project with ref. TIC2001- 3530-C02-01 and the Polytechnical University of Valencia, Spain.

N. Koch, P. Fraternali, and M. Wirsing (Eds.): ICWE 2004, LNCS 3140, pp. 98–102, 2004.

page only as a view of the conceptual schema makes difficult to specify aggregation of contents, where web pages are built as a composite of several conceptual schema views (see each numbered area in Figure 1). In this way, although some of the approaches mentioned above provide support in the design and/or implementation steps, none of them explicitly supports the specification of web applications with aggregation of contents in the conceptual modelling step.

In this work, we present conceptual modelling techniques that extend the OOWS (Object-Oriented Web Solution) [4] navigational modelling by refining the navigational context definition and introducing the concept of information abstraction unit in order to specify the contents for web applications of this kind. This new expressive capacity makes it easy to describe at a higher level of abstraction of web applications with content aggregation. It also provides powerful reuse mechanisms that

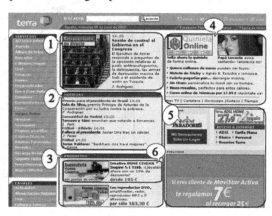

Fig. 1. Terra Home Page

can reduce development time and effort. Following a Model-Driven Development (MDD [6]) approach, the paper presents some ideas to implement web applications that support content aggregation by taking these enhanced navigational models as input.

This paper is organized in the following way: section 2 introduces the OOWS method which presents the proposed extensions at a conceptual modelling level using the Terra web site as a case study. Conclusions and future works are commented on in section 3.

2   Content Aggregation in OOWS

OOWS (Object-Oriented Web Solutions) [3] is the extension of an object-oriented software production method (OO-Method [4]) that introduces the required expressivity to capture the navigational requirements of web applications. In order to do this, OOWS introduces the **Navigational Model** that allows for capturing the navigation semantics in two steps: the "Authoring-in-the-large" (global view) and the "Authoring-in-the-small" (detailed view).

The *Authoring-in-the-large* step refers to the specification and design of global and structural aspects of the web application. These requirements are specified in a *Navigational Map* that provides a specific kind of user with its system view. It is represented using a directed graph whose nodes denote navigational contexts and whose arcs denote navigational links or valid navigational paths.

These navigational contexts (graphically represented as UML packages stereotyped with the «context» keyword) represent the user interaction units that provide a set of cohesive data and operations. The navigational links (navigational map arcs) represent context accessibility or "navigational paths". Figure 2 shows a piece of the navigational map for the Terra web site related to an anonymous *Internet user*.

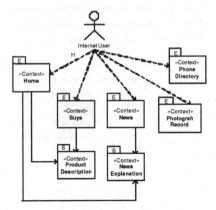

Fig. 2. Terra navigational map

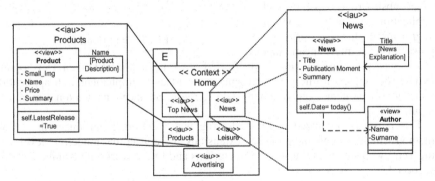

Fig. 3. *Home* navigational context and *News* and *Products IAUs*

The *"Authoring-in-the-small"* step refers to the detailed specification of the contents of the navigational contexts. The following section presents how these contexts must be defined in order to achieve content aggregation.

2.1 Navigational Contexts with Content Aggregation

In order to support content aggregation, navigational contexts should be considered as user interaction units which provide access to several information abstraction units. An information abstraction unit (IAU), stereotyped with the «iau» keyword, represents a specific view on the class diagram. Each IAU is made up of a set of *navigational classes* that represent class views (including attributes and operations). These classes are stereotyped with the «view» keyword. Moreover, selection filters (expressions that allow us to select specific objects) can be defined in OCL upon an object population which has been retrieved by a navigational class (see Figure 3, "self.latestRelease=True" at *Products* class and "self.Date=today()" at *News class*).

Navigational classes must be related by unidirectional binary relationships, called navigational relationships. They are defined over existing aggregation/association/composition or specialization/generalization relationships.

Figure 3 shows an example of the Home navigational context. This context is defined using five IAUs: *Top News, News, Products, Leisure* and *Advertising*. Figure 3 also shows the *News* IAU definition (that provides the news of the day) and the *Products* IAU definition (that provides information about the latest product releases). In Figure 1 we can see the implementation of this navigational context. In areas 1, 2, 3, 4 and 5 we can see the IAUs implementation corresponding each one to a different section of the home page.

2.2 Reuse Mechanisms

Introducing IAUs into the OOWS navigational model allows us to provide some mechanisms to reuse contents at a high level of abstraction. These mechanisms allow us (1) to specify new navigational contexts and/or (2) to specify new IAUs taking a predefined IAU as an input.

1. Specifying New Navigational Contexts: an IAU specified in a navigational context can be used to define other new contexts by means of a reference to it in the new definition. In this way, a new navigational context can be made up of: (1) new IAUs (mandatory option for the navigational context which is specified first) or (2) IAUs specified in other navigational contexts.

2. Specifying New IAUs through specialization: new IAUs can be defined taking an already defined one as a basis. We do this by extending the IAU definition by

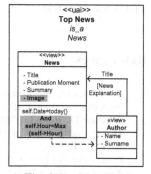

Fig. 4. Top News IAU

means of specialization mechanisms: the specialized IAU inherits a parent IAU definition. It can be refined

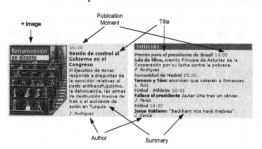

Fig. 5. *Top News* and *News* IAUs implementation.

to adapt the retrieved information, services and navigation capabilities to the needs of a particular navigational context, carrying out the following operations: Adding or removing attributes, adding or removing services, adding or removing navigational classes, adding or removing navigational relationships and adding, removing or redefining population selection filters.

IAU specialization is performed by means of some kind of **is_a** operator, allowing the analyst to refine the specialized IAU using the previous operations. Figure 4 shows the *Top News* IAU definition. This IAU has been specialized from the *News* IAU (see the top of the Figure 4). In this case, it has been refined by adding the *Image* attribute and redefining its population selection filter (only the last news item is retrieved at this moment). These refinements have been highlighted in Figure 4. Figure 5 shows sections 1 and 2 of Figure 1 corresponding to the implementation for both *Top News* and *News* IAUs.

3 Conclusions

In this paper we have proposed a solution from the conceptual modelling perspective in order to give methodological support for the development of web applications with content aggregation.

This solution redefines the navigational context as a conceptual abstraction that can be built using multiple information abstraction units (IAUs). Each IAU represents at the conceptual modelling step a specific content and the use of IAUs allows us to carry out content reuse mechanisms.

As future work, it would be necessary both to extend the presentation patterns that OOWS Presentation Model provides to attach them to the IAUs and to detect presentation relationships and dependencies between different IAUs in the same navigational context.

References

1. De Troyer O. and Leune C. WSDM: A user-centered design method for Web sites. In Proc. of the 7th International World Wide Web Conference, 1998.
2. Schwabe D., Rossi G., "An Object Oriented Approach to Web-Based Application Design", Theory and Practice of Object Systems 4(4), 1998. Wiley and Sons, New York, ISSN 1074-3224).)
3. Joan Fons, Vicente Pelechano, Manoli Albert y Oscar Pastor. Development of Web Applications from Web Enhanced Conceptual Schemas. Springer-Verlag, Lecture Notes in Computer Science. Proc. Of the International Conference on Conceptual Modelling, 22nd Edition, ER'03, pp 232-245. Chicago, EE.UU, 13 - 16 October 2003.
4. Pastor O., Pelechano V., Insfrán E,. and Gómez J. From Object Oriented Conceptual Modeling to Automated Programming in Java. 17th International Conference on Conceptual Modeling (ER'98). Springer-Verlag, LNCS 1507, pp. 183-196. Singapore, November, 1998.
5. Ceri S., Fraternali P., Bongio A. Web Modeling Language (WebML): a Modeling Language for Designing Web Sites. In WWW9, Vol. 33 (1-6), pp 137-157. Computer Networks, 2000.
6. Mellor, S.J.; Clark, A.N.; Futagami, T. "Model-driven development" – Guest editor's introduction. IEEE Software, p. 14-18, Sept.-Oct. 2003.

Exception Handling Within Workflow-Based Web Applications

Marco Brambilla and Nicola D'Elia

Dipartimento Elettronica e Informazione, Politecnico di Milano,
Via Ponzio 34/5, 20133 Milano, Italy
mbrambil@elet.polimi.it, nd636136@polimi.it

Abstract. As the Web becomes a platform for implementing B2B applications, the need arises of extending Web conceptual modeling from data-centric applications to data- and process-centric applications. New primitives must be put in place to implement workflows describing business processes. In this context, new problems about process safety arise, due to the loose control on Web clients. Indeed, user behavior can generate dangerous incoherencies for the execution of processes. This paper presents a proposal of workflow-enabling primitives for Web applications, and a high level approach to the management of exceptions that occurs during execution of processes. We present a classification of exceptions that can occur inside workflow-based Web applications, and recovery policies to retrieve coherent status and data after an exception. An implementation experience is briefly presented too.

1 Introduction

In recent years, the Web is more and more being used as the implementation platform for B2B applications, whose goal is not only the navigation of content, but also supporting business processes, content management, value-added services and so on. Conceptual modeling expertise from other fields (database, object-orientated programming, hypermedia applications) has been widely recognized as valid starting point for defining conceptual aids for Web application development too [7]. The first generation of conceptual models for the Web [1, 2, 5, 6] essentially focus on capturing the structure of data to be published, and the navigation primitives, represented by such concepts as pages, content nodes, and links.

To cover business processes support, a second generation of conceptual models is required. These new models should cope with process and workflow modeling, support Web service interaction, and integrate data-centric and process-centric modeling primitives into a mix suited to the development of advanced B2B Web applications. In this context, it is important to address the critical cases that can occur in the enactment of business processes on a Web-based platform.

This paper presents an extension to a first-generation Web modeling language [5, 6] to support the specification, design and implementation of B2B applications, and

N. Koch, P. Fraternali, and M. Wirsing (Eds.): ICWE 2004, LNCS 3140, pp. 103–117, 2004.
© Springer-Verlag Berlin Heidelberg 2004

offers an high-level analysis of critic aspects and exception management issues within Web applications exploiting business processes. Exceptions that can happen in a Web based application have peculiar characteristics with respect to traditional workflow applications. This is due to two main aspects: (i) interaction options provided by browser-based interfaces are very powerful, but they are more oriented to free navigation than strict processes adherence(e.g., user is enabled to jump back and forth on navigated pages, thus introducing dangerous repetition of process activities); (ii) user cannot be forced to perform any action or task (e.g., he can stand on a page for long time, or even close the browser and disconnect at any time).

Our approach is lightweight: we are interested in extending Web modeling to cope with process and exception modeling, not to adapt workflow management systems to the Web; about exceptions, we aim at defining a modeling paradigm for critical cases, not to build transactional systems or low level exception handling mechanisms.

Many works have addressed the problem of exception interception and compensation. They mainly studied transactional properties for activities, which is not in our scope. However, some works deals with weaker properties. For example, [8] is based on the concept of spheres, to make use of only those transactional properties that are actually needed; [12] is one of the first works that address the problem in the Web context.

The paper is organized as follows: Section 2 briefly outlines the main concepts about workflow and Web application modeling; Section 3 introduces the study of exception and critical situations that can occur in the execution of processes on the Web; Section 4 presents our approach to management and recovery of exceptional situations within process execution; finally Section 5 reviews implementation experience and Section 6 draws some conclusions and presents our ongoing and future work.

2   Conceptual Modeling of Web Applications and Workflows

Conceptual design consists in high-level, platform-independent specification of the application, which can be used to drive the subsequent implementation phase. In this section we focus on two aspects of conceptual design: (i) Web application design, briefly describing the WebML model, that will be used in the sequel to describe our proposals; (ii) Workflow modeling concepts and primitives.

It is important to point out that, although the paper uses the WebML notation to describe our contribution, the proposed approach is independent from the specific language or notation that is adopted. Our approach to conceptual design relies on the following guidelines: an Entity-Relationship diagram models the data stored, manipulated, and exchanged by the application actors, plus the metadata required for the management of the business processes; *process diagrams* are treated as a higher-level specification and are used to derive a set of hypertext models that "realizes" them. These hypertext models belong to the site views of the user groups involved in the process and must offer them the interface needed for performing their activities.

2.1 Process Modeling

For specifying processes, we adopt the terminology and notation defined by the Workflow Management Coalition [16], which provides a workflow model based on the concepts of *Process* (the description of the supported workflow), *Case* (a process instance), *Activity* (the elementary unit of work composing a process), *Activity instance* (an instantiation of an activity within a case), *Actor* (a user role intervening in the process), and *Constraint* (logical precedence among activities and rules enabling activities execution). Processes can be internally structured using a variety of constructs: sequences of activities, AND-splits (a single thread of control splits into two or more independent threads), AND-joins (blocking convergence point of two or more parallel activities), OR-splits (point in which one among multiple alternative branches is taken), OR-joins (non-blocking convergence point), iterations for repeating the execution of one or more activities, pre- and post-conditions (entry and exit criteria to and from a particular activity).

Fig. 1 exemplifies a WfMC workflow specifying the process of online purchase, payment and delivery of goods. The customer can choose the products to purchase, then submits his payment information. At this point, two parallel tasks are executed by the seller employees: the warehouse manager registers the shipping of the order, and a secretary prepares a bill to be sent to the customer.

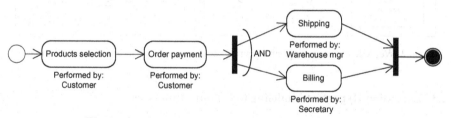

Fig. 1. Workflow diagram of the refunding request process

2.2 Hypertext Modeling

For hypertext modeling, we use the WebML notation[5, 6, 14], a conceptual language for specifying Web applications developed on top of database content described by a E-R diagram. A WebML schema consists of one or more *site views*, expressing the Web interfaces that allow the different user roles to browse or manipulate the data specified in the underlying E-R schema. A *site view* contains *pages*, possibly clustered in *areas*, typically representing independent sections of the site. Pages enclose *content units*, representing atomic pieces of information to be published (e.g., indexes listing items from which the user may select a particular object, details of a single object, entry forms, and so on); content units may have a *selector*, which is a predicate identifying the entity instances to be extracted from the underlying database and displayed by the unit. Pages and units can be connected through *links* of different types to express all possible navigation.

Besides content publishing, WebML allows specifying *operations*, like the filling of a shopping cart or the update of content. Basic data update operations are: the creation, modification and deletion of instances of an entity, or the creation and deletion of instances of a relationship. Operations do not display data and are placed outside of pages; user-defined operations can be specified (e.g., e-mail sending, e-payment, ...), and operation chains are allowed too.

Fig. 2 shows a simplified version of the two areas of the Customer site view of the e-commerce site example, whose workflow have been illustrated in Fig. 1: the *Products* area allows guests to browse products, by selecting in the *Home* page the product group from an index (*ProductGroups*). Once a group is selected, all the products of that group are shown in page *Products*. The *Mailing List Subscription* area allows the user to subscribe to a mailing list through a form. The submitted data are used to modify the profile of the User, by means of a modify operation called *Modify Subscr*, which updates the instance of entity *User* currently logged.

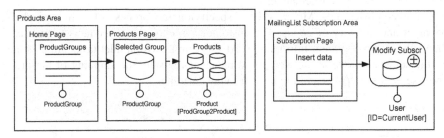

Fig. 2. WebML site view diagram featuring areas, pages, content units, and operations.

2.3   Extending Hypertext Modeling to Capture Processes

In the specification of a Web application supporting business processes[3], the data model, which is normally used to describe the domain objects, is extended with user-related and workflow-related data, and the hypertext model is enriched by a set of primitives enabling workflow dependent content of pages and navigation.

Process metadata. Data modeling is extended with the metadata used to represent the runtime evolution of processes as shown in Fig. 3. The schema includes entities representing the elements of a WfMC process model, and relationships expressing the semantic connections between the process elements.

Entity *Process* is associated with entity *ActivityType*, to represent the classes of activities that can be executed in a process. Entity *Case* denotes an instance of a process, whose status can be: initiated, active, or completed. Entity *ActivityInstance* denotes the occurrence of an activity, whose current status can be: inactive, active and completed. Entities *User* and *Group* represent the workflow actors, as individual users organized within groups (or roles). A user may belong to different groups, and one of these groups is set as his default group, to facilitate access control when the user logs in. Activities are "assigned to" user groups: this means that users of that group can perform the activity. Instead, concrete activity instances are "assigned to" individual users, who actually perform them. If needed, the model can be enriched at will with new relationships to represent more complex assignment rules.

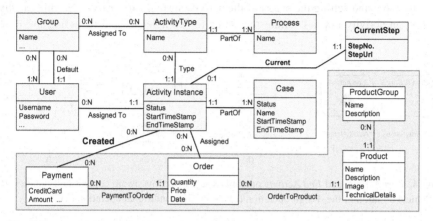

Fig. 3. Data model incorporating workflow concepts and exception handling information

Application data is described by a usual E-R model representing information involved in the current application. In our example, as depicted in the boxed part of Fig. 3, we model a catalog (in which each *Product* belongs to a *ProductGroup*), the *Orders* that the user submits and the *Payment* details. Orders are *assigned* to Activity Instances in which will be processed, whilst Payments are connected to the Activity Instances in which they are created. These relationships associate metadata concepts to application information. In general, the designer can specify an arbitrary number of relationships between the application data and the workflow data, which may be required to connect the activities to the data items they use. Note that minimum cardinality of these relationships is typically 0, since in most cases each activity instance is not associated to all the application data, but only to a very small set of objects.

This schema already includes metadata for supporting exception handling information. Such data are represented in bold face. In particular, the *Created* relationship and the *CurrentStep* entity are needed for supporting recovery policies for exceptions. Their use will be explained in the sequel of the paper.

Workflow hypertext primitives. In order to enact the process, some workflow-specialized hypertext primitives are also necessary to design interfaces capable of producing and consuming such metadata. At this purpose, a few additional primitives are introduced in WebML for updating process data as a result of activity execution, for accessing the data associated with a specific activity instance, and for expressing the assignment of data objects to an activity instance eventually to be executed.

The portion of hypertext devoted to the execution of an activity must be enclosed between the two workflow-related operations shown in Fig. 4(a): *start activity* and *end activity*. These operations are triggered respectively by incoming and outgoing links of the activity and have the side effect of updating the workflow data. Specifically, starting an activity implies creating an activity instance, recording the activity instance activation timestamp, connecting the activity instance to the current case (relationship PartOf), to the current user (relationship AssignedTo), and to the proper activity type, and setting the status of the activity instance to "active". Symmetrically, ending an activity implies setting the status to "completed" and recording the time-stamp.

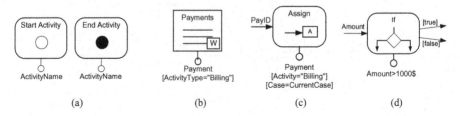

(a)   (b)   (c)   (d)

Fig. 4. *Start Activity* and *End Activity* operations (a); workflow-aware content unit notation(b); graphical notation of the *Assign* operation (c) and of the conditional operation (d)

The *Start Activity* operation can also be marked as the *starting case activity*, when the activity to start is the first one of the entire process; dually, the *End Activity* operation can be tagged as the *end of the case*, thus recording the general status of the process.

Workflow-aware content units can be used for retrieving the data objects related to a particular activity. These units are like the regular WebML content unit but are tagged with a "W" symbol denoting a simplified syntax for their selector, which shortens the expression of predicates involving both application data and workflow data. For example, Fig. 4 (b) shows a workflow-aware index unit that retrieves all the instances of entity *Payment* that have been assigned to an activity of type "Billing".

The *assign operation* is a WebML operation unit that connects application object(s) to an activity instance, for which an activity type, a case and possibly a user are specified. Fig. 4(c) shows the graphical representation of the assign operation, which assigns a *Payment* to the activity called "Billing" for the current process case.

The navigation of a hypertext may need to be conditioned by the status of activities, to reflect the constraints imposed by the workflow. Two dedicated operations called *if* (see Fig. 4(d)) and *switch* operations allow conditional navigation, performing the necessary status tests and deciding the destination of a navigable link.

Mapping rules have been defined from WfMC-based workflow description to WebML hypertexts enhanced with workflow primitives [3].

2.4   Fine Grained Description of Activities

To study in a simple and effective way the exception handling problem, we define some new concepts that describe the structure of activities.

We call *step* a hypertext page belonging to an activity. Steps are univocally numbered within an activity. Between two subsequent steps there can be a chain of operations, which is not relevant for our purposes. Indeed, since we do not consider server-side failures, a chain of operations can be seen as an atomic element that never fails (server-side failure is addressed by standard WebML mechanisms, like KO links [6]). We define the *current step* of an active activity as the last page that the server has generated after a request by the client. This information is stored into the *CurrentStep* entity of the workflow metadata schema (Fig. 3). Within a process case, it is always possible to retrieve the currently active activities, and for each of them the current step.

The current step has 2 important properties: *(i)* it is always uniquely defined for an active activity; *(ii)* it gives us a correct idea of the progress of the activity.

It is important to notice that if the client uses the back and forward buttons of the browser, the current step of the activity does not change, since the client does not make any request to the server. Moreover, by clicking the *back* button we do not roll back the operations between consecutive steps, we just reload an old page.

3   Critical Situations and Exception

Within the execution of a process, exceptional situations can occur, due either to user behavior or to system failures. We define a critical situation as an incorrect browsing behavior of the user (*user-generated exceptions*) or a technical failure of the system (*system failures*).

3.1   User-Generated Exceptions

This section presents the critical situations that can arise from wrong browsing behavior. For Web context, this problem is much more relevant than for traditional applications. The most evident examples are *back* and *forward* buttons of a Web browser, that allow the user to explore the hypertext of the Web application in a free way, while a workflow scenario has usually a strictly forced execution/ navigation structure, and its steps must be executed in the proper order. Moreover, the user is able to jump without restrictions from an application to another. Back and forward buttons let the user go outside the pages of an activity still active or move back to a completed activity and try to resume its execution. With respect to workflow activities, improper browsing can be of three types:

(i)   *improper inbound browsing:* the user gets into a workflow activity without executing the *Start activity* operation, for example by clicking repeatedly on the *back* browser button, until a previously executed activity is reached;

(ii)   *improper outbound browsing:* the user, during the execution of an activity, follows a *wrong* navigational path, exiting the activity without passing by the *End activity* operation. In this case the user leaves the pages of the current activity, either by pressing repeatedly the back browser button or by following a landmark link (i.e., a link which is always clickable within the whole Web application). In this way, the user can potentially start an arbitrary number of activities, since he can try to start a new activity beside the current one. Moreover, the user left an activity in status Active, which cannot proceed, and thus remains halted;

(iii) *improper internal browsing:* the user, during the execution of an activity, presses the back button of the browser one or more times reaching a previous page of the same activity, and then clicks on a link, trying to repeat part of the activity. In this way, the user is in a page that is different from the current step of the activity, since the page from which the user resumes the browsing is different from the last page requested to the server;

(iv) *wait:* the user does not request a page to the server for a given amount of time, after which a timeout expires and the user session ends up. A *Session End* exception is generated, and this behavior collapses in a system failure.

3.2   System Failures

System failures can occur both at client and at server side. *Client-side failures* are problems that are generated by system breakdown, that is either a client crash or a network failure. We do not consider server-side failures, since this problem for Web-based workflows can be addressed in the same way of traditional workflow systems, and several recovery theories and techniques already exist for this context (e.g., rules based on active rules [4]). System failures result in a Session end exception at server-side. To discover client-side failures, HTTP session is a standard technique employed in Web applications. After a session has been established, a network failure or a client failure will result either in the client not performing a request to the server for a given amount of time, or in the server being unable to send the response back to the client. When the server recognizes that the client is no more reachable, it will end up the user session: client-side failures can be captured at application level by generating a *Session End* exception. In this sense, client failure and network failure will be indistinguishable and will be collectively denoted also as *Crash* situations.

After a crash situation the activity instance executed by the user remains in Active status, but is not completed. This means that the activity execution cannot proceed, since the user lost his session, and if he tries to login he can only see the activities that are in Inactive status (ready to be executed). Typically he is not allowed to perform activities potentially in execution (i.e., in Active status).

If the activity instance is not recovered, the whole process case will possibly be stopped, if there are other activities waiting for the completion of the crashed one.

A thrown Session End exception will help to track the crash for later recovery

3.3   Inconsistencies

Data and process inconsistencies can arise from system failure and incorrect browsing behavior. Each of them will be addressed with a different approach:

1) *activity/process halt:* one or more activities (and the processes they belong to) get halted and cannot be resumed or concluded by the user. These problems are detected after they take place and are recovered by means of appropriate policies;

2) *inconsistent database:* one or more database tuples are created or destroyed in an unexpected way, resulting in an inconsistent database and workflow application; these problems are caused by incorrect browsing behavior, and will be handled in a preventive way, by detecting the user faults and generating an exception before they result in a failure.

4 Exceptions and Recovery Policies

As we have seen in previous sections, if a critical situation occurs, the workflow application might be in an inconsistent state due to the presence of a halted activity, i.e. an activity in status Active that cannot proceed. The need arises to recover the halted activity to bring the workflow application back to a correct state and let the process execution proceed. To address the problem, we define the concepts of exception and recovery policy.

4.1 Exceptions

To manage critical situations and to prevent/recover inconsistencies, we introduce the concept of exception. An *exception* is an event that is thrown by the system, as a consequence of a critical situation that is occurred.

An exception is either synchronous, if it is thrown after a page request, or asynchronous, if it is not tied to a page request but can occur independently. In case of synchronous exceptions, the user navigation can be immediately affected since the server can decide to provide the user with a different page depending on the caught exception. On the other hand, the only asynchronous exception that we will consider is Session End. It cannot influence immediately the user browsing, since he already disconnected from the application (his session is no more valid). Table 1 resumes the characteristics of exception types.

Table 1. Types and properties of the exceptions

Exception Type	Session Status	Addressed Problem
Asynchronous	Inactive	Technical Failure Incorrect Browsing Behavior
Synchronous	Active	Incorrect Browsing Behavior

Exceptions to be managed in order to guarantee the correctness of workflow-based Web applications are the following:

1) *Session End:* the user disconnected the client, or a failure happened on the network or at client-side. These events are undistinguishable from server side;

2) *Activity Already Active:* the user is trying to start an activity when there is another activity already active in his session;
3) *Wrong Starting Page:* inside an activity, an action has been performed in a page that is not the last one that the user has visited;
4) *Action By completed Activity:* an action has been performed within an activity that has been already closed.

In the following section we will discuss all possible critical situations and exceptions that can be generated.

4.2   Recovery Policies

We define a *recovery policy* (for a halted activity) as a collection of operations that we perform on the activity and on the related data in order to bring the workflow application to a correct state and to let the process proceed.

Policies can be classified with respect to three orthogonal dimensions:

- **policy direction**, that considers the way in which a coherent status of the process is reached: the policy can try to recover a correct status that was previously visited by the workflow application (*backward policy*), or can try to move to a new correct status that was not previously visited by the workflow application (*forward policy*).

- **policy definition**, that considers who defined the policy. In this sense, we can have policies defined either by the workflow design framework (*predefined policy*) or by the web designer (*user-defined policy*, also known as *compensation chain*).

- **policy execution**, that considers whether the policy is applied in an automated way (*automatic policy*) or in a manual way (*manual policy*). In the former case the policy is automatically applied by the workflow engine after an exception is caught and the engine detects a halted activity. In the latter case a user (the activity executor or another suitable user) can choose the policy to execute through a Web interface (*recovery page*), which is eventually reached after the activity interruption, through an explicit login of the user (Fig. 5).

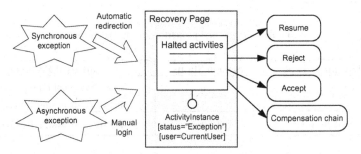

Fig. 5. Manual policies for synchronous and asynchronous exception management

Policies for Synchronous and Asynchronous Exceptions. Policy application can be affected by the type of the exception to be managed. In particular, we will apply different policies depending on the fact that exceptions are synchronous or not.

When a synchronous exception occurs the user session is still active. To take advantage of this fact we consider only manual policy for synchronous events: when the exception occurs the user will be redirected to a recovery page and will choose the most appropriate policy(either predefined or user-defined) for the halted activity.

When an asynchronous exception (i.e., a Session End) occurs, the user session is not connected any more and it is not possible to immediately apply manual policies. Therefore we consider both automatic and manual policy for asynchronous events.

Automatic policies are applied automatically and transparently to the user, while manual policies are applied by the user itself, when he starts a new session through a new login. At that point the user can go in a recovery page and choose the best policy to apply. This behavior is depicted in Fig. 5, together with the predefined policies that are described in next section.

4.3 Predefined Policies

Our framework offers three predefined policies: Accept, Reject and Resume. To better understand their behavior, we consider a very simple example, consisting in the order payment activity, as described in Fig. 6: the activity starts, a payment is created and connected to the order, and the user fills up a form with his credit card data. Then, the payment is performed (through a black-box service) and the payment status is updated. If an exception occurs the current step of the activity will be step 1 (since it's the only step of the activity).

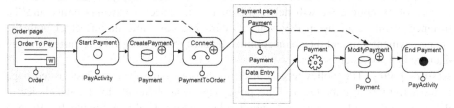

Fig. 6. Payment activity. There is just one step (the payment page), a preceding chain of operation (comprising the create payment unit and the connect unit) and a following chain (comprising the unit for the payment and the modify payment)

Accept policy. It accepts the operations already done by the halted activity, setting the activity status to Completed, executing all the data assignment and activating all the proper following activity. The process can proceed, but it may happen that part of the halted activity was not executed. The accept policy is a forward policy, since it tries to bring the workflow application to a correct status not previously visited, by simply assigning the status Completed to the halted activity.

This policy is suitable only for activities that have some non critical parts, that can be omitted. In all the other cases, it has resulted ineffective, since it leaves the activity results meaningless, thus damaging the whole process case execution. For example, suppose that an exception occurs in the payment activity in Fig. 6. Current step is 1, and if we apply an accept policy, we will consider the activity executed even if the payment unit has not been performed. The process will be enabled to continue, even if the payment has not been performed. Therefore, in this case the accept policy is not a correct choice.

Reject policy. It deletes the data created by the activity, trying to recover the initial state of the database before the activity execution, and assigns the Inactive status to the activity. The reject policy is a backward policy, since it removes the data created by the activity (and all the relationships with connected objects), tries to recover the initial state of the database before the activity execution, and assigns the Inactive status to the activity. Reject policy is not a full rollback mechanism, since not all the operations executed by the activity are undone (i.e., deletion and modification results are kept as they are). Indeed, we don't want to implement a transactional system, with data versioning and so on. In this way, this policy can be implemented simply by means of a "*Created*" relationship, that connects the Activity Instance to the objects created in the activity itself (an example can be seen in Fig. 3). Once the reject is invoked, the activity is set to Inactive (ready to start) and all the *Created* objects are removed. Thus, reject is an approximate recovery of the initial state of the activity. This behavior partially limits the effectiveness of the policy but improves its efficiency, avoiding a performance burden resulting from a complete track of all the operations of the activity. Reject policy is suitable for all the activities that should be completely performed, and whose core task consist in creation of objects. With this policy, users can be asked to complete the activity repeatedly, until it is successfully finished. From empiric evaluations, this case results to be very frequent.

If we go back to the payment activity example (Fig. 6), by applying the reject policy in case of exception, we will delete the created instance of payment entity and the instance of the relationship PaymentToOrder, thus canceling the effect of both the create payment unit and the connect unit. The activity is ready to be restarted and the data are in a consistent status.

Resume policy. This policy lets the user resume browsing from the last visited page of the activity before the failure. This policy can be applied only by manual choice of the user, while the first two can be applied both automatically and manually. Browsing is resumed from the last page of the activity generated by the server, i.e. the current step. Note that operations with side effect are not improperly triggered by this policy: if the side effect occurs between the previous and the current page, it is not executed twice, because the user is provided with the url pointing directly to the page; if the side effect occurs after the current page, it has not been executed yet, otherwise the current page should point to the next one.

Resume is a backward policy, since it brings the application and the workflow to a correct state that was previously visited. Indeed, if an exception occurs, either the user session is expired or the page that is shown to the user is different from the current step. The user cannot proceed with the execution of the correct activity, and the whole process status is incorrect. As we said before, the resume policy can only be applied through manual intervention by the user. This can be achieved by providing to the user a recovery page, in which he can see the activities in incorrect status, and can decide to resume them. By reloading the last page generated by the server on the user browser, the activity execution can proceed (e.g., in Payment activity example in Fig.

6, the resume policy lets the user reload the payment page and complete the payment).

4.4 Compensation Chains

To allow a more fine-grained exception handling, we allow the designer to define his own recovery policies (e.g., sending warning emails to users, or implementing full rollback capabilities for specific activities). This solution will be adopted to manage the most critical activities only. The user can define operation chains that are triggered by exceptions. We provide a new unit (called CatchEvent unit), with the following parameters: ExceptionType, ActivityType, ActivityInstance. Exception type and Activity type are specified at design time and define the situation in which the compensation chain is triggered. Activity instance is a runtime parameter, whose value is available to operations of the chain, for retrieving further related data. Note that, since triggering and execution of compensation chains is completely automatic, no pages involving user interaction are allowed within chains. Fig. 7 shows a sketched example of compensation chain for the Payment activity depicted in Fig. 6.

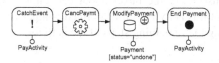

Fig. 7. Payment exception compensation chain. The payment is canceled and the information about it are update into the database

5   Implementation Experience

The concepts presented in this paper have been proved valid on the field, since a prototype implementation has been developed and used to design sample applications. The implementation extends a commercial tool called WebRatio[15], which allows to design and automatically generate Web applications from WebML models. Our extension provides the workflow metadata schema and all the units presented in Section 2.3. Moreover, new units for granting automatic policies enactment are available (Accept, Reject and Resume units).

Several case studies exploiting exception handling capabilities have been implemented, thus validating and refining the approach. The results of this research, which is part of the WebSI project, funded by the EC's 5th framework, has been used by the partners of the WebSI project for pilot applications, and by other projects.

Among them, Acer Business Portal (that includes remote service calls for providing location and driving information to users, and workflow-based interaction between Acer and its commercial partners), and MetalC project[11], which is the most complex among the application we have developed, since it includes a set of B2B portals (one for each business partner). The purpose of the project is to allow business interactions between Italian companies of the mechanical field by means of their respective Web portals, through Web services calls. In this context, complex workflow interactions have been put in place, to grant reliable cooperation. For example, the purchasing process in a B2B scenario consist of a very complex set of interactions, since the buyer typically asks for a quote, the seller makes his offer, then the buyer sends his order for the best offer. In this context, exceptions management becomes very critic. In the implemented communication platform all the discussed recovery policies have been used. Some examples follows: *(i)* if an exception occurs within the AskForQuote activity, an accept policy is performed, and the request is sent even if not all the data are submitted (less relevant data are left in the last steps of the activity); *(ii)* if an exception occurs within the SendOrder activity, the reject policy is applied: data created within the activity is deleted, and the user is asked to restart it; *(iii)* in case of exception within the self-registration activity, which is a long sequence of data submission by the partners, resume policy is exploited, to allow the user resume the self-registration from the point in which he left the application.

An example of user defined recovery becomes necessary within the shipping confirmation activity: once the order has been confirmed and the goods are ready to be shipped, the seller must notify the buyer about the sending. If an exception occurs during the execution of this activity, a user-defined compensation chain is performed, automatically executing the remaining steps of the activity.

6   Conclusions

In this paper we proposed a conceptual approach to exception handling within workflow-based Web applications, described through a metadata model and a set of primitives to be used into hypertext specification. To manage critical situations, we proposed an approach based on exception handling (some Java implementation already exists that could be used to support this approach [17]), and definition of predefined and user-defined policies, that have been tested on the field.

The main advantage of our approach stands in allowing to define exception handling and compensation chains without lowering the abstraction level of the design.

Future work will address refinement of the implementation, to allow a more seamless and transparent integration of exception handling within WebML specification, to avoid the need of explicitly specifying in WebML all the basic steps of exception handling. A second research direction is towards study of exception handling in remote service calls. Some preliminary considerations have been done, and we expect an approach similar to the one we have studied for workflow-based Web applications.

References

1. Atzeni, P., Mecca, G., Merialdo, P.: Design and Maintenance of Data-Intensive Web Sites. EDBT 1998: 436-450.
2. Baresi, L., Garzotto, F., Paolini, P.: From Web Sites to Web Applications: New Issues for Conceptual Modeling. ER Workshops 2000: 89-100.
3. Brambilla, M., Ceri, S., Comai, S., Fraternali, P., Manolescu, I.: Specification and design of workflow-driven hypertexts, Journal of Web Engineering, Vol. 1, No.1 (2002).
4. Casati, F., Ceri, S., Paraboschi, S., Pozzi, G., Specification and implementation of exceptions in workflow management systems. ACM Transactions on Database Systems, Sept. 1999, (Vol. 24, No. 3), pp. 405-451.
5. Ceri, S., Fraternali, P., Bongio, A.: Web Modeling Language (WebML): a modeling language for designing Web sites. WWW9/Computer Networks 33(1-6): 137-157 (2000).
6. Ceri, S., Fraternali, P., Bongio, A., Brambilla, M., Comai, S., Matera, M.: Designing Data-Intensive Web Applications, Morgan-Kaufmann, December 2002.
7. Conallen, J.: Building Web Applications with UML. Addison Wesley (OTS), 2000.
8. Hagen, C., Alonso, G.: Exception Handling in Workflow Management Systems, IEEE Transactions on software engineering, October 2000 (Vol. 26, No. 10), pp. 943-958
9. IBM MQSeries Workflow Homepage: http://www.ibm.com/software/ts/mqseries/workflow/v332/
10. Oracle Workflow 11i: http://www.oracle.com/appsnet/technology/products/docs/workflow.html
11. MetalC project Homepage: http://www.metalc.it
12. Miller, J. A., Sheth, A. P., Kochut, K. J., Luo Z. W.: Recovery Issues in Web-Based Workflow, CAINE-99, Atlanta, Georgia (November 1999) pp. 101-105.
13. Schwabe, D., Rossi, G.: An Object Oriented Approach to Web Applications Design. TAPOS 4(4): (1998).
14. WebML Project Homepage: http://www.webml.org
15. WebRatio Homepage: http://www.webratio.com/
16. Workflow Management Coalition Homepage: http://www.wfmc.org
17. Ofbiz WF Java implementation: http://www.ofbiz.org/api/components/workflow/build/javadocs/

Loosely Coupled Web Services in Remote Object Federations

Uwe Zdun

Department of Information Systems, Vienna University of Economics, Austria
zdun@acm.org

Abstract. Loosely coupled services are gaining importance in many business domains. However, compared to OO-RPC middleware approaches, emerging technologies proposed to implement loosely coupled services, such as Web services or P2P frameworks, still have some practical problems. These arise in many typical business domains, for instance, because of missing central control, high network traffics, scalability problems, performance overheads, or security issues. We propose to use ideas from these emerging technologies in a controlled environment, called a federation. Each remote object (a peer) is controlled in one or more federations, but within this environment peers can collaborate in a simple-to-use, loosely coupled, and ad hoc style of communication. Our design and implementation relies on popular remoting patterns. We present a generic framework architecture based on these patterns together with a prototype implementation.

1   Introduction

Loosely coupled (business) services are nowadays propagated and/or enabled by many different technologies, including Web services, P2P systems, coordination and cooperation technologies, and spontaneous networking. Compared to OO-RPC middleware approaches, such as CORBA, RMI, or DCOM, these approaches promise loose coupling, a service-based architecture, ease of use, and ease of deployment. However, as we will point out in Section 2, today all these technologies have their limitations in the context of business-critical systems, for instance, regarding central control tasks, network traffics, scalability, performance, or security.

Typical applications of loosely coupled (Web) services in different business domains are workflows, groupware, legacy integration, or coordination of business components. When we offer loosely coupled (Web) services in these business domains, there are some specific, recurring requirements. For instance, if spontaneous connections are allowed, we require some level of control to ensure that a business service cannot be misused. Consider an e-commerce service that should be provided only to service users who have paid for the service. One business peer can play more than one role in different contexts. Consider a peer that represents the delivery service of a content provider: it also has to provide a contract engine and handle rights enforcement. To model such situations, we cannot use the "all peers are equals" model of current P2P environments in the whole system. However, it would be useful, if peers that are actually equals in a certain situation can be handled as such. As we could use a very simple remoting model in such cases, this would ease the development of distributed programs significantly.

N. Koch, P. Fraternali, and M. Wirsing (Eds.): ICWE 2004, LNCS 3140, pp. 118–131, 2004.

Moreover, service-based architectures and ad hoc connectivity may ease deployment in a controlled environment, say, within a company.

We propose a federated model of remote objects as a solution. Within a federation, each peer offers Web services (and possibly other kinds of services) to its peers, can connect spontaneously to other peers (and to the federation), and is equal to its peers. Each remote object can potentially be part of more than one federation as a peer, and each peer decides which services it provides to which federation. Certain peers in a federation can be able to access extra services that are not offered to other peers in this federation via its other federations. A semantic lookup service allows for finding peers using metadata, exposed by the peers according to some ontology. Thus it enables loosely coupled services and simple self-adaptations for interface or version changes.

We present a framework for loosely coupled Web services built internally with well known (OO-)RPC remoting patterns (from [21,22,23]). We will discuss a reference implementation written in the object-oriented Tcl variant XOTcl [18] using SOAP-based communication. The pattern-based design has the aim that a similar framework can be implemented in any language with any Web service framework. The framework is designed to be extensible and implementation decisions, such as using a particular SOAP implementation as the communication protocol, can be exchanged, if required.

In this paper, we first discuss prior work in the areas of Web services, P2P systems, coordination technologies, and spontaneous networking. Then we discuss open issues in these approaches regarding loosely coupled services. Next, we discuss a generic framework design and a prototype implementation in XOTcl on top of SOAP, called Leela. Finally, we discuss in how far the open issues are resolved in our concepts and conclude.

2   Related Work

In this section, we discuss related work in the areas of Web services, P2P systems, coordination technologies, and spontaneous networking. We will see that all of these concepts implement some of the desired functionalities, but leave a few issues open.

2.1   Web Services

Web service architectures center around the service concept, meaning that a service is seen as a (set of) component(s) together with a providing organization. Thus Web services are a technology offering both, concepts for deployment and providing access to business functions over the Web. Technically, Web services build on different Web service stacks, such as IBM's WSCA [15] or Microsoft's .NET [17]. These have a few standard protocols in common, but the Web service stack architectures are currently still diverse. At least, HTTP [11] is usually supported for remote communication. Asynchronous messaging protocols are also supported. SOAP [4] is used as a message exchange protocol on top of the communication protocol. Remote services can be specified with the Web Service Description Language (WSDL) [7]. WSDL is an XML format for describing Web services as a set of endpoints. Operations and messages are described abstractly, and then bound to a concrete communication protocol and message format to define an endpoint. Naming and lookup is supported by UDDI [19].

Each Web service can be accessed ad hoc, and services are located and bound at runtime. Additional composition of services is supported by business process execution languages, such as BPEL4WS [1]. Such languages provide high-level standards for (hierarchical) flows of Web services.

Web services are providing a loosely coupled service architecture and a service deployment model. However, today's Web service stack architectures are already relatively complex and have a considerable overhead, especially for XML processing. Federated or grouped composition is not yet in focus, even though technically possible.

2.2   Peer-to-Peer Systems

Peer-to-Peer (P2P) computing refers to the concept of networks of equal peers collaborating for specific tasks. P2P environments allow for some kind of spontaneous or ad hoc networking abilities. Typical applications of P2P are file sharing, grid computing, and groupware. P2P computing is a special form of distributed computing that has gained much attention in recent times, especially P2P systems for personal use, like Gnutella, Napster, and others.

Technically there are still quite diverse views on P2P. For instance, P2P can be interpreted as a variant of the client/server paradigm in which clients are also servers; it can also be interpreted as a network without servers. Often P2P is referred to as a type of network in which each peer has equivalent capabilities and responsibilities. This differs from client/server architectures, in which some computers are dedicated to serving the others. Note that this is only a distinction at the application level. At the technology level both architectures can be implemented by the same means.

Basic functionalities shared by most current P2P systems are that they connect peers for a common purpose, permit users to lookup peer services, and provide a way to exchange data or invoke remote services. These basic properties are still quite vague – and do also apply for many client/server architectures. There are many optional properties, one can expect from a P2P system, but none is a single identifying property – that is, all can also be missing [8]:

- usually there is some kind of sharing of resources or services,
- there is an ease-of-use for users or developers,
- there is a direct exchange between peer systems,
- usually clients are also servers,
- load distribution may be supported in some way, and
- there is a notion of location unawareness regarding a used service – provided mainly by the lookup service used to locate a desired service.

Regarding remote business services, P2P offers a set of potential benefits: it can be used to provide a very simple remoting infrastructure and loose coupling is inherently modeled. However, missing central coordination may cause problems regarding security, performance, scalability, and network traffic.

2.3   Coordination Models

Coordination models are foundations for a coordination language and a coordination system, as an implementation of the model. A coordination model can be seen as a formal framework for expressing the interaction among components in a multi-component system [9]. As related work for our work, especially coordination of distributed and concurrent systems is of interest. The coordination language Linda [13] introduced the view that coordination of concurrent systems is orthogonal to the execution of operations (i.e. calculations) in this system. Linda can be used to model most prevalent coordination languages. It consists of a small number of coordination primitives and a shared dataspace containing tuples (the tuplespace).

The original Linda has no notions of multiple federations; a single tuplespace is used for all processes. However, this has its practical limitation regarding distributed systems, as the single tuplespace is a performance bottleneck. Moreover, there is no structuring of sub-spaces and scalability is limited. Bauhaus [6] introduces the idea of bags that nest processes in tuplespaces. A process can only be coordinated with other processes in the bags, or it has to move into a common bag to coordinate with other processes. PageSpace [10] structures Linda spaces by controlled access using different agents for user representation, interfaces to other agents, administrative functionality, and gateways to other PageSpaces.

2.4 Spontaneous Networking

Spontaneous networking refers to the automatic or self-adaptive integration of services and devices into distributed environments. New services and devices are made available without intervention by users. Services can be provided and located in the network. Providing means that they can be dynamically added to or removed from the network group without interfering with the global functionality. Failure of any attached service does not further affect the functionality of the network group. Failing services are automatically removed and the respective services are de-registered.

Jini [2] is a distributed computing model built for spontaneous networking. Service providers as well as clients firstly have to locate a lookup service. A reference to the lookup service can be received via a multicast. Service providers register with the lookup service by providing a proxy for their services as well as a set of service attributes. Each service receives a lease that has to be renewed from time to time. If a lease expires, the service is automatically removed from the network. Clients looking for a service with particular attributes send a request to a lookup service for such a service. In response the client receives all those proxies of services matching the requested service attributes.

The Home Audio Video interoperability (HAVi) standard [14] is designed for networking consumer electronics (CEs). Especially, self-management and plug & play functionalities are provided for spontaneous networking. Remote services are registered using a unique Software Element Identifier (SEID) with a system-wide registry for service lookup. HAVi specifies the communication protocols and access methods for software elements in a platform-independent way.

2.5 Open Issues for Loosely Coupled Service Architectures

The concepts, described in the previous sections, can be used to implement loosely coupled service architectures. However, all have different benefits and liabilities in the context of business systems, such as information systems within an organization (for workflows, groupware, etc.) or information systems offering services to the outside (such as e-commerce environments). In this paper, we propose to combine some ideas of these approaches to resolve the following open issues:

- *Control of Peers and Access to the Network:* If a peer offers a vital service that should not be visible to everyone (for instance, only to those who have paid), we have to control access in business environments. The idea is to combine the grouping concepts of coordination models, such as tuplespaces, with basic networking properties of the P2P model.
- *Dynamic Invocation:* If static interface descriptions are mandatory for remote invocations, ad hoc connectivity is hard to model. In the context of loosely coupled Web services we propose the use of dynamic invocation mechanisms (on top of SOAP).
- *Simplicity:* For the application developer, remoting technologies should be in first place simple. In a coordinated group, where we can be sure that access can be granted, developers of remote objects accessing the service should be able to use a very simple remoting model with direct interactions.
- *Security:* Access to coordinated groups and the permissions what a peer can do within a group have to be secured.
- *Performance and Scalability:* The internal protocols used should be exchangeable to deal with performance and scalability issues. It should be possible to replace performance-intensive (or memory-intensive) framework parts transparently and provide means for QoS control.
- *Deployment:* Each accessible remote object should provide services that expose the ease of deployment and access known from Web services.

3   Peer Federations

In this section, we will step-by-step discuss our concepts for peer federations. These are combining concepts from the different approaches, discussed in the previous section, to resolve (some of) the named open issues. We illustrate our concepts with examples from our prototype implementation Leela. Leela is implemented in XOTcl [18], an object-oriented scripting language based on Tcl. Our framework is designed with the remoting patterns[1] from [21,22,23]. We illustrate our designs with UML diagrams.

Before we describe the peer and federation concepts, we describe the basic concepts of the communication framework of Leela. The communication framework's model is tightly integrated with the higher-level peer and federation concepts. Therefore, it is important to understand its design before we go into details of the peer and federation concepts.

3.1   Basic Communication Framework

As its basic communication resource, each Leela application uses two classes implementing a CLIENT REQUEST HANDLER [23] and a SERVER REQUEST HANDLER [23] (see Figure 1). The CLIENT REQUEST HANDLER pattern describes how to send requests across the network and receive responses in an efficient way on client side. On the server side,

---

[1] We highlight pattern names in SMALLCAPS font.

the requests are received by a SERVER REQUEST HANDLER. This pattern describes how to efficiently receive request from the network, dispatch the requests into the server application, and send the response back to the client side. Each Leela application instance acts as a client and server at the same time. The Leela application instance and its request handlers can be accessed by each peer.

The request handlers contain PROTOCOL PLUG-INS for different protocols that actually transport the message across the network. Currently, we support a SOAP [4] protocol plug-in. However, any other communication protocol can be used as well. As described below, Leela supports different invocation and activation styles (see Sections 3.4). Thus the specialties of most protocols supporting mainstream communication models, such as remote procedure calls (RPC) or messaging, can be supported. It is expected from the protocol that it can – at least – transport any kind of strings as message payload, and that one of the invocation and activation styles, supported by Leela peers, can be mapped to the protocol. For most protocols, it should be possible to map all invocation and activation styles of Leela to the protocol – of course, with different trade-offs.

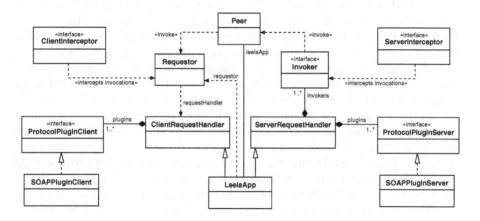

Fig. 1. Structure of the Leela Communication Framework

Remote invocations are abstracted by the patterns REQUESTOR [23] and INVOKER [23]. A REQUESTOR is responsible for building up remote invocations at runtime and for handing the invocation over to the CLIENT REQUEST HANDLER, which sends it across the network. The REQUESTOR offers a dynamic invocation interface, similar to those offered by OO-RPC middleware such as CORBA or RMI. Leela also supports peer and federation proxies that can act like a CLIENT PROXY, offering the interfaces of a remote peer or federation.

The INVOKER gets the invocation from the SERVER REQUEST HANDLER and performs the invocation of the peer. In Leela, there are different INVOKERS for different activation strategies (see Section 3.4). The SERVER REQUEST HANDLER is responsible for selecting the correct INVOKER. The INVOKER checks whether it is possible to dispatch the invocation; in Leela only exported objects and methods can be dispatched. This way, developers can ensure that no malicious invocations can be invoked remotely.

The Leela invocation chain on client side and server side is based on INVOCATION INTERCEPTORS [23]. That is, the invocation on both sides can be extended transparently with new behavior. Interceptors are used in Leela to add information about the Leela federation to the invocation (see below). Also, a client-side INVOCATION INTERCEPTOR can add security attributes and similar information to the invocation. A server-side interceptor can read and handle the information provided by the client.

The REQUESTOR, INVOKER, and request handlers handle synchronization issues on client and server side. The request handlers handle the invocations according to the invocation and activation styles used. On server side, the SERVER REQUEST HANDLER receives network events asynchronously from a REACTOR [20]. The SERVER REQUEST HANDLER can have multiple different PROTOCOL PLUG-INS at the same time. That is, network events can come in from different channels concurrently. The SERVER REQUEST HANDLER queues the network events in an event loop.

The actual invocations of peers are executed in a separate thread of control. The access of a particular peer can either be queued (synchronized) or handled by a multi-threaded OBJECT POOL [23]. The results are queued again, and handed back to the receiving thread.

On client side, different styles of asynchronous invocation and result handling are supported. Because in Leela each client is also a server, synchronous invocations – that let the client process block for the result – are not an option: if the Leela application blocks, it cannot service incoming requests anymore. Instead, Leela implements a variety of asynchronous invocation styles with a common callback model. The request handlers work using an event loop that queues up incoming and outgoing requests in a MESSAGE QUEUE. Client-side invocations run in a separate thread of control.

The result arrives asynchronously and has to be obtained from the receiving thread. This is done by raising an event in the CLIENT REQUEST HANDLER's event loop. This event executes a callback specified during the invocation. An ASYNCHRONOUS COMPLETION TOKEN (ACT) [20] is used to map the result to its invocation. Using this callback model we can implement different asynchronous invocation styles, described in [22,23]. We can send the invocation and forget about the result as described by the pattern FIRE AND FORGET. SYNC WITH SERVER is used, when a result is not needed, but we want an acknowledgment from the server. Finally, the patterns POLL OBJECT and RESULT CALLBACK allow us to receive the result asynchronously. POLL OBJECT lets the callback write the result to an object that is subsequently polled by the client for the result. RESULT CALLBACK propagates the callback to the client – that is, it informs the client actively of the result.

3.2 Invocation Types

A remote invocation consists of a number of elements. Firstly, the actual invocation data consists of method name and parameters. Secondly, a service name is required – it is an unique OBJECT ID that enables the INVOKER to select the peer object. Thirdly, protocol-specific location information is required – in the case of SOAP over HTTP this is the host and the port of the SERVER REQUEST HANDLER. The OBJECT ID plus location information implement the pattern ABSOLUTE OBJECT REFERENCE – an unique reference for the particular service in the network. Finally, the invocation might contain INVOCATION CONTEXT data. The INVOCATION CONTEXT [23] contains additional parameters of the invocation, such as information about the federation or security attributes. In Leela, the INVOCATION CONTEXT is extensible by peers and INVOCATION INTERCEPTORS.

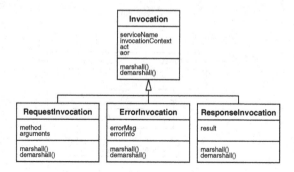

Fig. 2. Invocation Types and Marshallers

Leela sends the message payload as a structured string (we use Tcl lists). These strings are different for different invocation types. Currently, we support request, response, and error invocation types. The scheme is extensible with any other invocation type. The error message type is used to implement the pattern REMOTING ERROR [23] – we use it to signal remoting-specific error conditions in the Leela framework.

As shown in Figure 2 the different invocation types contain different information. Converting invocations to and from byte streams that can be transported across the network is the task of the pattern MARSHALLER [23]. The invocation classes shown in Figure 2 are able to marshal and demarshal the information stored in them; thus they implement the main part of the MARSHALLER pattern for the Leela framework.

3.3   Federations and Peers

A federation is a concept to manage remote objects in a remote object group (here federation members are called peers). Each federation has one central federation object that manages the federation data consistently. To allow peers to connect to a federation, the federation itself must be accessible remotely. Thus the federation itself is a special peer. Peers can be added and removed to a federation.

A federation can be accessed remotely by a federation proxy. This is a special CLIENT PROXY [23] that enables peers to access their federation, if it is not located on the same machine. The federation proxy is a local object that implements the federation interface. In principle, it sends each invocation across the network to the connected federation.

Similar to federations, there is also a CLIENT PROXY for peers, the peer proxy. The peer proxy basically implements the peer interface and sends all invocations to the connected peer of which it holds the ABSOLUTE OBJECT REFERENCE. Thus, using the peer proxy, a local peer can interact with any remote peer that is part of its federation as if it is another local peer. The peer can invoke other local and remote peers using location information (with the method send) or using an ABSOLUTE OBJECT REFERENCE (with the method sendAOR). The federation and peer structures are shown in Figure 3.

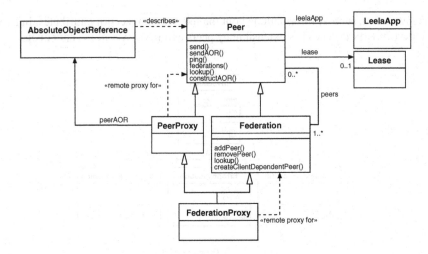

Fig. 3. Peer Federations Structure

Federations can be introspected for their peers and properties using a semantic lookup service (see Section 3.6). Peers can also perform a lookup: here all federations of the peer are queried.

3.4 Peer Activation

In a loosely coupled remoting environment, activation of remote objects is a critical issue. Activation means creation and initialization of a remote object so that it can serve requests. Some peers are long living and/or persistent entities. Others are perhaps client-dependent such as peers that represent some session data. A client-dependent peer should be removed from the federation, at least, when the last peer that uses it, is destroyed or leaves the federation. In such cases, a LIFECYCLE MANAGER [23] has to ensure that these peers are removed from the federation, if they are not required anymore. We support the following activation STRATEGIES [12] (see Figure 4):

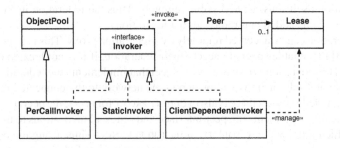

Fig. 4. Activation Strategies Implemented on Invokers

- STATIC INSTANCE: The peer is already activated before it is exported and survives until it is explicitly destroyed or the Leela process stops.
- PER-CALL INSTANCE: The class of the peer is exported and the peer is activated when the request arrives. Then this peer serves the request and is de-activated again. Per-call activated peers apply the pattern OBJECT POOLING [23] – that is, they are pre-initialized in a pool to reduce the activation overhead for instantiation.
- CLIENT-DEPENDENT INSTANCE: A factory operation is provided by the federation to create client-dependent peers, e.g. to store session data. In a remote environment, however, it is unclear, when a client-dependent object is not needed anymore, except the client explicitly destroys it. If a given object is not accessed for a while this can mean that the client has forgotten to clean up the instance, that it requires a longer computation time till the next access, that network latency causes the delay, or that the client application has crashed. The pattern LEASES [23] helps the federation to decide whether a certain client-dependent peer is still required. For each client-dependent peer a lease is started when it is created. The activating peer has to renew the lease from time to time. The lease is automatically renewed, when the peer is accessed. The client can also renew the lease explicitly using the operation ping of the peer. When the lease expires and it is not renewed, the client-dependent peer is removed from the federation.

In Leela the LIFECYCLE MANAGER pattern – implementing the management of the activation STRATEGIES – is implemented by different elements of the framework. Peers are registered with an activation strategy. There are different INVOKERS for the different activation STRATEGIES. The appropriate INVOKER is chosen by the SERVER REQUEST HANDLER.

3.5   Peer Invocation and Federation Control

A peer may be invoked only by the federation, or by a peer in one of its federations, or by a local object in its own scope (e.g. a helper object the peer has created itself). Peers are executed in their own thread of control, and each of these threads has its own Tcl interpreter as THREAD-SPECIFIC STORAGE [20]. Thus peers have no direct access to the main interpreter. The threaded peer interpreters are synchronized by MESSAGE QUEUES [23] implemented by event loops of the interpreters. That is, the peer threads can only post "send" and "result" events into the main interpreter – and the request handlers decide how to handle these events.

In other words, each federation controls its peers. These cannot be accessed from outside of the federation without a permission of the federation. Of course, some peers in a federation need to be declared to be publicly accessible. For instance, the federation peer is accessible from the outside – otherwise remote peers would not be able to join the federation.

Control of remote federation access is done by INVOCATION INTERCEPTORS [23] (see Figure 5). On client side, an INVOCATION INTERCEPTOR intercepts the construction of the remote invocation and adds all federation information for a peer into the INVOCATION CONTEXT. On server side this information is read out again by another INVOCATION IN-TERCEPTOR. If the remote peer is not allowed to access the invoked peer, the INVOCATION

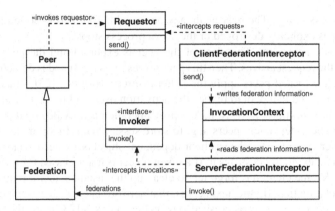

Fig. 5. Peer Federation Interceptor Structure

INTERCEPTOR stops the invocation and sends a REMOTING ERROR to the client. Otherwise access is granted.

Peers within a federation can access their services with equal rights. Per default each peer is allowed to freely send invocations to each other peer in its federation and access exported services. Each service offered in a federation must be explicitly exported by a peer. Only exported services can be accessed by other peers. By introducing INVOCATION INTERCEPTORS for particular peers, peer types, INVOKERS, or REQUESTORS we can fine-tune the control how these elements can be accessed. For instance, we can introduce an interceptor that only grants access if some security credentials, such as user name and password, are sent with the invocation.

Some peers are members of multiple federations. Thus they are able to access services of peers in other federations, something the other peers in the federation cannot do. Optionally, peers can act as a "bridge" to another federation – offering some of that federation's services in the context of another federation.

Figure 6 shows an example sequence diagram of an invocation sequence with a static INVOKER. Details, such as marshaling and demarshaling, are not shown here. The two other activation strategies just require some additional steps for interacting with the object pool or dealing with the lease.

3.6 Semantic Lookup Service

The idea to provide loosely coupled business services is often not easy to implement because dynamic invocation of these services requires us to know at least the object ID, operation name, and operation signature. To enable ad hoc connectivity this information can potential be unknown until runtime. Therefore, compile time INTERFACE DESCRIPTION [23] approaches (like interface description languages) are not enough. Instead a dynamic INTERFACE DESCRIPTION is required as well.

The pattern LOOKUP [23] is implemented by many discovery or naming services. These provide the necessary details of any remote object that is matching a query. Here, often another problem is that the designers of the lookup services cannot know in

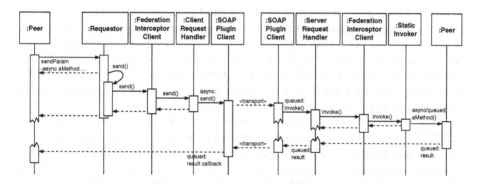

Fig. 6. Sequence Diagram for a Simple Invocation with a Static Invoker

advance how the query might look like and which strategies should be applied to retrieve the results. For instance, always searching for all matching peers can be problematic regarding performance; always (deterministically) returning the first matching peer can cause problems regarding load balancing. Thus we propose a lookup service that is extensible regarding the provided information and the possible queries.

The basic concept of the Leela lookup service is that each peer provides semantic metadata about itself to its federation's lookup service. Peers can perform lookups in all lookup services of their federations. We use RDF [24] to describe the peers. RDF supports semantic metadata about Web resources described in some ontology or schema. For instance RDF-Schema [5] and OWL [16] support general relationships about resources, like "subclass of". Developers can also use RDF ontologies from other domains; for instance, in an e-learning system probably an ontology for learning materials will be used.

The federation provides metadata about all its peers, such as a list of ABSOLUTE OBJECT REFERENCES and OBJECT IDS (the service names). Each peer adds information for its exported methods, their interfaces, and their activation strategy. This information can be introspected by clients.

Leela currently implements a distributed interface for the Redland RDF library [3] and its interface abstractions. Peers of a federation can read from and write to this metadata repository. As query abstractions, Redland supports the lookup of specific resources and sets of resources, the generation of streams, and iterators. The actual query is thus constructed on client side. In the future we plan to support a more powerful query engine on top of Redland.

4   Discussion and Conclusion

We have presented an approach for service-based remote programming based on remote object groups, called federations. The approach has similarities to Web services, P2P systems, coordination technologies, and spontaneous networking, but can also resolve some apparent open issues of these approaches. The most important design goal is ease-of-use regarding the development, use, and deployment of remote services. In many business scenarios often a certain level of control is required. For this goal, we have provided a simple control model introduced by the concept of peers that can join multiple federations. Only those services that should be accessed by a remote peer are exported. Interceptors can be used to fine-tune the remote access. Services can be introspected for metadata using a semantic lookup service. Thus we can deal with unexpected lookup information and query types; services just have to expose additional metadata and the appropriate queries can be constructed on client side.

Our design and implementation are based on well-known remoting patterns (from [21,22,23]) and follow the pattern language quite closely. Therefore, many underlying parts of our framework can be exchanged with other (OO-)RPC middleware or be implemented in other programming languages – a benefit of the pattern-based design. We are currently working on a Java implementation using the Apache Axis Web service framework, and we are implementing more protocol plug-ins. Thus we believe our results as generally applicable. Moreover, we can potentially deal with scalability and performance problems, as the framework is designed in such a way that the internal protocols and technologies are exchangeable. Our deployment model is similarly simple as Web service and P2P models; however, we require to know the location of at least one "well-known" federation to connect to a business service environment. We consider this not as a drawback, but an incentive in many business scenarios. Note that this "well-known" federation might just provide a lookup service. Thus the activities how objects are initially located are quite similar to lookups in other middleware environments, such as CORBA or Web service frameworks – but they are different to those P2P environments that are exploiting broadcasts and similar means.

The security aspect is handled by controlling which objects can join a federation and that only exported methods can be invoked. Each peer executes in its own interpreter and thread of control – thus peers cannot interfere with each other. All other security issues can be handled by INVOCATION INTERCEPTORS and PROTOCOL PLUG-INS.

We believe our framework design to be usable in many (business) scenarios and plan to apply it for different applications as future work. Especially, we want to use the framework as a very simple remoting infrastructure. The federation model can be used for simple role modeling in a company; on top of such models, workflows and groupware applications can be implemented. As the scripting language XOTcl is primarily designed for component composition, we also want to use the Leela framework for distributed component gluing and coordination, especially in the context of legacy system integration.

Most of the ingredients of our approach are already known from other approaches, but we combine them in an easy-to-use remoting concept. The framework can be extended with add-on functionality. There are also some liabilities of the current prototype implementation: the current prototype does not allow for structured federations (like hierarchical federations), is implemented with SOAP only, and offers no QoS or failover control features (except those of the used Web server). We plan to deal with these issues in future releases of the Leela framework.

References

1. T. Andrews, F. Curbera, H. Dholakia, Y. Goland, J. Klein, F. Leymann, K. Liu, D. Roller, D. Smith, S. Thatte, I. Trickovic, and S. Weerawarana. Business process execution language for web services version 1.1. http://www-106.ibm.com/developerworks/library/ws-bpel/, 2003.
2. K. Arnold, A. Wollrath, B. O'Sullivan, R. Scheifler, , and J. Wald. *The Jini Specification*. Addison-Wesley, 1999.
3. D. Beckett. Redland RDF Application Framework. http://www.redland.opensource.ac.uk/, 2004.
4. D. Box, D. Ehnebuske, G. Kakivaya, A. Layman, N. Mendelsohn, H. F. Nielsen, S. Thatte, and D. Winer. Simple object access protocol (SOAP) 1.1. http://www.w3.org/TR/SOAP/, 2000.
5. D. Brickley and R. V. Guha. RDF Vocabulary Description Language 1.0: RDF Schema. http://www.w3.org/TR/2004/REC-rdf-schema-20040210/, 2004.
6. N. Carriero, D. Gelernter, and L. Zuck. Bauhaus linda. In P. Ciancarini, O. Nierstrasz, and A. Yonezawa, editors, *Object-Based Models and Languages for Concurrent Systems: Proc. of the ECOOP'94 Workshop on Modles and Languages for Coordination of Parallelism and Distribution*, pages 66–76. Springer, Berlin, Heidelberg, 1995.
7. E. Christensen, F. Curbera, G. Meredith, and S. Weerawarana. Web services description language (WSDL) 1.1. http://www.w3.org/TR/wsdl, 2001.
8. E. Chtcherbina and M. Voelter. P2P Patterns – Results from the EuroPLoP 2002 Focus Group. In *Proceedings of EuroPlop 2002*, Irsee, Germany, July 2002.
9. P. Ciancarini. Coordination models and languages as software integrators. *ACM Computing Surveys*, 28(2):300–302, 1996.
10. P. Ciancarini, A. Knoche, R. Tolksdorf, and F. Vitali. Pagespace: an architecture to coordinate distributed applications on the web. *Computer Networks and ISDN Systems*, 28(7-11):941–952, 1996.
11. R. Fielding, J. Gettys, J. Mogul, H. Frysyk, L. Masinter, P. Leach, and T. Berners-Lee. Hypertext transfer protocol – HTTP/1.1. RFC 2616, 1999.
12. E. Gamma, R. Helm, R. Johnson, and J. Vlissides. *Design Patterns: Elements of Reusable Object-Oriented Software*. Addison-Wesley, 1994.
13. D. Gelernter and N. Carriero. Coordination languages and their significance. *Commun. ACM*, 35(2):97–107, 1992.
14. HAVI. HAVI specification 1.1. http://www.havi.org, May 2001.
15. H. Kreger. Web service conceptual architecture. IBM Whitepaper, 2001.
16. D. L. McGuinness and F. van Harmelen. Web Ontology Language (OWL). http://www.w3.org/TR/2004/REC-owl-features-20040210/, 2004.
17. Microsoft. .NET framework. http://msdn.microsoft.com//netframework, 2003.
18. G. Neumann and U. Zdun. XOTcl, an object-oriented scripting language. In *Proceedings of Tcl2k: The 7th USENIX Tcl/Tk Conference*, Austin, Texas, USA, February 2000.
19. OASIS. UDDI. http://www.uddi.org/, 2004.
20. D. C. Schmidt, M. Stal, H. Rohnert, and F. Buschmann. *Patterns for Concurrent and Distributed Objects*. Pattern-Oriented Software Architecture. J. Wiley and Sons Ltd., 2000.
21. M. Voelter, M. Kircher, and U. Zdun. Object-oriented remoting: A pattern language. In *Proceedings of VikingPLoP 2002*, Denmark, Sep 2002.
22. M. Voelter, M. Kircher, and U. Zdun. Patterns for asynchronous invocations in distributed object frameworks. In *Proceedings of EuroPlop 2003*, Irsee, Germany, Jun 2003.
23. M. Voelter, M. Kircher, and U. Zdun. Remoting patterns. To be published by J. Wiley and Sons Ltd. in Wiley's pattern series in 2004, 2004.
24. W3C. Resource Description Framework (RDF). http://www.w3.org/RDF/, 2004.

MDA Applied: From Sequence Diagrams to Web Service Choreography

Bernhard Bauer[1] and Jörg P. Müller[2]

[1] Programming of Distributed Systems, Institute of Computer Science,
University of Augsburg, D-86135 Augsburg, Germany
bernhard.bauer@informatik.uni-augsburg.de
[2] Siemens AG Corporate Technology, Intelligent Autonomous Systems,
Otto-Hahn-Ring 6, D-81739 München, Germany
joerg.p.mueller@siemens.com

Abstract. Web Services and Web Service composition languages for Web Service choreography are becoming more and more important in the area for inter-enterprise application and process integration. However the aspects of modeling these software systems have not been studied in detail, in contrast to the definition of business processes where well-known techniques exist. The model-driven architecture (MDA) approach of the Object Management Group is a good starting point for the development of Web Services and Web Service choreography. In this paper we show how platform independent models specified by UML 2 sequence diagrams can be automatically transformed in a Web Service composition language representation.

1 Introduction

Over the past few years, enterprises are currently in a thorough transformation process as they encounter the necessity to react to challenges such as globalization, unstable varying demand, and mass customization. A most important factor to maintaining competitiveness is the ability of an enterprise to describe, standardize, and adapt the way it reacts to certain types of business events, and how it interacts as well as its procedures for interaction with suppliers, partners, competitors, and customers. Today, virtually all larger enterprises describe these procedures and interactions in terms of *business processes,* and invest huge efforts to describe and standardize these processes. Web Services are the key technology for Enterprise Application Integration (i.e. EAI; see e.g. [3] for details, [16]) and Inter Enterprise Integration. IBM defines Web Services as [1]: *"Web services are self-contained, self-describing, modular applications that can be published, located, and invoked across the Web* (see e.g. [17])." It is possible to combine them to added-value Web Services offering more functionality than the original ones. This process is called Web Service Choreography or - composition depending on the point of view of the description. Several standards are under development for the definition of languages for Web Service composition or Web Service Choreography, typical examples are BPEL4WS [4], BPML [9], XPDL [13]. ebXML [8] with ebXML *Business Process Specification Schema* [7].

The **Model Driven Architecture (MDA)** (for details see [10, 11]) is a framework for software development driven by the OMG. The following models are at the core of the MDA: **Computational Independent Model (CIM):** This model describes the business logic and domain model; **Platform Independent Model (PIM):** This model is defined at a high level of abstraction; it is independent of any implementation technology. **Platform Specific Model (PSM):** It is tailored to specify a system in terms of the implementation constructs available in one specific implementation technology, e.g. Web Services. **Code**: The final step in the development is the transformation of each PSM to code. Based on OMG's model-driven approach, our objective is to demonstrate a mapping of platform independent models based on UML 2 sequence diagrams [12] (triggered by e.g. [15]) to a platform dependent model based on the Business Process Execution Language for Web Services (BPEL4WS). This paper can be seen as part of a series of papers dealing with software engineering starting from business processes and transforming them into web services choreography, see [19, 18].

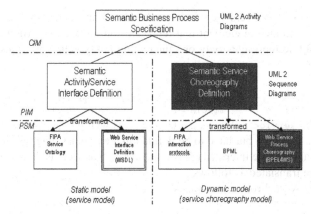

Fig. 1. Web Service enabled business processes

2   Conceptual Methodology

Figure 1 (an updated version of Figure 3 of [18]) illustrates the top-down development process starting with a semantic business process specification using and extending UML 2.0 activity diagrams. This specification is refined into two models: a **static model**, which is essentially the service model in our conceptual methodology, even though enhanced with metadata, such as the description of pre- and post-conditions for service invocation, and with exception definitions; a **dynamic model**, which is essentially the service choreography oriented layer in the conceptual methodology. Each of these two models is described by a platform independent model and one or more platform specific models. In this paper we will focus on the mapping of UML 2 Sequence Diagrams to BPEL4WS as a part of the development process. Readers interested in the other parts are referred to [18, 19].

3   From Sequence Diagrams to BPEL4WS

As a next step we will now go into the details of UML 2 sequence diagrams and define informally[1] by induction the mapping of sequence diagram elements to BPEL2WS, i.e. a mapping

$$\text{transform: Sequence Diagram Element} \to \text{BPEL4WS}$$

A sequence diagram defines an interaction denoted as $\boxed{}$. Thus a complete sequence diagram is transformed into a process definition of BPEL4WS:

transform ($\boxed{}$) = <process name = "EventOccurence" >

   transform(inner_part($\boxed{}$))</process>

where inner_part delivers the sub-diagram defined in the overall sequence diagram. Lifelines are a modeling element that represents an individual participant in an interaction. A lifeline represents only one interacting entity. They are transformed by the following rule:

transform ($\boxed{}$ ...) = <partners> partner name = "Lifeline" serviceLinkType = "..."
   partnerRole = "..." myRole = "..." </partner> ... </partners>

Note, that the serviceLinkType, partnerRole as well as myRole are not specified in the sequence diagram, but have to be defined in a e.g. class diagram defining the role of a participant and the interface (serviceLinkType) as well as the partner role.

Messages are translated as follows

Synchronous/Asynchronous messages:

Transform($\xrightarrow{\text{operation}}$) = <receive partner = receiver($\xrightarrow{\text{operation}}$)
   portType = "..." operation = "operation" inputContainer = "operationInC"
   outputContainer = "operationOutC" </receive>

where receiver calculates the name of the right-hand-side lifeline name and operationInC and operationOutC are automatically generated tokens for the input and output container of the operation, for aynchronous messages an output container is not specified since no result is transported back to the sender.

Reply messages:

Transform($\circ\!\!\!\!-\!\!\!\!-\!\!\!\!-\!\!\!\!-\!\!\!\circ$) = <reply partner = receiver($\circ\!\!\!\!-\!\!\!\!-\!\!\!\!-\!\!\!\!-\!\!\!\circ$) portType = "..."
operation = "operation" container = "operationC"</reply>

where receiver calculates the name of the left-hand-side lifeline name and operationC is an automatically generated token for the container of the operation.

---

[1] Note that, a formal definition of the mapping can be based on the MOF/XMI for data exchange of models; however for the sake of readability we use the graphical notation of the elements instead.

Lost and *found* messages are specified as usual messages with the exception of applying the wait-construct. *Co-regions* are constructed with the `flow`-construct and the messages of the co-region are transformed in the usual way.

One of the newest aspect of UML 2 sequence diagrams is the possibility to define

combined fragements, depicted as . UML 2 distinguishes between:

- `alt` – at most one of the operands will execute, this can be transformed using the `switch`-construct

```
transform (  [alt diagram]  ) =
  <switch> <case condition="bool-expr">  transform(operand_1) </case>
                     ...
            <otherwise>? transform(operand_n+1) </otherwise>
  </switch>
```

  in this case the alternatives in the sequence diagram have to be annotated with specific conditions for each case (as in our application example in one case).

- `opt` – either the (sole) operand happens or nothing happens, this is modeled similar to the `alt`-operator, where we have two cases, one case is the transformed operand and the other one is the distinguished no-operation of BPEL4WS.

- `loop` – repeated a number of times, transformed using the while-construct
```
<while condition="myConstraint"> transform(operand_loop) </while>
```
  where `myConstraint` is the translated constraint of the sequence diagram.

- `par` – parallel merge between the behaviors of the operands, this can easily be transformed with the flow-construct.
```
<flow> transform(operand_1) ... transform(operand_n) </flow>
```

- `seq` – weak sequencing depending on lifelines and operands and strict – strict sequencing not depending on lifelines and operands can be modeled with
```
<sequence> transform(operand_1) ... transform(operand_n) </sequence>
```

`critical` – critical region, this is handled by the transaction mechanism; `assert` – assertions are translated into boolean expressions which are evaluated during runtime; `ignore` – message types are not shown within `fragment`; `consider` – messages considered within fragment; and interaction reference – a `reference` to another interaction, can be seen as abbreviations and need not be transformed; `neg` – invalid traces, have not been transformed. Another novelty is the usage of continuations which can be seen as conditional "goto" statements. These continuations can be mapped to BPEL4WS by applying while-loops and a boolean global variable stating if the jump has to performed or not. The while-statement has to be placed at the maximal comprehensive block of the operands where the jump is performed.

4   Conclusions and Outlook

The main contribution of this paper is that it elaborates the relationship between the platform independent model of service choreography and its mapping to BPEL4WS a specific business process execution language. The work is part of a larger project depicted in Figure 1. The informal definition of a mapping between the two representation shows that such a step can be automated. However additional information concerning the Web Services has to be at hand. This can be the WSDL definition of the Web Service interfaces specified with UML class diagrams as used e.g. by [20]. The next steps are the definition of a formal mapping between both representations; looking at a inverse mapping to allow reverse engineering; taking the "other" aspects of BPEL4WS into consideration, i.e. modelling of the context of the Web Service choreography; integration with the mapping from the computational independent model to the platform specific model, and integration into a development tool.

References

1. IBM (2003) 'Web Service Tutorial',
    http://www-106.ibm.com/developerworks/web/library/w-ovr/?dwzone=ibm
2. WebServices (2003) http://www.webservices.org
3. Sun (2002) 'Powering the Collaborative Enterprise Sun ONE and Java Technology in the Extended Supply Chain',
    http://www.sun.com/products-n-solutions/automotive/docs/sunarc.pdf
4. IBM (2003) 'BPEL4WS',
    http://www-106.ibm.com/developerworks/webservices/library/ws-bpel/
5. IBM (2003)' WSCI', http://wwws.sun.com/software/xml/developers/wsci/
6. WFMC (2003) 'XPDL', 10 June, http://www.wfmc.org/standards/docs.htm
7. ebXML (2003) 'Business Process Specification Schema', 10 June,
    http://www.ebxml.org/specs/ebBPSS.pdf
8. ebXML (2003) 'Enabling global electronic markets', http://www.ebxml.org
9. BPMI (2003) 'BPML', 10 June, http://www.bpmi.org/
10. MDA homepage. The Object Management Group (OMG). http://www.omg.org/
11. Kleppe M., Warmer J., Bast W. MDA Explained – The Model Driven Architecture: Practice and Promise, Addison Wesley, 2003
12. UML Homepage. The Object Management Group. http://www.omg.org/uml/
13. WFMC (2003) 'XPDL', 10 June, http://www.wfmc.org/standards/docs.htm
14. FIPA (2003), FIPA specifications, 10 June, http://www.fipa.org/specs/fipa00030/
15. Bauer, B., Müller, J.P., Odell, J.: Agent UML: A Formalism for Specifying Multiagent Software Systems, International Journal on Software Engineering and Knowledge Engineering (IJSEKE), Vol. 11, No. 3, 2001 Engineering, 2001.
16. Fuchs, I. (2002) 'Web Services and Business Process Management Platforms – Understanding Their Relationship and Defining an Implementation Approach',
    http://www.ebpml.org/ihf.doc
17. W3C Web Services glossary. http://www.w3.org/TR/ws-gloss/
18. Müller, J.P., Bauer, B., Friese, Th.: Programming software agents as designing executable business processes: a model-driven perspective, in Proceeding PROMAS 03, 2004.
19. Bauer, B., Marc-Philippe Huget: Modelling Web Service Composition with (Agent) UML, Special Issue of Journal of Web Engineering, 2003
20. Armstrong, Ch. (2002) 'Modelling Web Services with UML', Talk given at the OMG Web Services Workshop 2002.

A Three-Level Architecture for Distributed Web Information Systems

Markus Kirchberg[1], Klaus-Dieter Schewe[1],
Bernhard Thalheim[2], and Richard Wang[1]

[1] Massey University, Information Science Research Centre,
Private Bag 11 222, Palmerston North, New Zealand
{M.Kirchberg|K.D.Schewe|R.B.Wang}@massey.ac.nz
[2] Christian Albrechts University Kiel,
Institute of Computer Science and Applied Mathematics,
Olshausenstrasse 40, 24098 Kiel, Germany
thalheim@is.informatik.uni-kiel.de

Abstract. In this article we present a three-level architecture for distributed web information systems (WISs) based on media objects. We distinguish between a service level, a database level and an operational level. The media objects serve as a mediator between the service requested by users and the database. The operational level is based on communicating agents that realise the functionality of a distributed database.

1   Introduction

Media objects [1] support tight integration between a global data and operations level and a local interface and dialogue level in WISs. Roughly speaking a media object abstracts from the content and functionality of a web-page in a WIS including the navigation links. Using classification abstraction we define media types the instances of which are the media objects. The core of the definition is formed by a view on some underlying database schema. This view is extended by operations and by features that allow media objects to be tailored to different user needs as well as limitations arising from different end-devices or communication channels. We present a brief overview of media types in Section 2.

As media types provide a formal framework for WIS, the challenge in WIS engineering is to develop adequate system support for the storage and maintenance of media objects. In this article we address this problem and link media objects with a physical architecture, in which media objects can always be constructed and personalised at a server receiving a request from a user. In other words, the media objects will act as mediators between the service level that is available to the WIS users and a physical database level.

In case of database distribution we obtain a further separation between a global database level and an operational level, which will become available locally at each node of a network. Using this idea we exploit the well known approach of two-stack machines to realise this operational level. The major addition is

N. Koch, P. Fraternali, and M. Wirsing (Eds.): ICWE 2004, LNCS 3140, pp. 137–141, 2004.

to extend the two-stack machines in such a way that distribution, generalised remote procedure calls, parallelism and communication are supported. In Section 3 we introduce the three-level architecture for distributed WIS.

2   Media Types

A *view* V on a database schema $\mathcal{S}$ consists of a view schema $\mathcal{S}_V$ and a defining query q_V, which transforms databases over $\mathcal{S}$ into databases over $\mathcal{S}_V$.

The defining query may be expressed in any suitable query language, e.g. query algebra, logic or an SQL-variant. For our purposes, however, this is yet not sufficient, since in all these cases the query result will be a set of values. One key concept that is missing in the views is the one of *link*.

In order to introduce links, we must allow some kind of "objectification" of values in the query language. This means to transform a set $\{v_1, \ldots, v_m\}$ of values into a set $\{(u_1, v_1), \ldots, (u_m, v_m)\}$ of pairs with new created URLs u_i of type *URL*. In the same way we may objectify lists, i.e. transform a list $[v_1, \ldots, v_m]$ of values into a list $[(u_1, v_1), \ldots, (u_m, v_m)]$ of pairs. We shall talk of *query languages with create-facility*. This leads to the definition of *raw media type*.

A *raw media type* has a name M and consists of a content data type $cont(M)$ with the extension that the place of a base type may be occupied by a pair $\ell : M'$ with a label ℓ and the name M' of a raw media type, and a defining query q_M with create-facility such that $(\{t_M\}, q_M)$ defines a view. Here t_M is the type arising from $cont(M)$ by substitution of *URL* for all pairs $\ell : M'$.

Finite sets $\mathcal{C}$ of raw media types define *content schemata*. Then a database $\mathcal{D}$ over the underlying database schema $\mathcal{S}$ and the defining queries determine finite sets $\mathcal{D}(M)$ of pairs (u, v) with URLs u and values v of type t_M for each $M \in \mathcal{C}$. We use the notion *pre-site* for the extension of $\mathcal{D}$ to $\mathcal{C}$. The pair (u, v) is called a *raw media object* in the pre-site $\mathcal{D}$.

Raw media objects are not yet sufficient for information service modelling. In order to allow the information content to be tailored to specific user needs and presentation restrictions, we must extend raw media types.

Cohesion introduces a controlled form of information loss. Formally, we define a partial order $\leq$ on content data types, which extends subtyping [1]. If $cont(M)$ is the content data type of a raw media type M and $sup(cont(M))$ is the set of all content expressions exp with $cont(M) \leq exp$, then a partial order $\preceq_M$ on $sup(cont(M))$ extending the order $\leq$ on content expressions is called an *cohesion order*. Clearly, $cont(M)$ is minimal with respect to $\preceq_M$. Small elements in $sup(cont(M))$ with respect to $\preceq_M$ define information to be kept together, if possible.

Another possibility to tailor the information content of raw media types is to consider dimension hierarchies as in OLAP systems. Flattening of dimensions results in information growth, its converse in information loss.

For a raw media type M let $\bar{H}(M)$ be the set of all raw media types arising from M by applying a sequence of flat-operations or their converses to raw media types or underlying database types. A *set of hierarchical versions* of M is a finite subset $H(M)$ of $\bar{H}(M)$ with $M \in H(M)$. Each cohesion order $\preceq_M$ on M induces an cohesion order $\preceq_{M'}$ on each element $M' \in H(M)$.

A *media type* is a raw media type M together with an cohesion order $\preceq_M$ and a set of hierarchical versions $H(M)$. A *media schema* is defined in the same way as a content schema replacing raw media types by media types. A database $\mathcal{D}$ over the underlying database schema $\mathcal{S}$ extends to a unique pre-site. Furthermore, we may extend $\mathcal{D}$ to all hierarchical versions $M' \in H(M)$ and all $M'' \succ_{M'} M'$ defined by the cohesion orders. This wide extension of $\mathcal{D}$ will be called a *site*.

Finally, we collect all media types $M_1, \ldots, M_k$ together with their hierarchical versions and types defined by the cohesion order such that $(u, v_i) \in \mathcal{D}(M_i)$ holds for a given URL u. The pair $(u, (M_1 : v_1, \ldots, M_k : v_k))$ will be called a *media object* in the site $\mathcal{D}$.

3   The Physical Architecture

Let us now look at the architecture that will support WIS based on media-objects. This architecture is illustrated in Figure 1 and we will refer to this figure to explain details of the architecture.

On the top we have the *service level* that is formed by the provision of tailored media objects to various servers. The middle level is the *database level*, which is realised by a distributed database system. The lowest level is the *operational level*. The media objects are defined by views on the database, thus mediate between the service and the database level.

The distributed database can be seen as a collection of physical objects stored on a physical storage device. These objects can be accessed through the System Buffer and Record Administration Server (SyBRAS). It provides efficient access to physical objects (synchronised by latches) and physical data independency, guarantees persistency for objects, etc.

The Persistent Object Store (POS) resides on top of SyBRAS. It provides another level of abstraction by supporting storage objects. Storage objects are constructed from physical objects, e.g., records. POS maintains direct physical references between storage objects, and offers associative, object-related and navigational access to these objects. Associative access means the well-known access via key values. Object-related access refers to direct object access using object identifiers. Navigational access is related to the propagation along physical references [6,3].

Communicating agents implement the functionality of the whole system. They integrate the processing of queries, methods assigned to objects and trans-actions. Furthermore, they are responsible for distributing requests to (remote) agents that store corresponding objects or process requests more efficiently.

These communicating agents are realized as two-stack abstract machines (2SAMs). Each agent consists of two levels. Lower levels link with POS and employ 2SAMs that deal with logical local objects. Higher level machines act as coordinators for transactions and, thus, deal with logical global objects that are constructed from logical 'local' objects. On both levels multiple 2SAMs may process concurrently. In order to take advantage of concurrent processing and the distributed architecture 2SAMs can distribute requests to 2SAMs employed on the same level. However, only those machines on the higher level are equipped with an extended RPC enabling them to distribute requests to remote agents.

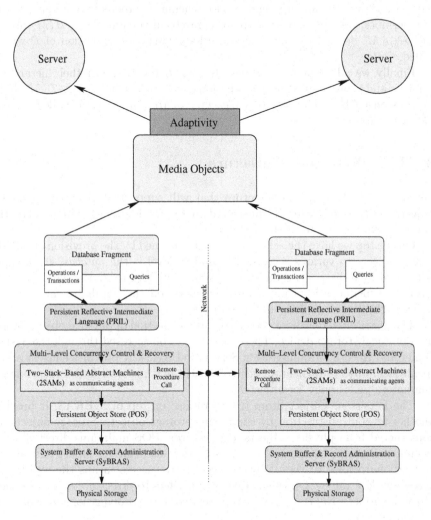

Fig. 1. General Architecture

Having these multiple object levels we can take advantage of a more sophisticated transaction management system. It is based on the multi-level transaction model [4,2] which is counted as the most promising transaction model in theory. It is combined with the ARIES/ML recovery mechanism.

Local objects do not correspond directly to logical global objects as processed by the communicating agents. Furthermore, high-level queries, transactions, object methods, etc need to be translated into code that can be interpreted by communicating agents. This conceptual gap between the logical level and the communicating agents is bridged by a persistent reflective intermediate language (PRIL).

PRIL will support linguistic reflection [5]. We provide a macro language, in which the high-level constructs in transactions such as generic update operations and the high-level algebra constructs for querying can be formulated.

4   Conclusion

The challenging engineering question in the area of WISs concerns system architectures that support WISs that are modelled as collections of media objects. In this article we presented a three-level architecture as an answer to this question. We argued that the materialisation of media objects in the underlying database reduces the problem to the integrated support of queries and operations, which both arise from the definition of media types. Our architecture is centered around two-stack abstract machines (2SAM), but the original idea of such machines has been extended in a way that communication between such machines, parallelism and distribution are supported. This defines three-levels: a service level addressing the services offered to WIS users, a database level addressing standard schema issues, and an operational level based on 2SAM as communicating agents.

References

1. FEYER, T., KAO, O., SCHEWE, K.-D., AND THALHEIM, B. Design of data-intensive web-based information services. In *Proceedings of the 1st International Conference on Web Information Systems Engineering (WISE 2000)*, Q. Li, Z. M. Ozsuyoglu, R. Wagner, Y. Kambayashi, and Y. Zhang, Eds. IEEE Computer Society, 2000, pp. 462–467.
2. KIRCHBERG, M. Exploiting multi-level transactions in distributed database systems. In *Proc of the Workshop on Distributed Data & Structures* (2002), Carleton Scientific.
3. KUCKELBERG, A. The matrix-index coding approach to efficient navigation in persistent object stores. In *Workshop on Foundations of Models and Languages for Data and Objects* (1998), pp. 99–112.
4. SCHEWE, K.-D., RIPKE, T., AND DRECHSLER, S. Hybrid concurrency control and recovery for multi-level transactions. *Acta Cybernetica 14* (2000), 419–453.
5. STEMPLE, D., SHEARD, T., AND FEGARAS, L. Reflection: A bridge from programming to database languages. In *Proc of the Hawaii Conf on System Sciences* (1992).
6. ZEZULA, P., AND RABITTI, F. Object store with navigation acceleration. information systems. *Information Systems 18*, 7 (1993), 429–459.

Modeling and Analysis of Contract Net Protocol

Fu-Shiung Hsieh

Overseas Chinese Institute of Technology
407 Taichung, Taiwan, R.O.C.
shie1210@ocit.edu.tw

Abstract. Contract net protocol can be implemented by exploiting the Web Service technologies. However, the lack of a process model in contract net protocol to capture the interactions between the bidder and manager agents makes it difficult to analyze the feasibility of the resulting contracts. We proposed a framework to execute contract net protocol based on Web Services technologies and a Petri net model to analyze the contract net negotiation results.

1 Introduction

Contract net protocol [1] is a negotiation and task distribution mechanism to optimize the performance in multi-agent systems (MAS) [2]. Contract net protocol can be implemented by exploiting the Web service discovery, invocation, selection and execution mechanism. In this paper, we focus on modeling and analysis of contract net protocol that can be implemented based on Web Services technologies [3]. Given a set of tasks, a set of agents, a cost function, contract net protocol finds the globally optimal task allocation based on distributed algorithms. In contract net protocol, there are two types of agents: manager and bidder. Four stages are involved to establish a contract between a manager and the best bidders. To apply Web Services technologies to execute contract net protocol, each manager is mapped to a Web services requester whereas each bidder is mapped to a Web services provider. Each bidder (which is a service provider) publishes the Web services by registering through a Web services broker. A manager (which is a service requester) looks up the registries of a Web service broker to discover qualified Web services provided by the potential bidders. Fig. 1 (a) illustrates our concept. Once the required qualified Web services have been found, the manager executes the contract net protocol to award the contract to the best bidder as shown in Fig. 1(b)~(e). By combining the contract net protocol with Web services technologies, it is possible to automate negotiation process.

A major drawback of the original contract net protocol is the lack of a formal model to capture the interactions between bidders and managers as well as the negotiation results. This makes it difficult to analyze the feasibility of the contract net negotiation results. For example, in real world, several contracts may need to be established between a company and his business partners to achieve a certain business objective. The lack of a model makes it difficult to efficiently evaluate the feasibility of the contracts. In this paper, we will propose a Petri net [4] model to model the

N. Koch, P. Fraternali, and M. Wirsing (Eds.): ICWE 2004, LNCS 3140, pp. 142–146, 2004.

interactions between the bidders and the managers in contract net protocol and facilitate the feasibility analysis of the contract net negotiation results.

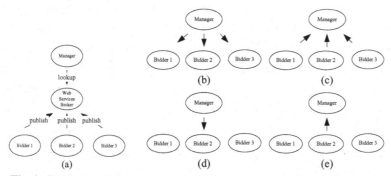

Fig. 1. Execution of contract net protocol based on Web Services technologies

2 Petri Net Model for Evaluating Contracts

To model the interactions between the bidders and the managers in contract net protocol, we adopt a bottom-up approach using Petri nets, which can be broken down into three steps: (1) modeling of bidders' proposals, (2) modeling the workflow of tasks and (3) modeling the overall system. We assume there is a set B of bidders in the system and each bidder $b \in B$ has a set R_b of type-b resources available to bid for several contracts. We use P_b to denote the states of type-b resources and place p_{b0} to denote the idle state of type-b resources. Allocation and de-allocation of the resources by bidder b are represented by a circuit that starts and ends with place p_{b0}. The Petri net G_b to describe a bidder's proposal is defined as follows.

Definition 2.1: The Petri net $G_b = (P_b, T_b, I_b, O_b, m_{b0}, F_b)$ of a bidder $b's$ proposal is a strongly connected state machine (SCSM) with any two circuits in G_b having only one common place p_{b0} but having no common transitions.

The Petri net $G_b = (P_b, T_b, I_b, O_b, m_{b0}, F_b)$ represents a proposal submitted by the bidder $b \in B$. Fig. 2 illustrates seven bidders' proposals using Petri nets. We assume that there is a set J of different types of tasks in the system. A type-j task, $j \in J$, is modeled by a Petri net to executing a sequence of operations.

Definition 2.2: The Petri net $G_j = (P_j^w, T_j^w, I_j^w, O_j^w, m_{j0}^w, F_j^w)$ of the workflow of a type-j task, $j \in J$, is a strongly connected state machine (SCSM). Every circuit in G_j contains the idle state p_{j0}, the starting transition t_j^r, the final transition t_j^f, the initial state place p_{ji} and the final state place p_{jf}, with $p_{j0}^{\bullet} = \{t_j^r\}$, $^{\bullet}p_{j0} = \{t_j^f\}$, $t_j^{r^{\bullet}} = \{p_{ji}\}$ and $^{\bullet}t_j^f = \{p_{jf}\}$. As each transition represents a distinct operation in a task, we assume $T_j \cap T_k = \Phi$ for $j \neq k$.

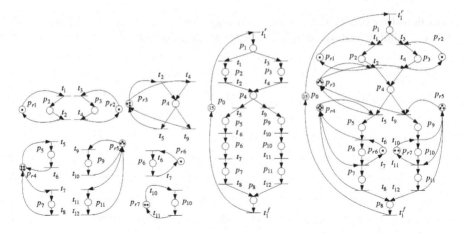

Fig. 2. Bidders' Proposals   **Fig. 3.** A Task Workflow   **Fig. 4.** Petri net Model

Fig. 3 illustrates the Petri net model of a task workflow. Place p_1 represents the initial state place while place p_8 represents the final state place. All the other places in this Petri net represent the states of the task. Each directed path from place p_1 to p_8 represents an execution sequence for the task. The Petri net models for the bidders' proposals and the task workflow are merged to form a Petri net $N_j(m_{j0}) = \|_{b \in B} G_b \| G_j = (P_j, T_j, I_j, O_j, m_{j0}, F_j)$ to model the interactions between resources and a task, where $\|$ is an operator to merge a number of different Petri net models with common transitions, places and/or arcs.. The Petri net model in Fig. 4 is obtained by merging the proposals in Fig.2 with the task in Fig. 3.

3   Feasible Condition to Award Contracts

The Petri net N_j provides a model for a manager to award contracts. To characterize the condition to complete a type-j task, we define a feasible execution sequence as follows.

Definition 3.1: Given a Petri net N_j with initial marking m_{j0}, a feasible execution sequence $s = t_1 t_2 t_3 ... t_{|s|}$ with $t_1 = t_j^r$ and $t_{|s|} = t_j^f$ is a firing sequence such that firing s brings a token from the initial state place p_{ji} to the final state place p_{jf}.

As $N_j = \|_{b \in B} G_b \| G_j$ and G_j is a connected state machine, there may be more than one execution sequence for a type-j task. However, an arbitrary execution sequence might not be a feasible one. For example, in Fig. 5, $t_1 t_2 t_9 t_{10} t_{11} t_{12}$ is not a feasible execution sequence due to the lack of a type-7 resource in place p_{r7}. In Fig. 5,

$t_1 t_2 t_5 t_6 t_7 t_8$ and $t_3 t_4 t_5 t_6 t_7 t_8$ are feasible execution sequences. A feasible execution sequence can be characterized based on the minimal resource requirement (MRR) concept.

Definition 3.2: The MRR of an execution sequence $s = t_1 t_2 t_3 .... t_{|s|}$ is denoted by a marking m_s^* of N_j with

$$m_s^*(p) = \begin{cases} N_s^*(b) & \text{if } p = p_{b0} \text{ for some } b \in B \\ 0 & \text{otherwise} \end{cases},$$

where $N_s^* = R_{t_1} \oplus R_{t_2} \oplus R_{t_3} \oplus ... \oplus R_{t_{|s|}}$, a vector in $Z^{|B|}$, denotes the set of resources required to fire s, R_t, a vector in $Z^{|B|}$, denotes the resource requirement to fire t only, and $\oplus$ is an operator that takes the larger of two vectors element by element.

Existence of a feasible execution sequence for $N_j(m_{j0})$ is as follows.

Property 3.1: Given $N_j(m_{j0})$, s is a feasible execution sequence if and only if $m_{j0} \geq m_s^*$.

Remark that N_j is constructed by merging G_j with G_b for all $b \in B$. Each execution sequence of N_j must be an execution sequence of G_j. Each execution sequence $s = t_1 t_2 t_3 ... t_{|s|}$ of G_j corresponds to a directed path γ_s from t_j^r to t_j^f in G_j. Therefore, to find a feasible execution sequence for a type- j task, it is sufficient to find a directed path γ_s from t_j^r to t_j^f with $m_{j0} \geq m_s^*$.

To award the contracts for a type- j task, we find the minimum cost feasible execution sequence for a Petri net $N_j(m_{j0})$. The problem is formulated as follows. Let c_t denote the cost to fire a transition t, where $t \in T_j$. The cost to fire the sequence $s = t_1 t_2 t_3 ... t_{|s|}$ of transitions is then $c(s) = \sum_{t \in s} c_t$. Let S_j denote the set of all feasible execution sequences of $N_j(m_{j0})$. The optimization problem can be formulated as the problem to find $\min_{s \in S_j} c(s)$. The problem to find $\min_{s \in S_j} c(s)$ is equivalent to solve $\min_{\gamma \in \Gamma_j^{feasible}} c(\gamma)$, where $\Gamma_j^{feasible} = \{ \gamma | \gamma \text{ is a directed path from } t_j^r \text{ to } t_j^f \text{ and } m_{j0} \geq m_\gamma^* \}$ denotes the set of all feasible directed paths in N_j.

Definition 3.3: Let $T_j^{feasible} = \{ t | t \in T_j, R_t \leq m_{j0} \}$ and $T_j^{\text{inf } easible} = T_j \setminus T_j^{feasible}$ be the set of transitions that cannot be fired due to insufficient resource tokens in m_{j0}.

The problem $\min_{\gamma \in \Gamma_j^{feasible}} c(\gamma)$ can be converted to a shortest path problem by constructing a weighted directed graph $\tilde{G}_j$ based on G_j and $T_j^{\text{inf } easible}$, where $\tilde{G}_j$ can be constructed by removing p_{j0} and the set $T_j^{\text{inf easible}} \cup \{t_j^r, t_j^f\}$ of transitions from G_j, and then convert-ing each transition in the resulting graph into a directed arc and assigning a weight to it. The weight w_t of a transition t is c_t for each $t \in T_j^{\text{feasible}}$. The shortest path problem described by $\tilde{G}_j$ can be solved by applying the Dijkstra's algorithm with polynomial complexity. Fig. 6 illustrates the Petri net $\tilde{G}_j$ obtained based on G_j in Fig. 3 and $T_j^{\text{inf easible}} = \{t_{10}, t_{11}\}$. Existence of a shortest path depends on $\tilde{G}_j$ and marking m_{j0}.

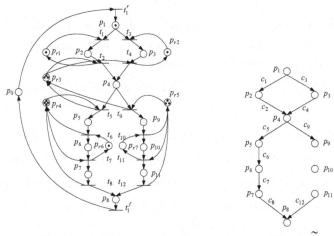

Fig. 5. An N_j with Infeasible Execution Sequence   **Fig. 6.** $\tilde{G}_j$

4   Conclusion

We focused on modeling and analysis of contract net. We identified a feasible condi-tion to award contracts and formulated an problem to find a minimal cost feasible execution sequence for a task based on Petri net. The optimization problem can be converted to a shortest path problem, which can be solved efficiently.

References

1. R.G. Smith, "The Contract Net Protocol: High-Level Communication and Control in a Distributed Problem Solver", *IEEE Trans. On Computers* Vol. 29, pp. 1104-1113, 1980.
2. Jacques Ferber, "Multi-Agent Systems, An Introduction to Distributed Artificial Intelli-gence," Addison Wesley, 1999.
3. S. McIlraith, T.C. Son, H. Zeng: Semantic Web Services, IEEE Intelligent Systems, Special Issue on the Semantic Web, 16 (2) (2001) 46-53.
4. Tadao Murata, "Petri Nets: Properties, Analysis and Applications," *Proceedings of the IEEE*, vol. 77, No. 4, April 1989.

A Web Metrics Survey Using WQM

Coral Calero, Julián Ruiz, and Mario Piattini

ALARCOS Research Group
Computer Science Department. University of Castilla-La Mancha
Paseo de la Universidad, 4
13071, Ciudad Real (Spain)
{Coral.Calero, Julian.Ruiz, Mario.Piattini}@uclm.es

Abstract. Quality is an essential characteristic for web success. Several authors have described different methodologies, guidelines, techniques and tools in order to assure the quality of web sites. Recently, a wide ranging set of metrics has been proposed for quantifying web quality attributes. However, there is little consensus among them. These metrics are sometimes not well defined, nor empirically or theoretically validated. Moreover, these metrics focus on different aspects of web sites or different quality characteristics, confusing, rather than helping, the practitioners interested in using them. With the aim of making their use easier, we have developed the WQM model (Web Quality Model), which distinguishes three dimensions related to web features, lifecycle processes and quality characteristics. In this paper we classify the most relevant web metrics using this framework. As a result of this classification we obtain that most of the metrics are classified into the "usability / exploitation / presentation" cell. Another conclusion obtained from our study is that, in general, metrics are automated but not validated formally nor empirically which is not a good way of doing things.

1 Introduction

Nowadays web technology is of paramount importance in Information Systems. In fact, the world economy's slowdown has not affected the web field because large firms stopped expanding, and began consolidating and moving to the web, to cut costs [45]. Over the next few years, the web is expected to increase by a factor of 20, growing to 200 million sites by 2005, and the number of actual web pages will increase even more [42].

The ever increasing presence of web technology and its importance for the survival of organizations make it essential to develop a complete Web Information Systems Engineering (WISE), meant as a collection of sound principles, methods, techniques and tools for developing web-based information systems, which differ from traditional information systems in their unique technological platform and design philosophy [37] and quality assurance is one of the challenging processes to the Web Engineering as a new discipline [11]. WISE aims improve and achieve quality web sites. Despite discussion of sticky web sites and development of mechanisms to encourage users to return, thus far the only mechanism that brings repeat users to web sites is quality [36].

N. Koch, P. Fraternali, and M. Wirsing (Eds.): ICWE 2004, LNCS 3140, pp. 147–160, 2004.
© Springer-Verlag Berlin Heidelberg 2004

However, and perhaps because the quality of web sites is not universally definable and measurable [9] their quality is not always assured [2, 10].

In recent years several experts have worked on different proposals to improve web quality: methodologies [39], quality frameworks [13, 25], estimation models [28], criteria [50], usability guidelines [34], assessment methods [49] and metrics.

In fact, web metrics is a particularly valuable area of ongoing commercially relevant research [47]. Since the nineties, a wide ranging set of metrics has been proposed for quantifying web quality attributes [1, 3, 5-7, 12, 14, 17, 18, 22-24, 26-31, 33, 38-41, 44-46, 51].

However, these metrics are sometimes not well defined and neither empirically nor theoretically validated. All these metrics, focused on different aspects of web sites or different quality characteristics, can confuse, rather than help, the practitioners interested in using them.

With the aim of classifying these metrics and making their use easier, we have elaborated the WQM model (Web Quality Model), which distinguishes three dimensions related to web features, lifecycle processes and quality characteristics [48].

Recently, Dhyani et al. [12] proposed a web classification framework using different categories: web graph properties, web page significance, usage characterization, web page similarity, web page search and retrieval, and theoretical information. The authors try to determine how the classified metrics can be applied to improving web information access and use. However they discard other important dimensions such as lifecycle and web features which are included in our model. Moreover in this survey they do not consider some very interesting metrics such as [24, 28, 38].

In the following section we present the WQM model explaining each of its dimensions. In the third section we will summarize the result of the classification of the most relevant web metrics. Conclusions and future work will appear in the last section.

2   Dimensions in Web Quality

In Ramler et al. [43] the authors define a cube structure in which they consider three basic aspects when making a test of a web site. Following this idea, in Ruiz et al. [48] we proposed another "cube" in which the three dimensions represent those aspects that must be considered in the evaluation of the quality of a web site: features, life cycle processes and quality aspects, which can be considered orthogonal. We have used this model to classify different studies on web engineering and we have refined our dimensions. In this section we will summarize the last version of the WQM, which is represented in figure 1.

2.1   Web Features Dimension

In this dimension we include the three "classic" web aspects: *Content*, *Presentation* and *Navigation* [6, 15, 16]. Navigation is an important design element, allowing users

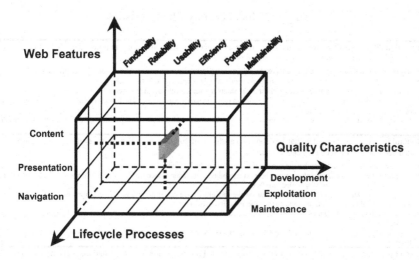

Fig. 1. Graphic representation of the model.

to acquire more of the information they are seeking and making that information easier to find. Presentation and content are prime components in making the page easier to use [42].

In *Content* we have included not only data such as text, figures, images, video clips, etc, but also programs and applications that provide functionalities like scripts, CGI programs, java programs, and others. *Content* also deals with structure and representation issues. Due to the close intertwining of functions and data the border between them is not clearly drawn, and we consider them the same feature.

Navigation concerns the facilities for accessing information and for moving around the web.

Presentation is related to the way in which content and navigation are presented to the user.

2.2 Quality Characteristics Dimension

For the description of this dimension we use as a basis the Quint2 model [35] based on the ISO 9126 standard [20]. We have decided to use Quint2 instead of the standard because this model extends the ISO standard with new characteristics very appropriate for web products. Quint2 is a hierarchical model that fixes six basic characteristics, each one of them with a set of subcharacteristics, to which a set of attributes is associated. These are the basic elements. Table 1 shows the characteristics of Quint2, indicating, if necessary, those subcharacteristics added or removed respect to ISO 9126.

There is also a *compliance* subcharacteristic for all characteristics (attributes of software that make it adhere to application related standards, conventions in laws and similar prescriptions).

Table 1. Model Quality Characteristics

Functionality. A set of attributes that bear on the existence of a set of functions and their specified properties. The functions are those that satisfy stated or implied needs.
▪ *Suitability*: Attribute of software that bears on the presence and appropriateness of a set of functions for specified tasks. ▪ *Accuracy*: Attributes of software that bear on the provision of right or agreed results or effects. ▪ *Interoperability*: Attributes of software that bear on its ability to interact with specified systems. ▪ *Security*: Attributes of software that bear on its ability to prevent unauthorized access, whether accidental or deliberate, to programs or data. ▪ *Traceability* (Quint2): Attributes of software that bear on the effort needed to verify correctness of data processing on required points.
Reliability. A set of attributes that bear on the capability of software to maintain its level of performance under stated conditions for a stated period of time.
▪ *Maturity*: Attributes of software that bear on the frequency of failure by faults in the software. ▪ *Fault tolerance*: Attributes of software that bear on its ability to maintain a specified level of performance in cases of software faults or of infringements of its specified interface. ▪ *Recoverability*: Attributes of software that bear on the capability to re-establish its level of performances and recover the data directly affected in case of a failure and on the time and effort needed for it. ▪ *Availability* (Quint2): Attributes of software that bear on the amount of time the product is available to the user at the time it is needed. ▪ *Degradability* (Quint2): Attributes of software that bear on the effort needed to re-establish the essential functionality after a breakdown.
Usability. A set of attributes that bear on the effort needed for use, and on the individual assessment of such use, by a stated or implied set of users.
▪ *Understandability*: Attributes of software that bear on the users' effort for recognising the logical concept and its applicability. ▪ *Learnability*: Attributes of software that bear on the users' effort for learning its application (for example, control, input, output). ▪ *Operability*: Attributes of software that bear on the users' effort for operation and operation control. ▪ *Explicitness* (Quint2): Attributes of software that bear on the software product with regard to its status (progression bars, etc.). ▪ *Attractivity* (*Attractiveness* in Quint2): Attributes of software that bear on the satisfaction of latent user desires and preferences, through services, behaviour and presentation beyond actual demand. ▪ *Customisability* (Quint2): Attributes of software that enable the software to be customized by the user to reduce the effort required for use and increase satisfaction with the software. ▪ *Clarity* (Quint2): Attributes of software that bear on the clarity of making the user aware of the functions it can perform. ▪ *Helpfulness* (Quint2): Attributes of software that bear on the availability of instructions for the user on how to interact with it. ▪ *User-friendliness* (Quint2): Attributes of software that bear on the users' satisfaction.
Efficiency. A set of attributes that bear on the relationship between the level of performance of the software and the amount of resources used, under stated conditions.
▪ *Time behaviour*: Attributes of software that bear on response and processing times and on throughput rates in performing its function. ▪ *Resource behaviour*: Attributes of software that bear on the amount of resources used and the duration of such use in performing its function.
Portability. A set of attributes that bear on the ability of the software to be transformed from one environment to another.
▪ *Adaptability*: Attributes of software that bear on the opportunity for its adaptation to different specified environments without applying other actions or means than those provided for this purpose for the software in question. ▪ *Installability*: Attributes of software that bear on the effort needed to install the software in a specified environment. ▪ *Replaceability*: Attributes of software that bear on the opportunity and effort of using it in the place of specified other software in the environment of that software. ▪ *Co-existence* (not included in Quint2): The capability of the software to co-exist with other independent software in a common environment sharing common resources.
Maintainability. A set of attributes that bear on the effort needed to make specified modifications.
▪ *Analysability*: Attributes of software that bear on the effort needed for diagnosis of deficiencies or causes of failures, or for identification of parts to be modified. ▪ *Changeability*: Attributes of software that bear on the effort needed for modification, fault removal or for environmental change. ▪ *Stability*: Attributes of software that bear on the risk of unexpected effect of modifications. ▪ *Testability*: Attributes of software that bear on the effort needed for validating the (modified) software. ▪ *Manageability* (Quint2): Attributes of software that bear on the effort needed to (re)establish its running status. ▪ *Reusability* (Quint2): Attributes of software that bear on its potential for complete or partial reuse in another software product.

2.3 Life Cycle Processes Dimension

By introducing this dimension, we believe that we are also considering the people involved in the development who have different skills and therefore different priorities and attitudes [32] are included. For example, the developer's interests are considered in the development process.

So, in this dimension we include the diverse processes of the web site life cycle following the ISO 12207-1 standard [19]. In the current version of the model we only included three main processes: the development process, the exploitation process (which includes the operative support for users) and the maintenance process (which includes the evolution that the web site undergoes).

It is important to emphasize that the activities of these processes must not be developed sequentially, because, due to the characteristics of web development, it will be necessary to use more iterative models and even more flexible developments without following formal methodologies [4].

3 Analysis of Existing Metrics

3.1 Surveyed Metrics

For the present study, we have surveyed different studies of metrics related in some manner with web topics. We have reviewed about 60 papers, from 1992 to 2003. From all these we have selected the ones (about 40) where metric proposals (considered useful for classification purposes on WQM) were included, discarding some others where the proposed metrics were not really applicable in our context or did not provide any relevant information. Examples of the discarded metrics include all the process metrics, focusing our work only on product metrics. We also discarded repeated metrics, i.e., those metrics proposed by more than one author.

We included each metric only once. 326 metrics were selected, and are listed at the end of this paper. Finally, we wish to note that the process of classifying metrics is not a simple task and we are conscious that some of the assignments may be arguable.

3.2 Filling the Cells of the Cube

Although the model does not restrict the number of cells that can be assigned to a given metric m, for the sake of simplicity and practicality we tried to minimize this number by assigning the metrics to the cells where they could be most useful. To avoid unnecessary complexity, we decided to show in the WQM only the quality characteristic assigned, instead of the precise sub-characteristic.

Assigning metrics to life cycle processes was not easy. We have given some special consideration to exploitation and maintenance. In the web world, where typical timeline in web development is 3-6 months [44], it is difficult to distinguish when exploitation finishes and maintenance begins. In case of doubt we have classified metrics in both processes.

3.3 The Resulting Cube

Due to the extent of the detailed assignments of metrics to cells, this information is included at the end of this paper.

In this section we will summarize the main figures of our classification shown in table 2. The "% Absolute" row shows the percentage of metrics classified on each value dimension and the sum of these values is greater than 100% because, as we have already explained, a metric can be classified in more then one cell in the cube. Because of this we have extracted prorated values shown in the "% Prorated" row.

Table 2. Metrics Classification.

	Web Features			Quality Characteristics						Lifecycle Processes		
	Content	Presentation	Navigation	Functionality	Reliability	Usability	Efficiency	Portability	Maintainability	Development	Exploitation	Maintenance
Total	99	179	67	50	21	263	47	40	79	64	267	162
% Absolute	30%	55%	21%	15%	6%	81%	14%	12%	24%	20%	82%	50%
% Prorated	29%	52%	19%	10%	4%	53%	9%	8%	16%	13%	54%	33%

Figure 2 shows metric distribution over the three dimensions of the model: web features, quality characteristics, and lifecycle processes, using prorated figures. The next subsections present several conclusions that we can extract from it.

3.3.1 Web Features Dimension

About 52% of the metrics were "presentation" metrics. This value confirms the tendency in the web world to give it the greatest importance, making the sites as attractive as possible for the end user.

At this point it is convenient to remark that usually there is a confusion between presentation and navigation [6] so, perhaps the results of the navigation could vary depending on the person who makes the classification.

3.3.2 Quality Characteristics Dimension

Most of the metrics (53%) are usability metrics. We have to take into account that this data is prorated, because if we examine absolute data (table 2) we can see that 81% of metrics are related to usability. Again this value confirms the end-user focus trying to design usable web sites that attract users.

However, it is curious that only 4% of metrics focus on reliability, when this characteristic it is also extremely important for customer acceptance of web sites.

Finally, we think that the appearance of new devices (such as PDA, mobiles, ...) will encourage the definition of new portability metrics.

3.3.3 Life-Cycle Dimension

With respect to life cycle, the exploitation and maintenance processes are the ones with most metrics. These results can be justified by taking into account the evolutionary nature of the web. The fact that there are not too many metrics defined

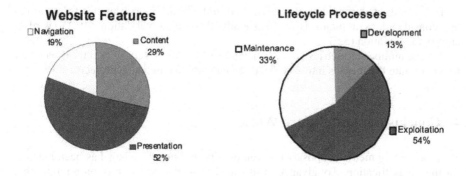

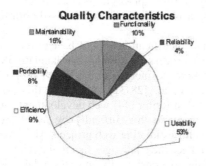

Fig. 2. Metric Distribution across the Model Dimensions

for the development process can be explained because getting their software to the market first is the top priority for firms doing business on the web and so, rather than develop software from requirements through the waterfall, web developments firms try to use rapid application development methods and continuous prototyping [44].

3.4 Metrics Properties

We have also evaluated the metrics considering the following properties [8]:

- *Granularity Level*, depending on whether the metric focuses on a single web page or on a web site.
- *Theoretical Validation* helps us to know when and how to apply metrics.
- *Empirical Validation*, with the objective of proving the practical utility of the proposed metrics.
- *Automated Support*, i.e., whether or not there is a support tool that facilitates the calculation of the metrics.

The results of this evaluation are shown at the end of this document.

As we can see there is a balanced distribution of metrics defined for web pages (47%) and web sites (53%).

The results of the validation confirm that, unfortunately, web metric validation is not considered as a major issue, especially theoretical validation (4%) but also, empirical validation (32%).

A large number of metrics are automated (79%). This is very important if we want to incorporate the metrics into web development and maintenance projects.

4   Conclusions and Future Work

There are many metric proposals for web quality, but no consensus has been reached for their classification. To advance in this area, it is essential to rely on a model that allows us to classify and systematize metric use. In this paper we have presented the WQM and we have surveyed the most relevant web metrics.

Nevertheless, this is only a first approach that needs to be reviewed until a definitive and complete version is reached that can be used with total reliability and guarantee of success.

Regarding the model, some modifications could be carried out in the life cycle dimension including a project process (following the standard ISO 15288, System Life Cycle Processes [21] in order to include in the WQM proposals related to web estimation effort like Mendes et al. [28-31]. We think this point is particularly interesting because as remarked in Reifer [44] web developments are hard to estimate and many professionals try to avoid this difficulty by using the more traditional processes, metrics and models for estimating web projects. However, these traditional approaches do not seem to address the challenges facing the field.

It could also be interesting to consider the metrics related to cost estimation because this is an essential element for providing competitive bids and remaining successful in the market [47].

Regarding the metrics classified in this study, we do not claim this survey to be complete. It would be necessary to make an even more exhaustive study of the state of the art. We also intend to define new metrics in those "cells" in which the nonexistence of metrics is detected.

Acknowledgements. This research is part of the TAMANSI project (PCB-02-001) and the MESSENGER project (PCI-03-001) supported by the Consejeria de Ciencia y Tecnología of Junta de Comunidades de Castilla-La Mancha (Spain) and the CALIPO project (TIC 2003-07804-C05-03) supported by the Ministerio de Ciencia y Tecnologia.

References

1.   Abrahão, S., Condori-Fernandez, N., Olsina, L., Pastor, O. (2003a) *Defining and Validating Metrics for Navigational Models*. Ninth International Software Metrics Symposium (METRICS'03), IEEE. pp. 200-210
2.   Abrahão, S., Pastor, O. (2003b) *Calidad de Sistemas Web. En: Calidad en el Desarrollo y mantenimiento del software*. Madrid, Ed. Ra-Ma (spanish).

3. Alves de Silva, E.A., Ponti de Mattos Fortes, R. (2001) *Web Quality Metrics: An Analysis Using Machine Learning Systems*. International Conference on Information Systems, Analysis and Sintesis. World Multiconference on Systemics, Cybernetics and Informatics. Information Systems Technology. SCI 2001/ ISAS 2001. Volumen XI.
4. Avison, D. E., Fitzgerald, G. (2003). *Where Now for Development Methodologies?* Communications of the ACM, 46 (1). pp 79-82.
5. Bajaj, A., Krishnan, R. (1999) *CMU-WEB: A Conceptual Model for Designing Usable Web Applications*. J. Database Manag. 10(4). pp 33-43
6. Baresi, L., Morasca, S., Paolini, P. (2003) *Estimating the Design Effort of Web Applications*. Proc. 9th International Metrics Symposium (METRICS'03) IEEE. pp. 62-72
7. Botafogo, R., Rivlin, E., Shneiderman, B. (1992) *Structural analysis of hypertexts: Identifying hierarchies and useful metrics*. ACM Trans. Inform. Systems, 10(2). pp 142--180, Apr.
8. Calero,C., Piattini, M., and Genero, M. (2001). *Empirical Validation of Referential Integrity Metrics*. Information Software and Technology. Special Issue on Controlled Experiments in Software Technology. Vol. 43, N° 15. 2001. pp. 949-957
9. Ciancarini, P. and Moretti, R. (2003) Towards a framework for web sites quality evaluation. 15th International conference on Software Engineering and knowledge Engineering. 1-3 July 2003. San Francisco, California. pp 721-725
10. Cutter Consortium, (2000) *Poor Project Management – Problem of E-Projects*. October 2000, http://www.cutter.com/press/001019.html
11. Deshpande, Y., Murugesan, S., Ginige, A., Hansen, S., Schwabe, D., Gaedke, M. And White, B (2002). Web Engineering. Journal of Web Engineering, Rinton Press, US, 1(1), pp. 61-73.
12. Dhyani, D., NG, W.K. and Bhowmick, S.S. (2002). *A Survey of Web Metrics*. ACM Computing Surveys, 34 (4). pp 469-503.
13. Donaldson, A.J.M., Cowderoy, A.J.C. (1997). *Towards Multimedia Systems Quality*. ESSI-SCOPE conference, Dublin.
14. Fink D. (2001) *Web Site Effectiveness: A Measure of Information and Service Quality*, Information Resource Management Association International Conference, Toronto, Canada. pp. 144-147
15. Fraternali, P. (1999) *Tools and Approaches for Developing Data-Intensive Web Applications: A survey*. ACM Computing Surveys, Vol 31, No. 3, Sept. pp. 227-263
16. Gómez, J., Cachero, C., Pastor, O. (2001). *Conceptual Modeling of Device-Independent web applications*. IEEE Multimedia. April-June 2001. pp. 26-39
17. Herder, E. (2002) *Metrics for the Adaptation of Site Structure*. Proc. of the German Workshop on Adaptivity and User Modeling in Interactive Systems ABIS02 - Hannover, pp. 22-26
18. Herzinger M. (2001) *Hyperlink Analysis for the web*. IEEE Internet Computing, Jan-Feb.
19. ISO/IEC (1995) ISO/IEC 12207. *Information Technology*. Software Life Cycle Processes.
20. ISO/IEC (2001a) ISO/IEC 9126. *Software Product Evaluation-Quality Characteristics and Guidelines for their Use*.
21. ISO/IEC (2001b) ISO/IEC 15288. *Systems Engineering – System Life Cycle Processes*.
22. Ivory, M., Hearst, M. (2001) *The State of the Art in Automating Usability Evaluation of User Interfaces*. ACM Comput. Surv. Vol. 33, No. 4. pp 470-516.
23. Ivory, M.Y., Sinha, R.R., Hearst, M.A. (2001) *Empirically Validated Web Page Design Metrics*, SIGCHI. Conference on Human Factors in Computing Systems, March 2001 pp. 53-60
24. Ivory, M.Y. (2001) *An Empirical Foundation for Automated Web Interface Evaluation*. PhD Thesis, University of California, Berkeley, Computer Science Division, 2001.
25. Katterattanakul, P. and Siau, K. (2001). *Information Quality in Internet Commerce Design*. In "Information and database quality". Kluwer Academic. pp. 45-56

26. Lafuente, G., González, J., Olsina, L. (2001) *Automatizando Métricas Web*, 4° Encontro para a Qualidade nas Tecnologias de Informação e Comunicações (QUATIC), Lisboa, Portugal, pp.17-24.
27. Mendes, E., Counsell, S. (2000) *Web Development Effort Estimation using Analogy*. Proceedings of the 2000 Australian Software Engineering Conference - ASWEC 2000, April 28-April 30, Australian National University, Canberra, ACT, Australia, IEEE CS Press. pp. 203-212.
28. Mendes, E., Mosley, N., Counsell, S. (2001) *Web metrics - Metrics for estimating effort to design and author Web applications*. IEEE MultiMedia, special issue on Web Engineering, January-March, pp. 50-57.
29. Mendes, E, Mosley, N., Counsell, S. (2002a) *Comparison of Web size measures for predicting Web design and authoring effort*. IEE Proceedings - Software 149(3). pp 86-92.
30. Mendes, E., Watson, I., Trigss, C., Mosley, N., Counsell, S. (2002b) *A Comparison of Development Effort Estimation Techniques for Web Hypermedia Applications*. Proceedings IEEE Metrics June, Ottawa, Canada. pp. 131-140.
31. Mendes, E., Mosley, N., Counsell, S. (2003) *Early Web Size Measures and Effort Prediction for Web Costimation*. Proc. 9th International Metrics Symposium (METRICS'03). pp. 18-29.
32. Mich, L., Franch, M. and Gaio, L. (2003) *Evaluating and Designing Web Site Quality*. IEEE Multimedia. January-March 2003. pp. 34-43.
33. Morisio, M., Stamelos, I., Spahos, V. Romano, D. (1999). *Measuring Functionality and Productivity in Web-Based Applications: A Case Study*. Sixth IEEE International Symposium on Software Metrics, November. pp. 111-118
34. Nielsen, J. (2000). Designing web usability. Ed. New Riders.
35. Niessink, F. (2002) *Software Requirements: Functional & Non-functional Software Requirements*. www.cs.uu.nl/docs/vakken/swa/ Slides/SA-2-Requirements.pdf
36. Offutt (2002). Quality attributes of web software applications. IEEE Software. March-April, pp. 25-32
37. Oinas-Kukkonnen, H., Alatalo, T., Kaasila, J., Kivelä, H and Sivunen, S. (2001) Requirements for web engineering methodologies. In Information Modelling in the New Millenium. Rossi and Siau (eds). Idea Group Publishing. Pp. 360-382
38. Olsina, L. (2000) Quantitative Methodology for Evaluation and Comparison of Web Site Quality, PhD Thesis, Ciencias Exactas School, UNLP, La Plata, Argentina, 2000.
39. Olsina, L., Lafuente, G., Rossi, G. (2001) *Specifying Quality Characteristics and Attributes for Websites*. Web Engineering: Managing Diversity and Complexity of Web Application Development. Springer-Verlag, June, pp. 266-277.
40. Olsina L., Rossi G. (2002) *Measuring Web Application Quality with WebQEM*, IEEE Multimedia, October-December, pp. 20-29.
41. Olsina, L., Martín M., Fons, J., Abrahão, S., Pastor, O. (2003) *Towards the Design of a Metrics Cataloging System by Exploiting Conceptual and Semantic Web Approaches*. Proc. of the International Conference on Web Engineering (ICWE 2003), LNCS 2722, pp. 324-333.
42. Palmer, J. (2002) *Web Site Usability, Design and Performance Metrics*, Information Systems Research, June, 13(2), pp. 151-167.
43. Ramler, R., Weippl, E., Winterer, M., Shwinger, W., Altmann, J. (2002). *A Quality-Driven Approach to Web Testing*. Iberoamerican Conference on Web Engineering, ICWE'02. Argentina. September. Vol. 1. pp. 81-95.
44. Reifer, D. (2000) *Web Development: Estimating Quick-to-Market Software*. IEEE Software, Nov-Dec. pp. 57-64.
45. Reifer, D. (2002) *Ten Deadly Risks in Internet and Intranet Software Development*. IEEE Software, March-April. pp. 12-14.
46. Rivlin, E., Botafago, R., Shneiderman, B. (1994) *Navigating in hyperspace: Designing a structure-based toolbox*, Communications of the ACM, Vol. 37, No. 2, February, pp. 87-96.

47. Ruhe, M., Jeffery, R., Wieczorek, I. (2003) *Using Web Objects for Estimating Software Development Effort for Web Applications*. Proc. 9th International Metrics Symposium (METRICS'03) IEEE. pp. 30-39

48. Ruiz, J., Calero, C. and Piattini, M. (2003). *A Three Dimensional Web Quality Model*. Proc. of the International Conference on Web Engineering (ICWE'03), LNCS 2722, pp. 384-385.

49. Schubert, P. (2003). Extended Web Assessment Method (EWAM) – Evaluation of Electronic Commerce Applications from the Customer's viewpoint. International Journal of Electronic Commerce, Vol. 7, No. 2, Winter 2002-2003, pp. 51-80. www.e-business.fhbb.ch/eb/publications.nsf/id/118

50. W3C (1999) WWW Consortium: *Web Content Accessibility Guidelines 1.0*, W3C Working Draft. http://www.w3.org/TR/WCAG10/

51. Warren, P., Gaskell, C., Boldyreff, C., *Preparing the Ground for Website Metrics Research*. Proc. 3rd International Workshop on Web Site Evolution (WSE'01). IEEE 2001.

Second (lower) table — metrics 1–62:

#	Metric	Ref
1	Distance	17
2	Depth	17
3	Breadth (Width)	17
4	Perimeter	17
5	Radius	17
6	Converted Out Distance (COD)	7
7	Converted In Distance (CID)	7
8	Converted Distance (CD)	7
9	Relative Out Centrality (ROC)	7
10	Relative In Centrality (RIC)	7
11	Status	7
12	Compactness	7
13	Stratum	7
14	Connectedness	3
15	Stratum	3
16	Impurity Tree	3
17	Number IN Links (NIL)	3
18	Number OUT Links (NOL)	3
19	Connectivity Density	28
20	Structure	28
21	Total Link Count (NL)	38
22	Number Broken Links (NBL)	38
23	Number Link (OLB)	38
24	Number of Different Broken Links	38
25	Different Broken Links	38
26	Images Count	38
27	Link Image Count	3
28	Surface of Images	3
29	Different Image Count	38
30	Different Image Count	38
31	Image Redundancy	38
32	Page Count	28
33	Media Complexity	28
34	Media Duration	38
35	Quick Access Pages	38
36	Program Complexity	28
37	Program Count	28
38	Page Allocation	28
39	Total Page Allocation	28
40	Total Media Allocation	28
41	Total Code Length	28
42	Total Code Allocation	28
43	Media Allocation	28
44	Video Complexity	28
45	Animation Complexity	28
46	Code Length (LOC)	28
47	Code Comment Length	28
48	Image Allocation	28
49	Reused Media Count	28
50	Image Allocation	28
51	Reused Program Count	28
52	Total Reused Media Allocation	28
53	Total Reused Code Length	28
54	Reused Comment Length	28
55	Reused Code Length	28
56	Total Page Complexity	28
57	Cyclomatic Complexity	28
58	Graphic Complexity	28
59	Suitable Information	14
60	Isolated Information	14
61	Degree of Interest	16
62	Formatted Docs (doc, pdf, ...)	27

First (upper) table — metrics 63–115:

#	Metric	Ref	Granular Level
63	Size Formatted Docs (.doc, .pdf)	28	Web
64	% Text	38	Web
65	% OLT Text	38	Web
66	Num. Panes Regarding Frames	38	Web Page
67	Avg. Broken Links per Hit Page	39	Web
68	Images per Page	38	Web Page
69	Coherence	5	Web Page
70	Local Coherence	5	Web Page
71	Global Coherence	5	Web
72	Cognitive Overhead	5	Web Page
73	Local Coherence due to Relationario	5	Web Page
74	Between Information Chunks (LORIC)	5	Web Page
75	Local Coherence due to Short Term Memory (LCSTM)	5	Web Page
76	Within Adjacent due to Hyperlink Within Attention (GCHLWA)	5	Web
77	Global Coherence due to Cognitive Jumps (GCCJ)	5	Web
78	Cognitive Overhead due to Inconsistency (COG)	5	Web
79	Cohesion (COH)	5	Web
80	Download Time	5	Web Page
81	Download Links Count	38	Web
82	Unimplemented Link Count	38	Web
83	Spelling Errors	3	Web
84	Deficiencies or absent features due to different browsers	38	Web
85	Deficiencies or unexpected results in properties of browsers	38	Web
86	Destination Pages	38	Web Page
87	Destination Nodes Under Construction	38	Web
88	Support for Text-Only Version	38	Web Page
89	Image Title	38	Web
90	Global Readability (without browsing images)	38	Web Page
91	Non-Frames Version	38	Web
92	Table of Contents	38	Web
93	Site Map	38	Web
94	Subject Index	38	Web
95	Alphabetical Index	38	Web
96	Chronological Index	38	Web
97	Geographical Index	38	Web
98	Other Indexes (audience, format,etc.	38	Web
99	Quality Labeling Systems	38	Web
100	Audience-Oriented Guided Tour	38	Web
101	Conventional Tour	38	Web
102	Guided Tour	38	Web
103	Global Help	38	Web
104	Specific Help	38	Web
105	Email Directory	38	Web
106	Phone-Fax Directory	38	Web
107	Post mail Directory	38	Web
108	FAQ Feature	38	Web
109	What's New Feature	38	Web
110	Questionnaire Feature	38	Web
111	Subject-Oriented Feedback	38	Web
112	Guided Book	38	Web
113	Completeness by Grouping Main Control	38	Web

Table (upper) — columns: Metric | Ref | WQM Quality Characteristic (Ref | Rel | Usa | Effic | Port | Main) | WQM Lifecycle Process (Des | Exp | Main) | WQM WebSite Feature (Cont | Pres | Nav) | Granularity Level | Theo Valid | Emp Valid | Auto

Metric	Ref	Ref	Rel	Usa	Effic	Port	Main	Des	Exp	Main	Cont	Pres	Nav	Granular. Level	Theo Valid	Emp Valid	Auto
Semantics Association Centers	6		X	X						X				Web		X	X
Segments	6		X	X						X				Web		X	X
Nodes	6		X	X						X			X	Web		X	X
Navigational Slots	6		X	X						X			X	Web		X	X
Nodes Cluster	6		X	X						X			X	Web			X
Slots Node	6		X	X						X			X	Web		X	X
Clusters	6		X	X						X				Web		X	X
Publishing Units	6	X	X							X		X		Web		X	X
Presentation Links	6		X							X		X		Web		X	X
Sections	6		X							X		X		Web		X	X
Word Count	24		X							X		X		Web Page		X	X
Page Title Word Count	24		X				X	X			X		X		Web Page		X	X
Overall Page Title Word Count	24		X				X	X			X		X		Web Page		X	X
Visible Word Count	24	X	X							X		X		Web Page		X	X
Meta Tag Word Count	24	X	X							X		X		Web Page		X	X
Body Word Count	24		X							X		X		Web Page		X	X
Display Word Count	24		X				X	X			X		X		Web Page		X	X
Display Link Word Count	24		X							X		X		Web Page		X	X
Link Word Count	24		X							X		X	X	Web Page		X	X
Average Link Words	24		X							X		X		Web Page		X	X
Graphic Word Count	24		X							X		X		Web Page		X	X
Alt Word Count	24		X				X	X			X		X		Web Page		X	X
Exclamation Point Count	24		X							X		X		Web Page		X	X
Spelling Error Count	24		X							X		X		Web Page		X	X
Word Variation	24		X							X		X		Web Page		X	X
Good Body Word Count	24		X							X		X		Web Page		X	X
Good Display Word Count	24		X							X		X		Web Page		X	X
Good Display Link Word Count	24		X							X		X		Web Page		X	X
Good Link Word Count	24		X							X		X		Web Page		X	X
Average Good Kin Words	24		X							X		X		Web Page		X	X
Good Graphic Word Count	24		X							X		X		Web Page		X	X
Good Page Title Word Count	24		X							X		X		Web Page		X	X
Overall Good Page Title Word Count	24		X							X		X		Web Page		X	X
Good Meta Tag Word Count	24		X							X		X		Web Page		X	X
Reading Complexity	24		X							X		X		Web Page		X	X
Overall Reading Complexity	24		X							X		X		Web Page		X	X
Big Word Count	24		X							X		X		Web Page		X	X
Big Big Word Count	24		X							X		X		Web Page		X	X
Overall Big Big Word Count	24		X							X		X		Web Page		X	X
Big Sentence Count	24		X							X		X		Web Page		X	X
Overall Big Sentence Count	24		X							X		X		Web Page		X	X
Text Link Count	24		X							X		X	X	Web Page		X	X
Page Link Count	24		X							X		X	X	Web Page		X	X
Redundant Link Count	24		X							X		X	X	Web Page		X	X
Graphic Ad Count	24		X							X		X		Web Page		X	X
Graphic Link Count	24		X				X	X			X		X		Web Page		X	X
Animated Graphic Ad Count	24		X							X		X		Web Page		X	X
Animated Graphic Link Count	24		X							X		X		Web Page		X	X
Bolded Body Word Count	24		X							X		X		Web Page		X	X
Average Length Audio Clips	24		X				X	X			X		X		Web Page		X	X
Centralized Body Word Count	24		X							X		X		Web Page		X	X
Colored Body Word Count	24		X							X		X		Web Page		X	X
Italicized Body Word Count	24		X							X		X		Web Page		X	X
Reclaimed Body Word Count	24		X							X		X		Web Page		X	X
Italicized Body Word Count	24		X							X		X		Web Page		X	X
Undefined Word Count	24		X							X		X		Web Page		X	X
Serif Word Count	24		X							X		X		Web Page		X	X
Sans Serif Word Count	24		X							X		X		Web Page		X	X
Incolor Font Style Word Count	24		X							X		X		Web Page		X	X
Font Style	24		X							X		X		Web Page		X	X
Minimum Font Size	24		X							X		X		Web Page		X	X
Maximum Font Size	24		X							X		X		Web Page		X	X
Average Font Size	24		X							X		X		Web Page		X	X

Table (lower) — columns: Metric | Ref | WQM Quality Characteristic (Ref | Rel | Usa | Effic | Port | Main) | WQM Lifecycle Process (Des | Exp | Main) | WQM WebSite Feature (Cont | Pres | Nav) | Granularity Level | Theo Valid | Emp Valid | Auto

Metric	Ref	Ref	Rel	Usa	Effic	Port	Main	Des	Exp	Main	Cont	Pres	Nav	Granular. Level	Theo Valid	Emp Valid	Auto
Direct Control Permanence	38		X	X								X		Web			
Indirect Control Permanence	38		X	X								X		Web			
Stability	38		X	X								X		Web			X
Link Color Style Uniformity	38		X	X								X		Web			X
Global Style Uniformity	38		X	X								X		Web			X
Foreign Language Support	38		X	X								X		Web			X
Global	38		X	X								X		Web			X
Screen (sub-site or page)	38		X	X								X		Web			X
Screen Resolution Indicator	39		X	X								X		Web			X
Global Screen	38	X												Web			X
Level of Retrieving Customization	38	X		X										Web			X
Level of Retrieving Feedback	38	X		X										Web			X
Indication of Path	38	X						X	X				X	Web			X
Extent of Current Position	38	X						X	X				X	Web			X
Contextual Permanence Controls	38	X						X	X				X	Web			X
Contextual Stability Controls	38	X						X	X				X	Web			X
Vertical Scrolling	38	X						X	X				X	Web			X
Horizontal Scrolling	38	X						X	X				X	Web			X
Link Titles (with explanatory help)	38	X		X					X			X		Web			X
Quality of Link Phrase	38	X		X					X			X		Web			X
Quick Browse Controls	38	X		X										Web			X
Number of Navigational Contexts	1					X	X			X			X	Web	X	X	X
Number of Navigational Links	1					X	X			X			X	Web	X	X	X
Density of a Navigational Map	1					X	X			X			X	Web	X	X	X
Depth of a Navigational Map	1					X	X			X			X	Web	X	X	X
Breadth of a Navigational Map	1					X	X			X			X	Web	X	X	X
Minimum Path Between Navigational Contexts	1		X						X				X	Web	X	X	X
Compactness	1		X						X				X	Web	X		X
Stratum	1		X						X				X	Web	X	X	X
Depth of a Navigational Context	1		X						X				X	Web	X	X	X
Fan-Out of a Navigational Context	1		X						X				X	Web	X	X	X
Number of Attributes	1		X						X				X	Web	X	X	X
Number of Methods	1		X						X				X	Web	X	X	X
Number of Building Blocks	44	X	X						X		X	X		Web	X		
Number of COTS Components	44	X	X						X		X	X		Web	X		
Number of Object or Applicat. Points	44	X	X						X		X	X		Web	X		
Number of XML, SGML, HTML, and	44	X						X		X	X			Web	X		X
XSL Lines																	
Number of Web Components	44	X						X		X	X			Web	X		X
Number of Scripts (Visual Language, Audio, Motion)	44	X						X		X	X			Web	X		X
Function Points	33		X		X									Web		X	
Object-Oriented Function Points	33		X		X									Web		X	
Reuse Level LOCs	33		X		X									Web		X	
Reuse Level DOFPs	33		X		X									Web		X	
Total Number Flash Animations	31		X				X	X				X		Web		X	X
Total Number of Icons/Buttons	31		X				X	X				X		Web		X	X
Average Length Audio Clips	31		X				X	X				X		Web		X	X
Total Number Video Clips	31		X				X	X				X		Web		X	X
Total Embedded Code Length	31		X						X			X		Web		X	X
Size CPU	31		X						X			X		Web Page		X	X
Number of Entities	6	X	X						X			X		Web		X	X
Number of Components	6	X	X						X			X		Web		X	X
Number of InfoSlots	6	X	X						X			X		Web		X	X
Slots Semantic Association	6	X	X						X			X		Web		X	X
Slots Collection Center	6	X	X						X			X		Web		X	X
Components Entity	6	X	X						X			X		Web		X	X
Slots Components	6	X	X						X			X		Web		X	X
Semantics Associations	6	X	X						X			X		Web		X	X

Table (upper): Metrics 299–326

	Metric	Ref	WQM Quality Characteristic						WQM Lifecycle Process			WQM Website Feature			Granular Level	Theo. Valid	Emp. Valid	Auto
			Fun	Rel	Usa	Effic	Port	Maint	Dev	Exp	Maint	Cont	Pres	Nav				
299	All Unique Page Text Terms	24			X					X		X			Web Page			X
300	All Page Text Hits	24			X					X		X			Web Page			X
301	All Page Text Score	24			X					X		X			Web Page			X
302	Visible Link Text Terms	24			X					X		X			Web Page			X
303	Visible Unique Link Text Terms	24			X					X		X			Web Page			X
304	Visible Link Text Hits	24			X					X		X			Web Page			X
305	Visible Link Text Score	24			X					X		X			Web Page			X
306	All Link Text Term	24			X					X		X			Web Page			X
307	All Unique Link Text Term	24			X					X		X			Web Page			X
308	All Link Text Hits	24			X					X		X			Web Page			X
309	All Link Text Score	24			X					X		X			Web Page			X
310	Page Title Terms	24			X					X		X			Web Page			X
311	Unique Page Title Terms	24			X					X		X			Web Page			X
312	Page Title Hits	24			X					X		X			Web Page			X
313	Page Title score	24			X					X		X			Web Page			X
314	Page Title Variation	24			X					X		X			Web Page			X
315	Text Element Variation	24			X					X		X			Web Page			X
316	Link Element Variation	24			X					X		X			Web Page			X
317	Graphic Element Variation	24			X					X		X			Web Page			X
318	Text Formatting Variation	24			X					X		X			Web Page			X
319	Link Formatting Variation	24			X					X		X			Web Page			X
320	Graphic Formatting Variation	24			X					X		X			Web Page			X
321	Page Formatting Variation	24			X					X		X			Web Page			X
322	Page Performance Variation	24			X					X		X			Web Page			X
323	Overall Element variation	24			X					X		X			Web Page			X
324	Overall Formatting Variation	24			X					X		X			Web			X
325	Overall Variation	24			X					X		X			Web			X
326	Median Page Breadth	24			X					X		X		X	Web			X

Table (lower): Metrics 237–298

	Metric	Ref	WQM Quality Characteristic						WQM Lifecycle Process			WQM Website Feature			Granular Level	Theo. Valid	Emp. Valid	Auto
			Fun	Rel	Usa	Effic	Port	Maint	Dev	Exp	Maint	Cont	Pres	Nav				
237	Body Color Count	24			X					X			X		Web Page			X
238	Display Color Count	24			X					X			X		Web Page			X
239	Text Positioning Count	24			X					X			X		Web Page		X	X
240	Text Column Count	24			X					X			X		Web Page		X	X
241	Text Cluster Count	24			X					X			X		Web Page			X
242	Link Text Cluster Count	24			X					X			X		Web Page			X
243	Border Cluster Count	24			X					X			X		Web Page			X
244	Color Cluster Count	24			X					X			X		Web Page			X
245	Text Cluster Count	24			X					X			X		Web Page			X
246	Link Cluster Count	24			X					X			X		Web Page			X
247	Link Color Count	24			X					X			X		Web Page			X
248	Non-underlined Text Links	24			X					X	X		X		Web Page			X
249	Standard Link Color Count	24			X					X	X		X		Web Page			X
250	Minimum Graphic Height	24			X	X				X	X		X		Web			X
251	Maximum Graphic Height	24			X	X				X	X		X		Web			X
252	Average Graphic Height	24			X	X				X	X		X		Web			X
253	Minimum Graphic Wide	24			X	X				X	X		X		Web			X
254	Maximum Graphic Wide	24			X	X				X	X		X		Web			X
255	Average Graphic Wide	24			X	X				X	X		X		Web			X
256	Color Count	24			X					X			X		Web Page		X	X
257	Minimum Color Use	24			X					X			X		Web Page			X
258	Maximum Color Use	24			X					X			X		Web Page			X
259	Good Text Color Combination	24			X					X			X		Web Page			X
260	Neutral Text Color Combination	24			X					X			X		Web Page			X
261	Bad Text Color Combination	24			X					X			X		Web Page			X
262	Good Panel Color Combinations	24			X					X			X		Web Page			X
263	Neutral Panel Color Combinations	24			X					X			X		Web Page			X
264	Bad Panel Color Combinations	24			X					X			X		Web Page		X	X
265	Font Count	24			X					X			X		Web Page			X
266	Serif Font Count	24			X					X			X		Web Page			X
267	Sans Serif Font Count	24			X					X			X		Web Page			X
268	Undefined Font Style Count	24			X					X			X		Web Page			X
269	Page Height	24			X					X			X		Web Page			X
270	Page Width	24			X					X			X		Web Page			X
271	Page Pixels	24			X					X			X		Web Page			X
272	Vertical Scrolls	24			X					X			X		Web Page			X
273	Horizontal Scrolls	24			X					X		X	X		Web Page			X
274	Interactive Element Count	24	X		X					X		X			Web Page			X
275	Search Element Count	24	X		X					X		X			Web Page			X
276	Minimal Style/well Use	24			X					X		X			Web Page			X
277	Good Page Width Use	24			X					X		X		X	Web Page			X
278	Page Width Use	24			X					X		X			Web Page			X
279	Page Type	24			X					X		X			Web Page			X
280	Self Containment	24			X					X		X	X		Web Page			X
281	Scanning Use	24			X					X		X	X		Web Page			X
282	Table Count	24			X					X		X	X		Web Page			X
283	Script File Count	24			X					X		X	X		Web Page			X
284	Script Bytes	24			X					X		X	X		Web Page			X
285	Object File Count	24			X					X		X	X		Web Page			X
286	Object Bytes	24			X					X		X			Web Page			X
287	Object Count	24			X					X		X			Web Page			X
288	Body Approved	24			X					X		X			Web Page			X
289	Body Priority 1 Errors	24			X					X		X			Web Page			X
290	Body Priority 2 Errors	24			X					X		X			Web Page			X
291	Body Priority 3 Errors	24			X					X		X			Web Page			X
292	Body Browser Errors	24			X					X		X			Web Page			X
293	Website Errors	24		X	X					X		X			Web Page			X
294	Visible Page Text Terms	24			X					X		X			Web Page			X
295	Visible Unique Page Text Terms	24			X					X		X			Web Page			X
296	Visible Page Text Hits	24			X					X		X			Web Page			X
297	Visible Page Text Score	20			X					X		X			Web Page			X
298	All Page Text Terms	24			X					X		X			Web Page			X

A COSMIC-FFP Based Method to Estimate Web Application Development Effort

Gennaro Costagliola, Filomena Ferrucci, Carmine Gravino, Genoveffa Tortora, and
Giuliana Vitiello

Dipartimento di Matematica e Informatica, Università degli Studi di Salerno
Via Ponte Don Melillo, 84084 Fisciano (SA), Italy
{gcostagliola, fferrucci,gravino,tortora,gvitiello}@unisa.it

Abstract. In the paper we address the problem of estimating the effort required
to develop dynamic web applications. In particular, we provide an adaptation of
the *Cosmic Full Function Point* method to be applied on design documents for
counting data movements. We also describe the empirical analysis carried out
to verify the usefulness of the method for predicting web application development effort.

1 Introduction

In the present paper we address the problem of estimating the effort required to develop web applications. This represents an emerging issue in the field of web engineering, due to the dramatic increasing of complexity and size of web applications,
and the consequent demand for tools supporting project development planning with
reliable cost and effort estimations [2,6,7,8,9,10,11].

In [9] Rollo employed *COSMIC-FFP* (*Cosmic Full Function Point*) [5], an adaptation of *Function Points* [1] originally defined for real-time applications, to measure
the functional size of an Internet bank system. Following his suggestion in [6] Mendes *et al.* provided a formal method which adopts *COSMIC-FFP* to measure size of
static hypermedia web applications. In the paper we propose to apply the *COSMIC-
FFP* method also to dynamic applications. Indeed, since *COSMIC-FFP* measure is
focused on the counting of data movements, it turns out to be suitable for client-
server applications, which are characterized by large amounts of data movements. To
provide an early size estimation, we propose to apply the method on design documents. In particular, we extend the proposal by Mendes *et al.,* by defining some rules
that allow us to measure functional size of client-server applications, using class diagrams. Moreover, we also report on an initial empirical validation of the approach
performed on a set of dynamic applications developed by undergraduate students of
two academic courses on web engineering.

The paper is organized as follows. In Section 2 we describe the rules to adapt
COSMIC-FFP counting to class diagrams describing dynamic web applications. Section 3 presents the results of the empirical analysis carried out so far. Section 4 concludes the paper giving some final remarks and discussion on future work.

N. Koch, P. Fraternali, and M. Wirsing (Eds.): ICWE 2004, LNCS 3140, pp. 161–165, 2004.
© Springer-Verlag Berlin Heidelberg 2004

2 Applying COSMIC-FFP to Dynamic Hypermedia Applications

The *COSMIC-FFP* method is focused on counting data movements from *Functional User Requirements* to obtain the functional size of the software, expressed in terms of *CFSU (Cosmic Functional Size Unit)* [5]. Each *CFSU* corresponds to either an *entry*, or an *exit*, or a *read*, or a *write*.

In the sequel, suitable rules are given for counting data movements of dynamic web applications using class diagrams, expressed in terms of the UML notation for the web proposed in [3].

1. For each static web page count 1 *entry* + 1 *read* + 1 *exit*. Indeed, an entry is sent to the application by requesting the client page (*entry*), the page is read from the web server (*read*) and then shown to the user (*exit*).
2. For each multimedia component, which is visualized after an explicit request of the client, count C*(1 *entry* + 1 *read* + 1 *exit*). C denotes a weight associated to the component and is determined by considering its influence on the development process. In particular, C=1, means little influence; C=2, means medium influence; C=3, means strong influence.
3. For each script used to provide a functionality to manipulate document on the client side (i.e., in the web browser), count 1 *entry*.
4. For each application executed on the client side, count C*(1 *entry* + 1 *exit*), where C denotes again a weight. The *entry* is considered to run it and the *exit* to show it.
5. For each server side interpreted script or compiled module used to produce a dynamic web page, count 1 *entry* + 1 *read* + 1 *exit*. In this case, a form allows users to input data and request a dynamic page (*entry*). The web server elaborates the input of the user through the server-side script or module (*read*) and produces a web page which is sent to the user (*exit*). Moreover, count an additional *read* if an access control is first performed and then the input is elaborated to generate the web page.
6. For each server side script modifying persistent data through the web server, count 1 *entry* + 1 *write* + 1 *exit*. The user inputs data through a form (*entry*), the data is written through the web server (*write*) and the result is shown to the user (*exit*). Count an additional *read* if an access control is first performed.
7. For each web page that contains confirmation, alert or error messages sent by the web server to the browser, count 1 *read* + 1 *exit*.
8. For each reference to external applications such as commercial package, library routine, count 1 *entry* + 1 *exit*.

Let us note that rules 5, 6, 7, 8 were specifically conceived to consider dynamic aspects of web applications, rule 2 refers to multimedia components and rules 1, 3, 4 take into account elements common to static web applications. In particular, the latter rules are analogous to the ones provided by Mendes *et al.* in [6] to measure hypermedia web applications. The sum of the identified data movements is expressed in terms of *CFSU*.

In the sequel we show the application of some rules. To this aim, let us consider the class diagram depicted in Fig. 1, which is referred to a web application designed for e-learning purposes and is concerned with the final test. The user requests the final test by specifying his/her data through the HTML form *UserRegistration* contained in the client page *FinalTest*. The server page *UserIdentification* verifies whether or not the user is registered and the server page *TestCreation* prepares the form *TestForm* by using the information of the class *Test*. The user fills in the form by answering the questions and submits his/her test. Then, the server page *Scoring* interacts with the database and determines the score which is sent back to the user as an HTML page (i.e., *Score*). Moreover, the server page *DBUpdating* inserts the score into the database by using the user data contained in the object *Session*. The presence of the server pages *UserIdentification*, *TestCreation*, *Scoring* determines the application of rule 5, resulting in 9 *CFSUs*. Rule 6 is instead applied considering the server page *DBUpdating*, determining other 3 *CFSUs*. Finally, the presence of the static web page *FinalTest* which contains the HTML form *UserRegistration*, causes the application of rule 1, counting further 3 *CFSUs*. Thus, the total counting for the considered piece of design documentation is 15 *CFSUs*.

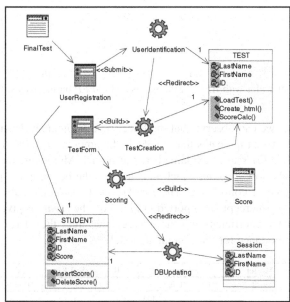

Fig. 1. The UML class diagram modelling the final test within an e-learning course

3 Empirical Evaluation

A statistical analysis has been performed to establish whether the proposed application of *COSMIC-FFP* can be used to predict the development effort of web based systems. We have exploited data coming from 32 web projects developed by students during the course on Web Engineering of two subsequent academic years. In both cases, the most skillful students were equally distributed among the groups in order to allow uniformity. Table 1 provides the descriptive statistics performed both for the variable *Effort* (*EFH*), expressed in terms of person-hours, and the variable *COSMIC-FFP* (*C-FFP*), expressed in terms of *CFSUs*.

Table 1. Descriptive statistics of *EFH* and *C-FFP*

	Obs	MIN	MAX	MEAN	STD. DEV.
EFH	32	62	172	117.6250	33.6699
C-FFP	32	84	833	346.4688	225.6862

In order to perform the empirical validation of the proposed method, we have applied an Ordinary Least-Squares regression analysis. The scatter plot of Fig. 2.a exposes a positive linear relationship between the variables *EFH* and *C-FFP*. From the Q-Q plot of Fig. 2.b we can observe that the residuals are normally distributed.

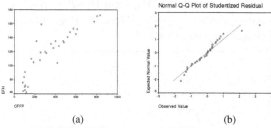

(a)   (b)

Fig. 2. (a)The scatter plot with *EFH* on the *y*-axis and *C-FFP* on the *x*-axis. (b) The Q-Q plot of the residuals.

From Fig. 3.a, we can observe that the linear regression analysis shows a high adjusted R^2=0.763, which indicates that 76.3% is the amount of the variance of the dependent variable *EFH* that is explained by the model. Moreover, we can observe a high *F* value and a low *p-value*, which indicate that the prediction is indeed possible with a high degree of confidence. The *p-values* and *t-values* for the corresponding coefficient and the intercept are reported in Fig. 3.b. The *p-values* give an insight into the accuracy of the coefficient and the intercept, whereas their *t-values* allow us to evaluate their importance for the generated model.

Prediction Model	adjusted R^2	R	Std Err	F	p-value
EFH=0.131*C-FFP +72.254	0.763	0.878	16.3978	100.699	0.000

(a)

	Value	Std. Err	t-value	p-value
Coefficient	0.131	0.013	10.035	0.000
Intercept	72.254	5.371	13.453	0.000

(b)

Fig. 3. The results of the OLS regression analysis for evaluating the *EFH* using *C-FFP*

In order to assess the acceptability of the derived effort prediction model, we have considered the *Mean of Magnitude of Relative Error* (*MMRE*) [4] over the 32 observations. The model exhibits an *MMRE* = 0.1151, which is less than 0.25, the threshold suggested by Conte *et al.* for an effort prediction model [4]. Moreover, we have evaluated the *prediction at level 0.25* [4], which has turned out to be 0.8438. According to Conte *et al.* a good effort prediction model should exhibit a value not less than 0.75, which is the case for the derived model.

4 Final Remarks

In this paper we have proposed an approach for estimating the functional size of dynamic web applications, exploiting the *COSMIC-FFP* method, during design phase. The results of the empirical analysis that we have carried out are encouraging, and suggest several research directions for future work. First of all, further analysis is planned for the assessment of the method. Indeed, the empirical evaluation provided in the paper has to be considered a preliminary analysis since the use of students' projects may threat the external validity of the experiment and hence data coming from the industrial world are presently being collected, in order to obtain more reliable results. Such data will be also used to perform a comparative analysis with respect to other proposals, such as *Web Objects* [10,11], and to refine the current proposal by considering other features, such as the complexity of the data structure and algorithm behind the data movement. We finally plan to automate the application of the proposed rules on the class diagrams in order to integrate such functionality in a suitable CASE tool.

References

1. A.J. Albrecht, "Measuring Application Development Productivity", in *Proceedings of the IBM Application Development Symposium*, Monterey, 1979, pp. 83-92.
2. L. Baresi, S. Morasca, P. Paolini, "Estimating the Design Effort of Web Applications," in *Procs. IEEE Software Metrics Symposium*, Sydney, 2003, pp. 62-72.
3. J. Conallen, *Building Web Applications with UML*, Addison-Wesley, 1999.
4. D. Conte, H.E. Dunsmore, V.Y. Shen, *Software Engineering Metrics and Models*, The Benjamin/Cummings Publishing Company, Inc., 1986.
5. COSMIC: COSMIC-FFP Measurement Manual, vers. 2.2, http://www.cosmicon.com, 2003.
6. E. Mendes, N. Mosley, S. Counsell, "Comparison of Web Size Measures for Predicting Web Design and Authoring Effort", *IEE Proceedings-Software* 149 (3), 2002, pp. 86-92.
7. E. Mendes, I. Watson, C. Triggs, N. Mosley, S. Counsell, "A Comparative Study of Cost Estimation Models for Web Hypermedia Applications", *Empirical Software Engineering* 8(2), 2003, pp. 163-196.
8. M. Morisio, I. Stamelos, V. Spahos, D. Romano, "Measuring Functionality and Productivity in Web-based Applications: a Case Study", in *Procs. 6th Intern. Software Metrics Symposium*, Boca Raton, 1999, pp. 111-118.
9. T. Rollo, "Sizing E-Commerce", in *Procs. Australian Conference on Software Measurement*, Sydney, 2000.
10. D. Reifer, "Web-Development: Estimating Quick-Time-to-Market Software", *IEEE Software*, 17 (8), 2000, pp. 57-64.
11. M. Ruhe, R. Jeffery, I. Wieczorek, "Using Web Objects for Estimating Software Development Effort for Web Applications", in *Procs. IEEE Software Metrics Symposium*, Sydney, 2003, pp. 30-39.

Evaluation of Commercial Web Engineering Processes

Andrew McDonald and Ray Welland

Department of Computing Science, University of Glasgow, Glasgow, Scotland. G12 8QQ.
{andrew, ray}@dcs.gla.ac.uk, http://www.dcs.gla.ac.uk/

Abstract. Over the past five years a small number of specific commercial processes and evolutions to traditional software engineering processes for Web Engineering have been proposed. The existing Web engineering literature focuses mainly on techniques and tools that underpin the process of building Web applications, with little or no focus on the commercial suitability of the Web Engineering processes themselves. Based on our experience and surveys of Web engineering in practice, we have defined a set of essential criteria to be addressed by a commercial Web engineering process. In this paper we present a systematic evaluation of a sample of commercial Web engineering processes against these criteria. None of the commercial Web engineering processes evaluated addresses all the identified criteria. Ultimately to address the criteria for a Web engineering process there is a need for a different type of process.

1 Introduction

Our experience and that of others suggest that Web engineering requires different software development processes from traditional software engineering. From October until December 2000 we carried out a survey of commercial organisations involved in Web-based application development [1, 2]. Based on our personal experience, this survey and other surveys of Web engineering in practice, we have identified seven characteristics of Web engineering that we believe must be addressed by a Web engineering processes. These are support for:
1. Short development life-cycle times
2. Different business models (Business Process Re-engineering)
3. Multidisciplinary development teams
4. Small development teams working in parallel on similar tasks
5. Business Analysis and Evaluation with End-Users
6. Explicit Requirements and rigorous Testing against requirements
7. Maintenance

Koch [3] in her comparative study paper identified several differences between the development of hypermedia systems and traditional software development. These included: different developer skills, taking into account aesthetic and cognitive aspects; augmented user role; and the more important role of the maintenance phase. She concluded "in particular, some research is needed to improve and test methods that cover the complete life cycle of hypermedia applications" and argued for better requirements capture and more focus on validation, verification and testing.

N. Koch, P. Fraternali, and M. Wirsing (Eds.): ICWE 2004, LNCS 3140, pp. 166–170, 2004.

2 Evaluating Commercial Web Engineering Processes

Over the past five years a small number of specific processes and evolutions to traditional software engineering processes for Web Engineering have been proposed. Processes specifically for Web engineering include Collaborative Web Development [4] and Crystal Orange Web [5]. Evolutions to traditional software engineering process include extensions to OPEN [6] and to The Rational Unified Process [7].

This section provides a short introduction to each process, followed by a table describing our analysis of how each of the processes supports our criteria for Web engineering processes. Each process evaluated is given a rank against each of the criteria, points 1-7, listed above, indicating how strongly a particular process supports each criterion under the following scheme: *none, weak, partial, strong* or *very strong*.

The **Collaborative Web Development** (CWD) process [4] is based on Burdman's extensive experience of developing Web-based applications. However, she comes from a technical and creative writing background and this is strongly reflected in the process she describes. The CWD process life-cycle is plan-driven, with four phases: 'Strategy'; 'Design and Specification'; 'Production'; and 'Testing and Launch'. The communications model proposed is very hierarchical and appears rather heavyweight for Web-based applications. Table 1 describes our analysis of CWD's support for the criteria for a Web Engineering Process.

Table 1. Collaborative Web Development's support for the Criteria for a Web Engineering Process

No.	Support	Comments
1.	*Partial*	CWD prohibits any changes being incorporated during the production phase without cost implications. This approach is only suitable within contracting projects with fixed requirements.
2.	*None*	No support for impact into business and domain models from the software model.
3.	*Partial*	CWD only supports the creative design and development roles, ignoring the business and domain experts.
4.	*Weak*	Team structure is the same regardless of the size of the project and there is no inter-team communication model for parallel development.
5.	*Weak*	There is some support for business analysis in the Strategy phase but a lack of explicit focus on Evaluation within CWD.
6.	*Weak*	The Design and Specification phase, combining requirements and design to produce a technical specification in CWD is known to be problematic [1, 2]. Conventional testing by development team only.
7.	*Partial*	CWD maintenance focus is on software and creative design models, ignores business and domain models.

Crystal Orange Web (COW) [5] is part of a family of agile processes developed by Alistair Cockburn. Crystal processes are: "people- and communication-centric"; intended for development teams that are collocated within the one building and are not designed for safety critical systems. Crystal methodologies should be adjusted to fit a particular setting and Crystal Orange Web is an application of the Crystal methodology used to deliver a Web-based application for eBucks.com. Table 2 describes our analysis of COW's support for our criteria.

Table 2. Crystal Orange Web support for the Criteria for a Web Engineering Process

No.	Support	Comments
1.	*Strong*	COW recommends two-week development cycles, with a further recommendation that "each team must deliver something useful to the public every four weeks".
2.	*Weak*	COW encourages "business owners" to consider the business processes required for software failure or errors. However there is no explicit encouragement to discuss the potential benefits that may be derived by re-engineering business processes.
3.	*Strong*	One of the objectives of COW is that ideally, the programmers, user interface designers, testers, business owners, marketing experts, et al. should sit in cross-functional teams.
4.	*Weak*	There is an absence of support for concurrent development in COW, although other Crystal processes show strong support for this criterion.
5.	*Weak*	Business analysis involves the business owner writing a business use case and a system use case brief. COW does not mention end-user involvement during the development life-cycle before live delivery of software.
6.	*Partial*	Requirements are supported by business analysts producing detailed use cases and data descriptions. COW emphasises support for testing by the developers.
7.	*Partial*	There is no mention of long term maintenance and evolution issues within COW, the focus is on rapid short-term evolutionary steps.

Web OPEN is based on Object-oriented Process, Environment and Notation (OPEN) [8], an object-oriented process framework developed and maintained by over thirty five members of the OPEN Consortium. A recent paper [6] describes how OPEN can be extended to "fully support the new demands of website construction and the delivery of business value on the Web".

In assessing the suitability of Web OPEN we have considered the explicit extensions to the basic process [6] and also where the extended process depends upon the foundations of the OPEN process framework. Table 3 describes our analysis of Web OPEN against our criteria.

There are extensions for Web application development with IBM's **Rational Unified Process** (RUP) [9], a well known plan-driven software process product which is widely used for the development of object-oriented systems. A Rational white paper [7] describes how the RUP can be extended for Web-based application development. This paper *"focuses particularly on the front-end of the lifecycle, and how to integrate the creative design process with the software engineering process of the Rational Unified Process"*.

In assessing the suitability of the extended form of RUP we have considered the explicit extensions to the basic process [7] and also where the extended process depends upon the foundations of the RUP process. Table 4 describes our analysis of how the proposed extensions to RUP support the criteria for a Web Engineering Process.

3   Conclusions

Using the criteria for the evaluation of Web engineering processes we have evaluated a number of commercial Web engineering processes using the available literature.

Table 3. Web OPEN support for the Criteria for a Web Engineering Process

No.	Support	Comments
1.	*Weak*	The OPEN framework requires process engineers to create a process instance particular to their project or organization. There is therefore a strong dependency on a skilled process engineer, Cockburn level 3 [5], to ensure that the process is sufficiently tailored to deal with the time-to-market pressures experienced in Web engineering. It is unlikely that most Web projects will have access to such a skilled process engineer.
2.	*Weak*	The Web OPEN process does not address impact from software model back into the business and domain models nor does it not mention business process re-engineering. The OPEN process framework does however provide a Phase within the Enterprise Lifecycle known as Business Reengineering.
3.	*Partial*	Web OPEN includes the creative design and developer roles but there is no mention of the business or domain expert roles.
4.	*None*	There is no mention of how teams are coordinated or work together within a large Web engineering project.
5.	*Partial*	The OPEN framework includes business modelling but it is not clear how this relates to business analysis. Web OPEN does not mention an Evaluation phase or the involvement of end-users during development. However, OPEN provides a number of work products for Usability Testing, although we could find no discussion of where, how or when these should be applied in Web development.
6.	*Strong*	OPEN provides a focus on requirements engineering and Web OPEN provides specific focus on testing through the Web Site Testing Task.
7.	*Strong*	There is explicit focus in Web OPEN on a new Activity known as Web Site Management dealing with the bringing *"together of all the issues regarding the development, maintenance and management of a corporate website which may or may not include access to back-end transaction processing systems"*

Table 4. RUP and extensions support for the Criteria for a Web Engineering Process

No.	Support	Comments
1.	*Weak*	Process is too predictive and heavy weight, requiring the development of a 'Full Web User Interface prototype', (six documented deliverables), to be produced covering all use-cases, before the construction phase. Recommends re-use of use cases from previous Web projects to address time-to-market.
2.	*None*	The impact reflected within the process is from the business and domain model to the software and creative design models, as opposed to just the software model as in vanilla RUP. There is no mention of impact back into the business and domain models from the software model.
3.	*Partial*	Focus on the increased visibility of the creative design role when building Web solutions. There is explicit mention of a wider diversity of stakeholders required to build Web solutions than in traditional software engineering, but no integration of these roles into the development process.
4.	*Weak*	No mention of parallel activities or coordinating many small teams.
5.	*Partial*	RUP includes business modelling workflow before deriving software requirements. No explicit mention of evaluation with end-users or how to support this activity within the process.
6.	*Strong*	Explicit focus on capture of all types of requirements including functional (use case model) and non-functional, including those specifically relevant to the creative design model. The testing element is contained within vanilla RUP but there is no explicit mention of Web site testing.
7.	*Partial*	No explicit mention of maintenance issues. However a number of documented deliverables are produced within the creative design and software models.

Our analysis shows that Crystal Orange Web is the only process that explicitly addresses the crucial criterion of short development life cycles. There is clearly a need for stronger support for different business models and business process re-engineering, reflecting impact back from the software model into the business and domain models. COW is the only process to incorporate the wide range of development roles required in Web engineering. None of the processes provide a mechanism to support scalability to a number of small teams working in parallel. There is a need for stronger focus on addressing the customer community view (end-users and those impacted by the project deliverables) within commercial Web engineering processes and particularly end-user participation throughout development and evaluation. With respect to requirements, testing and maintenance the extensions to traditional software engineering processes provide stronger support because of their software engineering process foundations.

Our original motivation for doing this work was to identify criteria for Web engineering processes that would underpin our research in developing a new Web engineering process. Our work on the Agile Web Engineering (AWE) process has been described elsewhere [10]. However, we believe that these criteria for evaluating Web engineering processes are much more widely applicable. Further empirical evidence will either strengthen or modify our assessment of the essential criteria, which can then be used to evaluate other Web engineering processes, both commercial processes and those proposed by other researchers in the field. They can also be used as the starting point for further research into Web engineering processes.

References

1. McDonald A. and Welland R. (2001) 'A Survey of Web Engineering in Practice', Department of Computing Science Technical Report TR-2001-79, University of Glasgow, Scotland, 01 March.
2. McDonald A. and Welland R. (2001) 'Web Engineering in Practice', Proceedings of the Fourth WWW10 Workshop on Web Engineering, Page(s): 21-30, 01 May.
3. Koch, N. 'A Comparative Study of Methods for Hypermedia Development', Technical Report 9905, Ludwig-Maximilians-Universität München, November 1999.
4. Burdman J., 'Collaborative Web Development: Strategies and Best Practices for Web Teams', Addison-Wesley, 1999, ISBN: 0201433311
5. Cockburn A., 'Agile Software Development', Pearson Education, Inc, Feb 2002, Page(s): 117, ISBN: 0201699699
6. Haire B., Henderson-Sellers B., and Lowe D., 'Supporting web development in the OPEN process: additional tasks', Proceedings of COMPSAC'2001: International Computer Software and Applications Conference, Chicago, Illinois, USA, October 8-12, 2001.
7. Ward S. and Kroll P., 'Building Web Solutions with the Rational Unified Process: Unifying the Creative Design Process and the Software Engineering Process', Rational Software Corporation, 1999, http://www.rational.com/media/whitepapers/76.pdf
8. Henderson-Sellers B., 'The OPEN Website', OPEN Consortium, Feb 2004, http://www.open.org.au/
9. Kruchten P., 'The Rational Unified Process: An Introduction', Addison Wesley Longman, Inc., 2nd ed. March 2000, ISBN: 0-201-70710-1
10. McDonald A. and Welland R. 'Agile Web Engineering (AWE) Process', Department of Computing Science Technical Report TR-2001-98, University of Glasgow, Scotland, December 2001.

A Roadmap Towards Distributed Web Assessment

Arno Scharl

University of Western Australia, Business School
35 Stirling Highway, Crawley, WA 6009, Australia
arno.scharl@uwa.edu.au

Abstract. The webLyzard project generates empirical Web data by processing large samples of Web sites automatically. It mirrors more than 5,000 international Web sites in monthly intervals and has amassed Web data in excess of one terabyte since 1999. Structural and textual analyses convert the wealth of information contained in the sample into detailed site profiles and aggregated content representations. A distributed approach promises to increase both sample size and the frequency of data gathering. This paper presents a roadmap towards distributed Web assessment, extending and revising the current system architecture to enhance its scalability and flexibility for investigating the dynamics of electronic content.

1 Introduction and Methodology

Software agents extracting and processing Web sites automatically ensure scalability, speed, consistency, rigorous structure, and abundant longitudinal data. They alleviate methodological limitations of subjective impressions and anecdotal evidence [1-3]. Judged against human evaluation, automated approaches are more efficient at handling dynamic Web data, and immune to inter- and intra-personal variances. These advantages come at the expense of sacrificing recipient-dependent attributes, which are difficult to quantify. Domain knowledge and expert opinions, therefore, play an important role when interpreting and applying the results.

This paper presents a roadmap towards distributed Web monitoring in terms of analytical objectives, process and data structures, and interface representation. Higher demands on transparency, flexibility and portability require new structures for data representation and transformation based on XML schemas and XSLT stylesheets, respectively. These data structures will pave the way for advanced visualisations. Topographic information mapping and geo-referenced projections will encourage the interactive exploration of Web resources.

2 Methodology

The webLyzard project has built the foundation for regularly sampling thousands of Web sites [2, 3]. As the volume and constantly changing char- acter of Web data entails ongoing analysis, a crawling agent mirrors the Web sites in monthly intervals, aptures their characteristics and stores the resulting profiles in a relational database.

N. Koch, P. Fraternali, and M. Wirsing (Eds.): ICWE 2004, LNCS 3140, pp. 171–175, 2004.

The move from centralised to distributed data gathering will not only increase the frequency of data gathering (weekly or daily intervals, depending on the site's characteristics), but also put samples of 100,000 sites and more within reach by leveraging spare bandwidth and previously unused computing resources from geographically dispersed clients.

The methodology considers both visible (raw text including headings, menus, or link descriptions) and invisible text (embedded markup tags, scripting elements, and so forth). Ignoring graphics and multimedia files, the agent follows a site's hierarchical structure until reaching 10 megabytes for regular sites, or 50 megabytes for online media. The size restriction helps compare systems of heterogeneous size, and manage storage capacity. Documents found in lower hierarchical levels are not part of the main user interface and can be disregarded for most analytical objectives.

2.1 Sample specification includes adding new Web sites, updating external rankings, and regularly checking the validity of addresses. The current sample of more than 5,000 Web sites comprises the Fortune 1000 (www.fortune.com), international media sites, environmental non-profit and advocacy organisations, European tourism sites, and nominees of the 2003 Webby Awards.

2.2 Data extraction processes and automatically codes the mirrored data. Automated coding attenuates subjective interpretations and many of the questionable aspects of manual coding. It renders the problems of time-consuming and expensive coder training or intra- and intercoder reliability obsolete, as the process measures variables directly and does not involve individuals who could disagree on particular attribute values. The variables constituting the site profiles fall into one of four categories: *navigational mechanisms, interactive features, layout and multimedia characteristics,* and *linguistic descriptives.*

2.3 Data representation of the current system needs a fundamental revision in order to meet the requirements of distributed Web monitoring (see Section 2.8). Currently, the variables are stored in a relational database and exported as comma-separated text files for further processing by external applications. The revision aims at replacing the current structures with a modular and reusable repository of Web metrics based on XML technologies. The flexibility of data definitions via XML schemas will provide the foundation for the envisioned distributed architecture. XSLT stylesheets will transform structural site metrics into diverse output formats such as XML, X(HTML), .CSV, and .PDF. The portability of XML-encoded data will encourage collaborative development of analytical modules.

2.4 Structural analysis relies upon multivariate statistical techniques or supervised neural networks to determine success factors by correlating the site profiles (set of independent variables) with measures of online success such as network statistics, server log-files, and questionnaire data (dependent variables). Important aspects of the proposed research are evaluating the availability and suitability of external rankings, and utilising third-party data such as Google Page Ranks (www.google.com), Alexa traffic statistics (www.alexa.com), and organisational details from Internet registrars (www.internic.net). The increasing availability of Application Programming Interfaces (APIs) and specialised scripting languages such as the Compaq Web Language [4] and the HTML Extraction Language [5] should facilitate these tasks.

2.5 Textual analysis converts the raw data into adequate representations, assigns languages to each document, and eliminates ambiguities in order to provide linguistic site metrics and identify focal points of environmental Web coverage. Most methods for analysing textual Web data originate from corpus linguistics and textual statistics [6, 7]. The type token ratio, for example, indicates the richness of the vocabulary of a given text by dividing the number of distinct words (types) by the total number of words (tokens) encountered when processing the text file.

The study of multicultural Web samples requires explicit attention to the role of language. *Trigrams* (three letter sequences within a document) and *short words* (determiners, conjunctions or prepositions) are good clues for guessing a language. As the results of both methods are nearly identical for textual segments comprising more than ten words [8], the computationally less intensive short word technique has been chosen for the current prototype. The proposed research aims to evaluate algorithms for document classification and employ more advanced parsing of sentence structures to eliminate ambiguities concerning the syntactic function or semantic nature of words, and explore knowledge representations such as XML topic maps [9] to handle dynamic and often redundant content segments.

2.6 Topic detection and tracking identifies semantic clusters in continuous streams of raw data that correspond to previously unidentified events [10]. Web-based tracking of events and public opinion on environmental issues complements and enhances traditional questionnaire surveys. Presenting news items culled from approximately 4,500 sources worldwide, Google News (news.google.com) demonstrates that automatic content classification by computer algorithms without human intervention can produce viable results. Standardised document type definitions – e.g., the News Markup Language (www.newsml.org), which is used by major international content providers such as *Reuters* or *United Press International* – facilitate classifying and aggregating content from multiple sources.

2.7 Visualisations of environmental Web content incorporates knowledge from cartography and geo-informatics [11], allowing visual recognition of document similarity by spatial cues and increasing the accessibility of complex data sets. The project will evaluate visualisation techniques and automate the creation of perceptual maps, currently performed manually by post-processing the output of statistical standard software. Scalable Vector Graphics (SVG), a modularised language for describing two-dimensional vectorial graphics in XML syntax [12], will be used to generate on-the-fly representations of Web content including frequency, context, geographic distribution, and hierarchical position of characteristic terms.

2.8 Distributed Web monitoring applies emerging computing frameworks that have revolutionised the processing of complex information. As some simulations are beyond the reach of current supercomputers, *Seti@Home* (setiathome.berkeley.edu), *Climateprediction.net* or *LifeMapper.org* exploit spare computer cycles by breaking down the calculations into parallel units that are processed by networks of volunteers (Seti@home scans radio signals from space to search for extraterrestrial intelligence;

Climateprediction.net explores climate change caused by manmade atmospheric pollutants; Lifemapper maps ecological profiles based on records of the world's natural history museums). As participating in active research attracts a large number of users, these projects often scale to thousands or millions of nodes. With the support of nearly 4.8 million users, Seti@Home executes more than 60 trillion floating point operations per second (TeraFLOPS) as of January 2004. This surpasses the capacity of the world's fastest supercomputer – i.e., the *Earth Simulator,* a Japanese climate modelling project generating a maximum of 36 TeraFLOPS (www.es.jamstec.go.jp).

There are two main approaches to the distributed processing of information. *Peer-to-Peer (P2P) computing* has been popularised by file sharing and the highly parallel computing applications described above. *Grid computing*, by contrast, serves smaller communities and emphasises large-scale systems with fixed or slowly changing node populations in environments of at least limited trust [13, 14].

Migrating from centralised to distributed system architectures is complex and labour-intensive. Therefore, the project will utilise a standard service layer to collaborate with other projects, streamline system implementation, and manage computing resources more effectively. Examples of P2P service layers are the *Berkeley Open Infrastructure for Network Computing* (boinc.berkeley.edu), *XtremWeb* (www.lri.fr/~fedak/XtremWeb), and *JXTA* (www.jxta.org). The *Open Grid Services Architecture* (www.globus.org/ogsa) is based on Web service technologies to provide a more service-oriented platform, allowing computational services providers to register within known registries that can be browsed and searched by clients [15]. This achieves a cleaner middleware layer for individual applications based on industry standards such as the *Web Services Description Language* (WSDL) and the *Universal Description Discovery and Integration* (UDDI) protocol (www.w3.org/TR/wsdl; www.uddi.org).

While the project will benefit from the scalability and fault tolerance of P2P computing, its data-intensity suggests exploring light-weight Grid frameworks – as exemplified by the *Knowledge Grid* [16], a knowledge extraction service on top of the *Globus* (www.globus.org) grid architecture.

Distributed Web crawling permits gathering data in weekly or daily intervals, depending upon the media's dynamic characteristics. Leveraging spare bandwidth and previously unused computing resources from geographically dispersed clients, samples of 100,000 sites and more become feasible, limited only by the number of participating individuals and institutions. As this process consumes lots of bandwidth but demands less resources in terms of processing capacity, it complements computation-intensive projects such as Seti@home and Climateprediction.net.

3   Conclusion

The roadmap presented in this paper incorporates knowledge of multiple disciplines to better understand the determinants, structure and success factors of Web content. The project builds upon the technology of the webLyzard project, which analyses more than 5,000 international Web sites in monthly intervals. Distributed data gathering will allow running the crawling agent in weekly or daily intervals. Leveraging spare bandwidth and previously unused computing resources from geographically dispersed clients, samples of 100,000 sites and more will become feasible, limited only by the number of participating individuals and institutions.

The use of open standards for encoding both structural and textual site data will enable other disciplines and stakeholders to effectively leverage the gathered information, which will be available via the collaborative environment of the Web portal (www.ecomonitor.net). A combination of the content management platform's core components and customised modules will facilitate the exchange of information with the research community, international and regional media, and the general public. This ensures a broad and international base of active researchers who are likely to contribute computational resources to the data gathering process, access and use the provided Web services, and promote the project among their peers.

References

[1]   Ivory, M. Y.: Automated Web Site Evaluation: Researchers' and Practitioners' Perspectives. Kluwer Academic Publishers, Dordrecht (2003)

[2]   Bauer, C., Scharl, A.: Quantitative Evaluation of Web Site Content and Structure. Internet Research: Networking Applications and Policy 10 (2000) 31-43

[3]   Scharl, A.: Evolutionary Web Development. Springer, London (2000)

[4]   Compaq Web Language. http://www.research.compaq.com/SRC/WebL/.

[5]   Sahuguet, A., Azavant, F.: Building Intelligent Web Applications using Lightweight Wrappers. Data & Knowledge Engineering 36 (2001) 283-316

[6]   McEnery, T., Wilson, A.: Corpus Linguistics. Edinburgh University Press, Edinburgh (1996)

[7]   Biber, D., Conrad, S., Reppen, R.: Corpus Linguistics - Investigating Language Structure and Use. Cambridge University Press, Cambridge (1998)

[8]   Grefenstette, G.: Comparing Two Language Identification Schemes. In: Proc. 3rd International Conference on Statistical Analysis of Textual Data (JADT-95) (1995) 263-268

[9]   Le Grand, B.: Topic Map Visualization. In: J. Park and S. Hunting, (eds.): XML Topic Maps - Creating and Using Topic Maps for the Web. Addison-Wesley (2003) 267-282

[10] Chang, G., Healey, M. J., McHugh, J. A. M., Wang, J. T. L.: Mining the World Wide Web - An Information Search Approach. Kluwer Academic Publishers, Norwell (2001)

[11] Dodge, M., Kitchin, R.: New Cartographies to Chart Cyberspace. GeoInformatics 5 (2002) 38-41

[12] Quint, A.: Scalable Vector Graphics. IEEE Multimedia 10 (2003) 99-102

[13] Milenkovic, M., Robinson, S. H., Knauerhase, R. C., Barkai, D., Garg, S., Tewari, V., Anderson, T. A., Bowman, M.: Toward Internet Distributed Computing. Computer 36 (2003) 38-46

[14] Foster, I., Iamnitchi, A.: On Death, Taxes, and the Convergence of Peer-to-Peer and Grid Computing. In: F. Kaashoek and I. Stoica, (eds.): Peer-to-Peer Systems II: Second International Workshop, IPTPS 2003 Berkeley, CA, USA. Springer (2003) 118-128

[15] Giannadakis, N., Rowe, A., Ghanem, M., Guo, Y.-k.: InfoGrid: Providing Information Integration for Knowledge Discovery. Information Sciences 155 (2003) 199-226

[16] Cannataro, M., Talia, D.: The Knowledge Grid. Communications of the ACM 46 (2003) 89-93

Ontology for Software Metrics and Indicators: Building Process and Decisions Taken

Luis Olsina and María de los Angeles Martín

Department of Informatics, Engineering School at UNLPam, Argentina.
{olsinal,martinma}@ing.unlpam.edu.ar

Abstract. There are various useful ISO standards related to software quality models, measurement, and evaluation processes. However, we observe sometimes a lack of a sound consensus among the same terms in different documents or sometimes absent terms. In [7, 10], our ontology for software metrics and indicators was detailed. In this article, the process and decisions that have been taken during the construction of the ontology are highlighted.

1 Introduction

Software measurement and even more web measurement are currently in a stage in which terminology, principles, models, and methods are still being defined and consolidated. In order to promote a more mature discipline, it has becomes mandatory to start reaching a common agreement between researchers and other stakeholders about primitive terms such as attribute, metric, measure, measurement and calculation method, scale, elementary and global indicator, calculable concept, among others.

One key factor for the success of our proposed cataloging web system [9] was the conceptualisation of the software metrics and indicators domain formalized by an ontology. Then, our aim was to construct an explicit specification of the conceptualisation for this domain, where concepts, attributes, and their relationships were clearly represented. In this paper, the process and decisions that have been taken during the construction of the ontology are highlighted. We explain why the meaning from one proposal and not from the others was chosen, or why new terms were needed. For this end, the main steps for building the ontology using the *Methontology* strategy [1] is presented in Section 2. In Section 3, a discussion about decisions taken in choosing the terms is presented. Finally, concluding remarks are drawn.

2 Methodology for Building the Ontology

A considerable number of methodologies to build ontologies have been published so far in which different design principles and stages for ontology development were reported. One of the well-known methods is the *Methontology* strategy [1]. It proposes an effective, generally applicable method for domain knowledge model construction and validation as well. At least, it distinguishes the following steps: *Specification, Conceptualisation, Implementation,* and *Evaluation.*

N. Koch, P. Fraternali, and M. Wirsing (Eds.): ICWE 2004, LNCS 3140, pp. 176–181, 2004.

Specification Step. In a general sense, a sound metrics and indicators specification, flexible documentation, consultation, and retrieval mechanisms are needed in order to contribute to the comprehension and selection process whether metrics and indicators can be useful, easy to collect, and understand. For this end, we argued that a well-designed repository of metrics and indicators and a semantic web-based cataloging system [9] can be effectively used to support quality assurance processes such as nonfunctional requirement definition and specification, metrics and indicators understanding and selection, amongst others. Therefore having an explicit ontology was a key requirement for our cataloging system.

On the other hand, the sources of knowledge for the proposed metrics and indicators ontology came from our own experience backed up by previous works in metrics and evaluation processes and methods, from different software-related ISO standards, and also from recognized research articles. Taking into account some of his own previous works, Olsina [8] authored the _Web Quality Evaluation Method_ (WebQEM), which is grounded on the design, selection and implementation of metrics, elementary and global indicators and their associated decision criteria, starting from a calculable concept (e.g. quality), and its model. A further research was aimed to specify web metrics, and to develop a conceptual model just for metrics and its cataloging system [9]. Mainly, our ontology has also been inspired in sources as ISO standards and other recognized research articles and books. To quote just a few: The terminology provided in the ISO 15939 standard [5], as well as in the ISO 9126-1 [4], and in the ISO/IEC 14598-1 standards [3].

Conceptualisation Step. Conceptualisation helps to organize and structure the acquired knowledge using external representation languages (such as UML diagrams, tables, classification trees, etc.) that are independent of implementation languages and environments. As results of this step, the metrics and indicators knowledge using a UML conceptual model was yielded, where the main domain concepts, attributes, and relationships were represented (see details in [7, 10]). In table 1 the glossary of terms for the metrics and indicators ontology is explicitaly described.

Implementation Step. To implement the ontology in a formal language, we mainly used RDF/S, since it is the associated language for ontology implementation with semantic web capability. Implementing the metrics and indicators ontology with semantic web technologies provides more interoperability, automateability, and scalability to our cataloging web system, as discussed elsewhere [9, 10].

3   Discussion About Decisions Taken in Choosing Some Terms

It is worthy of mention that there are various useful recently issued ISO standards related to software quality models [4], measurement [5], and evaluation processes [3]. The primary aim of these standards was to reach a consensus about the issued models or processes together with a consensus about the used terms; however, they do not constitute themselves a formal or a semiformal ontology.

The ontology for software metrics and indicators we are discussing was based as much as possible on the defined terms of the ISO standards. Specifically, eight terms and their exact meaning out of twenty seven terms of our proposal were fairly used, namely: the attribute [3], decision criteria [5], entity [5], information need [5], measurable concept [5] (we used the "calculable" word instead of "measurable" as we discuss later on), measure [3], scale [3], and unit [5] terms. In addition, we employed almost the same meaning to the metric term as in [3], i.e., "the defined measurement *and calculation* method and the measurement scale". We argue that a direct metric uses just a measurement method meanwhile an indirect metric can use both measurement and calculation methods –an indirect metric is represented by a function or formula that specifies how to combine metrics.

Considering these ISO standards, we have very often observed a lack of sound consensus among the same terms in different documents or sometimes absent terms. For instance, the "metric" term is just used in [3, 4] but not in [5]. Even more, [3, 4] use the terms "direct measure" and "indirect measure" (instead of direct or indirect metric), meanwhile [5] uses "base measure" and "derived measure". In some cases we could state that they are synonymous terms, but in other such as metric, which is defined in [3] as "the defined measurement method and the measurement scale", there is no term with exact matching meaning in [5]. Furthermore, we argue that the measure term is not synonymous with the metric term. The measure term defined in [3] (the meaning we adopted) as "the number or category assigned to an attribute of an entity by making a measurement" or in [5] as "variable to which a value is assigned as the result of measurement" reflects the fact of the measure as the resulting value or output for the measurement activity (or process). Thus, we claim the metric concept represents the specific and explicit definition of the measurement activity.

Besides, we observe some absent terms in these standards such as "elementary indicator" and "global indicator" (even though in [5] the "indicator" term is defined with similar but not equal meaning as in our proposal), as well as the "calculation" and "calculation method" terms that are totally absent. For us, the intended objective for using a measurement method is slightly different for that of using a calculation method. The former is just intended for a measurement activity; the latter, just for a calculation activity.

Focusing us again on the metric term, the metric **m** represents the mapping **m:A ->X**, where **A** is an empirical attribute of one or more entities (the empirical world), **X** the variable to which categorical or numerical values can be assigned (the formal world), and the arrow denotes a mapping. In order to perform this mapping a sound and precise measurement (activity) definition is needed by specifying explicitly the method and scale.

On the other hand, a semantic distinction between metric and indicator concepts should be raised. The indicator represents a new mapping coming from the interpretation of the metric's value (formal world) into the new variable to which categorical or numerical values can be assigned (the new formal world). In order to do this mapping a model and decision criteria for a specific user information need is considered. It is interesting to observe the definition of the "rating" term in [3] that says "the action of mapping the measured value to the appropriate rating level" in addition to the "indicator" term in the same document that says "a measure that can be used to estimate or predict another measure". However our meaning for the indicator term (see table 1) is broader in the sense of an explicit definition of the calculation activity needed to produce an indicator value.

Table 1. Software metrics and indicators ontology: Glossary of Concepts.

Concept Name	Description
Attribute	A measurable physical or abstract property of an entity [3].
Calculable Concept	Abstract relationship between attributes of entities and information needs [5].
Calculation	Activity that uses an indicator definition in order to produce an indicator's value.
Calculation Method	The particular logical sequence of operations specified for allowing the realisation of a formula or indicator description by a calculation.
Categorical Scale	A scale where the measured or calculated values are categories, and cannot be expressed in units, in a strict sense.
Concept Model	The set of sub-concepts and the relationships between them, which provide the basis for specifying the concept requirement and its further evaluation or estimation.
Decision Criteria	Thresholds, targets, or patterns used to determine the need for action or further investigation, or to describe the level of confidence in a given result [5].
Direct Metric	A metric of an attribute that does not depend upon a metric of any other attribute.
Elementary Indicator	An indicator that does not depend upon other indicators to evaluate or estimate a calculable concept.
Elementary Model	Algorithm or function with associated decision criteria that model an elementary indicator.
Entity	Object that is to be characterised by measuring its attributes [5].
Function	Algorithm or formula performed to combine two or more metrics.
Global Indicator	An indicator that is derived from other indicators to evaluate or estimate a calculable concept.
Global Model	Algorithm or function with associated decision criteria that model a global indicator.
Indicator	The defined calculation method and scale in addition to the model and decision criteria in order to provide an estimate or evaluation of a calculable concept with respect to defined information needs.
Indicator Value	The number or category assigned to a calculable concept by making a calculation.
Indirect Metric	A metric of an attribute that is derived from metrics of one or more other attributes.
Information Need	Insight necessary to manage objectives, goals, risks, and problems [5].
Measure	The number or category assigned to an attribute of an entity by making a measurement [3].
Measurement	Activity that uses a metric definition in order to produce a measure's value.
Measurement Method	The particular logical sequence of operations and possible heuristics specified for allowing the realisation of a metric description by a measurement.
Method	Logical sequence of operations and possible heuristics, specified generically, for allowing the realisation of an activity description.
Metric	The defined measurement or calculation method and the measurement scale.
Numerical Scale	A scale where the measured or calculated values are numbers that can be expressed in units, in a strict sense.
Scale	A set of values with defined properties [3].
Software Tool	It is a tool that automates partially or totally a measurement or calculation method.
Unit	Particular quantity defined and adopted by convention, with which other quantities of the same kind are compared in order to express their magnitude relative to that quantity [5].

In addition, we would like to remark the introduction of the terms categorical and numerical scale to our ontology (that are not explicitly specified in the ISO standard). This distinction is important to understand the unit concept associated to scales (see definitions in table 1). Particularly, a categorical scale is a scale where the measured or calculated values are categories, and cannot be expressed in units, in a strict sense. Instead, in a numerical scale the values are numbers that must be expressed in units.

Lastly, at the moment of publishing our ontology the closest related work was the recent proposal of the software measurement ontology documented by Genero *et al.* [2], which was inspired mainly in the terms of the ISO 15939 standard. This work had been a consultation source for our proposal, nevertheless, we have aimed mainly to the metrics and indicators ontology rather than to the measurement process ontology. Our ontology could serve as a subontology for that. In the same direction, with the aim to reach a consensus in a measurement ontology, we were maintaining discussions with different Ibero-American research groups, where a final technical report containing the glossary of terms will be published in 2004 (we held three physical meetings in 2003). As results of the joint discussions we have not yet reach a total agreement in all the terms so far. The main discrepancies are in the metric and indicator terms. Some participants claim that the definition of the metric term is as follows: "a defined measurement form -i.e., a measurement method, or a function, or an analysis model-, and a scale in order to perform measurements of one or more attributes". Moreover, an indicator is a kind of metric (an inheritance relationship). For instance, under this consideration (likewise in [2]), the double mapping for an indicator is not clearly represented. Despite these enriching discrepancies a final joint report will be issued, which could be referenced as another source of knowledge.

4 Concluding Remarks

As Kitchenham *et al.* say [6], without sound and agreed definitions it is difficult to assure metadata consistency and, ultimately, data values are comparable on the same basis. We hope our proposal will have a good diffusion within the software and web communities, and also can serve as a trigger for new enriching discussions as well. The stability and maturity of an ontology can also be judged by the level of agreement reached in a domain-specific international community. This involves the evolveability and perfectibility features of any consensuated knowledge building process.

References

1. Fernández López, M., Gómez-Pérez, A. and Juristo, N., "METHONTOLOGY: From Ontological Art Towards Ontological Engineering", *Proceed. of the AAAI Symposium*, California, US, 1997, pp. 33-40.
2. Genero, M.; Ruiz, F.; Piattini, M.; García, F.; and Calero, C.; "An Ontology for Software Measurement", *In proceed. of SEKE'03, 15th Int'l Conference on Software Engineering and Knowledge Engineering*, San Francisco, US, 2003, pp 78-84.
3. ISO/IEC 14598-1:1999 "International Standard, Information technology - Software product evaluation - Part 1: General Overview".
4. ISO/IEC 9126-1: 2001 "Int'l Standard, Software Engineering - Product Quality - Part 1: Quality Model".
5. ISO/IEC 15939: 2002 "Software Engineering - Software Measurement Process".
6. Kitchenham B.A., Hughes R.T., Linkman S.G., "Modeling Software Measurement Data", *IEEE Transactions on Software Engineering*, 27(9), 2001, pp. 788-804.

7. Martín, M.; Olsina, L., "Towards an Ontology for Software Metrics and Indicators as the Foundation for a Cataloging Web System", *In proceed. of IEEE Computer Society (1st Latin American Web Congress),* Santiago de Chile, 2003, pp 103-113, ISBN 0-7695-2058-8.
8. Olsina L., Rossi G., "Measuring Web Application Quality with WebQEM", *IEEE Multimedia,* 9(4), 2002, pp. 20-29.
9. Olsina, L.; Martin, M. A.; Fons, J.; Abrahao, S.; Pastor, O., "Towards the Design of a Metrics Cataloging System by Exploiting Conceptual and Semantic Web Approaches", *In LNCS of Springer, Int'l Conference on Web Engineering (ICWE'03)*, Oviedo, Spain, LNCS 2722, 2003, pp. 324-333.
10. Olsina, L.; Martín, M.; Ontology for Software Metrics and Indicators, To appear in the *Journal of Web Engineering*, Rinton Press, NJ, US, 2004.

Measuring Semantic Relations of Web Sites by Clustering of Local Context

Carsten Stolz[1], Vassil Gedov[2], Kai Yu[3], Ralph Neuneier[3], and Michal Skubacz[3]

[1] University of Eichstätt-Ingolstadt, Germany, `carsten.stolz@ku-eichstaett.de`
[2] University of Würzburg, Germany, `gedov@informatik.uni-wuerzburg.de`
[3] Siemens AG, Corporate Technology, Germany,
{`kai.yu, ralph.neuneier, michal.skubacz`}`@siemens.com`

Abstract. Our contribution in this paper is an approach to measure semantical relations within a web site. We start with a web page description by key words. The implementation of structural and content information reduces the variety of key words. Thereby, the document-key-word-matrix is smoothend and similarities between web pages are emphasized. This increases the possibility of cluster key words and identif topics successfully. To do so, we implement a probabilistic clustering algorithm. To assess semantic relations, we introduce a number of measures and interpret them.

1 Introduction

Facing a huge, complex corporate web site, it is difficult to keep track of daily changing web pages and their relationship to the rest of the web site. Therefore, it is helpful to provide an insight into the content structure of a web site. With this semantic information it would be possible to improve the web site design and its usability.

In order to create a semantical overview of a web site, the first step should be the analysis of the web content. In a second step we should analyze the structure of the web site. Based on the assumption that the link structure provides useful semantic clues [2], it is important to integrate these implicit information. Additional insight into the semantical structure can be provided if each page is integrated into its context [3]: If a page is not regarded as a solitaire, the information of its neighborhood is relevant for its understanding.

In contrast to this approach, **related work**, done in this area of research[2] uses a pre-defined set of topics. Chakrabati et al. [2] argues that predefined topic taxonomies circumvent key word ambiguity. For their purpose, it is reasonable since they do not focus on huge corporate web sites. In contrast we do and aim to create a generic solution. Like them, we do not rely on well-kept meta information. Including an identification of hubs and authorities [1] has to be analyzed whether it can improve our results. Reasonable results of document clustering incorporating hyperlink structures can be found in He et al. [4]. The usage of the folder structure like Sun et al. describe in [5] is not possible for our target sites. Modern content management systems prevent from the use of the folder structure by cryptic URLs.

N. Koch, P. Fraternali, and M. Wirsing (Eds.): ICWE 2004, LNCS 3140, pp. 182–186, 2004.

2   Algorithm

The **structure** of a web site is determined by the link structure between its web pages. A link in this context is considered to be a link encoded as a HTML tag. We do not consider the anchor text of a link as structural information since we believe it belongs to the content information. Excluding self-references, we focus on hard coded inter-page links represented by a directed cyclic graph. In order to create single page descriptions, a crawler extracts key words and follows all web-site-internal links in a breadth-first mode. The words are stemmed in order to reduce key word diversity by applying the Porter Stemming Algorithm. We assume that the most frequent words define the content of the web page. The highest ranked words are said to be key words, where their number is proportional to the text length. Very frequent key words like the company's name, occurring virtually on all pages, are pruned. In [3] we empirically determined the usable HTML tags, which we believe to reflect author's focus.

2.1   Local Context Page Description

In order to include the link structure, we combine a page's set of key words with the key words of its direct neighborhood like [1]. The latter is defined as the pages, having a direct link to (inedges) or from (outedges) the page in focus. We call it the **local context (LC)** of a page. We perform the combination of structure and content by generating a new set of key words. We add the key words from the LC to the processed page and accumulate the frequencies over the entire key word set including the anchor tags as key words, ordered by frequency. The number of words is kept proportional to the text length. We perform this process bottom-up with respect to the minimal click path. We interpret the results of our algorithm as an intersection between the contents of the LC and the particular page. Moreover, we assume that salient words ascend towards the root page.

2.2   A Topic Discovery Algorithm

By clustering key words we are trying to identify topics. In other words, we consider word classes (topics) $\{z_j\}_{j=1}^{L}$, and model the likelihood of a document d (web pages) as follows,

$$p(\mathbf{w}_d) = \prod_w \left(\sum_z p(w|z, \beta) p(z|\theta_d) \right)^{n_{d,w}} \qquad (1)$$

where β are parameters specifying the probability of words given topics, θ_d are document-specific parameters that indicate the topics mixture for document d, $\mathbf{w}_d$ is the word list of this document and $n_{d,w}$ is the number of occurrences of word w in $\mathbf{w}_d$. Then given a corpus of documents $d = 1, \ldots, n$, we have the following EM algorithm to estimate the parameters:

- E-step: for each document d, we estimate the posterior distribution of topics given each word w in it:

$$p(z|w,d) = \frac{p(w|z,\beta)p(z|\theta_d)}{\sum_z p(w|z,\beta)p(z|\theta_d)} \qquad (2)$$

- M-step: we maximize the log-likelihood of "complete data" for the whole corpus:

$$\sum_d \sum_{\mathbf{Z}} \left(\prod_w p(z|w,d) \log \prod_w \left(p(w|z,\beta)p(z|\theta_d) \right)^{n_{d,w}} \right) \qquad (3)$$

with respect to parameters β and $\{\theta_d\}_{d=1}^N$, which gives rise to

$$\beta_{i,j} = p(w_i|z_j) \propto \sum_d n_{d,w_i} p(z_j|w_i,d) \qquad (4)$$

$$\theta_{j,d} = p(z_j|d) \propto \sum_w n_{d,w} p(z_j|w,d) \qquad (5)$$

We perform the E-step and M-step iteratively and at the convergence obtain the final estimate of $p(w|z)$ and $p(z|d)$. $p(w|z)$ indicates the probability of occurrence of word w given topic z. The algorithm groups semantically related words into topics. Intuitively, if several words often occur together (in the same documents), then these words are likely to be associated with one topic. $p(z|d)$ indicates the probability of topic z for document d. The parameters transform documents, which are originally distributed in high-dimensional but low-level word space, into low-dimensional and high-level topic space.

3   Evaluation and Case Study

We describe measures to evaluate the improvements by the LC. Therefore, we evaluate each measurement for both key word descriptions: stand alone and the LC. We performed our clustering algorithm on our data with 100 topics (word clusters). Where the number was determined by applying SVD on our data. First, we provide some **basic definitions**: The relevant topics for a specific document are the topics with the highest probability $topn(p(z_j|d)$, given document d_i, called *topic mixture* for d. The number of documents in LC with respect to a particular document is $|LC(d_i)|$. We are also interested in the number of distinct topics which are most relevant for each document in the LC. The number may vary from 1 to $|LC(d_i)|$, respectively.

3.1   Evaluation of Topic Clustering

For our analysis we have used Siemens' corporate web site: *www.siemens.com*. We crawled 1569 web pages, extracted key word sets (stand alone description)and derived key word set involving the LC. Regarding a particular document, we are now able to determine which topic is the most relvant one. Having this topic, we then select the documents which are most similar with respect to it. We observed in table 1, that the number of shared relevant topics has increased by using the LC: instead of one, now 3 of 4 topics are shared. **Topic mixture key words**: For a given document d_i, we determine the topic mixture. Each document d_i is represented by a topic vector $v_{d_i} = p(z|d_i) = \{z_1...z_n\}$. For all elements in the vector $(z_j \in v_d)$ we select the topic key words. They are weighted with their corresponding probabilities for that topic. Finally, the probabilities of all topic key words are proportionaly accumulated which form the topic mixture key words: $\sum_z p(w|z)p(z|d_i)$. This mixture is supposed to describe the document which contains one to several topics with different importance. We are now interested in the most important key words for this mixture. A word is said to be a key word for the topic mixture, if it has a high accumulated value.

Table 1. Topic document rate in the LC for our sample.

	stand alone	LC
Number of documents of the LC	21	21
Number of distinct topics of the LC	20	4
Number of occurrences of topic 3 in the LC	-	11 of 21
Topic document rate	0,048	0,809

Topic document rate in LC: In order to evaluate the impact of the LC based key word sets, we compare the number of distinct topics for the pages in the specific LC. As we discussed above, the number of topics in a LC may vary from 1 to the number of documents in the local context. So, the topic document rate is defined as $1 - \frac{\#\text{topics} \in LC(d_i)}{|LC(d_i)|}$. Consequently, the more topics are found the less is the rate. Note, that in both cases the pages within the LC are the same, but in the stand alone description the LC based algorithm from [3] is not applied. In table 1 we see that there are almost as many distinct topics as documents in the LC of our sample page. Furthermore, the most relevant topic of our test page does not occur at all. The number of distinct topics in the LC based description (table 1) has decreased significantly, and thus the topic document rate for the LC based description is very high. In addition, the most relevant topic for the sample page (topic ID 3) occurrs eleven times as most relevant topic for pages in the LC. Obviously, our LC based approach reduces key word diversity between linked documents.

3.2   Case Study for LC-Interpretation

By applying our measures on the data we have shown that the LC based description improves the result of our clustering algorithm. Now we want to exploit the additional information revealed by the local context. The LC of a selected page consists of 21 pages. We compare the most relevant topics for each page of the LC - one topic per page. The table shows that from these 21 topics topic no. 3 is the most relevant topic. It occurred 11 times representing more than half of the pages. Regarding the variety of topics, one sees that the most relevant topics for 21 pages consist of 4 different topics. This observation is supported by analysis of the LC key words. Out of 215 key words one finds 65 distinct key words. Concluding these observations, one can characterize this LC as *homogeneous*. A manual inspection of the LC pages affirms this conclusion.

4   Conclusion

This paper describes and evaluates the concept of the local context (LC). First, we use the LC successfully to smoothen the stand alone key words what we have shown empirically. Furthermore, we have shown that by using the LC the web site structure gets incorporated into the key word description of a page. Consequently, the clustering algorithm benefits from these information which identifies topics successfully. In the case study, we have described one application of the results: We are able to characterize a web page and its surrounding pages in terms of their content homogenity. This is only a part of the potential applications. Consequently, we will compare structure and content of a web site intensively and combine them with an user behaviour analysis.

Since this approach does not rely on predefined topics, it can be used generically. Additionally, we attempt to give more emphasis to the web site structure by using an adjacency matrix in the cluster algorithm.

References

1. K. Bharat and M. Henzinger; Improved algorithms for topic distillation in a hyperlinked environment Proc. of SIGIR-98, p. 104–111, ACM Press, 1998
2. S. Chakrabarti; Mining the Web - Discovering Knowledge from Hypertext Data. Morgan Kaufmann, 2002
3. V. Gedov, C. Stolz, R. Neuneier, M. Skubacz, D. Seipel, Matching Web Site Structure and Content, WWW04, New York (2004)
4. X. He, H. Zha, C. Ding, and H. Simon Web document clustering using hyperlink structures Computational Statistics and Data Analysis, 41:19-45, 2002
5. A.Sun and E.-P. Lim. Web unit mining, In Proc. Int. Conf. on Information and Knowledge Manag. p. 108–115. ACM Press, 2003.
6. W. Wong and A. Fu, Incremental Document Clustering for Web Page Classification, IEEE 2000 Int. Conf. on Info. Society (IS2000)

Interplay of Content and Context

Rudi Belotti, Corsin Decurtins, Michael Grossniklaus,
Moira C. Norrie, and Alexios Palinginis

Institute for Information Systems, ETH Zurich
8092 Zurich, Switzerland
{belotti,decurtins,grossniklaus,norrie,palinginis}@inf.ethz.ch

Abstract. We examine general and abstract approaches to web engineering and context-awareness and how they interact with each other. This involves considering the appropriateness of approaches to context when used by a complex application such as a content management system, while, at the same time, presenting how a content management system can use context information to enrich its functionality. We show that the integration of such systems is feasible only if, in both fields, we make use of approaches based on strong information models. Last but not least, we show that the relationship between context engines and content management systems is not at all a one-sided client-server scenario, but rather a mutually important symbiosis.

1 Introduction

As the amount of available digital data continues to grow, vast quantities of information surround us in our everyday life. With the abundance of information that is accessible to us, the problem no longer is whether information is within reach, but rather whether the right information can be delivered in the right form to the right person at the right time. Hence, the value of information is no longer solely dependent on the quality of the information itself, but is influenced by other factors as well. Emerging from classical information systems, content management systems have been developed to attain the goal of adequate information delivery. These systems extend the traditional functionalities of organising and accessing data with means to publish, present and deliver content. Even though content management systems were originally developed for the administration of large websites, they have proven to be so successful that a wide range of other applications use content delivery technologies nowadays.

At the same time, a shift in applications to mobile and ubiquitous information environments is clearly noticeable. Applications within this domain require highly situation-aware computing and it no longer suffices to simply present the information to the user in the right form. Depending on the user's situation, the information must be filtered according to what is important for the user. Information is no longer static, but highly dynamic as the situation of the user is altering continually according to an ever-changing environment. Context and context-aware computing have been recognised as key concepts in reaching this

N. Koch, P. Fraternali, and M. Wirsing (Eds.): ICWE 2004, LNCS 3140, pp. 187–200, 2004.

goal and a lot of research has been invested in this topic. Today, application-specific solutions and context frameworks exist, but a generic context engine with a semantic model for context is still lacking.

We have developed such a context engine for the management of context information that can be coupled with existing applications to augment them with the notion of context. We have also developed a content management system that supports the delivery of context-dependent content, but does not specify its own model for context. In this paper, we present the integration and interplay of these two aspects and components and how they complement each other. As we will see, the interplay between content and context is not a client-server relationship, but rather a symbiosis where both counterparts profit from each other.

Sect. 2 presents an overview of related work that has been done in the field of context-aware computing in general and specifically in the area of content management systems. In Sect. 3 we then describe our context engine. Our content management system that is used to demonstrate the interplay of content and context is outlined at the beginning of Sect. 4 followed with a discussion of how context influences the content management system. The opposite direction—how the content management system influences the context engine—is presented in Sect. 5. Finally, future directions and conclusions are given in Sect. 6.

2   Related Work

From the very beginning of the batch processing era, programs have been designed to produce and present an appropriate output to some given input. Although nowadays the input could be issued interactively and an application may even accept input from arbitrary sources, the principle of the black-box still holds. The output is completely determined by the given input. In contrast, context-aware applications also use implicit information hidden in the application's and user's environment [1], in addition to explicit input, to determine the output.

The influence of user behaviour and, in general, the situation of the environment where an interaction is taking place has been identified as context and studied by different communities including philosophy, linguistics and social sciences. Later people in the field of computer science borrowed the term and applied it in various applications [2,3,4]. With the rise of ubiquitous and pervasive computing, context has strongly been associated with information extracted from the physical environment. Spatial information such as location, orientation and speed or environmental information such as temperature, light and noise level are commonly sensed context properties for this application domain.

Context-aware applications have been designed and implemented such as office and meeting tools [5], tourist guides [6,7] and specific fieldwork enhancements [8]. All those examples propose context models specifically tailored to each application domain and directly implemented in the application logic. Many common concepts and components had to be implemented in isolation for each application. At the same time, some researchers wanted to provide a reusable and helpful infrastructure and proposed general context frameworks [9,10].

Based on such a framework, a context-engine can be created to acquire, manage and offer context-relevant information. Applications can then use the engine to gather context information which enriches their behaviour. Furthermore, the proposals offer an infrastructural solution to the architecture, based on either a transparent host/port distributed communication [9] or CORBA [10]. Further, [9] separates the actual sensor from the abstract context which allows the decoupling of context acquisition and the application using the context.

Although the functionality and infrastructure offered by such context frameworks simplifies the implementation of context-aware applications, they still lack a clear information and conceptual model that describes the context engine. Such a metamodel can be used as a reference model for context-engines, increasing the understanding of different approaches and enabling a comparison based on the concepts introduced in the metamodel. Context information exchange is also facilitated by using appropriate mappings to transform context-engine specific data to the metamodel. In [11], we present a general information model for context and, in the next section, we describe a context engine based on that model.

A general purpose context-engine can be used by any type of application. Nowadays, web-based applications represent a major and common class of applications as web technologies and infrastructure have become defacto standards for many application environments. In the field of web engineering, the first steps towards context-awareness were made by introducing adaptation concepts directly into hypertext models [12,13]. Such Adaptive Hypermedia Systems (AHS) are based on various user characteristics presented in a user model. Most of the early examples focus on information collected from the user's click stream. In [14], user data, usage data and environment data is distinguished. An extensive discussion on the field of AHS and related work can be found in [15]. We should mention here that user characteristics such as presented in AHS are not always necessarily describing context, but rather the user profile in general. For example, user preferences such as colours, styles and interests might be part of the current context, i.e. they contribute to the dynamic characterisation of an interaction situation, but this does not have to be the case.

AHS employs a user model to capture the adaptive relevant properties. After each interaction, the user model is updated and, based on adaptation rules, appropriate output is generated. Adaptation is applied to the basic concepts of hypermedia models, namely, component and link. Rules are defined to control the composition of components (fragments) or even alter link presentation.

Due to the fact that components encapsulate both notions of content and presentation in an indistinguishable manner, it is not possible to adapt only one of them in isolation. This is unfortunate if one considers that a major adaptation requirement of web applications is context-dependent presentations. When evaluating AHS, we are confronted with the situation found in other application-specific approaches. The user model is inspired and specified with the browser/server environment in mind. Thus, no general approach to context is taken with important properties such as context history, sensor generality, quality etc.

To provide a better solution, model-based approaches to web site development have recently been studied with respect to adaptation [16] and context-awareness [17,18,19]. Based on strong and abstract information models, these approaches have the potential to exploit context-awareness in many dimensions, keeping the solutions as simple as possible. In [16], delivery channel characteristics can be used to influence the hypertext and navigational model of the original WebML model [20]. In this approach, no explicit context model is used. Instead, general data modelling techniques are made available to manage context information. Although the presentation cannot be adapted explicitly, it can be influenced by adapting similar content units bound to different presentation templates.

In OMSwe [17], the database management system OMS Pro [21] is extended with versioning and basic content and presentation management facilities to empower a web development environment. All relevant information, from the development process to implementation and application data, is managed by the database system. Context information is provided in the form of characteristic/value pairs from a context gateway component. This information builds the request state, based on which, the database will retrieve the most appropriate versions of the objects involved in the response. eXtensible Content Management (XCM) [22] takes the approach one step further and defines a full-strength content management system with well defined general information concepts. Based on this approach, we present here the interplay between this system and the general context engine that we developed. Details of XCM are given in Sect. 4.

3   Context Engine

In [11], we consolidated research in the field of context and context-awareness and presented a model for a generic context engine. The basic and abstract concept of context is influenced both by the application and framework requirements, as well as the problems presented by Dourish in [23]. In this section, we use an example to describe how our context engine works and how application-specific models can be specified.

Each entity of an application can potentially have a context. An application schema, for instance, could define the concept of a room. The context of a room could be described by its physical properties such as the temperature and the light intensity. For each point in time, the room's context is composed of the set of values over its context properties: e.g. `temperature=30` and `light=40`.

Obviously, the values 30 and 40 do not provide any information about the scales that are used. Moreover, a context engine supplies context information to many different applications, thus making a quantification even more important. We therefore use a type system to define concepts within the context engine.

The system distinguishes four kind of types. *Base types* define common values such as `string`, `integer`, `boolean` etc. The model allows base type restrictions as used in XML Schema. Hence, we can create base type restrictions with new names that represent values with specific semantics. In the example below, we define a base type `celsius` as a restriction of `real`. Restrictions of a type are expressed through a constraint that checks the validity of the values acceptable for the defined type.

```
btype celsius is real {
        constr: 'self(S), S > -273.16';
};
```

Our prototype system is implemented in Prolog and the context definition language (CDL) used here has been developed to define concepts and their types for an application-specific context schema. Operational components of CDL are defined in Prolog. For the above example, the constraint is a predicate that evaluates to *true* if the given value is legal. To check if a value is appropriate as a `celsius` temperature, the value is first retrieved using the predicate `self/1` and then checked to be greater than -273.16.

Apart from the base types, the context model uses references to application-specific types to define and control application entities. Apart from a uniquely identifiable *application type*, the context engine does not deal with, and has no control over, the values composing an application entity. Thus an application reference type is sufficiently defined by the pattern `applicationID:typeID`. The third class of types are the *bulk types* which designate sets of values of a given member type. Finally, the model supports context types which define the composition of the context itself rather than its values. As a common composite type, *context types* are defined over a set of attributes of a given type. In the following example, we define a context type `ctx_temperature` with one attribute `temperature` of type `celsius`.

```
contextType ctx_temperature characterises app:physical_obj {
        temperature: celsius;
};
```

Optionally, the context type designates the type of entity to which it can be bound. In the above example, the defined context poses the constraint to characterise application entities of the type `physical_obj` defined in application `app`. Application types could be defined in an is-a hierarchy, designating a compatibility among them (not shown in this example).

After declaring the types, an application can create context elements and bind them to some application entity. In the following example we create the temperature context for `app:roomA32`, which is an instance of `app:room`, subtype of `app:physical_obj`.

```
context c_roomA32_temp: ctx_temperature describes app:roomA32
```

Context elements are either queried directly from client applications or received through an event notification mechanism. Such clients play the role of consumer with respect to the context engine. On the other hand, a sensor abstraction exists that encapsulates the context acquisition mechanism. Sensors are well defined components that are initialised with some parameters and bound to context elements. Sensors could either be hardware or software in nature. A hardware sensor could be a thermometer and a software sensor could be a program that extracts the current application status with respect to an interaction.

To allow reusability and separation of concerns, we introduced the concept of a *sensor driver*. It holds the acquisition logic of the sensor. Multiple sensors can be instantiated based on a single sensor driver. The next example defines a temperature sensor that is connected to the serial port of a computer and provides temperature context information based on the `ctx_temperature` context type. The last statement initialises the actual thermometer based on the given sensor driver, providing context information to the `c_roomA32_temp` context.

```
sensorDriver tempSensor(serial_port: integer): ctx_temperature;
sensor s_thermo1: tempSensor(1) provides c_roomA32_temp;
```

In addition to the sensor driver definition, an implementation is necessary. For our prototype, it is coded in SICStus Prolog [24] and bindings to Java are used in cases where the actual sensor offers a Java API. Examples of such sensors are software sensors that use information collected from the content management system. More details on such sensors will be given in Sect. 4. For a context-aware news application, we have developed a prototype sensor driver for the recognition of people in a room. It is based on the ARToolKit [25] augmented reality library and recognises people through special tags that are recognised by the ARToolKit in a stream from a small video camera.

Having presented our context engine, we now go on to explain in the next section how it can be used to make an existing application context-aware.

4   From Context to Content

To demonstrate the interworking of the previously described context engine with an application system, we show in this section how it can be integrated with a content management system. Further, we outline how information flows from the context engine to the content management system and vice versa. As a content management system, we have chosen our own eXtensible Content Management (XCM) [22,18]. The current version of XCM is implemented in Java and based on OMS Java [26], an object-oriented database management system based on the Object Model (OM) [27], a model that integrates object-oriented and entity-relationship concepts. The original version of XCM supports only a rather simple implementation for context. We are currently working on the extension of XCM for support of the context engine that we have described in the previous section.

XCM has been designed as a platform that provides support to applications requiring features typical of content management such as user management, workflows, personalisation, multi-channel delivery and multi-variant objects. At the heart of the system stands the separation of content, structure, view and layout. The concept of *content* allows data to be accumulated into content objects and stores metadata about this content. As it is often required that the same content object may be delivered in different variations, the system supports what we call "multi-variant objects". For example, a news article may have multiple variants that correspond to the different languages in which it is available. Multi-variant objects however can comprise much more than the simple dimension of language. Other dimensions are often required, such as the target group of users or whether it is free or premium content for which users have to pay. Our system does not predefine the possible dimensions, but rather provides support to handle any annotation of content variants that makes sense in a given application domain. To achieve this, the concept of a content object is separated from its actual representation while still allowing for strict typing. In Fig. 1, a metamodel is displayed that shows how XCM represents multi-variant objects. The notation and semantics is that of the previously mentioned Object Model (OM).

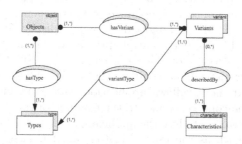

Fig. 1. Metamodel for XCM Multi-Variant Objects

At the top of the figure, the separation of the concept of an object and its actual content is clearly visible in the form of `Objects` linked to a non-empty set of `Variants` by means of the association `hasVariant`. Each variant of a multi-variant content object can be described by `Characteristics` that are linked to the variant over the association `describedBy`. A characteristic is simply represented as a (`name, value`) tuple. For example, to annotate a variant for english, one would simply associate it with the tuple (`language.name, english`). As we will see later, characteristics play an important role in context-aware content management applications. XCM also manages metadata about the types of content objects and their variants. Thus, in the metamodel, objects as well as variants are associated with `Types` using the `hasType` and `variantType` associations, respectively. This information can then be used by the system to determine whether the type of a variant matches the type of the corresponding object. As the cardinality constraints indicate, an object can have more than one type to support polymorphism and multiple instantiation.

XCM uses the concept of *structure* to build content hierarchies from multi-variant content objects. In a content management system, structures are required to build complex objects such as pages, collection of pages or "folders". Our system uses the very simple component-container approach to build these structures. As a container can hold a number of components and other containers as well, arbitrary tree-based structures can be represented. Structure objects, i.e. containers, form the inner nodes of the tree, whereas the actual content is located in the leaves. Separating the structure from the content makes possible different access patterns to the same content.

Personalisation in XCM is achieved through the concept of a *view*. A view decides which aspects of a multi-variant content object are presented to the user. Further, it can aggregate other information to the object based on the schema of the content, thereby augmenting it. Hence, our view concept is not unlike that found in relational database systems. Managing different views for different users or situations effectively provides support for personalisation and custom content delivery.

Finally, the concept of *layout* encapsulates the graphical representation of the content. The layout is applied to container and content objects by means of templates that match the type of the target object. As for all four basic concepts of our system, layout objects can have multiple variants for different requirements. For example, a template to render a news article can have one variant to produce HTML and another variant to display WML. Hence, layout objects are required to support multiple presentation channels.

Based on this overview of the basic elements of XCM, we now go on to describe the integration of the context engine into the system. As mentioned before, our context model allows application entities to be linked to context elements within the context engine. In the example of the content management application, it is intuitive to link the application concept of Sessions to various context elements such as the user's identity and language, the version of the browser and other information about the current situation of the requestor. As sessions are already used in content management systems to store values essential to the current user, it is only natural to use this concept and augment it with context information.

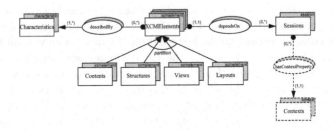

Fig. 2. Conceptual Model for the Context Binding

Figure 2 shows the model of the binding between XCM and the context engine. The parts that physically belong to the context model of our context component are represented with dashed lines. The four basic concepts have been unified with a common super concept XCMElements which depends on the values of a given session. The separation between an object and its variants has been collapsed into a box with multiple shades to indicate that these objects can have multiple variants. From the model, it is apparent that not only content, but also structure, view and layout can have multiple variants and thus adapt to context. Again, each variant can be described with characteristics as shown on the left-hand side of the figure.

This conceptual link between context elements and the application concept of a session is materialised using the context type definition given in the example below. The displayed Prolog code first creates a base type for physical internet addresses by means of a restriction on the type **string**. Then a context type is created to represent the browser that is used in a given context. The actual binding is defined by the third declaration. It defines a type **ctx_session** which is linked to the concept **xcm:session** within XCM. It comprises four attributes that represent the context information available from the sensors. The attribute **user** provides the identity of the user of the current session, **lang** its language and **browser** the name and version of the browser used. Finally, the attribute **host** gives information about the physical address from which the content management system is accessed.

```
btype ip is string {
       constr: 'self(S), split(S,".",L), \+ (member(X,L), \+ conv_integer(X,_))';
};

contextType ctx_browser {
       name: string;
       version: string;
};

contextType ctx_session characterises xcm:session {
       user: xcm:user;
       lang: language;
       browser: ctx_browser;
       host: ip;
};
```

Having explained how the context engine is bound to the content management application, we now go on to discuss how such a system reacts to the information supplied by the context component. In XCM, context information is used to select the appropriate variant of an object, i.e. the context information is compared to the characteristics of each variant of such an object and the best matching version is selected. In practice, this can prove to be quite difficult, as the characteristics available to the system need not fully match the incoming context information. It is often the case that the context information comes at a higher level of detail than the metadata stored in the content management system. Of course, the opposite case that the metadata is more precise is also possible. In these cases of "under-" and "over-specified" context information, the matching process uses heuristics to select from the set of possible variants or to select a default variant if no match is found at all. A similar matching process together with heuristics is used in [17,28].

For the mapping of context information to characteristics to work, the names of the (**name**, **value**) tuples have to match. This means that some sort of convention, taxonomy or ontology has to be used that assures a uniform naming scheme. As the definition of such conventions is clearly beyond the scope of this work, we adopt the simple approach of what we call "property paths". A property path locates a value inside a context element and can be derived from its context type definition, e.g. the value of the browser version in the current session would be identified by the path `ctx_session.browser.version`.

Further complexity arises from the fact that XCM supports not only simple values for characteristics, but also sets and ranges. This is used to specify, for instance, a set of matching browser versions with the characteristic (`ctx_session.browser.version`, [`5.0`, `5.5`, `6.0`, `6.1`]) or a time period when a variant of an object is valid with (`valid`, [`1/1/2004..31/1/2004`]). XCM also provides the notion of *mandatory* and *"show-stopper"* characteristics. In contrast to *unconstrained* characteristics, these categories of properties are not freely matched to the context information, but instead are treated specially. A mandatory characteristic takes precedence over all other non-mandatory values, whereas a "show-stopper" property would not allow a certain variant to be selected if the context value does not match that of the characteristic.

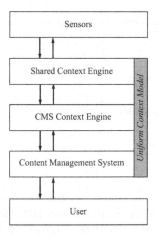

Fig. 3. Overview of the Architecture

Having discussed the integration of the context component into our content management system, we can finally give an architectural overview of the whole system. Figure 3 shows a graphical representation of all components. At the bottom, the user is shown that communicates with the content management system through a browser requesting pages. The content management system then interworks with a private context component to manage the context proprietary to the system. Further, the private context component is connected to a shared context component that manages context for several applications and provides a global notion of context. This shared context component is connected to the sensors as shown at the top of the figure. The two context components and the content management application are conceptually connected by the model that is common to all three of them. As the figure also indicates, information can always flow in both directions. We discuss the opposite flow of information in the next section.

5   From Content to Context

In the previous section, we described how the content management system can use the context engine to provide context-aware content for a user. In this section, we describe the reverse relationship. The content management system can also act as a provider of information for the context engine. This context information can then be used either by the content management system itself, or by another context-aware application of an information environment.

In Sect. 3, we introduced the abstract concept of a sensor. A sensor is basically any piece of software or hardware that generates context values for a given context element. Sensors can be classified into two categories, depending on the environment that they target: *Physical sensors* acquire context information from the physical environment, e.g. from a room, the human body or a physical object. *Software sensors*, on the other hand, gather information from the virtual environment formed by the logic and data of an application. The content management system is such an application to which software sensors can be applied. As XCM is implemented in Java, the corresponding software sensors would be implemented in the same language. The binding of the sensors to the context engine is done through the mechanism of a sensor driver as mentioned in Sect. 3.

The concepts of interest are the same for both physical and software sensors. From the main areas described in [29], the *user environment* is of special importance for information environments. Whereas the physical part of the user environment (e.g. location and orientation of a person) is usually relatively easy to acquire with appropriate sensors, the mental state of a user is much harder to obtain. The content management system is able to provide very valuable context information in this area such as what the user is currently working on, which topics are of interest, how busy the user is and whether they are currently working on a precise topic or just browsing an information space.

Context information can be extracted from application data, content data, the local context model of the content management system or the user sessions. Some of this context information, e.g. the level and type of activity, is independent of the actual application data in the content management system and relies only on its metadata. Software sensors can be provided that extract this context information in a generic way. However, for the other examples mentioned above, the actual data model of the application is very important. The fact that we have an expressive semantic data model in our content management system greatly simplifies the task. Actually, the extraction of semantic context information would be very difficult, if not impossible, without a proper application model in the content management system. Imagine, for instance, a news application where individual news messages are categorised with respect to their topics. In some traditional content management systems that do not support customised data models, this could be modelled with a page for each topic containing a list of news messages in the form of paragraphs, links etc. and a page for each news message with more details. In this setup, it is not possible to extract the topics in which the user is currently interested. As we have described in Sect. 3, in our content management system, the application data is not stored in the form of paragraphs, links and pages, but rather according to a semantic application model. A customised software sensor could thus easily retrieve the categories of the news messages that the user is currently browsing and store corresponding entries in the context engine. In contrast to other context frameworks such as [9], as described in Sect. 3, we are also able to use application objects as context values through reference types. This means that the content management system can store the actual object that represents the category in the context engine, rather than just the name of the category.

It is important not to confuse the extraction of context information with general data mining, e.g. for user profiling. Similar technologies and algorithms can be used for both of them, but whereas data mining focusses on general facts and information, for example about users, *context mining* is only concerned with the current state of the user. This might include historical information, but usually, context information is of interest for a limited time only.

The extracted context information can be used for a variety of applications. Of special interest to us are information environments and corresponding platforms that integrate multiple context-aware applications for a physical location or virtual community. We have implemented a context-aware news application for such an information environment that uses a content management system for the delivery of information and adapts according to the people in a room. Currently, we are working on the extension of this news application towards the inclusion of virtual rooms and the integration of the context engine described previously.

Another example are community awareness applications that visualise the presence and activities of other users. This is context information of the user. A content management system as part of an information environment of a community could provide some of this context information, for example, for an application such as the context-aware instant messaging and chat application described in [30]. It visualises a list of users that are present along with their current state (present, busy, free-for-chat etc.). Another interesting example is the area of Computer-Supported Cooperative Work (CSCW) or collaborative systems in general. In this context, the content management system could also provide context information for a community of users, such as users working on specific topics, rather than just for individuals. This information could be displayed by other context-aware applications or the context management system itself.

6   Conclusions and Future Work

We have discussed the interplay between context and content in terms of the relationship between the basic concepts of context engines and content management systems, respectively. We used the example of our own content management system to demonstrate how our generic context engine enabled us to seamlessly adapt all dimensions of content delivery—content, view, structure and presentation—through a process of matching context to multi-variant objects for these dimensions.

Moreover, we showed that a content management system can be, not only a client to the context engine, but also a potential provider of context information.

Our system XCM exhibits two features that make it an ideal component for determining the computation context: It consolidates well organised information from arbitrary sources and acts as a bridge between the user and the organisation through multiple communication channels. We showed how this crucial and complete information provides context and how we use XCM as a software sensor to the context engine.

We are currently working on a platform for a context-aware information environment (SOPHIE) that combines features from pervasive computing and information systems. The SOPHIE platform is based on content management technologies and context engines and represents an important step forward in the integration and extension of these technologies to cater for information delivery and interaction in environments that span the physical and digital worlds and involve multiple interrelated users and devices.

References

1. Lieberman, H., Selker, T.: Out of Context: Computer Systems that Adapt to and Learn from Context. IBM Systems Journal **39** (2000)
2. Brown, P.J.: The Stick-e Document: a Framework for Creating Context-aware Applications. In: Proc. EP'96, Palo Alto. (1996)
3. Dey, A.K., Salber, D., Abowd, G.D., Futakawa, M.: The Conference Assistant: Combining Context-Awareness with Wearable Computing. In: ISWC. (1999)
4. Chen, G., Kotz, D.: A Survey of Context-Aware Mobile Computing Research. Technical Report TR2000-381, Dept. of Computer Science, Dartmouth College (2000)
5. Want, R., Hopper, A., Falc o, V., Gibbons, J.: The Active Badge location system. ACM Transactions on Information Systems **10** (1992)
6. Abowd, G., Atkeson, C., Hong, J., Long, S., Kooper, R., Pinkerton, M.: Cyberguide: A mobile context-aware tour guide (1997)
7. Davies, N., Mitchell, K., Cheverst, K., Blair, G.: Developing a Context Sensitive Tourist Guide (1998)
8. Ryan, N.S., Pascoe, J., Morse, D.R.: Enhanced Reality Fieldwork: the Context-aware Archaeological Assistant. In Gaffney, V., van Leusen, M., Exxon, S., eds.: Computer Applications in Archaeology 1997. British Archaeological Reports, Oxford (1998)
9. Salber, D., Dey, A.K., Abowd, G.D.: The Context Toolkit: Aiding the Development of Context-Enabled Applications. In: Proceedings of the 1999 Conference on Human Factors in Computing Systems (CHI '99), Pittsburgh, PA (1999)
10. Hess, C.K., Ballesteros, F., Campbell, R.H., Mickunas, M.D.: An Adaptive Data Object Service Framework for Pervasive Computing Environments (2001)
11. Belotti, R., Decurtins, C., Grossniklaus, M., Norrie, M.C., Palinginis, A.: Modelling Context for Information Environments. In: Ubiquitous Mobile Information and Collaboration Systems (UMICS), CAiSE Workshop Proceedings. (2004)
12. Brusilovsky, P.: Methods and Techniques of Adaptive Hypermedia. User Modeling and User-Adapted Interaction **6** (1996)
13. Brusilovsky, P.: Adaptive Hypermedia. User Modeling and User-Adapted Interaction **11** (2001)

14. Kobsa, A., Müller, D., Nill, A.: KN-AHS: An Adaptive Hypertext Client of the User Modeling System BGP-MS. In: Proc. of the Fourth Intl. Conf. on User Modeling, Hyannis, MA (1994)
15. Wu, H.: A Reference Architecture for Adaptive Hypermedia Systems. PhD thesis, Technical University Eindhoven (2002)
16. Ceri, S., Daniel, F., Matera, M.: Extending WebML for Modeling Multi-Channel Context-Aware Web Applications. In: Proc. MMIS'2003, Intl. Workshop on Multichannel and Mobile Information Systems, WISE 2003. (2003)
17. Norrie, M.C., Palinginis, A.: Empowering Databases for Context-Dependent Information Delivery. In: Ubiquitous Mobile Information and Collaboration Systems (UMICS 2003), Klagenfurt/Velden, Austria (2003)
18. Grossniklaus, M., Norrie, M.C., Büchler, P.: Metatemplate Driven Multi-Channel Presentation. In: Proc. MMIS 2003, Intl. Workshop on Multi-Channel and Mobile Information Systems, WISE 2003, Roma, Italy (2003)
19. Perkowitz, M., Etzioni, O.: Towards adaptive Web sites: conceptual framework and case study. Computer Networks (1999)
20. Ceri, S., Fraternali, P., Bongio, A.: Web Modeling Language (WebML): A Modeling Language For Designing Web Sites. Computer Networks (2000)
21. Norrie, M.C., Würgler, A., Palinginis, A., von Gunten, K., Grossniklaus, M.: OMS Pro 2.0 Introductory Tutorial. Inst. for Information Systems, ETH Zürich. (2003)
22. Michael Grossniklaus and Moira C. Norrie: Information concepts for content management. In: Proc. DASWIS 2002, Intl. Workshop on Data Semantics in Web Information Systems, WISE 2002, Singapore, Republic of Singapore (2002)
23. Dourish, P.: What We Talk About When We Talk About Context. Personal and Ubiquitous Computing 8 (2004)
24. Swedish Institute of Computer Science S-164 28 Kista, Sweden: SICStus Prolog User's Manual. (1995)
25. Kato, D.H., of Washington, H.L.U., of Canterbury, H.L.U.: Artoolkit. http://www.hitl.washington.edu/artoolkit/ (2003)
26. Kobler, A., Norrie, M.C.: OMS Java: Lessons Learned from Building a Multi-Tier Object Management Framework. In: Proc. OOPSLA'99, Workshop on Java and Databases: Persistence Options. (1999)
27. Norrie, M.C.: An Extended Entity-Relationship Approach to Data Management in Object-Oriented Systems. In: Proc. ER'93, 12th Intl. Conf. on the Entity-Relationship Approach. (1993)
28. Norrie, M.C., Palinginis, A.: Versions for Context Dependent Information Services. In: Proc. COOPIS 2003, Conf. on Cooperative Information Systems. (2003)
29. Schilit, B.N.: A System Architecture for Context-Aware Mobile Computing. PhD thesis, Columbia University (1995)
30. Ranganathan, A., Roy H. Campbell, A.R., Mahajan, A.: ConChat: A Context-Aware Chat Program. Pervasive Computing 1 (2002)

Model-Driven Design of Web Applications with Client-Side Adaptation

Stefano Ceri[1], Peter Dolog[2], Maristella Matera[1], and Wolfgang Nejdl[2]

[1] Dipartimento di Elettronica e Informazione - Politecnico di Milano
Via Ponzio, 34/5, 20133 Milano, Italy
{ceri, matera}@elet.polimi.it

[2] Learning Lab Lower Saxony - University of Hannover,
Expo Plaza 1, 30539 Hannover, Germany,
{dolog, nejdl}@learninglab.de

Abstract. In this paper, we integrate WebML, a high-level model and technology for building server-side Web applications, with UML-Guide, a UML-based system that generates client-side guides for the adaptation of Web applications. The combination of the two systems is shown at work on an e-learning scenario: WebML is the basis of the specification of a generic e-learning system, collecting a large number of learning objects, while UML-Guide is used for building company-specific e-learning curricula. The resulting system can be considered an "adaptive hypermedia generator" in full strength, whose potential expressive power goes beyond the experiments reported in this paper.

Keywords: Personalization, UML, WebML Modeling, Web Engineering.

1 Introduction

In recent years, the control of Web applications has moved from the client to the server side, leading to more economical, structured, and well engineered solutions. In particular, the model-driven approach, as advocated in [3,6,11,17] has proved very effective in extending the classical methods and best practices of Software Engineering to the Web. Design methods now concentrate on content, navigation, and presentation design, which are orthogonally developed by means of specialized abstractions and techniques.

While server-side solutions are dominant, yet bringing some intelligence to the client may be highly beneficial in some cases [16,18]. Client-side solutions can reveal as being more dynamic, more adaptive, and protective for sensitive user data. They may be very effective for "remembering" the local context or being aware of the local peculiarities of the interaction. Also, a clear separation of concerns between the client and the server may lead to interesting business opportunities and models.

This paper explores the combination of two existing approaches to the engineering of Web applications. We use the WebML method [3] and its development support environment [4] for generating the application server-side "backbone". We then integrate such a backbone with UML-Guide [9], a client-side personalization engine that dynamically generates additional interfaces and user guides for personalizing the application's fruition, by managing user profiles and context-sensitive data at client side.

N. Koch, P. Fraternali, and M. Wirsing (Eds.): ICWE 2004, LNCS 3140, pp. 201–214, 2004.
© Springer-Verlag Berlin Heidelberg 2004

The proposed approach capitalizes on the use of two systems that both start from high-level abstractions, and are both capable of automatic deployment of the implementations:

- The WebML method is based on the use of high-level concepts, such as the notions of entity and relationship to denote content, and of page, unit, and link to denote hypertexts. These abstractions are automatically turned into implementation artifacts by means of WebRatio, a tool for the automatic deployment of Web applications [3].
- UML-Guide is based on the use of UML state diagrams, whose nodes and arcs—representing states and transitions—are turned into XMI specifications. A client-side translator, written in XSL, turns such specifications into a user interface facilitating the adaptive use of the application [9].

Coupling WebML and UML-Guide yields the following advantages:

- The use of high-level WebML abstractions in the context of UML-Guide enables the specification of a powerful client-side personalization engine. The resulting application generator can be considered an "adaptive hypermedia generator" in full strength, whose potential expressive power goes well beyond the experiment reported in this paper.
- The tools prove to be highly complementary and easily integrated, as it is sufficient to reuse concepts of WebML inside UML-Guide to provide concept interoperability, and the URL generation technique of the WebML runtime inside the UML-Guide XSL code to provide systems interoperability.
- The use of UML-driven methods in conjunction with WebML is by itself a very interesting direction of research, aiming at the integration of UML, the most consolidated software engineering method (and related technology), with WebML as a representative case of new, hypertext-specific models and techniques.

1.1 Driving Scenario

In order to exemplify the integration of the two methods, we refer to an e-learning scenario, in which a courseware company develops and distributes a vertical application for e-learning, running on the company's server, specified and developed through WebML[1]. The vertical incorporates learning objects in the format of lessons, exercises, tests, definitions and examples for computer science, arranged according to the ACM categories[2], and learning paths with checkpoints for the learner. Thus, such a vertical has learning objects as content, and navigation mechanisms, such as guided tours or indexed accesses to pages based on broad categories, enabling a generic user to access such a content though predefined navigation paths.

The vertical is used by Small-Medium Enterprises (SMEs) wishing to build personalized e-learning curricula, to be used by their employees for focused training activities. We assume that each SME has a clear instruction goal (for example, teaching its employees how to integrate Java programming into Oracle 9i), and that it can use UML-Guide

---

[1] This scenario is suggested by the ProLearn Network of Excellence, whose main focus is the enhancement of professional e-learning methods and technology; see
http://www.prolearn-project.org.

[2] See http://www.acm.org/class/1998/

to specify it in UML; we assume that UML state diagrams, together with a vocabulary listing all the learning objects available in the vertical, may be an easy-to-use interface for the SME designer. UML-Guide specifications select the concepts to be covered in the learning paths, as well as the workflow driving the student in the learning process. We also assume that each SME has a clear view of its employees' competencies, and thus is able to constrain possibilities in the learning paths by adaptation rules based on such competencies. These rules enable adaptive content selection from the WebML vertical and also enable to adaptively indicate, show, and hide links in the learning path, and adaptively customize their targets.

1.2 Paper Organization

The paper is organized as follows. Section 2 introduces the WebML component, by providing an overview of the WebML method and the WebML-based specification of the vertical e-learning application. Section 3 introduces the UML-Guide method, and the specification of the client-side personalization for the vertical e-learning. Section 4 illustrates the integration of the two methods by means of an architecture where the application server-side code is generated through WebML, while personalization with respect to specific learning goals is managed at client-side through UML-Guide. Section 5 then describes the user interface generated for the integrated application. Sections 6 and 7 illustrate some related work and draw our conclusions and future work.

2 WebML Component

WebML is a visual language for specifying the content structure of a Web application and the organization and presentation of contents in one or more hypertexts [3]. The design process based on WebML starts with the specification of a data schema, expressing the organization of contents by means of the Entity-Relationship primitives. The *WebML Hypertext Model* allows then describing how contents, previously specified in the data schema, are published into the application hypertext.

The overall structure of the hypertext is defined in terms of *site views*, *areas*, *pages* and *content units*. A *site view* is a hypertext, designed to address a specific set of requirements. It is composed of *areas*, which are the main sections of the hypertext, and comprise recursively other sub-areas or pages. *Pages* are the actual containers of information delivered to the user; they are made of *content units* that are elementary pieces of information, extracted from the data sources by means of queries and published within pages. In particular, as described in Table 1, content units denote alternative ways for displaying one or more entity instances.

Their specification requires the definition of a *source* (the name of the entity from which the unit's content is extracted) and a *selector* (a condition, used for retrieving the actual objects of the source entity that contribute to the unit's content).

Within site views, links interconnect content units and pages in a variety of configurations yielding to composite navigation mechanisms. Besides representing user navigation, links between units also specify the transportation of some information (called *context*) that the destination unit uses for selecting the data instances to be displayed.

Table 1. Some basic WebML content units. The whole set of units is described in [3].

Unit name	Visual Notation	Description
Data unit		It displays a set of attributes for a single entity instance.
Multidata unit		It displays a set of instances for a given entity.
Index unit		It displays a list of properties, also called *descriptive keys*, of a given set of entity instances.
Hierarchical Index unit		A variant of the index unit, which displays list of properties of instances selected from multiple entities, nested in multi-level three.
Scroller unit		It represents a scrolling mechanism, based on a block factor, for the elements in a set of instances.

WebML-based development is supported by a CASE tool [4], which offers a visual environment for drawing the WebML conceptual schemas, and then supports the automatic generation of server-side code. The generated applications run in a standard runtime framework on top of Java 2 application servers, and have a flexible, service-based architecture allowing components customization.

2.1 WebML Specification for the Vertical E-learning

The data schema of the vertical e-learning application is centered on the concept of learning object. As reported in Figure 1, the LO entity represents descriptions of learning objects, by means of attributes inspired by the LOM standard[3]. Among them, the attribute type expresses the different types of LOs (e.g., lectures, lecture modules, definitions, exercises, tests) published by the vertical application. Each LO has associations with other LOs: for example, a lecture module can be associated with some related definitions, exercises, examples, or tests. The entity Content then represents the contents (texts, images, files) LOs consists of. In order to facilitate LO access, the schema also includes the entity Category: it stores the ACM categories that classify the LOs published by the e-learning application.

---

[3] http://ltsc.ieee.org/

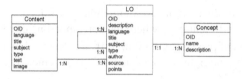

Fig. 1. WebML Data schema for the vertical e-learning application.

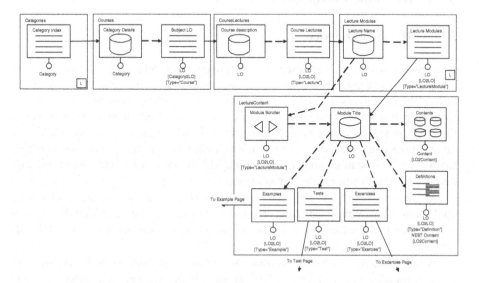

Fig. 2. The WebML specification of the hypertext interface for the vertical e-learning application.

Figure 2 reports a simplified excerpt of the WebML hypertext schema defined for the vertical e-learning application; it refers to pages for selecting a lecture module, and accessing its contents as well as associated definitions, exercises examples, and tests. The lecture module selection is operated by means of a navigation chain, in which users progressively select a subject category (Categories page), then a course that refers to the selected category (Courses page), then a lecture (CourseLectures page), and finally the lecture module they are interested in (LectureModules page). Pages Categories and LectureModules are marked with an "L" label, which indicates that they are *landmark* pages. This property represents that the two pages will be reachable from any other page of the hypertext, by means of landmark links.

Contents of the selected lecture module are shown in page LectureContent. As represented by the Module Scroller unit, users can browse lecture modules in a *Guided Tour* navigation that allows moving forward and backward in the (ordered) set of modules available for the currently selected lecture. For each module, the data unit Module Title shows the title and a short description of the learning object, the Contents multidata unit shows texts and images that compose the module, while the Definitions hierarchical index shows titles of the definitions associated with the module and, nested, the corresponding contents. Three index units then show the lists of examples, tests and exercises available for the current lecture module. The selection of one item from such lists leads users in a different page where the corresponding contents are displayed.

The presentation of page LectureContent, as generated by the WebML code generator, can be seen in the right frame of the Web page depicted in Figure 7.

3 UML-Guide Component

3.1 UML-Guide Overview

UML State diagrams [12] are used in UML-Guide for modelling the user navigation in a hypertext. Each *state* represents the production of a given information chunk on the device observed by a user, and each state *transition* represents an event caused by user interaction that leads to the production of a new chunk of information. State diagrams therefore provide an abstraction of *hypertext trails*, where each trail can be adapted by taking into account the user background, level of knowledge, preferences and so on [9]. In this way, UML state diagrams are a suitable interface for UML-Guide, whose primary purpose is to build adaptive hypermedia systems.

Atomic states can be grouped into *superstates*. States usually refer to concepts of an application domain; thus, they can correspond to the representation of WebML pages or page units, which enable the viewing of the information entities within the WebML data schema.

Parallel substates represent information chunks to be presented simultaneously. *Fork* and *join* pseudostates are used respectively for splitting and joining computations and enabling parallelism. The *SyncState* pseudostate is used for synchronizing substates of parallel regions.

Transitions represent active interconnections between information chunks, and usually correspond to associations in the application domain model (thus, they can correspond to WebML links, that interconnect pages and units, and in turn depend upon the relationships of the WebML data model). *Events* raise transitions in a state machine; they include user-generated or system-generated events, and the latter include time events. *Guards* can be used to constrain transitions by adaptation rules. Usually, they consist of a predicate over user profile attributes or context information.

Actions can be performed after a transition is raised and before entering a state. Also, transitions can be associated with *side effect actions*, whose effect is, for example, the modification of a user profile, or the choice of presentation styles for a given chunk of information. Actions can also process parameters used in guards of outgoing part of branches. Side effect actions, as well as adaptation rules, can be assigned to *entry*, *exit*, and *do* actions of states.

Tagged values are domain-specific properties used to extend the semantics of elements in UML diagrams. These values can refer, for example, to concepts of the structural model of the application domain, or to specific terminologies which might be useful to identify additional navigation requirements. We will make extensive use of tagged values for linking UML diagrams of UML-Guide to WebML concepts, as illustrated in Section 4.

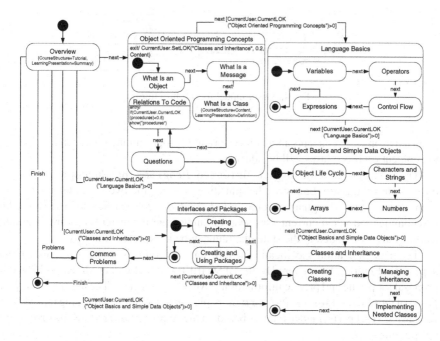

Fig. 3. A navigation model for a Java tutorial in the UML state diagram notation.

3.2   UML-Guide State Diagram for E-learning

The UML-Guide state diagram of Figure 3 illustrates a personalized learning environment for teaching object-oriented programming in JAVA, borrowed from a well-known Sun tutorial [4]. The chosen personalization example focuses on link adaptation; other adaptation aspects are covered in [9].

The tutorial starts with an overview of available lectures, as represented by the Overview state, which summarizes the available lectures in the tutorial, as specified by the Summary value in the LearningPresentation tagged value. It also presents the high level tutorial steps (Tutorial value in the CourseStructure tagged value). Links from the overview point not only to the first section of the tutorial, but also to the other main sections; all these links, except the first one, are associated with guard conditions that check that the user has enough knowledge to jump directly to the respective lectures.

The next step from the Overview is a lecture on the Object Oriented Programming Concepts. This state is accessible without any prerequisite on background knowledge; it is a composite state, containing five steps, represented by four substates: What is an Object, What is a Message, What is a Class, Relations to Code, and Questions. The Relations to Code state also shows an entry procedure addressing *content level adaptation*. The procedure applies to a learning step about building programs; it states that if the current user does not have sufficient

---

[4] See http://java.sun.com/docs/books/tutorial/java/index.html.

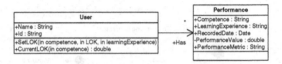

Fig. 4. A user model for the Java tutorial.

knowledge on basic concepts about object-oriented programming procedures, then learning content on procedures will be added.

The next step from the `Object Oriented Programming Concepts` is the composite state `Language Basics`. The transition between the two states features a `next` event and a guard. The guard specifies a *link level adaptation* rule, saying that the link is recommended when current user level of knowledge is greater then zero. The other learning steps modelled in the state diagram can be interpreted similarly.

The personalization specification within state diagrams is based on the user model depicted in Figure 4. It is inspired by the LTSC IEEE 1484.2 Learner Model WG Standard proposal for public and private information (PAPI) for learner[5],[6]. The user model is composed of the classes `User` and `Performance`, plus an association expressing that a learner can have several performance records based on the acquired `LearningExperience` and `Competence`.

The `Performance` class stores the user's level of knowledge about the concepts described by the tutorial. This value is the one used for determining if a transition into a new state is appropriate and must be suggested to a given user. For example, the following condition:

```
[CurrentUser.CurrentLOK(''Classes and Inheritance'')>0]
```

is a guard that in the state diagram determines wether a link can be followed between the `Classes and Inheritance` state and the `Interfaces and Packages` state, based on current user level of knowledge. The `Performance` class maintains as well the value of competence, recorded date, and metrics used to measure level of competence.

The `User` class provides operations to set and get the acquired level of knowledge or level of competence. These operations are used in guards and actions for adaptivity rules, and for updating learner profile. For example, in the state diagram of Figure 3, the user level of knowledge about "Classes and Inheritance" can be acquired either in the `Object Oriented Programming Concepts` lecture or in the `Classes and Inheritance` lecture. Exit procedures of these states indeed contain similar update operations, as the one which follows:

```
CurrentUser.SetLOK(''Classes and Inheritance'',0.2,Content).
```

---

[5] http://ltsc.ieee.org/archive/harvested-2003-10/working_groups/wg2.zip

[6] For a more detailed learner profile, used e.g. in EU/IST Elena (http://www.elena-project.org), the reader is referred to the learner RDF bindings web site at http://www.learninglab.de/~dolog/learnerrdfbindings/.

In UML-Guide, state diagrams are used as input for visualizing navigation maps, whose structure is made of documents (nodes), composite nodes (folders), links (arrows), and parallel regions (dashed boxes). State diagrams are edited by means of the commercial tool Poseidon[7]). The navigation map is then generated through a transformation method [9], whose input is the state diagram encoded in XMI (as produced by Poseidon), and whose output is the map.

4   Integration of WebML and UML-Guide

The integration of WebML with UML-Guide proposed in this paper aims at composing a generic "vertical e-learning" WebML application with a UML-Guide that is focused on a specific learning goal. We offer to the users of the composite system the standard, WebML-generated interface of the vertical, populated by content spawning a large body of knowledge; but we also offer to the focused learners a guide, available on an interface that can be opened "aside" the main one, and that points to pages and contents published by the WebML-generated interface, according to a specific learning objective and user experience.

The integration is loose and preserves the distinctive features of the two systems. In particular, some nodes and links in a UML-Guide state diagram point to content which is managed in the WebML e-learning vertical; therefore, the integration of UML-Guide with WebML requires UML-Guide adopting WebML concepts, such as page identifiers and content identifiers. In this way, concepts used as state names or as tagged values within UML-Guide are mapped to learning resources stored in the database generated from the WebML data model.

In the resulting application, the user-specific adaptation occurs in UML-Guide. This separation of concerns represents an extreme solution, as it is possible to support personalization [5] and adaptation [2] directly in WebML. However, the proposed solution is an example of how client-side computations, specified at high-level in UML, can integrate WebML-designed solutions. As such, this experiment can be replicated for many other applications and the focus on UML-Guide can pursue different objectives.

Figure 5 describes the system architecture. The high-level WebML and UML-Guide specifications are mapped into XML-based internal representations, respectively built by the Code Generator component of WebRatio [4] and by the XMI [13] Generator of Poseidon.

The WebML run-time component runs JSP templates (also embedding SQL), and uses XSL style sheets for building the application's presentation. The XMI representation of a UML-Guide drives a run-time adaptation engine, written in XSLT, which dynamically changes the content of the profile variables and produces the UML-Guide user interface. The WebML and UML-Guide interfaces are then composed and presented to the user.

In this architecture, the main integration issue is concerned with the generation of WebML links "pointing" to the WebML-controlled portion of the application, to be addressed while building the UML-Guide interface. WebML links take the format:

---

[7] http://www.gentleware.com/

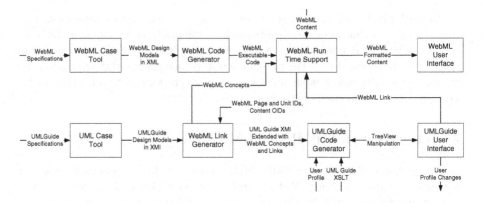

Fig. 5. Architecture of the composed system.

```
ApplicationURL/page_identifier.do?ParameterList
```

where `page_identifier` denotes a WebML page and `ParameterList` is a list of tag-value pairs, in the form `entity_id.attribute=parameter`. Thus, UML-Guide state diagrams must be extended with tagged values to be used as pointers to WebML concepts.

Figure 6 depicts an excerpt of state diagram extended with tagged values for WebML concepts, needed for computing WebML links. This work must be performed by UML-Guide designers, typically in the course of the transformations required for "implementing" UML-Guides starting from their high-level descriptions (as illustrated in Figure 3).

For instance, `Object Oriented Programming Concepts` is a lecture. The corresponding page name is `LectureModules` from WebML hypertext model. The entity used to store lectures in the WebML data model is `LO`. The title used as an attribute to identify the lecture is the same as the state name. Entry and exit actions are transformed if they send parameters in WebML links, as it is in the case of `Relations To Code` (where the parameter of the `show` method is replaced by specific WebML parameter `&LO.Title=Procedures`). It is worth noting that, although in our example tagged values for page and entity names are constant values, in more complex cases they can be specified as well as parametric selectors, so as to automatically retrieve their values from the WebML XML specification based on specific conditions. Also, more tagged values can be needed, for example for identifying content units IDs, in situations where the selection of pages is based upon the content units they include.

Queries for retrieving OID's of the WebML concepts and content are submitted through a specifically designed interface to the WebML run-time components. The interface consists of the two functions `GetWebMLConcept(Type, Name)` and `GetWebMLRecordOID(Entity, Attribute, Value)`.

5   Generation of the Integrated E-learning Application

Figure 7 presents the user interface of the integrated application. The UML-Guide generated map, obtained as a transformation of the UML state diagram depicted in Figure 3,

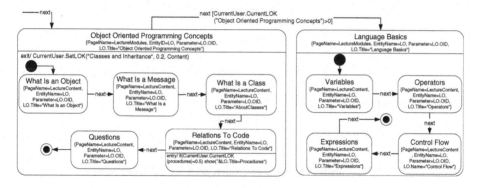

Fig. 6. Excerpt of the UML-Guide state diagram extended with tagged values representing WebML concepts.

is on the left; the WebML application, generated from the specification of Figure 2, is on the right. While the WebML application has an arbitrary interface, which depends on content composition within pages and on the adopted presentation style, the UML-Guide interface has a given structure that includes the following elements:

– *Folder symbol*—represents a composite information fragment composed by other (simple or composite) information fragments and links. The *composition* is visually represented by the plus/minus symbol, for showing/hiding enclosed items, and by the left hand indent of enclosed items. A content can be associated to each symbol.
– *Dashed box symbol*—represents a composite information fragment, which has to be presented concurrently with other composite information fragments (the dashed boxes) depicted on the same level.
– *Document symbol*—represents a simple information fragment; only links can be nested under it.
– *Arrow symbol*—represents a link to another composite or simple information fragment; the arrow symbols can be nested under the folder when they represent different alternatives of suggested links starting from a particular document. Each arrow is associated with a content and a name of the corresponding target node. Also, the "/next" string is added to names of arrows representing guidance to the next fragment according to the course sequence.
– *Grayed background of nodes*—represents the currently presented node, i.e., the position reached by a user in the navigation map.

Presentation for the adaptive navigation support depends on the generator settings. For example, according to the traffic light metaphor, adaptive recommendations may be represented through different colors (green for nodes appropriate with respect to the current state of the user profile, red for not appropriate nodes, yellow for other situations—e.g. a node that has been already visited). Also, other metaphors might show, hide, or sort the nodes.

Profile records are maintained at the client side. When users begin a new session, their profile is initialized from a client-side XML-based database. The navigation map is

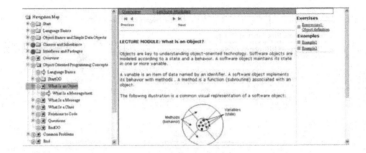

Fig. 7. Visualization of the navigation graph for the Java e-lecture.

manipulated at the client side as well. Javascript is used to implement the user interface control and user profile manipulation. The events generated by user actions on the user interface invoke profile adaptation actions, which possibly process and add new values to the user profile. They also trigger regeneration of the navigation map, according to the newly computed values.

The navigation map responds to changes in user profile by changing recommendation annotations (e.g., changing colors of nodes or showing/hiding nodes). When specific requirements, for example those set by conditions in entry actions of states, are met, the WebML vertical adapts delivered content based on additional parameters that UML-Guide is able to send to the server-side application.

6   Related Work

Model-driven development of Web applications has been intensely investigated during last years [6,10,11,17]. WebML has been proposed for the model-driven design of "data-intensive" Web applications. Its distinguishing feature is that the proposed design method is also supported by XML- and Java-based technologies, which enable the automatic generation of the application code [4].

During last years, some approaches have been proposed for extending traditional development methods by means of features enabling one-to-one personalization [1,15, 17]. The aim is to customize the applications contents and the hypertext topology and presentation with respect to user preferences and needs, so as to offer an alternative to the traditional "one-size-fits-all" static approach in the development of Web systems [1]. Some proposals cover the adaptivity of Web applications with respect to some other dimensions characterizing the context of use (see [14] for a complete survey). WebML also offers some constructs for personalization. In particular, the application data schema can be extended through some entities representing user profiles and user access rights over the application content [5]. Recently, WebML has also been extended with some primitives for modelling context-aware applications, i.e., mobile, personalized applications that are also able to adapt to the current situation of use [2]. However, WebML, as well as the majority of Web personalization and adaptivity approaches so far proposed, manages personalization at server-side, and does not offer the alternative of managing user profiles and personalization policies at client side. Conversely, the UML-Guide approach establishes model-driven design for adaptive applications, by considering link level adaptation and content level adaptation at the client side, where adaptation is computed according to the UML design specifications. First, requirements are modelled as variation points with mandatory and optional features in application domain models [7]. Guard logical expressions and adaptivity actions are used in navigation specifications [9]. A rule based approach has been also employed in more open environment based on semantic web models [8].

7 Conclusions and Further Work

This paper has shown the integration between WebML and UML-Guide; the proposed approach demonstrates that server-side and client-side technologies can coexist and that it is possible, for both of them, to use model-driven code generation techniques starting from high-level requirements, expressed in graphical form. The proposed application scenario augments an 'e-learning" vertical so as to make it adaptable and personalisable.

In our experiments, we moved especially user dependent functionality to the client side which allowed us to leave control over sensitive user data to the user. Users can decide on their own which information will be disclosed and which they will deny access to. On the other hand, this increases requirements for client-side tools to be able to interpret a database with information about a user and process it for purpose of adaptation and personalization. As client machines are usually less powerful, this might result in some lacks of performance. We will further investigate and experiment with the approach proposed to find a good balance between client-side and server-side processing.

We regard this work as the first step of a deeper methodological inspection of the interactions between UML and WebML, and more specifically of the possibility of using state diagrams, which best represent the modeling of dynamic interfaces, for collecting the requirements that can naturally evolve into WebML specifications. The experiments described in this paper, and specifically the mechanisms for rendering state transitions as WebML links, will be extended and reused. In this paper we showed an integration of the two methods on an application where the state diagram is used to model interaction over information from one class. As a part of the deeper investigation, more complex applications will be studied where interaction between objects of several classes implies a need to use other behavioral techniques (collaboration and sequence diagrams) together with state diagrams.

We are also planning an extension of the WebML CASE tool and of UML-Guide for providing automatic support to the integration of the two methods.

References

1. P. Brusilovsky. Adaptive Hypermedia. *User Modeling and User-Adapted Interaction*, 11(1-2):87–100, 2001.
2. S. Ceri, F. Daniel, and M. Matera. Extending WebML for Modeling Multi-Channel Context-Aware Web Applications. In *Proceedings of WISE—MMIS'03 Workshop, Rome, Italy, December 2003*, pages 615–626. IEEE Computer Society, 2003.

3. S. Ceri, P. Fraternali, A. Bongio, M. Brambilla, S. Comai, and M. Matera. *Designing Data-Intensive Web Applications*. Morgan Kauffmann, 2002.

4. S. Ceri, P. Fraternali, et Al. Architectural Issues and Solutions in the Development of Data-Intensive Web Applications. In *Proc. of CIDR'03, Asilomar, CA, USA*, 2003.

5. S. Ceri, P. Fraternali, and S. Paraboschi. Data-Driven One-To-One Web Site Generation for Data-Intensive Web Applications. In *Proceedings of VLDB'99, September 1999, Edinburgh, UK*, pages 615–626. IEEE Computer Society, 1999.

6. J. Conallen. *Building Web Applications with UML*. Object Technology Series. Addison Wesley, 2000.

7. P. Dolog and M. Bieliková. Towards Variability Modelling for Reuse in Hypermedia Engineering. In Y. Manolopoulos and P. Návrat, eds., *Proc. of ADBIS 2002, LNCS*, vol. 2435, pages 388–400. Springer, 2002.

8. P. Dolog, N. Henze, W. Nejdl, and M. Sintek. Personalization in Distributed e-Learning Environments. In *Proc. of WWW2004*, May 2004. To appear.

9. P. Dolog and W. Nejdl. Using UML and XMI for Generating Adaptive Navigation Sequences in Web-Based Systems. In P. Stevens, J. Whittle, and G. Booch, eds., *Proc. of UML 2003—The Unified Modeling Language, LNCS*, vol. 2863, pages 205–219. Springer, 2003.

10. P. Fraternali. Tools and Approaches for Developing Data-Intensive Web applications: A survey. *ACM Computing Surveys*, 31(3):227–263, September 1999.

11. F. Garzotto, P. Paolini, and D. Schwabe. HDM—a Model-Based Approach to Hypertext Application Design. *ACM Transactions on Information Systems*, 11(1):1–26, January 1993.

12. O. M. Group. OMG Unified Modelling Language Specification, version 1.3, Mar. 2000. Available at http://www.omg.org/. Accessed on June 1, 2001.

13. O. M. Group. OMG XML Metadata Interchange (XMI) Specification, ersion 1.1, Nov. 2000. Available at http://www.omg.org/. Accessed on June 1, 2002.

14. G. Kappel, B. Proll, W. Retschitzegger, and W. Schwinger. Customization for Ubiquitous Web Applications: a Comparison of Approaches. *International Journal of Web Engineering and Technology*, 11, January 2003.

15. N. Koch and M. Wirsing. The Munich Reference Model for Adaptive Hypermedia Applications. In P. D. Bra, P. Brusilovsky, and R. Conejo, eds., *Proc. of AH2002—Adaptive Hypermedia and Adaptive Web-Based Systems, LNCS*, vol. 2347. Springer, 2002.

16. K. Marriott, B. Meyer, and L. Tardif. Fast and Efficient Client-Side Adaptivity for SVG. In *Proc. of WWW 2002, May 2002, Honolulu, Hawaii, USA*, pages 496–507. ACM Press, 2002.

17. D. Schwabe, R. Guimaraes, and G. Rossi. Cohesive Design of Personalized Web Applications. *IEEE Internet Computing*, 6(2):34–43, March-April 2002.

18. G. South, A. Lenaghan, and R. Malyan. Using Reflection for Service Adaptation in Mobile Clients. Technical report, Kingston University-UK, 2000.

Personalisation Services for Self E-learning Networks*

Kevin Keenoy[1], Alexandra Poulovassilis[1], Vassilis Christophides[2],
Philippe Rigaux[3], George Papamarkos[1], Aimilia Magkanaraki[2],
Miltos Stratakis[2], Nicolas Spyratos[3], and Peter Wood[1]

[1] School of Computer Science and Information Systems, Birkbeck, University of
London {kevin,ap,gpapa05,ptw}@dcs.bbk.ac.uk
[2] Institute of Computer Science, Foundation for Research and Technology – Hellas
(FORTH-ICS) {christop,aimilia,mstratak}@ics.forth.gr
[3] Laboratoire de Recherche en Informatique, Universite Paris-Sud
{rigaux,spyratos}@lri.fr

Abstract. This paper describes the personalisation services designed
for *self e-learning networks* in the SeLeNe project. These include personalised search results, view definition over learning object metadata, metadata generation for composite learning objects and personalised event
and change notification services.

1 Introduction

Life-long learning and the knowledge economy have brought about the need
to support diverse communities of learners throughout their lifetimes. These
learners are geographically distributed and have heterogeneous educational backgrounds and learning needs.

The SeLeNe (*self e-learning networks*) project is investigating the feasibility
of using semantic web technology to support learning communities and match
learners' needs with the educational resources potentially available on the Web.
SeLeNe relies on semantic metadata describing educational material, and is developing services for the discovery, sharing, and collaborative creation of *learning objects* (LOs). A SeLeNe will facilitate access to LOs by managing their
metadata descriptions. In order to enable effective search for LOs in a SeLeNe,
LO descriptions conform to e-learning standards such as IEEE/LOM (Learning Object Metadata), and also employ topic-specific taxonomies of scientific
domains such as ACM/CCS (Computing Classification System) or taxonomies
of detailed learning objectives. LO schemas and descriptions are represented in
the Resource Description Framework/Schema Language (RDF/S), which offers
advanced modelling primitives for the SeLeNe information space.

The diversity and heterogeneity of the communities we envisage using Se-
LeNes means that no single architectural design will be suitable to support all of

---

* A longer version of this document that includes detailed examples is available from
the SeLeNe project website: http://www.dcs.bbk.ac.uk/selene.

N. Koch, P. Fraternali, and M. Wirsing (Eds.): ICWE 2004, LNCS 3140, pp. 215–219, 2004.
© Springer-Verlag Berlin Heidelberg 2004

them. We have thus defined a service-based architecture that can be deployed in a centralised, mediation-based or peer-to-peer fashion, so the deployment option best addressing the needs of any particular learning community can be chosen (see [1]). Figure 1 illustrates the service architecture of a SeLeNe. The facilities that are the focus of this paper are provided by the User Registration, LO Registration, Trails and Adaptation, Event and Change Notification, and View services.

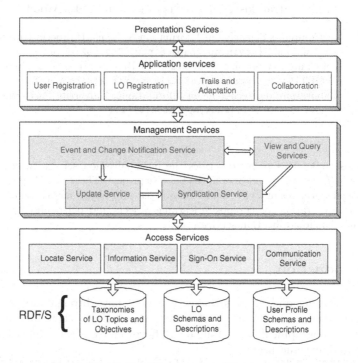

Fig. 1. SeLeNe service architecture

The users of a SeLeNe will include *instructors, learners* and *providers* of LOs. When registering, users will supply information about themselves and their educational objectives in using this SeLeNe, which forms the basis of their *personal profile*. LO authors maintain control of the content they create and will be free to use any tools they wish to create their LOs before registering them. We call such LOs, created externally to SeLeNe, *atomic LOs*. Users will also be able to register new *composite LOs* that have been created as assemblies of LOs already registered with the SeLeNe. The taxonomical descriptions for these LOs can be automatically derived by the SeLeNe from the taxonomical descriptions of its constituent LOs and this process is discussed in Sect. 2. The SeLeNe will provide facilities for defining personalised *views* over the LO information space, discussed in Sect. 3, and also personalised searching facilities, discussed in Sect. 4. Provision of automatic change detection and notification facilities allowing personalised notification services depending on users' profiles is discussed in Sect. 5.

2   Registration of LOs

Registration of a LO with a SeLeNe consists of providing a metadata description including the URI of the LO. An important feature of SeLeNe's LO Registration service will be the ability to automatically infer the *taxonomical* part of the description for a composite LO o, from the taxonomical descriptions of its component LOs $o_1, \ldots, o_n$. This description, which 'summarises' the taxonomical descriptions of the parts of o, is called the *implied taxonomical description* (ITD) of o. This is used to augment the *publisher taxonomical description* (PTD) – the set of terms supplied by the LO's provider (which can be empty) – to derive the final taxonomical description used to register the composite LO.

The ITD of a composite LO o expresses what its parts have in common – only terms reflecting the content of all parts are included in the ITD. A LO may thus generate different ITDs depending on what its 'companion' parts are within a composite LO.

The ITD of a composite LO o composed of parts $o_1, \ldots o_n$ with descriptions $D_1, \ldots, D_n$ is computed by a simple algorithm that takes the cartesian product of $D_1, \ldots, D_n$, computes the least upper bound of each n-tuple and then 'reduces' the resulting set of terms by removing all but the minimal terms according to the subsumption relation $\preceq$ between the terms of the taxonomy. The overall taxonomical description of a LO o is computed by another simple algorithm: if o is atomic then its taxonomical description is just its PTD. Otherwise its taxonomical description is recursively computed from its PTD and the taxonomical descriptions of its constituent parts. Readers are referred to [2] for more details of both algorithms.

3   Declarative Queries and Views

Finding LOs in a SeLeNe will rely on RQL [3], a declarative query language offering browsing and querying facilities over the RDF/S descriptions that form the SeLeNe information space.

As well as the advanced querying facilities provided by an expressive RDF/S query language such as RQL, personalisation of LO descriptions and schemas is also needed. For instance, a learner might want LOs presented according to his/her educational level and current course of study. To enhance the SeLeNe user's experience we need the ability to personalise the way the information space can be viewed, by providing simpler virtual schemas that reflect an instructor's or learner's perception of the domain of interest. This will be done by using the RVL language [4], which provides this ability by offering techniques for the reconciliation and integration of heterogeneous metadata describing LOs, and for the definition of personalised views over a SeLeNe information space.

One of the most significant features of RVL is its ability to create virtual schemas by simply populating the two core RDF/S metaclasses *Class* and *Property*. A SeLeNe user can then easily formulate queries *on the view* itself. RVL can also be used to implement advanced user aids such as *personalised navigation* and *knowledge maps*.

4   Trails and Query Adaptation

Personalisation of query results will rely on the *personal profile*. This is an RDF description of the user including some elements from existing profile schemas (PAPI-Learner and IMS-LIP), some of our own elements (we have defined RDF schemas for expressing competencies, learning goals and learning styles), and a history of user activity that will allow the profile to adapt over time.

Although the underlying query mechanism in SeLeNe is RQL, users will mostly search for LOs using simple keyword-based queries. Search results will be personalised by *filtering* and *ranking* the LOs returned according to the information contained in the user's personal profile. This is done by the Trails and Adaptation service, which constructs personalised RQL queries for execution and generates personalised rankings of query results by matching the personal profile against relevant parts of the LO descriptions.

SeLeNe will give the user the option of having their query results presented as a list of *trails* of LOs, suggesting sequences of LO interaction. These trails will be automatically derived from information contained in the LO descriptions about the semantic relationships between LOs. We have defined an RDF representation of trails as a sub-class of the RDF *Sequence* (a sequence of LOs) with two associated properties, *name* and *annotation*.

5   Event and Change Notification

We provide SeLeNe's reactive functionality by means of event-condition-action (ECA) rules over SeLeNe's RDF/S metadata. This includes features such as:

- automatic propagation of changes in the description of one resource to the descriptions of other, related resources (e.g., propagating changes in the taxonomical description of a LO to those of any composite LOs depending on it; propagating changes in a learner's history of accesses of LOs to the learner's personal profile; automatic generation and update of 'emergent' trails);
- automatic notification to users of the registration of new LOs of interest to them;
- automatic notification to users of changes in the description of resources of interest to them.

SeLeNe's RDF ECA rules will be automatically generated by the higher-level Presentation and Application services, and may be resource-specific or generic (i.e., they might or might not reference specific RDF resources).

Peers that support the Event and Change Notification service will run an *ECA Engine* consisting of three main components: an *Event Detector*, *Condition Evaluator* and *Action Scheduler*. The Query service is invoked firstly by the Event Detector to determine which rules have been triggered by the most recent update to the local description base, and again by the Condition Evaluator to determine which of the triggered rules should fire. The Action Scheduler generates a list of updates from the action parts of these rules, which are then passed to the Update service for execution. We refer the reader to [5] for a description of the syntax and semantics of our RDF ECA rules, and some examples.

6   Concluding Remarks

This paper has described several novel techniques for providing the personalisation services of *self e-learning networks*. The novel aspects of SeLeNe compared with other related systems[1] include:

- collaborative creation and semi-automatic description of composite LOs;
- declarative views over combined RDFS/RDF descriptions (i.e. over both the LO descriptions and their schemas);
- personalised event and change notification services;
- automatic generation of trails of LOs from their descriptions.

We are currently implementing and integrating the components of SeLeNe. A number of open issues remain. Firstly, there is as yet no standard query or update language for RDF, although we believe that the RQL, RVL and RDF ECA languages we have described here provide sound and expressive foundations for the development of such standards. Secondly, whatever standards eventually emerge for such RDF languages, if ECA rules are to be supported on RDF repositories then the event sub-language for RDF ECA rules needs to be designed so that it matches up with the actions sub-language; another important open area is combining ECA rules with transactions and consistency maintenance in RDF repositories. Thirdly, our algorithms for personalised ranking of query results need to be empirically evaluated. Finally, the design of user interfaces enabling easy and intuitive access to SeLeNe's advanced personalisation services will be crucial – users will need to be shielded from the complexities of RDF and the RQL, RVL and ECA languages, and also from the complex taxonomies of topics, competencies and goals in use by the system.

References

1. The SeLeNe Consortium: An architectural framework and deployment choices for SeLeNe. See http://www.dcs.bbk.ac.uk/selene/reports/Del5-1.0.pdf (2004)
2. Rigaux, P., Spyratos, N.: Generation and syndication of learning object metadata. See http://www.dcs.bbk.ac.uk/selene/reports/Del4.1-2.2.pdf (2004)
3. Karvounarakis, G., Alexaki, S., Christophides, V., Plexousakis, D., Scholl, M.: RQL: A declarative query language for RDF. In: Proceedings of the Eleventh International World Wide Web Conference 2002, Honolulu, Hawaii, USA (2002) 592–603
4. Magkanaraki, A., Tannen, V., Christophides, V., Plexousakis, D.: Viewing the semantic web through RVL lenses. In: Proceedings of the Second International Semantic Web Conference (ISWC'03), Sanibel Island, Florida, USA (2003)
5. Papamarkos, G., Poulovassilis, A., Wood, P.T.: RDFTL: An Event-Condition-Action language for RDF. In: Proceedings of the 3rd International Workshop on Web Dynamics. (2004) See www.dcs.bbk.ac.uk/webDyn3/.

---

[1] Such as UNIVERSAL (www.ist-universal.org), Edutella (edutella.jxta.org), Elena (www.elena-project.org), SWAP (swap.semanticweb.org).

Personalizing Web Sites for Mobile Devices Using a Graphical User Interface

Leonardo Teixeira Passos[1] and Marco Tulio Valente[2]*

[1] Department of Computer Science, Catholic University of Minas Gerais, Brazil
[2] Department of Computer Science, FUMEC University, Brazil
ltpassos@pucmg.br, mtov@pucminas.br

Abstract. Despite recent advances in wireless and portable hardware technologies, mobile access to the Web is often laborious. For this reason, several solutions have been proposed to customize Web pages to mobile access. In this paper, we describe a wrapper system that targets the personalization of Web pages to mobile devices. A personalization is a subpage of a given web page containing just the information that mobile users would like to access using a PDA.

1 Introduction

Mobile access to the web is often laborious, since most of the web content was not produced for mobile devices. In the last few years, several solutions have been proposed to customize and adapt Web pages to mobile access. In general, these solutions can be disposed on three categories: (i) redesign of web sites for use in mobile devices; (ii) usage of transcoders, i.e., proxies responsible for reformatting web pages, such as Digestor [2] and PowerBrowser [3]; (iii) usage of wrappers, i.e., programs that automatically retrieve and extract particular content from Web documents, such as Lixto [1], WebViews [4] and Smartview [6].

In this paper, we describe a wrapper system that targets the *personalization* of Web pages to mobile computing devices. A personalization is a subpage of a web page that contains just the information a given user would like to access using a PDA. The proposed personalization system – called PWA – meets the following requirements: (i) it supports personalization of standard web pages, despite if they are well-formed or not; (ii) it supports personalizations that are robust to common changes in Web pages; (iii) it supports the creation of personalizations using a GUI, requiring no pattern matching language programming.

The rest of this paper is organized as follows. In Section 2 the architecture of the system is described, along with its algorithms and data structures. Section 3 presents the first results we have obtained in the creation of personalizations and Section 4 concludes the paper.

---

* This research was supported by FAPEMIG (grant CEX488/02).

N. Koch, P. Fraternali, and M. Wirsing (Eds.): ICWE 2004, LNCS 3140, pp. 220–224, 2004.

2   The PWA System

The PWA system has two basic modules: the personalization definition system and the personalization server. These two modules are described next.

2.1   Personalization Definition System

The personalization definition system is in charge of creating extraction expressions, i.e., expressions that when applied to a web page return the corresponding subpage.

User Interface: In the PWA system the creation of extraction expressions happens in a desktop computer. The following steps are required:

1. The user should accesses the web page he want to personalize using a standard browser.
2. Using the mouse, the user should select the components of the page he wants to access later in his mobile device. The selection process is identical to the one used to select texts in standard editors.
3. The user should copy the selected text to the clipboard.
4. The user should start the personalization definition system and choose the option *New Personalization* in its main menu. From the text saved in the clipboard, the system will generate an extraction expression and will present the personalization associated to this expression to the user.
5. If the user is satisfied with the personalization, he should choose the *Export Personalization* option in the main menu. The personalization will be saved in the personalization server.

This process is fully based on standard browsers and in the built-in *copy-and-paste* facility provided by common window systems.

Data Structures: In order to create an extraction expression, the personalization definition system relies on the following data structures: (i) *list of tags*, i.e., a linear list whose nodes store information about the tags and the text of the target web page; (ii) *buffer*, i.e., an array containing just the raw text of the target web page. (iii) *mapper*, i.e., a function from $Int \rightarrow Int$. A mapping like $i \rightarrow k$ means that the text stored in the i-th position in the buffer comes from the k-th text node in the list of tags.

Figure 1 describes the previous data structures for the fragment of a simple web page. The design of the PWA system was inspired in the MVC architecture [5]. The previous data structures represent the model in the MVC architecture, the browser represents the view and the clipboard the controller.

Extraction Expression: The algorithm used to create the extraction expression has as input value the text T that the user has selected and copied to the clipboard. First, T is matched against the *buffer*, resulting in the range of buffer indexes $[ib, jb]$. If T occurs more than once in the buffer, the intervention of the

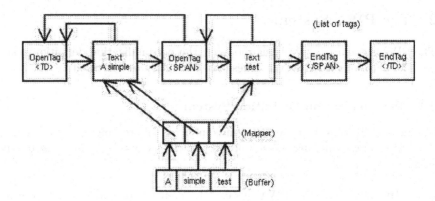

Fig. 1. *List of Tags, buffer* and *mapper* structures

user is requested to select the appropriate match. Next, using the *mapper* function, the range $[ib, jb]$ is translated to indexes $[i, j]$ in the *list of tags* containing the nodes where T is stored. The sublist of the list of tags defined by indices $[i, j]$ is called S. The extraction expression is composed by the tuple: (N, U, T, i, j, S), where N is the name given to the expression by the user and U is the URL from the associated web page. This tuple is exported to the personalization server.

2.2   Personalization Server

The PWA server performs the following tasks: (i) it receives requests for personalizations from mobile users; (ii) it retrieves the web page associated to the requested personalization; (iii) using the extraction expression previously informed by the personalization definition system, it extracts the requested personalization from the retrieved web page; (iv) it sends the personalization to the device of the mobile user.

Data Structures: Besides the data structures described on Section 2.1, the personalization server makes use of an extra structure, called *Skeleton*. The skeleton is a copy of the *list of tags* except by the fact that tags that only provide formatting information (such as <B>, <I> etc), programs (such as <APPLET>, <SCRIPT>) and images (such as <IMG>) are purged. Tags not presented in the skeleton are called *volatile*. Volatile tags are often removed and inserted in web pages. Therefore, expression extractions that consider them can easily break.

Extraction Algorithm: The extraction algorithm has as input value the extraction expression (N, U, T, i, j, S) previously saved in the personalization server by the personalization definition system. The algorithm has the following steps:

1. The page associated to URL U is retrieved and the *buffer*, *mapper* and *list of tags* data structures described on Section 2.1 are created for this page.

2. The text T is matched against the *buffer*. If this match succeeds and the matched indexes are the same indexes $[i, j]$ saved in the extraction expression, the personalization is the sublist S. This happens when the associated web page is static (i.e., its content does not change with the time) and its structure has also not changed since the time the extraction expression was created.

3. If the previous step fails, this means that the page has changed. Then, the idea is to verify if the change is restricted to the content of the personalization, i.e., if the tags (or the structure) of the personalization remains unchanged. Therefore, the sublist S is matched against the full *list of tags* created in the step 1. A sublist S' located in the indexes $[i', j']$ of the list of tags is the returned personalization if it matches S. In case of multiple matched sublists, we chose the one closest to the original position of S, i.e., the match where $|i - i'|$ is minimum.

4. If the previous step fails, this means that both the content and the structure of personalization have changed. The idea is to verify if the changes were restricted to the insertion or removal of volatile tags. First, the *skeleton* data structure is created. Next, the volatile tags of S are removed and a new sublist S' is created. This new sublist is matched against the skeleton. A sublist S'' located in the indexes $[i'', j'']$ of the skeleton is the returned personalization if it matches S'. In case of multiple matches, we chose the one closest to the original position of S, i.e., the match where $|i - i''|$ is minimum.

Table 1. Experimental Results. Column *Success* contains the number of days the personalization was extracted successfully. Column *Changes Inside* contains the number of days the original page has undergone changes inside the area of the personalization. Column *Changes Outside* contains the number of days the original page has undergone changes outside the area of the personalization.

Site	Success	Changes Inside	Changes Outside
Bloomberg (Insight & Commentary)	13	13	13
Bloomberg (Market Snapshot)	13	0	13
Yahoo Sports	13	13	13
Google News	12	13	13

Suppose that P is the personalization returned by the previous algorithm. This personalization is a list containing tags and text. Most of the time, this raw list cannot be directly transmitted to mobile devices, since it does not contain appropriate *context tags*. For example, maybe the first tag of P is a <TD>. However, a <TD> can never appear without an enclosing <TR>, and this last cannot exist without an enclosing <TABLE>. Thus, the personalization P is augmented with appropriate context tags before it is sent to the mobile user.

3   Experimental Results

In order to validate the PWA system, we have created personalizations associated to the following sites: www.bloomberg.com (two personalizations, comprising the *Market Snapshot* and the *Insight & Commentary* sections of the page), news.google.com, (one personalization comprising the *Top Stories* section of the page) and sports.yahoo.com (one personalization comprising the top headline section). We have accessed these personalizations during 13 days, in order to verify the robustness of the proposed extraction algorithm. Table 1 summarizes the results we have obtained in this experiment.

As described in Table 1, the personalizations for the Bloomberg and Yahoo Sports web page have remained working for the whole duration of the experiment. The only personalization that has broken during the test was the one associated to the Google News page. This personalization has not produced the expected content in the 13th day of the experiment. The reason was a radical change in the structure of the personalization.

4   Concluding Remarks

We consider that the PWA system presents the following contributions:

- The definition of personalizations by end-users is fully based on a GUI, integrated to a standard browser and to the system clipboard. This GUI is structured according to the well-known MVC model.
- Our first experiments have shown that the proposed extraction algorithm is robust to a considerable types of changes. Particularly, it is fairly robust to changes outside the personalization area. Moreover, its is robust to changes inside the personalization if they affect only volatile tags.

As part of future work, we will focus on the definition of personalizations including different and non-continuous sections of the same web page. Finally, more extensive experiments will be performed.

References

1. R. Baumgartner, S. Flesca, and G. Gottlob. Visual web information extraction with Lixto. In *The VLDB Journal*, pages 119–128, 2001.
2. W. Bickmore and B. Schilit. Digestor: Device-independent access to the world-wide web. In *6th World Wide Web Conference*, 1997.
3. O. Buyukkokten, H. Garcia-Molina, A. Paepcke, and T. Winograd. Power browser: Efficient web browsing for PDAs. In *Conference on Human Factors in Computing Systems*, pages 430–437, 2000.
4. J. Freire, B. Kumar, and D. F. Lieuwen. Webviews: accessing personalized web content and services. In *10th World Wide Web Conference*, pages 576–586, 2001.
5. G. E. Krasner and S. T. Pope. A cookbook for using the model–view–controller user interface paradigm in smalltalk-80. In *Journal of Object Oriented Programming*, pages 26–49, Aug. 1988.
6. N. Milic-Frayling and R. Sommerer. Smartview: Flexible viewing of web page contents. In *11th World Wide Web Conference (poster presentaion)*, 2002.

Personalizing Digital Libraries at Design Time: The Miguel de Cervantes Digital Library Case Study*

Alejandro Bia, Irene Garrigós, and Jaime Gómez

Web Engineering Group. DLSI
University of Alicante, Spain
{abia, igarrigos, jgomez}@dlsi.ua.es

Abstract. In this article we describe our experience in the development of a personalizable dissemination model for the Miguel de Cervantes Digital Library's Web-based newsletter-service, which combines adaptive with adaptable personalization techniques, being capable or ranking news according to navigation-inferred preferences and then filter them according to a user-given profile. We explain how Web engineering design techniques have been applied to make that service evolve into a more adaptive personalization approach obtaining more effective results. The work is presented in the context of the OO-H [5] web design method.

1 Introduction

The Miguel de Cervantes Digital Library (MCDL) of the University of Alicante is the biggest electronic publishing project in Spain, and perhaps the biggest digital library of Spanish texts on the Internet, currently with more than 10000 entries in its catalogue. One of the goals of the MCDL is to act as a communication channel for the academic community. In this sense we have implemented a number of communication services, and we try to maintain a permanent communication with our readers. It is obvious that the personalization of these services is a key issue in the management of the DL in order to get a better use.

The idea of giving the user the impression of interacting with the application by means of a dedicated interface, specifically tailored to the user's needs and preferences is a "must" in current Web development. Content personalization systems select, adapt and generate contents according to user models that define information needs. Dissemination models help to achieve this goal. In a dissemination model environment, users subscribe to an information dissemination service by submitting a set of personalization settings that describe their interests, which are usually called profiles. Then they passively receive information filtered according to such profiles. Enhanced dissemination models allows the sender of such information to get a feedback of the users interests, which may evolve with time, or to get a feedback of the users opinions on the information received. In this context, user profile and preferences can be acquired in three ways [1]: be set by the application designer by

---

* This paper has been partially supported by the Spanish Ministry of Science and Technology (Ministerio de Ciencia y Tecnología de España), project TIC2001-3530-C02-02.

N. Koch, P. Fraternali, and M. Wirsing (Eds.): ICWE 2004, LNCS 3140, pp. 225–229, 2004.

means of *stereotyped* techniques, be given by the users themselves by means of *interview* techniques (this includes input forms) or be automatically inferred by the application based on user activity (*observation* techniques). The applications of the second type are also referred to as "*adaptable*" while the third type are "*adaptive*", and when the origin of personalization information is a system event we talk about "*proactive*" applications [2, 3].

2   Personalization of the Newsletter Service: Ranking and Filtering

In the first stage, our profile was very simple and allowed only for the choice of one or more possible thematic newsletters out of five [4]. In the second stage of development, we have remodeled the personalization approach to both offer a finer granularity (more detailed personalization choices) and also obtain explicit (adaptable approach) and implicit (adaptive approach) feedback from users which allows for dynamic changes in personalization settings and will also provide, as said before, useful information on user navigation habits and preferences. The user model we have implemented for newsletters automatically and transparently incorporates information gathered from user navigation (adaptive part). In addition, the user can set-up some filtering restrictions and customization preferences when registering for this service (adaptable part). The final model is based both on implicit interests on certain digital library sections (information gathered during navigation) and on explicit preferences that compose the user profile.

News are classified by category and subject-matter. Categories are: new publications (new digital resources), future publications, new sections, chat announcements, call for papers, suggestions from our departments, letters from readers, visits of important people, contests, and the remainder are classified as general news. Subjects or matters are derived from the actual thematic structure of the DL. Each theme section or subcollection generates a subject-matter, as for instance: Latin-American literature, humanities research, history, children's literature, theatre, interactive services of the DL, computers and humanities, critical studies, tribute to Hispanists, Argentine Academy of Letters, PhD theses, movies, magazines/journals, recently printed books, law, and many more. This allows for a very fine granularity. Every time the user clicks on an entry of the newsletter's table of contents, the Web page jumps to a single piece of news, and the server increments in one the corresponding category and subject-matter counters. Only one category but multiple subjects can be assigned to a piece of news. Relative access frequencies can be computed for categories and for subjects. Then news can be given a ranking value for a given user for a given news-reading session, which is calculated as the sum of subject frequencies of the subjects corresponding to a given piece of news, multiplied by the frequency of its category. For instance, if a user has an access frequency of 0.3 for the "new-publications" category, and, 0.1 for the "history" and 0.2 for the "PhD-theses" subjects, then a piece of news announcing the publication of a PhD thesis on history will weight $(0.1 + 0.2)$ $0.3 = 0.09$, and will be ranked accordingly. On registration, the users can specify Boolean constraints for categories and subjects, saying which ones should be sorted out and which should be displayed. This profile can be modified by the user.

Newsletters are accessed through a monthly index, where news are ordered first by category and then by subject, according to the dynamically computed ranking. But not all the ranked news appear, they are filtered according to the user explicit profile. The first N^1 ranked entries that pass the filter are shown openly, and the rest appear as a collapsed "more news" button.

3 Adapting the MCDL Using the OO-H Personalization Frame-Work

The OO-H (*Object Oriented Hypermedia*) method [5] is a generic model, based on the object oriented paradigm that provides the designer with the semantics and notation necessary for the development of web-based interfaces. Web design modelling is achieved by means of the two complementary views, namely (1) the Navigational Access Diagram, that enriches a standard UML class diagram with navigation and interaction properties, and (2) the Abstract Presentation Diagram that gathers the concepts related both to structure of the site and specific presentation details respectively. OO-H also supports dynamic personalization (described in [6]), allowing the designer to better tailor the site to the particularities and needs of the individual user. This is done by means of a personalization framework that is a part of the model. That framework can be instantiated by the web designer, and connected to any OO-H based site to empower it with personalization support for (individual) users. The framework can be divided in two parts: (1) the user model, which allows to store the beliefs and knowledge the system has about the user, and (2) the personalization model, which is used to specify the personalization strategy for the different groups of users.

In the context of the MCDL, we have used this approach to personalize the newsletters. In Figure 1 we can see the user model for the MCDL case study.

The user model represents the variable part of the conceptual model. We have two association classes in which we store by *subject-matter* and by *category* the number of times that the user consults a piece of news. We also store the user preferences in a class that the user can change when desired.

The personalization model allows the designer to define a collection of rules that can be used to define a personalization strategy for a user or group of users. The rules are Event-Condition-Action [6] rules: they are triggered by a certain event (e.g. a browsing action, the start of a session) and if a certain condition is fulfilled, the associated action is performed. Figure 2 shows the NAD corresponding to this modeling example. The NAD's entry point is a link to a user-connection parameters form to access the system (login, password). Registered users are shown a link to access the newsletter. The personalization rule is attached to it. When the user clicks on it, a table of contents appears, showing the ranked and filtered list of news. To determine the user interest in a piece of news, we have the *Acquisition* rule that is attached to the "consult" service link. In this rule we'll acquire the number of times a user consults a piece of news and its related *subject-matters* and *category*, and using these two attributes together with the user-set preferences profile, we rank and filter

---

[1] N is a user given parameter.

228   A. Bia, I. Garrigós, and J. Gómez

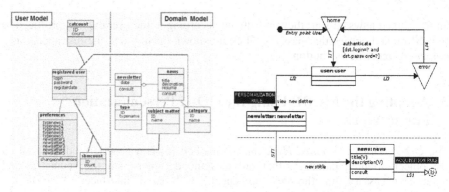

Fig. 1. User and Domain models   **Fig. 2.** NAD for the newsletters system

the news according to the user's interests. The ranking is computed with the above described algorithm. Later, this NAD is compiled to obtain the XML specification that is interpreted by a rules engine to give personalization support to our application. That compilation process produces 2 types of XML specs acquisition rules and personalization rules that are presented next.

Acquisition Rule: Below the dotted line of figure 2, we can see the part of the NAD diagram that holds the rule that stores the preferences information (acquisition rule). Every time a user consults a piece of news (event that triggers the rule), the corresponding subject-matters and category counters must be incremented. To store this information (in the user model), we need to check whether the subject-matter and category of the piece of news the user has consulted are the same we are going to update in the User model. With these data we can predict the user preferences. The XML specification of the acquisition rule defined by our system follows:

```
<rule type="acquisition" name="StorePreferences" >
  <params>
        <param name="idsbm"
  value="session.registereduser.newsletter.news.subjectmatter.id"/>
        <param name="idcat"
  value="session.registereduser.newsletter.news.category.id"/>
  </params>
        <event type="MethodInvocation" link="Consult"/>
  <condition "idsbm=newstittle.news.subjectmatter.id and
      idcat=newstittle.news.category.id"/>
  <action value="session.registereduser.sbmcount.count++
      and session.registereduser.catcount.count++" />
</rule>
```

We use the subject-matter and category identifiers of the piece of news as parameters of the rule, to simplify the expressions.

Personalization Rule: Above the dotted line of figure 2, we can see the part of the NAD diagram that holds the rule that models this requirement (personalization rule). When the link *View Newsletter* is activated the rule is triggered. In this case we have navigation personalization, because we have to sort the links the user is going to see. We have the two attributes as parameters (stored in the user model by the acquisition rule). The personalization event indicates that the link *View Newsletter* must be active. When this link is activated, the action will be executed: the news are sorted and shown.

```
<rule type="personalization:navigation" name="Recommendations" >
    <params>
        <param name="sbmcount" value="
session.registereduser.sbmcountcount "/>
        <param name="catcount" value="
session.registereduser.catcountcount "/>
    </params>
    <event type="Navigation" link="View newsletter"/>
    <action type="Sort" link="newstittle" byval1="sbmcount"
byval2="catcount" ORDER="DESC"/>
</rule>
```

4 Conclusions

Concerning the dissemination model for these newsletters, we have enhanced the granularity by offering more detailed personalization options, which allow us to rank the news based on preferences gathered from user navigation (observation model). The design of this solution was performed according to the OO-H Model. This technology can significantly increase the productivity at the time of developing Web applications. The MCDL, with this effort, struggles to fulfill its objective of spreading research knowledge to the global academic community through the Web. Our goal is not only the mere publication of research work, but to build a rich and open communication channel for the global scientific community. The newsletter service described here plays a key role in this communication effort.

References

1. Nora Koch. *Software Engineering for Adaptive Hypermedia Systems: Reference Model, Modeling Techniques and Development Process*. PhD thesis, Institut für Informatik, Ludwig-Maximilians-Universität München, December 2000.
2. Gerti, Kappel, Werner, Retschitzegger, Brirgit, Pöll, and Wieland, Schwinger. Modeling Ubiquitous Web Applications . Thw WUML Apporach. In: Proccedings of the International Workshop on Data Semantics in Web Information Systems. Yokohama, Japan. 2001 (11).
3. Wu, H. A Reference Architecture for Adaptive Hyermedia Systems. 2001.
4. Alejandro Bia and Jaime Gómez, Developing a simple production and dissemination model for a complex DL-news service using XML, XSLT and TEI., RCDL'03 Saint Petersburg State University, Moscow, 29-31 October 2003.
5. J. Gómez, C. Cachero. OO-H method: Extending UML to Model Web Interfaces. Information Modeling for Internet Applications. Pages. 50-72. Idea Group. 2002
6. .I. Garrigós, J. Gómez and C. Cachero. Modeling Dynamic Personalization in Web Applications. 'Third International Conference on Web Engineering (ICWE'03), LNCS 2722, pages 472-475. Springer-Verlag Berlin Heidelberg, 07 2003.

Comparison of Two Approaches for Automatic Construction of Web Applications: Annotation Approach and Diagram Approach

Mitsuhisa Taguchi, Kornkamol Jamroendararasame,
Kazuhiro Asami, and Takehiro Tokuda

Department of Computer Science, Tokyo Institute of Technology
Meguro, Tokyo 152-8552, Japan
{mtaguchi, konkamol, asami, tokuda}@tt.cs.titech.ac.jp

Abstract. In order to support development of consistent and secure Web applications, we have designed a number of Web application generators. These generators can be classified into two types of approaches: annotation approach and diagram approach. In this paper, we try to make the roles of these generators clear, and compare two approaches in terms of target applications, developing processes and target users. While both approaches are powerful and flexible enough to construct typical Web applications efficiently, we may select the most appropriate generator according to the characteristics of the application and the developing process.

1 Introduction

Today, Web applications such as database query systems and transaction systems are widely used especially on the Internet. The development of such applications, however, requires much cost and experience of developers because of the complexity of security checks and session management, which are unique to Web applications. In order to support development of consistent and secure Web applications, we have designed a number of Web application generators which generate source codes necessary to execute the application [1,2,3,4,5,6, 7,8,9]. Web application generators encapsulate the complexity unique to Web applications and make developers concentrate on the business logic of the application.

Our generators can be classified into two types of approaches. The first is annotation approach, which concentrates on input data and embedded values on each Web page [1,2]. Developers first compose Web page templates and give declarative annotations to them. And then the generator generates procedural program codes from Web page templates with annotations. The second is diagram approach, which concentrates on data-flow relationships in the application [3,4,5,6,7,8,9]. Developers first compose diagrams which describe overall data-flow relationships among Web components such as Web page templates, server

N. Koch, P. Fraternali, and M. Wirsing (Eds.): ICWE 2004, LNCS 3140, pp. 230–243, 2004.

side programs and databases. After developers select appropriate program templates and components, a generator can generate executable program codes from the diagrams.

Each approach has assumptions and roles in developing processes. Developers can select the most appropriate generator according to the characteristics of the application and the developing process. In this paper, we try to make the roles of these generators clear, and compare the two approaches in terms of target applications, developing processes and target users. We also give discussions on our future work based on this comparison.

The organization of the rest of this paper is as follows. In section 2 and section 3, we describe annotation approach and diagram approach, and give examples of our generator systems based on each approach. In section 4, we compare two approaches in terms of target applications, developing processes and target users. In section 5 we give related work. We finally give future work and concluding remarks in section 6.

2 Annotation Approach

2.1 Basic Idea of Annotation Approach

From the viewpoint of user interfaces, we can consider general Web applications as transitions between Web pages just like ordinary Web pages that have no server side programs. In most Web applications, the greater part of each Web page template is static, and a part of the template is dynamic where actual values are embedded by server side programs. Based on this idea, we present annotation approach to automatic construction of Web applications. In annotation approach, we describe dynamic part of Web page templates as declarative annotations. More precisely, the following steps are taken in the generation method.

1. We first construct Web page templates for intended Web applications. Web page composers and other support tools may be used to visually compose Web page templates efficiently. Dynamic part of the templates, where values are embedded at run time, may be described as special characters to distinguish from static part.
2. We give annotations to dynamic part of Web page templates. Our annotations are declaration of data processing which is executed on the server side. Their tasks are mainly related to data-flow relationships among Web components as follows.
   - For input data checking, such as checking acceptable types and length of input values and constraints between them.
   - For session management, such as checking the beginning and the end of the session.
   - For database handling, such as the access to database management systems using queres.
   - For communications with external programs, such as invocation of Web services, EJB components and other applications.

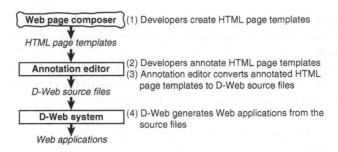

Fig. 1. The architecture of A-Web system

3. From Web page templates with annotations, a Web application generator automatically generates source codes of server side programs. Generated programs have consistency and the standard level of security because the generator checks transitions and parameters between Web page templates, and generates additional codes to prevent inconsistency.

2.2 Generator: A-Web System

Based on annotation approach, we designed and implemented a prototype generator called A-Web system which generates Web applications from Web page templates [1,2]. While our current prototype can generate only CGI programs, we may be able to generate Web applications based on other architecture by replacing part of the generator because annotation approach itself is independent of specific architecture.

The architecture of A-Web system is shown in Fig.1. A-Web system consists of two parts: an annotation editor and a Web application generator called D-Web system.

Web page templates. Before using A-Web system, Web page templates should be prepared as input of the system. We can compose Web page templates using visual composers and other support tools because A-Web system requires ordinary XHTML documents. Dynamic part of the templates should be represented by special characters ${scope.valiable}$. *Variable* is a name to distinguish from other variables among the application and should be unique in each *scope*. Because the special characters are ordinary strings, not extension of HTML tags, common tools can deal with these templates. Thus it is unnecessary for us to modify the source codes directly.

Fig.2 shows an example of Web page templates of a simple member registration system. This application first requires users to input id and password which the user chooses, a name, an email address and so on at a Web page 'Registration'. If the id is already registered or the input data don't satisfy specified conditions, a Web page 'Error' is generated. Otherwise a Web page

Fig. 2. An example of Web page templates

'Confirmation' is generated. After the confirmation, the registration becomes definite.

An annotation editor. An annotation editor is a part of A-Web system, which is an editor to annotate Web page templates and convert them to D-Web source documents. When the editor gets Web page templates, it analyzes the templates, points out where we can give annotations and allows us to give annotations visually. In our prototype, we introduce five types of annotations: input check, constraint, session, SQL and SOAP.

An input check annotation defines conditions for acceptable users' input. If the input is strings, we can define the length and types of acceptable characters. If the input is numbers, we can define a range of acceptable numbers.

A constraint annotation defines relations which must be satisfied among input data.

A session annotation defines the behavior of session management for each template. When a user accesses a Web page with a session annotation 'begin', the program starts the new session. In the case of 'check', the program checks whether the session is valid or not. In the case of 'end', the program terminates the session.

A SQL annotation describes SQL statements to access database management systems. We can deal with database transactions.

A SOAP annotation describes statements to invoke external Web services using SOAP protocol.

Fig.3 shows an annotation editor in A-Web system. It analyzes Web page templates and adds hyperlinks to special annotation pages automatically.

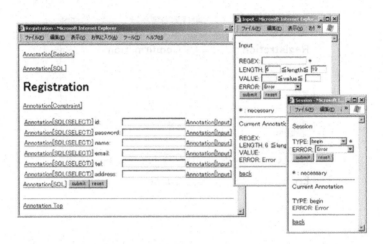

Fig. 3. An annotation editor of A-Web system

```html
<html>
<head>
  <title>Registration</title>
  <session type="begin" error="Error.html"/>
</head>
<body>
  <h1>Registration</h1>
  <form action="Confirmation.html" method="Post">
    id:<input type="text" name="id" length="[6,10]"/>
      ---- omit following parts ----
</body></html>
```

Fig. 4. An example of D-Web source codes

Fig.3 shows 'Registration' page, a session annotation page and an input annotation page. Fig.4 shows an example of D-Web source codes, which are generated by the annotation editor from a Web page template 'Registration' and its annotations. D-Web source codes have a number of extended tags.

D-Web system. D-Web system is a part of A-Web system, which gets D-Web source documents and generates source codes of Web applications. In our prototype, D-Web system generates XHTML documents and CGI programs written in Perl. To keep consistency of generated applications, D-Web system analyzes all variables in Web page templates and transitions between Web pages, and gives methods to pass the values between Web pages correctly. To keep the standard level of security, all generated programs have additional codes as follows.

1. After receiving input data, each program checks whether the user comes from correct Web page.

2. Then each program checks whether user's session id is valid.
3. Then each program checks whether input data are correct according to input check annotations.

If there is at least one error, the user's request is redirected to an error page.

3 Diagram Approach

3.1 Basic Idea of Diagram Approach

From the viewpoint of data-flow relationships among Web components such as Web pages and programs, we can consider Web applications as applications based on pipes and filters architecture. A filter corresponds to a server side program and a pipe corresponds to a Web page which passes data between programs. Based on this idea, we present diagram approach to automatic construction of Web applications. In diagram approach, we first compose diagrams describing overall behavior of the application and select general-purpose templates and components to generate executable applications. More precisely, the following steps are generally taken in the generation method using this approach.

1. We first compose directed graphs whose nodes represent Web components such as Web page templates, server side programs and databases, and whose edges represent data-flow relationships among the components. Most of our generators use diagrams called *Web transition diagrams* which we designed for the above purpose.
2. All generators based on diagram approach have predefined program templates and components which are independent of specific domains of applications, for example, for purposes of database manipulations, sending electronic mails. Referring specifications of these programs, we give correspondence between nodes in diagrams and the programs, and give values of parameters of them.
3. From the descriptions of diagrams and values of parameters, a generator automatically generates Web page templates and source codes of server side programs. Generated programs have consistency and the standard level of security, because the generator checks consistency of the diagrams, checks correspondence between diagrams and predefined programs, and then generates additional codes to prevent inconsistency.

3.2 Generator: T-Web System

Based on diagram approach, we designed and implemented a prototype generator called T-Web system which generates Web applications from directed graphs called Web transition diagrams [3,4,5,6,7,8,9]. While we have prototypes to generate CGI programs, JSP/Servlet programs and ASP programs respectively, we may be able to generate applications based on other architecture by replacing part of the generators because diagram approach itself is independent of specific architecture of Web applications.

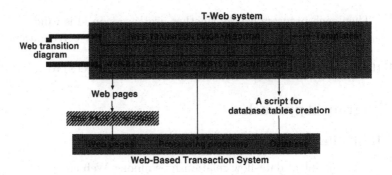

Fig. 5. The architecture of T-Web system

In this section, we explain the basic architecture of T-Web system on the basis of the generator for JSP/Servlet-based applications. The architecture of T-Web system is shown in Fig.5. T-Web system consists of two parts: a Web transition diagram editor and a Web application generator.

Web transition diagrams. In T-Web system, we describe overall behavior of intended application as directed graphs called Web transition diagrams. Basically, Web transition diagrams consist of four types of nodes and two types of links as follows.

- **A fixed Web page node** is a static Web page which can be reached by a certain URL. Its notation is a rectangle with its name, whose line is thick. It may have a number of page elements such as hyperlinks and input fields inside the rectangle.

- **A output Web page node** is a dynamic Web page which is generated by a server side program. Its notation is a rectangle with its name, whose line is thin. Like a fixed Web page node, it may have a number of page elements.

- **A processing node** is a server side program which is activated by users' requests to perform processing. Its notation is an oval with its name.

- **A database node** is a relational database table in a database server. Its notation is a cylinder with its name. The schema of the table is represented by a list of names between '{' and '}'.

- **A page transition link** is a hyperlink relationship between Web pages. Its notation is a directed line.

- **A data-flow link** is a data-flow relationship among Web components such as Web pages, programs and database tables. Its notation is a directed line with a blocked line.

Each generator may have some extension of Web transition diagrams according to the target architecture. Fig.6 shows an example of Web transition diagrams of a simple member registration system which is the same application as given in section 2.

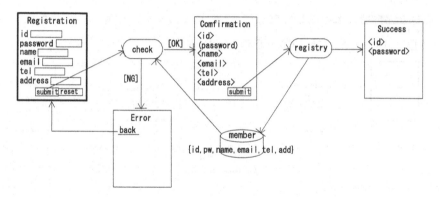

Fig. 6. An example of Web transition diagrams

A Web transition diagram editor. A Web transition diagram editor is a part of T-Web system, which is an editor to support composition of consistent Web transition diagrams. It allows users to do all operations visually. We compose Web transition diagrams as follows.

1. We start up the editor and the editor receives available program templates and components automatically.
2. We draw Web transition diagrams by selecting a node from a list, putting it on a drawing field and arrange nodes. A links is given by selecting the target node from a list so that we can give only syntactically correct links.
3. We specify details of each node using a window called *a property window*. When we specify details of a processing node, we should select the most appropriate program template from a list.

Fig.7 shows a Web transition diagram editor of T-Web system.

A Web application generator. A Web application generator is a part of T-Web system, which gets intermediate documents a Web transition diagram editor generates, and generates source codes of server side programs and Web page templates. Our prototype system shown in Fig.5 generates JSP documents written in HTML and servlet source codes written in Java.

Generators have general-purpose program templates which are independent of specific domains of applications so that we can widely reuse them. The above prototype has 16 program templates which are mainly for database manipulations, session management and sending electronic mails. Fig.8 shows an example of program templates in T-Web system. In our templates, a word between special characters '/*' and '*/' represents a parameter. Special characters '/**' and '**/' mean a repetition part. As the generator rewrites above parameters to corresponding values, the program template becomes a complete program.

To keep the standard level of security, all generated programs have additional codes as follows.

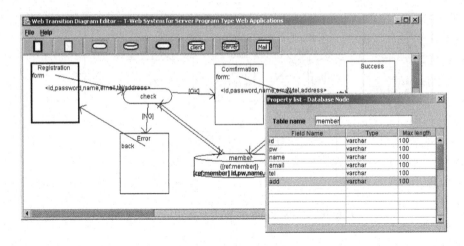

Fig. 7. A Web transition diagram editor of T-Web system

1. After activated by a user's request, each program checks whether user's session id is valid.
2. Then each program checks whether input data are correct according to specifications we give.
3. After processing of business logic, each program checks whether output data are correct according to database specifications. Especially when the program updates database tables, it checks consistency between output data and specifications of the database table.

If there is at least one error, the user's request is redirected to an error page.

4   Comparison of Two Approaches

We compare annotation approach and diagram approach in terms of target applications, developing processes and target users. We discuss target applications dividing into three viewpoints: application domains, flexibility and scalability. We discuss them according to the following criteria.

1. **Backgrounds** show why the viewpoint is important to select a generator.
2. **Characteristics** show the advantage and the disadvantage of two approaches and compare them.
3. **Examples** show our practical experience and other points to notice.

4.1   Application Domains

Backgrounds. Web applications can be generally classified into two types according to their functions: data-centric Web applications and control-centric

```
public class /*CLASSNAME*/ extends HttpServlet {
  public void doGet(HttpServletRequest request,
                    HttpServletResponse response)
                              throws ServletException, IOException {
    String myHttpsURL = "/*HTTPSBASEURI*/"+"/*PROGRAMURI*/"
                      +"/*PACKAGE.*/"+"/*CLASSNAME*/";
    String dbName = "/*DBNAME*/";
    String tbName = "/*TABLE1*/";
    String[] dbColNames = {/*"FIELDNAME1"*/};
    /**String PARAMETER = "";**/
    Connection con = TWeb.doConnect(dbName);
      --- omit following parts ---
  }
}
```

Fig. 8. An example of program templates

Web applications. Data-centric Web applications have side effect computations such as operations to update databases, while control-centric Web
applications concentrate on execution of complex business logic.

Characteristics. Both our annotation approach and diagram approach concentrate on data-centric Web applications. Our Web application generators
aim to encapsulate complex tasks unique to Web applications such as session
management and security checks, which are greater problems in data-centric
Web applications than in control-centric ones. In general, both approaches
can deal with applications having functions as follows: database manipulations, invocation of external programs and sending/receiving electronic
mails. On the other hand, both approaches are not good at dealing with
complex page transitions which depend on the results of programs.
Annotation approach is useful to generate Web applications whose structure
of Web page templates is complex, because we can use general Web page
composers and authoring tools to compose flexible page layouts before the
generation. Diagram approach is not good at developing such applications,
especially clickable maps and multiple frames, because it is complicated work
to connect data-flow relationships to the above components after the generation. On the other hand, diagram approach doesn't care a ratio of static
parts and dynamic parts in each Web page, while annotation approach is not
good at developing Web applications whose ratio of dynamic parts is high.

Examples. We are successful in developing typical data-centric Web applications using A-Web system and T-Web system respectively: shopping cart
systems, guestbook systems, glossary systems, schedule organizing systems,
member registration systems and reservation systems. The most appropriate generator mainly depends on the complexity of appearance of Web pages
but not on application domains. When we want to develop more complicated
Web applications, general software techniques such as object-oriented anal-
ysis/design and the extension of them may be helpful[11].

4.2   Flexibility

Backgrounds. When we need new business logic to generate an intended Web application, it is a big problem how to add new program templates and components into generators. It is also important what types of architectures it can deal with, because we often have constraints on the execution environment of the application.

Characteristics. In annotation approach, we can set new program components and give annotations to invoke the program. In diagram approach, we have only to add new program templates, program components and documents of their specifications, because the generators usually load specifications of all program templates and components automatically when it starts up. Diagram approach seems to be more flexible than annotation approach, because program templates encapsulate invocation of external programs and it is easier to add new program templates. When we want to generate Web applications based on various architectures, we can replace a part of generators in both approaches. Especially in diagram approach, we may have only to replace program templates to achieve the above goal.

Examples. Using our generators, typical data-centric Web applications are generated without new program templates and components. However, we possibly need new business logic in the case of a complex shopping Web site. In that case, it requires high programming skills and much cost to test them to produce new program templates and components. We have implemented generators and made sure that our approaches can deal with CGI, ASP and JSP/servlet architectures. When we extend a generator so that it can deal with new architecture, it requires very high programming skills. In that case, diagram approach may be easier than annotation approach.

4.3   Scalability

Backgrounds. The scale of the intended application is also an important problem as well as the complexity of Web page templates.

Characteristics. In annotation approach, we can basically concentrate on transitions between two Web pages, because the generator automatically gives a method to pass values of parameters from the origin page to the pages where they are used. Thus, even if the scale of an intended Web application becomes larger, the task of generation doesn't become so complicated. In diagram approach, however, the larger the scale of an intended Web application becomes, the more complex the management of diagrams becomes. While we can make diagrams nested, it is still a big program how to manage specifications of databases which are used in several diagrams.

Examples. Generators based on diagram approach can deal with no more than 15 Web page templates easily. While 15 Web page templates are enough for typical Web applications, a complex shopping Web site may exceed the number of templates. It may be helpful to use site diagrams which represent the structure of the Web site and static relations among Web page templates.

4.4   Developing Processes

Backgrounds. Web applications are characterized by three major design dimensions: *structure*, *navigation* and *presentation*[10]. We discuss effective developing processes in each approach taking notice of the order of these three design activities.

Characteristics. In annotation approach, we generally take the following developing process.

1. We first describe requirement specifications and analyze them.
2. We decide what Web pages are needed in the application, and design data structure (as a structure model) which the application deals with. From the above two models, we design Web page templates (as a presentation model) and implement them. We also design data-flow relationships among the application (as a navigation model) based on the above two models.
3. From the implementation of Web page templates and the navigation model, we generate server side programs using the generator.

In diagram approach, we generally take the following developing process.

1. We first describe requirement specifications and analyze them.
2. We decide what Web pages are needed, design data structure (as a structure model) and design data-flow relationships among the application (as a navigation model). From the above three models, we compose diagrams such as Web transition diagrams.
3. From the diagrams, we generate server side programs and prototypes of Web page templates using the generator. And then, we design Web pages (as a presentation model) and revise generated templates.

If we want to revise the appearance of Web pages after the generation easily, we should use XSLT and CSS to compose Web page templates in both approaches.

Examples. Annotation approach has the advantage of composing prototypes of Web page templates early in the process and reusing them for the final product. We can take an iterative and incremental process composing Web page templates. On the other hand, it is the disadvantage that it's hard to implement navigations as a prototype before composing Web page templates. Diagram approach has the advantage of designing and implementing structure and navigation iteratively and incrementally. On the other hand, it is the disadvantage that we cannot start implementation of Web page templates before the generation.

4.5   Target Users

Backgrounds. The knowledge a generator requires is important for developers to use the generator.

Characteristics. In annotation approach, Web page designers compose page templates before the generation. Users of the generator don't need knowledge of markup languages, because an annotation editor points out where and what types of annotations we can give. The users also don't need knowledge of architecture of Web applications. On the other hand, the annotation based generator requires knowledge of data types, regular expression and the concept of session management. To develop advanced Web applications, it may require knowledge of APIs to invoke external programs. In diagram approach, users don't need knowledge of markup languages and programming languages, because program templates and components encapsulate them. The generator requires knowledge of Web interfaces, the concept of session management and basic architecture of Web applications. It also requires a skill in selecting and using general-purpose programs.

Examples. Annotation approach is effective for programmers who have basic knowledge of software development. Diagram approach may be easier for inexperienced programmers, because most typical data-centric Web applications have database manipulations and input checks, which are encapsulated by the generator.

5   Related Work

Currently there are many languages and tools to support development of Web applications. One of the widely used server side technology is so-called server side scripting such as ASP, JSP and PHP. We give fragments of program codes into Web page documents to describe dynamic parts of the Web page. However, we still have to give processing steps of session management and security checks in detail, because most of the program codes are procedural. Similarly, most support tools to generate a part of the above program codes require procedural programming. Thus, the encapsulation of such techniques is not enough for inexperienced programmers.

We may observe that there are many types of diagrams used for design or construction of Web applications. The extension of UML diagrams is one possible approach [11]. These diagrams are available to describe not only data-centric Web applications but also control-centric Web applications. However, it is not easy to use such diagrams for automatic construction because the descriptions are too detailed for inexperienced programmers to understand them. The aims are different in such techniques and our software generators.

One of the systematic construction methods of Web applications is object-oriented hyper media design method [12]. This method is to produce interfaces of Web applications from abstract data types using three types of diagrams. It presents the developing process from requirements to the products and diagrams to use. While it is useful under specific conditions, it is not so flexible because the starting point of the developing process is always abstract data types.

6   Conclusion

We have presented two approaches to automatic construction of consistent and secure Web applications. We designed and implemented Web application generators based on each approach. In this paper, we showed the roles of these generators, and compared two approaches in terms of target applications, developing processes and target users. Both approaches are powerful and flexible enough to construct typical data-centric Web applications efficiently. Especially annotation approach has the advantage of developing applications whose Web page templates have flexible page layouts. On the other hand, diagram approach has the advantage of rapid and iterative/incremental development.

As our future work, we may try another approach which is based on the combination of two approaches. In this approach, we can develop programs and Web page templates concurrently. Such generator makes developing processes more flexible.

References

1. K. Asami, and T. Tokuda. Generation of Web Applications from HTML Page Templates with Annotations. *Proceedings of the IASTED International Conference, APPLIED INFORMATICS*, pp.295-300, 2002.
2. K. Asami and T. Tokuda. Generation of Web Applications from Annotation-Based Definitions. *Proc. of Engineering Information Systems in the Internet Context*, pp.69-79, 2002.
3. K. Jamroendararasame, T. Suzuki and T. Tokuda. A Generator of Web-based Transaction Systems Using Web Transition Diagrams. *Proc. 17th Japan Society for Software Science and Technology*, 2000.
4. K. Jamroendararasame, T. Matsuzaki, T. Suzuki, T. Tokuda. Generation of Secure Web Applications from Web Transition Diagrams. *Proc. of the IASTED International Symposia Applied Informatics*, pp.496-501, 2001.
5. K. Jamroendararasame, T. Matsuzaki, T. Suzuki, T. Tokuda. Two Generators of Secure Web-Based Transacion Systems. *Proc. of the 11th European-Japanese Conference on Information Modelling and Knowledge Bases*, pp.348-362, 2001.
6. K. Jamroendararasame, T. Suzuki, T. Tokuda. JSP/Servlet-Based Web Application Generator. *18th Conference Proceedings Japan Society for Software Science and Technology*, 2C-1, 2001.
7. K. Jamroendararasame, T. Suzuki, and T. Tokuda. A Visual Approach to Development of Web Services Providers/Requestors. *Proc. of the 2003 IEEE Symposium on Visual and Multimedia Software Engineering*, pp.251-253, 2003.
8. M. Taguchi, T. Susuki, and T. Tokuda. Generation of Server Page Type Web Applications from Diagrams. *Proc. of the 12th Conference on Information Modelling and Knowledge Bases*, pp.117-130m 2002.
9. M. Taguchi, T. Suzuki, and T. Tokuda. A Visual Approach for Generating Server Page Type Web Applications Based on Template Method. *Proc. of the 2003 IEEE Symposium on Visual and Multimedia Software Engineering*, pp.248-250, 2003.
10. Piero Fraternali. Tools and Approaches for Developing Data-Intensive Web Applications: A Survey. *ACM Computing Surveys Vol.31 No.3*, pp.227-263, 1999.
11. J. Conallen. Modeling Web Application Architectures with UML. *Communications of the ACM Vol.42 No.10*, pp.63-70, 1999.
12. G. Rossi and D. Schwabe. Designing Computational Hypermedia Applications. *Journal of Digital Information, Vol. 1, No. 4*, 1999.

Device Independent Web Applications –
The Author Once – Display Everywhere Approach

Thomas Ziegert[1], Markus Lauff[1], and Lutz Heuser[2]

[1] SAP AG, Corporate Research, Vincenz-Prießnitz-Str. 1,
76131 Karlsruhe, Germany
{Thomas.Ziegert, Markus.Lauff }@sap.com
[2] SAP AG, Global Research & Innovation, Neurottstraße 16,
69190 Walldorf, Germany
Lutz.Heuser@sap.com
http://www.sap.com/research

Abstract. Building web applications for mobile and other non-desktop devices
using established methods often requires a tremendous development effort. One
of the major challenges is to find sound software engineering approaches enabling the cost efficient application development for multiple devices of varying
technical characteristics. A new approach is to single author web content in a
device independent markup language, which gets then adapted to meet the special characteristics of the accessing device. This paper describes our approach
to single authoring, which was developed in the course a large European research project. The project has developed a device-independent language profile based on XHTML 2.0 and implemented a compliant rendering engine. We
focus on layout and pagination capabilities of the RIML (Renderer Independent
Markup Language) and show how authors can be assisted by development tools
supporting device independent authoring.

1 Introduction

The World Wide Web has established itself as one of the most important sources for
information as well as a perfect infrastructure for applications, which need to be accessible from anywhere. Web-enabled devices potentially offer access to globally
adopted infrastructure. But why is this offer just potentially? Currently, most web
content is optimised for the usage on a PC. This is still true despite the efforts of the
Web Accessibility Initiative [1] which set standards for universal accessibility of web
content. As more and more non-desktop devices enter the market, a convenient way
to access web content and web applications using such devices is required. The industry addressed that requirement for a limited set of applications particularly in the
B2E (Business-to-Employee) domain by developing device specific versions of such
applications. This application-specific approach tends to be too costly and not manageable if scaled to a large number of diverse devices and applications. Therefore,

N. Koch, P. Fraternali, and M. Wirsing (Eds.): ICWE 2004, LNCS 3140, pp. 244–255, 2004.

more generic ways to prepare web content in a device-independent way are necessary.

Various approaches have been proposed to address the challenge of high quality applications at minimal costs. Some approaches (e.g. [2, 3]) automatically compile web content to fit on a target device. These approaches are based on HTML and use heuristics in addition to tag information to extract structure information, due to the fact that HTML is lacking the necessary semantics which is needed to perform the conversion to other markup languages. Therefore, some approaches replace HTML by another markup language which is semantically rich enough to serve as a basis for conversion [4, 5, 6]. However, none of these proposals is standards-based and they were therefore not widely adopted in the marketplace. To open the path for a widely adopted device-independent markup language for authoring web content, two considerable efforts have been launched recently: a) The W3C chartered the Device Independence Group to establish specifications supporting single authoring, b) a consortium of six European companies, named CONSENSUS[1] [7], has built a prototype which implements authoring and conversion tools for a Renderer-Independent Markup Language (RIML), which was also developed by this consortium. Both efforts cooperate intensively. The ultimate vision of device independence as stated in the charter of the W3C Device Independence working group [8] is to provide "Access to a Unified Web from Any Device in Any Context by Anyone". In this paper we focus on layout and pagination capabilities of the RIML (Renderer Independent Markup Language) and show how authors can be assisted by development tools supporting device independent authoring.

2   Requirements for Device Independency

In this section we briefly cover the most important requirements for a device independent markup language and explain how the Consensus project has dealt with those in the RIML. Following the author once, display everywhere approach, an application is written once and gets then adapted to a particular device, which is accessing it.

A perfect solution according to [9] should offer:

> a device independent markup language preserving the intent of the author,
> an adaptation system transforming it into a device specific form,
> means to retain the authors control over the final result/presentation.

Concentrating on the developer's part item 1 and 3 are the most important ones. To keep the intent of the author the markup language should offer semantically rich

---

[1]   IST-Programme / KA4 / AL: IST-2001-4.3.2. The project CONSENSUS is supported by the European Community. This document does not represent the opinion of the European Community. It is also the sole responsibility of the author and not the responsibility of the European Community using any data that might appear therein.

markup elements. While XHTML 2.0 [10] provides certain means for device independent markup some necessary ingredients are missing. The RIML defines a language profile which is based on XHTML 2.0 and includes new elements for functionality, which was missing in current standards or proposals. In the reminder of this section we give a brief overview of these.

Due to the fact that devices widely vary in the amount of content their screens can accommodate there is a need for providing hints for content splitting and navigation between split up pieces of content. RIML therefore uses the `section` element of XHTML 2.0 as implicit hint for splitting and introduces new elements for combining layout with pagination and controlling the generation of navigation links between pages of split documents.

To provide means for the development of interactive web applications (business applications usually belong into this group) there is furthermore a need for elements dealing with form interaction. The XForms 1.0 [11] specification perfectly fulfills this requirement. The RIML language profile includes XForms 1.0, which strictly separates data from its presentation and keeps user interface elements device independent[2].

Apart from the fact that a device independent language allows for the generic description of a user interface for web applications, there should be means allowing for the inclusion of optional and alternative content. Even if this is somehow contradicting the author once approach, cause it allows for special versions of content for different devices, it enables the author to retain the control over the result of the adaptation process and allows him to consider the specialities of particular device classes (e. g. the support for certain audio or video formats). The RIML language profile therefore includes SMIL [12] Basic content control plus some extensions. Content control furthermore allows for the selection of device (class) specific style sheets. Style attributes like font sizes and weights tend to be very device specific, therefore RIML authors should provide different style sheets for different target markup languages and use the RIML content control mechanisms to select between them.

An optimal layout of a page or presentation unit on a certain device (class) heavily depends on the special characteristics of it. A generic layout specification, which then is adapted to the device accessing the content, is hardly to achieve. The layout should facilitate the usability of the particular application and therefore utilize the special characteristics of the device, e. g. the available screen size. Therefore RIML supports the authoring of different layouts for different device classes in a RIML document. Using content control the author is able to define when to use which layout.

---

[2] The latest draft of the XHTML 2.0 specification now also includes an XForms 1.0 module.

In this paper we focus on layout and pagination capabilities of the RIML (Renderer Independent Markup Language) and show how authors can be assisted by development tools supporting this novel features.

3 Layout and Pagination

Layout refers to the arranging pieces of content on a presentation unit PU[3]. The way layout is specified is a crucial problem when developing device-independent applications. Usually authors accomplish the layout by using frames and/or abusing tables for this purpose. Especially the latter is in conflict with the initial meaning of tables to serve as a structuring element, assembling multiple data records, each of which takes up exactly one row of the table. A generic layout specification, which then is adapted to the device accessing the content, is hardly to achieve. Automated layout generation, as described in [13, 14] might help for certain use cases, like assembling the layout of a remote control UI on several devices, but removes the author's control over the final result to a wide extent.

The layout should facilitate the usability of the particular application and therefore utilize the special characteristics of the device, e.g. the available screen size. Considering the limitation of the available screen size on certain devices another challenge of device independent authoring becomes apparent. Adapting to small screens requires the pagination (decomposition) of content, which in turn has to be taken into account, when specifying means for the layout of an authoring unit[4]. Usually some layout regions should be visible on all pages, e.g. menus and status bars; others include content, which should get split into a sequence of presentation units the pagination process generates.

Automated pagination support was a main design goal for RIML. Other approaches assume selectors that explicitly define device dependent breaks (like [15, 16]), in effect, falling back to device related authoring. In contrast, a RIML author requires a minimal knowledge of how a desired layout will be paginated by the RIML adaptation system. In this respect, RIML is related to other approaches [17, 18]. It differs from these in that it supports generic HTML like (row, column) constructs for adaptation, respectively applies adaptation to arbitrarily nested row and column structures.

---

[3] A presentation (PU) unit is this result of splitting the resource into a number of smaller units (PUs), which are presented to the user in a manner that is appropriate to the device (see DIWG2002]).

[4] An authoring unit is a piece of content the author is working with, but which is less than a document (see DIWG2002]).

Layout in RIML

Because of the reasons discussed in the last section RIML supports the specification of device (class) dependent layouts. Using Content Control the author is able to define when to use which layout. The overall layout of a RIML document is defined by using elements specified in the RIML layout module. The layout module defines a set of container types: rows, columns, grids, as well as frames. Whereas containers define the overall structure of a layout definition, frames are used to fill the several regions of the layout with content. Using different layouts and Content Control for layout selection allows content to be organized differently, depending on the target device and its unique properties. If a frame cannot simultaneously accommodate all of the content assigned to it in the target language, the content needs to be paginated. Pagination, the division of a RIML document into multiple pages, and navigation, the hyper linking among pages generated from a single authoring unit, are carried out automatically by the adaptation system.

RIML defines the following layout containers:

`grid`: A grid is a layout container allowing for the arrangement of container items in a grid layout. Container items can be (nested) other layout containers as well as frames. The parameter set of the grid element supports the specification of the maximum permissible number of columns in a grid and the direction into which grid items will be led out (either horizontally or vertically).

`column`: The column container is a special case of the grid container limiting the number of columns to one by definition.

`row`: The row container is a special case of the grid container forcing all contained items to be laid out in a single row.

`frame`: A frame is the only layout element content is assigned to, therefore a frame cannot contain any other layout elements. Each layout definition includes one or several frames. The assignment of content to a frame is done using the `riml:frameId` element.

Multiple frames can be used for the same presentation unit. Arranging frames differently in containers produces different layouts. RIML's Content Control gives the author a possibility for defining rules when to use which layout. While layout containers arrange the layout of frames in different ways, the actual content is assigned to frames only. All content in the body part of the document must be included into sections. Each section is assigned to a frame. The content of the section will be rendered within that frame (see Fig. 1). The content of a section will be ignored, whenever a section is not assigned to a frame or the frame does not exist. A RIML document should therefore define at least one frame in the document header. The overall layout of a document is defined by grouping multiple frames inside containers. RIML offers different container types with differing layout and paginating behavior. All frames must be placed inside a container. The nesting of containers is allowed, i.e. a container can include other containers, whereas the innermost container must always include a frame. Therefore, a frame is the only type of container, which can be associated with content.

```
<head>
  <riml:layout eccdc:deviceClassOneOf="DeviceClass2">
    <riml:column riml:id="root-col">
      <riml:frame riml:id="head" />
      <riml:frame riml:id="nav-menu " />
      <riml:frame riml:id="home" />
    </riml:column>
  </riml:layout>
</head>
<body>
    <section id="head-sec" riml:frameId="head">
      ...
    </section>
    <section id="menu-1sec" riml:frameId="nav-menu">
      ...
    </section>
    ...
</body>
```

Fig. 1. Assigning content to Frames

Pagination in RIML

XHTML 2.0 defines the block level element `section` as a means for structuring content. Apart from this a section defines an implicit page break, which is more "natural" than explicit page break markers. Therefore we decided to use sections as semantic hints for the adaptation system, when applying pagination. The author is therefore required to put all content, which should go onto the same screen (e. g. an input field and its label or a whole address form) into a section. Sections might be nested[5], whereas the innermost sections never get split. As every section moves into a certain frame defined by the layout in the head part of the RIML document, it is often the case, that certain regions of the layout should not get distributed over several pages, because they contain information, which should appear on every page, even if the document gets split. Taking Fig. 2 as an example, the LogoFrame as well as FrameB are defined as non-paginating frames (see also Fig. 3). For FrameA pagination was allowed (`paginate` is set to true).

---

[5] The current reference implementation does not support nested sections.

Fig. 2. Pagination and Layout Example

Therefore the content assigned to the LogoFrame and FrameB remains over the sequence of pages produced during adaptation. For FrameA the content gets distributed across all the pages the adaptation process produces. Fig. 3 shows a snippet of the markup, which was used to produce the results shown in Fig. 2. Section s10 contains special markup for guiding the automated generation of links between split pages. According to the definition used here, navigation elements should be generated for every page, showing a link to the previous and next page respectively. Navigation links are generated if and only if pagination occurs. The `navigation-links` element offers attributes allowing the author to define the type of link to be produced and to which Frame it is related. In Fig. 3 the scope attribute refers to FrameA, therefore navigation links are generated referring to pages containing sections from FrameA.

The size of a frame is determined by the adaptation system in order to accomplish pagination. However, the author should be able to provide the system with meta-information regarding the intended width of a frame. The pagination process considers the width of the virtual area on which the content gets finally rendered only (rendering surface), because this value can be reasonably defined. In case the browser supports no scrolling this value typically equals the physical screen width. Using the aforementioned frame elements the rendering surface can be divided into multiple parts. A frame serves as a bounding box in which the content will be laid out that it is assigned to. Using the following frame attributes the author is able to control the adaptation:

`minWidth` - the minimum width in pixels - the frame should never be smaller than this specified width.

`preferredWidth` - the recommended width of a frame is usually specified as a percentage in relation to the actual width of the rendering surface of the device. Absolute pixel values for preferredWidth are also supported.

```
<head>
  <title>Pagination and Layout</title>
  <riml:layout>
    <riml:column riml:id="col1">
      <riml:frame riml:id="LogoFrame" riml:paginate="false"
                  riml:minWidth="200"
riml:preferredWidth="400"/>
      <riml:frame riml:id="FrameA" riml:paginate="true"
                  riml:minWidth="200"
riml:preferredWidth="400"/>
      <riml:frame riml:id="FrameB" riml:paginate="false"
                  riml:minWidth="200"
riml:preferredWidth="400"/>
    </riml:column>
  </riml:layout>
</head>
<body>
  <section id="s1" riml:frameId="FrameA">
    ...
  </section>
  <section id="s2" riml:frameId="FrameA">
    ...
  </section>
  <section id="s10" riml:frameId="FrameB">
    <riml:navigation>
      <riml:navigation-links riml:scope="FrameA"
        riml:links="previous" riml:linksValue="relative-order"/>
      <riml:navigation-links riml:scope="FrameA"
        riml:links="next" riml:linksValue="relative-order"/>
    </riml:navigation>
  </section>
  <section id="s11" riml:frameId="LogoFrame">
    <strong>This is the sticky logo frame</strong>
  </section>
</body>
```

Fig. 3. Example Markup for Layout and Pagination

The preferredWidth attribute of a frame provides a hint to the adaptation process to determine the actual width of a frame. The author has to ensure that minWidth attributes in a RIML document layout can be obeyed for all devices. Therefore, the author should consider the device offering the smallest width of all targeted devices or better specify multiple layout definitions for different devices respectively device classes using Content Control.

Given those hints, a pagination algorithm has enough knowledge to paginate without exceeding the screen surface width. A similar approach cannot be applied with respect to container height, due to mentioned undetectable user preferences. The determination of optimal height is based on two observations.

First, we expect that most browsers support vertical scrolling. Vertical scrolling was shown to be acceptable from a usability point of view [19], in contrast to two-dimensional panning. Vertical scrolling was shown to be disturbing, if certain limits are exceeded [20]. To avoid the latter, we enable the user to reduce (resp. increase) the size limit which is applied during pagination. In support of this, the adaptation system is to insert corresponding control hyperlinks. In effect, the user exploits the visible outcome of pagination to avoid undue vertical scrolling depths.

Besides Frames, the RIML furthermore defines other types of paginating elements, which are: paginatingGrid, paginatingRow and PaginatingColumn. With respect to pagination all of these container types operate on their child nodes, which might be either other containers or frames and which might be either paginating or not. To preserve a useable result, the pagination of nested layout elements is allowed for one branch only. Assuming that the hierarchy of layout elements forms a tree, this means that two paginating elements must not have a common ancestor.

For non-interactive content i.e. printed pages, the content will be split when the page is full and page numbers are inserted to provide a basic means of navigation. Specifications such as XML Print [17], CSS3 Paged Media [13], and XSL-FO [12] address that.

4 Tool Support

One major issue with new language proposals like RIML addressing Device Independence is the learning curve they require. The necessary authoring environment is often neglected in similar projects. Therefore, we decided to put considerable effort into the development of an authoring environment containing innovative tools, enabling the application developer to easily author in a device-independent way. Based on the Eclipse [21] open source platform, this authoring environment has been developed as a plugin, gathering a set of views and editors, synchronised around a common document model. The Consensus authoring environment provides a whole set of tools.

Besides an XML Editor consisting of a source text editor, code completion based on the RIML schemas, RIML language validation, and an XML tree editor, the toolset also provides tools, helping the developer to cope with the new concepts RIML introduce in a visual way. A Frames Layout View allows the author to get a first impression how the document looks like, based oh the abstract layout he defined in the document. The concept of this view is to show an early version of the frames layout of the current RIML document. Depending on the device class one chooses, the view will show the frames layout, including in each frame the names (or ids) of the section that belong to this frame. The XML text in the text editor is highlighted depending on how the author places the focus in the Frames Layout View. Fig. 4 and 5 show the Frames Layout View for a PC and a smart phone, respectively.

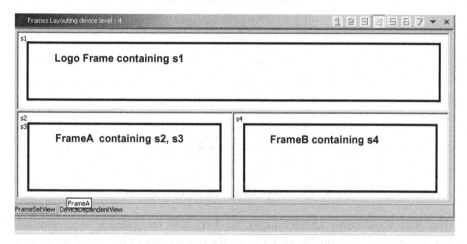

Fig. 4. Frames Layout View for Device Class 4

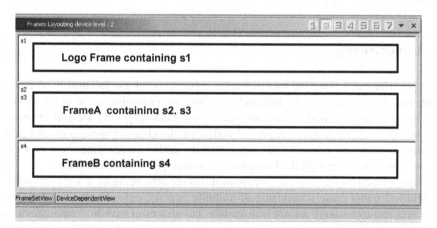

Fig. 5. Frames Layout View for Device Class 2

RIML authors often need to know how the developed document will be paginated depending on a device class. Therefore, the RIML Device Dependent View provides an overview of how the document is paginated, how many pages are created, and what they contain. The view was implemented similar to an XML tree view, presenting the split pages as a set of nodes. Fig. 6 shows an example of the device dependent view.

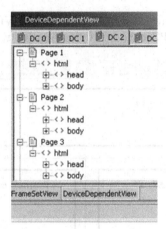

Fig. 6. Device Dependent View for Device Class 1

Apart from these rather abstract views, we have also integrated a set of available device emulators, allowing the author to see the actual result of the adaptation process on a particular device.

5   Conclusions

The paper has discussed the two particular aspects layout and pagination of content authoring for non-desktop devices and respective solutions developed in the Consensus research project. Rather than just specifying technology and markup to support single authoring, the Consensus project undertook the effort to implement a reference implementation and a set of tools supporting the author in applying these new concepts. Our experience with the Consensus prototype proved the feasibility of the concepts developed by the project. Test applications are now being built and will undergo a field test under close supervision of usability experts, ensuring that the developed concepts and technology are not just feasible, but also meet usability requirements. In parallel to that, the project works in close cooperation with the W3C to standardize key concepts explored in the project.

References

1. Web Accessibility Initiative, http://www.w3.org/WAI/
2. Bickmore, T.W.: Digestor: Device-independent Access to the World Wide Web, Proceedings of 6th International WWW Conference (1997)
3. Schilit, B.N., Trevor, J., Hilbert, D., Koh, T.K.: m-Links: An Infrastructure for Very Small Internet Devices. *Proceedings of the 7th Annual International Conference on Mobile Computing and Networking.* Rome, Italy, (2001) 122-131

4. Puerta, A., Eisenstein, J.: XIML: A Common Representation for Interaction Data, available at: http://www.ximl.org/documents/XIMLBasicPaperES.pdf
5. User Interface Markup Language, http://www.uiml.org
6. Eisenstein, J. et al.: Applying Model-Based Techniques to the Development of UIs for Mobile Computers, Proc. of the Conf. on Intelligent User Interfaces, Santa Fe, NM, USA, (2001)
7. Consensus Project Website, http://www.consensus-online.org
8. W3C's Device Independence Working Group, http://www.w3.org/2001/di/Group/
9. Butler, M., Giannetti, F., Gimson, R., Wiley, T.: Device Independence and the Web, IEEE Internet Computing, Sep./Oct. (2002) 81-86
10. McCarron, S., Axelsson, J., Epperson, B., Navarro, A., Pemberton, S. (eds): XHTML2, W3C Working Draft 5 August 2002, work in progress, http://www.w3.org/TR/xhtml2/
11. Dubinko, M., Klotz, L. L., Merrick, R., Raman, T. V.: XForms 1.0, W3C Recommendation 14. October 2003, http://www.w3.org/MarkUp/Forms/
12. Hoschka, P. (eds): Synchronized Multimedia Integration Language (SMIL) 1.0 Specification, http://www.w3.org/TR/1998/REC-smil-19980615 (1998)
13. Myers, B. A., Nichols, J.: Communication Ubiquity Enables Ubiquitous Control. 'Boaster' for Human-Computer Interaction Consortium (HCIC'2002). Winter Park, CO, Feb. (2002)
14. Nichols, J., Myers, B. A.: Automatically Generating Interfaces for Multi-Device Environments, Ubicomp 2003 Workshop on Multi-Device Interfaces for Ubiquitous Peripheral Interaction. Seattle, WA., October 12 (2003)
15. Adler, S. et al: Extensible Stylesheet Language (XSL), Version 1.0, http://www.w3.org/TR/xsl/
16. Lie, H. W., Bigelow, J. (eds): CSS3 Paged Media Module, work in progress, http://www.w3.org/TR/css3-page/
17. Mandyam, S. et al: User Interface Adptations, W3C Workshop on DI Authoring Techniques, http://www.w3.org/2002/07/DIAT
18. Keränen, H., Plomp, J.: Adaptive Runtime Layout of Hierarchical UI Components, Proceedings of the NordCHI 2002, Arhus, Denmark.
19. Giller, V. et al: Usability Evaluations for Multi-Device Application Development, Three Example studies, MobileHCI03, September (2003)
20. Baker, J. R.: "The Impact of Paging vs. Scrolling on Reading Passages", http://psychology.wichita.edu/surl/usabilitynews/51/paging_scrolling
21. The Eclipse Platform, http://www.eclipse.org/platform

WAPS: Web Application Prototyping System

Roberto Paiano and Andrea Pandurino

Set-lab, University of Lecce, Italy
{roberto.paiano,andrea.pandurino}@unile.it

Abstract. The growing demand for web applications and the new multi-user and multi-device requirements of these has led to the need for a structured and well-reasoned approach that helps both the application designer and the developer to produce a good quality product. On one hand we have the application designer, who has to describe all aspects of the application and manage the complexity of the tasks; on the other hand both the application customer and the developer need to validate and understand the designer's choices. To conciliate these needs, we propose a prototyping framework based on W2000 [1][2] methodology: in this way the designer has a powerful tool to keep control over the web application, the customer has a point of reference for evaluating the design, and the developer can better understand the design thanks to the prototyped application.

1   Introduction and Background

During the development and design of web applications (WAs) there are many critical factors to be considered; the designer has to manage the individual aspects and must be able to predict the inevitable interactions between them. In order to manage WAs fully, the production of a mock-up application that prototypes the most important aspects as quickly as possible, with minimum investment of time and resources, is desirable. Szekely stated that prototyping involves building a small scale version of a complicated system in order to acquire the critical knowledge required to build a complete system [3]. Considering the relation between requirement elicitation and the mock-up application [4], the first version of the prototype will rarely get the users excited but the developers should encourage the users to give feedback for the revision of the prototypes and let them know that their feedback will be considered in the redesign. It might seem like a large effort is being spent on something that will eventually be discarded but this upstream activity represents good investment as it will avoid costly problems downstream. In the past few years, web application engineering (and thus prototyping) has been synonymous with ad hoc development and a lack of any structured methodological approach. Thus, several methodologies, supported by a suite of tools, have emerged in order to simplify and automate the development of WAs. HDM [5] proposes a model for hypermedia application design, which divides the conceptual schema into two categories: structural and navigational. Starting from the HDM model, Autoweb [6] introduces a variant notation - HDM-Lite - that adds a presentation schema to design a WA and store the schema together with

N. Koch, P. Fraternali, and M. Wirsing (Eds.): ICWE 2004, LNCS 3140, pp. 256–260, 2004.

the data in a database. Jweb [7] provides a design/prototyping environment, integrating XML technology with HDM. In order to stay modular and flexible, one of the relevant features of the JWeb environment is the use of XML to the exchange of information among the different tools. RMM [8] methodology, HERA [9], ARANEUS project [10] and the WebRatio generation tool [11] represent other interesting approaches in a model-driven prototyping. Besides these approaches, UML [12] has been extended to model web specific elements [13]; starting from the use of UML as a language and the new WA features, HDM methodology has evolved into a W2000 approach. W2000 has been defined in response to the transformation of Web-based hypermedia from read-only navigational "repositories" to complex applications that combine navigational and operations in a sophisticated way. This paper describes a completely new prototyping architecture based on the W2000 methodology and the results of the UWA project.

The W2000 experience gave rise to the UWA Consortium [14], which in turn started the UWA project, which began in January 2000 and was completed in December 2002. This defines a set of methodologies, notations, and tools to tackle the main problems foreseen in the design of WAs. In addition, the project addresses the need for standard design and documentation to improve the possibility for exchanges and interoperability by extending the Unified Modeling Language (UML) as a design notation and using XML for internal representation. The project output, interesting for the purpose of prototyping, is the *unified software* environment, based on Rational Rose [15], which integrates the tools specific to each modeling activity.

2   WAPS: Web Application Prototyping System

In accordance with the W2000 methodology and the UWA design support environment, we propose a prototyping tool, called WAPS, which is able to understand the design model and create a mock-up application, with the benefits described above. Rose helps to design the WA in graphic format, using standard UML notation, in accordance with W2000 methodology; in order to obtain a "machine understandable" description we use another rational rose add-in: "Unisys Rose XML Tools" produced by Unisys [16] that exports the UML diagram into a standard XMI [17] output. Before choosing the XMI as the input format for WAPS, we considered two other reading model methods such as to read the rose petal file in raw mode or to produce an add-in to export the model into an xml-like format. The XMI solution seems the more standard, and appears to be suitable for our purpose; thus WAPS uses as input the XMI model description produced using the Unisys add-in which exports the Rational Rose W2000 model designed with the UWA add-in. As mentioned above, W2000 methodology and the UWA design tool were thought to be more appropriate for the design of WAs than for prototyping purposes. Therefore it is necessary to complete the WA model in order to support the prototyping process. It is clear that the complementary information tool must be a Rational Rose add-in (WAPS-Add-in), which provides a uniform environment for designing (with the UWA add-in) and prototyping WAs. The prototyping information is exported at the same time as the design information, in XMI format by the Unisys add-in.

The WAPS architecture is composed of several modules: for the most part they make up the run-time environment (WAPS-RT), the other part provides a set of tools (the *"InstanceDB Manager"* and all the *"Rational Rose Add-in"* in Fig. 1) to get WAPS-RT ready, such as the tool to insert the application data. The run-time environment, the WAPS core, has the main task of creating a mock-up application starting from the W2000 model in XMI format.

In accordance with the modular structure of the W2000 methodology and the various aspects of WA, it is possible to identify a clear n-tier architecture for the WAPS run-time environment. The architecture was born as a generalization of the three-layer software architecture used to develop a pilot application based on W2000 methodology [18]. This choice was highly suitable for the W2000 methodology: just as the model examines one by one the different aspects (information, navigation, publishing) of WAs in order to manage their complexity, each architecture layer manages a single aspect (or a pool of aspects), and provides services to the other levels. Since WAPS is based on an XMI description, it's clear that all the data managed in the modules are in XML format; furthermore, all interaction between modules must be in the same format; the XML verbosity and adaptability ensure good portability and scalability of the whole system; furthermore, after checking the environment, it is possible to distribute the modules on several machines using web service techniques based on XML messages.

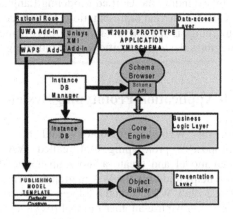

Fig. 1. WAPS architecture

In the WAPS-RT design, each level and thus each module manages a particular WA aspect; in detail:

- **Schema Browser**: WAPS uses the WA schema based on the W2000 model to prototype the WA. The schema is the XMI description exported from Rational Rose. This module allows a unique entry point to the WA schema, hiding the complexity in order to manage the XMI in raw mode. The module provides a set of schema APIs (S-API) to navigate the WA model via W2000 primitives.

- **Core Engine:** This module corresponds to the business level for a three-tier application. This module has the task of understanding the requests from the Object Builder, using the S-API of the schema browser to compose the reply schema that will contain the application data taken from the Instance DB. Since this module creates the reply schema (and thus the page that the user will see), it is clear that all design customizations take effect at this stage. Users not only access the information but interact through the operations. In the future, this module will provide standard methods to implement the operations. Obviously the operation will be expressed as manipulation of the W2000 model elements. Thus, the task of adding a product to the shopping bag is translated in WAPS as adding an instance of PRODUCT to the dynamic collection called "Shopping bag". In this way it is possible to describe complex operations as a sequence of basic ones performed on model elements. The importance of this piece of the framework is plain, if we consider its function, and it is so big that we may call it the "Core Engine".

- **Object Builder**: this module is the door to WAPS systems: the user request comes in, the prototyped page goes out. The module moves the request to the Core Engine and receives the response in XML-like format. Its main task is to apply a template to make the page visible. In order to manage several devices, WAPS uses the XSLT transformation to obtain HTML or WML pages in XHTML [19] format. XHTML is the keystone in W3C's effort to create standards that provide richer web sites on an ever increasing range of browser platforms. Browsers are not limited to desktops and include mobile phones and PDAs. Additionally, Cascading Style Sheets (CSS) can be used to control the content presentation. The use of CSS to manage the multi-device task is quite suitable for the prototyping purpose where the layout aspects are to provide an idea of the final layout.

WAPS uses several information repositories to store the data: the XMI schema described earlier, the Instance DB and the publishing model template.

The Instance DB is an E-R database that contains the data that will be showed to the user. The E-R schema stores the data in meta-structures derived from the W2000 model; thus the schema is fixed and doesn't change with the domain of the WA being prototyped. The Publishing Model Template is a E-R database which contains the references to the visualization template to create the page. There are two kinds of template: the default templates, which are generic and will be used to view the model structures such as the publishing unit, and the custom template, which the designer can create and associate with a specific page or publishing unit.

The Instance DB manager is a specific tool to populate the Instance-DB: it accesses the WA schema to understand the data structure in order to guide the operator through the schema to insert meaningful data.

3   Conclusion and Future Work

This paper has concentrated on the model-driven prototyping of web applications. We propose a prototyping system called WAPS that allows the designer to produce a WA mock-up starting from its W2000 model drawn up using Rational Rose. In accordance with the W2000 model structures, the multi-layer WAPS architecture encapsulates in each level a specific aspect; this, combined with the extensive use of XML-like format (to describe the model and the application data, and to exchange information between modules) ensures good scalability and adaptability of the environment.

Future work is evolving in two directions: the first aims to offer a better support for operation and customization and to improve the quality of the prototype; the second aims to produce support tools: considering the importance of application data in obtaining a good prototype, we are thinking of creating a tool that populates the

Instance-DB with data from statistics algorithms. As for the quality of application data, we are studying the features offered by the semantic web in order to add a new semantic layer to WAPS.

References

1. L. Baresi, F. Garzotto, Paolo Paolini, From Web Sites to Web Applications: New Issues for Conceptual Modeling, *Proceedings WWW Conceptual Modeling Conference*, Salt Lake City, October, 2000.
2. L. Baresi, F. Garzotto, and P. Paolini, Extending UML for Modeling Web Applications, *Proceedings of 34th Annual Hawaii International Conference on System Sciences (HICSS-34)*. IEEE Computer Society, 2001.
3. P. Szekely, User Interface Prototyping: Tool and Tecniques, 1994, USC/Information Sciences Institute
4. Steve McConnell, Software Project Survival Guide, *Microsoft Press*, 1998
5. F. Garzotto, P. Paolini, and D. Schwabe, HDM–A model Based Approch to Hypermedia Application Design, *ACM Transactions on Information Systems*, 11,1, pp 1-26
6. P. Fraternali and P. Paolini, Model-driven Development of Web Applications: The AutoWeb System, *ACM Transactions on Information System (TOIS)*, Vol. 18, Issue 4, October, 2000, pp. 323-382
7. Nicola Fiore, Leonardo Mangia, Roberto Paiano, Delivering Web Application: JWeb II Navigation Engine, *TELEC '02 International conference*, Santiago de Cuba (Cuba)
8. Isakowitz T., Stohr E.A. and Balasubramanian P., RMM: a methodology for structured hypermedia design, *Communications of the ACM 38 (8)*, Aug. 1995, pp. 33-44
9. Flavius Frasincar, Geert-Jan Houben, Richard Vdovjak , "Specification Framework for Engineering Adaptive Web Applications", *WORLD WIDE WEB CONFERENCE 2002*, Honolulu, Hawaii, USA
10. P. Atzeni, A. Masci, G.Mecca, P.Merialdo, G. Sindoni, " The Araneus Web-based Management Sistems", 1998
11. WebRatio site development studio, www.webratio.com, 2002
12. G. Booch, I. Jacobson, and J. Rumbaugh, *The unified modeling language user guide*, Addison-Wesley 1998, Readings, MA
13. J. Conallen, Modelling Web application achitectures with UML, *communication of the ACM*, Vol. 42, Iss. 10 Oct. 1999, pp. 63-70
14. UWA Consortium. General Definition of the UWA Framework. Technical report EC IST UWA Project, 2001.
15. IBM Rational Software, *www.rational.com*
16. Unisys Corporate, *www.unisys.com*
17. Object Management Group, *www.omg.org/technology/documents/formal/xmi.htm*
18. Paiano, A. Pandurino, From the Design to the Development: a W2000 Based Framework, Issues and Guidelines, *IRMA International Conference*, Philadelphia, 2003
19. XHTML 1.0 The Extensible HyperText Markup Language (Second Edition), www.w3.org/TR/xhtml1/

A Framework for the Simulation of Web Applications

Pedro Peixoto, K.K. Fung, and David Lowe

University of Technology, Sydney
PO Box 123 Broadway NSW 2007, Australia
{ppeixoto, kkf, david.lowe}@eng.uts.edu.au

Abstract. In recent years numerous Web application modeling languages have been developed and others improved. There has, however, been little research on how these languages may be simulated. Simulation of models constructed using design languages allows early evaluation and prevents unnecessary Web code development and implementation. It can therefore significantly reduce the design cycle time and cost. This paper introduces a Web application simulation model framework that was designed to be compatible with existing modeling languages. This was accomplished by specifically identifying the objectives of a simulation language and contrasting this with those of design models. The simulation model supports analysis of simulations from four key Web application perspectives (and hence the model is constructed around these perspectives) namely: presentation, navigation, functionality and content. We argue that with this approach substantial inferences about the quality of the design can be drawn from simulation of the Web application model.

1 Introduction

Web applications projects have reached a level of complexity that demand modeling techniques to tackle their design intricacies. Several modeling languages such as OOHDM [1], UML [2] and WebML [3] have been proposed as aids to Web application design, development, and implementation. Although these modeling languages provide an overview of the system, there is still the need for some coding to get a first glimpse of the interaction amongst the systems components.

A desirable approach would be to simulate the design without any implementation whatsoever. Simulation has been widely and successfully used in the hardware design field. In fact, Hardware Description Languages (HDLs) such as VHDL (Very High-Speed Integrated Circuit Hardware Description Language) [4,5], are considered an indispensable modeling tool. Simulation of VHDL models is performed without a physical implementation thereby reducing both cost and design time. But if modeling of Web applications has been thoroughly addressed, simulation of the models themselves is little researched. So far, simulation has only been used to evaluate Web systems performance [6,7,8].

N. Koch, P. Fraternali, and M. Wirsing (Eds.): ICWE 2004, LNCS 3140, pp. 261–265, 2004.
© Springer-Verlag Berlin Heidelberg 2004

We feel that Web modeling languages have reached a maturity level that permits the present attempt of defining a framework for Web application simulation. We aim to build the foundations of a simulation model based on a Web Description Language (WDL), developed specifically to assist on the simulation process, permitting the assessment of Web application designs regardless of the modeling language chosen.

The next section describes the WDL Simulation model, and in section 3 we outline the objectives, input stimuli, results, and analysis of the simulation. Finally Section 4 makes a brief summary and draws conclusions.

2   The WDL Simulation Model

Simulation consists on the observation of a system's response over time when a known set of stimuli is present at its inputs [9, 10]. In this paper, simulation is regarded as the evaluation of the extent to which the Web application design (represented using some modeling notation) supports interaction with the user, and aims to monitor and draw inferences of what occurs internally.

To simulate a design a description of its components has to be available. To deal with the specificities of Web applications a description language (WDL) was developed which captures both the structural and dynamics of each component, similar to VHDL, where for each component a definition of the interface and functionalities is explicitly declared. The main purpose of WDL is not to model the Web application but to enable the simulation.

For the designer the most important aspects of the application that need to be assessed are its graphical interface, the navigation network structure, the scripts interface and workflow, and data exchanged among the components. In fact, existing models such as the Dexter Hypertext Reference Model [11], HDM [12], and WebML [13, 14], tend to decompose systems along these lines [15] emphasizing the use of different layers to tackle distinct aspects of Web applications. For this reason, our simulation model focuses on four different perspectives corresponding to four different layers, namely: presentation, navigation, functional, and content, as Fig.1 shows. Also a *User Interaction Model* was considered to reflect the possible actions that may be undertaken by a user, restricting the simulation stimuli to a well known set. Each layer, being an orthogonal aspect of the design, enables analysis from a distinct point of view. Simulation on these four layers requires the ability of the modeling language to describe in detail components structure, workflow, and behavior, and, therefore, a set of requirements must be met for a high degree of accuracy simulation. If, however, the modeling language used does not encompass all the requirements, it does not automatically preclude simulation but will imply a lower simulation detail. The set of requirements the modeling languages should meet are enumerated and described in [16].

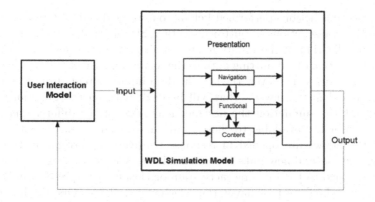

Fig. 1. The WDL Simulation Model

3 Layer Definition

The Presentation Layer – Simulation relies on its stimuli to evaluate the system under analysis. Since the system is a Web application, its change in state is essentially due to user inputs through the graphical interface – the Presentation layer. Our simulation model reflects this by wrapping the Presentation layer around the remaining preventing the user to directly interact with them.

This layer deals with the description of the page's look and feel, namely the user data input components, information components, and hyperlinks. However, it does not attempt to interpret the user actions; its semantics are dealt with on the remaining layers. As a consequence, user actions that potentially alter the state of the system are initiated on the Presentation layer but acquire significance and meaning on the remaining layers. Stimuli of this layer come mainly from the user interaction through interface components – concrete and clearly identified HTML elements with well-defined structure and behavior.

Results from the simulation are essentially the rendering of the model's graphical user interface description by displaying the active pages, and the interaction with the remaining layers – the navigational consequences of the user browsing, the functional script outcomes, and the data included and displayed. Assessment of the user interface is this layer's simulation main purpose, namely the graphical realization of hyperlinks and data input elements. Furthermore, the interface may pose some interaction limitations, namely on a data input level, which must be properly assessed by the designer.

The Navigation Layer – On this layer, pages are considered as macro blocks or abstractions of the pages displayed by the Presentation layer – they are simply containers of navigation components. Simulation of the navigation path through the Web pages set due to the user interaction with the interface via the Presentation layer is performed. It is on this layer that some of the signals that trigger script processing have their origin. Simulation performed on this layer is driven by user interaction with the displayed components of the Web application. The user interacts with the pages on the Presentation layer and the possible actions performed belong to a well-defined finite set - following hyperlinks, mouse actions or buttons selection. Stimuli that drive the simulation are a generalization of the inputs in stereotyped categories such as clicking on links or the action of submitting data to the server, and script actions that imply navigation changes. However, the specific data input contents from the user are not considered in this layer - that will be dealt with on the Functional layer. Throughout the simulation the designer may observe the different navigation paths the user has available to chose from due to changes in the active pages. Different windows are opened in response to diverging navigation trails and, consequently, several new links become available. The designer may trace which user actions led to the opening, activation or closing of a specific window, and the correspondingly set of navigation elements available. One of the goals of simulating this layer is the verification of the navigation flow and assertion of the navigation path due to user and script actions.

The Functional Layer – It is on this layer that the application acquires its dynamic aspect and where the client and server-side scripts are managed. Furthermore, this layer interacts with the Presentation layer for dynamic page construction, and with the Navigation layer for internal changes in the active pages. Data input in Web forms as well as any state information are the principal sources of information obtained from users. Scripts process this data from the Presentation layer and stored data from the Content layer, and are triggered by other scripts or by user action via the Navigation layer. Resulting from the simulation, data flow exchange between the script components and components on the remaining layers are observed. The data used by a specific script and its results are also displayed. What scripts are running at a particular point in time and their contribution to the overall Web application dynamics are another of the simulation results. Furthermore, the assessment of the process workflow assures that the Web application dynamics is in agreement with the design requirements.

The Content Layer – All data stored on the system is managed by this layer which is a main information resource of the Functional and Presentation layers. It manages all the data used by the Web application – whether from databases, files, or more volatile data such as Web session variables. The stimuli of the content layer simulation are the data write and read command set such as a database write operation or reading a client's cookie ID.

The information flow amongst the different layers and all the actions that involve data manipulation are displayed, enabling assessment of the Web application content management.

4   Conclusion and Future Work

A framework for the simulation of Web application design models is presented. By using a Web Description Language that maps the design into an enumeration of the structural and behavioral characteristics, the WDL Simulation model is able to evaluate the design from four orthogonal perspectives, namely: Presentation, Navigation, Functional, and Content, which relate to the four important analysis a designer has to conduct to verify the Web application and validate its requirements. By simulating the application directly from the model, and without any code implementation, substantial project time reduction is achieved. A prototype is being developed to simulate designs using several modeling languages such as UML or WebML. Furthermore, the next logical step is to use WDL to automatically synthesize the code. This, as it happens in the hardware design field, would provide designers with powerful tools for the development of complex Web applications. A fuller description of the layers and especially the interfaces between them is available in an extended version of this paper published as an Technical Report [16].

References

1. Schwabe, D., Rossi, G.: The object-oriented hypermedia design model. Communications of the ACM **38** (1995) 45–46
2. Conallen, J.: Building Web Applications with UML. Addison Wesley Object Technology Series. Addison-Wesley (1999)
3. Ceri, S., Fraternali, P., Bongio, A., Brambilla, M., Comai, S., Matera, M.: Designing Data-Intensive Web Applications. 1st edn. Morgan Kaufmann Pub. (2003)
4. Ashenden, P.: The Designer's Guide to VHDL. 1st edn. Morgan Kaufmann Publishers (2002)
5. Jerraya, A., Ding, H., Kission, P., Rahmouni, M.: Behavioral Synthesis And Component Reuse With VHDL. 1st edn. Kluwer Academic Publishers (1997)
6. Cohen, E., Krishnamurthy, B., Rexford, J.: Improving end-to-end performance of the web using server volumes and proxy filters. In: SIGCOMM. (1998) 241–253
7. Iyengar, A., MacNair, E., Nguyen, T.: An analysis of web server performance. Global Telecommunications Conference, GLOBECOM '97 **3** (2000)
8. Hadharan, R., Ehrlich, W.K., Cura, D., Reeser, P.K.: End to end performance modeling of web server architectures. SIGMETRICS Perform. Eval. Rev. **28** (2000) 57–63
9. Schriber, T.J., Brunner, D.T.: Inside simulation software: inside discrete-event simulation software: how it works and why it matters. In: Proc. of the 32nd conference on Winter simulation, Soc. for Comp. Sim. International (2000) 90–100
10. Banks, J.: Simulation fundamentals: simulation fundamentals. In: Proc. of the 32nd conference on Winter simulation, Soc. for Comp. Sim. Int'l (2000) 9–16
11. Halasz, F., Schwartz, M.: The Dexter hypertext reference model. Commun. ACM **37** (1994) 30–39
12. Garzotto, F., Paolini, P., Schwabe, D.: HDM - a model-based approach to hypertext application design. ACM Trans. Inf. Syst. **11** (1993) 1–26
13. Ceri, S., Fraternali, P., Bongio, A.: Web modeling language (WebML): a modeling language for designing web sites. In: Proc. of WWW9 Conf., Amsterdam (2000)
14. Bongio, A., Ceri, S., Fraternali, P., Maurino, A.: Modeling data entry and operations in WebML. Lecture Notes in Computer Science (**1997**)
15. Fraternali, P.: Tools and approaches for developing data-intensive web applications: a survey. ACM Comput. Surv. **31** (1999) 227–263
16. Peixoto, P., Fung, K., Lowe, D.: Simulating Web Applications - The Definition of a Framework. Technical report, University of Technology, Sydney, Faculty of Engineering, Sydney, Australia (2004)
http://www.eng.uts.edu.au/Research/Reports/UTS-Eng-TR-04-001.pdf.

ADVISOR SUITE: A Tool for Rapid Development of Maintainable Online Sales Advisory Systems

Dietmar Jannach and Gerold Kreutler

University Klagenfurt
Universitätsstraße 65
9020 Klagenfurt, Austria
0043 463 2700 3757
{dietmar.jannach, gerold.kreutler}@uni-klu.ac.at

Abstract. A sales advisory system is a tool supporting customers in the decision-making and buying process by interactive and personalized requirements elicitation and the provision of comprehensible product proposals and explanations. The particular challenges when building such systems lie in the strong interdependencies between the recommendation and personalization logic and the corresponding adaptive, web-based user interface. The ADVISOR SUITE tool described in this paper is a system that follows a consistent knowledge-based approach for all tasks that are required to build such intelligent sales advisory systems for arbitrary domains. The development of advisory applications is based on a conceptual model of online sales dialogues, a "Model-View-Controller" application architecture, a generic controller component, as well as (semi-)automatic, template-based web page generation. Experiences from various real-world applications show that the knowledge-based approach and the corresponding graphical tools of ADVISOR SUITE significantly accelerate the development and maintenance process for such applications.

1 Introduction and Overview

Online customers are increasingly overwhelmed by the variety of comparable products or services available on the online channel. Web-based sales assistance and recommendation systems are a means for supporting online customers in their product selection and decision-making processes. These systems provide the best value for the customers when they simulate the behavior of a real sales assistant. Therefore, they acquire the customer's real needs in a personalized dialogue ([1], [2]), and come up with a suitable set of proposals and provide adequate explanations for these proposals, which is required to increase the customer's confidence in his buying decision.

The purpose of the ADVISOR SUITE framework described in this paper is to provide a domain-independent tool for integrated development and maintenance of such web-based sales advisory applications. At the core, ADVISOR SUITE is an expert system where the knowledge of the domain expert is made explicit in a declarative knowledge base. This knowledge both comprises the recommendation guidelines of the domain, as well as information about *how* the real customer requirements have to be elicited, i.e., knowledge about efficient sales dialogues. The main challenge of

N. Koch, P. Fraternali, and M. Wirsing (Eds.): ICWE 2004, LNCS 3140, pp. 266–270, 2004.

such an approach is that there are strong interrelations between these two types of knowledge. Typically, the user's preferences are acquired by asking questions in an interactive dialogue. The user's answers (i.e., his/her profile) obviously influence the personalized set of products to be recommended, but also determine the further dialogue flow which should be adapted, e.g., to the user's skill level.

Consequently, the web pages used in the online dialogue must be extremely flexible and dynamic such that changes in the knowledge base are immediately taken into account and do not require manual adaptation of the dynamic HTML code. Nonetheless, the web pages have to be comprehensible and editable by a Web developer who aligns the pages' style to the corporate layout or integrates the application into an existing web site.

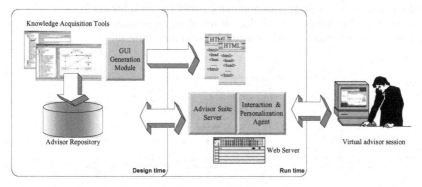

Fig. 1. Architecture of the framework

Fig. 1 shows the overall architecture of the ADVISOR SUITE framework. The required knowledge is acquired using graphical knowledge acquisition tools and stored in a common repository. The *server* component utilizes that knowledge and creates *interaction and personalization agents* that manage the user input for each advisory session. Before the system is started, the needed web pages for the dialogue and a generic controller component implementing the personalization logic are generated.

2   Combining the Recommendation Logic and Adaptation Logic

In our approach, the *customer properties* are the glue between the recommendation logic and the personalized adaptation of the user interface and the dialogue. First, these properties, i.e., the user's interests and preferences, determine the products to be proposed and their degree of fit with the requirements. The possible values (answers) for the properties are typically finite and pre-defined. The computation of suitable products is based on a priority-based filtering technique similar to [3] and declarative rules like,

"If the customer's experience in the domain is low and he has limited financial reserves, we propose low-risk investments."[1]

---

[1] Simplified example taken from the domain of online investment advisory.

Such advisory rules are modeled in a graphical tool and are expressed in a high-level, end-user oriented language; the individual ranking of the remaining products is based on a standard personalization technique [4] and the evaluation of the products' utilities for the customer. More details on the knowledge-based recommendation approach can be found in [5].

On the other hand, the customer properties also steer the interaction process, i.e., the sequence of the dialogue pages. In many cases, for instance, the interaction style depends on the user's self estimate of his knowledge level in the domain. Expert users can be asked fewer, but more complex and more technical questions, novice users might need more help and a different form of explanations. Within the ADVISOR SUITE framework, this adaptation and personalization knowledge that an experienced sales agent will have is also made explicit. Again, the personalization process is driven by the customer properties and made explicit with rules like,

"If the user has limited knowledge on the domain, proceed to a page where he is asked if he wants to have a look on more introductory material."

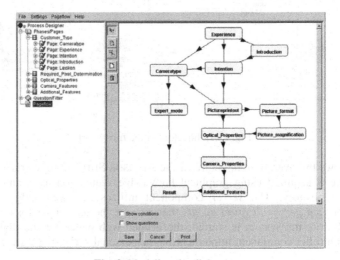

Fig. 2. Modeling the dialogue

These rules are maintained with the help of a special development tool which is depicted in Fig. 2. In particular, the used modeling approach is based on a simple but general *conceptual model* of a sales advisory dialogue, where the major concepts are chosen in a form such that they are close to the resulting web application and use a non-technical representation: Basically, sales assistance dialogues consist of dialogue steps (pages) that contain one or more questions on customer preferences or desired product properties. Each dialogue step can have a number of possible successor pages, whereby the actual successor page is determined dynamically based on the personalization rules described above. A dialogue can have "special steps", like hints on conflicting requirements or additional information or result and explanation pages. Our experiences from several practical applications show that domain experts are able to cope with this level of complexity and can describe the structure of a good dialogue using these concepts after a very short training phase. An important factor for user acceptance also lies in the conceptual integration of this knowledge with the recommendation logic, e.g., the same customer properties used for product filtering now appear as questions in the dialogue; the language for expressing complex conditions is the same as for page successor relations and for filtering rules.

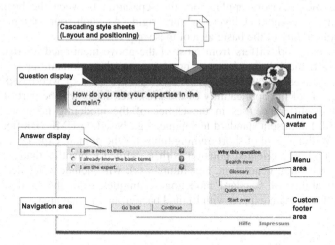

Fig. 3. Structure of a dialogue page

3 User Interface Generation

The dynamic HTML pages of the final application have to be very flexible and must immediately reflect changes in the knowledge base, e.g., when a new question is defined. Moreover, they have to be simple enough such that they can be easily adapted by a Web developer who for instance wants to change the layout of the pages. ADVISOR SUITE uses the following basic techniques to deal with that problem. First, we make extensive use of *Custom Tags* [6] which are syntactically similar to standard HTML tags, but implement application-specific functionality. The usage of these tags helps us both to avoid the problematic mixture of static HTML-code with procedural scripting code and also leads to a more clear and legible page source code. On the other hand, we also rely on automatic web page generation based on an elaborated template mechanism. Each dialogue page is actually built up from different, predefined areas and like question or explanation areas, headers and footers. The *GUI Generation Module* in Fig. 1 automatically assembles and parameterizes the needed web pages from small, pre-defined templates such that the basic dialogue can be generated (in a rapid prototyping process) without programming. Fig. 3 shows the layout and the different areas of such a generated page.

4 Conclusions

Over the last years, several approaches (e.g., [7], [8], [9], [10], and [11]) have been presented that aim at applying state-of-the-art Software Engineering practices to the specific requirements of the development of web applications. To some extent, our work can be seen as an implementation of best-practices from these approaches for a specific application domain: The design process is based on a generic, conceptual model of a sales advisory application; the separation between the business logic, controller, and presentation layers is very rigid. As such, our system shows the practical applicability of the basic idea of these approaches.

However, our work differs from most of the above-mentioned approaches as we want to support the full development process up to the automatic generation of the web pages; although we limit ourselves to a specific class of web-based systems, a broader analysis of the applicability of the presented ideas will be part of our future work. Another difference lies in the choice of the modeling notation, where we deliberately did not use a standard technique, e.g., based on UML (Unified Modeling Language). With the goal of short training times for the domain expert, we opted for a proprietary, end-user oriented notation with a defined semantics that is needed for automated application generation. Our future work will include a detailed evaluation of the applicability of standard modeling techniques from the field of Software Engineering for domain experts with limited background in that area.

References

[1]   Ardissono, L., Felfernig, A., Friedrich, G., Goy, A., Jannach, D., Petrone, G., Schäfer, R., and Zanker, M.: A Framework for the Development of Personalized, Distributed Web-Based Configuration Systems, *AI Magazine*, Vol. 24(3) Fall 2003, 93-110.

[2]   Ardissono, L., Felfernig, A., Friedrich, G., Goy, A., Jannach, D., Petrone, G., Schäfer, R., and Zanker, M.: Personalizing on-line configuration of products and services, *Proceedings 15th European Conference on Artificial Intelligence*, Lyon, France, IOS Press, 2000.

[3]   Schiex, T., Fargier, H., Verfaille, G.: Valued Constraint Satisfaction Problems: Hard and Easy Problems, *International Joint Conference on Artificial Intelligence*, Montreal, Canada, 1995, 631-639.

[4]   von Winterfeldt, D., Edwards, W.: *Decision Analysis and Behavioral Research*, Cambridge University Press, Cambridge, UK, 1986.

[5]   D. Jannach and G. Kreutler, Building on-line sales assistance systems with ADVISOR SUITE, *Proc. of 16th Intl. Conference on Software Engineering and Knowledge Engineering* (SEKE'04), Banff, CAN, 2004.

[6]   Goodwill, J.: *Mastering JSP Custom Tags and Tag Libraries*, Wiley Publishers, 2002.

[7]   Ceri, S., Fraternali, P., and Matera, M.: Conceptual Modeling of Data-Intensive Web Applications, *IEEE Internet Computing*, Vol. 6 , No. 4, pp. 20-30.

[8]   Conallen, J.: Building Web Applications with UML, Addison Wesley, Reading, MA, 2000

[9]   Rossi, G., Schwabe, D., Esmeraldo, L., Lyardet, F.: Engineering Web Applications for Reuse, *IEEE Multimedia* 8(1), 2001, pp. 20-31.

[10]   Jacyntho, M. D., Schwabe, D., Rossi, G.: A Software Architecture for Structuring complex Web Applications, *Journal of Web Engineering*, 1 (1), October, 2002, pp. 37-60.

[11]   Gomez, J., Cachero, C., Pastor, O.: Extending a Conceptual Modelling Approach to Web Application Design, *Proc. of the 1st International Workshop on Web-Oriented Software Technology*, Valencia, Spain, June 2001.

An Agent-Based Approach to Web Site Maintenance*

Wamberto W. Vasconcelos[1] and João Cavalcanti[2]

[1] Department of Computing Science, University of Aberdeen
AB24 3UE Aberdeen, United Kingdom
wvasconcelos@acm.org
[2] Department of Computer Science, University of Amazonas
69077-000 Manaus, AM, Brazil
john@dcc.fua.br

Abstract. Web sites are public representations of corporations, businesses and governmental bodies. As such they require proper maintenance to ensure that accurate and updated information is presented adequately. Dynamically created Web sites sometimes are not an option: they add a computational overhead on the server and make the automatic indexing of pages difficult. Static Web sites may grow to an extent that manually performing maintenance operations becomes unfeasible: automatic or semi-automatic means ought to be put in place. In this paper we explain one such approach, using software agents to look after large data-intensive Web sites. Our maintenance operations are performed by a team of autonomous agents that communicate with each other as well as with Web masters or other human agents. Our approach can be naturally incorporated into existing Web sites and its use can be gradually extended to encompass larger portions of the site. Because our agents are independent, their individual malfunctioning should not stop the maintenance effort as a whole.

1 Introduction

Web sites provide to the public at large representations of corporations, businesses and governmental bodies. Increasingly Web sites provide the first (and sometimes only) form of contact between the general public and the actual organisation. It is imperative that proper care and attention be placed into the *design* of the Web site: the look-and-feel of pages, the provision of maps for the site, the amount and positioning of information, and so on [1]. However, an independent and equally important (or even more important) issue concerns the actual *contents* of the Web site: how accurate and updated the information presented is and what mechanisms are in place to support their maintenance. This is a particularly sensitive issue in data-intensive Web sites, where data suffers constant or frequent updates and there may be many sources of data involved.

---

* Partially supported by the Brazilian Research Council (CNPq) grant no. 55.2197/02-5 (Project SiteFix – Adapting Web Sites to Perform Information Retrieval Tasks).

N. Koch, P. Fraternali, and M. Wirsing (Eds.): ICWE 2004, LNCS 3140, pp. 271–286, 2004.

We propose an automatic approach to Web site management via a team of software agents: a collection of independent and communicating pieces of software will share the responsibility and computational effort of looking after a large data-intensive Web site, managing static Web pages. We introduce an abstract and generic architecture and describe how it can be implemented using existing technologies and standards.

Dynamic-page techniques [2,3] have been used to tackle the contents maintenance problem. However, static pages still have an important place as they are simpler to manage, require less computational power and are visible to search engines. It should be clear that we do not propose a replacement for dynamic pages: information which usually resides in a database or that needs some computation before presentation are clearly better addressed via dynamic generation. Our approach targets pieces of information which do not require complex computations, changing only their values and, in many cases, not being stored in databases. Both approaches should co-exist and be used in a single Web site application.

This paper is organised as follows. In the next section we address some of the issues related with using agents to carry out Web site maintenance. In Section 3 we explain our proposed architecture and its components. In Section 4 we present an example to illustrate our approach. Section 5 contrasts our approach with existing work and in Section 6 we draw conclusions and discuss the work presented.

2   Web Site Maintenance with Agents

The idea to employ autonomous agents to perform Web site maintenance comes from the fact that maintenance tasks are usually small, well defined and recurrent. To our knowledge, no-one has attempted this before: simple and robust software agents can be designed to carry out stereotypical tasks and be reused and customised to suit particular needs.

Typical maintenance tasks our agents can handle are those involving updating a piece of information and publishing it on a Web page. In order to specify this sort of task, it is only necessary to specify the information item, its data source, the frequency of update and the page where it is published. As a result, the amount of knowledge agents need is relatively small. Agents can be implemented as simple lightweight programs, using only the necessary system resources. The main advantages of using agents are [4,5]:

- *proactiveness* – agents are proactive, *i.e.*, they take action when necessary.
- *autonomy* – each agent is autonomous, being able to perform its task on its own with little or no human intervention.
- *social ability* – agents can send and receive messages to the Webmaster, making it easier to follow maintenance activities.

It is important to note that the proposed approach is not a replacement for dynamic pages techniques, such as ASP [3] and JSP [2]. Dynamic pages comprises a widely adopted solution for maintaining the information updated. Although any piece of information that changes over time can be regarded as dynamic, we can make a distinction between two types of dynamic information: (1) pieces of information which result from a computation, often requiring parameters given by users or coming from other source. (2) pieces of information that only have their values changed periodically. Once instantiated, this sort of information can be presented in static Web pages, which are simpler to be served to users and easier to be found by search engines.

Our approach can co-exist with dynamic pages in a Web site, since the maintenance agents are designed only to maintain static Web pages. It is an alternative for maintaining static pages which contains dynamic pieces of information of type (2) as explained earlier. Note that we have not yet addressed other dynamic aspects that can appear in the navigation structure and presentation of a Web site application. Another important feature of our approach is the ability to update content and visualisation separately. That allows, for instance, changing completely the look-and-feel of a Web page without affecting the content specification or its data source. As benefits, our approach keeps Web pages automatically up-to-date, speeding up the maintenance process. Since it requires fewer technical personnel (Webmaster), it also helps to reduce the overall costs of maintaining a Web site.

3 An Agent-Based Architecture for Web Site Maintenance

In this section we describe the components of our architecture, their details, how they relate to each other and how we implemented them. It is worth pointing out that the architecture herewith described could have been implemented rather differently, using distinct communication infrastructures, different programming languages and even different notations to specify our agents with.

In Fig. 1 we show a diagrammatic account of our architecture. The Web Master is shown on the right-hand side interacting with the Web pages (white arrow): he/she annotates the HTML files with specifications of agents to be started up by the Scanner Agent, shown as a grey circle. The Scanner

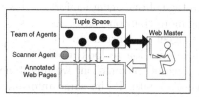

Fig. 1. Agent-Based Architecture

Agent is responsible for going through a given directory where the HTML files are stored and scans these for the annotations specifying agents. For each annotation found in the HTML file, a corresponding agent (black circles) is started up – the complete set of agents obtained at the end of the scanning process is called the Team of Agents looking after the Web site, updating the same Web pages that gave rise to them (vertical arrows in the diagram). The Web Master and the Team of Agents communicate via message-passing (black two-way arrow in the diagram). We explain below each component of the architecture.

3.1   Annotated Web Pages

The Webmaster adds annotations to individual Web pages, that is, to particular HTML [6] files. Since these annotations become part of an HTML file which Web browsers need to display, they must be *innocuous*, that is, they should not alter the rendering of the HTML by any browser. We achieve this by employing the HTML comment tag "<!-- ... -->" to wrap our annotations.

The actual annotations that go within the HTML comment tags are a special-purpose XML [7] construct of the form

    <agent info="*InfoId*" type="*AgType*" param="*AgParams*"></agent>

where *InfoId* is a label to uniquely identify the piece of information within the Web site, *AgType* is the type of agent to be started and *AgParams* is an optional attribute with any parameters which ought to be passed on to the agent being started up.

The information identification *InfoId* allows *content agents* (explained below) to refer to the particular portion of the page they should look after. A single agent, the *publisher agent* explained below, is responsible for updating the annotations of a Web page. The scanner agent assigns to each page with at least one annotation a publisher agent; the annotations themselves cause a number of content agents to be started up – these should look after particular pieces of information on the page. Whenever there are changes to be carried out on the HTML file, they are done via the publisher agent. This arrangement solves any issues arising from concurrent updates of a file and preserves the separation of contents and presentation matters. We exploit a fully distributed coordination mechanism, explained below, by means of which content agents independently offer their updates which are published by the publisher agent.

The information identification *InfoId* labels a piece
of information within a Web
site, allowing us to take advantage of one agent's effort
for more than one page. As
an agent is started up for
an annotation to look after

```
<html><head><title>Weather Forecast...</title></head>
<body>
...
Current Temperature
<!-- <agent info="temp" type="weatherAg"
              param="[every,15,min]"> -->
30 <!-- </agent> --> &deg;C
</body></html>
```

Fig. 2. Sample Annotation for Web Pages

a piece of information, we might need the same information elsewhere within the Web site. If the same information appears elsewhere in the site then the Webmaster should annotate it with the same label – the agent looking after the information will interact with the publisher agent of the pages where the information appears and that have been annotated. If, however, the Webmaster accidentally uses a new label for a piece of information already associated with an agent, a new agent will be started up and will look after the information. This will not affect the Web site as the agents will independently look after the same information, but there will duplication of effort.

Our annotations also work as delimiters for the HTML portion that the agents should be looking after, that is, the part of the page they are responsible for monitoring and/or updating. In order to tell agents where the portion they should be looking after ends, we split the "<agent ...>" and "</agent>" tags, (using HTML comments around them) and enclosing the portion of HTML within the two. We show in Fig. 2 a complete example of an annotation. In it, a specific item of information of an HTML file is enclosed within tags <agent...> and </agent>. We have associated the agent weatherAg with this portion of the HTML file which will be responsible for updating the information every 15 minutes. The actual kinds of agents and their parameters are extensible. Webmasters may create annotations and associate them to special purpose agents which they also develop. We have explored a class of such agents which we explain below.

The Scanner Agent – The scanning process is itself carried out by an agent. This agent is constantly running, checking for new annotations in the files or changes to existing annotations. When a new annotation is found the scanner agent starts up a corresponding agent which will be responsible for that annotation in the HTML file. If there is already an agent responsible for that piece of information, the scanner agent will skip the annotation. Changes to existing annotations (type of the agent or parameters) will cause the previously started agent to be killed and a new agent to be started up instead. The scanner agent parses a hierarchy of HTML files, starting up the team of agents that were specified by the Webmaster to look after the Web site. The Webmaster will include an annotation everywhere in the Web pages where there is a need for monitoring and updating of information and/or formatting. A special agent, the *publisher agent* is started up for each page with at least one annotation. This agent is responsible for collecting the updates on the pieces of information within its page and update them in the HTML file. The scanner agent does not abort when it finds ill-constructed annotations, but skips over them and tells the Webmaster about them. The scanning process does not check for the correctness of the HTML contents, simply concentrating on the annotations and their associated effects (*i.e.*, start up of agents).

Publisher Agents – The scanner agent starts up a *publisher agent* for each HTML file with at least one annotation. This publisher agent is responsible for collecting the information from other agents looking after particular portions of the file and updating it. An alternative to our approach would be to have one agent looking after all annotated pieces of information of a page as well as updating the HTML file. However, if the annotated pieces of information have different frequencies for updates, then this one single agent would need to assess the time elapsed for each previous update in order to perform the next update. Although this is not an impossible task, such an agent will be unnecessarily more complex.

Content Agents – For each piece of information annotated, a corresponding *content agent* is created. This agent's task is to access periodically the data source as defined by the task frequency checking for any update in the information content. Having a specific agent for each piece of information isolates the details of the access to each data source, supporting multiple data sources and facilitating changes in the data source of any information.

Hence, content agents manage and access data only and publisher agents manage the Web pages visualisation (HTML files).

3.2   A Team of (Logic-Based) Agents

Each annotation may give rise to one or more agents, if the piece of information has not already got an agent started up. All our agents are self-contained processes with which Webmasters can communicate via message passing. The type of agent specified in the annotation informs the scanner agent which contents (functionalities) the agent ought to have. Each type is associated with a file containing the source code the agent will use once started up. The parameters in the annotation are passed to the agent which will use its source code with them.

In principle, any programming language can be used to represent the code. We have employed a simple executable temporal logic called TeLA (Temporal Logic of Assertions) [8] that confers a clean design on our agents and makes it possible to formally verify them with temporal theorem provers [9] as well as with model-checking tools such as SPIN [10] and LTSA [11]. The temporal dimension is also required to cope with the issues of frequency. We have used SICStus Prolog [12] to implement all our agents and infrastructure.

Our simple executable temporal logic has only one operator, the next time operator $\bigcirc$, and our formulae have a very restricted syntax, of the form *Present Conditions* $\Rightarrow$ $\bigcirc$*Assertions*, the meaning of which is, if it can prove *PresentConditions*, a conjunction of non-temporal (ordinary) literals, at the current state of affairs (current state of the system), then *Assertions*, a conjunction/disjunction of (possibly temporal) literals will be made to hold in the next state. This simple temporal logic is a practical compromise between the expressiveness of full first-order temporal logic [13] and an efficient means to

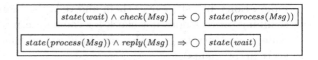

Fig. 3. Sample TeLA Agent

compute models for its formulae. The creation of such models guides the execution of temporal logic programs. We show in Fig. 3 a simple agent in TeLA. The execution changes between two states, *wait* and *process(Msg)*, where *Msg* is a variable (we adopt Prolog [14] conventions) to be instantiated to a message. Our simple agent switches between these two states: it stays in the *wait* state until a message *Msg* arrives (predicate *check* succeeds if a message is available for the agent). When a message arrives it moves to state *process(Msg)* (first axiom) – a state in which the agent will handle the message it just got. The second axiom allows the agent to reply to the message it has received and the agent goes back to the *wait* state.

We have enclosed the left and hand sides of the formulae in boxes to improve visualisation. The formulae show an agent that keeps an account of its current state, one of the set {*wait*, *process(Msg)*}, and the conditions that ought to hold in order for the states to change. Actions can be conveniently encoded as conditions: when a predicate like *check*/1 is attempted to be proved, it causes the execution of a routine to check if a message is available for the agent. A set of temporal formulae such as those above is put to use by means of a proof procedure that tries to build a model that satisfies all the formulae. The formulae depict the program and the proof procedure its interpreter. When agents are started up their corresponding program is the union of temporal formulae and the proof procedure.

The proof procedure works by checking if the atomic formulae on the left-hand side hold true. If they do, then the right-hand side is used to build a model for the next state of the computation. The proof procedure builds a model for the next state in which *all* formulae hold. In order to prove the left-hand side, the proof procedure checks the model for the current state for all those atomic formula that hold. However, the proof procedure also keeps a conventional (atemporal) logic program in which auxiliary predicates are defined – in our example above, the *check* and *reply* predicates are proved by means of one such program. The separation between temporal and atemporal aspects provides neater programs.

3.3   Communication Among/with Agents

Our agents are started up and run as independent Prolog processes which exchange messages by means of the Linda process communication mechanism available in SICStus Prolog [12]. Linda [15] is a concept for process communication, consisting of an area, the *tuple space* (shown in Fig. 1) where data from a number of different processes can be stored and a few basic operations (write, read and delete) can be performed on this area. The Linda concept has proven very successful due to its simplicity and flexibility, being incorporated into a number of programming languages, including Java [16]. SICStus Prolog incorporates a Linda library and offers a repertoire of built-in predicates with which one can write programs that run independently and exchange data. The messages our agents exchange via the tuple space are variants of the FIPA-ACL [17] standard adapted to Prolog's syntax. The information within messages are XML constructs [7] transferred as strings. This standardisation allows for changes in our infrastructure: for the sake of simplicity, we have used Prolog to implement all components of our architecture. However, we could move to a more standard and popular multi-agent platform like JADE [18] without much reimplementation.

Webmasters can communicate with agents, to find out about their status and follow their activities. A simple interface allows communication between the Webmaster and the team of agents. When agents encounter problems they can send messages to the Webmaster alerting to the difficulties they meet and whether they require intervention. Ideally, such interactions should be kept to a minimum, conferring as much autonomy to the agents as possible when they are being designed.

4   Working Example

In this Section we describe three maintenance agents as an example of the use of our approach for automated Web site maintenance. In this example there is one publisher agent and two content agents. For simplicity, it is assumed that all Web site content is kept in a database and all agents have access to this database. Let us consider a Web site for weather forecast having the following information for each location: day of the week, minimum temperature, max-

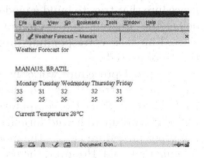

Fig. 4. Weather Forecast Page

imum temperature and current temperature. This database can be represented by the Prolog [14] facts weather($Location, Day, MinTemp, MaxTemp$) and current_temp($Location, CurrentTemp$). The information content in this database is constantly updated from multiple sources. The agents' task is to keep this information updated on a page for a chosen location. Figure 4 illustrates a Web page of this sort. Given that this sort of information is volatile, the content agents need to check the database periodically – for example, every hour the database is checked for a new current temperature. The forecast for maximum and minimum temperatures for the next 5 days does not change in the same frequency, for that reason there is another content agent responsible for keeping track of that particular information.

```
<html><head><title>Weather Forecast...</title></head>
<body>
...
<!-- <agent info="days_temp" type="weather_ag1"
          param="[every,12,hour]"> -->
<table><tr><td>Monday</td><td>Tuesday</td>...
<tr><td>33</td><td>31</td>... </table> <!-- </agent> -->
<br> Current Temperature
<!-- <agent info="curr_temp" type="weather_ag2"
          param="[every,1,hour]"> -->
30 <!-- </agent> --> &deg;C ...
```

Fig. 5. Annotation for Web Page Maintenance

In order to specify the content agents, the portion in the Web page code where the information about current temperature and the 5-day forecast appears must be annotated as presented in Fig. 5. These are identified, respectively, as agents weather_ag1 and weather_ ag2. Note that a publisher agent is automatically created for every page with an annotation. In this example we will identify this agent as pub_ag.

A typical content update agent behaviour can be illustrated by a state transition diagram, depicted in Fig. 6. From the initial state (start), the agent immediately moves to the check state, where it checks the data source for an

information update. At this point there are two possibilities: there is an update
to perform and the agent moves to state **update**, or there is no update to be
performed and the agent goes to state
sleep. Yet another possibility is a problem state, caused by unavailability of the
data source, for example. In this case the
agent should notify the Webmaster and
finish its execution accordingly. We omitted this state for simplicity.

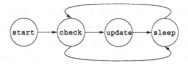

Fig. 6. Content Agent Behaviour

When an agent is in state **update** it puts the new information on the tuple
space and notify all publisher agents that are expecting that message – we explain
below how this notification is done. After sending the information, the content
agent goes to sleep. The details of this coordination among agents is explained
in Section 4.1.

State **sleep** cor-
responds to a time
(defined by the fre-
quency of the task)
in which the agent re-
mains inactive. When
the agent gets active
again it moves back
to state **check**. Fig. 7

```
start ⇒ ○ state(check)
(state(check) ∧ check_info(nil)) ⇒ ○ state(sleep)
(state(check) ∧ check_info(I) ∧ I ≠ nil) ⇒
                                 ○ state(update,I)
(state(update,I) ∧ notify_publishers(I)) ⇒
                                 ○ state(sleep)
(state(sleep) ∧ sleep(1,hour)) ⇒ ○ state(check)
```

Fig. 7. Content Agent for Current Temperature

shows the specification of a content maintenance agent using TeLA. Predicate
check_info(I) encapsulates all necessary steps to access the data source and
retrieve the latest data. If there is no new information available, the predicate
returns **nil**. Predicate **notify_publishers(I)** makes the updated information
available to the publisher agent. Predicate **sleep** makes the agent inactive for a
specific duration of time, which is also specified in the Web page annotation.

The specification of the five-day forecast agent **weather_ag1** is basically the
same. The only differences are the piece of information the agent is interested in
and the frequency of its update. In this case the agent looks after the information
with label **days_temp**, defined in the page annotation.

The publisher
agent is, however,
rather different as
it needs to know
about the Web
page visualisation
style, the actual
page layout and

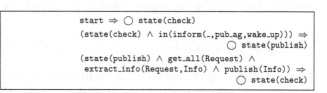

Fig. 8. Publisher Agent

the specific place where the information managed by the content agents will
be published. It works by placing an information request on the tuple space
and it waits for a signal from the content agent responsible for that piece
of information. Once the content agent has placed an updated information,

the publisher receives a "wake up" signal and updates the Web page. Fig. 8 shows the publisher agent specification. In state check the publisher agent waits for a "wake up" message from a content agent, denoted by predicate in(inform(_,ag_pub,wake_up)). In state publish the publisher gets all updated information it needs via predicate get_all(Request), then it extracts the value of the pieces of information from the messages using predicate extract_info/2, and finally publishes the Web page via publish(Info). Details of the implementation of these predicates and those predicates used in the content agents are given in Section 4.1 below. Note that the page layout is associated with the publisher agent. It is encapsulated by predicate publish(I) which inserts the updated piece of information I in its right place as defined in the annotation.

Changing the style is also possible, via the publisher agent. This is possible because of an important feature of our approach: keeping content and visualisation management separate. We can define individual styles for pieces of information as a set of predicates where, given a piece of information, it produces a corresponding publishable piece of code in a target mark-up language, such as HTML. For example, itemize(L) where L is a list of items with the form [$item_1$,$item_2$, ..., $item_n$] results in the HTML code <ul><li>$item_1$</li><li>$item_2$</li>... <li>$item_n$ </li></ul>. Similarly, other style predicates are defined as table(LL), paragraph(P), enumerate(L), bigText(P), and so on, each resulting in a piece of code which is placed in a page template. As a result the visualisation style of a particular data is changed. This allows the publisher agent to change a piece of information presentation style without affecting its content and completely independent of content maintenance agents and data sources. This also reinforces the idea of separation between information content and visualisation details.

Another use of the publisher agent is to re-publish a corrupted or deleted page, as the agent includes the layout and all static information of a Web page. The content maintenance agents provide the dynamic information of a page and once with all this information a new page can be produced.

The agents presented in this example keep the Web page presented in Fig. 4 automatically updated. Whenever the current temperature or the 5-day weather forecast changes in the database the content agents capture the new values and send them to the publisher agent, which in turn updates the HTML file.

4.1   Agent Coordination

The maintenance agents are coordinated in a particular way, in order to provide independence between content and publisher agents, allowing the same piece of information to be used by more than one publisher agent and to minimise overhead in message exchanging.

A major concept used in our agent architecture is the tuple space. It works as a notice board where any agent can post and retrieve messages. Our coordination mechanism is defined by this order of events:

1. the publisher agents put a request for updated information on the tuple space;
2. the content agents, when they have new updates, look up the tuple space for requests for their pieces of information – each piece of information is identified by the label provided by the Webmaster;
3. the content agents add their new information to the requests and put a wake-up notice on the tuple space to alert the publisher agents there is something for them.

The request message format is request(Sender,Receiver,Info):Flag. In this notation, Sender and Receiver are agent identifications. Info has the form info(Label,Data), where Label is a unique identifier of a piece of information, as defined in the page annotation and Data is its corresponding value. The information label (originated in the Web page annotation) identifies a piece of information and is used by publisher agents to find the right place of the data on its Web page. Flag is used as an indication whether the information value Data has been updated by a content agent. Our convention is to set Flag to value 0 indicating that Data has not been updated yet and zero otherwise.

The second type of message is only a signal used to wake up publisher agents with the form inform(Sender, Receiver,Signal). This message is necessary to avoid unnecessary repeated verifications of the tuple space by publisher agents, checking for updated information. Fig. 9 illustrates the given example showing how agents communicate via the tuple space. The top half of the diagram illustrates the pub_ag writing on the tuple space the requests for the two pieces of informa-tion it needs in its Web page – the en-

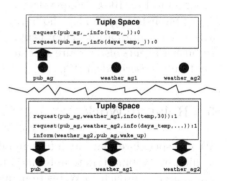

Fig. 9. Coordination via Tuple Space

tries have "_" (anonymous variables) in the fields whose value is to be supplied by a content agent.

The bottom half of the diagram of Fig. 9 depicts the content agents weather_ag1 and weather_ag2 independently accessing the tuple space and al-tering the requests with their information. The first agent to supply information to the publisher agent pub_ag also inserts the wake-up notice. In our example, weather_ag2 does this.

The agent implementation in TeLA presented in Figs. 7 and 8 makes use of auxiliary (atemporal) predicates which actually perform the maintenance tasks, such as accessing a database, checking messages on the tuple space and creating the HTML files. It is important to point out that these predicates also have the important role of hiding implementation details, keeping the agent specification clean and easier to read. It allows, for instance, changing the access to data sources, without changing the main specification in TeLA. We describe the implementation details of these predicates below. The content agents also include three such predicates:

1. check_info/1: succeeds if the data item has changed in the data source, returning its value, or succeeds if the data item has not changed, returning nil. The actual implementation might involve details for connecting and accessing a database, via SQL queries, for example.

2. sleep/1: succeeds if the execution of an agent is suspended for the duration specified by the arguments (number and time unit).

3. notify_publishers/1: succeeds if there are requests from publisher agents for the piece of information in the tuple space and sends the updated value of the information and a signal to wake up the publisher agents who have requested that information. The code in Fig. 10 illustrates this predicate implementation for the agent that updates the current temperature. Predicate bagof_rd_noblock(A,B,C) builds list C with all terms A that match term B in the tuple space. In the program in Fig. 10, AllRequest is a list of publisher agent ids, who have asked for information curr_temp. Publisher agents also require special predicates described in [19].

```
notify_publishers(I) :-
    bagof_rd_noblock(P,
        request_info(P,_,info(curr_temp,_)):0,
        AllRequest),
    my_id(Me),
    send_info(Me,AllRequest,I).

send_info(_,[],_).
send_info(Me,[P|RestP],I) :-
    out(request_info(P,Me,info(curr_temp,I)):1),
    out(inform(Me,P,wake_up),
    send_info(Me,RestP,I).
```

Fig. 10. Content Agent Implementation

5   Related Work

We can speculate that batch files and daemons have been employed in an ad-hoc fashion by Webmasters to automate repetitive tasks, but these have not led to a systematic approach to Web site maintenance. One major drawback with batch files and daemons is their lack of responsiveness: in order to find out about them (*i.e.*, whether they are alive and running), the Webmaster must look up their process identifications and their status or log files – scaling up clearly becomes a problem.

Similar annotations, the associated scanning process and the bootstrapping of agents were originally described in [20], using Java [21] as a programming language and JADE [18] as a communication platform. Each agent incorporated a particular functionality: a particular piece of information from *another* Web site was specified for the agent to monitor and periodically fetch, using it to update one's Web site [22]. These two references inspired our work herewith described and, apart from them, we have not been able to find any work on using multi-agent systems to look after Web sites.

A number of methods and techniques for Web site development have been proposed such as OOHDM [23], Araneus [24], Strudel [25], WebML [26], UWE [27], and the logic-based approaches of [28] and OMSwe [29], among others. The use of a formal approach for Web site modelling and development facilitates maintenance tasks as they usually provide a high-level view of the application and separation between content, navigation structure and visualisation. This allows, for instance, updating page templates or colour schemes without affecting the page content or links. Although these works have addressed the problem of Web site application development in the large, where maintenance is one of the issues involved, our work proposes an approach to static Web page maintenance which can also be adapted in order to be employed as part of a complete Web site application development method, as those mentioned above.

Specific automated maintenance is not addressed by most methods, although some claim support for it or offer some degree of automation. Given that there are certain maintenance tasks which are well defined and repetitive, it is possible to automate them in order to avoid human intervention, saving maintenance time and keeping the Web site continuously updated. With this respect, two work are closer to our proposed approach.

Sindoni [30] proposes an approach to enforce consistency between page content and database state. A specific algebra is proposed for defining views and views updates, which uses the Araneus Data Model as the reference model. Views updates are used by an algorithm that automatically updates the Web site from a set of changes on the application database. Maintenance is performed by removing or generating the appropriate sets of pages.

OntoWebber [31] is an ontology-based approach designed for the generation of data-intensive Web sites, in particular Web portals. It addresses the problem of multiple and heterogeneous sources of data by defining integration and articulation layers responsible for resolving syntactic and semantic differences between the different data sources. The composition layer includes a specification of a Web site view based on the Web site modelling ontologies. Ontologies are described using DAML+OIL [32], a semantic mark-up language for Web resources. A generation layer process queries the site specification to produce the Web pages. This approach offers some degree of automation by means of rules defined as triggers. These rules update the source data, meta-data, and site view specifications according to the fired triggers. However it is restricted to content maintenance.

6   Conclusions and Discussion

In this paper we introduce an agent-based approach to the maintenance of Web sites. Our approach caters for static Web pages whose contents require monitoring and updating. We offer a notation that Webmasters can use to annotate particular points of a Web page (an HTML file) in order to specify that an agent should monitor and update that portion of the page. The Webmaster can add as many annotations as required in one Web page. Our architecture associates, via a scanning process (carried out by an agent itself) an agent to each annotation. This agent is started up and autonomously looks after its prescribed piece of information. Any modifications to a Web page are centrally carried out by a publisher agent with whom all agents communicate – each annotated Web page has a publisher agent, started up by the scanning process.

It is important to decouple our proposed architecture and its implementation, as explained here. We do not suggest that ours is the only or the best means to implement the proposed architecture: our implementation should be considered as a proof-of-concept prototype used to exploit and refine our ideas. However, our implementation captures all basic functionalities of our architecture and is evidence that our architecture is feasible. Some features of our proposal worth pointing out are:

- *Scalability* – as many agents as required can be started up, provided that there are available computational resources. In our experiments, we used up to 250 agents in one single Pentium III PC (1GHz) running under Linux. However, the scanner agent can be programmed to start up agents in different machines. The SICStus Prolog tuple space employs a unique *host:port* addressing which allows agent anywhere in the Internet to access it.
- *Ease of use* – agents are now responsible for tasks that relied on humans or off-line daemons and batch files. Rather than keeping a record on the status of daemons and batch files or the actions of humans, the manager can now communicate with thousands of agents collectively or individually.
- *Robustness* – because the task of monitoring and updating the pages of the Web site is divided among independent agents, if individual components fail it is still possible to achieve some degree of overall functionality. Additionally, we can enable agents to perform failsafe operations when they encounter exceptional circumstances. For instance, if the data source an agent is using suddenly becomes unavailable, the agent could provide a "`Not Available`" default value to update the information on the Web page. The agent could also send a message to the Webmaster and wait for further instructions.
- *Backwards compatibility* – any existing Web site can incorporate our architecture, as the annotations are naturally accommodated within HTML files.
- *Extensibility* – the class of available agents and their functionalities can be gradually extended, and new annotations specifying them can be added at will. Web pages can be gradually annotated as the Webmaster becomes used to the new managerial style of administering a team of software agents.

Hyperlinks within Web sites may need constant monitoring as the objects they point at may move or disappear – we envisage employing software agents for constantly scanning the whole collection of HTML files, checking for broken references. These agents notify the Webmaster and isolate the offending reference, wrapping it as a comment. We are currently working on how these agents can be incorporated into our architecture.

Work is under way to integrate our proposal for agent-based maintenance with a high-level specification of Web sites, as described in [28,33]. This approach also uses logic to specify a Web application thus facilitating the desired integration. We notice that in a high-level specification of a Web site application the annotations for associating pieces of information to agents do not need to be made in the HTML files directly; rather they should become part of the site specification. This opens new possibilities to improve both approaches to Web site synthesis and maintenance.

References

1. Wang, P.S., Katila, S.S.: An Introduction to Web Design and Programming. Brooks/Cole-Thomson, U.S.A. (2004)
2. Hall, M.: Core Servlets & JavaServer Pages. Addison-Wesley (2000)
3. Weissinger, A.: ASP in a Nutshell, 2nd Edition. O'Reilly (2000)
4. Franklin, A. and Graesser, A.: Is it an Agent, or just a Program? In: LNAI. Volume 1193. Springer, Berlin (1997)
5. Wooldridge, M.: An Introduction to MultiAgent Systems. John Wiley & Sons Ltd., England, U.K. (2002)
6. Musciano, C., Kennedy, B.: HTML & XHTML: The Definitive Guide. 4th edn. O'Reilly, USA (2000)
7. Harold, E.R.: XML: Extensible Markup Language. IDG Books, U.S.A (1998)
8. Cavalcanti, J., Vasconcelos, W.: A Logic-Based Approach for Automatic Synthesis and Maintenance of Web Sites. In: Procs. of the 14th Int'l Conf. on Soft. Eng. & Knowl. Eng.(SEKE'02), ACM Press (2002)
9. Manna, Z., Pnuelli, A.: How to Cook a Temporal Proof System for your Pet Language. In: Proc. 10th POPL-ACM. (1983) 141–154
10. Holzmann, G.J.: The SPIN Model Checker. IEEE Trans. on Soft. Eng. **23** (1997)
11. Magee, J., Kramer, J.: Concurrency: State Models and Java Programs. John Wiley & Sons, England, UK (1999)
12. SICS: SICStus Prolog User's Manual. Swedish Institute of Computer Science, available at http://www.sics.se/ sicstus (2000)
13. Barringer, H., Fisher, M., Gabbay, D., Gough, G., Owens, R.: MetateM: an Imperative Approach to Temporal Logic Programming. Formal Aspects of Computing **7** (1995) 111–154
14. Apt, K.R.: From Logic Programming to Prolog. Prentice-Hall, U.K. (1997)
15. Carriero, N., Gelernter, D.: Linda in Context. Comm. of the ACM **32** (1989)
16. Freeman, E., Hupfer, S., Arnold, K.: JavaSpaces: Principles, Patterns and Practice. Addison-Wesley, U.S.A. (1999)
17. FIPA: The Foundation for Physical Agents. http://www.fipa.org (2002)
18. Bellifemine, F., Poggi, A., Rimassa, G.: JADE: A FIPA-compliant Agent Framework. Technical report, CSELT S.p.A (1999) http://sharon.cselt.it/projects/jade/.
19. Vasconcelos, W.W., Cavalcanti, J.: Agent-Based Web Site Maintenance. Technical Report 0401, Dept. of Comp. Science, Univ. of Aberdeen, U.K. (2004) Available at http://www.csd.abdn.ac.uk/~wvasconc/pubs/techreportAUCS0401.pdf.
20. Clarkson, D.: Agents for Web Management: An Architecture and its Implementation. MSc Report, MTP Programme in E-Commerce, Dept. of Computing Sci., Univ. of Aberdeen, U.K. (2003)
21. Spell, B.: Professional Java Programming. Wrox Press Inc (2000)
22. Shand, A.: Minion: An Approach to Automated Website Information Updating. MSc Report, MTP Programme in E-Commerce, Dept. of Computing Sci., Univ. of Aberdeen, U.K. (2003)
23. Schwabe, D., Rossi, G.: The Object-oriented Hypermedia Design Model. Comm. of the ACM **38** (1995) 45–46

24. Atzeni, P., Mecca, G., Merialdo, P.: Design and Maintenance of Data-Intensive Web Sites. In: Procs. of the Int'l Conf. on Extending Database Technology (EDBT), Valencia, Spain (1998)

25. Fernández, M., Florescu, D., Kang, J., Levy, A., Suciu, D.: Catching the Boat with Strudel: Experience with a A Web-site Management System. SIGMOD Record **27** (1998)

26. Ceri, S., Fraternali, P., Bongio, A.: Web Modeling Language (WebML): a Modeling Language for Designing Web Sites. In: Proceedings of the WWW9 conference, Amsterdam, the Netherlands (2000)

27. Hennicker, R., Koch, N.: A UML-based Methodology for Hypermedia Design. In: Procs. Unified Modeling Language Conference (UML'2000). Volume 1939 of LNCS. Springer-Verlag (2000) 410–424

28. Cavalcanti, J., Robertson, D.: Synthesis of Web Sites from High Level Descriptions. Volume 2016 of LNCS. Springer, Germany (2001)

29. Norrie, M., Palinginis, A.: From State to Structure: an XML Web Publishing Framework. In: 15th Conf. on Advanced Information Systems Engineering (CAiSE'03), Klagenfurt/Velden, Austria (2003)

30. Sindoni, G.: Incremental Maintenance of Hypertext Views. In: Procs. of the Int'l Workshop on the Web and Databases, Valencia, Spain (1998) 98–117

31. Jin, Y., Decker, S., Wiederhold, G.: OntoWebber: Model-driven ontology-based Web site management. In: Procs. of the 1st Int'l Semantic Web working symposium (SWWS'01), Stanford, CA, USA (2001)

32. W3C: DAML+OIL Reference Description (2001) http://www.w3.org/TR/daml+oil-reference.

33. Cavalcanti, J., Robertson, D.: Web Site Synthesis based on Computational Logic. Knowledge and Information Systems Journal (KAIS) **5** (2003) 263–287

From Maintenance to Evolutionary Development of Web Applications: A Pragmatic Approach

Rudolf Ramler[1], Klaus Wolfmaier[1], and Edgar Weippl[2]

[1] Software Competence Center Hagenberg GmbH,
Hauptstrasse 99, A-4232 Hagenberg, Austria
{rudolf.ramler, klaus.wolfmaier}@scch.at
[2] University of Vienna, Liebiggasse 4/3-4, A-1010 Vienna, Austria
weippl@acm.org

Abstract. Development of Web applications is dynamic by its very nature. Web development processes have to facilitate a Web application's continual refinement and evolution based on feedback from end-users. Evolutionary development can easily be achieved by end-user involvement through seamless integration of feedback and issue reporting mechanisms into Web applications. This paper discusses the use of conventional methods and tools for maintenance and change management as an infrastructure for evolutionary development of Web applications. An example demonstrates the feasibility of the proposed approach. It describes our experience from integrating the open source issue tracking system Bugzilla into a Web application.

1 Introduction

Today's economic realities pressure organizations to continuously adapt to shifting environments. Accordingly, "systems should be under constant development, can never be fully specified and are subject to constant adjustment and adaptation" [1]. "Web developers have the capability to modify their systems for all users immediately, without being impeded by the manufacturing, distribution and sales channel delays inherent in shrink-warp software development." [2] Web applications are installed on a central server and modifications are instantly propagated to all users. As a consequence, Web applications can be developed in an evolutionary process. Once a feature is implemented, end-users can start using it and their feedback can be quickly incorporated into new releases. This iterative process of delivering the application in multiple small steps allows immediate response to rapidly changing business needs while continually maturing and adapting the application over time. Refinement and adaptation are in many cases the only viable option in view of the fact that business needs often change as development proceeds, making a straight path to an end product unrealistic [3].

The goal of this paper is to present an easy yet effective approach to seamless end-user involvement into the evolutionary development process of Web applications. By relying on existing maintenance infrastructure, the users' feedback can be routed directly to the developers with little additional overhead. According to this goal, the remainder of this paper is structured as follows. In section 2 we present requirements

N. Koch, P. Fraternali, and M. Wirsing (Eds.): ICWE 2004, LNCS 3140, pp. 287–299, 2004.

for a Web development process. Section 3 outlines our conventional maintenance approach and the associated infrastructure (methods and tools), while section 4 describes how we enhanced the maintenance infrastructure to support evolutionary Web development. Section 5 gives an overview of related approaches that deal with rapid changes in Web development, and section 6 concludes the paper.

2   Requirements for a Web Development Process

From our experience in developing Web applications as well as from literature research, we have derived a list of requirements for our Web development process. The most important requirements are to provide (1) end-user involvement, (2) prototyping, (3) change management, (4) immediate response, (5) risk minimization, (6) no administrative overhead, and (7) transparency and overall guidance.

End-user involvement. Among the top three reasons for challenged or failed projects is the lack of end-user involvement [4]. Knowing the end-users' requirements is essential for the development of successful Web applications. The customer, although defining the main goals for the development of a Web application, usually is not the actual end-user and, therefore, he or she is not able to define all the requirements important to end-users. Involving actual end-users is most effective when uncertainty about requirements is high [5], but difficult to achieve in Web projects. The main reasons are the potentially high number of end-users, their geographical distribution (possibly all over the world), and their anonymity due to the lack of direct interaction.

Prototyping. End-users should be capable to provide all necessary requirements. However, as Web applications and their related concepts and metaphors are still new to many users, they have difficulties to develop realistic expectations and to express their needs [6]. Prototyping is used to leverage the involvement of end-users in Web application development. End-users are potentially highly skilled evaluators of product functionality [7]. Thus, we find it viable to prepare a first, stable prototype and present it to the end-users as a basis for feedback. Thereby, the users can refer to a clearly defined part of the application, which helps to avoid a plethora of (unrealistic) ideas and wishes. With emphasis on evolutionary prototypes of reasonable usability and reliability, we strive to establish continuity in development and avoid confusion and frustration of end-users – the main pitfall of rapid application development in Web development according to [8].

Change management. In many cases, it is not possible to fully specify the requirements of a Web application at the beginning of the project, because they will either evolve over time or change during development. Typical reasons are frequent changes in the environment (e.g. new business partners and competitors), new user requirements (stemming from intermediate development results presented to the user), the availability of new technologies, methods, and tools, or the need for refactoring and error correction throughout development. Thus, the incorporation of effective mechanisms to manage the Web application's change and maintenance is one of the key steps of successful development [9]. A single channel for requests and issues has to be defined and a change control board to prioritize requests and issues has to be established to allow for flexible and prompt reaction.

Immediate response. Developing Web applications means "internet-speed" software development [10]. Immediate response to changing requirements, to user feedback, and to market shifts is required. Regarding the aforementioned change management, immediate response relies mainly on immediate reaction to feedback from the end-users to intermediate development results, such as prototypes. Thereby, immediate feedback to the user is necessary in order to inform the end-user about the consecutive steps and to show that his/her effort is taken seriously, even if not all suggestions can be incorporated right away. In addition, immediate response to market situations provides the ability to tackle the demanding time-to-market problem in Web development. By employing evolutionary prototyping [7] it is feasible to go on-line with a first working solution that serves as a starting point for further development efforts and to exploit the opportunity of being a first-mover.

Risk minimization. Web projects have to deal with a high level of uncertainty and a large number of risks [12]. Typical examples are unrealistic schedules, misunderstood or frequently changing requirements, underestimated complexity of non-functional requirements, and unstable technologies. An ideal Web development process explicitly addresses these risks. Therefore, a realistic estimation of the project situation is necessary. This is possible through frequent feedback from customers and end-users on working examples and the continuous adaptation of previous estimations.

No administrative overhead. Typical Web projects have to cope with harsh limitations of financial resources, and – in addition – with restrictive schedules, often less than one or two months [11]. Thus, it is important to keep the administrative overhead at a minimum. Lightweight or agile approaches have to be applied and the often immense burden of (inappropriate) regulation and tool usage has to be avoided in order to keep both process costs and reaction time low. Yet, lightweight tools can significantly increase effectiveness and efficiency with simple, problem-specific solutions.

Transparency and overall guidance. In evolutionary Web development establishing a clear vision and long-term goals for the project is essential to unite the project team's efforts and to assure that all the efforts are aimed in the right direction. The product management, comprising the main stakeholders (e.g., customer and project manager), is responsible to outline a roadmap for future work and to align the project goals with business goals. A shared vision is required. Misalignment with business goals is quoted as one of the ten deadly Internet and Intranet project risks [12]. The collected and reviewed feedback from end-users serves as a decent controlling instrument. For effective guidance, the whole process has to be transparent for the team members as well as for the customers.

Most of these requirements have been frequently cited throughout the Web engineering literature ([8], [13], [14], [15], [3]) as prerequisites for the development of Web applications. For us, the question is not whether or not to incorporate these requirements, but how we could do this without the burden of changing existing processes and established structures or applying new methods and new tools. Yet, a rigorous reduction of development cycles resulting in a blend of development and maintenance activities proved as an effective and pragmatic approach towards an evolutionary development process. Tool support helped to make this approach efficient and systematic.

3   (Conventional) Maintenance and Change Management

Maintenance is the modification of a software product after it has been placed into production. Commonly, four different types of maintenance are distinguished [8]: (1) *Corrective maintenance* to fix bugs and design deviations, (2) *preventive maintenance* to avoid future bugs or maintenance, (3) *adaptive maintenance* when a system's environment changes, e.g. when a new Web browser is released and the application has to be modified to work properly within that browser, and (4) *perfective maintenance* to introduce enhancements such as new functionality or to increase efficiency.

Keeping track of changes and their effects on other system components is not an easy task. The more complex the system is, the more components are affected by each change. For this reason, change management [3] – important during development – is critical during maintenance. For conventional software development, our approach is to establish a change management process lead by a change control board to oversee this process. Open source tools, such as CVS and Bugzilla, are employed to support control and collaboration among team members.

CVS (Concurrent Versions System) [16] is used for version control. This tool keeps track of the different versions of all the files that are part of a project. CVS version control significantly eases the collaboration between developers and the authoring of Web sites [17]. In addition, we rely on Bugzilla [18] to report and track issues (e.g. requirements, bugs, user requests, or remarks). Bugzilla is a popular open source issue tracking system that derived from the open source project Mozilla. It provides an extensive set of features useful for distributed development teams and end-user involvement, such as a Web-based user interface or an email notification mechanism. As the source code is freely available, Bugzilla can easily be adopted and extended to meet specific organizational needs. Nevertheless, the predefined workflow introduces a flexible yet clear and systematic way to deal with issues. The state diagram in Figure 1 illustrates the basic steps of the workflow from the perspective of an issue's lifecycle. Further details can be found in [18] or [19].

Fig. 1. Bugzilla issue management workflow

4   Transition to Evolutionary Development

David Lowe compares the development of Web applications with town planning and landscape gardening: "The evolution of Web applications is analogous to a garden changing as a natural part of its cycle of growth." From this, Lowe draws the following conclusions: "... Web development tends to differ greatly in that we are no longer aiming to develop a 'finished' product. Rather, we are aiming to create an organic entity that starts with an initial consistent structure, but continues to grow and evolve over time. This evolution is much finer-grained than the maintenance changes that occur with more traditional software products, and tends to be an integral part of the lifecycle of the product. Compare this to conventional software maintenance, which tends to be a coarse-grained response to errors in the products, changes in requirements, or a changing environment." [20]

In conformance to Lowe's suggestions, we reviewed and aligned our development process. Instead of aiming towards a final product from the very beginning, we started with laying out a general, flexible fundament for a more generic Web application by modularizing functionality and by relying on component-oriented development. For our first projects, we used an in-house Web application framework, similar to the architecture described in [21], since other available solutions were still in their infancies. The framework allowed us to develop modular function blocks and to specify their coupling, parameters, error conditions, and access rights through XML configuration files. This framework was later on superseded by the freely available Struts framework [22], part of the Apache project. On the basis of this initial structure we developed the functionality in small increments to enable evolutionary growth. These increments did not encompass fully featured implementations of functions, but rather initial, stable, and useable prototypes to demonstrate the conceptual and technical feasibility. Only the feedback from the end-users facilitated the function's continual refinement and maturation.

In the remainder of this section we describe how we implemented such a feedback mechanism by means of the issue tracking system Bugzilla for a Web application for internal use, the lessons we learned, and further implications. The experience and data presented in this section is a summary of the project's final report, the usage analysis of Bugzilla, and the notes from periodical project and process reviews conducted by quality management.

4.1   Enabling End-User Involvement

At a first glance, the approach to evolve an application based on user feedback does not seem much different to any conventional (iterative) software development process that includes a beta testing and stabilization phase. For us, this was an advantage as no major changes to the underlying processes and no new methods or tools were necessary. However, there exists an inherent difference regarding the nature of the feedback that is often overlooked, especially by development: A comparison of conventional and evolutionary development shows a significant shift in the importance of the different types of maintenance. While conventional maintenance approaches tend to emphasize corrective maintenance, evolutionary development is characterized by a focus on adaptive maintenance [23]. This is an important finding, as it underlines that evolutionary development focuses on (new) requirements rather than on errors in existing functionality. Evolutionary development should therefore primarily address the problem that users are not able to fully specify their requirements at the beginning of the projects and, even if they do, requirements may still change over time as business procedures and technologies evolve. Furthermore, evolutionary development is often the preferable way to develop a common understanding about the goals of the project and the needs of the users [6]. "In other words, the specification of the system emerges from the design, rather than preceding and driving the design." [24]

Consequently, we used the maintenance infrastructure, namely the issue tracking system Bugzilla described in section 3, primarily to collect and maintain the continually evolving requirements of the application. Thereby, using the existing maintenance infrastructure for evolutionary development provided several benefits: First of all, a proven tool with a clear and systematic process was used. All the involved developers were familiar with the infrastructure. Thus, similar to the advantages initially mentioned, no radical changes of the underlying development process were necessary and overhead costs could be kept at a minimum. Second, as described below, the integration of the Bugzilla issue tracking system turned out as an effective vehicle to interact with end-users and to collect requirements. Third, it supported collaborative work throughout development as well as measuring and tracking the ongoing development effort.

To establish a single channel for end-user feedback, we made our maintenance infrastructure an integral part of the Web application. Beside the solution presented here, we also experimented with various other approaches that are commonly suggested in the literature for end-user integration (see [23]). Useful to stimulate feedback and discussion are, for example, annotation mechanisms to Web pages or Wiki-style authoring [25]. However, these approaches focus mainly on content – the data, its structure and presentation. We required a more general feedback channel amenable to the different functional and non-functional aspects of Web applications (e.g., correctness, security, usability, or performance issues related to functionality, content, or infrastructure aspects) as described in [26]. Nevertheless, an easy to use and seamless integrated solution was required. When, in a first step, Bugzilla was integrated solely via a link, we experienced little acceptance of the feedback mechanism because of major usability deficiencies: The access to Bugzilla was rather uncomfortable due to switching to a (very) different application. The users had to logon again and were confronted with the (non-intuitive) user interface of Bugzilla, data had to be copied manually into Bugzilla's report form, and the users were burdened with the concepts of Bugzilla's issue tracking process.

To overcome these drawbacks, we integrated a simple issue report and enhancement request form into the Web application, which forwarded the data entered by the user to the issue tracking system Bugzilla. Even though the form resembled the structure of a conventional Bugzilla issue report, it was aligned with the style of the Web application (see Figure 2 for an example). A few additional field values, e.g. *enhancement request* for the field *issue type*, had to be added to support not only issue tracking but also requests for enhancements and new features. Hence, the users were relieved from directly accessing the Bugzilla interface and we could still utilize our preferable issue tracking system in the background. Furthermore, the form was made available within a single click from every page of the Web application. On accessing the form, the context of use was analyzed and the fields of the form were automatically pre-filled with meaningful default values to minimize the amount of data the user had to enter. For example, the user's browser type was identified to easily reproduce issues related to the different behavior of the various Web browsers and the link referring to the page plus the name of the application module the user last accessed were automatically suggested.

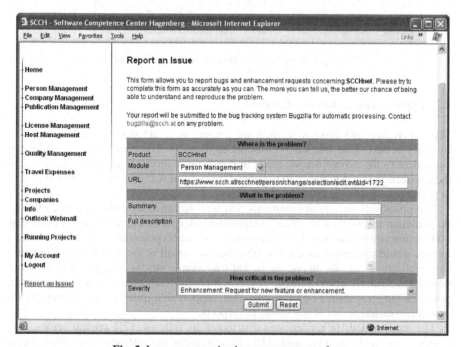

Fig. 2. Issue report and enhancement request form

To get a first version of the Bugzilla integration setup up and running, we relied on the Bugzilla email gateway. Technically spoken, the report form is submitted to a Java mailing servlet[1] part of our Web application. The servlet assembles an email containing the data from the report form structured according to the requirements of the Bugzilla email gateway and sends it to a dedicated email account on the Bugzilla server. There, the email is parsed, the report data is extracted and entered into the issue tracking system. Thus, we can easily access Bugzilla and initiate the issue tracking workflow. Bugzilla auto-assigns the report to the developer in charge for the affected module, tracks all changes, and sends email notifications on updates. Figure 3 illustrates the interaction between the user's Web browser, the Web application, and Bugzilla integrated via the email gateway.

---

[1] The Java source code of this servlet can be obtained from the authors.

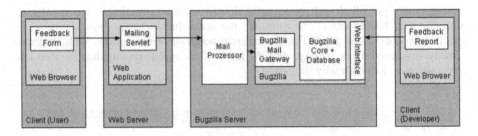

Fig. 3. Bugzilla Integration in Web Applications

4.2 Experience and Lessons Learned

The experience and lessons learned we present here are derived from integrating Bugzilla as part of an internal Web-based application. The main results were largely equivalent to the experience we made in consecutive projects. The target audience of the application was a group of experienced users from within our organization as well as partner companies at distributed locations.

The possibility to submit comments was well accepted by end-users. Even though no particular measures were taken to encourage user feedback, we received more than 100 reports within one month from a group of about 50 potential users. Many of these reports would otherwise have been submitted via email or through informal personal communication, e.g. by phone or in hallway conversations. Or, more likely, they would have simply been omitted. The development team greatly benefited from the issue tracking capabilities of Bugzilla that supported a quick triage as well as the systematic management of the submitted reports.

The total number of reports was distributed as follows: 17% critical errors, 41% errors of normal severity, and 42% improvement suggestions and enhancement requests. Critical and normal errors together made 58% of all collected reports, despite the fact that we estimated a much higher potential for improvement comments and enhancement requests than for error reports. The reason seems to be that the motivation to react and comment on problems increases with the perceived severity of the problem. From personal feedback we know that, in some cases, users even did not report obvious errors when they found easy workarounds. Thus, incentives may be necessary to motivate feedback and, furthermore, the costs for providing feedback must be kept at a minimum. The ease of use of the feedback mechanism is of uttermost importance. A short and concise form and a careful pre-selection of default values are required as lengthy forms to fill in deter many users.

However, including user session data in reports may possibly conflict with privacy, a major concern of many users. Therefore, we used only a few pre-filled entries and we did not log any usage data related to the reported issues. Rather, the user was asked to give a description of the issue and the necessary steps to reproduce it. The optional statement of an email address allowed us to contact the user in case of further questions. Besides, we were able to offer the user email notification on certain events, e.g., when the reported issue had been accepted or resolved. So we involved the end-users into the development process instead of frustrating them with the feeling as if reporting "into a black hole".

Two important lessons we learned were, first, that we could not expect users to positively confirm correctly working solutions. To some extent, the absence of comments may only indicate a correct working solution. Second, since we provide the feedback form for existing functionality only, users did not come up with new features or any "great new ideas". Hence, evolutionary Web development still requires a great deal of planning ahead and the proactive development of new functionality, e.g. motivated by competitive analysis [2]. In addition, careful analysis of the end-users' reports and a "creative mindset" are necessary to stimulate new ideas within the development team. A shared vision serving as overall guidance for the project team helped to direct these ideas into the right direction.

Furthermore, reports have to be brought in relation to overall usage statistics to evaluate the relative significance of the feedback. Other sources that provide an insight into the attitude and behavior of users should be included in the data collection to support the reasoning about improvements and to strengthen the conclusions drawn. Therefore, we are currently extending our feedback mechanism to allow real-time analysis of application logs as described in the following section.

4.3   Towards a Bugzilla Web Service

The approach described in section 4.1 allows a quick and easy integration of Bugzilla into any Web application. However, the Bugzilla email gateway is an extension to the Bugzilla project with some limitations regarding functionality and flexibility. It lacks full access to all of the features of Bugzilla. Currently, only a one-way access to the issue tracking system is possible – issues can only be submitted from the Web application to Bugzilla. Full access should permit creating new issues, adding comments, changing issue related metadata (e.g. priority or severity), querying for existing issues, or voting for issues (so the frequency of issues can be documented and the number of duplicate reports can be reduced).

In Figure 4, we outline an integration concept based on a SOAP (Simple Object Access Protocol) interface [27] to Bugzilla. Thus, the SOAP interface provides access to all of the Bugzilla functionality via a Web Service and enables communication in both ways – from the Web application to the Bugzilla issue tracking system (e.g. to submit an issue) and from Bugzilla to the Web application (e.g. to return the status information of an issue). The example of an automated issue reporting system, part of a Web application, illustrates the advantages of such an interface to Bugzilla. We are currently using the Log4J framework [28] for application logging. So, a log recorder/analyzer can be used to observe and analyze the activity and state of the Web application and react to certain events, e.g. application errors, in real-time by submitting appropriate reports directly into the issue tracking system without further human interaction.

We are currently evaluating the Jagzilla Web Service API, part of the Jagzilla System [29] as a way to realize an integration of Bugzilla into Web Applications like depicted in Figure 4. Jagzilla provides a simple re-implementation of the core functionality of Bugzilla while relying on the original database of the Bugzilla issue tracking system. By the date of writing, the Jagzilla Web Service API is still in early alpha status.

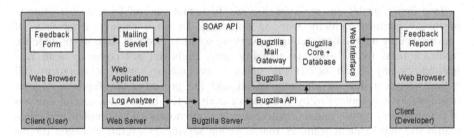

Fig. 4. Bugzilla integration based on Web Services

5   Related Work

Being in a constant state of flux, the adaptation and continuous evolvement of Web applications as an answer to rapidly changing requirements has long been a topic in Web engineering. Various approaches to deal with this problem have therefore been proposed. In this section, we give an overview of related work, which we consider as a prerequisite, a logical next step, or a useful basis in combination with the approach that has been described in this paper.

Modeling and design. Web applications must be built with a mindset towards frequent changes throughout the lifecycle. Development has to establish a basis for applications that can be modified, fixed, or maintained at little cost of time or money. Common approaches are modular architectures, e.g. based on re-useable components, Web application frameworks, or code generation from domain models. Various design methodologies support these strategies. An overview of methods and appropriate tools specific for Web applications can be found in [30], [20], [23], or [31]. From the maintenance perspective, re-engineering and reverse engineering are of particular interest. Methods and tools based on modeling and design strategies have been developed that support maintenance and evolutionary development. (Prominent examples are STRUDEL [32], ReWeb [33], WARE [34], or Rigi [35].) Evolutionary prototyping-based development, furthermore, has a rich tradition in User-Centered [36] and Participatory Design [37]. Participatory Design explicitly considers social, ethical, as well as political viewpoints in addition to technical issues and takes a "democratic" approach to system design by actively involving users. From our point of view, modeling and design techniques are a prerequisite for effective maintenance and, thus, complementary to our evolutionary development approach.

Adaptive and customizable Web applications. With the transition to dynamic Web sites and Web-based applications, where Web pages can be generated on the fly, the idea of self-adaptation in response to external changes emerged. Several approaches have been published that demonstrate this idea. For an overview of this topic please refer to [23], [38], [39], or [40]. In contrast, our approach requires a human (e.g. a programmer or product manager) to look at all submitted feedback reports, to validate them, and to initiate proper measures. The necessary changes – the adaptation and the extension of the Web application – are done by development, not by the system itself. However, an integration based on Web Services, as described above, may provide enough flexibility to serve as a first step towards adaptive applications.

Agile development. Agile development methods have successfully found their way into Web development processes [41, 42] and, conversely, agile processes have been developed for Web engineering [43]. There are a number of rapid development software methodologies all referred to as "agile development" [44]. Many of these methods explicitly address the requirements of an evolutionary Web development process as stated in Section 2. They offer, for example, rapid prototyping, comprehensive end-user involvement, support for frequent changes (e.g. by unit testing), and they emphasize low administrative overhead. As we do not prescribe any development process in our approach, the workflow and tools proposed in this paper may be combined with most of the agile development methods. Some processes, e.g. Feature-driven Development [45], even suggest similar ideas to cooperate with stakeholders or to organize work.

6   Conclusions and Future Work

Within this paper we first presented a requirement's perspective for an ideal Web development process. In order to address and fulfill the presented requirements, we then elaborated on how we successfully implemented a process for evolutionary development based on conventional maintenance concepts. Our pragmatic approach has the advantage that established development processes can be retained, no radical changes are necessary, and existing tools can be utilized. Furthermore, while maintenance such as adding new features or correcting errors may be initiated by the development team, in practice maintenance is often triggered by feedback, both direct and indirect, from end-users. The seamless integration of the issue tracking system Bugzilla into the Web application permits easy and flexible involvement of end-users and encourages the feedback necessary to adapt and grow Web applications. Thereby, the workflow implied by Bugzilla supports an ordered and systematic development process (as demanded in [9]), regardless of which particular process model is actually used. From our point of view, agile development processes conveniently harmonize with Web development and prevent ad-hoc approaches and undisciplined hacking (see also [46]).

In a next step, we will consider to integrate the interface to the Bugzilla issue tracking system into an existing Web application framework (e.g. Struts). This would considerably ease the automated collection of end-user feedback and, thus, further support the development of evolving Web applications as described in this paper.

Acknowledgements. This work has accrued in the framework of the K-plus Competence Center Program, which is funded by the Austrian Government, the Province of Upper Austria and the Chamber of Commerce of Upper Austria.

References

1. Truex D.P., Baskerville R., Klein H.: Growing Systems in Emergent Organizations. Communications of the ACM, vol. 42, no. 8, August 1999, pp. 117-123
2. Norton K.S.: Applying Cross-Functional Evolutionary Methodologies to Web Development. pp. 48-57, in: [13] pp. 48-57
3. Pressman R.S.: Software Engineering: A Practitioner's Approach. 5.Ed., McGraw-Hill, 2001
4. Standish Group International: Extreme Chaos. Update to the CHAOS Report, Standish Group International, Inc., 2001
5. Emam K.L., Quintin S., Madhavji N.Z.: User Participation in the Requirements Engineering Process: An Empirical Study. Requirements Engineering, 1996 (1), pp. 4-26
6. Lowe D.: Web System Requirements: An Overview. Requirements Engineering Journal, 8 (2), 2003, pp. 102-113
7. Pomberger G., Blaschek G.: Object Orientation and Prototyping in Software Engineering. Prentice-Hall, 1996
8. Powell T.A.: Web Site Engineering: Beyond Web Page Design. Prentice-Hall, 1998
9. Ginige A., Murugesan S.: The Essence of Web Engineering: Managing the Diversity and Complexity of Web Application Development. IEEE Multimedia, vol. 8, no. 2, April-June 2001, pp. 22-25
10. Baskerville R., Levine L., Pries-Heje J., Slaughter S.: Is Internet-Speed Software Development Different?. IEEE Software, vol. 20, no. 6, Nov.-Dec. 2003, pp. 70-77
11. Pressman, R.S.: What a Tangled Web We Weave. IEEE Software, Vol. 17, No.1, Jan-Feb 2000, pp. 18-21
12. Reifer D.J.: Ten Deadly Risks in Internet and Intranet Software Development. IEEE Software, vol. 19, no. 2, March-April 2002, pp. 12-14
13. Murugesan S., Deshpande Y. (Eds.): Web Engineering – Managing Diversity and Complexity of Web Application Development. LNCS 2016, Springer, 2001
14. Kappel G., Pröll B., Reich S., Retschitzegger W. (Eds.): Web Engineering – Systematische Entwicklung von Web-Anwendungen. d-punkt Verlag, 2003
15. Lowe D., Hall W.: Hypermedia & the Web. An Engineering Approach. Wiley, 1999
16. Concurrent Versions System. Web (http://www.cvshome.org)
17. Dreilinger S.: CVS Version Control for Web Site Projects. Technical report, 1999 (http://www.durak.org/cvswebsites/howto-cvs-websites.pdf)
18. Bugzilla Bug Tracking System. Web (http://www.bugzilla.org)
19. Allen M.: Bug Tracking Basics – A beginners guide to reporting and tracking defects. STQE Magazine, vol. 4, iss. 3, May-June 2002, pp. 20-24
20. Lowe D.: A Framework for Defining Acceptance Criteria for Web Development Projects. pp. 279-294, In: [13], pp. 279-294
21. alphaWorks: ServletManager. IBM, 2002 (http://alphaworks.ibm.com/tech/servletmanager)
22. The Apache Struts Web Application Framework. Web (http://jakarta.apache.org/struts)
23. Scharl A.: Evolutionary Web Development. Springer, 2000
24. Lowe D., Eklund J.: Client Needs and the Design Process in Web Projects. Proc. of the 11th Int. World Wide Web Conference, Hawaii, 2002
25. Leuf B., Cunningham W.: The Wiki Way – Quick Collaboration in the Web. Addison-Wesley, 2001
26. Ramler R., Weippl E., Winterer M., Schwinger W., Altmann J.: A Quality-Driven Approach to Web-Testing. Proc. of the 2nd Int. Conf. on Web Engineering, Santa Fe, Argentina, Sept. 2002
27. Gudgin M., Hadley M., Mendelsohn N., Moreau J.J., Nielsen H.F.: SOAP Version 1.2 Part 1: Messaging Framework. W3C Rec., June 2003 (http://www.w3.org/TR/SOAP)
28. Logging Services - Log4J. Web (http://logging.apache.org/log4j)

29. Jagzilla Home Page. Web (http://jagzilla.sourceforge.net)
30. Christodoulou S.P., Styliaras G.D., Papatheodrou T. S.: Evaluation of Hypermedia Application Development and Management Systems. Proc. of the 9th Conf. on Hypertext and Hypermedia, Pittsburgh, US, 1998
31. Schwinger W., Koch N.: Modellierung von Web-Anwendungen. In. [14], pp. 49-75
32. Fernandez M., Florescu D., Kang J., Levy A., Suciu D.: STRUDEL: A Web-site Management System. Proc. of the Int. Conf. on Management of Data, Tucson, US, May 1997
33. Ricca F., Tonella P.: Understanding and Restructuring Web Sites with ReWeb. IEEE MultiMedia, vol. 8, no. 2, April-June 2001, pp. 40-51
34. Di Lucca G.A., Fasolino A.R., Pace F., Tramontana P., De Carlini U.: WARE: A Tool for the Reverse Engineering of Web Applications. Proc. of the 6th Eur. Conf. on Software Maintenance and Reengineering, Budapest, Hungary, March 2002
35. Martin J., Martin L.: Web Site Maintenance With Software-Engineering Tools. Proc. of the 3rd Int. Workshop on Web Site Evolution, Florence, Italy, Nov. 2001
36. Vredenburg K., Isensee S., Righi C.: User-Centered Design: An Integrated Approach. Prentice Hall, 2001
37. Muller M.J., Kuhn S.: Participatory design. Communications of the ACM, vol. 36, no. 4, June 1993, pp. 24-28
38. Perkowitz M., Etzioni O.: Adaptive Web sites. Communications of the ACM, vol. 43, no. 8, August 2000, pp. 152-158
39. Brusilovsky P., Maybury M.T.: From Adaptive Hypermedia to the Adaptive Web. Communications of the ACM, special section: The Adaptive Web. vol. 45, no. 5, May 2002
40. Patel N.V. (ed.): Adaptive Evolutionary Information Systems. Idea Group Publishing, 2002
41. Engels G., Lohmann M., Wagner A.: Entwicklungsprozess von Web-Anwendungen. In [14], pp. 239-263
42. Hansen, Steve: Web Information Systems:- The Changing Landscape of Management Models and Web Applications. Workshop on Web Engineering, Proc. of the 14th Int. Conference on Software Engineering and Knowledge Engineering, Ischia, Italy, July 2002
43. McDonald A., Welland R.: Agile Web Engineering (AWE) Process, Department of Computing Science Technical Report TR-2001-98, University of Glasgow, Scotland, December 2001 (http://www.dcs.gla.ac.uk/~andrew/TR-2001-98.pdf)
44. Abrahamsson P., Warsta J., Siponen M.T., Ronkainen J.: New Directions on Agile Methods: A Comparative Analysis. Proc. of the 25th Int. Conf. on Software Engineering, Portland, US, May, 2003
45. Coad P., Lefebvre E., De Luca J.: Java Modeling Color with UML: Enterprise Components and Process. Prentice Hall, 1999
46. Boehm B.: Get Ready for Agile Methods, With Care. IEEE Computer, vol. 35, no. 1, January 2002, pp. 64-69

An MDA Approach for the Development of Web Applications

Santiago Meliá Beigbeder and Cristina Cachero Castro

Universidad de Alicante, España
{santi,ccachero}@dlsi.ua.es

Abstract. The continuous advances in Web technologies are posing new challenges to Web Engineering proposals, which now require the inclusion Software Architecture techniques in order to integrate the explicit consideration of non-functional features in the Web application design process. In this article we propose a new approach called WebSA, based on the the MDA (Model Driven Architecture) paradigm. WebSA specifies a model driven process that adds to the traditional Web-related functional viewpoint a new software architectural viewpoint that permits, by means of successive model transformations, to establish the desired target application structure.

1 Introduction

The high pace at which advances in Web technologies are taking place has changed the idiosyncrasy of Web applications, that now imply not only more complex functional requirements but also stricter constraints posed on features such as distributability, scalability, platform-independence or extensibility. In order to tackle such new requirements, several authors [1] propose the use of Software Architecture techniques. Following this trend, in this article we present WebSA (Web Software Architecture). WebSA is a Web model-driven approach that is based on the standard MDA (Model Driven Architecture) [5]. The MDA framework provides WebSA not only with the possibility to specify and formalize a set of Web-specific models by means of a UML profile, but also to specify each process step from the models to implementation by means of a set of transformation rules.

The remaining of the article is structured as follows: in section 2 we present briefly the WebSA Development process and its main views and models. From these views, the architectural viewpoint and, more specifically, its logical architectural view is discussed in section 3. Last, section 4 outlines the conclusions and further lines of research.

2 WebSA: Model Driven Architecture of Web Applications

As we stated above, WebSA is a proposal whose main target is to cover all the phases of the Web application development and to contribute to cover the gap existing between traditional Web design models and the application implementation. In order

N. Koch, P. Fraternali, and M. Wirsing (Eds.): ICWE 2004, LNCS 3140, pp. 300–305, 2004.
© Springer-Verlag Berlin Heidelberg 2004

to achieve this aim, it defines an instance of the *MDA Development Process* for the Web application domain. Also, it proposes the formalization of the models by means of a MOF-compliant repository (metamodel) and a set of OCL constraints (both part of the OMG proposed standards) that together specify (1) which are the semantics associated with each element in the models, (2) which are the valid configurations and (3) which constraints apply. This formalization is being performed, as other Web methodologies [14] have done before, by the definition of a UML [8] profile that gathers the main constructs of the models involved in the specification of applications in the Web domain.

In order to define a Web application System proposes a Web application view model that is made up of 8 *views*, grouped into three *viewpoints:* requirements, functional and architectural viewpoints. From them, the architectural viewpoint is a main contribution of WebSA. This viewpoint includes a logical architectural view that gathers the set of logical components (subsystems, modules and/or software components) and the relationships among them. Also, it includes a physical architecture view that describes the physical components that integrate the lower level specification of the application (clients, servers, networks, etc.). As we have stated above, and in order to shift from one view to the other, WebSA defines a process that is explained next.

2.1   The WebSA Development Process

The WebSA Development Process [3] is based on the MDA development process. In order to fulfill this goal, it establishes a correspondence between its Web-related artifacts and the MDA artifacts. Also, and as a main contribution, it defines a transformation policy partly driven by the architectural model that can be seen in Fig. 1. In this figure we observe how in the analysis phase the Web application specification is divided horizontally into two viewpoints. The functional-perspective models reflect the functional analysis, while the architectural models define the system architecture. Both of these models are PIMs in the context of an MDA framework. In this phase, the architectural models are based on the concept of *Conceptual Architecture* [4], and are made up of conceptual elements, obtained by abstraction of the elements found in the Web application domain. These models fix the application structure orthogonally to its functionality, therefore allowing their reuse in different Web applications.

The *PIM-to-PIM* transformation (see T1 in Fig. 1) of these models into platform independent design models (PIMs) provides a set of artifacts in which the conceptual elements of the analysis phase are mapped to concrete elements where the information about functionality and architecture is integrated. It is important to note how these models, being still platform independent, are the basis on which several new transformations, one for each target platform (see e.g. T2, T2' and T3 in Fig. 1), can be defined. The output of these *PIM-to-PSM* transformations is the specification of our Web application for a given platform. At this level of abstraction, the models can still endure a final *PSM-to-code* transformation, usually implemented in WebSA by means of templates. In this way, the WebSA process guarantees the traceability from analysis to code. In order to complete the specification of this process, WebSA formalizes the three transformations (PIM-to-PIM, PIM-to-PSM y PSM-to-code) by means of QVT (Query View Transformation) [6]. QVT defines a transformation language that is based on an extension of the MOF 2.0 metamodel and which allows to link models situated in different views and map them through the different life cycle phases. Also, QVT extends OCL for the specification of queries and filters over the models. The inclusion of an architectural view in this process has a preeminent role for the completion of the specification of the final Web application, and drives the refinement process from analysis to implementation. In the next section we will center on this *architectural viewpoint* and how it influences the refinement process.

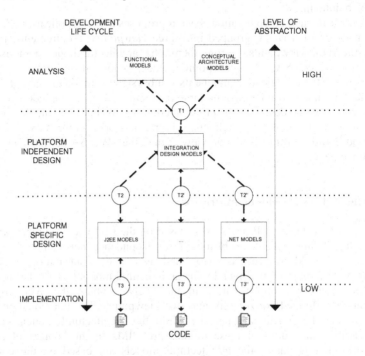

Fig. 1. WebSA Web Development Process.

3   Logical Architectural View for Web Applications

The logical architectural view is responsible for the definition of the logical components (subsystem, modules and/or software components) that collaborate in the system, as well as the relationship among them. In WebSA this view is made up of three models, namely (1) the *Subsystem Model* (SM), which determines the conceptual subsystems that make up our application, (2) the *Web Component Configuration Model* (WCCM), which decomposes each subsystem in a set of abstract components related by abstract connectors and (3) the *Web Component Integration Model* (WCIM) which, as its name may suggest, performs an integration of views.

3.1 Subsystem Model

Also known as structural design, the Subsystem Model determines which are the subsystems that make up our application.

This model is made up of two main constructs:

- **Subsystem**: element of coarsest granularity in any Web application architectural design. It defines a group of software components developed to support the functionality assigned to a given logical layer. Subsystems are depicted in WebSA by means of the UML package symbol.
- **Dependency Relationship**: link element that reflects the use dependencies between subsystems. In WebSA it is depicted as a UML dependency arrow.

This model provides the most abstract perspective of the logical architecture view, and the subsystems obtained during this phase will be later identified with each logic layer in the application. This separation on layers is essential to reduce the complexity of the system, as it is justified in the "layering approach" pattern presented in [2]. In this model, and in order to ease its construction, WebSA proposes the use of any of the five *distribution patterns* defined in [7].

The different layers identified for a given system are reflected in the Subsystem Model by means of a stereotype associated to the subsystem package symbol. WebSA defines nine subsystem stereotypes, namely: «user interface», «server», «business logic», «presentation», «dialog control», «process control», «business object», «data access» and «physical data». Additionally, WebSA provides a set of restrictions that apply to the possible relationships between subsystems.

Once the different subsystems have been identified, we must specify the contents of each subsystem, that is, the set of abstract components that configure them. Such contents are specified in the Web Component Configuration Model, which is introduced next.

3.2 Web Component Configuration Model (WCCM)

The second model of the logic Architecture view is the Web Component Configuration Model, which consists of a set of abstract components and connectors, particular to the Web domain. These abstract elements, also based on the Conceptual Architecture, are the result of a refinement process performed on each subsystem identified in the previous model. The main constructs of the Web Component Configuration Model are *abstract components* and *abstract connectors.*

- An *abstract component* represents an abstraction of one or more software components with a shared functionality in the context of a Web application. An example of it is a Client Page, which represents any artifact that contains information and/or interaction code relevant for the user. Note how this kind of component does not necessarily map to a single physical page but reflects a general task that must be performed by the application, such as showing certain information to the user. Abstract components are depicted with a UML class symbol.

- The *abstract connector* represents a dependency relationship between two abstract components in the system, and is depicted with a stereotyped UML dependency relationship. This relationship may affect either the interface or the whole component.

In order to construct a WCCM, the designer may use any of the architectural and design patterns. Such patterns provide powerful configurations that, applied to abstract components, not only provide a reuse mechanism but also contribute to a more efficient development process.

3.3   Web Component Integration Model (WCIM)

The last model defined as part of the logical architectural view is the Web Component Integration Model (WCIM). This view is also known as *integration model*, as it connects the functional and architectural views under a common set of concrete components, modules and connectors which will eventually make up the Web application. This model is defined during the WebSA Platform Independent Design phase, and still centers on design aspects (components, their interfaces and their relations).

The WCIM includes three main constructs: concrete components, modules and concrete connectors. *Concrete Components* (CC) are the smallest unit in the context of the integration model. It represents a software component in a given application domain, and it is obtained as an instance of an abstract component. A module (M) is a container of one or more concrete elements in the context of a given Web application. Such elements can be either other modules, concrete components or concrete connectors. *Modules* condense the functionality of a set of elements, reducing in this way the complexity of the models, and are depicted by means of a UML package metaclass. Last, *Concrete Connectors* (CN) express a relationship between two concrete components or modules of the system. It can be regarded as an instance of a dependency relationship defined in the WCCM. The number of instances (concrete connectors) generated for each abstract connector depends both on the cardinality of such abstract connector and on the existing relationships between those abstract components and the functional side of the application. Concrete connectors belong, just as modules and concrete components, to a given application domain.

4   Conclusions

In this paper we have presented a Web development approach called WebSA. WebSA fosters the use of the MDA philosophy to define a set of suitable models and a complete refinement process to cover the Web application domain. In this way, WebSA adds a new architectural viewpoint to explicitly address the architectural issues. This view is made up of three models, and its construction follows a top-down process that goes from the Subsystem Model, where the layers of the application are defined, to the Web Component Integration Model, where the designer determines the low level platform-independent components that make up the final application. In each phase WebSA promotes the use of a set of reuse practices and provides the mechanisms to reflect different sets of requirements. Currently, we are working on a formal definition of the UML 2.0 profile and metamodel for WebSA, and also on the set of QVT transformation models that support the WebSA refinement process, which we expect to be incorporating in the VisualWADE Development Enviroment [9] in the near future.

References

1. Bass, L., Klein, M., Bachmann, F. "Quality Attribute Design Primitives" CMU/SEI-2000-TN-017, Carnegie Mellon, Pittsburgh, December, 2000.
2. Buschman F., Meunier R., Rohnert H., Sommerlad P., Stal. M.: "Pattern-Oriented Software Architecture – A System of Patterns"; John Wiley & Sons Ltd. Chichester, England, 1996.
3. Santiago Meliá, Cristina Cachero y Jaime Gomez. Using MDA in Web Software Architectures. 2nd OOPSLA Workshop in "Generative Techniques in the context of MDA". http://www.softmetaware.com/oopsla2003/mda-workshop.html. October, 2003.
4. Nowack, P.: "Structures and Interactions – Characterizing Object-Oriented Software Architecture" PhD thesis. The Maersk Mc-Kinney Moeller Institute for Production Technology, Univertity of Southern Denmark".
5. Model-Driven Architecture (MDA) Home Page: http://www.omg.org/mda/index.htm.
6. Object Management Group. Request for Proposal: MOF 2.0 Query / Views / Transformations RFP,2002. ad/2002-04-10.
7. Renzel K., Keller W. Client/Server Architectures for Business Information Systems. A Pattern Language. PLoP'97 Conference.
8. UML 2.0 Standard, OMG (2003). http://www.omg.org.
9. VisualWADE. http://www.visualwade.com

RetroWeb: A Web Site Reverse Engineering Approach

Sélima Besbes Essanaa and Nadira Lammari

CEDRIC Laboratory, CNAM,
292 rue Saint Martin 75141 Paris Cedex 03, France
Besbes_s@Auditeur.Cnam.fr, Lammari@cnam.fr

Abstract. Most of Web sites are built as a matter of priority. Therefore, to reduce the development time, the conceptualization phase is often put aside and the associated documentation is neglected. Moreover, during the exploitation phase, Web sites suffer the effects of a rapid and unstructured evolution process. Their reconstruction encompasses inevitably a reverse engineering process. In this paper, we propose RetroWeb, a reverse engineering approach of semi-structured Web sites. It aims to provide a description of the site informative content at the physical, logical and conceptual levels. This approach uses, at each level, a meta-model which is instantiated using reverse engineering rules.

1 Introduction

In spite the effort and the generated high costs for their development and maintenance, most enterprise Web sites are not suitable. The traditional principles of the information systems design and documentation are often neglected on behalf of the visual and esthetic aspects. The lack of conceptualization during the development leads to maintenance problems and to a bad structuring of the information over the Web site pages. To reconstruct already existing Web sites that do not respect the development life cycle, the reverse engineering is essential. It aims to extract, in a clear and formal way, at various abstraction levels, all available information in order to understand the site functionalities.

This paper presents an approach, called RetroWeb, to reverse engineer the informative content of semi-structured Web sites. Besides the EER conceptual model, two meta-models are proposed to describe, at three abstraction levels, the semi-structured data coded on the Web site HTML pages. The first one is used to represent the Web site through its physical views. It is instantiated using the semi-structured data extracted from each HTML page. The second one is used to describe the Web site through its logical views. Mapping rules are proposed for the translation of physical views into logical views and then into conceptual ones. The whole site conceptual description is obtained by merging the generated conceptual views.

The remainder of the paper is organized as follows. Section 2 describes RetroWeb. Section 3 discusses the related works. Section 4 concludes and presents future work.

N. Koch, P. Fraternali, and M. Wirsing (Eds.): ICWE 2004, LNCS 3140, pp. 306–310, 2004.

2   RetroWeb Approach

RetroWeb is an approach to reverse engineer the informative content of semi-structured Web sites[1]. It is built on the inversion of the life-cycle design process. Starting from web site HTML pages, it deduces an EER conceptual description of its informative content. It encompasses three steps: the extraction, the conceptualization and the integration steps. The following paragraphs describe each of these steps.

The Extraction Step. It aims to the retrieval of the semi-structured data coded on the site HTML pages and to describe them through physical views (one physical view per page). Its result is the instantiation of the meta-model describing the extracted physical views. For instance, let us consider a Web site for academic journal publications. The left part of Fig. 1 presents a Web page that displays, for each volume of the academic journal, its authors. The right part of the same figure gives its corresponding physical view.

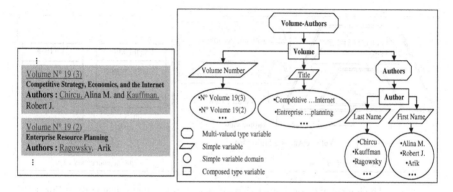

Fig. 1. An academic journal publications Web site page and its corresponding physical view

The concepts used to build physical views are: simple variable, simple variable domain, composed type and multi-valued type variables. A simple variable is an atomic structure that can hold an atomic piece of data. Simple variable domain is the values set (data) that can be hold by a simple variable in a page. A composed type variable is a data record build by one or more simple variables. A multi-valued variable is a set of composed type variables.

The extraction step is performed into three phases: pre-processing, extraction and naming phases. The pre-processing phase takes as an entry HTML pages, corrects them, proceed to some cleaning, executes some transformations and then returns, for each page, a coded sequence describing the page structure. In this sequence, the structure tags are codified using the same number of positions. All textual data that are not identified as tags are replaced by a token "Text". The second phase deduces pattern expressions that will be used by the wrapper to extract data from pages. It uses the DeLa system technique described in [1]. The last phase assigns significant names

---

[1] Semi-structured web sites are in majority data-rich and display data in contiguous blocks. These blocks are ordered and aligned such that they exhibit regularity.

to variables of the physical views. It uses an algorithm that improves the labeling itself by reducing the number of concepts to name. It first defines classes of concepts that may be assigned the same label. Then, it assigns to any concept, not yet labeled, a name and gives this name to its family (i. e. to all concepts sharing the same class). It uses, to that end, some heuristics. More details about this phase can be found in [2].

The Conceptualization Step. It aims to produce the EER schemas associated with the physical views. In order to reach this result, the conceptualization step translates first the physical views into logical ones, constructs for each logical view its corresponding EER schema and then, affects, according to the same naming process used in the precedent step, significant labels to entity-types and relationship-types of the obtained conceptual schemas. Consequently, it generates successively an instance of the meta-model describing the logical views of the web site pages and an instance of an EER model. For our example, the physical view described in Fig. 1 is transformed into the logical view of Fig. 2a and then into the EER schema of Fig. 2b.

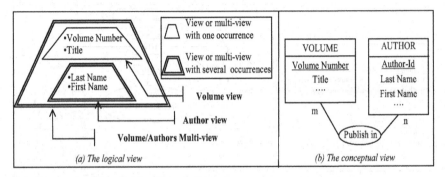

Fig. 2. The logical and conceptual views deduced from the physical view of Fig. 1

A logical view is described through three concepts: the property, the view and the multi-view concepts. A property is a logical representation of a variable. A view is a logical representation of a composed type variable. It groups properties that describe an object represented in a web page. It can have one or several occurrences. A multi-view is obtained by assembling all deduced views. It can also have several occurrences.

The different schema transformations are performed thanks to reverse engineering rules. For example, among rules used to translate logical views into conceptual ones, we can quote:

- Rule 1: every logical view becomes an EER schema
- Rule 2: each view of a multi-view becomes an entity-type of the EER schema
- Rule 3: if two views V1 and V2 belong to the same multi-view then the entities that they represent are linked by a relationship-type. If the two views have a number of instances higher than 1 then the cardinality of this relationship-type is M: N. In contrary, if one of the two views has a number of instances equal to 1, then the cardinality of this relationship-type is 1: N.

The Integration Step. It merges the portions of EER schemas into a global one in order to give a global conceptual description of the whole web site informative content. This step is based on integration techniques well known in the information systems context. The majority of these techniques propose an integration in 4 phases: (i) a pre-integration phase which aims to standardize the schema sources by translating them into a common conceptual model, (ii) a comparison phase whose aim is to identify the relations between schema sources, (iii) a fusion phase which allows the merging of the schema sources in an integrated one according to the results of the precedent phase and to the existing integration rules and finally (iv) a reorganization phase that improves the quality of the integrated schema. We re-use these phases. We choose the EER model as a common conceptual model.

3 Related Works

The evolution of Web sites has been addressed from various ways. Some research works take an interest to the evolution of the presentation [3, 4] and others to the restructuring of the HTML code [5, 6, 7]. [2] proposes an approach that allows small display units, like PDA and WAP, to access to the Web site content. [5] describes a clustering technique to translate static pages into dynamic ones. [6] uses a slicing technique to reduce the site size. [7] applies re-writing rules to the HTML code.

The literature also supplies approaches that aim to obtain Web sites abstract representation [8, 9, 10, 11, 12]. [8] presents a framework to deduce, from XML pages, the corresponding DTD. [9] analyzes web site code in order to automatically reconstruct the underlying logical interaction design. [10] translates the visual layout of HTML forms into a semantic model. [11] produces HTML UIs by integrating data of several web pages. [12] uses UML diagrams to model views of web applications, at different abstraction levels.

Other related works concern data extraction from HTML code. Their principal concern is the retrieval of data concealed in semi-structured data-rich pages. The way in which these data will be displayed, and the models to which they will be mapped, are left to the user.

Through RetroWeb, we wish to recover the informative content of the whole site. Thanks to the proposed meta-models, RetroWeb supplies, at physical, logical and conceptual levels, a clear and semi-formal description of the web site informative content. This extracted description is useful for its re-documentation, re-structuring or integration with other Web sites.

4 Conclusion

In this paper we have proposed a reverse engineering approach of semi-structured and undocumented Web sites, called RetroWeb. RetroWeb gives a description of the informative content of the site at various abstraction levels: physical, logical and conceptual levels. Reverse engineering rules are defined to map the physical description into the logical one and then into the conceptual one.

According to the type of needed evolution, the web site maintainer can execute totaly or partially the reverse engineering process. For instance, RetroWeb can be used either for the integration of Web sites or for the translation of HTML sites into XML sites. In the firts case, the conceptual description of the informative content of the two sites must be retreived. In the second case, the retrieval of physical views can be enough.

Our current work involves implementing RetroWeb. Further works will mainly concern the enrichment of the set of heuristics used for the naming of concepts. We also expect to enrich the reverse engineering rules set in order to exhibit, for example, generalization-specialization links at the conceptual level. Finally, we wish to extend our process to other aspects like the site navigational structure.

References

1. Wang, J., Lochovsky, F.: Data extraction and label assignment for Web databases. Proc. of the 12th International Conference on World Wide Web, Hungary (2003) 187–196
2. Essanaa, S., Lammari, N.: Improving the Naming Process for Web Site Reverse Engineering. Proceedings of the 9th International Conference on Application of Natural Language to Information Systems, Manchester June (2004)
3. Vanderdonckt, J., Bouillon, L., Souchon, N.: Flexible Reverse Engineering of Web Pages with Vaquista. Proceedings of the 8th Working Conference on Reverse Engineering (WCRE'01), October (2001) 241–248
4. Lopez, J. F., Szekely, P.: Web page adaptation for universal access. In Stephanidis, C. (ed.) Universal Access in HCI: Towards an Information Society for All. In proceedings of the 1st International Conference on Universal Access in Human-Computer Interaction, New Orleans August (2001). Mahwah, N. J.: Lawrence Erlbaum Associates 690-694
5. Ricca, F., Tonella, P.: Using Clustering to Support the Migration from Static to Dynamic Web Pages. Proceedings of the 11th International Workshop on Program Comprehension, Portland Oregon USA May (2003) 207–216
6. Ricca, F., Tonella, P.: Construction of the System Dependence Graph for Web Application Slicing. Proceedings of SCAM'2002, Workshop on Source Code Analysis and Manipulation, Montreal Canada, October (2002) 123–132
7. Ricca, F., Tonella, P., Baxter, I., D.: Web Application Transformations based on Rewrite Rules. Information and Software Technology Volume 44(13) (2002) 811–825
8. Chuang-Hue, M., Ee-Peng, L., Wee-Keong, N.: Re-engineering from Web Documents. Proceedings of the International Conference on digital Libraries (2000) 148–157
9. Paganelli, L., Paterno, F.: Automatic Reconstruction of the Underlying Interaction Design of Web Applications. Proceedings of the 14th International Conference on Software Engineering and Knowledge Engineering (SEKE 02), Ishia Italy July (2002)
10. Gaeremynck, Y., Bergman, L. D., Lau, T.: MORE for less: model recovery from visual interfaces for multi-device application design. Proc. of the Int. Conf. on Intelligent user interfaces, Miami Florida USA January (2003), ACM Press, New York USA (2003) 69-76
11. Stroulia, E., Thomson, J., Situ, Q.: Constructing XML-speaking Wrappers for Web Applications: Towards an Interoperating Web. Proc. of the 7th Working Conference on Reverse Engineering (WCRE'2000), Queensland Australia (2000), IEEE Computer Society
12. Di Lucca, G. A., Fasolino, A. R., Pace, F., Tramontana, P., De Carlini, U.: WARE: a tool for the Reverse Engineering of Web Applications. Proc. of the European Conference on Software Maintenance and Reengineering (CSMR2002), Budapest March (2002)

Empirical Methodologies for Web Engineering

Briony J. Oates, Gary Griffiths, Mike Lockyer, and Barry Hebbron

School of Computing
University of Teesside
Middlesbrough
TS1 3BA, UK
B.J.Oates@tees.ac.uk

Abstract. We review a range of data generation methods and empirical research strategies of potential usefulness to web engineering research. The various strategies do not all share the same underlying philosophy about knowledge and how it can be acquired. We therefore explain two contrasting philosophical paradigms: positivism and interpretivism. We suggest that empirical web engineering should use a plurality of research strategies and data generation methods, and recognise the potential usefulness of both positivism and interpretivism. Finally we discuss the implications of such a plurality.

1 Introduction

The majority of web engineering research, like software engineering research, concentrates on design research i.e. developing new concepts, models, methods or instantiations [1]. However, there have been strong criticisms of software engineering researchers for under-usage of empirical studies and failing to validate their research ideas [e.g. 2]. There is therefore increasing interest in empirical software engineering. If web engineers are to avoid similar criticisms, they must be able to both perform empirical studies and also assess the empirical research findings of others. We therefore review a range of empirical strategies and data generation methods of potential usefulness to web engineering research and summarize two contrasting philosophical paradigms: positivism and interpretivism. We argue that both philosophies and all the strategies and methods are relevant to web engineering research.

2 Data Generation Methods and Research Strategies

Data and data analysis can be either quantitative (i.e. numeric), or qualitative (i.e. textual, verbal or visual). Data generation methods available for gathering evidence include questionnaires, interviews, observations and documents (which include multimedia 'documents': non-textual artifacts such as photographs, videos and screenshots). Research strategies are the ways in which data generation methods are used and combined. One strategy can use many data generation methods, although

N. Koch, P. Fraternali, and M. Wirsing (Eds.): ICWE 2004, LNCS 3140, pp. 311–315, 2004.

particular strategies may be associated with particular methods, and typically one research strategy addresses one research question.

Strategies for using and combining data generation methods include experiments, surveys, case studies, action research and ethnography. Table 1 below summarizes each strategy, provides references where more information about each strategy can be found, and gives examples of its use in web-related research.

Table 1. Summary of research strategies for web engineering

Strategy	Brief description	Examples
Experiments	Use observations to look for evidence of cause and effect, so can confirm or refute a hypothesis [3]	[4, 5]
Surveys	Systematic gathering of information from a large sample, looking for general trends or patterns via statistical analysis [6]	[7-9]
Case studies	Rich account of particular experience, event or situation, often longitudinal view [10, 11]	[12, 13]
Action research	Developers research iteratively into own practice, with twin aims of contributing to practical concerns of people in a situation and to the goals of science [14]	[15, 16]
Ethnography	Researchers immerse themselves in lives of the people under study, experience the same as them, and place phenomena they observe in their social and cultural context [17]	[18, 19]

3 Philosophical Paradigms

The strategies in Table 1 are based on different philosophical assumptions about the nature of 'reality' (i.e. ontological assumptions) and about the nature of 'knowledge' and how it can be obtained (i.e. epistemology). These are summarized in Table 2.

Positivism underlies the scientific method, which has been developed by the natural sciences [e.g. 20]. Many people know of only this approach to research, and our modern daily discourse is frequently based, often unthinkingly, on a positivist worldview, with politicians and journalists demanding 'proof' and 'the truth'. Interpretivism [eg. 21] has been developed by the social sciences, and recognises that the social world has few equivalents to the 'laws of nature' in the physical world. For example, there is no guarantee that two people joining in with the life of a web development department as ethnographers would gather the same data and interpret it in the same way to draw the same conclusions.

Table 2. Summary of positivism and interpretivism

	Positivism	**Interpretivism**
Strategies	Experiments and surveys	Ethnography, most action research and many case studies
Ontological assumptions	Physical and social world exists independently of humans; exists 'out there' to be studied, captured and measured. Researcher 'discovers' this world by measurement, modeling and observations.	Whatever 'reality' is, it can only be accessed through social constructions such as language and shared meanings.
Aims	Generalizations – irrefutable objective facts and fundamental laws	Understanding, how people make sense of their perceived worlds, and how those perceptions change over time and differ from one person or group to another
Researcher	Must be neutral, objective detached	Can never be neutral: their assumptions, beliefs, actions inevitably shape research process and affect situation.
Epistemology	Empirical testability of hypotheses and theories, leading to verification or refutation, and a search for universal laws or principles	Studying people and practices in their natural social or work settings
Evaluation criteria	Internal and external validity, reliability and replication	Plausibility and cogency of the reasoning and the evidential data

4 The Need for Plurality

Our literature searches have confirmed the findings of Bahli and Di Tullio [22]: most empirical web engineering research has used surveys or experiments and a positivist perspective. In Section 2 we had to suggest web research examples for some strategies from the information systems, social sciences and education disciplines.

Members of the web engineering community *could* decide that only positivist research is appropriate to their discipline. Or they could decide that an interpretive case study is only appropriate as an exploratory method of investigation prior to a more 'scientific' approach. We suggest, however, that web engineering should accept both positivism and interpretivism and recognise a wide range of research strategies [cf. 23]. Web engineering is dependent on the people and the environment in which it is practised, making it difficult or impossible to design and implement carefully controlled and repeatable experiments. Where such experiments can be achieved, a positivist approach could provide some truths on which to build the discipline. Where this is not possible, interpretivist approaches such as ethnographies and case studies can help us to explore particular situations and contexts, in order to understand better how people understand, engineer and use web-based artifacts in the real world. Rich and detailed understanding from a series of case studies of web engineering might, but not necessarily, gradually accumulate into a generally applicable body of knowledge.

5   Implications

We are not proposing that everyone has to abandon positivism and adopt interpretivism. But our argument for plurality does mean that researchers and reviewers should not automatically reject a as 'unscientific' work which does not fit the positivist paradigm. On the other hand, researchers and reviewers do not automatically have to accept qualitative, interpretive evidence. They should know enough about the tenets of interpretivism to accept or reject the validity of such evidence on its own terms.

Web engineering practitioners may also need educating in the different types of data generation methods and strategies and underlying philosophies of empirical research, especially if they are to be persuaded to adopt new practices on the basis of qualitative, interpretive evidence. Their own educational background might have only introduced them to the positivist scientific method, and, as we noted earlier, our modern daily discourse is frequently unthinkingly based on a positivist worldview.

By using a wide range of strategies and data generation methods, and both positivist and interpretivist approaches, empirical web engineering research can increase our knowledge and understanding of how to develop, deploy and maintain high quality Web-based systems and applications.

References

[1]   S. March and G. Smith, "Design and natural science research on information technology," *Decision Support Systems*, vol. 15, pp. 251-266, 1995.
[2]   M. V. Zelkowitz and D. Wallace, "Experimental validation in software technology," *Information and Software Technology*, vol. 1997, pp. 11, 1997.
[3]   B. A. Kitchenham, S. L. Pfleeger, L. M. Pickard, P. W. Jones, D. C. Hoaglin, K. El-Emam, and J. Rosenberg, *Preliminary Guidelines for Empirical Research in Software Engineering*: National Research Council of Canada, 2001.
[4]   C. Rumpradit and M. L. Donnell, "Navigational Cues on User Interface Design to Produce Better Information Seeking on the World Wide Web," presented at 32nd Hawaii International Conference on System Sciences (HICSS-32), Hawaii, USA, 1999.
[5]   S. Grazioli and A. Wang, "Looking without seeing: Understanding unsophisticated consumers' success and failure to detect Internet deception," in *Proc. 22nd International Conference on Information Systems*, 2001, pp. 193-203.

[6]   S. L. Pfleeger and B. A. Kitchenham, "Principles of survey research, Part 1: Turning lemons into lemonade," *Software Engineering Notes*, vol. 26, pp. 16-18, 2001.

[7]   M. Lang, "Hypermedia systems development: A comparative study of software engineers and graphic designers," *Communications of the AIS*, vol. 12, pp. 242-257, 2003.

[8]   D. Gehrke and E. Turban, "Determinants of successful web site design: relative importance and recommendations for effectiveness," in *Proc. 32nd Hawaii International Conference on Systems Sciences*, 1999.

[9]   A. S. Huarng, "Web-based information systems requirement analysis," *Information Systems Management, 2003*, vol. 20, pp. 49-57, 2003.

[10]   R. K. Yin, *Case Study Research. Design and Methods*, Third ed. Thousand Oaks, Calif.: Sage Publications, 2003.

[11]   R. K. Yin, *Applications of Case Study Research*, Second ed. Thousand Oaks, Calif.: Sage Publications, 2003.

[12]   E. Mendes, N. Mosley, and C. Steve, "Web metrics - Estimating design and authoring effort," *IEEE Multimedia*, vol. 8, pp. 50-57, 2001.

[13]   C. Hine, "Web pages, authors and audiences. The meaning of a mouse click," *Information, Communication & Society*, vol. 4, pp. 182-198, 2001.

[14]   R. L. Baskerville and A. T. Wood-Harper, "A critical perspective on action research as a method for information systems research," *Journal of Information Technology*, vol. 11, pp. 235-246, 1996.

[15]   R. Vidgen, "Constructing a web information system development methodology," *Information Systems Journal*, vol. 12, pp. 247-261, 2002.

[16]   G. Griffiths and B. J. Oates, "Lecture-free teaching for systems analysis: An action research study," in *Proc. INSITE Informing Science and Information Technology Education conference, 24-27 June*. Pori, Finland, 2003, pp. 355-365.

[17]   J. Van Maanen, *Tales of the Field: On Writing Ethnography*. Chicago: University of Chicago Press, 1988.

[18]   N. Hayes, "Boundless and bounded interactions in the knowledge work process: The role of groupware technologies," *Information and Organization 11 (2001) 79-101*, vol. 11, pp. 79-101, 2001.

[19]   C. Hine, *Virtual Ethnography*. London: Sage Publications, 2000.

[20]   K. Popper, *The Logic of Scientific Enquiry*. London: Harper, 1959.

[21]   N. K. Denzin and Y. S. Lincoln, "Handbook of Qualitative Research." Thousand Oaks, Calif.: Sage Publications, 1994.

[22]   B. Bahli and D. Di Tullio, "Web engineering: An assessment of empirical research," *Communications of the AIS*, vol. 12, pp. 203-222, 2003.

[23]   R. Dawson, P. Bones, B. J. Oates, P. Brereton, M. Azuma, and M. L. Jackson, "Empirical methodologies in software engineering," in *(Under review)*: Springer Verlag, 2004.

Using RDF to Query Spatial XML

Jose Eduardo Córcoles and Pascual González

LOuISE Research Group. Dept. Informática.
Universidad de Castilla-La Mancha
02071, Albacete (Spain)
{corcoles, pgonzalez}@info-ab.uclm.es

Abstract. In tackling the *Semantic Web*, a rich domain that requires special attention is the Geospatial Semantic Web. A contribution to the Geospatial semantic Web is the definition of an approach for integrating non-spatial resources like HTML, PDF, GIF, etc., with spatial XML resources represented by Spatial XML [4]. However, in order to put this approach into practice it is necessary to solve the problem of developing an integration system for querying spatial XML resources stored in different sources. In this paper, we have implemented an approach for querying spatial and non-spatial information represented in the Geographical Markup Language (GML). The approach uses RDF to integrate the spatial XML documents. A performance study has been carried out and the results are given.

1 Introduction

A rich domain that requires special attention is the Geospatial Semantic Web [1]. The enormous variety of encoding of geospatial semantics makes it particularly challenging to process requests for geospatial information. In the future, the Geospatial Semantic Web will allow the returning of both spatial and non-spatial resources to simple queries, using a browser. For example, a query *"lakes in Maine"* should return all relational resources with lakes in Maine (pictures, text, ...) in different formats (XML, HTML, JPG, PDF, References, ...) [1].

However, in the same way as with the Semantic Web, in order to approach the Semantic Geospatial Web it is necessary to solve several problems. One of these is the integration of spatial and non-spatial resources with different schemas stored in different sources.

Tackling the integration of spatial information on the Web is not a simple task since there are several High level problems (e.g. heterogeneity for representing spatial information, for using spatial operators, for defining the semantic of the objects, etc. [2]) and Low level problems (e.g. the sources may store large amounts of incomplete spatial data, which may make it necessary to join the results of queries with spatial joins [3]).

In order to contribute to the Geospatial Semantic Web, in this paper we study a prototype for querying spatial XML resources. The main task of this approach is to provide users with a unique interface for querying spatial XML resources with different schemas, independently of their actual organization and location. It provides

N. Koch, P. Fraternali, and M. Wirsing (Eds.): ICWE 2004, LNCS 3140, pp. 316–329, 2004.
© Springer-Verlag Berlin Heidelberg 2004

the infrastructure for formulating structured spatial queries by taking into consideration the conceptual representation of a specific domain in the form of an ontology. The resources are integrated using RDF. This work is based on [4], and we detail how to use RDF for integrating non-spatial resources (HTML, PDF, etc.) with spatial XML resources represented by GML. The most novel and critical feature of this approach is the querying of spatial XML resources, because it uses a different way from that of querying and relating non-spatial resources. Therefore, our prototype is focused on this alone. After proving the viability of this prototype, making a prototype in accordance with [4] is a simply task.

In our study the spatial information is represented by GML because it is an XML encoding for the transport and storage of spatial/geographic information, including both spatial features and non-spatial features. The mechanisms and syntax that GML uses to encode spatial information in XML are defined in the specification of OpenGIS [5]. Thus, GML allows a more homogeneous and flexible representation of the spatial information.

Query mediation has been extensively studied in the literature. Directly concerned with the integration of XML resources, it is worth noting C-Web Portal [6] and [7]. C-Web Portal supports the integration of non-spatial resources on the Web, and it provides the infrastructure for formulating structured queries by taking into consideration the conceptual representation of a specific domain in the form of an ontology. On the other hand, [7] proposes a *mediator* architecture for the querying and integration of Web-accessible XML data resources (non-spatial data). Its contribution is the definition of a simple but expressive mapping language, following a *local as view* approach and describing XML resources as local views of some global schema. Both of these approaches have aims in common with our approach, but they are only focused on non-spatial information.

In relation to spatial XML integration, the approaches developed by [8], [9] and [10] stand out. [8] presents a mediation system that addresses the integration of GIS data and tools, following a *global-as-view* approach. It has a multi-tier client-server architecture based on WFS and uses standard wrappers to access data, extended by derived wrappers that capture additional query capabilities. [9] extends the MIX wrapper-mediator architecture for integrating information from spatial information systems and searchable databases of geo-referenced imagery. MIX is focused on integrating geo-referenced imagery but our approach is focused on spatial geometries. On the other hand, [10] designed a novel approach for integrating GML resources. The proposed architecture uses a Catalog expressed by RDF to relate the GML resources. Although [10] has the same aims as [4], it has a different focus.

An overview of the architecture offered in this work is detailed in Section 2, which contains the most important features of our prototype. Section 3 provides some results from our performance studies. Section 4 contains conclusions and projected future work.

2 Overview

The main task of an integration mediator is to provide the users with a unique interface for querying the data, independently of its actual organization and location [11]. This interface, or global schema, is described as an *ontology* expressed with

RDF(S). As used here, an *ontology* denotes a light-weight conceptual model and not a hierarchy of terms or a hierarchy of concepts [7]. The global schema can be viewed as a simple object-oriented data model. Hence, a global schema can be viewed as defining a database of objects, connected by roles, with the concept extents related by subset relationships as per the *isA* links in the schema. Since it is an integration schema, this is a *virtual* database. The actual materialization exists in the resources.

Users pose queries in terms of global schema (RDFS). As a consequence, the mediator system must contain a module (*Solve mapping*) that uses the resource descriptions in order to translate a user query into a query that refers directly to the schemas of the GML resources. For this purpose, we establish a correspondence between each resource and the global schema using RDF instances. In the *Solve mapping* module, an execution plan is not necessary because a query will be executed over a source if it fully satisfies all attributes of the query.

In addition, this approach supplies *descriptions* of the resources and specifies constraints on resource contents (e.g. contains information about "Madrid"). These *descriptions* are stored as alphanumeric data in RDF instances (Filter Resources).

A Wrapper receives a query over a schema of the resources from the mediator system. Here, the query is executed and the results of the query are expressed in GML format, which are then returned to the mediator.

This process is a well-known pattern in applications over non-spatial XML documents. However, to apply this architecture efficiently over spatial XML documents it is necessary to take into account the following points:

1. The spatial query language used for the users should have the same semantic as the query language used in the sources, so the translation between both languages is easier. Because of this, we have used the same spatial language to query the ontology and the GML data model on the sources[4]. This query language was born as a spatial query language over spatial semi-structured XML documents. The data model and the algebra underlying the query language are defined in [12]. The query language has a familiar *select-from-where* syntax and is based on SQL. It includes a set of spatial operators (disjoint, touches, etc.), and includes traditional operators (=, >, <, ...) for non-spatial information.

2. Unlike XML, it is very difficult to make efficient queries over GML because the spatial operator requires a spatial index that cannot be created directly over GML. Due to this an efficient method for storing GML documents is necessary. In [13] we studied three storage models for storing and retrieving GML documents over RDBMS. This work concluded that the LegoDB approach [14] obtains the best performance. We have therefore used this approach in our implementation.

3. Obviously, in schema integration the mediator can know when a resource has schema to satisfy a query. However, only when the query is executed in the resources does the mediator know whether the information stored in the resource satisfies the *where clause*. Thus, for example, it is possible that 100 resources have schema to satisfy the query, but only 10 have the information that the user wants. In this case, posting the query to each resource (100) is inefficient. To solve this, our approach uses the above-mentioned *description* to obtain *a priori* a set of candidate resources (in the same way as a *Catalog* in [15]).

In the following section the most important features of our prototype are detailed.

2.1 Ontology

The solution proposed in this paper is based on [4], which details how to use RDF(S) for querying spatial XML resources (GML). [4] is based on *Community Web Portal (C-Web)* [16]. *C-Web* essentially provides the means to select, classify and access, in a semantically meaningful and ubiquitous way, various information resources for diverse target audiences. However, in [4] we do not only use the RDF(S) to relate resources (html, pdf, jpg,...) situated in different web sites; we also use it to know how a schema satisfies an ontology. These schemas are always expressed as DTDs for each source. Each site can offer the schemas that satisfy, fully or partially, the ontology defined for an interest community. Therefore, unlike the original C-Web, it is possible to apply spatial operators (comparatives: cross, overlap, touch; analysis: Area, Length) over the resources provided that they represent geometry information with GML.

In Figure 1an example of the *Portal Schema* and its instances is shown. Due to RDF's capability for adding new feature and geometry types in a clear and formal manner, this example has been carried out extending the geospatial ontology defined by OpenGIS [5], where the class (*Geometry, LineString, etc*) and properties (*coordinates, PolygonMember, etc*) are defined. The example shows a simplification of a City Model. In this, *CityModel* contains *Blocks* and a *Block* contains *Parcels*, and a *CityModel* has the properties *name, population* and *Category*.

The most important feature of this approach is that there are two kinds of properties: (1) properties that describe the data offered by the resources (*descriptions*), represented by a rectangle filled with white; (2) properties that represent the name of the attributes of a schema (DTD) that have the same semantic, represented by a rectangle filled with gray.

The first set of properties such as *Name* and *Category* in *CityModel* or *Type* in *Parcel* make the *Catalog*. It allows a spatial query to be refined before it is posted to the sources. For example, if we wanted to execute a query about parcels in "Albacete", it would not be necessary to execute the query in all the resources with information about parcels, but only in those resources related to the *CityModel* called "Albacete". At the beginning, users filter resources in accordance with their description in order to get the candidate resources, and then users can apply a spatial query over these alone.

Evidently, a large *Catalog* allows better filtering of a query, but it leads to difficult management. Owing to this, the size of the *Catalog* should be defined by consensus for each problem.

With regard to the second set of properties, in our prototype the attributes are referenced by beginning with the root of the XML documents. For instance, the resource &r2 (*Block*) located in *www.cities.com/Blocks.gml* represents in a DTD the *"Boundary"* property with the attribute *"world.city.BoundaryCity"*, and the same property is represented by &r3 with *"Block.BoundaryBy"*. Figure 2 shows an example of a data model for the resource &r3. This data model is obtained to start from a GML document [12]. Note that *dot notation* is used to describe the attributes in the spatial XML data model. It is the same syntax used in our query language mentioned above. Thanks to this, a translation between notations (query and mapping) is not necessary. In addition, *wildcards* and other features related to semi-structures can be used to define attributes [12].

Portal Schema

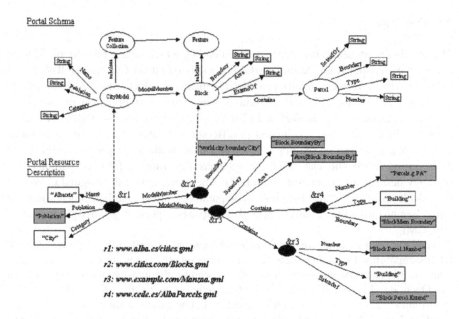

Fig. 1. Portion of Catalog of a CityModel.

On the other hand, spatial operators defined with the syntax of our query language can also be used to enrich the meaning of a property in a resource. Thus, for example, the property *Area* in the concept *Parcel* is defined in &r3 as a function *"AREA[Block.BoundaryBy]"*. In this case, &r3 does not have an attribute to describe the property *Area*, but it is possible to obtain data with the same meaning applying an operator *Area[]* over *Block.BoundaryBy*. In this way, operators like *Length, Area, Buffer, ConvexHull, Union, Intersection*, etc. can be used. This feature can only be used when it is applied over attributes in the same resource.

With the Portal Schema and the Portal Resources Description we have all the information necessary to know what resources there are and how to satisfy a query. For example, we define the following query over the ontology shown in Figure 1: *"Obtain the Area of a Block where the Parcel(extendof) touches Block(boundary) and the Parcel(Number) > 20"*. This query is represented in our query language over a data model query language in Table 1(a).

According to Figure 1 the only resource that can satisfy all the properties defined in the query is &r3. Table 1(b) shows the results of applying translation of the properties in the ontology to real attributes in the resource &r3 (Figure 2). Note that it is a very simple translation because we use the same query language and we do not have to adapt the semantic between them. Note that the relation between *Parcel* and *Block* in the Resource &r3 is not included in the query. This relation is established on the Wrappers.

Table 1. Example of translation

SELECT *Block.Area* **FROM** *Block contains Parcel* **WHERE** *Parce.Number > 20 AND Block.extendof_B* *TOUCHES Parcel.extendOf*	SELECT *AREA[B.boundaryBy]* **FROM** *Block AS B , Block.Parcel AS P* **WHERE** *P.Number>20 AND B.extendof_B TOUCHES* *P.extendOf*
(a)	(b)

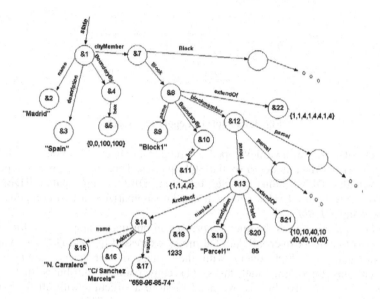

Fig. 2. Example of Data model – Resource &r3

Note that the queries are executed firstly over the *catalog* to filter the resources that have useful *descriptions* for the user. Finally, the user makes a spatial query over these resources. However, the description of the user interface for carrying out these queries is not the aim of this paper.

2.2 Wrapper

Generally speaking, a wrapper should execute the query and generate the results as a GML document. However, as is mentioned above, the query over GML in each source must be efficient. The spatial operator requires a spatial index that cannot be created directly over a spatial XML document. Thus, an efficient method for storing GML documents is necessary. In [13] we studied the behavior of different alternatives over XML documents (non-spatial data) applied to GML documents (spatial and non-spatial data). As a result, we selected a RDBMS model called LegoDB[14] because it obtains the best results in the study. In Figure 3, an example over the data graph in Figure 2 is shown. It is the simplest mapping proposed, usually called *inlining*.

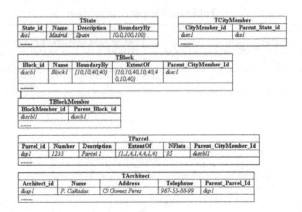

Fig. 3. Example of LegoDB approach

In view of this, we have developed a wrapper architecture to convert our query language over our data model to spatial SQL queries. This approach is not dependent on a particular DBMS, thus Oracle, Informix, DB2 or any spatial RDBMS or ORDBMS may be used. This approach can be summarized in two components: *T-Relational* and *T-DBMS*.

T-Relational transforms the query expressed in our query language (following our data model) to a query over a Relational model expressed by *LegoDB*. The output of this component is a SQL query with the syntax of our query language. This component has three important tasks: (1) conversion of attributes that contain wildcards (%,#)[12]. To do this, we need to store a structure with all the possible paths of the data model for each document that is queried. This structure is obtained from the XML Schema (DTD) of the documents; (ii) transforming each attribute of the query expressed in a data model (e.g. *block.parcel.extentof*) in the real name in the relational schema (e.g. TParcel. *extentof*); (iii) the automatic generation of *From* clause in the final SQL query, according to relations involved in the query. The relations included in the *From* clause are obtained from the attributes used in the query. In order to carry out this transformation, a definition of a mapping for the relation of our data model and the relational model is necessary. This mapping (expressed in XML) relates the semantic relation between a path in our data model with a pair (relation, attributes) in the relational model.

T-DBMS transforms the result of the *T-Relational* component to a SQL query in the syntax and semantic of a particular DBMS. This component depends on the DBMS used in the implementation. The complexity of this component depends on how to satisfy a DBMS with the OpenGIS specifications [13]. In this implementation we have used *Oracle 9i*, which follows most of the specifications defined in OpenGIS.

In Table 2 a translation of a query in Table 1(b) to a SQL query is shown. This query has the syntax of Oracle 9i. Note that the relations between relations are included.

Table 2. SQL query

```
SELECT
MDSYS.SDO_GEOM.SDO_AREA(TBLOCKS.BOUNDARY,MDSYS.SDO_DIM_ARRAY(MDSYS.SDO_DIM_ELEM
ENT('X', 0, 10000, 0),MDSYS.SDO_DIM_ELEMENT('Y', 0, 10000, 0)))
FROM TBLOCKS,TPARCEL,TBLOCKMEMBER
WHERE ((((TBLOCKMEMBER.P_BLOCK_ID = TBLOCKS.BLOCK_ID AND TPARCEL.P_BLOCKMEMBER_ID
= TBLOCKMEMBER.BLOCKMEMBER_ID)) AND ((TPARCEL.NUMBER > 20) AND
MDSYS.SDO_RELATE(TBLOCKS.EXTENDOF,TPARCEL.EXTENDOF,'mask=TOUCH querytype =
JOIN')='TRUE')))
```

3 A Performance Study

In this section, we describe the experimental studies that were conducted in order to assess the efficiency of querying a GML document with our approach. We focus on the effectiveness of this approach in terms of translation of queries over an ontology into queries supported by the wrappers, translation of these queries into spatial SQL queries, query processing and generation of GML documents from the results. All the experiments were conducted on an 2300Mhz PC with 512Mb RAM, 40Gb hard disk with operating system Windows XP professional. The RDBMS used was *Oracle9i Spatial 9.0.1*, which we selected because it allows the storage of spatial objects and the application of spatial operators over them. Oracle's Spatial object-relational model was used (SDO_GEOMETRY object) [17] for simplicity. However, as mentioned above, Oracle's relational model or another RDBMS may be used. All experiments were conducted on the same computer, using different databases to the mediator and the wrappers in the same Oracle DBMS. In this way, we obtained a greater system load.

The data set used in these experiments respects the data set used in [13]. This data set represents a *City model* where a city has several blocks, each block has several parcels and each parcel has an owner. We used a data set with 7.1 Mb approx. and 5000 rectangular parcels. In the mediator, we used three data sets: D1 (2.1Mb approx.) with 1250 resources, D2 (4.4Mb) with 2500 resources and D3 (8.4Mb approx.) with 5000 resources.

For this test, on the DBMS the same relations shown in [13] were created. We used the simplest mapping proposed by [14]. The relations stored the data model shown in Figure 3. Indexes on relational tables were also properly built to improve query processing as follows: the attributes: *TState(state_id), TCitymember(Citymember_id), TBlock(block_Id), TBlockmember(blockmember_id), TParcel (parcel_id), TArquitet (arquitect_id)* are primary key. *TCitymember(parent_state_id), TBlock(parent_Citymember_id), TBlockmember(parent_block_id), TParcel (parent_blockmember_id), TArquitet (Parent_parece_id)* are foreign key. The Spatial Attributes *TState(BoundaryBy), TBlock(BoundaryBy,Extendof)* and *TParcel (extendof)* have been indexed with *R-Tree* [17]. In order to carry out this mapping efficiently the RDF is stored in a RDBMS following [15].

3.1 Elapsed Time

In our study, we have focused our attention on the following aspects involved in assessing performance:

1. Translating queries over an ontology into queries supported by the wrappers has an elapsed time that should be studied [11].
2. Translating queries from our data model to the relational model (spatial SQL) needs a mapping process. It depends on the path length between the entities in the GML document [13].
3. Since we are dealing with an XML query language, a very large number of joins is necessary. It is one of the more important performance problems in the relational implementation of these query languages [18]. In addition, storing and querying spatial data requires a larger amount of resources than storing and querying alphanumeric data [19]. This elapsed time was studied in [13] in isolation from a real system, but now we study how it works inside our system.
4. Generating GML documents from the results. This process can be very expensive because a spatial query can return a very large amount of spatial objects.

For these aspects we have studied the following elapsed times: T1 is associated to the translation of queries over an ontology into queries supported by the wrappers (parser and mapping). T2 is associated to translation of these queries into spatial SQL queries (parser, mapping, generation of *from* clause and translation to SQL). T3 is the elapsed time for the execution of SQL sentences, and T4 is the elapsed time for the generation of GML documents from the result set.

Firstly, a set of queries is used to study the behavior of these approaches, involving only alphanumeric data (users may only wish to query alphanumeric data of a GML document). Secondly, a set of queries with spatial and alphanumeric operators is used. We define the complexity of a query according to the number of properties included in the query, the number of relations involved in the final spatial SQL and the number of joins in SQL. Table 4 shows the number of joins and relations involved in the final SQL query. All queries return 2500 objects approx. We have used the data set D2 in the mediator. In the execution of the query only one resource satisfies the query.

Table 3. Number of joins and relations in each query

Query	N° Joins	Relations		Query	N° Joins	Relations
Q1	0	1		Q7	5+1+1	6
Q2	4	5		Q8	5+1+1	6
Q3	4+1	5		Q9	3+1+1	4
Q4	5+1+1	6		Q10	3+1+1s	4
Q5	2+1	3		Q11	5+1+1s	6
Q6	5+1+1	6		Q12	5+1+1s+1	6

The elapsed query times for these queries are shown in Figure 4. Q1-Q4 are queries with only alphanumeric operators. For Q1-Q2 additional joins are not included. They have a progressive number of joins and relations. Q3-Q4 are queries with more properties in *Select* and *Where* clause and 1 additional *joins* in Q3 and 1 additional *joins* and 1 *none equi-joins* in Q4.

Q5-Q12 are queries with spatial operators, some of which have spatial and alphanumeric operators. Q5-Q6 are spatial queries with spatial operators (*Area, Length* and *Buffer*). The number of joins and relations is doubled in Q6.

The elapsed query times for these queries are shown in Figure 4. The elapsed time for the first mapping (mapping mediator - T1) depends on the number of resources and the number of properties involved in each query. However, the results are not very sensitive to the increment in the number of properties. The second mapping (mapping wrapper – T2) has a longer elapsed time than the first mapping. The most expensive function in this mapping is looking for all relations involved in the query and the relations between them to construct the from *clause*. However, the depth of our data model limits this elapsed time. Note that Q4 and Q6 have the highest elapsed time because they have the highest number of properties and involve entities that are highly-nested in the schema. The time of Execution (T3) of the SQL statement depends on the number of joins and the number of spatial operators involved. Note that this elapsed time increases with several joins and spatial operators. However, as is mentioned above, the number of joins can be limited by applying more specific heuristics [20]. Finally, the elapsed time to create GML documents is highest. This elapsed time increases with the adaptation of spatial objects to GML. This process was carried out following a process outside the DBMS. The process used the *Oracle sdoapi* to adapt Oracle Geometries to XML (we explore the record set to adapt the objects). In this way, we do not depend on a particular DBMS and simplify the translation to SQL. In addition, in this process a conversion between names of the relational attributes to GML attributes is carried out.

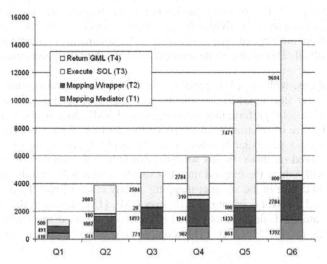

Fig. 4. Elapsed query time (Q1-Q6)

Q7-Q12 use spatial operators which are more expensive in time than Q5-Q6. Q7 uses a spatial *Union* and has a high number of joins. Q8-Q9 use spatial operators in *select* clause (*Union, Area*) and comparison with spatial operators (*Length*) in *where*

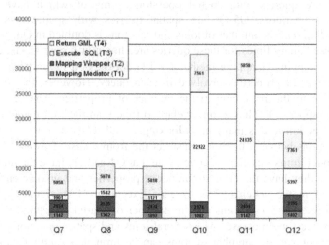

Fig. 5. Elapsed query time (Q7-Q12)

clause. Q10-Q12 are the most complex queries with a high number of joins and spatial joins. Q12 has *Union* and comparison with spatial operators (Area) in *where* clause for the spatial joins.

The elapsed query times are shown in Figure 5. Note that when there are complex spatial operators with a higher number of joins, execution time increases. Q7, Q8 and Q9 include, in the *select* clause, *Union* operators, combined with *Area* operator in Q8 and Q9. The elapsed time of these queries is greater than the previous set. Q10-Q12 use spatial joins (*Intersect*). Evidently, this kind of queries gets the worst elapsed time. In addition, the elapsed time to generate GML documents increases when spatial joins are involved. This is due to the process used to adapt the geometries mentioned above.

In view of this, with complex spatial queries, applying a specific study (following on from [14]) for storing GML documents over relational databases is necessary. In order to obtain a good performance querying spatial XML documents, it is preferable to increase the size of relations, and to reduce the number of joins between relations. For each source a particular heuristic must be applied, depending on the kind of information stored on them. In this way, we can reduce the number of joins in each query. This will reduce the elapsed time to execute spatial SQL and the elapsed time to get the *from* clause in the wrapper mapping. In any case, T2 plus T3 is much lower than the elapsed time for querying directly over GML [13]. However, the high elapsed time to generate GML documents could be reduced if we used specific tools offered by the DBMS (SQL/XML[17]). (This comparative is not included for reasons of space).

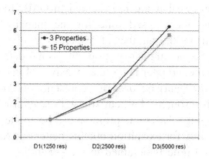

Fig. 6. Scalability Test

3.2 Scalability Test

With regard to scalability, three studies can be carried out: (i) scalability over the spatial Data, (ii) scalability over the mapping in the wrapper, and (iii) scalability of the translation of the query languages in the mediator. The first study does not depend on either the data in the mediator or the data in the wrapper; it just depends on the DBMS. A study with these features was carried out in [13]. The second study is not relevant because the size of the data needed to translate the queries in the translator is very small. Consequently, we only deal with the third study.

In order to do this, we used the D1, D2 and D3 data sets detailed above. Over these data sets we translated two queries with few attributes (3 attributes, Q1) and queries with a lot of attributes (15, it is not included in table 2). Thus, we can study the influence between the mapping over lots of resources involved in the query and the number of attributes of the query. In our test we suppose all resources stored in the data set satisfy the query (so, 1250 resources satisfy the queries in D1, 2500 in D2 and 5000 in D3).

Figure 6 shows the elapsed time ratios for the two kinds of queries. The elapsed query times ratios are defined as follows. Assuming the elapsed time of a query using D1 is treated as scale t_a, and the elapsed time of the same query is t_b, using either D2 or D3, the elapsed time ratio is t_b/t_a. The study shows the difference in the number of attributes is not relevant with respect to the number of resources that satisfy the query. The elapsed time of the parse is inconsiderable.

In conclusion, in our prototype the elapsed time of the mapping depends on the number of resources that satisfy the query and not on the number of attributes involved in the query. In the same way, as shown above, if there are 2500 resources but only one satisfies the query, the most significant elapsed time depends on the time to translate this query over this resource.

4   Conclusions

In this paper a prototype of a mediation system for querying XML spatial resources is studied. The main feature of this approach is the possibility of applying spatial operators over the resources that are represented in GML format. We studied four elapsed times: regarding the elapsed time for the mapping in the mediator, we concluded that it depends on the number of resources involved in the query. For the same number of resources, the number of properties is not determinative. The elapsed time for the mapping in the wrapper is more expensive. Moreover, it is more variable because it depends on the heuristic used to represent a GML data model over the relational model in each resource. An heuristic with several relations offers a worse elapsed time in the mapping . The same problem can be applied over the execution of the query. The elapsed time for execution obtains better results with fewer relations. Finally, the worst elapsed time is obtained in the generation of GML. However, we can improve this elapsed time using specific tools offered by the DBMS.

Future work foresees the development of a prototype to allow the splitting of a query between different sources, and the joining of the result in the mediator. The study presented in this paper will be used to check the efficiency of this future approach. In addition, we are developing a prototype to integrate GML resources and any other kind of resource (HTML, PDF, etc). Thus, with this approach it is possible to discover spatial and non-spatial resources which are interrelated semantically on the Web. In this way, this work represents a small step towards the Semantic Geospatial Web.

Acknowledgment. Research Project: "Metodologías de desarrollo de interfaces de usuario dinámicas" – (JCCM PBC-03-003). Junta de Comunidades de Castilla-La Mancha.(Spain)

References

[1]   J. Egenhofer. Toward the Semantic Geospatial Web. ACM-GIS 2002. 10th ACM International Symposium on Advances in Geographic Information Systems. McLean (USA). 2002.

[2]   OpenGis Consortium. Specifications. http://www.opengis.org/techno/specs.htm.1999

[3]   H. Samet. Applications of spatial data structures. Computer Graphics, Image processing and GIS. Addison – Wesley. 1990.

[4]   J. Córcoles and P. González. Querying Spatial Resources. An Approach to the Semantic Geospatial Web. CAiSE'03 workshop "Web Services, e-Business, and the Semantic Web (WES): Foundations, Models, Architecture, Engineering and Applications". To Appear in Lecture Notes in Computer Science (LNCS) *by Springer-Verlag.* 2003.

[5]   OpenGIS. Geography Markup Language (GML) v3.0. http://www.opengis.org/techno/documents/02-023r4.pdf. 2003

[6]   B. Amann, I. Fundulaki and M. Scholl, C. Beeri, A-M. Vercoustre. Mapping XML Fragments to Community Web Ontologies. In Proc. Fourth International Workshop on the Web and Databases. 2001

[7]   B. Amann, C. Beeri, I. Fundulaki, and M. Scholl. Ontology-Based Integration of XML Web Resources. In *International Semantic Web Conference (ISWC)*, Sardinia, Italy, 2002.

[8]   O. Boucelma, M. Essid and Z. Lacroix. A WFS-Based Mediation System for GIS Interoperability. ACM-GIS 2002. 10th ACM International Symposium on Advances in Geographic Information Systems. McLean (USA). 2002

[9]   A. Gupta, R. Marciano, I. Zaslavsky and C. Baru. Integrating GIS and Imagenery through XML based information Mediation. Integrated Spatial Databases: DigitalImages and GIS. Lecture Notesin Computer Science. Vol1737. Pp. 211-234. Springer-Verlag. 1999

[10]   J. Córcoles, P. González and V. López-Jaquero. Integration of Spatial XML Documents with RDF. International Conference on Web Engineering. Spain. To Appear in Lecture Notes in Computer Science (LNCS) *by Springer-Verlag*. 2003.

[11]   A.Y. Levy. Logic-Based Techniques in Data Integration. In Jack Minker, editor, Logic Based Artificial Intelligence, pages 575-595. Kluwer, 2000.

[12]   J. Córcoles and P. González. A Specification of a Spatial Query Language over GML. ACM-GIS 2001. 9th ACM International Symposium on Advances in Geographic Information Systems. Atlanta (USA). 2001

[13]   J. Córcoles and P. González. Analysis of Different Approaches for Storing GML Documents ACM-GIS 2002. 10th ACM International Symposium on Advances in Geographic Information Systems. McLean. (USA) 2002

[14]   P. Bohannon, J. Freire, P. Roy and J. Simeon. From XML Schema to Relations: A Cost-Based Approach to XML Storage. 18th International Conference on Data Engineering (ICDE2002). 2002.

[15]   S. Alexaki, V. Christophides, G. Karvounarakis, D. Plexousakis, K. Tolle. *"The ICSFORTH RDFSuite: Managing Voluminous RDF Description Bases"*. In Proceedings of the 2nd International Workshop on the Semantic Web (SemWeb'01), in conjunction with WWW10, pp. 1-13, Hong Kong., 2001.

[16]   Karvounarakis, G., Christophides, V., Plexousakis, D., and Alexaki, S. Querying community web portals. Technical report, Institute of Computer Science, FORTH,Heraklion, Greece. 2000 http://www.ics.forth.gr/proj/isst/RDF/ RQL/rql.pdf.

[17]   Oracle9i Database Documentation. http://otn.oracle.com:80/docs/products/oracle9i/content.html. 2002.

[18]   S. Abiteboul, P. Buneman and D. Suciu. Data on the Web. From Relations to Semistructured Data and XML. Morgan Kaufmann Publishers. 2000.

[19]   P. Rigaux, M. Scholl and A. Voisard. Spatial Databases with Application to GIS. Morgan Kaufmann Publishers. 2002.

[20]   J. Shanmugasundaram, K. Tufte, G. He, C. Zhang, D. DeWitt, and J.Naughton. Relational Databases for Querying XML Documents: Limitations and Opportunities. In Proc. of the Int'l. Conf. On Very Large Data Bases, pages 3002-314. 1999.

Extending Policy Languages to the Semantic Web

Ernesto Damiani, Sabrina De Capitani di Vimercati, Cristiano Fugazza, and
Pierangela Samarati

DTI - Università di Milano
26013 Crema - Italy
{damiani,decapita,samarati}@dti.unimi.it, fugazza@dsi.unimi.it

Abstract. In the semantic web environment it is important to be able
to specify access control requirements about subjects accessing the information and about resources to be accessed in terms of the rich ontology-
based metadata describing them. In this paper, we outline how current
standard policy languages such as XACML can be extended to address
this issue. Then, we describe a reference architecture for enforcing our
semantics-aware policies.

1 Introduction

Current web-based applications describe resources (including users) and services via a number of XML-based standard protocols [10]. Among those, XML-
based standard definitions for policies and credentials have recently received an
increased interest [5,13]. *Semantic web technologies* are changing this picture,
using advanced knowledge representation techniques for enriching e-business environments. The semantic web is built around the notion of representing shared
knowledge via standard *ontologies*, that are used by intelligent agents to understand the nature of the information they are processing [6]. In an interoperable
e-business architecture based on the semantic web vision, *ontology-based domain
models* are therefore used as controlled vocabularies for resources description,
allowing users to obtain the right resources at the right time [3]. While research
on developing standards and tools that ultimately will lead to the existence of
the semantic web is increasing [16], security impacts of these new technologies
have not been addressed sufficiently. On the semantic web, writing access control
policies where subjects and objects are pointed at via data identifiers or simple
predicates is not enough. Rather, it is important to be able to specify access
control requirements about subjects and resources in terms of the rich metadata
describing them.

Some researchers have recently investigated security within the semantic web
for the purpose of either expressing security policies or protecting semantically
rich data. As an example of the two, [4,7] develop security ontologies that allow
parties to share a vocabulary to exchange security-related information using a
common language; while [9,12] present policy languages to specify access restrictions over concepts defined in ontologies. Another line of work merging security

N. Koch, P. Fraternali, and M. Wirsing (Eds.): ICWE 2004, LNCS 3140, pp. 330–343, 2004.

and semantic web concepts is presented in [14] as an approach for identifying Web inference channels due to ontology-based inference attacks. There, an ontology is used to detect tags appearing in different XML documents that are *ontologically equivalent* (i.e., can be abstracted to the same concept in the ontology), but which have contradictory security classifications.

Although these approaches represent a first step toward the definition of a semantics-aware access control process, they do not completely exploit the power of the semantic web. Neither semantic web-based proposals nor emerging stateful attribute-based security languages (e.g., XACML) allow support of access restrictions on resources according to complex semantics-aware assertions.

In this paper we bring forward the idea of exploiting the semantic web to extend current policy languages to allow the definition of access control rules based on generic assertions defined over concepts in the ontologies that control metadata content and provide abstract subject domain concepts, respectively. These rules are then enforced on resources annotated with metadata regulated by the same ontologies. Our proposal allows for specifying access control requirements about: *i)* subjects accessing the information and *ii)* resources to be accessed in terms of rich ontology-based metadata associated with them. The result is a powerful policy language exploiting the high expressive power of ontology-based models.

The contribution of this paper can be summarized as follows. First, we make the point for the need of more expressive policy languages and show how semantic web metadata formats can be exploited to this end. Second, we show how current standard security languages can be extended to include semantic-aware specifications. Third, we illustrate our architectural solution, including a semantic-aware authentication tool, called OntoPassport. Our proposal extends the eXtensible Access Control Markup Language (XACML) [5] by adding the capability to designate subjects and objects via generic RDF statements [15]. Our extensions to XACML introduce the following capabilities.

– *Semantic-aware subject description.* Semantic web applications need to easily operate on subject descriptions to determine whether a policy rule is applicable to a user.
– *Canonical metadata syntax.* The high expressive power of semantic web metadata allows for using different syntax to carry the same semantics. While no constraints can be posed apriori on the content of resources' descriptors, a standard syntax could be adopted for metadata used to describe subjects and objects within access control policies. Also, a standard syntax could be used for subjects' descriptions.

2   Basic Concepts

In this section, we briefly overview the main standards on which our proposal is based, namely, XACML, SAML (the XML standard for encapsulating access requests) and RDF, highlighting the features relevant to our research.

XACML

XACML is the result of a recent OASIS standardization effort proposing an XML-based language to express and interchange access control policies. XACML is designed to express authorization policies in XML against objects that are themselves identified in XML. The language can represent the functionalities of most policy representation mechanisms. An XACML policy consists of a set of rules whose main components are: a target, an effect, and a condition.[1] The target defines the set of resources, subjects, and actions to which the rule is intended to apply. The effect of the rule can be **permit** or **deny**. The condition represents a boolean expression that may further refine the applicability of the rule. A request consists of attributes associated with the requesting subject, the resource involved in the request, the action being performed and the environment. A response contains one of four decisions: **permit**, **deny**, **not applicable** (when no applicable policies or rules could be found), or **indeterminate** (when some errors occurred during the access control process). A request, a policy, and the corresponding response form the **XACML Context**.

The subjects and resources to which a rule applies are defined by using a set of pre-defined functions (e.g., equality, set comparison, arithmetic) and datatypes (e.g., string, boolean, integer). To illustrate, consider the following portion of a rule.

```
......
<Subject> <!-- match role subject attribute -->
  <SubjectMatch
    MatchId= "urn:oasis:names:tc:xacml:1.0:function:string-equal"> <!-- function -->
    <AttributeValue DataType= "http://www.w3.org/2001/XMLSchema#string">
      physician
    </AttributeValue>
    <SubjectAttributeDesignator AttributeId=
      "urn:oasis:names:tc:xacml:1.0:example:attribute:role"
      DataType= "http://www.w3.org/2001/XMLSchema#string" />
  </SubjectMatch>
</Subject>
......
```

This rule matches requests where the subject has an attribute **role** whose value is **physician**. While these functions and datatypes can be used to define many access control policies, XACML also specifies an extension mechanism for defining additional datatypes and functions. Our proposal makes use of such a mechanism to accommodate semantically rich constraints.

SAML

On corporate networks as well as on the global Net, access to services by single-sign-on authentication is becoming a widespread way to authenticate users.

---

[1] We keep at a simplified level the description of the language and refer the reader to the OASIS proposal [5] for the complete specification.

Single-sign-on authentication relying on digital certificates is currently the most popular choice for e-business applications. In this area, the most successful standard is SAML [13], an authentication protocol handling authentication information across transactions between parties. SAML uses tagged sets of user attributes to represent subject-related information encapsulated inside service requests. One might wonder whether the semantics of user credentials could be represented directly by the standard XML schemata describing SAML. Unfortunately, standard XML schema definitions need to cover a wide repertoire of possible user attributes. For this reason, optional elements are widely used, thus decreasing the expressiveness of the schema as a descriptor of single instances. The goal of authentication standards is to carry information according to a protocol, rather than describing a domain; also, a considerable number of SAML tags have a structural function and do not describe specific subjects.

RDF

RDF is a model to express generic assertions (RDF statements) associated with resources. An RDF statement is a triple of the form (*subject*, *predicate*, *object*), where subject[2] is the resource being described, predicate is a property associated with the resource, and object is the value of the property. For instance, statement `"index.html has been created by Lucy"` can be represented by the triple (index.html, created_by, Lucy). Due to the fact that the subject of a statement can be any resource, it is possible to make statements about statements in RDF. This technique is called *reification*. To clarify this important concept, consider the following statement:

"Video `http://www.acme.com/medical.avi` shows Dr. Harry Morris assisting patient Carl Smith"

To state this in RDF one must define several RDF statements:

```
(Harry Morris, is-a, physician);
(Carl Smith, is-a, patient);
(Harry Morris, assists, Carl Smith);
(http://www.acme.com/medical.avi, is-a, Video);
(http://www.acme.com/medical.avi, shows, ''Harry Morris, assists, Carl
Smith'').
```

Reification is represented by splitting a statement into three different parts (subject, predicate, and object) and asserting these parts. By reification, the previous sentences can be expressed as the following set of triples.[3]

```
(http://www.acme.com/medical.avi, type, Video)
(Harry Morris, type, Physician)
(Carl Smith, type, Patient)
(assists, type, relation)
(shows, type, relation)
```

---

[2] This is not to be confused with the use of subject in the authorization model.

[3] For the sake of clarity, we shall use an informal syntax where capital letters represent URIs and drop the use of XML namespace prefixes.

```
(A, type, statement)
(A, subject, Harry Morris)
(A, predicate, assists)
(A, object, Carl Smith)
(B, type, statement)
(B, subject, http://www.acme.com/medical.avi)
(B, predicate, shows)
(B, object, A).
```

Reification is used often and, in our approach, a uniform RDF based on reification simplifies the evaluation procedure.

3   Towards Semantic-Aware Access Control Language

In this section we show how current XML-based standards can be extended to seamlessly incorporate metadata-based designations of subjects and objects.

3.1   Including Assertion-Based Metadata in XACML

The design of a policy evaluation and enforcement engine exploiting semantic web metadata needs to be based on a sound model and language for expressing authorizations in term of metadata. To this purpose, we chose to exploit the *extensibility points* already built in the XACML language rather than redesigning a policy language from scratch. Our extension points can be summarized as follows.

- Extend the XACML Context to include metadata associated with both subjects and resources.
- Extend the AttributeValue XACML element (used in XACML to qualify both subjects and objects) capability of specifying auxiliary namespaces.[4] Auxiliary namespaces to be added are at least two: the rdf: one, allowing for using RDF assertions as values for the XACML AttributeValue element and another one (in our example, md: and ms:) enabling using properties and class names from a user ontology within those assertions.
- Extend the MatchID attribute by introducing a new function, called metadataQuery, expressing the processing needed for policy enforcement.

Although our proposed extensions to XACML rely on standard RDF syntax, some precautions should be taken to keep enforcement possible; namely, we prescribe that attribute values written in RDF use a RDF reification technique.

---

[4] Such additional attribute values are optional and do not disrupt parsability of standard XACML policies using our extended schema.

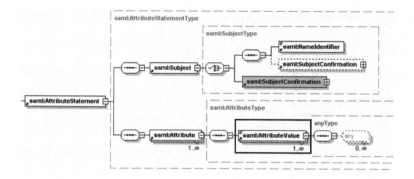

Fig. 1. The Schema for a SAML assertion

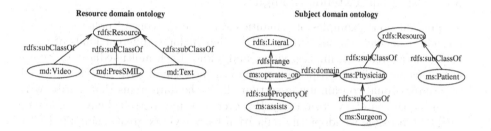

Fig. 2. An example of resource and subject domain ontology

3.2 Incapsulating Semantics-Aware Credentials in SAML

Figure 1 shows the portion of SAML-XML Schema specifying the structure of an authentication assertion, the boxed element shows our proposed extension point. Basically, the SAML schema defines a subject identification and associate it with a set of attributes. The attribute definition is extremely open, leaving it to application-specific XML schemata to specify the actual set of attributes identifying the user. We extend the attributes allowed for the `AttributeValue` element to enable content including RDF assertions using suitable ontology concepts as predicate names.

In the simplest case, the subject metadata can assert that the user holding the certificates belongs to a certain type such as (thisRequestUser, type, Physician), or more complex ones such as

```
(thisRequestUser, type, Person)
(thisRequestUser, buys , "Resource")
(Resource, type, MovieDVD)
(Resource, title, "Lord of the Rings")
```

However, once again we use a canonical reified syntax.

```
<rdf:RDF
  xmlns:rdf="http://www.w3.org/TR/WD-rdf-syntax#"
  xmlns:md="http://ourdomain.it/MD/Schema/md-syntax#"
  xmlns:ms="http://ourdomain.it/MS/Schema/ms-syntax#">
  <rdf:Description
    rdf:about="http://ourdomain.it/MD/Video/video010234.avi">
    <rdf:type rdf:resource="http://ourdomain.it/MD/Schema/md-syntax#Video" />
    <md:title>Treatment of Diseases</md:title>
    <md:duration>1054067</md:duration>
    <md:format>avi</md:format>
    <md:shows_how rdf:nodeID="content"/>
  </rdf:Description>
  <rdf:Description rdf:nodeID="content">
    <ms:surgeon>Sam</ms:surgeon>
    <ms:operates_on>Patient</ms:operates_on>
  </rdf:Description>
</rdf:RDF>
```

Fig. 3. An example of RDF metadata associated with a video presentation

3.3 Using the Extended Language

To illustrate our examples of semantics-aware access control policies, we shall consider a *medical digital library* (MDL) that includes different kinds of multimedia data: free text, images, video, and audio. Each multimedia data item is complemented with descriptive metadata in the form of RDF descriptors. RDF descriptors could contain any assertion about the data items that can be written using the ontology vocabulary. However, in some controlled environments it might be possible to adopt the reification-based syntax greatly simplifying the evaluation procedure. In the following, we shall assume that the reified format of RDF statements is used. Note that however conversion tools are available capable to translate a variety of RDF syntax into the reified ones.

To express the statements in our descriptors, we use three vocabularies. The first vocabulary contains standard terms such as **predicate**, **statement**, **subject**, **object** and standard relations such as **is-a**. This vocabulary is the RDFS base namespace (whose formal definitions can be found in [15]) containing the elements **rdf:statement**, **rdf:subject**, **rdf:predicate**, **rdf:object**, **rdf:type** that have a self-explanatory semantics. The second vocabulary, called *resource domain ontology*, contains domain-specific terms that are used to describe the resource content such as **Video** and **shows_how**. The third vocabulary, called *subject domain ontology*, contains terms that are used to make assertions on subjects such as **Physician**, **Patient**, **assists**. Figure 2 illustrates the resource domain ontology and subject domain ontology where, for the sake of simplicity, we only report the main concepts that will be used to show the expressive power of our proposal. Note that generally speaking no assumption can be made about the format of RDF descriptors associated with resources. Figure 3 illustrates an example of RDF descriptor where, in addition to the classical **rdf:** namespace, we use namespace **md:** for describing multimedia data and namespace **ms:** for describing medical staff. The RDF descriptor, associated with a video (**video010234.avi**), comprises of two sections: the first one expresses the document type according to a domain ontology and to some additional simple metadata (e.g., format of the document, title); the second one contains more complex metadata expressing the fact that "Video **video010234.avi** shows how surgeon **Sam** operates on a patient". Note that while the simple metadata in the first section could be expressed by a usual attribute-value pair, this is not the case for advanced metadata, to which our approach applies. Consider now the following protection requirement:

> Physicians of the **Trauma Therapy Center** department are allowed to see video presentations that show physicians assisting patients

This requirement is composed of two assertions stating, respectively, *1)* who can access the resource (Physicians of the **Trauma Therapy Center** department) and *2)* the kind of resources involved (Video presentations that show physicians assisting patients). Such assertions are used to define the target of the XACML rule as illustrated in Figure 4. Consider now a request to see video **video010234.avi** submitted by a user who presents to our system subject metadata stating that the requester is **Sam**, a surgeon of the **Trauma Therapy Center** Department (see RDF description in Figure 5). Intuitively, by exploiting the hierarchical organization of the concepts defined in the domain ontologies, the evaluation of this access request should return a permit decision because both **Sam** and the video involved in the request satisfy the subject and resource conditions specified in the rule, respectively. This is the result of the two following subsumptions:

- **Surgeon** is a sub-class of **Physician**
- **assists** is a sub-property of **operates_on**.

We will see in more details the policy evaluation process in the next Section.

4   Policy Evaluation

When a policy involving metadata needs to be evaluated, the subject context already contains the RDF description of the requester, taken from the SAML request. Our policy evaluation engine works as follows.

1. The semantic assertions about the requester that are included in the subject field of our policy rules and the metadata about the requester in the access request are compared to identify the policy rules that apply to the requester.
2. The semantic assertions that are included in the resource context of applicable policy rules are used to query the descriptive metadata of the requested resource, to verify whether the requested resource satisfies the rules selected in the previous step.

Both these selection steps involve RDF queries, where the assertions in the policy rules are used to query metadata associated with the requester and the involved resource.[5] A suitable query language is DQL, a logic-based query language

---

[5] Such querying can be tackled by means of two different techniques: *reasoning* based on metadata and *database-like* querying. The former approach considers RDF metadata as a knowledge base that can be translated into logic programming clauses and applies reasoning techniques to them.

```xml
<?xml version="1.0" encoding="UTF-8"?>
<Rule
  xmlns="urn:oasis:names:tc:xacml:1.0:policy"
  xmlns:xsi= http://www.w3.org/2001/XMLSchema-instance
  xmlns:ctx="urn:oasis:names:tc:xacml:1.0:context"
  xmlns:rdf="http://www.w3.org/TR/WD-rdf-syntax#"
  xmlns:md="http://ourdomain.it/MD/Schema/md-syntax"
  xmlns:ms="http://ourdomain.it/MS/Schema/ms-syntax"
  RuleId="urn:oasis:names:tc:xacml:examples:ruleid:1"
  Effect="Permit">
  <Target>
    <Subjects>
      <Subject>
        <SubjectMatch
          MatchId= "urn:ourdomain:function:metadataQuery">
          <AttributeValue
            DataType="http://">
            <rdf:Statement rdf:about="thisRequestUser" >
              <rdf:subject rdf:resource="http://ourdomain.it/MS/Schema/ms-syntax#Physician" />
              <rdf:predicate rdf:resource="http://ourdomain.it/MS/Schema/ms-syntax#belongs"/>
              <rdf:object rdf:datatype="http://www.w3.org/2001/XMLSchema#string">
                Trauma Therapy Center
              </rdf:object>
            </rdf:Statement>
          </AttributeValue>
          <SubjectAttributeDesignator
            AttributeId="urn:ourdomain:attribute:metatag"
            DataType="http://www.w3.org/2001/XMLSchema#string"/>
        </SubjectMatch>
      </Subject>
    </Subjects>
    <Resources>
      <Resource>
        <ResourceMatch
          MatchId="urn:ourdomain:function:metadataQuery">
          <AttributeValue
            DataType="http://">
            <rdf:Statement rdf:about="thisRequestUrl">
              <rdf:subject rdf:resource="http://ourdomain.it/MS/Schema/md-syntax#Video"/>
              <rdf:predicate rdf:resource="http://ourdomain.it/MD/Schema/md-syntax#shows_how"/>
              <rdf:object rdf:nodeID="content"/>
            </rdf:Statement>
            <rdf:Statement rdf:nodeID="content">
              <rdf:subject rdf:resource="http://ourdomain.it/MS/Schema/ms-syntax#Physician"/>
              <rdf:predicate rdf:resource="http://ourdomain.it/MS/Schema/ms-syntax#assists"/>
              <rdf:object rdf:datatype="http://www.w3.org/2001/XMLSchema#string">
                Patient
              </rdf:object>
            </rdf:Statement>
          </AttributeValue>
          <ResourceAttributeDesignator
            AttributeId="urn:ourdomain:attribute:metatag"
            DataType="http://www.w3.org/2001/XMLSchema#string"/>
        </ResourceMatch>
      </Resource>
    </Resources>
    <Actions>
      <Action>
        <AnyAction />
      </Action>
    </Actions>
  </Target>
</Rule>
```

Fig. 4. An example of access control policy in extended XACML

for the semantic web proposed in [2]. Here, however, we follow an SQL-like or an XQuery approach, assuming that RDF metadata about resources are stored as a relational or an XML database.

First, let us examine the rule selection step. Suppose a request comes in whose encapsulated metadata are:

```
(A, type, statement)
(A, subject, thisRequestUser)
(A, predicate, type)
(A, object, Physician)
```

```
<rdf:RDF
  xmlns:rdf="http://www.w3.org/TR/WD-rdf-syntax#"
  xmlns:ms="http://ourdomain.it/MS/Schema/ms-syntax#">
  <rdf:Statement
    rdf:about="http://ourdomain.it/MS/medstaff/11234">
    <rdf:subject rdf:resource="http://ourdomain.it/MS/Schema/ms-syntax#Surgeon" />
    <rdf:predicate rdf:resource="http://ourdomain.it/MS/Schema/ms-syntax#belongs"/>
    <rdf:object rdf:datatype="http://www.w3.org/2001/XMLSchema#string">
      Trauma Therapy Center
    </rdf:object>
  </rdf:Statement>
  <rdf:Statement
    rdf:about="http://ourdomain.it/MS/medstaff/11234">
    <rdf:subject rdf:datatype="http://www.w3.org/2001/XMLSchema#rfc822Name" >
      http://ourdomain.it/MS/Schema/ms-syntax#Surgeon"
    </rdf:subject>
    <rdf:predicate rdf:resource="http://ourdomain.it/MS/Schema/ms-syntax#name"/>
    <rdf:object rdf:datatype="http://www.w3.org/2001/XMLSchema#string">
      Sam
    </rdf:object>
  </rdf:Statement>
</rdf:RDF>
```

Fig. 5. An example of RDF description associated with a requester

Then all XACML rules R whose subject metadata include (?, subject, Surgeon) will be selected.

Let us assume that the resource metadata mentioned in the context of the policy rule R is the following:

```
(?, type, Statement)
(?, subject, Physician)
(?, predicate, assists)
(?, object, Patient)
```

These metadata can now be used to build a query on the resource descriptors, to identify the objects to which the rule applies. For instance, the policy will apply to the video presentation with the metadata shown in Figure 3.

The reified statement contained in the policy is used to construct the query which is submitted to the set of resource descriptors. Therefore, to evaluate the feasibility of our approach, the complexity of RDF query answering must be taken into account. RDF query evaluation process is composed of three main phases [8]: matches computation, minimization of queries, and redundancy elimination in answers. Here we shall only discuss the first contribution since some theoretical results are available from RDF querying research. The other two phases will need to be addressed with ad hoc solution for policy evaluation.[6] In [8] the authors used the simpler problem of testing emptiness of the query answer as an approximation of the complexity of computing the matches. Distinguishing between *query complexity*, considering the evaluation time as a function of query size for a given database, and *data complexity*, considering the evaluation time of a given query as a function of database size for a fixed query, they find out that evaluation is NP-complete for the query complexity and polynomial for the database complexity version. Furthermore, the size of the set of answers of a query q issued against a database D is bounded by $|D||q|$, where $|D|$

---

[6] Since query evaluation is often exponential in query size, static optimization of queries is an important goal.

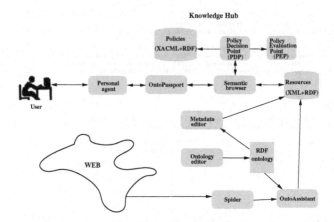

Fig. 6. Our reference semantic web architecture

is the size of the database (number of triples) and $|q|$ is the number of symbols in the query.

5   Our Architecture: The OntoPassport

To present our architecture we will focus on our semantic web system, called *Knowledge Hub* (KH) [1], illustrated in Figure 6. In the KH, network resources are first downloaded in their native XML/XHTML format[7], tidying them up if necessary. Then, a special-purpose tool, called *OntoAssistant*, is used to produce RDF descriptions of their content. Such descriptions are written exploiting the standard vocabulary provided by a business ontology, written in the RDFS standard language. While more structured ontology description languages such as OWL [17] are now available, the KH setting is general enough for our current purposes. Users connect to the KH system via a Semantic Navigator that allows them to navigate/query metadata as well as the data themselves. Thanks to the body of knowledge comprising the ontologies and the metadata, the Semantic Navigator can act as a logic program, performing more sophisticated reasoning than a conventional query engine. Also, the Semantic Navigator can use the available metadata about resources and users themselves to customize their navigation experience and data presentation. To present a semantic web application like our KH with a semantics-aware description of a user, we can encapsulate ontology-based metadata about the user within a SAML request. Our

---

[7] Of course, it would be perfectly feasible to associate metadata with external resources without downloading them; however, this would bring up the problem of keeping data and metadata consistent, which is outside of the scope of this paper.

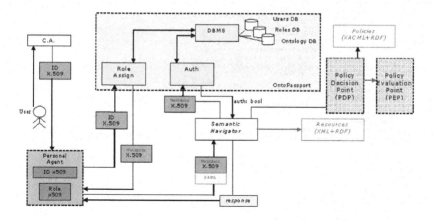

Fig. 7. The architecture of a security solution including the OntoPassport component

OntoPassport tool was designed to handle this approach by encoding metadata in a X.509 certificate that can be carried by SAML.[8]

Figure 7 shows a closer view of our evaluation architecture. Figure 8 shows the WSDL interface definition for the OntoPassport implemented as a web service. The input datatypes correspond to the XML encoding of a generic certificate, while the return datatype is designed to cointain a set of RDF assertions that qualify the user with respect to a suitable role ontology. We could substitute the username-password authentication scheme with a traditional certificate. In this case the OntoPassport acts as a "translator" of an authentication certificate into a digital identity according to an ontology.

The OntoPassport also includes in the certificate the name, URL and version of the RDFS Schema specifying the ontology it used to build the subject metadata. This makes the type hierarchy used for subjects (and, more generally, the entire metadata vocabulary used to talk about them) easy to share and maintain across an organization. We are currently working on the implementation of a PEP component including a fully featured RDF query engine.

6   Conclusions

Traditional access control models and languages result limiting for emerging Web applications. Although recent advancements allow the specifications of access control rules with reference to generic attributes/properties of the requestor

---

[8] Alternatively, our semantics-aware metadata can be saved in a secure cookie [11] on the user's machine.

```xml
<?xml version="1.0" encoding="UTF-8"?>
<definitions name="MyWebService"
  targetNamespace="http://MyServer/OntoPassport.wsdl"
  xmlns="http://schemas.xmlsoap.org/wsdl/"
  xmlns:xsd="http://www.w3.org/2001/XMLSchema"
  xmlns:soap="http://schemas.xmlsoap.org/wsdl/soap/"
  xmlns:tns="http://MyServer/OntoPassport.wsdl"
  xmlns:ns1="http://MyServer/MyWebService.xsd">
  <types>
    <schema targetNamespace="http://MyServer/MyWebService.xsd"
      xmlns="http://www.w3.org/2001/XMLSchema"
      xmlns:SOAP-ENC="http://schemas.xmlsoap.org/soap/encoding/">
      <complexType name="OntoPassportToken">
        <all>
          <element name="name" type="string"/>
          <element name="idCode" type="string"/>
          <element name="surname" type="string"/>
          <element name="mail" type="string"/>
          <element name="privilege" type="string"/>
          <element name="ttl" type="int"/>
          <element name="timeStamp" type="int"/>
        </all>
      </complexType>
    </schema>
  </types>
  <message name="tokenRequestRequest">
    <part name="usr" type="xsd:string"/>
    <part name="pwd" type="xsd:string"/>
  </message>
  <message name="tokenRequestResponse">
    <part name="return" type="ns1:OntoPassportToken"/>
  </message>
  <portType name="OntoPassportType">
    <operation name="tokenRequest">
      <input name="tokenRequestRequest" message="tns:tokenRequestRequest"/>
      <output name="tokenRequestResponse" message="tns:tokenRequestResponse"/>
    </operation>
  </portType>
  <binding name="OntoPassportBinding" type="tns:OntoPassportPortType">
    <soap:binding style="rpc" transport="http://schemas.xmlsoap.org/soap/http"/>
    <operation name="tokenRequest">
      <soap:operation soapAction="" style="rpc"/>
      <input name="tokenRequestRequest">
        <soap:body use="encoded" namespace="MyWebService"
        encodingStyle="http://schemas.xmlsoap.org/soap/encoding/"/>
      </input>
      <output name="tokenRequestResponse">
        <soap:body use="encoded" namespace="MyWebService"
        encodingStyle="http://schemas.xmlsoap.org/soap/encoding/"/>
      </output>
    </operation>
  </binding>
  <service name="MyWebService">
    <port name="OntoPassportPort" binding="tns:OntoPassportBinding">
      <soap:address location="http://OntoServices/MyWebService"/>
    </port>
  </service>
</definitions>
```

Fig. 8. The OntoPassport WSDL interface

and the resources, they do not fully exploit the semantic power and reasoning capabilities of emerging web applications. We have presented a semantics-aware approach aimed at controlling access to resources on the basis of complex assertions about subjects seeking access as well as about resources, stated by means of semantic web metadata standards. We have also shown how this expressive power can be easily accommodated by proper extensions of available XML-based policy languages, like XACML. While several aspects (including efficient techniques for performing enforcement) are still to be investigated, our proposal provides a clear problem statement and a first step toward its solution.

Acknowledgments. This work was supported in part by the European Union within the PRIME Project in the FP6/IST Programme under contract IST-2002-507591 and by the Italian MIUR within the KIWI and MAPS projects.

References

1. A. Corallo, E. Damiani, and G. Elia. A knowledge management system enabling regional innovation. In *Proc. of the International Conference on Knowledge-Based Intelligent Information Engineering Systems & Allied Technologies (KES 2002)*, Crema, Italy, September 2002.
2. DAML query language (DQL), April 2003. http://www.daml.org/2003/04/dql/.
3. J. Davies, D. Fensel, and F. van Harmelen. *Towards the Semantic Web: Ontology-Driven Knowledge Management*. John Wiley & Sons, Ltd, 2002.
4. G. Denker, L. Kagal, T. Finin, M. Paolucci, and K. Sycara. Security for DAML web services: Annotation and matchmaking. In *Proc. of the 2nd International Semantic Web Conference (ISWC2003)*, Sanibel Island, Florida, USA, October 2003.
5. eXtensible Access Control Markup Language. http://www.oasis-open.org/committees/tc_home.php?wg_abbrev=xacml.
6. D. Fensel. *Ontologies: A Silver Bullet for Knowledge Management and Electronic Commerce*. Springer-Verlag, 2003.
7. T. Finin and A. Joshi. Agents, trust, and information access on the semantic web. *ACM SIGMOD*, 31(4):30–35, December 2002.
8. C. Gutierrez, C. Hurtado, and A. Mendelzon. Formal aspects of querying RDF databases. In *Proc. of First International Workshop on Semantic Web and Databases*, Berlin, Germany, September 2003.
9. L. Kagal, T. Finin, and A. Joshi. A policy based approach to security for the semantic web. In *Proc. of the Second International Semantic Web Conference (ISWC2003)*, Sanibel Island FL, October 2003.
10. R. Khosla, E. Damiani, and W. Grosky. *Human-centered E-business*. Kluwer Academic Publisher, 2003.
11. J.S. Park and R.S. Sandhu. Secure cookies on the web. *IEEE Internet Computing*, 4(4):36–44, 2000.
12. L. Qin and V. Atluri. Concept-level access control for the semantic web. In *Proc. of the ACM Workshop on XML Security 2003*, Fairfax, VA, PA, October 2003.
13. Security assertion markup language (SAML) v1.0. http://www.oasis-open.org/committees/download.php/3400/oasis-sstc-saml-1.1-pdf-xsd.zip.
14. A. Stoica and C. Farkas. Ontology guided security engine. *Journal of Intelligent Information Systems*, 2004.
15. World Wide Web. *RDF Vocabulary Description Language 1.0: RDF Schema*, December 2003. http://www.w3.org/TR/rdf-schema/.
16. World Wide Web Consourtium. *Semantic Web*. http://www.w3.org/2001/sw/.
17. World Wide Web Consourtium. *OWL Web Ontology Language – Overview*, December 2003. http://www.w3.org/TR/owl-features/.

HyCo – An Authoring Tool to Create Semantic Learning Objects for Web-Based E-learning Systems[*]

Francisco J. García[1,2], Adriana J. Berlanga[2], Maria N. Moreno[1], Javier García[2], and Jorge Carabias[1]

[1] Department of Computer Science – University of Salamanca (Spain)
JORGECARABIAS@telefonica.net
[2] Institute of Educational Sciences – University of Salamanca (Spain)
{fgarcia, solis13, mmg, carrasco}@usal.es

Abstract. In this article we introduce HyCo (Hypertext Composer), an authoring tool devoted to create semantic learning objects. This authoring tool uses learning technology standards or specifications to save these semantic objects, which will be delivered in Web e-learning environments as encapsulated packages in order to ensure their reusability, interoperability, durability and accessibility. These learning objects are closed to the Semantic Web field because they combine hypermedia and semantic capabilities. Our research work is directed to use these semantic learning objects in order to define learning domains for an Adaptive Learning Environment. The aim of this system is to provide an e-learning environment where teachers have tools to create didactic materials and students carry out their knowledge acquisition through the most suitable adaptive learning technique giving the student's characteristics, the learning activities provided, and the learning objects' features.

Keywords: Hypermedia Authoring Tools; Semantic Web Applications; Learning Technologies Standards; IMS; E-Learning.

1 Introduction

The use of Internet as an instructional media not only has brought new ideas and thoughts around learning and teaching, but also a new conception about learning elements through WWW: they should be reusable, interoperable, durable and accessible.

To accomplish these requirements, several education institutions had incorporated information and communication technologies in the learning and teaching process in order to increase the quality, efficiency, and dissemination of the education. Consequently, learning domains have been passed thru a reconfiguration process where defining metadata for learning objects has a central role. Metadata guarantees interoperation, reusability, and interchange among e-learning systems, as well as a cost-effective development.

[*] This study was partly financed by the Regional Government of Castile and Lion through research project SA017/02. Also, it is supported by the European Union Project ODISEAME, ref. EUMEDIS B7-4100/2000/2165-79 P546.

N. Koch, P. Fraternali, and M. Wirsing (Eds.): ICWE 2004, LNCS 3140, pp. 344–348, 2004.
© Springer-Verlag Berlin Heidelberg 2004

Several LTS (Learning Technology Standards) have been defined, which are agreements about the characteristics a learning element should have in order to be compatible, interchangeable and interoperable into other learning systems [9].

If web-based e-learning systems fulfill a LTS, they are able to work with other systems (interoperability), follow-up information about learners and contents (manageability), generate learning objects that are usable in other contexts (reusability), and avoid obsolescence (durability). From students' point of view, standards ensure they get the right content at the right time (accessibility) and obtain a variety of knowledge resources (interchange of learning objects).

In our research work, we are interesting in defining SLOs (Semantic Learning Objects) that will be compliant with these LTSs and will be integrated or deployed in an ALE (Adaptive Learning Environment). The aim of an ALE system is to provide an e-learning environment where teachers have tools to create didactic materials and students carry out their knowledge acquisition through the most suitable adaptive learning technique giving the student's characteristics, the learning activities provided, and the learning objects' features [1].

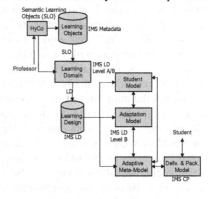

The proposed ALE architecture is composed of five subsystems: Learning Domain Model, Adaptive Model, Student Model, Adaptive Meta-model, and Deliver and Packing Model, as it is shown in Figure 1.

Fig. 1. ALE Architecture

The system pretends to be an open tool that differentiates between educative contents and learning process. The ALE system structures its semantic elements following the IMS specifications. Namely, to describe Learning Objects it uses IMS Metadata [6], to describe the Deliver and Packing Model it uses IMS Content Packaging (IMS CP) [4], and to describe the learning domain model, it uses IMS Learning Design (IMS LD) [5].

The rest of the paper is organised as follows. Section 2 gives a general introduction of the HyCo authoring tool. Section 3 is focused on the definition of the SLOs in HyCo. Finally, section 4 provides remarks and further work.

2 An Overview of the HyCo Authoring Tool

HyCo [3] is a powerful **authoring tool for educational purposes**; this means that an author can create hypermedia educational resources with it. But also the same tool could be used to access to the created contents in a read-only mode by a student or reader.

HyCo is a **multiplatform** tool. It does not force to use one concrete platform. The idea is that if we want the teachers use it, they should work in the context they feel good. The actual version of HyCo works in the wider range of operating systems, for this reason Java 2 Standard Edition technology was chosen as development base.

The main goal of the HyCo is the creation of **educational contents**, but trying to achieve an independence of the final format publication. There exits a clear separation between the contents and its presentation. This way the educator writes the contents once, and reuses them every time he/she needs. In order to achieve this goal, HyCo tool uses an internal XML-based format [2] to store the educational contents of the produced electronic books. Precisely, the HyCo XML-based format allows the introduction of the LTSs in this authoring tool, specifically HyCo supports IMS specifications [4, 5, 6] and EML (Educational Modelling Language) [8].

The fact of separating the content and the presentation forces to offer to the authors a way to generate an **independent result** of the authoring tool. In this way HyCo has an output gallery that supports HTML, PDF, TXT, RTF, SVG and PS output formats.

Following **pedagogical criteria**, HyCo reproduces the process that an author would follow to create a linear educational resource, but it channels it, at the same time as it organizes it, through the metaphor of the content index, adding the facilities for including multimedia elements as well as hyperlinks. This way a hierarchical structure is obtained that guides us in our creative process, which would consist in associating contents with each index entry, an index that may vary as the contents take shape, by inserting, eliminating or changing entries. In a nutshell, then, HyCo faithfully reproduces the process previously explained. This indexed or tree structure facilitates the authoring of the hypertext, but having only an index as navigation tool is not acceptable in order to create real pedagogical hypermedia resources where the student may construct its own knowledge. This way, the hyperdocuments should be designed in such a way as to encourage the readers to see the same text in as many useful contexts as possible. This means placing texts within the contexts of other texts, including different views of the same text [7]. For this reason HyCo also allows associating links to the multimedia elements that compose an index entry, i.e. a hypertext node. Thus, the hypertext can be followed by its index-structure, but when a node is selected, the reader may choose navigating by an existing link. Thus, HyCo documents combine both content index and Web-like structures.

3 Definition of Learning Resources in HyCo

When organizations, schools and teachers started to use the Web as an instructional media, almost the only way to publish educational contents was in HTML format, where e-learning elements were presented without any division between content and its meaning. This syntactic presentation prevents to automatically extract data, not to mention the definition of learning elements were as heterogeneous as existing e-learning designs. In this context, interoperability, reusability, and interchange among e-learning systems are impossible. Moreover, the idea of a cost-effective e-learning development is far away.

Several organizations have been working to define specifications and standards to design instructional elements, known as Learning Technologies Specifications. EML and IMS Specifications are LTSs that are now supported in HyCo authoring tool.

As we stated before, HyCo is an authoring tool to create SLOs, which are the learning resources that will be available in the instructional design process that defines the ALE learning domain.

3.1 Definition of Learning Resources

To create the learning domain model, the first step is to generate SLOs. Every SLO should be compliant with IMS Metadata [6]. Every section of every educational resource or e-book created in HyCo can be converted to a SLO.

To do it, HyCo executes a two-step process where the first step is an automatic process, while the second step is a manual process. In the automatic process, HyCo sets all the IMS Metadata elements that can be inferred from other data or that are liable to have default values.

Once this process is over, HyCo executes the manual process where it presents to the user the elements that can not be automatically generated and/or require reexamination, modification, or addition.

When the two-step process is finished a XML file is generated for each new SLO (each one of them corresponds to each educational resource, section, or subsection) and stored in an IMS Metadata SLO repository. This repository will allow us to have learning objects that can be attached to learning activities of the learning designs created in ALE.

3.2 Definition of Learning Components

The learning components design includes the definition of roles, learning activities and learning activities sequences.

Two steps are needed to define the learning components. First the addition and definition of roles and learning activities, and then connect these elements by means of an activity sequences.

The definition of roles includes elements as title, metadata and information. The definition of learning activities includes elements as title, metadata, learning objectives, prerequisites, description, feed back description, and so on. Also SLO can be included.

In order to ensure efficiency and simplicity in the authoring process, repositories of learning objects and learning designs, as well a set of selectors and creators will be provided. For example, to define learning activities the author can choose one learning object (i.e. SLO) from its repository and use selectors for describe elements as metadata, prerequisites, and learning objectives. Moreover, these selectors will be used reiteratively within the different definitions, where the same elements exist. The most representative case of this is the metadata selector that will be used when defining roles, learning activities and sequences of activities.

In addition, in the creation of learning activities, ALE will be able to propose learning objects taking into account the metadata stored in other elements as prerequisites, objectives, and so on.

After the author has defined the learning components, the next phase is to design the learning method where conditions and attributes will be delimited. Finally, the learning components and the learning method have to be integrated into the definition of the learning design, where general prerequisites and objectives are added, as well as roles, activities (that group learning activities and sequences), and the learning method.

4 Conclusions and Further Work

In this paper we have introduced HyCo as an authoring tool that allows the definition of both learning resources and learning components or SLOs, i.e. semantic educational resources based on XML specifications, which could be delivered in diverse Learning Management Systems. Specifically, HyCo supports EML and IMS.

The success of the HyCo authoring process has been proved with three educational web-based systems. Two of them are drafts devoted to test the authoring tool, one about computer history and other one about a software engineering course. But the third one is a complete electronic book in hypermedia format about cardiovascular surgery that is formed by 14 chapters, more than 500 sections and over 1000 images. This book is successfully used in the lectures of this subject in the University of Salamanca.

HyCo is an open system in which too much further work is going to be done, especially in adaptive hypermedia systems. Now the next step is to make the necessary changes and modifications to HyCo in order to turn it into the learning domain authoring tool of the ALE System.

Also, we are working in defining two more phases for the learning domain. Namely, a definition of a learning style theory and the definition of the adaptive rules the ALE system will follow. The first will be necessary to setup the students' characteristics that will be considered. The second will be helpful to define the adaptation rules the system will take into account to perform the adaptation of contents and links.

References

[1]   Berlanga, A., Morales, E., García, F. J.: Learning Technology Standards: Semantic Objects for Adaptive Learning Environments. In A. Méndez, J. A. Mesa, J. Mesa (Eds.), *Advances in Technology-Based Education: Toward a Knowledge-Based Society. Proceedings of the 2nd International Conference on Multimedia and Information & Communication Technologies in Education m-ICTE2003.* Consejería de Educación, Ciencia y Tecnología de la Junta de Extremadura. (2003) Vol. II, 860-864.

[2]   Bray, T., Paoli, J., Sperberg-MacQueen, C. M., Maler, E., Yergeau, F. (Eds.): Extensible Markup Language (XML) 1.0 (Third Edition). World Wide Web Consortium. http://www.w3.org/TR/2004/REC-xml-20040204. (2004).

[3]   García, F. J., García, J.: Educational Hypermedia Resources Facilitator. *Computers & Education.* In press. (2004).

[4]   IMS: IMS Content Packaging. http://www.imsglobal.org/content/packaging/index.cfm. (2003).

[5]   IMS: IMS Learning Design Specification. http://www.imsglobal.org/learningdesign/index.cfm. (2003).

[6]   IMS: IMS Learning Resource Metadata Specification. http://www.imsglobal.org/metadata/index.cfm. (2003).

[7]   Jones, R. A., Spiro, R.: Imagined Conversations: The Relevance of Hypertext, Pragmatism, and Cognitive Flexibility Theory to the Interpretation of "Classic Texts" in Intellectual History. In D. Lucarella, J. Nanard, M. Nanard, P. Paolini (Eds.), *Proceedings of the 4th ACM Conference on Hypertext – ECHT'92.* ACM Press (1992) 141-148.

[8]   Koper, R.: Modelling Units of Study from a Pedagogical Perspective. The Pedagogical Meta-model behind EML. http://eml.ou.nl/introduction/docs/ped-metamodel.pdf. (2001).

[9]   Wiley, D.: Connecting Learning Objects to Instructional Design Theory: A Definition, a Metaphor, and a Taxonomy. In D. Wiley (Ed.), *The Instructional Use of Learning Objects.* On line version: http://reusability.org/read/chapters/wiley.doc. (2000).

Annotation for the Semantic Web During Website Development

Peter Plessers and Olga De Troyer

Vrije Universiteit Brussel, Department of Computer Science, WISE, Pleinlaan 2, 1050
Brussel, Belgium
{Peter.Plessers, Olga.DeTroyer}@vub.ac.be

Abstract. While introducing the HTML standard to present information on the
World Wide Web, the importance of being able to express the deep structure
and meaning of the information was neglected. This has lead to some of the
limitations of the current web (e.g. its restricted query possibilities). Work has
started in the domain of the semantic web which tries to solve this problem by
annotating web pages with semantic information. A crucial aspect to the success of the semantic web is that we have methods available to create, integrate
and use this semantic information. In this paper, we present a new approach to
generate semantic information by taking the annotation process to a conceptual
level and by integrating it into an existing website design method.

1 Introduction

The large majority of current information available on the web is presented using the
standard HTML format. Emphasis was put in this standard on layout possibilities but
the importance of being able to express the meaning of the presented information was
neglected. The lack of semantic information in current websites is addressed by the
vision of the Semantic Web [1]. This vision states that the information available on
the WWW should be defined such that it remains usable for human interpretation, but
also becomes usable for machines. In this way, we can solve some of the limitations
of the current web (e.g. its restricted query possibilities, intelligent agents, ...).

A crucial aspect to realize the vision of the Semantic Web in practice is that we
have methods available to create, integrate and use semantic information and this, as
much as possible, in a transparent and automatic way. As mentioned in [7], the generation of semantic markup should be a by-product of normal computer use. A step
towards this goal has been taken in recent years by annotation approaches such as
SHOE [6], MindSwap [4] and CREAM [5]. While such tools solve a number of issues
like syntactic mistakes or inconsistencies with the used ontology, a number of fundamental problems still remain. The main reason for these problems is that current tools
define a linkage between an ontology and the actual data of the website on an implementation level resulting in a strong weaving of semantics and implementation. We
list some of the problems we encounter in current annotation approaches:

- Despite the introduction of supporting tools, the annotation process remains a very
  heavy and time consuming task. In addition, in most current approaches this proc-

N. Koch, P. Fraternali, and M. Wirsing (Eds.): ICWE 2004, LNCS 3140, pp. 349–353, 2004.
© Springer-Verlag Berlin Heidelberg 2004

ess is an additional activity and the ones that will benefit from the annotations are usually not the ones that should accomplish the job. Therefore, the motivation for performing the annotation process is low.

- It is usually assumed that the granularity of the concepts defined in the ontology matches exactly the granularity of the data on the website, although this assumption cannot be taken for granted. It must therefore be possible to define a link between semantically equivalent concepts but with a different level of granularity.
- Most of the supporting tools only allow annotating static websites, page by page on an implementation level. Even approaches that support the annotation of dynamic generated websites (by annotating the database) create a direct link between the implementation structure of the database (i.e. tables and columns for a relational database) and concepts in the ontology. For static web pages this has as consequence that the work done for one page needs to be repeated for similar structured web pages and that the maintenance of the metadata becomes a heavy task with a huge cost. Also note that for both static and dynamic websites, every time one changes the implementation of the website or database, even though nothing has changed to the semantics of the presented data, the defined linkage between the web pages or database and the ontologies can be affected.

In this paper we present initial ideas for annotating websites during their design. The presented approach tries to solve the problems mentioned earlier by elevating the annotation process to a conceptual level. It is also our belief that (whenever possible) the annotation is best done while designing the website, not after it is implemented. In this way we can take advantage of the information available during the website design process to ease and improve the annotation process. Therefore, we propose to integrate the annotation process into an existing website design method. Several website design methods have already been proposed in literature. We will use WSDM (Web Site Design Method) [2] in our approach as this method is well suited for our purpose as it proposes an explicit information-modeling step at a conceptual level.

2 Approach Overview

2.1 Architecture

Figure 1 gives an overview of the global architecture of our annotation approach. The different phases of WSDM that are relevant for our annotation approach are at the left: Task Modeling, Navigational Design, Page & Presentation Design, Database Design and finally the Implementation. Our approach is integrated into the original phases of the WSDM design method. A short overview of each step of the WSDM method, together with the enhancements (if any) we made for our annotation approach, is given below.

- *Mission Statement Specification:* Specifies the subject and goal of the website and declares the target audience. No enhancements are needed in this step.
- *Audience Modeling:* In this phase the different types of users are identified and classified into audience classes. For each audience class, the different requirements

and characterizations are formulated. Also in this step, nothing additional is needed.

- *Task Modeling:* A task model is defined for each requirement of each audience class. Each task defined in the task model is elaborated into elementary tasks. For each elementary task a data model (called 'object chunk') is created, which models the necessary information and/or functionality needed to fulfill the requirement of that elementary task. ORM (Object Role Modeling) is used as the representation language for the object chunks. For our purpose, we added an annotation process to the Task Modeling phase. This results in the creation of a linkage between the object types and roles of the different object chunks and the concepts of one or more ontologies. This annotation is called the *conceptual annotation* (arrow A in Figure 1) because it is performed on a conceptual level. In this way we define the semantic meaning of the object types and roles used in the object chunks. This conceptual annotation is performed for static as well as dynamic websites.

- *Navigational Design:* In this phase of WSDM the navigational structure of the website is described by defining components, connecting object chunks to those components and linking components to one another.

- *Page Design:* During Page Design, the components of the navigational structure and their associated object chunks are mapped onto a Page structure defining the pages that will be implemented for the website. We determine which object chunks will be placed on a certain page. Using this step as well as the previous one (the navigational design) we can identify which object chunks will be placed on a page. This is necessary to know for the actual implementation which annotations we have to add to a page.

- *Presentation Design:* For each page defined in the Page Design a page template is created defining the layout of the page. This layout is defined in an implementation independent way. To implement the actual web pages making use of a chosen implementation language (e.g. HTML, XML, ...), an instantiation of these page templates can be generated. For this, the templates are filled using the proper data to obtain the actual pages.

- *Data Design:* As explained in [3] we can derive an integrated conceptual schema from the object chunks made during Task Modeling. This integrated object schema is called the Business Information Model (BIM) and can be used as the basis for a database schema from which an underlying database can be created. The Data Design is only done when we deal with dynamically generated websites querying a database. For static web pages the data design step is omitted as the actual data will not originate from a database, but will be supplied by the designer during implementation. For our approach, we need to keep track of two mappings: 1) the mapping from the object types and relationships of the different object chunks to their correspondence in the integrated BIM (called *object chunk mapping*) (B in Figure 2); and 2) the mapping between the BIM, used as the conceptual database schema, and the actual implementation (called *database mapping*) (C in Figure 2). In this way we are able to determine the mapping between the queries specified at the (conceptual) level of the object chunks, and the actual database.

- *Implementation:* In this phase of WSDM the actual implementation of a website, based on the models created in the previous phases, is generated. To this step we added the generation of the actual annotation of the website (called the *page annotation*) (D in Figure 2). Here we have to distinguish between static websites and dynamically generated websites. For static websites only the conceptual annotation is needed. For dynamic websites also the chunk integration and the database mapping have to be taken into consideration.

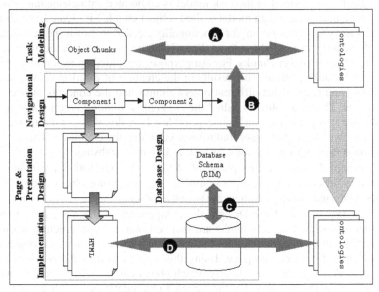

Fig. 1. Architectural overview

2.2 Advantages

The goal of our approach is to add semantic knowledge to the web pages of a new to create website. Opposed to current approaches, which perform the annotation on the web page level or on the database level (for dynamic websites), we define the annotation on a conceptual level. Web designers will provide the annotation during the conceptual design. Compared to currently existing annotation methods, this approach has a number of advantages:

- *The annotation is implementation independent.* Current methods define the annotations directly in the implementation of the website. Using our approach, an implementation will be generated (HTML, XML, ...) and changes can be generated without breaking the annotation, resulting in a greater level of maintainability of the annotation.
- *The annotation process is uniform for static and dynamic websites.* In current approaches the annotation for static and dynamic websites is done in a different way: respectively annotating web pages or a database. In our approach, the annotation step is done at the conceptual design which is independent on whether the website will be static or dynamic.
- *Reuse of the annotations.* In current annotation methods (for static websites), if a certain concept is used on different pages, the annotation has to be repeated for each page. In our approach, the annotation has to be defined only once and the same concept can be reused in different object chunks. Moreover, all copies of an

entity used over several Object Chunks will be updated automatically if the annotation of one copy has changed.

- *Improvement of the design process.* An important aspect of integrating the annotation into the design process is that it enables us to improve the consistency during this website design process and to speed it up by making use of the metadata already provided. It is for example possible to make suggestions to the designer about information to be included based on earlier conceptual annotations made.

3 Conclusion

In this paper, we presented an approach for the semi-automatic annotation of static as well as dynamic websites. The actual annotation process is performed during the design phase of the website. We presented the proposed approach integrated into an existing website design method, WSDM. This design method provides us a conceptual model of the website that can be used to annotate (at a type level) the information that will be available on the website, with concepts from an ontology. This is done by annotating the entities (Object Types and roles) used in the conceptual model of the website. Next, this "conceptual" annotation can be used to generate the actual page annotation by keeping track of the different transformations performed during the development process to derive an implementation.

References

1. Berners Lee, T., Hendler, J., Lassila, O.: The semantic web: A new form of web content that is meaningful to computers will unleash a revolution of new possibilities. Scientific American (2001) 5(1)
2. De Troyer, O., Leune, C.: WSDM: A User-Centered Design Method for Web Sites. Computer Networks and ISDN Systems, proceedings of the 7th International World Wide Web Conference, Brisbane Australia (1998) 85–94
3. De Troyer, O., Plessers, P., Casteleyn, S.: Solving Semantic Conflicts in Adience Driven Web Design. Proceedings of the WWW/Internet 2003 Conference, Algarve Portugal (2003)
4. Golbeck, J., Grove, M., Parsia, B., Kalyanpur, A., Hendler J.: New Tools for the Semantic Web. Proceedings of EKAW 2002, LNCS 2473. Springer (2002) 392–400
5. Handschuh, S., Staab, S., Maedche, A.: CREAM – Creating Relational Metadata with a Componentbased, Ontology Driven Framework. Proceedings of K-Cap, Victoria Canada (2001)
6. Heflin, J., Hendler, J.: Searching the web with SHOE. Artificial Intelligence for Web Search. Papers from the AAAI Workshop. WS-00-01, AAAI Press (2000) 35-40
7. Heflin, J., Hendler, J.: Agents and the Semantic Web. IEEE Intelligent Systems Journal 16(2) (2001) 30–37

Lifting XML Schema to OWL

Matthias Ferdinand[1], Christian Zirpins[1], and David Trastour[2]

[1] VSIS Group, University of Hamburg, Germany
{6ferdina,zirpins}@informatik.uni-hamburg.de
[2] Hewlett-Packard Laboratories Bristol, UK
david.trastour@hp.com

Abstract. The Semantic Web will allow software agents to understand and reason about data provided by Web applications. Unfortunately, formal ontologies, needed to express data semantics, are often not readily available. However, common data schemas can help to create ontologies. We propose mappings from XML Schema to OWL as well as XML to RDF and show how web engineering can benefit from the gained expressiveness as well as the use of inference services.

1 Introduction

The Semantic Web will allow software agents to understand, share and reason about data that is provided by Web application systems. Formal conceptual models, or ontologies, are necessary to express the semantics of the data. Unfortunately, semantic information is not usually available in such a form, but scattered across documentation and various software components. Because developing ontologies from scratch is costly and difficult, one should try to reuse this semantic information as much as possible. Thanks to their formal nature, document schemas like XML Schema provide a good basis for developing or re-engineering ontologies (see e.g. [1,2] for a comparison of ontology languages, web standards and markup languages).

In this work, we focus on extracting semantic information out of document schemas and propose a mechanism to lift XML Schema to the Web Ontology Language (OWL). While, for example, concrete translation procedures from OIL or XOL to XML Schema have been developed by [3,4], we specify and implement a mapping in the reverse direction producing an OWL ontology. In order to apply this semantic meta-information for reasoning on instance data, XML documents have to be mapped to RDF, bridging the gap between those models. General solutions typically require changes to XML or RDF: Melnik [5] developed an RDF interpretation for XML documents. In [6,7] a formal model and an architecture have been developed that allow uniform access to both types of documents. We propose another such mapping that does not require changes to the standards and incorporates XML Schema type information. Subsequently, based on our two mappings, we show that the engineering of XML based web applications can benefit from the high expressive power OWL has to offer and from inference services such as classification or satisfiability checking.

N. Koch, P. Fraternali, and M. Wirsing (Eds.): ICWE 2004, LNCS 3140, pp. 354–358, 2004.
© Springer-Verlag Berlin Heidelberg 2004

In the following, sect. 2 proposes two mapping concepts from XML to RDF and from XML Schema to OWL that allow lifting data from syntax to representation. Sect. 3 shows how reasoning techniques on such representations can be applied in web engineering. Finally, sect. 4 concludes.

2   From Syntax to Representation: Mapping Concepts

In this section, we propose a general binding of XML structured data to Semantic Web languages. The approach is twofold: XML documents are translated into RDF graphs and XML Schemas are lifted to OWL ontologies. This applies to all XML documents that conform to an XML Schema.

The first part of the concept concerns the *XML to RDF mapping*. XML is a language that defines a generic syntax to store and exchange documents by means of a tree-based structure. Although RDF has an XML-based syntax, XML and RDF serve different purposes and have been developed separately within the W3C, which lead to different modelling foundations.

XML is based on a tree model where only nodes are labeled and the outgoing edges are ordered. This model originates from semi-structured data and databases. In contrast to this, RDF is based on a directed graph model where edges have labels but are unordered. It distinguishes between resources (e.g. car) and properties (e.g. car color) while XML does not (e.g. both would be elements). This model originates from knowledge representation languages such as Frames [8] and description logics (DL).

To bridge the gap between both forms of data representation, we developed a procedure that transforms XML documents to RDF data models. In order to keep compatibility with existing documents and applications, this mapping does not require any change on either XML or RDF specifications (however, so-called mixed content models of XML are not fully supported). Structural differences of the data models represent no obstacle, as trees are a specialisation of graphs. We make a distinction between (1) elements that have sub-elements and/or attributes, and (2) attributes and elements that carry only a data type value. These two categories of components correspond respectively to XML Schema declarations associated with a `complexType` or a `simpleType`. The mapping is performed by the following procedure:

Initially, an RDF resource `Document` is created – representing the XML document itself. Then, for each sub-element and attribute of the element that is currently processed (starting with the root element), an RDF property on the RDF resource created before in the previous step is created. If we encounter a data type component (2nd category above), its data value is represented as an RDF literal on the respective property. If we encounter an object component (1st category above), an anonymous RDF resource is created and assigned as the value of the respective property. Then, this component is processed recursively.

As we also want to map XML Schema, it is desirable to transparently incorporate the type information specified in the corresponding schema. To facilitate this, we presume that an XML Schema-aware processor has validated the XML document, which results in type information represented in a Post-Schema Validation Infoset (PSVI). We will see that each XML Schema `complexType` is mapped into an OWL class. Hence each mapped RDF resource is of `rdf:type` the OWL class corresponding to the PSVI retrieved `complexType`.

The second part of the concept concerns the *XML Schema to OWL mapping*. XML Schema and OWL solve different problems: XML Schema provides means to express and constrain the syntax and structure of XML documents. OWL, in contrast, is intended for modelling the semantic relationships of a domain. However, there is an interesting overlap between the two, as both of them have an object-oriented foundation. XML Schema has the notion of class hierarchy and specialisation, and OWL is based on the notion of Frames. Although they accomplish it at two different levels of abstraction, the languages share the goal of defining common vocabularies and structures to support electronic exchange of information. Our mapping approach that complements the one seen before, capitalizes on these similarities. In the following, we give an overview of the fundamental choices. The mapping procedure of a complete XML Schema is composed of the mapping of its different components.

Main Concepts: Each XML Schema `complexType` is mapped to an `owl:Class`. Each `element` and `attribute` declaration is mapped to an OWL property. More precisely, elements of `simpleType` and all attributes are mapped to an `owl:Data typeProperty`; elements of `complexType` are mapped to an `owl:ObjectProperty`. Finally, the `schema` root element of a schema is mapped to an OWL `Class` of name 'targetNamespace + #Schema'.

Model Groups: Model group definitions and attribute group definitions are specialisations of complex types since they only contain element respectively attribute declarations. Hence, they are also mapped to OWL classes.

Specialisation: In object-orientation, inheritance mechanisms represent a central modelling tool which is used to express "is-a" relationships between classes. The literature differentiates between various types of inheritance, two of the most important ones are inheritance by restriction and inheritance by extension. XML Schema supports both of these ways by corresponding type derivation constructs and we both map them to `rdfs:subClassOf` in OWL, its only inheritance mechanism. XML Schema offers the `substitutionGroup` construct which specifies that an element can be replaced by a set of other elements in the instance document. Analog to the type derivation mechanisms, this construct can be interpreted as a way to express a specialisation of elements and thus is mapped to an OWL `subPropertyOf`.

Type and Cardinality: In XML Schema, "Particles" (resp. "AttributeUses") are used to associate a type and cardinality to a local element (resp. a local attribute).Because these definitions have a local scope, we map them to the intersection of two property restrictions: one restricting the type with `owl:allValuesFrom`, the other restricting the cardinality with either `owl:minCardinality`, `owl:maxCardinality`, or `cardinality`. The two restrictions apply to the same property (i.e. the one corresponding to the element or attribute).

Compositors: XML Schema offers three compositors to combine elements, `sequence`, `all` and `choice`. They are mapped to appropriate OWL boolean expressions. The difference between `sequence` and `all` is purely syntactic; semantically they are both conjunctions and are both mapped to an `owl:intersectionOf` constructor. The mapping of the `choice` compositor is more verbose since there is no direct equivalent in OWL to an exclusive-OR. Hence, it needs to be constructed with a boolean expression (with `owl:intersectionOf`, `owl:unionOf` and `owl:complementOf`).

Global Elements: Global element and attribute declarations are mapped similarly to local ones. Associated restrictions are added to the `Schema` class.

Identifiers are mapped from XML Schema to URIs by concatenating the `targetNamespace` URI, the `#` character and the component's local name. Problems can occur due to the fact that XML Schema partitions the `targetNamespace` into distinct so-called symbol spaces, one for each kind of definition or declaration. To prevent naming conflicts in OWL, the mapping process applies an appropriate renaming pattern to the affected components.

As a detailed discussion is out of scope here, we can only briefly note that we also found mappings for other language constructs of less common interest. However, because of a limited expressiveness in OWL or because the construct would not be appropriate, we also had to skip some non-essential language components like `abstract`, `final`, `block`, `default`, `form`, wildcards, identity-constraint definitions and `complexTypes` derived by restriction from `simpleTypes`.

3 Reasoning Support for Web Engineering

There are a number of promising applications for the mapping concept in Web engineering. In particular, it allows enhancing traditional XML languages and tools by the capabilities of OWL reasoners. Here, we distinguish support capabilities at design time and runtime of web applications. At *design time*, we see two principal usages for the mapping. On the one hand, ontologies can be extracted out of existing XML Schemas. This skeleton ontology can then be extended using OWL expressions. On the other hand, the mapping can support schema design. Analogous to the use of reasoners to design ontologies [9], they are useful to design XML Schemas. By using `owl:equivalentClass` instead of `rdfs:subClassOf` for the mapping of `complexType`, an OWL reasoner can infer implicit subsumption relationships, thus identifying super-types of some `complexTypes`. This fosters reuse and limits the class proliferation when large number of classes are encountered. An OWL reasoner could also help to check the compatibility of two independently developed schemas. DL based reasoners are the most suited for this type of operation as they can do efficient inference on classes. At *runtime*, the XML mapping into RDF can be used to do inference and semantic validation of XML data. Once translated into RDF, the data can be classified with an OWL reasoner. The classification could lead to discover implicit class membership or implicit relationships between objects. Finally, semantic validation can be performed by looking for unsatisfiable concepts.

4   Conclusion

We have proposed a general solution for automated binding of XML structured data to Semantic Web languages. General procedures have been shown to map XML documents to RDF graphs and XML Schemas to OWL ontologies. Subsequently, supporting techniques for the engineering of web applications have been presented that get possible by integrating mapping results with OWL reasoners.

To underpin the concepts, we offer a Java software toolkit that implements the mapping process [1]. In terms of engineering concepts, we note that we incorporated the RACER DL reasoner [10] and used its inference services to realise a real-world e-business Web application in the context of RosettaNet [11].

By automatically generating formal conceptual models from semi-structured data, our approach supports the automated bootstrapping of ontology development from existing XML Schemas, speeding up the adoption of Semantic Web technologies. It opens up to a wide range of XML based web applications the expressive power of OWL as well as the potentials of inferencing services. Unlike most traditional techniques (e.g. hard coded validation), semantic constraints can be written in a formal, well-documented and reusable fashion that can be applied to various tasks such as semantic validation of XML instances.

References

1. Fensel, D.: Relating Ontology Languages and Web Standards. In: Modelle und Modellierungssprachen in Inf. und WiInf., St. Goar, Fölbach-Verlag (2000)
2. Gil, Y., Ratnakar, V.: A comparison of (semantic) markup languages. In: Proc. 15th Intl. Florida Artificial Intelligence Research Society Conf., May 14-16, 2002, Pensacola Beach, AAAI Press (2002) 413–418
3. Klein, M., Fensel, D., van Harmelen, F., Horrocks, I.: The Relation between Ontologies and XML Schemas. Linköping Electr. Art. in Comp. and Inf. Sci. 6 (2001)
4. Rami, R., Nabila, B.: Translation Procedure to Clarify the Relationship Between Ontology and XML Schema. In: Proc. Intl. Conf. on Internet Computing (IC'2001), Las Vegas, CSREA Press (2001) 164–170
5. Melnik, S.: Bridging the Gap between RDF and XML (Accessed 1 Feb 2004) http://www-db.stanford.edu/~melnik/rdf/fusion.html.
6. Patel-Schneider, P., Sim on, J.: The Yin/Yang Web: XML Syntax and RDF Semantics. In: Proc. 11th Intl. WWW Conf. (WWW11), ACM (2002)
7. Patel-Schneider, P.F., Sim on, J.: Building the Semantic Web on XML. In: Proc. 1st Intl. Semantic Web Conf. 2002 (ISWC'02). (2002)
8. Minsky, M.: A Framework for Representing Knowledge. Technical report, Massachusetts Institute of Technology (1974) MIT-AI Laboratory Memo 306.
9. Bechhofer, S., Horrocks, I., Goble, C., Stevens, R.: OilEd: a reason-able ontology editor for the semantic web. In: Proc. DL-2001, CEUR Elct. Proc. vol. 49 (2001)
10. Haarslev, V., Möller, R.: Description of the RACER system and its applications. In: Proc. DL-2001, CEUR Elct. Proc. vol. 49 (2001)
11. Trastour, D., Preist, C., Coleman, D.: Using Semantic Web Technology to Enhance Current Business-to-Business Integration Approaches. In: Proc. EDOC 2003, IEEE (2003) 222–231

---

[1] http://www.servicecompostion.org/owlmap.php

Accelerating Dynamic Web Content Delivery Using Keyword-Based Fragment Detection

Daniel Brodie, Amrish Gupta, and Weisong Shi

Department of Computer Science
Wayne State University
Detroit, Michigan 48202

Abstract. The recent trend in the Internet traffic is increasing in requests for dynamic and personalized content. To efficiently serve this trend, several server-side and cache-side fragment-based techniques, which exploit reuse of Web pages at the sub-document level, have been proposed. Most of these techniques do not focus on the creation of the fragmented content from existing dynamic content. Also, existing caching techniques do not support fragment movement across the document, a common behavior in dynamic content.

This paper presents two proposals that we have suggested to solve these problems. The first, DyCA, a dynamic content adapter, takes original dynamic Web content and converts it to fragment-enabled content. Thus the dynamic parts of the document are separated into separate fragments from the static template of the document. This is dependent on our proposed keyword-based fragment detection approach that uses predefined keywords to find these fragments and to split them out of the core document. Our second proposal, an augmentation to the ESI standard, allows splitting the information of the position of each fragment in the template from the template data itself by using a mapping table. Using this, a fragment enabled cache can have a more fine grained level of identifying fragments independent of their location on the template, which enables it to take into account fragment behaviors such as fragment movement.

We used the content taken from three real Web sites to achieve a detailed performance evaluation of our proposals. Our results show that our keyword-based approach for fragment extraction provides us with cacheable fragments that, when combined with our proposed mapping table augmentation, can provide significant advantages for fragment-based Web caching of existing dynamic content.

1 Introduction

Researchers have recently proposed several server-side and cache-side mechanisms to improve the generation and serving of dynamic Web content. Server-side techniques, exemplified by techniques such as delta encoding [1], data update propagation [2], fragment-based page generation [3,4], reduce the load on the server by allowing reuse of previously generated content to serve new requests. Cache-side techniques, exemplified by systems such as Active Cache [5], Gemini [6], CONCA [7], and the content assembly technique proposed by Wills *et al.* [8], attempt to reduce the latency of dynamic content delivery by moving some functionality to the edge of network. Similar trends are also visible in commercial caching and edge server products, most notably

N. Koch, P. Fraternali, and M. Wirsing (Eds.): ICWE 2004, LNCS 3140, pp. 359–372, 2004.

IBM's WebSphere [9] and Akamai's Edgesuite [12]. Despite their difference in focus, both server-side and cache-side approaches share the same rationale, specifically that it is possible to view the document in terms of a quasi-static *template* (expressed using formatting languages such as XSL-FO [10] or, what is currently becoming the *de facto* standard, edge-side include (ESI) [11]), which is filled out with multiple individually cacheable and/or uncacheable *objects*[1]. This object composition assumption enables surrogates and downstream proxy caches to reuse templates and cached objects to efficiently serve subsequent requests and additionally reduce server load, bandwidth requirements, and user-perceived latencies by allowing only the modified or unavailable objects to be fetched.

Although the above techniques appear promising, there are a number of issues that are not addressed in these current infrastructures. Even though there might techniques used by certain companies [12], due to their closed nature we cannot check them, and so to the best of our knowledge, there is no open and free method of separating objects from existing dynamic document, except from our existing work on DYCE [13]. Also, current technologies for supporting dynamic objects do not differentiate between the location of the objects in the document, and object itself. This makes it impossible to efficiently implement the situations where the object can move between different places in the document without changing data, which is common in certain news Web sites [17].

This paper describes our efforts on addressing these shortcomings. We are proposing two methods that should solve these shortcomings. The first is an augmentation to the ESI standard, the most used method for specifying the format of the templates, to allow the fragment locations to be specified in a mapping table that is sent with the template. This allows the objects to move across the document without needing to re-serve the template. Our second proposal, DyCA, a Dynamic Content Adapter, is a two part model for creating object-based content from original dynamic content. The first part extracts the objects from the original content, giving us the needed separation between template, objects, and object location by using our mapping table approach. The second part of DyCA delivers the content to a fragment-enabled client, like a caching proxy server. A Python-based fragment-enabled caching proxy, named CONCA-Lite was developed to allow the testing of the object extraction, and content delivery modules of DyCA.

Our method for creating the dynamic content from the original Web content is based on a simple and effective keyword based object extraction technique to find dynamic objects inside a static Web page. The dynamic content can then be served by our DyCA server, which can serve fragments from the document as needed, enabling a client to support template and object caching. Our proposed ESI-extended format allows for caching of both the objects and the template and allows for object movement. This type of concept, where the object in the template maps, based on a mapping table, is, to our knowledge, introduced here for the first time. By having a fully functional fragment-enabled content server and client, and by testing on real world data, we have gotten accurate results, beyond regular experiments done in the field. These results have shown that our proposed method for fragment extraction based on the keywords in the document can allow us to cache existing non-fragmented content and achieve significant performance improvements by utilizing our proposed augmentation for a mapping-table based template.

---

[1] The terms *objects* and *fragments* will used interchangeably in this paper.

The rest of the paper is organized as follows. Section 2 describes the related background for this field. Section 3 addresses problems with the current infrastructures. Section 4 shows the design and implementation of the system. Section 5 presents the evaluation and results of the testing of our architecture. Section 6 concludes the paper and discusses our planned future work.

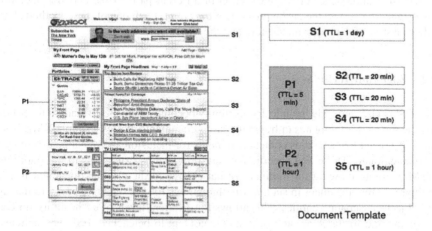

Fig. 1. Dynamic content can be viewed in terms of a quasi-static document template and individual objects, which exhibit different sharing, cacheability, and freshness time characteristics.

2 Background

2.1 Fragment Based Caching

One fundamental block in caching dynamic content is allowing to split up a document into different static and dynamic parts. By doing this, parts of the document, called *fragments*, can be treated separately rather then treating the document as a whole. Thus each fragment can have its own behavior allowing more fine-grained control over caching behavior and data sharing of the different segments of a document. Certain fragments of a document can be shared between different clients whereas some clients want different information in other fragments. Also, some parts of a document change more frequently than others, while other parts are completely static. By treating the document as a whole rather then separating it into fragments a page cannot be partially shared between users nor can it be partially cached. Rather, when a little part of the document changes the whole document needs re-fetching, and if parts of the document can't be shared, then the document can't be shared at all. For example, consider a popular customizable Web site with content that gets continuously updated with information such as news and weather. Figure 1 shows the snapshot of a personalized my.yahoo.com page, which fits in such an example, and what the corresponding document template and component objects might look like. S* and P* represent objects that are shared and private respectively, and

TTL captures the length of time this object remains valid. The contents of fragments on the page can change as new stories develop or as the weather changes, leaving other fragments unchanged and with no need to re-fetch the data. Users that are viewing sports stories can share those fragments, and if some of those users are also viewing the economic section, then that can be shared by all the people viewing that fragment as well. There currently are a number of ways to split a document into fragments and reconstruct it. Different approaches do reconstruction in different parts of the network, including the originating server, the cache proxy, and the client. Each one of these methods has a different way of dealing with caching and the fragments.

2.2   Edge-Side Includes

The ESI [11], Edge-Side Include, has currently become the de facto standard in specifying the format for templates in fragment based documents. It uses a simple XML-based markup format that specifies content fragments for inclusion and dynamic assembly in a base template. These ESI specific tags are provided as extensions to the traditional HTML format allowing for minimal format change to the original document format. It separates the document in such a way that allows for the server or proxy to manage the objects as separate entities. This allows for different levels of cacheability for each fragment, and for large amount of dynamic content to be cached. ESI also includes a very complete framework for conditional getting of fragments, cookie support, and error control. Every `esi:include` tag references a specific URI with a TTL, all of this is included in the template file which gives the layout and aesthetic look to the document. Thus, all the information regarding the fragments and the template are actually sent in the template itself. For a client to support the ESI framework all that it needs to do is to implement support for parsing and acting based on the template format. Thus, ESI's simplicity is a very strong point.

CONCA [7] allows for additional client information, such as the type of device of the client, to modify the returned content, based on a different template yet reusing the same objects.

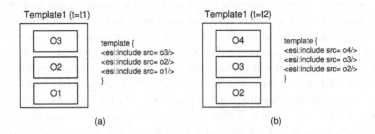

Fig. 2. An example of template caching problem.

3   Existing Problems of ESI

An important factor of the efficiency of fragment based documents is the method used to update it. One of the popular uses in fragment documents is for object movement. This type of behavior, as can be seen in Figure 2, is represented when one or more fragments from a dynamic document move between the different available positions on the template. A good example is a news Web site where old stories (represented as fragments) move down the document and new ones are added from the top. If we use ESI to construct our document then there are two possible ways to update the document so that the objects can move across the document. Since in ESI the document is split up into two parts, the template, and the fragments, then one possibility will be to update the fragments where the object moved to where it moved from. Another possibility is to update the template such that the updated template has the URL of the new locations in the template pointing to the correct fragment.

3.1   ESI – Static Template

One obvious solution to fragment movement, which we will call *static template*, is to update the fragments themselves, leaving the template completely static. Using our news Web site example from earlier, the news template points to a series of objects, and when a new story gets added to the page it pushes the old one out of the page. All the objects in the page need to expire, be invalidated, and be re-retrieved as the fragments lower down on the page. Considering that a document, like a news Web site, that has most of its objects moving around the Web page, this means invalidating most of the objects on the page and fetching them from the server on a regular basis. The biggest problem with this method is that most of these fragments are already present on the client just in a different location, and re-fetching them in a different place means a lot of wasted data transfer that could otherwise be cached.

3.2   ESI – Static Objects

A different approach to solve this problem, which we will call *static objects*, is to in-validate the template and re-fetch it for spatial changes, leaving the objects static for such a change. The fragments will still contain only dynamic data and would need to be re-fetched for a data change. The new template will have the object in the first position pointing to the new objects, and all the other positions pointing to the moved objects. This seems to solve the problem since the objects are unmodified do not need to be re-fetched. Supposedly, this saves a lot of data transfer by transferring only the new objects and not requiring all the objects to be re-fetched as in our earlier example. Since the only things that has actually changed in the template is the URL of a few of the fragments, this means that most of the transferred template, which would still contain only static data, is already on the client. Considering that the template can be very large, as we show later in section 5, doing this on a regular basis, and transferring all this data that could otherwise be cached, this is not a very efficient solution as it might seem at first.

3.3   Mapping Table

There is no way to solve the problem of object movement in the current ESI infrastructure. Either you will be invalidating many objects that really are valid, or you will
be invalidating a template which has very little data actually modified. That is why a
proposed solution needs to make additions to the ESI infrastructure. These additions,
a mapping table that gets sent along with the template and an addition to the template
format to allow inclusion of objects from the mapping table, allow for a new method
of fragment-based caching, which we will denote as *mapping table*, which does not
requires either the objects or the templates to be invalidated for spatial changes. Thus,
when a client retrieves a template, the client will also cache the mapping table that was
sent with the template. When this client needs to fetch a fragment from the template,
the identifier in the template is looked up in the mapping table, and then the fragment
is fetched from the appropriate URL. The mapping table is relatively a small amount of
data compared to the template and object sizes. When an object needs to be moved across
a document, from one locations in the template into another, the only thing that needs to
be updated is the mapping table. Thus, both the template and the objects continue to be
cached and treated efficiently, while still allowing for object movement. The mapping
table's small size and ease of use makes it optimal for these cases.

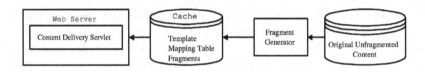

Fig. 3. The general architecture of DyCA.

4   DyCA: Dynamic Content Adapter

4.1   Design

As mentioned earlier, DyCA, our proposed **Dynamic Content Adapter**, has been designed
to augment the existing servers to serve dynamic content efficiently. In the client-proxy-
server model it sits on the front-end of the server and can then take existing Web content
that is requested from the server and process it to serve the dynamic content instead. So
when the original content changes, DyCA will regenerate its fragment-enabled content.
This allows it to be deployed anywhere from the same location as the actual Web server
or to the ISP level. As shown in Figure 3, DyCA is actually split up into 2 separate
but very important parts, the Dynamic Content Generator module, and the Dynamic
Content Delivery module. The generator module deals with taking the existing dynamic
content and converting it into fragmented content. The delivery module can then take
the dynamic Web pages generated by the earlier module, and serve them to the client
appropriately.x These two modules together let us take an existing static Web site and
easily change it into a fragment-based dynamic Web site, that can be cached properly.

The content generation module generates the objects and template from the original dynamic Web content. It uses a keyword based approach to split up the dynamic content into fragments. The keyword based approach works by building an XML of the Web site and searching this XML tree for specific tags that can signify a different object. These tags are set separately for different Web site based on the structure of the HTML and the content. By looking at popular Web sites, such as the personalized my.yahoo.com page shown earlier in figure 1, it is fairly simple to see the implicit fragments contained in the document. Fragments can be easily distinguished based on certain differences such as a different font or a table tag, and based on certain predefined keywords, such as the TV Listings headlines, or the Weather headlines. Once the tags in the XML tree are identified, the children XML tags and the rest of the XML content contained in the identified tags is extracted to create the objects. A special include tag, that has a special object id for each object, will be placed in the position where the object was extracted from the main document. The mapping table is just a list of the object ids and their corresponding URLs in a parse-able file.

Additional information for each object, such as the TTL of the object, is calculated by looking at a long term overview of the Web site. Numerous instances of the Web page are collected over a regular period of time. Each instance is parsed and separated into the different objects, template, and mapping table by the content generation module. By comparing the objects and their position over the period of time, an accurate dynamic behavior can be seen that allows the correct generation of the mapping table to be most efficient with regards to object movement. It also allows the TTL for each fragment location in a document to be generated. Since the location in the TTL of a location in the template remains mostly the same, this TTL is then reused later as the TTL for each fragment location in the document. In our news Web site example, the sidebar listing all the news from yesterday will always have a TTL of 24 hours.

The content delivery module is responsible for serving the template, objects, and mapping table to the fragment-enabled proxy cache. The content delivery module uses the data created by the content generation module. The content delivery module needs to implement the extensions to the protocols in order to send the data created by the content generation module in an appropriate way. It needs to add information regarding the mapping table, and so notify its client, the fragment-enabled proxy cache, when a request is dynamic and has a template or when it is static. By sending the mapping table to the client, the client can then get the static URLs of the objects to be able to access them from the template. The content delivery module also needs to support the client updating only its mapping table, so that bandwidth would not need to be wasted with already cached objects, or templates. This module can be backwards compatible with existing technologies and can support serving to both client level caching [14], and proxy level caching [7,12].

4.2 Implementation

The dynamic content generator is program that parses existing Web sites and outputs a dynamic, fragment based, cacheable, Web page. Three Web sites, New York Times [15], India Times [16], and Slashdot.com [17], were chosen due to their dynamic nature, and since none of them supported any form of cacheable dynamic data. The Web sites were

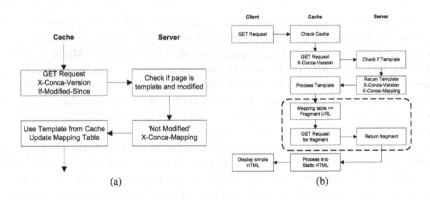

Fig. 4. (a) Process of initial retrieval (b) Process of cached retrieval.

constantly monitored for changes during an extensive period covering 2 weeks. This data was then passed through the keyword based object extraction. Each object was extracted from each instance of the Web site by finding appropriate, predefined tags in the document. Once each object was extracted and the ESI-based template was constructed, the resulting fragmented documents were compared across their time element to calculate the TTL and the mapping table. Object movement across the document is taken into account and allows for the object to not be replaced too soon, and remain in the mapping table. An object was considered expired once it wasn't in any part of the document. Once the template, objects, and mapping table are in place from the generator module, the dynamic content delivery module just needs to serve them. Implemented as a server extension using servlets in Java and sitting on top of popular Web servers such as the Apache Web Server [18] or the Jigsaw Web Server [19], this module appears as a traditional Web server to regular clients, but provides the dynamic content ability to able clients. This module uses information from the generator module to build up information such as which pages are templates, the TTL for certain objects, and the mapping table. Figure 4 shows the process of events when a client request for a Web page. When a CONCA-enabled request from a proxy for a document is made, if the document has fragments then the mapping table is looked up and added as an X-CONCA-MAPPING HTTP header to the response. The expiration of the object is set based on the TTL contained with the mapping table. The body of the response is just the ESI augmented template. Once the cache has the template, it will go on and request the fragment as needed from the server. The cache can then build up the proper final document and send that off to the client. The servlet's support of the If-Modified-Since HTTP header when requesting the template is crucial to the efficiency of the mapping table. When the template expires on the cache, the cache will request the template over again using the If-Modified-Since HTTP header. Since the template rarely changes, this will mean that the cache will usually get a '304 Not Modified' response. This response will contain the new mapping table, allowing the cache to update it's mapping table without having to re-transfer the template. If a static document, or a static fragment is requested from the content delivery module, then the content delivery module will behave just like a regular Web server.

4.3 ESI Augmentation

As explained earlier, ESI provides and extensive range of existing technology to support a wide range of uses in structuring a template file and specifying things like TTL and so forth. In trying to remain as standard compliant as possible, the ESI format was picked to represent the structure of the template. Yet the ESI standard only supports document fragments identified by static URLs, which will not suffice in our case. Thus we needed to augment the ESI standard by adding the `esi:xconca-include` tag. This tag allows the specification of an ID number that can be looked up by the client in the mapping table and retrieve the object's static URL.

5 Performance Evaluation

The experimentation of our proposed method for object extraction and object delivery required simulating a fragment-enabled client-cache-server model. Using this model we can compare different types of performance for the different types of fragment-enabled dynamic content behaviors. The experiments we used to test the performance of the different caching systems targeted user-perceived latency and bandwidth usage specifically.

5.1 CONCA-Lite

The experiments in our client-cache-server model required a proxy that supported our proposed augmentation to the ESI and supported the dynamic assembly of the final content for the client. To achieve this, a simple cache proxy, called CONCA-Lite, was implemented using Python and its `asyncore` modules to create a simple extensible proxy. It was designed such that testing different caching methods would require little or no change on the proxy side. Thus, allowing us to make fair and accurate comparisons between the different caching methods, which are tested on the same caching framework. This CONCA-Lite proxy, which implemented a minimalistic version of the CONCA proposal [7], was then used to test the different dynamic caching methods described later.

5.2 Evaluation Platform

We simulated the client-cache-server model using three machines, all connected on a 100Mbit/s LAN, at most, separated by a switch. The server, a 2.0 Ghz Pentium 4 machine with 512 MB RAM with Linux, ran the Jigsaw Java server to host the DyCA servlets. The cache, a 2.4 Ghz Pentium 4 machine with 1 GB RAM with Linux, ran the CONCA-Lite. The client, a 2.2 Ghz machine with 512B of RAM with Linux, ran a Python-based simulation of a client accessing Web pages in a predefined order.

We modeled 4 different caching behaviors using our experimentation. To test each approach, the client was set up to request the Web page of the server from the cache at request intervals of 10 seconds, for a total of 10 minutes. The cache would check to see if it has the needed document, request the document from the server if it needs to, and return the document to the client. When testing a caching behavior that has a fragment enabled template, it would request all of the objects in the template, it would construct the final document, and return it to the client. Thus the client does not need to implement anything beyond the standardized HTTP protocol. The first method, using no fragment caching, was implemented by disabling caching in the proxy, and having the server send the original Web page. This is consistent with the behavior of real dynamic content using static pages in today's Internet, due to cookies, and other such information, that render a page uncacheable. In the second method the template of the document remains static, while the fragments of the objects are updated for content change. The template was cacheable for the whole testing session, while the objects were cacheable for as long as their TTL was valid. In the third caching behavior, the template is updated when a fragment moves between locations in the document, and the objects change due to data changes only, and not spatial changes. The last model represents our proposed mapping table approach. When the template is returned a mapping table is returned with it in the HTTP header, the proxy can then cache the mapping table, and update the mapping table when a spatial change happens. The template remained static for the testing session, while the objects only changed for data changes.

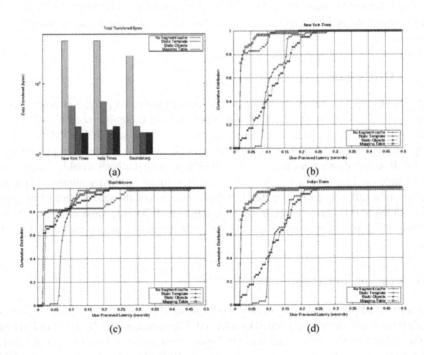

Fig. 5. Evaluation results: (a) total data transfer between server and cache, and user perceived latency for: (b) New York Times, (c) Slashdot, and (d) India Times.

5.3 Experimentation

Three Web sites, New York Times [15], India Times [16], and Slashdot.com [17], were used for testing each approach. Two types of measurements were taken during the testing to evaluate the performance, the total amount of data transfered between the client and the server, and the user perceived latency per user request. The first type of measurement is important to show what method performs best as a cache, with the least data transfer between the cache and the server. There is no need to check for the data transfer between the client and the cache, since in all four models it should remain roughly the same. The generation of the final non-fragmented Web page by the cache that gets sent to the client, and the method it is updated, is what changes between each method. The second measurement type is important to show how an improved Web caching architecture will benefit the client as well, and not only the server.

5.4   Results and Analysis

Figure 5(a) demonstrates the total bytes used in transferring data in all of the methods mentioned. As can be seen from the graphs, using a static template and updating the objects to support object movements requires considerable more data transfer between the server and the proxy. This is the method that is most commonly used today in dynamic Web sites. Using static objects and a dynamic template to achieve a dynamic Web page might seem efficient enough when looking at the bytes transfered, but, as we will see later, this efficiency is lost when looking at the user perceived latency. There is no comparison, though, between any of the dynamic methods and using traditional static objects. The amount of data transfer when not using a fragment based architecture can be more then 10 times the amount of data transfer when using a good fragment based caching. When using a mapping table to transfer the data, the amount of bytes transfered is considerably smaller. In fact, the total bytes transfered with a mapping table is little over the total size of the initial site and the size of the changes, meaning a minimal amount of wasted data is being transfered. This should considerably reduce the server load when using such an architecture. Figures 5 (b)(c)(d), show the user perceived latency in seconds for New York Times, Slashdot, and India Times respectively. This figure shows that the user has to wait the least amount of time for the Web site when the mapping table architecture is used. With regard to user perceived latency, the static object method's performance is almost as bad as the performance of using regular static Web pages. The only method that comes close to the method of using a mapping table is the static template method, which as we saw before performed badly when looking at the amount of bytes transfered. This type of optimization is very important for the client so it may receive its data in a timely manner, especially clients that use slower connections such as dialup. Otherwise, from the users prospective, the actual retrieval of the page is slower. From these figures we can conclude that the mapping table method has performed better then all of the other proposed methods in all of our tested fields.

We can see some unaccounted behavior in how the 2nd and 3rd method flip in their efficiency between the results of the amount of bandwidth used, and the user latency done. When the template is static and there is no mapping table, the objects get transfered at a higher request rate since the proxy can't cache them due to object movement. This extra data transfer has little effect on the user perceived latency in our testing environment due to it being a high speed network. Yet this extra data transfer is significant in terms of amount of data transfered, as can be seen in the earlier figure. Since the only thing that needs to get updated every once in a while is the transferring of the template, in terms of latency, this is very close to transferring a mapping table at about the same interval. Yet by looking at Table 1 you can see that the template is considerably larger then the mapping table in most cases. This is what causes the large amount of bytes to be transfered. Had we artificially slowed down the network, the user perceived latency for static objects would have been much greater. In the case of static objects, the templates is considered dynamic, and gets updated every time there an object moves. Every such template fetch requires the cache to re-parse the template, which can be very large as seen in Table 1, and recheck it's cache for every single object, in some cases this requires the cache to send HTTP request to see if the data was modified. This type of overhead causes the extra latency seen in the graph.

Table 1. The comparison of template and object sizes for the different Web sites.

	New York Times	India Times	Slashdot
Template Size	17 KB	15 KB	1.7 KB
Avg. Object Size	3.6 KB	4.8 KB	0.6 KB
Mapping Table Size	1.0 KB	0.8 KB	2.2 KB

6   Related Work

Dynamic Web content delivery have increasingly becoming an important Web engineering issue as more and more Web content are generated in a dynamic and personalized way. Fragment-based techniques have received considerable attention from the research community in recent years [2,3,4,8,14]. Most of these approaches either assume the fragment-based content is served by Web server automatically, or look at server-side caching only.

To our knowledge, few of existing work discuss the manner of how to generate fragment from existing legacy Web servers without server-side information. One of the first effort is DYCE [13], which is model-based dynamic Web content emulator. Recently, Ramaswamy *et al.* proposed a novel scheme to automatically detect and flag fragments [20], which share the similar goal of this paper. However, there are three differences between us: First, although both of our work intends to automatic detection of fragments, our keyword-based is simple and easy to implement, while their approach is complex and has theoretical analysis. However, which one is better is still not clear. Second, in our work we focus on engineering implementation of DYCA, while their work focuses on automatic detection. In this sense, their work is a good complement to DYCA. Third, the mapping table based fragment delivery proposed in this paper is novel.

Edge Side Includes [11] is becoming one of the foundation blocks in specifying a common format and method for fragments and templates in this field. It is popular among many different existing methods. Naaman *et al.* [21] have done studies comparing ESI to delta encoding, finding ESI to have possible performance advantages.

Automatic detection of templates from Web pages has been studied from data mining field as well [22,23]. They discuss the problem of template detection through discovery of pagelets in the Web pages. However, our work differs from the work on template detection both in context and content. First, the work on template detection is aimed towards improving the precision of search algorithms. While our aim is improving dynamic content delivery. Second, only template is interested in their work, while we care both template and fragments. Therefore, the method used in these two approaches are different too. The method presented there to finding fragments is done based on amount of hyperlinks present in certain parts of the document. They do not build up an XML tree, nor treat anything more then hyperlinks, unlike we have done in our approach. This method applies better to search algorithms rather then to dynamic fragment extraction.

Our current research differentiates from earlier work done on DYCE [13], the Dynamic Web Content Emulator. With DYCE, we were attempting to build up general models for usage to describe the behavior of current fragment-based caching. Although it looked promising at the time, it generated too many objects and didn't match up to actual real world designs. Our current research was an attempt to try and continue that same research using real world Web sites so as to get more correct results.

Other research groups [24,25] have also defined other criteria for finding objects in documents. While they have focused on content of the fragments and of the Web pages themselves, we have focused on their existence on a spatial, and location axis in the document.

7   Conclusions and Future Work

We have shown our proposed solution for keyword based object extraction, and object delivery. We have also explained our proposal of augmenting the ESI to include support for a mapping table. We have implemented these proposals into DyCA and then by taking actual Web pages and running through DyCA's keyword-based extraction to transform them into fragment-enabled content we have been able to run simulations between our sample proxy and the DyCA adapter. These simulations allowed us to compares our proposals to the current available methods of serving dynamic content on the Web. Our keyword-based approach allows for creation of dynamic content in such a way as to maximize the cache-ability of the content in a fragment-enabled caching system. Using the mapping table approach in the cache proxy which, according to our results, will give the best performance for both the server and the client, together with our DyCA adapter we can effectively cache in an efficient way Web sites that currently use non-fragmented content. Currently our DyCA and CONCA-Lite implementations are very young, and could still be further optimized. Our future work consists of continuing testing of these implementations to further refine the design of our CONCA prototype [7], which incorporates a novel design for efficient caching of dynamic and personalized content.

References

1. Mogul, J.C., Douglis, F., a. Feldmann, Krishnamurthy, B.: Potential Benefits of Delta-Encoding and Data Compression for HTTP. In: Proc. of the 13th ACM SIGCOMM'97. (1997) 181–194
2. Challenger, J., Iyengar, A., Dantzig, P.: A scalable system for consistently caching dynamic Web data. In: Proc. of IEEE Conference on Computer Communications (INFOCOM'99). (1999)

3. Challenger, J., Iyengar, A., Witting, K., Ferstat, C., Reed, P.: A publishing system for efficiently creating dynamic Web content. In: Proc. of IEEE Conference on Computer Communications (INFOCOM'00). (2000)

4. Douglis, F., Haro, A., Rabinovich, M.: HPP:HTML macro-pre-processing to support dynamic document caching. In: Proc. of the 1st USENIX Symposium on Internet Technologies and Systems (USITS'97). (1997) 83–94

5. Cao, P., Zhang, J., Beach, K.: Active cache: Caching dynamic contents on the Web. In: Proc. of IFIP Int'l Conf. Dist. Sys. Platforms and Open Dist. Processing. (1998) 373–388

6. Myers, A., Chuang, J., Hengartner, U., Xie, Y., Zhang, W., Zhang, H.: A secure and publisher-centric Web caching infrastructure. In: Proc. of IEEE Conference on Computer Communications (INFOCOM'01). (2001)

7. Shi, W., Karamcheti, V.: CONCA: An architecture for consistent nomadic content access. In: Workshop on Cache, Coherence, and Consistency(WC3'01). (2001)

8. Wills, C.E., Mikhailov, M.: Studying the impact of more complete server information on Web caching. In: Proc. of the 5th International Workshop on Web Caching and Content Distribution (WCW'00). (2000)

9. IBM Corp.: http://www.ibm.com/Websphere (Websphere platform)

10. http://www.w3.org/Style/XSL/ (W3C XSL Working Group)

11. Tsimelzon, M., Weihl, B., Jacobs, L.: ESI language specification 1.0 (2000)

12. http://www.akamai.com/ (Akamai Technologies Inc.)

13. Shi, W., Collins, E., Karamcheti, V.: DYCE: A synthetic dynamic Web content emulator. In: Poster Proc. of 11th International World Wide Web Conference. (2002)

14. Rabinovich, M., Xiao, Z., Douglis, F., Kamanek, C.: Moving edge side includes to the real edge – the clients. In: Proc. of the 4th USENIX Symposium on Internet Technologies and Systems (USITS'03). (2003)

15. http://www.nytimes.com (Nytimes Web site)

16. http://www.indiatimes.com (Indiatimes Web site)

17. http://www.slashdot.com (Slashdot Web site)

18. http://httpd.apache.org (Apache HTTP Server Project)

19. http://www.w3.org/Jigsaw (Jigsaw Project)

20. Ramaswamy, L., Iyengar, A., Liu, L., Douglis, F.: Automatic detection of fragments in dynamically generated Web pages. In: Proc. of the 13th International World Wide Web Conference (2004). (2004)

21. Naaman, M., Garcia-Molina, H., Paepcke, A.: Evaluation of esi and class-based delta encoding. In: Proc. of the 8th International Workshop on Web Caching and Content Distribution (WCW'03). (2003)

22. Arasu, A., Garcia-Molina, H.: Extracting structured data from Web pages. In: Proc. of ACM SIGMOD'03. (2003)

23. Bar-Yossef, Z., Rajagopalan, S.: Template detection via data mining and its applications. In: Proc. of the 11th International World Wide Web Conference (2002). (2002)

24. Butler, D., Liu., L.: A Fully Automated Object Extraction System for the World Wide Web. In: Proceedings of ICDCS-2001. (2001)

25. Gu, X., et al.: Visual based content understanding towards Web adaptation. In: Proceedings of AH-2002. (2002)

SIE – Intelligent Web Proxy Framework

Grzegorz Andruszkiewicz, Krzysztof Ciebiera, Marcin Gozdalik, Cezary Kaliszyk, and
Mateusz Srebrny

Institute of Informatics
Warsaw University
Banacha 2, 02-097 Warsaw, Poland

Abstract. In this paper we would like to present and describe *SIE*, a transparent, intelligent Web proxy framework. Its aim is to provide efficient and robust platform for implementing various ideas in broad area of Web Mining. It enables the programmer to easily and quickly write modules that improve pages on that site according to personal characteristics of the particular user. *SIE* provides many features including user identification, logging of users' sessions, handling all necessary protocols, etc. *SIE* is implemented in OCaml – a functional programming language – and has been released on GPL.

1 Introduction

We live in the era of information. The rapid development of computer and communication technologies enabled people to quickly exchange data at a low cost. Probably the most popular source of information is the Internet, and the most commonly used service is WWW. HTML pages are a universal way of publicizing knowledge, but it is very difficult to find the exact piece of information we are looking for. In our paper we would like to focus on one given Web site, containing various pages. The webmaster always tries to optimize the structure of the service in order to help users navigate. But different users have different preferences. When reading a page one user may next want to see page X, another one page Y, etc. When typing a keyword into the search engine, e.g. "chaos", one user wants to read about mythology, another one about fractals, and so on. Sometimes a user does not know which page exactly she is looking for, because she had not visited it yet. One static structure will not fully satisfy all users' needs.

That is why *dynamic page personalization* is so important. It is often possible to predict the interests of the user, analyzing for example the history of her choices. In this case it would probably be helpful for the user if she was provided, on the page she is currently using, with the most important links. It may be even more useful if she had some links to pages similar to the current page to minimize time spent on searching. Of course the better the algorithms to *predict interests* and to *find similar pages* the better the page personalization process.

The main problem with algorithms which try to understand human behavior and predict users' actions is that it is extremely difficult to develop them only theoretically. Humans are often irrational and their language is ambiguous. On many pages considerable amount of information is not only in written words but in pictures, animations or even sounds and these are still nearly impossible to analyze automatically. That is why

N. Koch, P. Fraternali, and M. Wirsing (Eds.): ICWE 2004, LNCS 3140, pp. 373–385, 2004.

most algorithms are heuristics based on empirical experiments and developed through testing. To advance the level of research in this field, scientists need to have possibility to test their algorithms and to tune their parameters quickly and cheaply.

Having made this observation we have decided to create a simple, yet powerful framework for constructing intelligent Web proxies. We called it *SIE – Site Improving Engine* and we wanted it not to be limited to personalizing alone – hence "Improving" and not "Personalizing". *SIE* relieves module writers from re-implementing user identification, network protocols handling, collection of statistics, etc. *SIE* gives users the opportunity to focus on the concept alone and enables them to quickly and comfortably write a new testing module.

In addition we include a few interesting modules showing the variety of *SIE* features.

It is worth mentioning that *SIE* and the modules are written exclusively in *OCaml* functional language. It gives the programmer many interesting possibilities characteristic for functional languages and provides very good performance. *SIE* has been released on GPL. Sources can be found at http://sie.mimuw.edu.pl.

2 Solution

We would like to present a framework supporting programmers in creating, changing, testing and fine-tuning intelligent Web proxies – including Adaptive Web systems. Our system – *SIE* – implements basic features, essential for intelligent Web proxy to function properly. In this section we will mention all these features and in the next one we will present related work. Further we will discuss the architecture of the system. Then we will present already implemented modules, their functionality, some theoretical analysis and the way they are integrated with the *SIE* framework. In the last two sections we will discuss possibilities of further development and summarize the paper.

SIE is implemented as a proxy server, transparent to the end user. It intercepts all HTTP messages that are sent to the server (requests) and its responses to the user. Our system interprets these messages and identifies the user. The identification process consists of two stages: when the user first sends HTTP request, the system finds out if she already has special cookie set, containing a unique ID value. If she does, *SIE* can identify and associate current session with the stored history. If she does not the system provides her with a new ID number. In the second stage, when the user fetches WWW pages, *SIE* does not employ the cookie mechanism. Instead it rewrites all the links pointing to the server, which are on the pages sent to the user, in such a way that they uniquely identify the user and the link followed. Uniqueness is achieved by generating 256-bit numbers and storing generated values in hash tables, which are then periodically purged of stale entries. For example the link pointing to http://www.i cwe2004.org could be rewritten as: http://sie.mimuw.edu.pl?SIE_SESSION=AF 387GZ2&SIE_LINK=2YUZ19A0&SIE_ORIGINAL=www.icwe2004.org. The purpose of each parameter is summarized in Table 1. With this method we can identify the user throughout each session, even if her web browser does not support (or has disabled) the cookie mechanism.

The core of the whole system is constituted by modules. A module usually consists of two parts: offline and online. Online parts of every module is invoked whenever

Table 1. Parameters added by *SIE*

Parameter	Purpose
SIE_SESSION	Identifies the session (and thus the user).
SIE_LINK	Identifies the exact link which has been followed by the user – the page which contained the link and the page the link was leading to.
SIE_ORIGINAL	Original link – in case the link is followed after appropriate hash-table is purged (e.g. if it was stored in bookmarks)

a request or response is processed by *SIE*. Upon registration in the framework the online part specifies:

- supported content types (e.g. text/html or image/png) (in case of text/html the module may also request a parsed HTML tree instead of pure text)
- callbacks provided (request modifier, response modifier)
- priority (used to determine the order in which modules are called)

When the HTTP message contains a HTML document and there is at least one module which requested to receive parsed HTML documents instead of pure text *SIE* interprets HTML and constructs a parse tree, which is a very convenient form for further analysis and modifications.

When modules are called back by *SIE*, they are provided with all the data they need in an appropriate form:

- HTTP parameters
- parsed HTML contents (when appropriate)
- user identification
- current trail in the traversal tree of current user [1]

Fig. 1. Example traversal tree representing user session. Solid lines are regular clicks. Dotted lines represent pushing "Back" button in the browser

Modules can modify HTML tree using received information – e.g. choose an appropriate model of user behavior basing on the user's ID, find out which pages may

---

[1] Formally this would be defined as the shortest path from the root to the current node in the tree (e.g. in Figure 2 when user visited "C" current trail would be given as list: A → B → C)

potentially be useful for the user and insert appropriate links into HTML tree. At the end *SIE* deparses HTML back to plain text and passes this new version of the document to the original destination.

Other content may be modified as well – e.g. images may be scaled down to size suitable for small, portable displays found in PDAs[2] or mobile phones. Modules may even generate responses themselves – allowing for custom pages generation.

Before processing the request all important properties of the HTTP request are logged. Apart from the fields found in CLF[3], there are two fields which together make up the strength of *SIE*. These are:

- user ID
- previous node in the traversal tree

Both of these fields are taken from the rewritten link (described above), which allows any module written for *SIE* to easily obtain traversal tree similar to the one presented in Figure 2 from logs. Constructing trees from logs is usually done by module's periodically executed part[4], which can prepare aggregated data for the online part. A traversal tree is a natural representation of behavior of a user visiting a Web site. Many papers dedicate whole chapters to techniques of extracting information about "user sessions" [5] and "episodes" [6] from a CLF-compliant log (e.g. Apache access log). Users of *SIE* are relieved from reimplementing those algorithms and can focus on their modules alone.

We are fully aware that sometimes CLF logs are the only source of information available but we also feel that widespread use of systems like *SIE* can quickly change this situation. Deploying *SIE* in front of a Web site – without any additional modules – can gather information useful for analyzing the site and testing new algorithms on it. The next step would be implementing a module which would use data collected previously.

SIE can be easily scaled thanks to its cluster architecture. It is able to distribute the servicing of different clients to separate computers in the cluster. It enables the administrator to increase performance with the growth of a Web site. In addition, thanks to the *Watchdog* function, the system is safe and easy to maintain. It automatically disables the parts which do not function correctly, or shuts itself down completely when the whole cluster has broken down. In such cases the WWW service functions unhindered, but without any additional features provided by *SIE* modules.

SIE has been tested on the server of the Programming Olympiad (http://sio.m imuw.edu.pl). We have collected some statistical data concerning the processing of requests by *SIE*. On average the preparation of the request (HTTP parsing, creating threads, etc.) took about 1% of the total processing time of the request. ESEE module took 2%. Then the request has been sent to the web server and 88% of processing time was spent on waiting for reply. Afterward BM used 5%, and the remaining 4% was used by *SIE* to prepare the reply for BM, and to send it back to the user. These results prove that *SIE* has a small time overhead over the web server and LAN connection.

---

[2] Portable Digital Assistants

[3] Common Log Format, *de facto* logging standard in WWW servers

[4] We call these parts *offline analyzers*

[5] Defined in [17] as "a delimited set of user clicks across one or more Web servers"

[6] Defined in [17] as "a subset of related user clicks that occur within a user session"

During the tests (about 3 months) the system was stable and fully functional all the time.

Unfortunately, due to organizational and financial constraints no tests of the "intelligence" of the modules have been performed. Such tests should be done on a large Web site, and should include some kind of opinion poll in order to estimate the effectiveness of our ideas. We hope we will manage to realize large-scale tests shortly.

3   Similar Systems

An impressive review of implementations of Web Usage Mining systems has been given by Robert Cooley in his PhD thesis [9]. It includes a systematic classification of reviewed systems into five categories:

1. Personalization
2. System Improvement
3. Site Modification
4. Business Intelligence
5. Usage Characterization

SIE with its current suite of modules (*Adapter* and *SEE*), would probably fit into "Personalization" and "Site Modification". Adding other modules (as described in section 6) could spread *SIE* also to other categories. In [7] authors present system called WebCANVAS which analyzes Web server's logs and displays visualization of navigation patterns on a Web site. It is accomplished by automatic clustering of users and manual clustering of pages on the Web site into categories. For every cluster of users, navigational patterns between categories are shown. These patterns represent habits of Web site's users and can be used for improving high-level structure of the site.

In [13] the author has presented IndexFinder – a tool which assists webmasters in adding so-called "index pages" to the site. An index page consists of links to similar pages. IndexFinder employs *conceptual cluster mining* to cluster pages not only visited together, but also having similar content. Proposed index pages are presented to the Webmaster which chooses if they should be added to the site.

Corin Anderson in his PhD thesis ([4]) described two systems: PROTEUS and MONTAGE. The former is used to adapt Web pages to the needs of electronic devices with small displays, such as PDAs or modern mobile phones. MONTAGE, on the other hand, does not modify content. Instead, it builds personalized web portals, consisting of content and links from sites the user had visited previously.

IBM has created its own framework for creating Web proxies called WBI – Web Browser Intermediaries[7]. Currently WBI is part of the WebSphere Transcoding Publisher and the Development Kit is no longer available for download. [5] introduces concept of intermediaries as "computational elements that lie along the path of a web transaction". This paper also describes WBI as a framework for building and running intermediaries. WBI supports five type of intermediaries: request editors, generators, document editors, monitors and autonomous. WBI, being a framework for creating intelligent proxies is,

---

[7] previously Web Browser Intelligence

in many aspects, similar to *SIE* . The main difference between them is the placement of the system between user and the Web server. As described in [6] WBI is placed between the user and the Internet (all servers), whereas *SIE* has been thought as a proxy between the Web site and the Internet (meaning here users visiting the site). Additionally, *SIE* includes several features (briefly mentioned in Section 2 and described in more details in following sections) which would have to be implemented as modules in WBI.

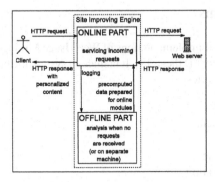

Fig. 2. *SIE* architecture.

4   Architecture

As mentioned before, *SIE* is divided into two parts with different functionality:

Online – this part serves the client directly, analyzes the information flow between client and server, updates the log file and invokes online parts of modules.

Offline – this part is active only periodically – it performs some time-consuming analyses for the online part.

SIE is just a framework to run special modules, which constitute the core of an intelligent Web proxy. Usually every module consists of an *online part*[8], which is executed for every request, and an *offline part* – the *analyzer*.

4.1   The Online Part

To make *SIE* as robust as possible, it is crucial to have the lowest possible overhead in request processing and achieve maximum throughput. That is why it is very important to make as many calculations as possible in the offline part, and to use the computed results online.

When a request is received by *SIE* it is processed by *Request Broker*, which chooses a *Box* and forwards the request to it. There may be many concurrently running Boxes,

---

[8] Sometimes we will use the term *module* – when we do, it will be clear from the context what we are referring to.

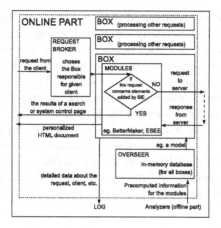

Fig. 3. Processes in online part. Arrows indicate information flow (data, document, message, etc.)

each of them on a different computer in the network. We have implemented a cluster architecture, which means the workload is divided among several computers functioning in parallel, all of them performing the same task. Performancewise, it is crucial to send all requests from a particular user to the same Box during one session. Otherwise computers in the cluster would have to utilize some kind of a shared memory which would hold all information about sessions. This could easily became a bottleneck of the whole system. Therefore we have decided that Boxes should run completely separate, and logs they generate should then be combined into one big log periodically by *Gatherer* (e.g. via NFS).

Gatherer is an external program, which reads logs generated by different Boxes and outputs a combined log. All concurrency issues emerging from accessing one shared log file in Boxes (lock contention, network issues originating from the use of a distributed file system, etc.) are thus avoided.

On the other hand, there has to be centralized configuration so that every module that runs inside Box uses the same model and parameters. This task is fulfilled by *Overseer* – a simple in-memory database. Analyzers insert models, needed by online parts, into the Overseer. Some modules may query Overseer about specific information they need on demand and some read the current version of the model contained in Overseer when Boxes are starting up. Later, when new models are calculated by offline analyzers, a special signal is generated, which informs all Boxes that objects in Overseer have been changed. Upon receival of that signal modules can update local copy of the model. As a result all Boxes have up-to-date versions of model.

At the beginning of the processing of every message, the Box logs appropriate properties of request (as described in Section 2). Then the request is passed to registered modules, which may modify it or even generate response without involving the WWW server. SEE[9] (a personalized search engine and *SIE* control center) takes advantage of this functionality. SEE checks whether the request refers to Web site's search engine.

---

[9] Details concerning the example modules can be found in the next section.

When it does – a response is produced and returned to user. Otherwise request is forwarded to the WWW server. Similarly, the check if the request is for the *SIE* control page is conducted. Control page is a place where the user can modify individual parameters for different modules. For example, she can set how many links will be added by BM to every page or set the favored search criterion described in section 5.2.

When response arrives from the WWW server, the same Box which processed the request modifies all the links found in the HTML document sent in the response, so they uniquely identify user and her session. Additionally a parse tree of the HTML page is constructed if any of the modules uses this form. The tree is then passed to all active modules. In current implementation, only module called *BetterMaker*[10] uses this functionality and adds personalized links to every page. BetterMaker uses data prepared by *eXPerimenter*, an offline analyzer described below.

4.2   The Offline Part

Offline parts are run periodically (e.g. using standard UNIX `cron` daemon) during low system load or on a computer dedicated to this task. The main idea is to perform some calculations using a log produced by Gatherer, which would be impossible or too expensive to do online. In addition *SIE* provides the modules with the current, analyzed content of the web server. A special program called *Robot* is responsible for preparing this data.

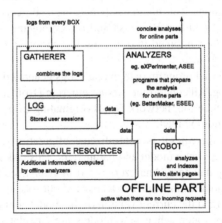

Fig. 4. Offline part as a support for online part. Arrows indicate information flow.

Offline parts should analyze the log and information about all the pages on the site in order to produce data, which would be useful for their respective online parts. For example, running an analyzer which would generate a model of Web site users' behavior every night would make the site truly adaptive, as the model would be updated daily.

Currently there are two analyzers implemented:

---

[10] See next section for more information.

eXPerimenter - analyzes traversal trees generated by Web site users. Then it generates a model for BetterMaker (the online counterpart), which uses this model online to personalize pages (by adding potentially interesting links to them).

A-SEE - analyzes features of pages which have been visited by all users. E-SEE (the online counterpart) uses generated model to personalize search results for users by appropriately reordering links returned by search engine.

A more detailed description of the example modules can be found in the next section.

5   Modules

5.1   Adapter

Adapter consists of two parts

- eXPerimenter (XP) – offline analyzer
- Better Maker (BM) – online module

The most visible to the end user is a little table with links predicted to be most useful to her. BM as an online module modifies responses sent back to the user and adds the table to the page. To generate this table, BM uses a model prepared periodically (e.g. daily) by XP. Model is stored as an object in Overseer and therefore when a new version is generated by XP it is automatically updated in all computers in the cluster. Number of links generated by system can be controlled by the user through a special control panel. In current implementation, the number of links chosen by the user is not stored in any persistent storage, so it is lost upon restart of *SIE*.

To effectively render such table two problems had to be solved. First, basing on previous traversal patterns of users of the Web site, given current user's trail, the algorithm has to predict which pages the user might visit next and with what probability. We chose for that task error-pruned Selective Markov Models described in [10]. The model contains k distinct Markov models, where k is the maximum episode length taken into account. k-th Markov model contains probabilities of visiting page j, having previously visited pages $i_1, i_2, \ldots, i_k$. For $k = 0$ the model reduces to unconditional probability[11] of visiting given page in the Web site. With the growth of k, the model would grow enormously, so *pruning* technique had to be applied. Currently, it is done using a subset of logs, which is not used for calculating Markov models. For details on the exact method of *overall error pruning* please refer to [10].

Attributing web pages with probabilities is not enough. Some pages may be buried down in the site's structure (i.e. to reach them user has to click on many links) whereas some others may be easily accessible. To compensate this, BM ranks links using expected number of saved clicks, i.e. the product of probability of visiting the page the link points to and number of clicks that would be saved had the link been put on the current page. To estimate this value, BM uses MINPATH – a simple recursive algorithm given in [2]. The algorithm takes as an input current user's trail and the model generated by XP and returns list of links ranked by the expected amount of saved clicks to the user. Carefully

---

[11] To be exact instead of probability we use frequency – the maximum likelihood estimator.

selected maximal recursion depth and great OCaml run-time performance allows for executing MINPATH for every response which is sent to the user.

Currently, Adapter does not distinguish between users – i.e. the same model is used for every user visiting Web site. Of course this approach may cause poor personalization on large sites with many different types of users. In such situation, a more sophisticated model needs to be used. We discuss possible improvements in the next section.

5.2 SEE

Another module is SEE – a search engine which aims at personalizing search results. More precisely, even though all searching users receive the same list of links, they get them in a different order. The order is set by SEE's knowledge about a specific user. To illustrate this, let us refer back to the example mentioned in the introduction. Let us assume that the user is concerned about "chaos" meaning a mythological phenomenon. Therefore she should find pages on ancient gods before those concerning fractals. First the *SEE analyzer* (A-SEE) indexes the Web site's resources rating each page according to a number of criteria (e.g. amount of text and pictures, number of links, etc.). The value of each criterion is represented by an integer between zero and ten. The criteria vector which is thereby computed describes the characteristics of each page.

SIE is then employed to provide the history of the user's searches. Not only does SEE focus on the keywords the user is searching for, but, more importantly, it takes into account which pages she chooses from the results suggested. This analysis shows which criteria are important for this particular user when she is looking for this particular keyword. It works like this: when the user looks for a word some results are provided by SEE or by any other search engine. The user clicks on one of the links provided. SEE assumes the user has chosen this particular page because she prefers it for some reason. After a period of time, the analyzer computes an arithmetical mean for the criteria values of such chosen pages. This results in SEE obtaining a set of weights for each user-keyword combination. These weights indicate which criteria are important (and to what extent) to this particular user when she is searching for this particular keyword.

The analyzer's task ends here. SEE comes back into action whenever the user searches the Web again. The resulting list of pages is sorted according to the criteria earlier identified as the ones preferred by the *SIE* user. More precisely, each resource containing the keyword has its criteria vector. For each page SEE multiplies this vector by adequate (for this particular user and keyword) weights and, thus, the ranking is computed.

The more the user searches, the wider SEE's knowledge about her and, thus, the more accurate the search results the user receives.

To provide the user with more control over her searches, SEE allows her to choose one criterion to be used individually. Should the user employ this feature, her lists of links will always begin with pages favored by the criterion.

6 Possible Improvements

SIE is in an early development stage and there are many features still to be added. For us, it is most important to develop *SIE* itself as a platform for building intelligent

Web proxies. However, we have also a few ideas for the improvement of the already implemented modules and adding of new, equally interesting ones.

6.1 SIE Itself

SIE is a framework created to aid the programmers. This is why it is crucial to develop additional technical documentation, tutorials, easy and well-commented example modules, etc. to make learning *SIE* as easy as possible. In the future, we are planning to create a graphical system to automatize basic tasks or to enable them to be performed by mouse drag-and-drop operations.

On the other hand every computer system should be easy to install and maintain. That is why we would like to add an automatic installer as well as create ready-to-use compiled packages for MS Windows and popular Linux distributions. In addition, a graphical user interface is needed for administrative purposes. It would be also very useful to enable the administrator to load/unload the modules without restarting the whole system. To accomplish this the usage of Overseer has to be enhanced. It can be used to provide communication between central administration console and Boxes. The infrastructure is present and working (i.e. the Overseer itself) but there is no code in Box that would allow for remote administration and feedback (e.g. sending of warnings and system logs describing error conditions).

In order to make *SIE* used in practice, we must improve the graphical aspect of our system. Elements added by our modules are readable, but they are behind the aesthetic standards imposed by modern HTML documents.

6.2 Modules

New modules. We hope to extend *SIE* by writing new modules ourselves and to encourage others to contribute their ideas as new modules as well. Currently, we see immediate need to add two modules which would show:

1. Top k most popular pages
2. k most recently added pages

We are also developing a module to record and save user session (as in a sequence of user clicks) as a program in *WTL*. WTL is a new script language, developed by us specially for describing user behavior on a web page. Such a program can be executed later, simulating user actions. This simulation could be used as a test, resembling real scenarios of Web site usage allowing to measure Web server's performance or find broken links. It can be also used to automatize some routine tasks done using a HTML interface.

Adapter. As mentioned in section 5.1 is a fairly simple module, which was implemented rather as proof of a theoretical concept than a module intended to be used in reality. Many features can be, however, improved or added.

First of all, BM constructs – and XP uses – only one model. For large Web sites it is obvious that no single model could be appropriate for all users. Therefore, basing on clustering of users, Adapter has to use many models, one for every user cluster. Possible approaches to user clustering are described e.g. in [7] and [12].

Another technique, which could prove useful for Adapter, is *page clustering*. Basing on words (terms) contained in the documents from the Web site, the module could group those documents into clusters of pages with similar content. Alternatively such classification could be done manually or semi-automatically (with the help of someone, who would provide keywords for every page). Especially appealing in this context seems to be the algorithm called *Concept Indexing* (described in [11]). For every page, it devises a list of terms (called *concepts*), which best describe the page's content. Having concepts attributed to every page, it is possible to create, for each user, a list of concepts she (or cluster of users) is interested in. Such information can be valuable from the marketing point of view (directing advertisements or communication to the user) and can also help resolve the problem of new pages – when a new page is added to the Web site it is not added to as a suggested link by BM because it is not yet seen in logs. With the help of concepts, BM can find all users potentially interested in reading the new page, and include link to the page on pages viewed by them.

Additionally, concepts could allow for creating models on a higher level of abstraction than URLs – namely clusters of pages. Such models could be used for visualization of user access patterns (as in [7]) or, as noted in [3], to predict Web page entries on a different Web site but with similar structure.

SEE. The way we developed SEE imposed on us the assumption that, before everything else, the general mechanism was needed. Now, when the module sorts links individually for each user, the lack of strong criteria has proved to be its main flaw. The criteria we have implemented only indicate how powerful SEE could be. They mainly test the percentage, on each rated page, of certain HTML tags, inside which are the keywords. The concept of semantics-driven criteria has accompanied the whole process of developing SEE. In other words, SEE could immensely benefit from clustering pages which cover the same topics.

Another issue which SEE should deal with is the size of the model. SEE attempts to store information in pairs: the user and a given keyword. Hence the need for grouping users sharing common interests (in terms of criteria). SEE could also do with a way of clustering keywords that the users perceive as similar.

7   Conclusion

Adaptive web and personalizing Web servers are relatively young fields of computer science. In spite *SIE* is still an immature system, we hope it will help the scientists to test their ideas and develop new modules. Such a framework could prove very useful in social sciences, or in fields that include interaction with humans, as it is impossible to model their behavior in absolutely abstract way. We were not able to find any similar framework freely available on the Internet. We hope *SIE* will fill this gap and make future research easier.

Acknowledgments. First of all we would like to thank Krzysztof Ciebiera, who had the main idea of the project. Without his irreplaceable help as our tutor the project would probably not succeed. *SIE* itself was developed by many authors. Detailed list can be found at http://sie.mimuw.edu.pl.

References

1. R. Agrawal, T. Imielinski, and A. Swami. Mining Association Rules between Sets of Items in Large Databases. In *Proceedings of SIGMOD-93*, pages 207–216, 1993.
2. C. Anderson, P. Domingos, and D. Weld. Adaptive web navigation for wireless devices, 2001.
3. C. Anderson, P. Domingos, and D. Weld. Relational markov models and their application to adaptive web navigation, 2002.
4. C. R. Anderson. *A Machine Learning Approach to Web Personalization*. PhD thesis, University of Washington, 2002.
5. R. Barrett and P. P. Maglio. Intermediaries: New places for producing and manipulating web content. In *World Wide Web*, 1999.
6. R. Barrett, P. P. Maglio, and D. C. Kellem. How to personalize the web. In *Proceedings of the Conference on Human Factors in Computing Systems CHI'97*, 1997.
7. I. V. Cadez, D. Heckerman, C. Meek, P. Smyth, and S. White. Visualization of navigation patterns on a web site using model-based clustering. In *Knowledge Discovery and Data Mining*, pages 280–284, 2000.
8. S. Chakrabarti. *Mining the Web*. Morgan Kaufmann Publishers, San Francisco, 2003.
9. R. Cooley. *Web Usage Mining: Discovery and Application of Interesting Patterns from Web Data*. PhD thesis, University of Minnesota, 2000.
10. M. Deshpande and G. Karypis. Selective Markov Models for Predicting Web-Page Accesses, 2001.
11. G. Karypis and E.-H. Han. Concept indexing: A fast dimensionality reduction algorithm with applications to document retrieval and categorization. Technical report tr-00-0016, University of Minnesota, 2000.
12. B. Mobasher, H. Dai, and M. Tao. Discovery and evaluation of aggregate usage profiles for web personalization, 2002.
13. M. Perkowitz. *Adaptive Web Sites: Cluster Mining and Conceptual Clustering for Index Page Synthesis*. PhD thesis, University of Washington, 2001.
14. M. Perkowitz and O. Etzioni. Adaptive Web Sites: an AI Challenge. In *IJCAI (1)*, pages 16–23, 1997.
15. M. Perkowitz and O. Etzioni. Towards adaptive Web sites: conceptual framework and case study. *Computer Networks (Amsterdam, Netherlands: 1999)*, 31(11–16):1245–1258, 1999.
16. P. Pirolli, J. Pitkow, and R. Rao. Silk from a sow's ear: Extracting usable structures from the web. In *CHI-96*, Vancouver, 1996.
17. W3C. Web characterization activity. http://www.w3.org/WCA.

Wide Area Performance Monitoring Using Aggregate Latency Profiles*

Vladimir Zadorozhny[1], Avigdor Gal[2], Louiqa Raschid[3], and Qiang Ye[1]

[1] University of Pittsburgh Pittsburgh, PA
{qye,vladimir}@sis.pitt.edu
[2] Technion – Israel Institute of Technology Haifa, Israel
avigal@ie.technion.ac.il
[3] University of Maryland College Park, MD
louiqa@umiacs.umd.edu

Abstract. A challenge in supporting Wide Area Applications (WAA) is that of scalable performance management. Individual *Latency Profiles (iLPs)* were proposed in the literature to capture latency distributions experienced by clients when connecting to a server; it is a passive measurement made by client applications and is gathered on a continuous basis. In this paper, we propose a scalable technique for managing *iLPs* by aggregating them into aggregate *Latency Profiles (aLPs)*. We use measures such as mutual information and correlation to compare the similarity of pairs of iLPs.

1 Introduction

Wide area applications (WAAs) utilize a WAN infrastructure, e.g., the Internet, to connect a federation of hundreds of servers, typically content providers, with tens of thousands of clients. Servers provide services that may range from simple downloads of digital content to complex Web services with multiple interchanges between client and server. It is expected that WAA must scale to millions of client and server pairs. As an example, consider a global name service such as the Handle protocol, an IETF/IRTF standard from CNRI- Corporation for National Research Initiatives [13]. Handle provides a namespace, a name resolution service, and protocols for digital object location and access. The International Digital Object Identifier (DOI) Foundation (www.doi.org) and the community of publishers utilize handles to facilitate the identification and exchange of intellectual property in the digital environment. It is expected that such applications must scale to tens of millions of Handles and thousands of content servers, representing the digital content managed by the publishing community, and large numbers of Handle clients.

A significant challenge in deploying WAA is that of scalable performance management for large numbers of clients. The unpredictable behavior of a dynamic WAN [11, 12] results in a wide variability in access latency (end-to-end delay). There has been extensive research in the networking literature to develop metrics and models to predict latencies, including *Internet distance* and *points of congestion* [1,4,9,11,12]. There has been research on route aggregation based on IP prefixes exchanged via the Border Gateway Protocol (BGP) and exploiting BGP information to monitor and predict

---

* This research is supported by NSF Grants IIS0219909 and EIA0130422.

N. Koch, P. Fraternali, and M. Wirsing (Eds.): ICWE 2004, LNCS 3140, pp. 386–390, 2004.

performance [5,7]. BGP routes expressed as paths via Autonomous Systems (ASes). However, an entire AS may not demonstrate homogeneous behavior, *e.g.*, whenever it spans a large geographic area. Further, the effort to acquire knowledge of the BGP paths between different clients and servers may vary, since some clients and servers do not provide a looking glass service. Finally, while network topology is often a good predictor of latency, it may be the case that there is no available latency data for a closely matching client and server pair. Alternately, a client and server pair with similar BGP routing may not always be a good predictor of latency for the client and server of interest, e.g., if the two servers experience dissimilar workloads, or were associated with dissimilar points of congestion. Latency prediction models based on network characteristics alone would not be appropriate, or would not differentiate the cases described above. This too motivates the complementary need for a management tool and measures that do not rely on extensive (and sometime unavailable) knowledge of the network and its characteristics.

In [10], we proposed *latency profiles* as a conceptual model to characterize the behavior of sources over a WAN. Latency profiles (LPs) are time-dependent latency distributions that capture the changing latencies clients experience when accessing a server; it is measured by client applications or middleware and is gathered passively and on a continuous basis. Latency profiles can be utilized as a WAA monitoring tool, to predict latencies that clients should expect in response to requests, using historical data and recurrent behavior patterns. However, in the presence of hundreds of servers and tens of thousands of clients, managing millions of latency profiles cannot scale. Therefore, we explore in this paper a method for aggregating latency profiles. We propose information theoretic and statistical measures such as mutual information and correlation to compare the similarity of pairs of iLPs. Individual latency profiles (iLPs) will be aggregated into an *aggregate latency profile (aLP)*. A representative latency profile for this aggregate will then be maintained. Whenever a request for service arrives, a prediction will be based on the representative latency profile. Using aLPs allows us to discover aggregate performance patterns that would have been difficult to obtain using network topology and characteristics alone. We empirically show that there is a considerable amount of non-random associations between iLPs. While some of the strong associations can be explained based on physical network topology and characteristics, our experiment also shows that given a group of client and server ASes, with similar (overlap) of BGP routes, there may be a wide variation of the strength of non-random associations between pairs of iLPs.

2 Wide Area Performance Monitoring

Figure presents a WAA performance monitoring architecture. There are three types of nodes, namely clients, content servers, and performance monitors (PMs). Clients continuously download data from content servers and passively construct individual iLPs. PMs manage large collections of iLPs; this is done by aggregating iLPs into a smaller number of aLPs; PMs then manage some number of aLPs and the associated iLPs. Clients consult PMs to obtain a prediction. The scope of an aLP is depicted in Figure 1 by elipses, where each elipse contains clients and servers for each an iLP can be constructed.

Suppose a latency prediction is requested for a pair (c, s) respresenting client c and server s. Suppose also the PM does not have an associated iLP, from the same

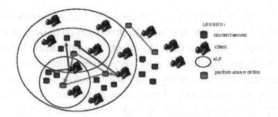

Fig. 1. WAA monitoring architecture based on performance profiles

client AS of c to the same server AS of s, that can be directly used to predict latency. Alternatively, the system does not have sufficient resources to continuously maintain all profiles. Assume further that there exist an iLP_1 associated with a client/server pair (c_1, s) for a different client AS than that of c, but to the same server AS as of s. Similarly, there is an iLP_2 for client/server pair (c, s_1) (same client AS as c and different server AS) and iLP_3 for client/server pair (c_1, s_1) (different client AS as c and different server AS as s). Now the PM can choose either iLP_1 or iLP_2 to make a prediction for the client/server pair (c, s). It is also possible that there exists strong non-random associations between iLP_1, iLP_2 and iLP_3. In this case, the best estimate of access latency for (c, s) is possibly obtained by aggregating iLP_1, iLP_2 and iLP_3 into an aggregate latency profile aLP, and choosing a representative profile.

2.1   Individual and Aggregate Latency Profiles

Given a client c, a server s, an object of size b, and a temporal domain T, an *individual latency profile* is a function $iLP_{c,s} : T \times \mathcal{N} \to \Re^+ \cup \{\mathcal{TO}\}$. $iLP_{c,s}(t, b)$ represents the end-to-end delay for a request from server s at time t, given as either a real number or using TO to represent a timeout. $iLP_{c,s}$ comes in two flavors, similar to [3]. One flavor measures time-to-first, which depends on factors such as workload at the server and size of the requested object. The other flavor measures time-to-last, which has a greater dependency on network bounds. Due to the stochastic nature of the network, $iLP_{c,s}$ is clearly a random variable.

An *aggregate latency profile* aLP_{iLP} combines a set of n individual latency profiles $iLP = \{iLP_{c_i,s_i}\}_{i=1}^n$. We construct an aLP by grouping iLPs with similar characteristics that are non-randomly associated with each other; this will ensure that the grouping will benefit the prediction ability of the aLP. For this grouping, we rely on information theoretic and statistical measures computed for the pair-wise association of iLPs. In particular, we use mutual information [2], and correlation [8]. A higher mutual information between two iLPs means that those iLPs are non-randomly associated. Conversely, a mutual information of zero means that the join distribution of iLPs holds no more information than their individual distributions. A higher correlation between two iLPs can also indicate that those iLPs are non-randomly associated. In general, there is no straightforward relationship between correlation and MI [6]. While correlation captures linear dependence, mutual information is a general dependence measure.

After constructing an aLP from a set of non-random associated iLPs, we can improve the prediction of an iLP by using observations of other iLPs in the aLP. Recall that using an observation of a random variable Y which is related to a random variable X in some way, *e.g.*, Y is non-randomly correlated with X, an optimal mean-square-error estimator of X given Y is the conditional expectation of X given Y, $E(X|Y)$ [8]. We use conditional expectation to utilize the meaningful relationships within an aLP in order to improve latency prediction.

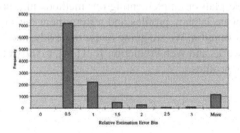

Fig. 2. Distribution of Average Relative Estimation Error

3 Experiments

In this section we report on part of our experiences with constructing $aLPs$. The experimental data was collected over the CNRI Handle testbed [13], – an emerging IETF/IRTF standard that provides a global name service for use over WANs. We gathered data from November to December 2002. The data is typically PDF files that are reachable via Handle resolution. We report on the performance of 22 clients (2 each on 11 client ASes) accessing 10 servers, yielding 220 *iLPs*. We explored two approaches for grouping *iLPs* in $aLPs$, namely using mutual information and using correlation.

We group strongly related *iLPs* in aLP. We applied conditional expectation to esimate individual latencies using observations of latencies from a representative *iLPs* within one aLP. All our $aLPs$ in this experiment consisted of two *iLPs*. For each aLP $\{iLPi, iLPj\}$ we esitmated latencies of $iLPi$ using observations of $iLPj$, i.e., we choose $iLPj$ as a representative profile.

We computed the average relative estimation errors for all iLP pairs ($aLPs$) considered in our experiment. Relative estimation error is defined as $abs(x - x_{est})/x$, where x and x_{est} are actual and estimated latencies correspondingly. For each aLP $\{iLPi, iLPj\}$ we average the relative errors of estimation of all individual latencies from $iLPi$. Figure 2 plots the distribution of the average relative estimation error. We observe that variability of the relative error is considerable. Figure 2 shows that major part of estimation errors (about 9000 estimations) is in a good range of $[0, 1]$. However, more then 1000 estimation errors are large (above 3), and as we see from Figure 2, they can be as much as 75. Meanwhile, from our experiments we found that *practically all of the large estimation errors spread over areas of low MI (< 0.4) and low correlation (< 0.2)*.

We observed that using MI and correlation to construct $aLPs$ does not always guaranty the best latency estimation, but it helps to maintain good estimation quality. Moreover, avoiding non-related representative $iLPs$ effciently eliminates large estimation errors. We conclude that aggregating non-randomly associated latency profiles can practically assist in wide area performance monitoring.

4 Conclusion

We have presented the concept of an aggregate latency profiles as a scalable methodology for utilizing latency profiles. Mutual information and correlations are compared in their ability to explore useful aggregate latency profiles. Our experiments show that in general correlation serves better is generating aggregate latency profiles and in predicting latencies. We plan on implementing our methods in a prototype, allowing the generation of aggregate latency profiles and testing them out in retrieving documents based on handle information. We are going to use more advanced prediction techniques such as Neural Networks and Web Prediction Tool [14], to fully utilize prediction power of aggregate latency profiles.

References

1. P. Francis, S. Jamin, V. Paxson, L. Zhang, D. Gryniewicz, and Y . Jin. An architecture for a global internet host distance estimation service. 1999.
2. F.Reza. *An Introduction to Information Theory.* McGraw-Hill, 1961.
3. J.-R. Gruser, L. Raschid, V. Zadorozhny, and T. Zhan. Learning response time for websources using query feedback and application in query optimization. *VLDB Journal*, 9(1):18–37, 2000.
4. S. Jamin, C. Jin, Y. Jin, D. Raz, Y. Shavin, and L. Zhang. On the placement of internet instrumentation. In *Proceedings of IEEE InfoComm*, 2000.
5. B. Krishnamurthy and J. Wang. On network-aware clustering of web clients. In *Proc. SIGComm*, pages 97–110, 2000.
6. W. Li. Mutual information functions versus correlation functions. *Journal of Statistical Physics*, (60), 1990.
7. Z. Mao, C. Cranor, F. Douglis, M. Rabinovich, O. Spatscheck, and J. Wang. A precise and efficient evaluation of the proximity between web clients and their local dns servers, 2002.
8. W. Mendenhall and T. Sincich. *Statistics for Engineering and the Sciences.* Macmillan Publishing, 1985.
9. V.N. Padmanabhan and L. Subramanian. An investigation of geographic mapping techniques for internet hosts. *Proceedings of the SIGCOMM*, 2001.
10. L. Raschid, H.-F. Wen, A. Gal, and V. Zadorozhny. Latency profiles: Performance monitoring for wide area applications. In *Proceedings of the Third IEEE Workshop on Internet Applications (WIAPP '03)*, San Jose, CA, June 2003.
11. D. Rubenstein, J. Kurose, and D. Towsley. Detecting shared congestion of flows via end-to-end measurement. *Proceedings of the ACM SIGMETRICS Conference*, 2000.
12. M. Stemm, S. Seshan, and R. Katz. A network measurement architecture for adaptive applications. In *Proceedings of IEEE InfoComm*, 2000.
13. S. Sun and L. Lannom. Handle system overview. *IRDM/IRTF Draft, 2001*, http://www.idrm.org/idrm_drafts.htm, 2001.
14. V. Zadorozhny, L. Raschid, T. Zhan, and L. Bright. Validating an access cost model for wide area applications. *Proceedings of the International Conference on Cooperative Information Systems (CoopIS 2001)*, pages 371–385, 2001.

Workload Characterization of Uncacheable HTTP Content

Zhaoming Zhu, Yonggen Mao, and Weisong Shi

Department of Computer Science
Wayne State University, Detroit, MI 48202, USA
{zhaoming,ygmao,weisong}@wayne.edu

1 Introduction

The rapid growth of uncacheable content over the HTTP protocol [1,2] necessitates the further investigation and exploitation of its properties. In this paper, we intend to answer these following questions: Among the huge HTTP content delivered on the Internet, which parts are cacheable and which parts are uncacheable? What are their characteristics, especially for uncacheable content? Is there any difference among different uncacheable HTTP content? Is there any cacheable possibility for these conventional uncacheable content? How about the cacheability of personalized content? Is there some relationship between uncacheable content and HTTP persistent connection?

To answer these questions, we sniffed and analyzed all inbound and outbound HTTP traffic on all possible TCP ports at a medium-size education institution. By analyzing an one-day trace, we observed the following: (1) uncacheable data have dominated today's HTTP traffic and multimedia type content transferred by P2P applications (35.5%) and graphic type (jpeg and gif) content (17.3%) are top two in the uncacheable HTTP objects; (2) compared with cacheable content, uncacheable content consumes more server-processing time, but due to network latency, the client-perceived response time tends to be close to that of cacheable content; (3) on average, uncacheable content has an larger object size than that of cacheable objects (13 K bytes vs. 7K bytes); (4) clients accessing personalized content and servers providing personalized content are more concentrated than general clients and server groups, while the total online personalized content occupies only a smaller percentage (less than 10%), far below than previous observations from [2]; (5) a considerable (50%) portion of HTTP objects have their TTL values equal to zero. Among these objects, we observed that the URL aliasing contributes 20% of total requests; (6) P2P traffic is increasingly scattered among multiple ports (only 13% on default ports for KaZaA traffic), which is a big challenge for deployment of P2P traffic caching. Several implications could be derived based on above observations: (1) a considerable portion of uncacheable HTTP content is cacheable; (2) domination of network latency factor motivates the moving of functionality for uncacheable HTTP content generation to the edge of networks; (3) prefetching for personalized Web content is promising because of the concentrated popularity of clients and servers; (4) convinced by the observed P2P request popularity, we believe that the content-based caching is significant to the ever-increasing P2P traffic; (5) exploiting URL-alias is a promising direction to improve cacheability of uncacheable content.

N. Koch, P. Fraternali, and M. Wirsing (Eds.): ICWE 2004, LNCS 3140, pp. 391–395, 2004.
© Springer-Verlag Berlin Heidelberg 2004

2   Analysis Results

2.1   Trace Collection

We collected one-day period (12:00 pm, Mar 18 -12:00pm Mar 19, 2003) HTTP traffic, rebuilt and investigated the contained content. To capture all possible HTTP traffic, TCP packets on all ports were sniffed. We have developed WebTACT, an Web Traffic Analysis and Characterize Tool, to extract the complete HTTP information, including both header and content. Analysis results and observations are depicted in the following. Due to space limitation, we present high level results only, more detailed data and analysis can be found in the technical report version of this paper [3].

From the viewpoint of proxy caching, generally HTTP object could be broadly categorized as uncacheable content or cacheable content. The cacheable HTTP objects refer to those infrequently changed HTTP objects (also known as static HTTP content), and the uncacheable HTTP content could be further classified into uncacheable subtypes one to seven respectively: NonGet, DynGen, Pragma, CacheCtl, Personalized, AbnormalStatus and ZeroTTL, based on the HTTP protocol specification [4].

2.2   High Level Characteristics

Table 1 lists the high level statistics for both cacheable and uncacheable content. For each content type, we detail them in different traffic directions. The inbound traffic means that the response objects are targeted to clients inside the campus, while the outbound traffic means that the response objects are targeted to clients outside the campus. The total distinct client number inside the campus is 9,053, and that outside campus is 93,250. The total server (host providing HTTP content) number inside the campus is 1,930, and that outside the campus is 114,416.

From Table 1, we can see that, the captured-reconstructed gross HTTP traffic (include HTTP headers and bodies) is around 117.5 GB. For the total objects size (or the total size of transferred HTTP response objects),[1] the uncacheable content outnumbers the cacheable content (72 GB vs. 2.7 GB). The servers that providing uncacheable content outnumber those providing cacheable content (116,149 vs. 7,518), while the clients accessing dynamic content also largely outnumber the clients accessing cacheable content(101,971 vs. 14,674). These data exemplify that the uncacheable content dominates today's HTTP traffic and the necessity of efficient delivery of uncacheable content. The majority of HTTP uncacheable traffic is multimedia audio/video type. This is because that: (1) the huge volume of P2P (KaZaA) application traffic focuses mainly on multimedia file exchange; (2) 99.6% KaZaA HTTP objects are categorized into uncacheable type by our analyzer. Comparing our data with previous results in [2], we observe an increase in the uncacheable request/response for image (gif and jpeg) content type, and a decrease in text (html and plain) content type. The possible reason is the widely acceptance of cache busting technologies [4]. The multimedia type objects (video/x-msvideo, video/mpeg and audio/mpeg), which contribute to a large percentage of total bytes and a small percentage of total number of responses, implies a larger average size of these kinds of objects.

---

[1] Hereafter, all the traffic mentioned in this paper are referring to total objects size.

Table 1. High-level statistics of HTTP traffic.

Type	Cacheable		Uncacheable	
HTTP Traffic Direction	Inbound	Outbound	Inbound	Outbound
# of Servers	7,345	173	114,221	1928
# of Clients	7,007	7,667	9,050	92,921
Total Gross Traffic(MB)	2,177	875	66,278	51,017
Total Object Size (MB)	1,917	825	42,209	31,619
# of Requests	309,616	73,662	6,688,378	2,181,252

2.3 Detailed Characteristics of Uncacheable HTTP Content

Uncacheable Content Breakdown. Table 2 lists the absolute numbers for each of the seven uncacheable subtypes, by their total object size and request/response number. The "mixed" type means the uncacheable subtype is a combination of this subtype and at least one other uncacheable subtype, while the "pure" type means the request belongs to this subtype only. We find that the personalized objects (subtype 5) occupy less than ten percent of all uncacheable content in terms of both bytes and number of requests, not as large as previous observation. We do not know the exact reason for this low percentage of personalized HTTP objects. A distinguished portion, ZeroTTL (subtype 7), implies a promising probability of caching performance improvement that we will give more detail analysis later.

Table 2. Detail breakdown for all seven uncacheable subtypes.

Subtype	ZeroTTL	AbnormalStatus	Personalized	CacheCtl	Pragma	DynGen	NonGet
pure requests	4,413,886	2,067,218	71,634	104,186	80,947	1,274,334	69,767
pure size(MB)	58,182	1,167	541	974	2926	6,493	276
mixed requests	0	574,645	92,989	402,960	232,048	476,420	80,710
mixed size(MB)	0	348	398	2,360	72	2,819	352

Response Time and Breakdown for Uncacheable Content. For further analysis, we first want to know, whether the cacheability of objects affects their response time, on both server side (processing time) and client side (latency). Because of the sniffing point location of our study, we could assume that for the inbound traffic, the response time is close to client-perceived latency, and for the outbound traffic, the response time is close to server-processing time. For the inbound HTTP traffic, the difference between the response time of uncacheable and cacheable objects is not so much. This implies that the time difference caused by dynamic/static content generation has been blurred by the network latency on their route. For the outbound HTTP traffic, there is a difference between the response time of uncacheable and cacheable content, this is probably caused by the time necessary to dynamically generate the uncacheable content. The response times for different dynamic types do not show much difference, especially for inbound traffic. These phenomena show the need to migrating the dynamic generation functions to the network edge.

Object Size Distribution. The distribution of object size is also an interesting topic, especially when HTTP objects are classified into two major classes: cacheable and uncacheable. Intuitively we believe that, on average, uncacheable object size is smaller than cacheable size, but our analysis gives contrary result. 90% of cacheable objects smaller than 14,860 bytes, while same percentage uncacheable objects are smaller than 18,694 bytes. The average size is 7K bytes (cacheable) vs. 13K bytes (uncacheable).

Amazingly, the largest HTTP object size we observed is 252 M bytes for uncacheable object and 12M bytes for cacheable objects. These numbers are much smaller than those appear in [5]. The possible reasons are: (1) our data collecting period is relatively short (24 hours vs. 9 days data collecting period [5]); (2) the object size is calculated based on the bytes on the wire, instead of the HTTP headers. As more and more applications (e.g., KaZaA) adopt parallel downloading or other segment-based content delivery techniques, supported by the HTTP protocol, we believe the size of individual HTTP objects will not be larger any more. So the real reconstructed (fragmented) objects reflecting only a fraction of total size is a reasonable explanation.

Is Uncacheable Content Really Uncacheable? Although the object composition technique, such as ESI, has been proposed, in this paper we are looking for URL-alias derived cacheable possibility. Totally, there are 4,413,886 objects belonging to ZeroTTL subtype. Among these we observe that many different URLs share the identical content digest. This is caused by the phenomenon called "URL-alias" [6]. Our analysis show that the number of requests targeting the top 1000 (less than 0.1% of total distinct digest value) rank digest value count for 18% of total number of requests. This observation reveals an opportunity for the future Web cache improvement if certain protocol could be designed to deal with ZeroTTL objects based on their digest value, rather than on their URLs only.

Client/Server Popularity. We assume that the personalized Web content would be more client/server-specific than general content, due to its "personalized" property and the analysis results do verify our assumption. Top 1% of clients that accessing personalized content bring about 20% of the total personalized content requests. However, unlike previous observations [2], we find that clients interested in personalized content only occupy 2% of the total client population. Some clients are much more likely to access personalized Web content. These clients are some public-access computers, located at public area like student dormitories, for students check updated personalized information like email or personal account on e-commerce Web sites. We also find that personalized content is provided by 1% of the total servers, and servers providing personalized content are also more concentrated than server providing general content. Top 1% of servers that provide personalized content handle 85% of the requests for personalized content requests. There are "hot" personalized Web servers and the top 30 of the servers contribute 95% of the total requests among the top 100 servers providing personalized content.

Object Popularity. Due to the personalized property, personalized HTTP objects might not be more concentrated than general objects and this is proved by our analysis. All these observations strongly suggest that personalized prefetching could be used to reduce the client perceived latency and network bandwidth equipment.

Persistent Connection vs. Uncacheable HTTP Objects. In our reconstructed HTTP data, there are totally 669,958 persistent connection sessions, consists of 3,411,741 HTTP request/response pairs. On average, a persistent session consists of 5.09 pairs. We have supposed that the uncacheable content would have some distribution patterns among multiple pairs within one persistent connection. One reasonable assumption is that, for a persistent HTTP connection, maybe the first object is an uncacheable dynamically generated page template, followed with embedded cacheable objects like graphics. But our analysis results deny this distribution pattern proposition and conclude that most of the uncacheable content does not appear in persistent connections.

Peer-to-Peer Traffic Analysis. We reconstructed all http-based P2P traffic by capturing all TCP traffic, instead of sniffing only some specific default ports (e.g., 1214 for KaZaA, 6346 and 6347 for Gnutella, used by previous work [5]). Generally, as observed earlier in this Section, P2P traffic contributes to a large portion of total HTTP traffic. For Gnutella type P2P applications, we aggregate several found Gnutella client applications (e.g., LimeWire, BearShare, Shareaza etc.) into a whole Gnutella division. For KaZaA type data, only the traffic from KaZaA client is calculated. The total HTTP object size transferred by Gnutella applications is 1,110,383,667 bytes, while that by KaZaA application is 26,659,686,069 bytes. The total object size transferred by P2P applications occupies 33.8% of the total observed HTTP object size while the corresponding percentage is over 75% in [5]'s work. With the evolution of P2P applications, P2P traffic ports are more distributed than before. For example, only 13% of KaZaA traffic is through its default port 1214. This phenomenon strongly implies the emergence of new mechanisms dealing with P2P traffic spreading on different TCP ports.

3 Summary

Implied by characteristics analysis of uncacheable HTTP traffic, we propose four promising directions to improve caching and content delivery of uncacheable HTTP content: first, pushing the functionality of uncacheable content generation to the network edges; second, applying the access pattern feature to prefetching schemes; third, implementing an efficient content-based P2P traffic caching; Finally combining content-based approach into current cache to exploit the prevailing URL-alias phenomenon.

References

1. Shi, W., Collins, E., Karamcheti, V.: Modeling object characteristics of dynamic web content. Journal of Parallel and Distributed Computing) **63** (2003) 963–980
2. Wolman, A., Voelker, G.M., Sharma, N., Cardwell, N., Brown, M., Landray, T., Pinnel, D., Karlin, A., Levy, H.M.: Organization-based analysis of web-object sharing and caching. In: Proc. of the 2nd USENIX Symposium on Internet Technologies and Systems (USITS'99). (1999)
3. Zhu, Z., Mao, Y., Shi, W.: Workload characterization of uncacheable http traffic. Technical Report MIST-TR-03-003, Computer Science Department, Wayne State University (2003)
4. Krishnamurthy, B., Rexford, J.: Web Protocols and Practice: HTTP/1.1, Networking Protocols, Caching and Traffic Measurement. Addison-Wesley, Inc (2001)
5. Saroiu, S., Gummadi, K.P., Dunn, R.J., Gribble, S.D., Levy, H.M.: An analysis of internet content delivery systems. In: Proc. of OSDI'02
6. Kelly, T., Mogul, J.: Aliasing on the world wide web: Prevalence and performance implications. In: Proc. of the 11th International World Wide Web Conference (2002). (2002)

A Scalable Component-Based Architecture for Online Services of Library Catalogs

Marcus Flehmig

University of Kaiserslautern, Department of Computer Science, P.O. Box 3049,
67653 Kaiserslautern, Germany
flehmig@informatik.uni-kl.de

Abstract. In recent years, more and more publications and material for studying and teaching, e.g., for Web-based teaching (WBT), appear "online" and digital libraries are built to manage such publications and online materials. Therefore, the most important concerns are related to the problem of durable, sustained storage and the management of content together with its metadata existing in heterogeneous styles and formats. In this paper, we present specific techniques, their use to support metadata-based catalog services deploying XML, and finally derive the concepts of a suitable component-based architecture.

1 Introduction

More and more e-learning material is produced for online services. In general, it is integrated into portal systems [1] and can be used via the Web. However, searching online material is not easy. Therefore, digital libraries and online catalog services have been built. First of all, information about online material has to be collected and made queryable. For this purpose, a metadata repository with search (full text) or query (structured) facilities has to be made available. Furthermore, online catalog services should deploy state-of-the-art frameworks and architectural concepts to deal with scalability requirements. Particularly with regard to the very central task of search and query support, scalability is essential. Finally, online catalog services stand for more than simple search engines. In fact, they provide search and query support, but additional sophisticated information about the query result is needed, which is presented in more detail in the next sections.

2 Requirements

To provide an online catalog, it first has to be filled with useful material. In an initial step, resources have to be found and identified. If acceptable, they have to be indexed and reviewed. All of these steps should be supported by an appropriate management system, for which the underlying process is illustrated in Fig. 1. The principal task consists of efficient query support. Short response time, high throughput, low resource consumption, integration of full-text search and structured queries, as well as support of highly concurrent user queries are requirements summarized by the term "efficient query support". In addition, various kinds of statistics – related to the original queries, the

N. Koch, P. Fraternali, and M. Wirsing (Eds.): ICWE 2004, LNCS 3140, pp. 396–401, 2004.
© Springer-Verlag Berlin Heidelberg 2004

most frequent subjects, the number of hits, or the variance of a distinct value distribution — are useful, e.g., to enable a comprehensive personalization concept, i.e., to provide navigational hints or help on choosing a good sorting or ranking method.

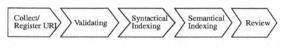

Fig. 1. Basic Indexing Process

The list of requirements of our project made it necessary to define a special set of metadata attributes tailored to its special needs. For this reason, we included special metadata attributes for online resources and peer reviews to deal with didactical issues and issues at law. In fact, for various reasons our project [2] has chosen Dublin Core and its meanwhile obsolete qualifier approach as a basis for defining a hierarchical scheme. This data model is aware of elements and attributes and a number of data types. It offers the specification of single-value elements, ordered lists, or unordered sets of elements. Metadata records are in relationship with other records. In this way, complex tree-like structures may result. A learning resource record, for example, may be in relationship with a user comment, a peer review, or again a learning resource, e.g., if the material occurs in different formats (like PostScript or the widespread PDF format). Deploying XML as formal representation makes it possible to describe the transformation of our metadata set representation into RDF or OAI-like (Open Archive Initiative) structures in a very formal way to easily support interoperability with other systems, e.g., within library consortia. The XML-based representation enables two distinct ways of processing the underlying data: element-based (fine-grained) or document-based (coarse-grained). Hence, especially in enterprise applications a document-centric, i.e., coarse-grained approach should be preferred. Therefore, the process model including definition, query, and retrieval of data is XML-based.

3   Basics

With the advent of object orientation (OO), many old software engineering problems could be solved, but some problems still remain. OO and the corresponding languages only support fine-grained concepts. Hence, scalability in large or data-intensive applications could become a problem. For this reason, components have emerged. Components are a coherent package of software that can be independently developed and delivered as a unit and that offers interfaces by which it can be connected with other components to compose a larger system. Its physical implementation is held in one place and components will often be larger-grained comparing to the traditional concept of objects. Because the standard Web-communication protocol HTTP is a request-response protocol, individual requests of Web-based applications are treated independently. For this reason, state management truly becomes an issue at the application layer. Sometimes it is advised to push state management completely back into the database tier [3]. With stateless implementations, resource sharing is easy, because they are exclusively used only by one component during a single method execution. Apparently, a centralized storage for component state seems to be very practical. The alteration from object orientation to component-based models is accompanied by a shift in paradigm related to the corresponding architectures. Traditional client/server architectures are displaced by enterprise application architectures. Even though enterprise application architectures could be considered as distributed n-tier client/server architectures, they are derived by the methodical appliance of engineering techniques and also by taking business application requirements into account. One of the most important techniques are design patterns.

4 Architecture Derivation

The main focus of our approach lies on the separation of concerns. Therefore, distinct tasks have to be identified and have to be separated. First of all, we have separated the data (i.e., the learning object) from its metadata and the metadata from its related metadata (so-called administrative metadata). Furthermore, beside the above separation of data and metadata we have made a strict distinction between three different main tasks: query processing, result set processing, and XML document processing.

Each of these tasks is realized by a separate component which places us in a promising position to achieve better scalability. As depicted in Fig. 2, the separation

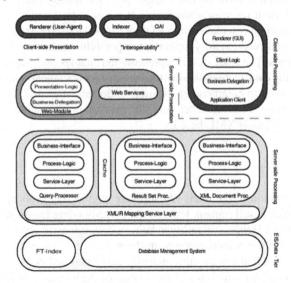

Fig. 2. Architectural overview

of business and application (i.e., framework-specific) logic is essential for enterprise programming. In the bottom tier (enterprise information system tier) data is managed. Unstructured data (or learning objects) are managed and indexed by a freely-available full-text indexing system, whereas structured metadata is stored in a relational database system (RDBS). Therefore, we need a transformation between the XML model and the relational data model with simultaneous consideration of the integration of the full-text index. Support for this transformation can be found in the XML/R mapping-support layer located at the server-side processing tier. It builds the foundation of the higher-level server-sided components which include services for meta model access, domain-value queries, or configuration management.

In addition, the server-side processing tier provides components for query processing which is separated into three distinct steps. In the first step, a client query against an XML schema is transformed into an equivalent SQL query by the query processor which provides methods to execute or refine queries and expects a descriptive query specification. The result of such a query is cached and processed by an additional component (result set processor). The XML documents qualified for a query could be modified by the third component (XML processor), if needed. These components act like a controller in accordance with the MVC pattern [4]. Thus, they mediate between the underlying data tier containing the models and the presentational views. The business interface implemented by its corresponding controller represents the distinct component interface and helps to abstract from the particular application-specific or frameworkspecific implementation details. The implementation of this interface realizes coarsegrained business methods by composition of less complex methods and is conceptually equivalent to SUN's Session Facade pattern [4].

The server-side presentation tier is located above the server-side processing tier. Web modules for supporting Web-based applications, for instance the Web-based search engine component, can also be found here as well as Web service connectors, which provide interoperability to special clients (e.g., in the case of OAI support, deployment of external indexing, or harvesting clients). Beside thin clients (i.e., user agents like Web browsers) fat clients for maintenance and indexing tasks are supported, too. Again, to abstract from particular application-specific or framework-specific implementation details, the business delegation pattern is deployed where all these details could be encapsulated. The business delegation pattern implementation builds a single point of communication between Web modules located in the server-side presentation tier and the various controllers in the server-side processing tier.

As a consequence of the above mentioned separation of concerns, query processing is separated from result set processing. This is achieved by caching the result set and providing a result set handle for identification purpose. But caching is also necessary to accomplish some reordering of the result set, because the full-text search engine does not support comprehensive sorting capabilities. However, caching even offers some more advantages. To determine the number of hits, the most frequently used terms or subjects, or to make helpful hints to determine appropriate search criteria by building the variance of distinct columns, it is not necessary to rerun the entire, typically very expensive, query. Beyond these so-called metaqueries it is feasible to use the cached results for query refinement, for reuse during processing of subsequent queries and for provision of a so-called stateless cursor. It is not feasible to hold a database cursor open all the time a user navigates through the result set pages, because open database connections are too expensive. In the case of stateful components, there exists a component instance for each single client request. An implementation has to be realized in a stateless manner and state can be managed by a distinct component or a RDBS. In our approach, the result set of a client query is stored into a separated (temporary) table of a RDBS together with additional administrative data (e.g., cursor position). Hence, concurrent queries and locks are no problem any longer and every subsequent query transformation or refinement of the result set could be locally executed in the cache.

5 Scalability

The trichotomy of the overall query process comes along with a very positive impact. By deploying such an architecture, we can cope with the typical workloads of digital library usage patterns and achieve better scalability. Typical workloads rely on the assumption that a user tries out some queries and refines a suitable query result by selecting a navigational hint to narrow the result set or by using one of the sort methods offered.

Additionally, information about the current query result should be presented to the user, e.g., the total amount of hits, how many documents are classified by a distinct subject, or information about the most frequent keywords. Though, evaluating such information is expensive. In most cases, a query has to be repeated more than one time to build suitable aggregated information about distinct columns of a result set. Regarding our requirements, a query has to be executed at least four times to aggregate all of the information needed. Incorporating the cache to evaluate, the above mentioned, metaqueries allows to specify very simple and inexpensive queries which get along with a few simple joins and which relieve the underlying RDBS. Furthermore, our approach yields another benefit regarding sort support. Consecutive queries differing solely in the sort criteria applied could be answered without the necessity to repeat the query.

In addition to caching operational data of a distinct user query, conversational state information is stored, too. For this reason, a stateless component architecture becomes feasible. The state is managed outside of the component and could be restored, before processing is continued regardless where the component resides, i.e., in the case of distributed processing, each node could answer any request. The query engine itself is implemented in a stateless manner and can be distributed, too. Result set processing is done by a separate component which operates on top of the cache. For this reason, initial queries are processed by the query engine and subsequent queries are performed locally. As a consequence, subsequent queries do not stress the underlying database system.

6   Conclusions and Outlook

In this paper, a scalable component-based architecture for online catalog services has been presented that can be used in the domain of digital libraries. In contrast to search engine services (e.g., Google or Altavista), appropriate products (e.g., ASPseek), directory services (e.g., Yahoo or DMOZ), or other digital library systems (e.g., MyCoRe), our approach is able to cope with a more comprehensive set of metadata attributes and uses standardized techniques as well as a component-based framework (J2EE). It is very flexible concerning the underlying metadata schema. In addition, automatic indexing services are integrated in our system. Thus, interoperability, scalability, process-oriented metadata management, and the integration of full-text search and structured queries are the outstanding characteristics of our approach. MyCoRe can be deployed for the development of Digital Library and archive solutions. Adjustability, extensibility, and open interfaces are fundamental design premises of MyCoRe, but, at the moment, it is dedicated to only a single database management system [5]. Therefore, the innovative aspect of our approach could be found in the segmentation of the query process. As a consequence, sophisticated caching becomes feasible. It is not necessary any longer to rerun expensive queries which could additionally include unstructured search to answer metaqueries and to accomplish the requirements of personalization. The concepts presented have been validated by realizing a prototype system[1]. Furthermore, in-memory cache management at the middle-tier may be considered which is similar to the approach described in [6].

---

[1] www.akleon.de (at the moment only available in German)

References

1. Flehmig, M.: Integration and Personalization – On Realization of Essential Aspects of Portal Systems, in: Proceedings of the International GI/OCG Computer Science Conference, Vienna, Sept. 2001, pp. 895–901 (in German).
2. META-AKAD: Metadata Element Set and Structure, in: Technical Report, University of Kaiserslautern, University of Regensburg, September 2003 (63 pages).
3. Intel e-Business Center: N-tier Architecture Improves Scalability, Availability and Ease of Integration, White Paper, 2001.
4. Alur, D., Crupi, J., Malks, D.: Core J2EE Patterns – Best Practices and Design Strategies, Prentice Hall / Sun Microsystems Press, 2001.
5. MyCoRe: The MyCoRe Project Homepage, `http://www.mycore.de/engl/index.html`, 2003.
6. Altinel, M., Bornhövd, C., Krishnamurthy, S.,Mohan, C., Pirahesh, H., Reinwald, B.: Cache Tables: Paving the Way for an Adaptive Database Cache, in: Proceedings of the 29th VLDB Conference, Berlin, 2003, pp. 718-729.

An XHTML 2.0 Implementation

Mikko Pohja, Mikko Honkala, and Petri Vuorimaa

Telecommunications Software and Multimedia Laboratory,
Helsinki University of Technology
P. O. Box 5400, FI-02015 HUT, Finland
Tel. +358-9-4515260
{mikko.pohja, mikko.honkala, petri.vuorimaa}@hut.fi

Abstract. The next version of XHTML is at work-in-progress stage
in the World Wide Web Consortium. It adds a lot of features to the
most used content language of the Web. The most notable change is the
addition of XForms, the next generation WWW forms language. This
paper describes the XHTML 2.0 specification and an XML user agent
implementation for it. The new features of the language are discussed
both from the author's and the user agent manufacturer's point of view.
In addition, it describes a case study, which takes advantage of the new
features.

1 Introduction

HyperText Markup Language (HTML) [1] is one of the greatest factors to the
success of the World Wide Web (WWW). It provides an easy way for authors to
create content to WWW. Originally, HTML was designed to describe structure
of the document. Later, a lot of presentational features were added into it.

To bring HTML back to its origin, it was redefined as an Extensible Markup
Language (XML) [2]. First versions of XHTML were just reformulation of HTML
4, but the newest version, XHTML 2.0 [3], which is at work-in-progress stage
in the World Wide Web Consortium (W3C), is no longer backward compatible
with the earlier versions. As a starting point to a design of XHTML 2.0 has
been experiences and problems of earlier web technologies, especially HTML.
The intention is to make XHTML 2.0 easy to adopt for authors and to match to
original purpose of HTML (i.e., describe the structure of hypertext documents).
For instance, XHTML 2.0 removes all presentation elements from HTML and
subordinates all presentation to stylesheets. In addition, a lot of functionality
has been added to XHTML 2.0. The objective is to reduce the use of scripting
languages within XHTML documents. Most common scripts have been replaced
by functional elements.

The success of the WWW is also largely based on interactive services such
as search engines, online banking, and e-commerce. A key technology used in
interactive Web applications is HTML forms. However, requirements for these
services have steadily increased since the advent of the technology. Today's high-
end forms use complex client-side ECMAScript [4] programming to achieve form

N. Koch, P. Fraternali, and M. Wirsing (Eds.): ICWE 2004, LNCS 3140, pp. 402–415, 2004.
© Springer-Verlag Berlin Heidelberg 2004

field validation and simple computations (or bounce the form back and forth to the server). Heavy use of scripting inevitably leads to low maintainability and accessibility. [5]

The HTML forms has been replaced by XForms in XHTML 2.0. That removes need for scripts from the forms and separates model and presentation of a form. Consequently completing the design principles of XHTML 2.0.

The transition to XHTML 2.0 will be more difficult than transitions between earlier HTML versions. XForms [6] will be the biggest change in XHTML 2.0, but there are also other changes, which are not backward compatible [7]. In this paper, we have assessed the impacts of the transition to both user agent developers and authors.

The paper describes XHTML 2.0 specification and an XML user agent implementation for it. Next section introduces XHTML and XForms modules of XHTML 2.0 and their integration. Sections 3, 4, and 5 discuss implementations of X-Smiles XML browser, XHTML module, and XForms module, respectively. A case study is described in section 6, while discussion about the transition to XHTML 2.0 is in section 7. Finally, section 8 gives the conclusions.

2   XHTML 2.0

XHTML 2.0, which is a W3C Working Draft, is a markup language, which describes structure of a document. It does not represent document's layout. XHTML 2.0 is successor of the earlier HTML languages, but it is not backward compatible with them.

XHTML 2.0 is supposed to be as generic XML as possible. Since XHTML 2.0 is an XML language, it can be combined with other XML languages and use their features. Only special-purpose XHTML features were included in XHTML 2.0. These are, for example, elements for images, tables, menus, etc. In addition, XHTML 2.0 uses facilities like XForms, XML Events [8], and XML Base [9]. In addition, layout of the document is defined by Cascading Style Sheets (CSS). All the presentational elements, such as *font* are removed from XHTML 2.0.

The separation of content and presentation has many advantages. Layout of the document can be easily changed, layout can be specified for different devices, documents are smaller, and user agents are easier to implement. For instance, from the user agent vendor's point of view the user agent's components can be separated and they can be smaller, while the author can more easily reuse styling. This also leads to better accessibility because it is easy to change the styling of a document without touching the contents.

Compared to earlier versions, XHTML 2.0 has better ability to make documents more structured. Content is intended to be divided into sections, which all can have titles and subsections. Sections within sections can nest indefinitely deep. As before, content in sections consist of paragraphs, tables, list, etc.

One aim of XHTML 2.0 is to reduce scripting from the documents. Many elements have now some kind of functionality as a default. That reduces device dependency and eases authors work, because they do not have care about script languages. It is still possible to use scripting via the Document Object Model (DOM) interfaces. Other benefits of moving from scripts to declarative languages are improved accessibility and device-independence. This results from the fact that it is easier to use automated tools to process declarative markup than scripted documents.

XHTML languages are divided into modules. XHTML 2.0 contains all the modules defined in XHTML Modularization 1.0 [10]. Although, content of the modules have been changed a bit. In addition, it uses modules from XForms, XML Events, and Ruby. XForms module is discussed in more detail in next subsection. XML Events provides an uniform way to integrate DOM Level 2 event interfaces with event listeners and handlers. Ruby module is used to add short annotations to the text. Usually it is used as pronunciation instructions with eastern languages. The Ruby module is out of scope of this paper.

The biggest changes in XHTML module are the addition of structural and functional elements. Functional elements had to be realized by scripts earlier. Now, there are elements, which have some default functionality. For instance, menus are common on the web pages. For that, there is navigation list in XHTML 2.0 [11]. Navigation list is like normal list, but only selected part of the list is shown at a time. The part can be selected for instance by moving cursor on it. It is possible to style such a list as a drop-down menu with CSS, as shown in Fig. 1. XForms specification also contains lot of features, whose intent is to replace scripting.

Fig. 1. Navigation list styled as a drop-down menu

Also, the use of attributes has changed. Attributes can be used more generally than before. For example, *href* attribute can be added to any element. That makes the *a* element useless. In addition, all the elements can have *src* attribute. That enables addition of external sources to the element. Element's normal content is shown, if source is not available or cannot be shown in the device in question.

2.1   XForms

HTML forms has many well-known shortcomings. It has no separation of data and presentation. Building anything more than a simple form requires excessive amounts of scripting, which is hard to implement and maintain. Another often-used approach is to send the form back and forth between the browser and the server, which leads to great amount of round-trips and reduced maintenance of the forms.

XForms 1.0 Recommendation is the next-generation Web forms language, designed by the W3C. It solves some of the problems found in the HTML forms by separating the purpose from the presentation and using declarative ways to describe the most common operations in form-based applications. It can use any XML grammar to describe the content of the form (the instance data). Thus, it is also possible to create generic editors for different XML grammars with XForms.

XForms separates the form into three main layers: Model, Instance Data, and User Interface (cf. Fig. 2 (a)). The Model layer includes the XML Schema and constraints. With the schema, it is possible to define the structure and the data types of the instance data, but XForms can also be authored without a schema. The schema can be processed via a normal XML Schema processor as shown in Fig. 2 (a).

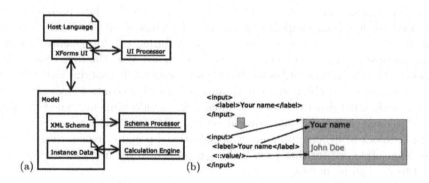

Fig. 2. (a) XForms layers and (b) the pseudo-class ::value inside a form control

It is possible to define dynamic relations (constraints) between parts of the instance data. These relations are defined using XPath expressions. Examples of dynamic relations include inter-field calculations and constraints, which dynamically set the state of an item in instance data to read-only or required. The calculation engine interacts with the instance data and it resolves and computes these relations dynamically while the user interacts with the form [5].

The User Interface is also bound to the instance data using XPath expressions. The choice of form controls covers the range of typical GUI widgets (although they are defined in higher level terms, such as select1 instead of menu).

Some form controls also adapt to the underlying XML Schema data type. For instance, an input control bound to a *date* data type will show a calendar picker instead of a text field. XForms also hosts a collection of dynamic user interface features, such as displaying and dynamically modifying collections of repeating items and switching parts of the user interface on and off. [12]

XForms exposes a lot of the processing to the author via DOM events. For instance, there are events that are thrown when the instance data becomes invalid, read only, required, etc. The author can catch these events declaratively using XML Events. The counterpart to XML Events are XForms actions, which can be executed when a certain event condition is met. This way it is possible to define, in a declarative fashion, certain actions to happen when the user interacts with the form. For instance, the form could be submitted partially when the user selects a certain item from a selection list.

2.2   Integration of XForms and XHTML

XForms is not a self-standing document type, i.e., it needs a host language to define the document's master layout. XHTML is a natural choice as a host language in Web context. The current version of the XHTML 2.0 Working Draft includes XForms as the forms module.

Since XHTML relies heavily on CSS2 layout, it is important that XForms also integrates to this model well. For instance, it uses the notions of pseudo-class, and pseudo-element from CSS. For instance, the "::value" pseudo-element is used to define the appearance of the UI widget itself (it would otherwise be hard to style just the widget, since in XForms, the form control element also encapsulates a label element). Fig. 2 (b) shows this; the first code snippet shows what the author writes to create a form control. It contains only the *input* element and a *label* child. To give the author better CSS control of the rendering, the specification describes an additional CSS pseudo-element, called "::value". The element *input* and *label* should be laid out using the CSS rules (such as display:block or display:inline) and the additional pseudo-element ::value is used to define style just for that part of the control, which the user can interact with; in this case an input box.

Other pseudo-elements defined non-normatively in the XForms specification are ::repeat-item and ::repeat-index. The ::repeat-item pseudo-element is used to style all the items in a repeating collection, while ::repeat-index pseudo-element is used to style the currently selected item.

3   The X-Smiles XML Browser

X-Smiles is an open source XML browser developed at the Helsinki University of Technology. The authors of this paper have implemented XHTML 2.0 and XForms support in the browser. In addition, the CSS layout implementation is done by the authors. The authors have also actively participated in the W3C XForms Working Group.

This section describes the main architecture of the browser. The main components of the X-Smiles browser can be divided into four groups: XML processing, Browser Core Functionality, Markup Language Functional Components (MLFCs) and ECMAScript Interpreter, and Graphical User Interfaces (GUIs).

3.1 Operation

The core of the browser controls the overall operation of the browser. It includes browser configuration, event handling, XML Broker, etc. MLFCs handle different XML languages and render the documents. There are several GUIs in the X-Smiles distribution. They are used to adapt the browser to various devices or as virtual prototypes, when prototyping content targeted to diverse range of devices. [13]

Basically, the X-Smiles operation consists of three steps: parsing, creating DOM, and rendering. Parsing and creating DOM are done concurrently. When reading new XML document, the X-Smiles browser first reads the document source. The file is accessed using either the file or http protocol. The Xerces XML parser and DOM implementation construct the DOM model of a document. Parser creates different Simple API for XML (SAX) events, which are used by DOM implementation. The MLFCs handle the presentation of the document. The MLFC layer is done in a modular way; it is possible to add and remove MLFCs for certain browser configurations without rebuilding the browser. It is also possible to show embedded documents. For instance, it is possible to use a SMIL presentation referenced by an object element in XHTML.

3.2 Hybrid Documents

Hybrid XML documents are documents, which contain several XML languages, separated by namespaces. Recently, the usage of hybrid documents has increased. The trend has been to specify XML languages as modules, which are combined to construct complete languages. This way, the modules can be reused across different languages, making implementations smaller and easier. It also reduces the number of different languages that the author must learn.

As the number of languages gets higher, a way to flexibly handle these kinds of documents is required. The X-Smiles browser has a framework that handles hybrid documents. This framework includes a component called XML Broker, which handles the registration of language implementations. A language implementation in the framework is called a MLFC (i.e., Markup Language Functional Component). An important concept in hybrid documents are *host* and *parasite* languages. There is always one *host* language in a document, usually determined by the namespace of the document element. The host language is used for the master layout of the document. Other languages that are embedded in the document are called *parasite* languages. In this paper, XHTML 2.0 is a *host* language, while XForms and XML Events are *parasite* languages. In an implementation, there is a need for communications between the *host* and *parasite* elements in the DOM. In X-Smiles, this is done by extending the DOM implementation and implementing general browser-defined interfaces. [14]

4   XHTML Module

The XHTML module handles XHTML documents. The documents can be styled by style sheets and contain elements from other XML languages. The operation of the XHTML module is depicted in Fig. 3. An XML parser parses a given XML document and creates DOM document, which is an object tree representation of the XML document. From each tag in the XML document, a node for DOM tree is created. The document is displayed by a layout document, which implements Java Swing's document model. The layout document is formed from DOM tree. Basically, every DOM element have respective layout element in layout document. Layout document is displayed by Swing Views. Each layout element has respective View, which defines its layout. Views render the document in browser window. [15]

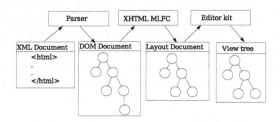

Fig. 3. Operation of the XHTML module

The XHTML elements can be divided into two groups: stylable and non-stylable elements. All the visible elements are stylable. A style is assigned for each stylable element after DOM has been created. Elements get their style from the style sheet object. It is possible to change the visual type of the element by using the CSS property "display" (e.g., inline/block).

Every DOM element has a respective layout element, which is used by layout document. In X-Smiles, XHTML elements and all the other elements in XHTML document have to have layout element in order to get rendered. In the case of XHTML, layout element is an instance of *AbstractElement*, which is an inner class of *XHTMLDocument2*. *AbstractElement* implements also Swing's *Element* interface, whereas *XHTMLDocument2* implements Swing's *StyledDocument* interface. That way they both can be used as a part of Swing document model. [16]

Views are also the part of the Swing document model. They define how elements are rendered in browser window. Views can contain content and other views and they are placed in a row either vertically or horizontally. For instance, inline elements are placed horizontally and paragraphs vertically. Every view has some basic layout, which can be modified by style sheet. Elements are associated with Views by editor kit, which ties the layout document and views together.

5 XForms Module

The XForms module was also implemented using the MLFC interfaces in the X-Smiles browser. It is an parasite MLFC and always needs a host MLFC (in this paper, XHTML2 MLFC). The host is responsible for the main document layout, while the parasite is responsible for rendering the host language elements.

5.1 Architecture

Fig. 4 depicts the architecture of the XForms MLFC in X-Smiles. There are three main layers in the implementation: XForms model, Meta UI and User Interface. At the lowest level of the XForms model, there are the XML libraries that the implementation uses. For XML parsing and XML Schema, we used the Xerces-J 2.4.0 implementation compiled with DOM level 3 support. DOM level 3 support was needed for Post Schema Validation Infoset (PSVI), which is used to get the data type information. For XPath, Xalan-J 2.5.1 was used. On top of the XML libraries lie the Instance document implementation, and the validation and calculation engine implementations. Data types are used in all layers, for instance to instantiate right types of form controls. The middle layer, Meta UI, contains high-level User Interface constructs, such as repeating items in a collection and switching parts of the User Interface on and off. The topmost layer is the User interface. To further enable multi-platform support, an additional layer, called Abstract Components was created. For each platform, an implementation, or wrappers, of the abstract components were included. Currently, we have support for AWT, Swing and Havi widgets.

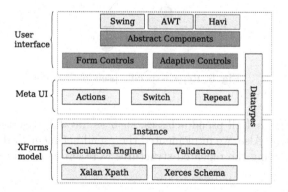

Fig. 4. XForms MLFC architecture in X-Smiles

XML Events was implemented by creating the XML Events MLFC into X-Smiles. The MLFC uses DOM events implementation in the Xerces-J parser to implement listeners and events. A general action interface was created for the browser, and all XForms action elements implement that interface.

5.2 CSS Integration

Because of the way XForms language was designed, it was not entirely trivial to integrate it with a CSS based layout engine, such as the XHTML+CSS engine in X-Smiles. For instance, there exists a notion of cursor inside a repeated construct, that has no correspondence in the DOM. Also, the element describing the form control contains a label element inside it, making it difficult to style just the form control itself, as discussed in section 2.2. Basically, the implementation of pseudo-classes was quite straight-forward, since it is a concept outside of the DOM tree. On the other hand, pseudo-elements are conceptually in the DOM tree for CSS styling and cascade purposes, and are therefore much harder to implement. For instance, the pseudo-elements ::repeat-item and ::repeat-index should be inserted in the middle of the DOM tree. Fig. 5 depicts this; a simple repeat construct bound to a nodeset containing two nodes leads to more complex run-time object tree containing several pseudo-elements. Note that some DOM elements are treated as children of the pseudo-elements for purposes of CSS styling and cascading.

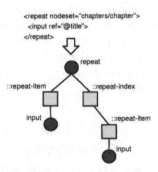

Fig. 5. Repeat-specific pseudo-elements

We implemented all pseudo-classes, such as :invalid, describing the state of the form control. Also, we implemented the pseudo-element ::value. The pseudo-elements for styling the repeated structures were left as a future work item.

6   A Case Study: Document Composition

In this section, we introduce a real-world example of how to use XHTML 2.0 to compose and navigate a large document. One of the shortcomings of XHTML 1.0 is that it does not support forms that edit repeating structures, thus requiring server-side or script processing to provide such functionality. Another shortcoming is the non-existing support for navigation lists, such as pull-down menus. Navigation lists show only the currently selected part of the list, thus helping the user to navigate more easily in a large document hierarchy. Navigation lists have to be implemented with complex scripting in XHTML 1.0, decreasing accessibility and device-independence. The example shows how to use the declarative features of XHTML 2.0 to implement both the structural editing and navigation. The whole example runs in the client and does not need server-side programming. It also does not use any scripting, thus making it accessible and device independent.

The document used in this case study is X-Smiles' Technical Specification document. It has been created using the Doc Book XML format. In this case study, we show how to present and navigate that document in XHTML 2.0 and even edit the document composition. The Doc Book source files are controlled by XForms and transformed to XHTML 2.0 using XSL Transformations.

The components of the example are shown in Fig. 6. The document consists of chapters, which each are in separate XML files. Headings, paragraphs, images, etc. are marked by specific tags in the chapter documents. All the chapter documents are included into a composition document by XML Inclusions (Xinclude)[1]. The composition document is edited by Edit document, which is an XHTML 2.0 document with XForms form. The composition document is an instance of the form. Through the Edit document, user can select, which chapters are included in the final document. The final document is transformed to XHTML 2.0 format by XSL style sheet. The document composition and structure are discussed in more detail below.

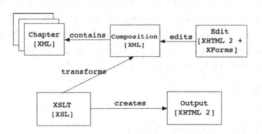

Fig. 6. Test case architecture

The editor document, which is depicted in upper-right corner of Fig. 6, is an XHTML 2.0 document, which includes embedded XForms elements. The XForms instance data is the Composition document. The editor document uses a XForms *repeat* element to create an editor for this document. It is possible to add new sections to the composition, or enable/disable them. The editor UI is depicted in Fig. 7 (a).

---

[1] XML Inclusions, http://www.w3.org/TR/xinclude/

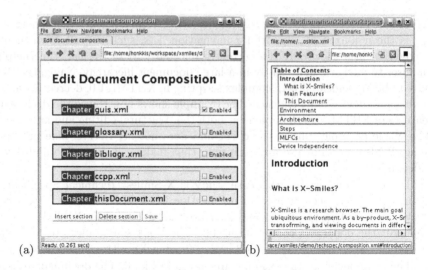

Fig. 7. (a) Editing the composition with XForms and (b) viewing the final document

The XSL style sheet converts all the elements from the composed file to XHTML 2.0 elements. Content of chapter documents is divided to sections, which can contain other sections, paragraphs, headings, etc. The XSL Transformation converts all the chapter and section elements to XHTML 2.0 sections. Therefore, document is structured automatically. In XHTML 2.0, all headings can be represented by h elements. Their style depends of amount of embedding sections. So, during transforming, there is no need to decide the level of headings.

The document has a menu in the beginning. It is realized using XHMTL 2.0 navigation list. Navigation list contains all the headings of the document. The navigation list shows only selected part of the list at the time. List items are also links, which refer to the heading in question in the document. Source code of the navigation list with few entries is shown below.

Source code of the navigation list

```
<nl>
  <label>Table of Contents</label>
  <li  href="#Introduction">
    <nl>
    <label href="#Introduction">Introduction</label>
    <li href="#WhatisX-Smiles?">What is X-Smiles?</li>
    <li href="#MainFeatures">Main Features</li>
    <li href="#ThisDocument">This Document</li>
    </nl>
  </li>
  <li  href="#Environment">
    <nl>
    <label href="#Environment">Environment</label>
```

```
    <li href="#RuntimeEnvironment">Runtime Environment</li>
    <li href="#Runningit">Running it</li>
    <li href="#BuildingwithAnt">Building with Ant</li>
    </nl>
  </li>
</nl>
```

The navigation menu could be styled like a regular pull-down menu as shown in Fig. 1, but due to limitations in the CSS layout in the current version of X-Smiles (0.82) that was not done. As discussed in Section 8, we are building a better CSS layout engine into the X-Smiles browser. The resulting document, viewed in the X-Smiles browser is shown in Fig. 7 (b). Part of the navigation list, whose source is shown above, is also visible.

7   Discussion

So far, the appearance of a new HTML version has not caused much headache for authors and user agent developers. Different HTML versions are backward compatible, which means that old documents do not need major revising. Even the transition to XHTML 1.0 is a straight forward process as it is basically a reformulation of HTML 4.01 in XML format. The new XHTML 2.0 specification will cause more problems, though. The biggest change is related to forms. The fifth Working Draft specifies that XForms will be used as the forms technology in XHTML 2.0.

XForms requires major changes especially in user agents. Old HTML form implementations cannot be used as a base for XForms, because the whole concept is different. XForms has a new data model and it contains more functionality than HTML forms. The new data model requires the use of XML Schema and XPath processors. Both of these are large components, which causes problems in restricted devices. W3C is aware of this problem, and thus it has defined the XForms Basic Candidate Recommendation. In XForms Basic, the data model is less advanced, requiring only support for certain data types, in effect removing the need for full XML Schema processor.

The transition to XHTML 2.0 causes also problems for authors. The main obstacle is that they have to learn a new forms language. Fortunately, they do not have to start from scratch. The reason is that XForms is based on XPath. Most XML developers use XSLT regularly. Since both XForms and XSLT are based on XPath, the developers already have a starting point. Another advantage is that XForms is declarative language. Current, HTML forms are heavily based on scripting, which makes updating and reusing of forms difficult. XForms is easier to maintain and it allows the reuse of forms in different XHTML documents.

Another major change in XHTML 2.0 is the real separation of content and presentation. XHTML 2.0 removes all the presentation related features from XHTML 1.0 and concentrates only on defining the structure of the document. All presentation related issues are defined using separate CSS style sheets. In addition, several XHTML 2.0 elements and attributes contain functionality, which before had to be realized using scripting. Therefore, authors do not have to use scripting as much as before and also their documents will be more widely accepted by the different user agents. Both of these features improve the maintenance of XHTML 2.0 documents.

Based on the above facts, our conclusion is that XHTML 2.0 is a major step in the development of web technology. The new features require major changes in user agents, though. In addition, the authors have to learn how to use the new features. In our opinion, the advantages brought by XHTML 2.0 outweigh the problems. For instance, XHTML 2.0 removes the need for heavy scripting and separates the content from presentation. Therefore, XHTML 2.0 documents are easier to maintain and reuse.

8   Conclusions

In this paper, we have discussed the new XHTML 2.0 specification and its user agent implementation. According to the previous section, the XHTML 2.0 documents are easier to maintain and reuse, because they require less scripting and the content is really separated from the presentation. The introduction of XHTML 2.0 requires major changes in user agents, though.

Our XHTML 2.0 implementation is part of the X-Smiles user agent. The implementation is modular and mainly based on already existing components. No changes had to be made to the parsing and processing of XML documents. The XHTML module uses the well established DOM interface to access the XML data. The DOM documents are rendered using Java Swing document model. The XHTML 2.0 documents can be styled by CSS style sheet and they can contain XForms elements. We reused an already existing CSS processor.

Unfortunately, we could not implement all XForms specific CSS features. Currently, we are removing the Swing dependency form the CSS layout engine. In future, we plan to use the new CSS layout engine with the XHTML 2.0 and XForms components. Then, we expect to be able to implement all XForms specific features. For instance, at the time of writing we have already implemented all the XForms pseudo-elements in the new version of the layout engine.

The results of this paper show that implementation of XHTML 2.0 requires further development of user agents, but is not unrealistic. User agents, which already support XHTML 1.0 can be updated to support XHTML 2.0. Already existing components can be used in most cases. Generally, changes below the DOM interface are not required, albeit XForms requires DOM Level 3 support. Also, existing XML Schema and XPath engines can be used. Some changes to the CSS layout model can be expected, though. In some cases, the XForms module is the only new component.

In our future work, we plan to study the use of XHTML 2.0 in restricted devices. The main research question is how all the components required by XHTML 2.0 can be fitted in to a restricted devices with less memory and processing power than desktop devices. Most problems are related to XForms. At the moment, it remains to be seen whether XForms Basic will help in this problem.

Acknowledgments. The author Mikko Honkala would like to thank to Nokia Oyj Foundation for providing support during the research. The research was funded by the XML Devices and GO-MM projects to whose partners the authors would like to express their gratitude.

References

1. Ragget, D. et al., "HTML 4.01 Specification," *W3C Recommendation*, December 1999. Available at http://www.w3.org/TR/html401/
2. Bray, T. et al., "Extensible Markup Language (XML) 1.0," *W3C Recommendation*, February 2004. Available at http://www.w3.org/TR/2004/REC-xml-20040204/
3. Axelsson, J. et al., "XHTML 2.0," *W3C Working Draft*, May 2003. Available at http://www.w3.org/TR/xhtml2/
4. ECMA-262, ECMAScript language specification, European Computer Manufacturers Association (ECMA), 1998.
5. Boyer, J., and Honkala, M., "The XForms Computation Engine: Rationale, Theory and Implementation Experience," in *Proc. of the 6th IASTED International Conference, Internet and Multimedia Systems, and Applications*, (IMSA 2002), August 12-14, 2002, Kauai, Hawaii, USA.
6. Dubinko, M. et al., "XForms 1.0," *W3C Recommendation*, October 2003. Available at http://www.w3.org/TR/2003/REC-xforms-20031014/
7. Pilgrim, M. The Vanishing Image: XHTML 2 Migration Issues," O'Reilly xml.com, July 02, 2003. Available at: http://www.xml.com/pub/a/2003/07/02/dive.html
8. McCarron, S. et al., "XML Events," *W3C Recommendation*, October 2003. Available at http://www.w3.org/TR/xml-events/
9. Marsh, J., "XML Base," *W3C Recommendation*, June 2001. Available at http://www.w3.org/TR/xmlbase/
10. Altheim, M. et al., "Modularization of XHTML," *W3C Recommendation*, April 2001. Available at http://www.w3.org/TR/xhtml-modularization/
11. Kendall, G.C., "XHTML 2.0: The Latest Trick," O'Reilly xml.com, August 07, 2002. Available at: http://www.xml.com/pub/a/2002/08/07/deviant.html
12. Honkala, M., and Vuorimaa, P., "Advanced UI features in XForms," in *Proc. of the 8th International Conference on Distributed Multimedia Systems*, September 25 - 28, 2002, pp. 715-722.
13. Vierinen, J., Pihkala, K., and Vuorimaa,P., "XML based prototypes for future mobile services," in *Proc. 6th World Multiconf. Systemics, Cybernetics and Informatics*, SCI 2002, pp. 135-140.
14. Pihkala, K., Honkala, M., and Vuorimaa, P., "A Browser Framework for Hybrid XML Documents," in *Proc. of the 6th IASTED International Conference, Internet and Multimedia Systems, and Applications*, (IMSA 2002), August 12-14, 2002, Kauai, Hawaii, USA, pp. 164-169.
15. Cogliati, A. et al., "XHTML and CSS Components in an XML Browser," in *Proc. of the 4th International Conference on Internet Computing*, IC 03, Las Vegas, USA, June 2003, pp. 563-569.
16. Pohja, M. and Vuorimaa, P., "Dynamic XHTML Layout Document for an XML Browser," in *Proc. of the 2nd IASTED International Conference on Communications, Internet, and Information Technology*, CIIT 2003, Scottsdale, AZ, USA, November 2003, pp. 355-360.

Semantic Matching of Natural Language Web Queries

Naouel Karam[1], Salima Benbernou[2], Mohand-Said Hacid[2], and
Michel Schneider[1]

[1] LIMOS (Laboratoire d'Informatique, de Modélisation et d'Optimisation des
Systèmes)
Université Blaise Pascal Clermont2,
Complexe Scientifique des Cézeaux 63177 Aubière, France
{karam, schneider}@isima.fr
[2] UFR Informatique
Université Claude Bernard Lyon1,
43 bd du 11 novembre 69100 Villeurbanne, France
{salima.benbernou, mshacid}@bat710.univ-lyon1.fr

Abstract. In this paper, we propose a method to automatically rank
documents returned by a search engine in the WWW with respect to a
query. The process consists in three steps, the first translates the query
and document descriptions into description logic terminologies. The
second computes a mapping between related elements in the query and
each document. This mapping matches concepts in the terminologies
based on their names and their definitions. The last step computes
the difference between the query (represented as a terminology) and
each document (also represented as a terminology) and ranks the
documents according this difference. To deal with linguistic information
when comparing description logic concepts, we propose a definition of
subsumption that takes into account names similarity between concepts
occurring in the descriptions being compared. We describe each step of
the method and show the intended results on a running example.

1 Introduction

This paper deals with the problem of ranking documents returned by a search
engine in the WWW. The ranking function involves a semantic comparison between the client query and the documents content. The document that best
matches the query is returned first. To perform this ranking we need:

- A formal description of the query and the documents content: the query and
  the documents are specified in natural language (NL), a formal description
  of their semantics is needed to achieve an automatic comparison.
- A matching algorithm that compares a query description and a document
  description and returns a set of matching elements between the query and
  the document.
- A ranking function that sorts the documents with respect to the size of the
  part of the query that is not covered by the documents.

N. Koch, P. Fraternali, and M. Wirsing (Eds.): ICWE 2004, LNCS 3140, pp. 416–429, 2004.
© Springer-Verlag Berlin Heidelberg 2004

The Proposed Approach

We propose to use description logics (DLs) [2] as a formal representation language for specifying documents and queries. The motivations are twofold: DLs come with well-defined semantics and correct inference algorithms and the formalization of a text in DLs has already been studied, see [8] for details about how we extract a terminology from a natural language document. As already stated in [14], not all aspects of a natural language can be captured by a formal description, we will restrict ourselves to a small fragment of NL that can be represented in DLs.

The matching step consists in comparing the two terminologies obtained from a query and a document. Given two terminologies $\mathcal{T}_Q$ and $\mathcal{T}_D$ describing a query Q and a document D respectively, our goal is to find the elements in $\mathcal{T}_Q$ and $\mathcal{T}_D$ that match. This is done by a *matching* function that takes two terminologies as input and produces a one to one *mapping* between defined concepts of the two terminologies that correspond semantically to each other.

Finally, the documents are ranked according to the size of the extra information contained in the query and not in the documents. The extra information is calculated with the help of the difference operation between pairs of mapped elements. We propose an algorithm that computes the difference between $\mathcal{ALE}$-concept descriptions. It is based on the work reported in [10], by taking into account linguistic relations (synonymy, hypernymy...) between concept names occurring in the two descriptions.

The paper is organized as follows. Section 2 presents the motivation behind this work. Section 3 gives a brief overview of description logics and the difference operator. We define the matching and the ranking problems in sections 4 and 5 respectively. We conclude in section 6.

2 Motivation

All major search engines available on the web rank web pages by determining relevancy through analyzing keyword location, frequency and through other methods, for example, by analyzing how pages link to each other. Non relevant pages appear frequently in the resulted rank and it may take time for the user finding out the intended information among this huge number of pages.

Our goal is to allow the user to describe his requirements by specifying a detailed description so that we can compare it semantically to the content of web pages. The most relevant page compared to the query needs comes first.

The proposed algorithm detects the parts of the documents that are semantically related to some parts of the query and then deduces the non covered part in the query. The most relevant match will be the one with the smallest non covered part.

Let us illustrate the practical interest of our method with an example.

Example 1. Consider the three simple NL texts depicted in Figure 1. The query Q describes the rooms of a hotel, D_1 and D_2 are documents returned by a research engine.

Q	All the rooms are comfortable and air conditioned. Each room is provided with a TV and a large bed. The hotel is located in Paris.
D_1	Located in the french capital, the hotel is convivial. Each bedroom is air conditioned and provided with a cable television. The breakfast is served in an elegant lounge.
D_2	The hotel is located in Paris. All our homelike rooms are provided with a queen size bed, a color TV and a private bathroom. The hotel accepts only credit card guarantee.

Fig. 1. Simple NL texts

By reading the documents, a user can see that the second document matches better the query needs than the first one. To do this, we need to be able to detect the related parts between the query and each document. The first document shares with the query the same information about hotel location, air conditioning and the existence of a television. For the second document, the common information concerns hotel location, comfort of the rooms and the existence of a television and a large bed.

This discovery is challenging because different words can be used to express the same semantic information. This can be done by synonyms (e.g. *comfortable* vs *homelike*, *french capital* vs *Paris*) or hypernyms (e.g. *bedroom* vs *room*, *cable television* vs *TV*).

Once this matching performed, the extra information contained in the query and not in the document can be computed easily. It is clear that the document that better meets the user needs is the one with the minimal extra information.

3   Preliminaries

In this section, we introduce description logics, the formalism used in our framework, the difference operator and the notion of size of a description.

3.1   Description Logics

Description logics (DLs, also called terminological logics) are a family of knowledge representation formalisms designed for representing and reasoning about terminological knowledge. In DLs, the conceptual knowledge of an application domain is represented in terms of *concepts* (unary predicates) that are interpreted as sets of individuals, and *roles* (binary predicates) that are interpreted as binary relations between individuals.

Starting with the set N_C of concept names and the set N_R of role names, complex concept descriptions are built inductively using concept constructors. The different description logic languages distinguish themselves by the kind of constructs they allow. In our framework we are going to use the $\mathcal{ALE}$ description logic. In this description logic, concept descriptions are formed according to the syntax rules depicted Figure 2. $A \in N_C$ denotes a concept name, $r \in N_R$ a role name, and C, D (complex) concept descriptions.

$$
\begin{array}{ll}
C, D \rightarrow \top \mid & \text{(top-concept)} \\
\bot \mid & \text{(bottom-concept)} \\
A \mid & \text{(concept name)} \\
\neg A \mid & \text{(primitive negation)} \\
C \sqcap D \mid & \text{(conjunction)} \\
\exists r.C \mid & \text{(existential restriction)} \\
\forall r.C \mid & \text{(value restriction)}
\end{array}
$$

Fig. 2. Syntax of some concept descriptions

Let $\mathcal{L}$ denotes some description logic, a concept built using the constructors of $\mathcal{L}$ is called an $\mathcal{L}$-concept.

The semantics of a concept description is defined by the notion of interpretation as given below.

Definition 1. *(Interpretation) An interpretation $\mathcal{I} = (\Delta^{\mathcal{I}}, .^{\mathcal{I}})$ consists of a non-empty set $\Delta^{\mathcal{I}}$, the domain of the interpretation, and an interpretation function $.^{\mathcal{I}}$ that maps each concept name $A \in N_C$ to a subset of $\Delta^{\mathcal{I}}$ and each role name $r \in N_R$ to a binary relation $r^{\mathcal{I}}$, subset of $\Delta^{\mathcal{I}} \times \Delta^{\mathcal{I}}$. The interpretation function can be extended to arbitrary concept descriptions as shown in Figure 3.*

$$
\begin{array}{l}
\top^{\mathcal{I}} = \Delta^{\mathcal{I}} \\
\bot^{\mathcal{I}} = \emptyset \\
(\neg A)^{\mathcal{I}} = \Delta^{\mathcal{I}} \setminus A^{\mathcal{I}} \\
(C \sqcap D)^{\mathcal{I}} = C^{\mathcal{I}} \cap D^{\mathcal{I}} \\
(\exists r.C)^{\mathcal{I}} = \{x \in \Delta^{\mathcal{I}} \mid \exists y : (x, y) \in r^{\mathcal{I}} \wedge y \in C^{\mathcal{I}}\} \\
(\forall r.C)^{\mathcal{I}} = \{x \in \Delta^{\mathcal{I}} \mid \forall y : (x, y) \in r^{\mathcal{I}} \rightarrow y \in C^{\mathcal{I}}\}
\end{array}
$$

Fig. 3. Semantics of concept descriptions

DL systems provide various reasoning services, the most important is the computation of the subsumption relation.

Definition 2. *(Subsumption) Let C, D be concept names, D subsumes C (noted $C \sqsubseteq D$) iff $C^I \subseteq D^I$ for all interpretation $\mathcal{I}$.*

Concept descriptions are used to specify terminologies that define the intentional knowledge of an application domain.

Definition 3. *(Terminology) Let A be a concept name and C a concept definition. Then $A \doteq C$ and $A \sqsubseteq C$ are terminological axioms. The first is a complete definition, the second an incomplete one. A terminology $\mathcal{T}$ is a finite set of terminological axioms such that no concept name appears more than once in the left-hand side of a definition. If a concept A occurs in the left-hand side of a definition, it is called* defined *concept. The other concepts are called* primitive *concepts.*

A terminology built using the constructors of some description logic $\mathcal{L}$ is called an $\mathcal{L}$-terminology.

An interpretation $\mathcal{I}$ is a model of a terminology $\mathcal{T}$ if it satisfies all the statements contained in $\mathcal{T}$:

- $A^{\mathcal{I}} = C^{\mathcal{I}}$ for all terminological axioms $A \doteq C$ in $\mathcal{T}$,
- $A^{\mathcal{I}} \subseteq C^{\mathcal{I}}$ for all terminological axioms $A \sqsubseteq C$ in $\mathcal{T}$.

In our work, natural language documents are represented by a DL terminology, NL statements are transformed into terminological axioms.

Example 2. The NL texts of example 1 are represented by the $\mathcal{ALE}$-terminologies $\mathcal{T}_Q$, $\mathcal{T}_{D_1}$ and $\mathcal{T}_{D_2}$ given in Figure 4.

$\mathcal{T}_Q$	Room $\doteq$ Comfortable $\sqcap$ Air-conditioned $\sqcap$ $\exists$provided-with.TV $\sqcap$ $\exists$provided-with.(Bed $\sqcap$ $\exists$has-size.Large) $\sqcap$ $\overline{\text{Room}_Q}$
	Hotel $\doteq$ $\exists$located-in.Paris $\sqcap$ $\overline{\text{Hotel}_Q}$
$\mathcal{T}_{D_1}$	Hotel $\doteq$ $\exists$located-in.French-capital $\sqcap$ Convivial $\sqcap$ $\overline{\text{Hotel}_{D_1}}$
	Bedroom $\doteq$ Air-conditioned $\sqcap$ $\exists$provided-with.Cable-television $\sqcap$ $\overline{\text{Bedroom}_{D_1}}$
	Breakfast $\doteq$ $\exists$served-in.(Elegant $\sqcap$ Lounge) $\sqcap$ $\overline{\text{Breakfast}_{D_1}}$
$\mathcal{T}_{D_2}$	Hotel $\doteq$ $\exists$located-in.Paris $\sqcap$ $\forall$accept.Credit-card-guarantee $\sqcap$ $\overline{\text{Hotel}_{D_2}}$
	Room $\doteq$ Homelike $\sqcap$ $\exists$provided-with.(Bed $\sqcap$ $\exists$has-size.Queen-size) $\sqcap$ $\exists$provided-with.Color-TV$\sqcap\exists$provided-with.(Bathroom$\sqcap$Private)$\sqcap$ $\overline{\text{Room}_{D_2}}$ $\sqcap$

Fig. 4. Examples of terminologies

The overlined concepts stand for the missing part of the definitions, we will ignore these concepts in the rest of the paper.

3.2 The Difference Operator

Informally speaking, the difference between two concept descriptions is the information contained in the first description and not in the second. The difference operator allows to remove from a given description all the information contained in another description. The difference operation between two concept descriptions was first introduced by Teege [15]. The difference between two concept descriptions C and D with $C \sqsubseteq D$ is given by

$$C - D := max\{E \mid E \sqcap D \equiv C\}$$

where max is defined with respect to subsumption.

[10] proposed a refinement of this definition by allowing the difference between incomparable descriptions (i.e. D is not required to subsume C) and taking the syntactic minimum (w.r.t a subdescription ordering $\preceq_d$) instead of a semantic maximum. The difference between two incomparable concept descriptions C and D is defined as

$$C - D := min\{E \mid E \sqcap D \equiv C \sqcap D\}$$

where *min* is defined with respect to a subdescription ordering.

This definition has two advantages, it does not contain redundancies and it is more readable by a human user. However, Tegee's difference captures the real semantic difference between two concept descriptions.

We use the second definition because it is defined for the DL $\mathcal{ALE}$ that allows us to represent a considerable number of NL semantics.

3.3   Size of a Concept Description

We define the size $|C|$ of an $\mathcal{ALE}$-concept description C as the number of conjuncts occurring on the top-level of C.

Example 3. The sizes of the concepts *Room* and *Hotel* of $\mathcal{T}_Q$ in Example 2 are 5 and 2 respectively.

4   The Matching Algorithm

In this section we introduce the matching operation. *Match* is an operation that takes a query description and a document description and returns a *mapping* that identifies corresponding elements in the two descriptions. This *mapping* consists of a set of mapping elements indicating that certain elements of the query Q are related to certain elements of the document D. By elements, we mean the defined concepts in the terminologies $\mathcal{T}_Q$ and $\mathcal{T}_D$. A concept A_i from $\mathcal{T}_Q$ is related to a concept B_i from $\mathcal{T}_D$ if their names and their definitions are similar.

In [11], a schema matching algorithm called Cupid was proposed. A schema consists of a set of related elements such as database or XML elements. The result of the match operation is a mapping indicating that certain elements of the first schema are related to certain elements of the second. Similarity coefficients are computed between elements of two schemas in two phases, a linguistic and a structural one. Then a mapping is deduced from those coefficients.

Following Cupid intuitions, we build an algorithm for matching a query description and a document description. First, it proceeds by computing similarity coefficients between defined concepts in the two terminologies and then deduces a mapping from those coefficients. The coefficients in the range [0,1] are calculated in two steps:

- **Step 1.** Matching of names : it is based on the notion of semantic relatedness introduced in [7] that measures the extent to which two lexicalized concepts are close. This measure is based on the semantic relations of Wordnet [6]. We will call the result the *name similarity coefficient (nsim)*.
- **Step 2.** Matching of description. it consists in comparing the concept descriptions occurring in the two terminologies. This phase uses name similarities between concepts appearing in the concept descriptions. We will call the result the *description similarity coefficient (dsim)*.

The weighted similarity ($wsim$) is a mean of $nsim$ and $dsim$, it is calculated as follows: $wsim = w \times nsim + (1 - w) \times dsim$, where w is a constant in the range [0,1]. We compute weighted similarity coefficients between defined concepts in the terminologies. A mapping ρ is deduced from those coefficients by choosing pairs of elements with maximal weighted similarity.

In the next two subsections, we detail name matching and description matching steps.

4.1   Name Matching

The first step of the matching is based on defined concept names. We need to determine the degree of semantic similarity between two concept names. We reuse the notion of semantic relatedness between two lexically expressed concepts [7]. This measure uses WordNet [6] as knowledge source. The idea behind this measure is that two concepts are close if the path relating them in WordNet is not long and does not change direction too often. We recall the definition of semantic relatedness and define the name similarity coefficient. It is expressed as function of the semantic relatedness since we require it to be in the range [0,1].

Definition 4. *(Semantic relatedness)[7] The semantic relatedness of two concept names c_1 and c_2 is given by:*

$$rel(c_1, c_2) = C - PathLength(c_1, c_2) - k * NumberOfChangesOfDirection(c_1, c_2),$$

where C and k are constants and PathLength denotes the length of the shortest path between two concepts. If no such path exists, $rel(c_1, c_2)$ is zero.

Definition 5. *(Name similarity coefficient) The name similarity of two concept names P_1, $P_2 \in N_C$ is given by:*

$$nsim(P_1, P_2) = \frac{rel(P_1, P_2)}{C}.$$

where C is the same constant used in the definition of the semantic relatedness.

4.2   Description Matching

The intuition behind the description matching is that two concept descriptions are similar if their difference is minimal. We estimate the description similarity coefficient as a function of the size of the difference between the two descriptions.

Definition 6. *(Description similarity coefficient) The description similarity between two concept descriptions C and D is given by:*

$$dsim(C, D) = 1 - \frac{|C - D|}{|C|}$$

The algorithm proposed in [10] that performs the difference between two $\mathcal{ALE}$-concept descriptions is based on the subsumption test. We propose a new definition of the subsumption, that takes into account linguistic information about concepts occurring in the descriptions being compared. It is denoted by $\sqsubseteq_S$. In order to exploit the graph-based subsumption reasoning, we are going to represent the concepts occurring in the terminologies as trees.

We know that a tree-based characterization of subsumption was stated in [1]. It works in three steps. First, concept descriptions are turned into normal forms, that makes the knowledge implicitly contained in a concept description explicit. Second, these normal forms are translated into description trees. Then subsumption is characterized in terms of graph homomorphism between the description trees.

We first recall the definition of normal forms and description trees, then we propose a definition of homomorphism taking into account name equivalence between concept names occurring in the descriptions.

Definition 7. *($\mathcal{ALE}$-normalization rules) Let C, D be two $\mathcal{ALE}$-concept descriptions and $r \in N_R$ a primitive role. The $\mathcal{ALE}$-normalization rules are defined as follows*

$$\forall r.C \sqcap \forall r.D \rightarrow \forall r.(C \sqcap D)$$
$$\forall r.C \sqcap \exists r.D \rightarrow \forall r.C \sqcap \exists r.(C \sqcap D)$$
$$\forall r.\top \rightarrow \top$$
$$C \sqcap \top \rightarrow C$$
$$P \sqcap \neg P \rightarrow \bot, \text{for each } P \in N_C$$
$$\exists r.\bot \rightarrow \bot$$
$$C \sqcap \bot \rightarrow \bot$$

If only the rule $\forall r.\top \rightarrow \top$ is applied to a concept description C, the resulting concept is called in $\top$-normal form and the corresponding description tree is noted $\mathcal{G}_C^\top$.

Definition 8. *($\mathcal{ALE}$-description trees) An $\mathcal{ALE}$-description tree is a tree of the form $\mathcal{G} = (N, E, n_0, \ell)$ where*

- N *is a finite set of nodes of $\mathcal{G}$;*
- $E \subseteq N \times (N_R \cup \forall N_R) \times N$ *is a finite set of edges labeled with role names r ($\exists$-edges) or with $\forall r$ ($\forall$-edges); $\forall N_R := \{\forall r \mid r \in N_R\}$;*
- n_0 *is the root of $\mathcal{G}$;*
- ℓ *is a labeling function mapping the nodes in N to finite sets $\{P_1, ..., P_k\}$ where each P_i, $1 \le i \le k$, is one of the following forms: $P_i \in N_C$, $P_i = \neg P$ for some $P \in N_C$, or $P_i = \bot$. The empty label corresponds to the top-concept.*

For $n, m \in N$ and $r \in N_R$, an $\exists$-edge from n to m labeled r is written as nrm, and a $\forall$-edge as $n\forall rm$.

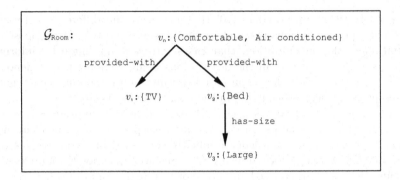

Fig. 5. an $\mathcal{ALE}$-description tree

Every $\mathcal{ALE}$-concept description C can be turned into an $\mathcal{ALE}$-description tree $\mathcal{G}_C$ (see [1] for a formal definition of this translation).

Example 4. The $\mathcal{ALE}$-concept description

$$\text{Room} \doteq \text{Comfortable} \sqcap \text{Air-conditioned} \sqcap \exists\text{provided-with.TV} \sqcap$$
$$\exists\text{provided-with.(Bed} \sqcap \exists\text{has-size.Large)}$$

yields the tree $\mathcal{G}_{Room}$ of Figure 5.

Definition 9. *(Name equivalence) Let P_1 and P_2 be two concept names in N_C, P_1 and P_2 are said to be equivalent, written $P_1 \equiv P_2$, if $nsim(P_1, P_2)$ exceeds a certain threshold th_{sim}.*

Given a set $\mathcal{S}$ of name equivalences between concept names and two $\mathcal{ALE}$-description trees, we define the notion of homomorphism between description trees w.r.t a name equivalence set as follows.

Definition 10. *(Homomorphism on description trees w.r.t a name equivalence set) A mapping $\varphi : N_H \rightarrow N_G$ from an $\mathcal{ALE}$-description tree $\mathcal{H} = (N_H, E_H, m_0, \ell_H)$ to an $\mathcal{ALE}$-description tree $\mathcal{G} = (N_G, E_G, n_0, \ell_G)$ is called homomorphism w.r.t a name equivalence set $\mathcal{S}$, if and only if the following conditions are satisfied:*

1. *$\varphi(m_0) = n_0$;*
2. *for all $n \in N_H$ we have, $\forall P_i \in \ell_H(n), \exists P_j \in \ell_G(\varphi(n))$ such that $P_i \equiv P_j$ is in $\mathcal{S}$ or $\perp \in \ell_G(\varphi(n))$);*
3. *for all $nrm \in E_H$, either $\varphi(n)r\varphi(m) \in E_G$, or $\varphi(n) = \varphi(m)$ and $\perp \in \ell_G(\varphi(n))$; and*
4. *for all $n\forall rm \in E_H$, either $\varphi(n)\forall r\varphi(m) \in E_G$, or $\varphi(n) = \varphi(m)$ and $\perp \in \ell_G(\varphi(n))$.*

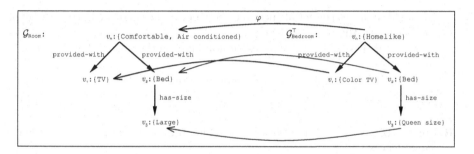

Fig. 6. Subsumption between $\mathcal{ALE}$-description trees

Theorem 1. *Let C, D be $\mathcal{ALE}$-concept descriptions. Then, $C \sqsubseteq_S D$ iff there exists a homomorphism w.r.t a name equivalence set S from $\mathcal{G}_D^\top$ to $\mathcal{G}_C$.*

Sketch of proof. The proof is based on the one given for the theorem 41 in [1]. The idea is to use at different stages of the proof the fact that if $P \equiv P'$ we have $x_0 \in P^I$ implies that $x_0 \in P'^I$ and vice versa.

Example 5. Let us illustrate Theorem 1 by two concept descriptions, namely Room and Bedroom

$$Room \doteq Comfortable \sqcap Air\text{-}conditioned \sqcap \exists provided\text{-}with.TV \sqcap$$
$$\exists provided\text{-}with.(Bed \sqcap \exists has\text{-}size.Large)$$
$$Bedroom \doteq Homelike \sqcap \exists provided\text{-}with.Color\ TV \sqcap \exists provided\text{-}with.(Bed \sqcap$$
$$\exists has\text{-}size.Queen\ size)$$

and the name equivalence set S

$$S = \{Comfortable \equiv Homelike,$$
$$TV \equiv Color\ TV,$$
$$Large \equiv Queen\ size\}$$

The descriptions are already in a normal form. A homomorphism from $\mathcal{G}_{Bedroom}$ to $\mathcal{G}_{Room}$ w.r.t S is depicted in Figure 6. From Theorem 1 we can conclude that $Room \sqsubseteq_S Bedroom$.

vvvvvvvv

Based on the algorithm proposed in [10] for computing the difference between $\mathcal{ALE}$-concept descriptions, we propose the algorithm diff$_{sim}$ depicted in Figure 7. Two changes have been made to the original algorithm. First, the definition of prim(C-D) has been changed since we are dealing with a name equivalence operator instead of equality of concept names. Second, the proposed subsumption over a set of name equivalence is used instead of the classical subsumption (line 6). The following notations are used:

- $prim(C)$ denotes the set of (negated) concept names and the bottom concept occurring on the top-level of C,
- $C.r = E$ if there exists a value restriction $\forall r.E$ on the top-level of C; $C.r = \top$ otherwise,
- $\exists r.C' \in C$ means that $\exists r.C'$ occurs on the top-level of C.

Require: $\mathcal{ALE}$-concept descriptions C and D in $\mathcal{ALE}$-normal form, a set S of name equivalences.

Ensure: $\text{diff}_{sim}(C, D)$

1: **if** $C \sqcap D \equiv \bot$ **then**
2:     $\text{diff}_{sim}(C, D) := \bot$
3: **else**
4:     $\text{diff}_{sim}(C, D) := \sqcap_{A \in prim(C-D)} A \sqcap \forall r.\text{diff}_{sim}(C.r, D.r) \sqcap \sqcap_{E \in \mathcal{E}'_r} \exists r.E$
      where $prim(C - D) := \{P \in prim(C) \mid$ there does not exist $P' \in prim(D)$ with $P \equiv P' \in S\}$ and the value restriction is omitted in case $\text{diff}_{sim}(C.r, D.r) \equiv \bot$ and $\mathcal{E}'_r$ is computed as follows:
      Let $\exists r.C_1, ..., \exists r.C_n \in C, \exists r.D_1, ..., \exists r.D_m \in D$ be all the existential restrictions in the top level of C and D, respectively, $\mathcal{E}_r = \{C_1, ..., C_n\}$.
5:     **for** $i = 1$ to n **do**
6:       **if** (i) there exists $j \in \{1, ..., n\}, j \neq i$, with $D.r \sqcap C.r \sqcap C_j \sqsubseteq_S C_i$, or
         (ii) there exists $j \in \{1, ..., m\}$, with $D.r \sqcap C.r \sqcap D_j \sqsubseteq_S C_i$, **then**
7:         $\mathcal{E}_r := \mathcal{E}_r \backslash \{C_i\}$
8:       **end if**
9:     **end for**
10:    $\mathcal{E}'_r = \{E^* \mid E \in \mathcal{E}_r\}$ where $E^* := \text{diff}_{sim}(E, C.r \sqcap D.r)$.
11: **end if**

Fig. 7. The algorithm diff_{sim}

Example 6. Computing the difference between the concept descriptions of Example 5 yields

$$\text{Room} - \text{Bedroom} = \text{Air-conditioned}$$

4.3 Mapping Generation

The set of mapping elements is deduced from the computed name and description similarities. Let $\mathcal{T}_Q = \{Q_i \doteq C_i, i \in [1, n]\}$ and $\mathcal{T}_D = \{D_j \doteq C_j, j \in [1, m]\}$ be two $\mathcal{ALE}$-terminologies describing a query Q and a document D respectively. A mapping ρ from $\mathcal{T}_Q$ to $\mathcal{T}_D$ is computed as follows:

- $\rho(Q_i) = D_j, 1 \leq i \leq n, 1 \leq j \leq m$, if $wsim(Q_i, D_j) \geq th_{map}$ and $wsim(Q_i, D_j) > wsim(Q_i, D_k)$ for all $D_k \in \mathcal{T}_D, k \neq j$,
- $\rho(Q_i) = \top$, if there is no $D_j, 1 \leq j \leq m$, with $wsim(Q_i, D_j) \geq th_{map}$.

Example 7. Let us illustrate the matching step on the terminologies $\mathcal{T}_Q$ and $\mathcal{T}_{D_1}$ of Example 2. The set of computed mappings is depicted in Table 1. The name similarity coefficients $nsim$ are computed with $C = 8$ and $k = 1$. The chosen thresholds th_{sim} and th_{map} are 0.75 and 0.5 respectively. For $wsim$, we take $w = 0.5$.

Table 1. The mapping generated from $\mathcal{T}_Q$ and $\mathcal{T}_{D_1}$

ρ	$nsim$	$dsim$	$wsim$
Room $\rightarrow$ Bedroom	0.87	0.5	0.68
Hotel $\rightarrow$ Hotel	1	1	1

5   The Ranking Problem

In this section we show how the mapping generated by the matching algorithm is used to compute the difference between a query terminology and a document terminology. Then we show how documents are ranked with respect to this difference.

Let $\mathcal{T}_Q = \{Q_i \doteq C_i, i \in [1, n]\}$ and $\mathcal{T}_D = \{D_j \doteq C_j, j \in [1, m]\}$ be two $\mathcal{ALE}$-terminologies describing a query Q and a document D respectively. The difference between the two terminologies is defined as follows:

Definition 11. *(Difference between terminologies) Given the mapping ρ resulting from the matching between $\mathcal{T}_Q$ and $\mathcal{T}_D$. The difference between the terminologies $\mathcal{T}_Q$ and $\mathcal{T}_D$ is the conjunction of the differences between each related pair of concepts in the two terminologies.*

$$diff_\rho(\mathcal{T}_Q, \mathcal{T}_D) = \sqcap_{Q_i \in \mathcal{T}_Q}(Q_i - \rho(Q_i))$$

With the notion of size of a description, we define the dissimilarity coefficient between two terminologies.

Definition 12. *(Dissimilarity coefficient) The dissimilarity coefficient between the terminologies $\mathcal{T}_Q$ and $\mathcal{T}_D$ is the size of their difference*

$$d(\mathcal{T}_Q, \mathcal{T}_D) = |diff_\rho(\mathcal{T}_Q, \mathcal{T}_D)|$$

Documents are ranked with respect to the dissimilarity coefficients between their descriptions and the query description. The more a document covers the query, the best is its rank.

Example 8. Let us now illustrate the ranking process on the terminologies $\mathcal{T}_Q$, $\mathcal{T}_{D_1}$ and $\mathcal{T}_{D_2}$ of Example 2. The differences between the terminologies are the following

$$diff_\rho(\mathcal{T}_Q, \mathcal{T}_{D_1}) = \text{Comfortable} \sqcap \exists\text{provided-with.}(\text{Bed} \sqcap \exists\text{has-size.Large})$$
$$diff_\rho(\mathcal{T}_Q, \mathcal{T}_{D_2}) = \text{Air conditioned}$$

We can deduce that the second document matches better the query than the first since its difference is the smallest one. Hence, we have the intended result described in Section 2.

6   Discussion

Nowadays, search engines sort their results according to number of criteria going from the number, proximity and location of terms matched, to pages related factors such as the number of links made to a page or the number of times a page is accessed from a results list. The ranking algorithms used by the search engines are not published and we know only a little about their ranking criteria [9]. The novelty of the approach proposed in this paper is that it allows the user to express his query as a natural language description. The criteria used when sorting the retrieved documents is their semantic relevancy w.r.t the query needs.

In the semantic web framework, an approach of ranking query results is proposed in the SEAL semantic portal [13]. Query results are reinterpreted as F-Logic knowledge bases. The semantic ranking is reduced to the comparison of two knowledge bases. A similarity is computed between the query and the knowledge bases, it serves as a basis for the semantic ranking. Their notion of similarity between two terminologies is reduced to the similarity between concept pairs.

Number of similarity measures for ontological structures were proposed in different domains like databases, artificial intelligence and semantic web [12,3, 5]. The work in [12] extends the comparison to semantic structures (set of super and sub-concepts of a concept) and relations between the concepts.

Our approach in matching terminologies is more complete since it operates in semantic descriptions expressed in description logics rather than structures. In addition, it involves both name and complex description matching.

Our name similarity measure is based on Wordnet. Different measures between lexicalized concepts in the Wordnet hierarchy have been proposed (see [4] for a survey). We choose to use the measure proposed by Hirst and St-Onge [7] because it uses all relations in Wordnet, the other measures are based only on hyponymy.

The constant and threshold values proposed in example 7 for computing the mapping between two terminologies are the typical values we have used in our experiments. Those values are subjective and depend on the intended results. For example, for additional restriction of the the mapping, th_{map} can be increased and allow only for synonyms and direct hypernyms in the set of equivalence names, th_{sim} have to be set to 0.87.

In real-life applications, often exact matching is not realistic. We will investigate in our future work an approximate matching of the query results.

References

1. F. Baader, R. Kusters, and R. Molitor. Computing Least Common Subsumers in Description Logics with Existential Restrictions. In T.Dean, editor, *Proceedings of the 16th International Joint Conference on Artificial Intelligence (IJCAI'99)*, pages 96–101. Morgan Kaufmann, 1999.
2. Franz Baader, Diego Calvanese, Deborah McGuinness, Daniele Nardi, and Peter F. Patel-Schneider, editors. *The Description Logic Handbook: Theory, Implementation and Applications*. Cambridge: University Press, 2003.
3. G. Bisson. Learning in FOL with a Similarity Measure. In *10th National Conference on Artificial Intelligence*. Morgan Kaufmann, 1992.
4. A. Budanitsky. Semantic Distance in WordNet: An Experimental, Application-oriented Evaluation of Five Measures, 2001.
5. A. Doan, J. Madhavan, P. Domingos, and A. Halevy. Learning to Map Between Ontologies on the Semantic Web, 2002.
6. C. Fellbaum. *WordNet An Electronic Lexical Database*. The MIT Press, 1998.
7. G. Hirst and D. St-Onge. Lexical Chains as Representation of Context for the Detection and Correction of Malapropisms. In C. Fellbaum, editor, *WordNet: An electronic lexical database and some of its applications. Cambrige, MA: The MIT Press*, 1998.
8. N. Karam and M. Schneider. Comparing Natural Language Documents: a DL Based Approach. In *International Workshop on Description Logics (DL2003)*, 2003.
9. M. Kobayashi and K. Takeda. Information Retrieval on the Web. *ACM Computing Surveys*, 32(2):144–173, 2000.
10. R. Kusters. *Non-Standard Inferences in Description Logics*, volume 2100 of Lecture Notes in Artificial Intelligence. Springer-Verlag, 2001.
11. J. Madhavan, P.A. Bernstein, and E. Rahm. Generic Schema Matching with Cupid. In *The VLDB Journal*, pages 49–58, 2001.
12. A. Maedche and S. Staab. Measuring Similarity between Ontologies. In *European Conference of Knowledge Acquisition and Management - EKAW2002*, Lecture Notes in Computer Science, Madrid, Spain, 2002. Springer.
13. A. Maedche, S. Staab, N. Stojanovic, R. Studer, and Y. Sure. SEAL – A Framework for Developing SEmantic Web PortALs. *Lecture Notes in Computer Science*, 2097, 2001.
14. R. A. Schmidt. Terminological Representation, Natural Language & Relation Algebra. In H. J. Ohlbach, editor, *Proceedings of the sixteenth German AI Conference (GWAI-92)*, volume 671 of *Lecture Notes in Artificial Intelligence*, pages 357–371, Berlin, 1993. Springer.
15. G. Teege. Making the Difference: A Subtraction Operation for Description Logics. In Jon Doyle, Erik Sandewall, and Pietro Torasso, editors, *KR'94: Principles of Knowledge Representation and Reasoning*, pages 540–550. Morgan Kaufmann, San Francisco, California, 1994.

From Relational Data to RDFS Models

Makym Korotkiy and Jan L. Top

Vrije Universiteit Amsterdam, Department of Computer Science, De Boelelaan 1081a,
1081 HV Amsterdam, The Netherlands
{maksym, jltop}@cs.vu.nl

Abstract. A vast amount of information resources is stored as relational-like data and inaccessible to RDFS-based systems. We describe FDR2 – an approach to integration of relational-like information resources with RDFS-aware systems. The proposed solution is purely RDFS-based. We use RDF/S as a mechanism to specify and perform linking of relational data to a predefined domain ontology. The approach is transformation-free, this ensures that all the data is accessible and usable in consistence with the original data model.

1 Introduction

The RDF and RDFS languages have been developed to express machine understandable semantics to facilitate more intelligent ways of information processing. RDF/S languages provide a unified syntax, data model, well-defined semantics and enable separation of data (RDF) from meta-data (RDFS). The formal acceptance of RDF/S by W3C [1] stimulates their utilization in many areas and by many organizations.

In spite of an increasing acceptance of RDF/S, this is still a new technology. Most information resources are not available in RDF/S-format. The relational data model, on the other hand, is widely accepted and currently supported by thousands of applications ranging from simple spreadsheets to complex relational databases.

Within this paper we use *relational data model* to refer to data presented as a collection of records usually depicted as a table. We would like to note that within the paper we differ between *relational data model* and *relational database model*. The latter extends the former by assuming that columns represent attributes, rows represent entities, and the table contains a set of attributes uniquely identifying each entity. We did not accept such assumptions because our experience indicated that very often the users organize data in an "intuitive" tabular way supported by spreadsheet applications but incompatible with these database-specific assumptions. This made us to focus on the less restricted *relational data model*.

Our application interest is to bring RDF/S technology to R&D companies and institutes as a part of what has been labelled as e-Science. The idea is that results of scientific experiments and computations as such should be shared within the (global) scientific community, in addition to communicating through

N. Koch, P. Fraternali, and M. Wirsing (Eds.): ICWE 2004, LNCS 3140, pp. 430–434, 2004.

traditional scientific publications. The latter do not contain sufficient details of the work done and the information presented by them cannot be machine processed.

Sharing is to be supported by an ontology-based information system. The primary goal of the system is to assist with the transition from traditional experimental science to e-Science facilitating large scale collaboration between scientists. Since we intend to bring benefits of ontologies into the e-Science environment, we have to find a way to link the relational data to an RDF/S model.

The main objective is to allow ontology-based querying of the relational data: the original relational data must be made available to an RDFS reasoner and become queryable with a vocabulary predefined in a domain ontology.

Our approach to the linking problem is explained in Sect. 2. Section 3 discusses the presented method and related research and Sect. 4 summarizes the results of this work.

2 *FDR2* Approach

We present our approach as a general procedure that can be modified and extended to fit particular needs. Let us assume that we have a set of data, expressed in a relational way (e.g., as a spreadsheet table where the first row is a header) and a domain ontology (DO) expressed in RDFS.

The general problem of linking relational and RDF/S models can be broken down into two subproblems:

1. Expressing relational data in an RDF/S format to enable syntactic and structural interoperability with DO.
2. Linking the newly created serialization to the RDFS representation of DO.

We approached the first subproblem by performing a two-step serialization of the relational data. On *Step 1* we automatically create a *relational schema* (RS) to express and preserve structure of the original data (*data representation level* on Fig. 1) and to provide a foundation for interoperability with DO (*pre-RDFS level* on Fig. 1). The data representation level contains notions common for all relational data sources (a header, rows, columns and cells). Concepts defined on the pre-RDFS level are shared between data sources with the same structure (table header). On *Step 2* we use RDF to express the actual content of the table according to the RS.

The second subproblem cannot be solved automatically due to the undefined semantics of the relational data. We leave it to the user to define the relationships between RS and DO (*Step 3*).

Our approach consists of three major steps. Additional actions (minor) are needed to exploit the RDF/S documents created during those steps to enable run-time interoperability (ontology-based querying).

Step 1: Build a relational schema to explicitly define the underlying relation. Since we cannot assume that every column represents an attribute and every row represents an entity, we have decided to build relational schemata upon a notion of class.

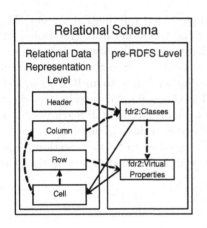

Fig. 1. The structure of the relational schema.

Every header cell represents a name of a class that is extensionally defined by the column cell values. An ordered set of all such classes C defines the underlying relationship R expressed within the table. RDFS models explicitly support binary relations only. Since any binary relation defined over a set A is a subset of $A x A$, where x denotes a Cartesian product, we have decided to use $C x C$ to obtain all binary *virtual relations (virtual properties)* defined over the classes presented in the relational schema.

After this step we have obtained the relational schema expressed in RDFS and containing a definition of all classes and all binary relationships between them. The resulting RS serves as a compact (intensional) representation of the data and can be directly connected to DO.

The structure of the relational schema is depicted on Fig. 1. Dashed arrows indicate transformation of simple concepts into more complex ones. For example, a collection of cells becomes a column which at the end is generalized into a class. Solid arrows explicitly indicate that classes and virtual properties enable access to the actual table data.

Step 2: Construct an RDF representation of the relational data. At this step we are dealing with the actual table content - the cell values. We consider every row as an instance of R, where every cell is represented as an instance of a class corresponding to its column. In addition, we instantiate all the *virtual relations* defined on the previous step.

This step provides us with instances representing table data and once hidden but now explicit relationships between cells of a row. At this point we have the advantage of being able to use general-purpose RDF/S repositories and querying engines but we still cannot employ the vocabulary defined in DO to access the relational data.

Step 3: Ask the user to link RS with the domain ontology. The user links concepts (classes and properties) from the relational schema to corresponding concepts in the domain ontology by identifying `rdfs:subClassOf` and `rdfs:subPropertyOf` relationships between corresponding classes and properties. A set of all such links constitutes an RDMap (Relational-RDFS Map). The RDMap directly links the relational schema to ontological definitions.

Having obtained the RDF/S serializations of the relational data and the RDMap, an RDFS reasoner will be able to deduct all necessary entailments to perform the actual linking of the relational schema and data with the concepts defined in DO. We will illustrate this with an example in the next subsection. The RDFS reasoner is required to merge the separate RDF/S documents and to generate the entailments.

To test the proposed technique and to provide basic support to the user we have developed **FDR2#Kit**[1] – a web-based toolkit consisting of a few utilities: **FDR2#Generator** takes a tab-delimited text file with tabular data and automatically generates RDF/S documents for the relational schema and relational data; **FDR2#Mapper** assists the user with linking the relational schema to DO; **FDR2#Tester** allows to run simple queries over the resulting combination of schema, data, RDMap and DO.

3   Discussion and Related Work

Over-generated *virtual relations* pose a serious performance problem. For example, a 10-column table will result in a RS with 90 *virtual relations* and quite significant portion of them may be redundant. Such a RS does not require a lot of resources to handle but a corresponding RDF-serialization of the table content will be polluted with irrelevant data. This problem can be handled by introducing a separate step between automatic generation of the RS and serialization of the table content. This stage is needed to enable the user to remove the redundant *virtual relations* from the original RS. Another option would be to swap steps 2 and 3 and to exploit a created RDMap to (semi)-automatically remove *virtual relations* not linked with DO. The modified RS will determine the final structure of the table content serialization preventing from polluting it with irrelevant data.

The relational schema facilitates analysis of the relational data on an abstract, intensional level. A possible practical applications of this is that an RDFS-based information system can keep track of known relational schemata and corresponding linking maps. This allows automating the whole process of handling complex input data. Since the RS is constructed automatically, it is quite likely that once created, the RDMap can be reused by many users who even do not know anything about the details of linking procedure and still able to take advantage of RDFS inference.

In [7] the authors describe a "naive" approach for mapping RDBMS schemata onto RDF (although we would rather call it RDBMS data mapping onto RDF). Our work takes it to the next level where we are focusing on linking relational and RDFS schemata. RDF serialization of actual data is quite straightforward and can be done in different ways according to application specific restrictions.

4   Conclusions

In this paper we have introduced **FDR2** – a technique that enables us to link relational and RDF/S data models. According to **FDR2** a relational schema

---

[1] http://www.cs.vu.nl/~maksym#tools

is automatically created to explicate the structure and internal relationships between elements of a relational collection of data. Explication of *virtual relations* allows the user to construct a relational schema specific RDMap by defining rdfs: [subClass|Property]Of relationships between concepts from the relational schema and a domain ontology. The actual relational data are automatically expressed in RDF according to the generated relational schema. Run-time integration is achieved by applying an RDFS reasoner to merge the above-mentioned components into a single RDFS model and to deduct necessary entailments. A resulting run-time model allows to access the relational data with queries termed according to the domain ontology. *FDR2* is purely RDF/S-based and does not require any additional software components except an RDFS reasoner.

References

1. W3C: Resource Description Framework (RDF). (http://www.w3.org/RDF/)
2. Omelayenko, B.: RDFT: A Mapping Meta-Ontology for Business Integration. In: Proceedings of the Workshop on Knowledge Transformation for the Semantic Web at the 15th European Conference on Artificial Intelligence (KTSW2002), Lyon, France (2002) 77–84
3. Bizer, C.: D2R MAP - Database to RDF Mapping Language and Processor. (http://www.wiwiss.fu-berlin.de/suhl/bizer/d2rmap/D2Rmap.htm)
4. aidministrator.nl: Sesame Project. (http://sesame.aidministrator.nl)
5. ICS-FORTH: The ICS-FORTH RDFSuite: High-level Scalable Tools for the Semantic Web. (http://139.91.183.30:9090/RDF/)
6. HP Labs Semantic Web Activity: Jena Semantic Web Toolkit. (http://www.hpl.hp.com/semweb/)
7. Beckett, D., Grant, J.: Semantic Web Scalability and Storage: Mapping Semantic Web Data with RDBMSes. SWAD-Europe deliverable, W3C (2003)

Automatic Interpretation of Natural Language for a Multimedia E-learning Tool

Serge Linckels and Christoph Meinel

Department for Theoretical Computer Science and New Applications, University of Trier
{linckels, meinel}@TI.uni-trier.de
http://www.informatik.uni-trier.de/~meinel

Abstract. This paper describes the new e-learning tool CHESt that allows students to search in a knowledge base for short (teaching) multimedia clips by using a semantic search engine. We explain the different steps to automatically describe the meaning of the clips with RDF (*Resource Description Framework*). The concept is based on graph theory and retrieval algorithms. Finally, we present rules how a human question can be transformed into a RDF query. Thus, the knowledge base and the query have the same format and can be compared.

1 Our Multimedia E-learning Tool

CHESt (*Computer History Expert System*) is the prototype of a new e-learning tool, see [7] for details. It focuses on three key features: the information is in a multimedia form, the content is split into small *clips* and a semantic search mechanism for information retrieval. We used *Tele-TASK* [1] [2] to record the lessons in order to create one well-structured multimedia stream. The result is a large number of *RealMedia* files that can be played with any compatible software, for example the free *RealOne Player* [5].

Essential in our concept is the length of the stored items in the knowledge base; the duration of the multimedia sequences. The younger the user, the shorter the time during which he/she will concentrate on the information displayed on the screen. Furthermore, it is easier to find the appropriate information inside a small piece of data than for example in an online lesson that lasts 90 minutes. Thus, we divided all our multimedia data into small *clips*. The duration of each clip varies from several seconds to 3 or 4 minutes. Each clip documents one subject or a part of a subject. Together, all the clips of the knowledge base cover one large topic; in our prototype we focus on computer history. We produced more than 300 clips about most important events in computer history. CHESt exists as standalone application (knowledge base and application software on one CD-ROM) and as online application. The later uses a streaming server to transmit the clips to the user's browser.

In this paper we present a retrieval mechanism where the user can enter a complete question. The tool "understands" that question and gives a small list of pertinent clips as answer, or better even just one clip.

N. Koch, P. Fraternali, and M. Wirsing (Eds.): ICWE 2004, LNCS 3140, pp. 435–439, 2004.

2   Describing the Meaning of the Clips

However, before the tool can even try to understand the user's question, it has to "know" what data are stored in the knowledge base. Therefore, we have to add metadata to each clip to describe its meaning. For this purpose we use the *Resource Description Framework* (RDF) [10]. In principle, this is done once, at the moment when the clip is added to the knowledge base. However, the computer can take on a part of this task.

We divided the CHESt knowledge base logically into two classes: clips that describe inventions (things) and clips that describe inventors (persons). Assertion: an invention was invented by one or more inventors. An invention and an inventor can be a *resource* (in our case: a clip) or a *literal* (just a textual information). Every resource is described with properties. An **inventor** has three properties (*predicates*): his name (vcard:FN), the year of his birth (chest:year_birth) and the year of his death (chest:year_death); if still alive, this property is left blank. As you see, we used the W3C recommendation v*Card* namespace property *full name* (FN) [9]. The class **invention** is divided into a number of subclasses to better organize the different resources (for example: Hardware, Software...). We used the *Dublin Core* (dc) namespace [3] to describe an invention with the following properties (*predicates*): its description (dc:title), its date of first appearance (dc:date) and its inventor (dc:creator). The complete CHESt RDF schema can be found at [6].

The next step is to search inside every clip for metadata. We applied an approved approach from the field of computer linguistics: create a dictionary of synonyms for every CHESt RDF element [4] [8]; in one column one will find the RDF elements and in the other column there is a list of natural language synonyms. For example, if we are scanning for dc:creator, we are searching for words like *creator*, *builder*, *constructor*, *inventor*, etc. The slides used to create the Tele-TASK clips are converted into pure text files. Then the *stemming process* can begin. All non-words and words with just one letter were eliminated from the generated text files because they have no semantic influence. All words are converted into lowercase and separation characters {, - . ? ! ( ) + * / & @} are replaced by a space. Then, a tree is built from those words, where every node represents one letter (see figure 1). This technique also allows to eliminate all double words. Each node contains the number of words that end with that particular letter.

The dictionary of synonyms is built from that tree. The idea is to regroup words with a similar spelling and thus with the same meaning (for example: build, built, builds). It is impossible to detect automatically all synonyms, because there are words that have a similar spelling, but not the same meaning. The aim of the stemming process is to limit human intervention by proposing clusters of generated synonyms. We got acceptable results with three simple rules. Two words are synonyms only if all three rules match.

- Firstly, the common part (*trunk*) of two words must have a length of at least 4 letters, for example: *trunk(begin, beginning)* = {*begin*} ≥4.
- Secondly, the remaining and not common part (*tail*) must not be longer than 5 letters, for example: *tail(begin, beginning)* = {*ning*}≤5.

- Thirdly, a different letter is only accepted if the common part has at least 3 letters, for example: *trunk(begin, began)* = {*beg*} ≥3.

Finally, RDF elements were affected to the concerned clusters, for example the cluster containing the words {*begin, begins, beginning, start, starting*} becomes synonym for dc:date and the words {*inventor, builder, constructor, inventors*} are affected to dc:creator. The final clustered dictionary is stored for later use (see section 3). The final step consists in scanning through the clips and searching for synonyms for the RDF elements. The result is a RDF/XML serialization for each clip.

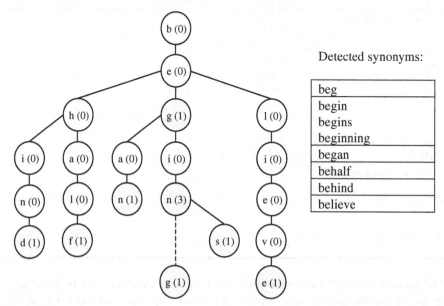

Detected synonyms:

beg
begin
begins
beginning
began
behalf
behind
believe

Fig. 1. Example of a generated tree of words. The number in brackets indicates the number of occurrences of the word. If the number is zero, then this node is no final letter. In this generated example, no wrong synonym is found. But one synonym was not clustered: {*began*} should be placed in the cluster {*begin, begins, beginning*}.

3 Understanding the User

To perform a semantic search, the question entered by the user must be transformed into RDF, in order to have the same structure for the question and for the database. The backbone of our semantic search is an inference engine which transforms a normal sentence (the user's question) into a well-formulated RDF query. For example: "Who invented the very first calculator" should become:

```
SELECT <?x> WHERE <chest:Computer>;<dc:creator>;<?x>
```

We will not describe details about representing RDF data in a database or how to launch a RDF query; see for example [11]. We will focus on the parsing of the sentence and the construction of the RDF query.

Table 1. Illustration of the basic rule for transforming a user's question into a RDF query.

Question	Subject	Predicate	Object
Who built the first calculator?	chest:Computer (*calculator*)	dc:creator (*built*)	?x
What does Zuse invent?	?x	dc:creator (*invent*)	chest:Person (*Zuse*)

Table 2. Illustration of several exceptions for transforming a user's question into a query.

Question	Subject	Predicate	Object
When was Aiken born?	chest:Person (*Aiken*)	chest:year_birth (*born*)	?x
What was the year Aiken died?	chest:Person (*Aiken*)	chest:year_death (*died*)	?x
What does ARPA mean and who founded it?	chest:Firm (*ARPA*)	dc:creator (*founded*)	?x
	chest:Firm (*ARPA*)	dc:title (*mean*)	?x
Who built the ENIAC and the EDVAC?	chest:Computer (*ENIAC, EDVAC*)	dc:creator (*built*)	?x
When did Zuse build his Z3?	chest:Computer (*Z3*)	dc:creator (*build*)	?x
	?x	dc:creator (*build*)	chest:Person (*Zuse*)
What is Linux?	chest:OS (*Linux*)		

The transformation of a common formulated sentence into RDF can be summed up by saying that the system has to replace all semantically important words by the RDF corresponding elements and to throw unimportant words away. For the question "Who invented the very first calculator?" the following words were replaced: {*invented*}→ dc:creator, {*calculator*}→ chest:Computer. All other words will not be considered. The missing part becomes the subject of the query. See table 1 for some general examples. But there are a lot of imaginable exceptions, for example:

- The predicate is not dc:creator (see table 2, lines 1+2). In that case, we are not in the basic assertion: "An invention was invented by an inventor", thus the general rule cannot be applied. It is a fact that the missing part must be the object. It is also a fact that the user is not searching for a person or an invention. There are several possible predicates depending on the class-membership of the subject: {dc:date and dc:title} if the subject is an invention or {chest:year_birth, chest:year_death and vcard:FN} if the subject is an inventor. The parser must choose the right predicate by analyzing the other found synonym(s), for example: words like "born" or "died" indicate a date.
- There is more than one predicate in the sentence. If the predicates are not concurrent then there will only be one query. If there are concurrent predicates (see table 2, line 3) then there will be as many queries as there are different predicates.

- There is more than one subject or object in the sentence. In analogy to the above exception, if the subjects or objects are not concurrent (see table 2, line 4), there will only be one query. If there are concurrent subjects or objects then there will be as many queries as there are different subjects or objects.
- There is no missing part. The question contains a predicate, a subject and an object (see table 2, line 5). This is the most complicated exception to handle. The system must find the best matching clip by associating the different queries.
- There are less than two known parts. In that case, the system lists all resources matching the keywords for the given class (see table 2, line 6).

4 Outlook

The prototype CHESt is tested with a simple keyword search in some selected schools in the summer term of the year 2004. Meanwhile, we are working on the improvement and development of the semantic search engine described in section 3. A prototype is to be tested in a larger pilot project in several schools and universities for the coming winter term (interested schools can contact us). The experience and empiric data that will be collected with the educational tool CHESt should then be the base of further research for a more general semantic search engine. One could imagine developing a generalized interface to access the knowledge base that contains clips of different topics: geography, French vocabulary, irregular English verbs, explanation of HTML tags, biography about famous actors, etc.

References

1. Chen T., Ma M., Meinel Ch., Schillings V.: Tele-TASK, Teleteaching Anywhere Solution Kit. Universität Trier. http://www.tele-task.de/
2. Meinel Ch., Schillings V.: Tele-TASK - Teleteaching Anywhere Solution Kit. In proceedings of ACM SIGUCCS 2002, Providence, USA (2002), pages 130-133
3. Dublin Core Metadata Initiative (DCMI). http://dublincore.org
4. Manning Ch., Schütze H.: Foundations of Statistical Natural Language Processing. The MIT Press, Cambridge London (2003)
5. Real.com: RealOne Player. http://www.real.com/
6. Linckels S.: CHESt namespace.
   http://www.linckels.lu/chest/elements/1.0/
7. Linckels S., Meinel Ch.: An Application of Semantics for an Educational Tool. In proceedings of IADIS International Conference of Applied Computing 2004, Lisbon, Portugal (2004), pages II-234 - II 239
8. Carstensen K.-U. et al.: Computerlinguistik und Sprachentechnologie. Spektrum Lehrbuch (2001)
9. World Wide Web Consortium: Representing vCard Objects in RDF/XML.
   http://www.w3.org/TR/2001/NOTE-vcard-rdf-20010222/
10. World Wide Web Consortium: Resource Description Framework (RDF) / W3C Semantic Web. http://www.w3.org/RDF/
11. Karvounarakis G. et al.: RQL, A Declarative Query Language for RDF. In proceedings of ACM WWW2002, Honolulu, USA (2002)

Representing XML Schema in UML –
A Comparison of Approaches

Martin Bernauer, Gerti Kappel, and Gerhard Kramler

Business Informatics Group, Vienna University of Technology, Austria
{lastname}@big.tuwien.ac.at

Abstract. There is a need to integrate XML schemas, i.e., schemas written in XML Schema, into UML-based software development processes. Not only the production of XML schemas out of UML models is required, but even more the integration of given XML schemas as input into the development process. In the model driven architecture, a two step integration is assumed, comprising a platform specific model and a platform independent model. Several approaches already exist addressing the problem of automatically creating a platform specific model for XML schemas. This paper contributes a comparison of these approaches, based on a comprehensive set of transformation patterns supporting creation of a platform specific UML model that is as concise and semantically expressive as possible without loosing XML Schema information.

1 Introduction

UML is being used as de-facto standard for software development, including web applications that exchange XML documents. Therefore a need arises to integrate XML schemas, i.e., schemas written in XML Schema, into UML-based software development processes. Not only the production of XML schemas out of UML models is required, but even more the integration of XML schemas as input into the development process, because standard data structures and document types are part of the requirements.

In the model driven architecture [9], a two step integration is assumed, comprising a platform specific model which abstracts from implementation language details, and a platform independent model which abstracts from technology details. For the platform independent model, plain UML is applied, whereas for the platform specific model, UML tailored to the target technology is employed. An evaluation of existing UML profiles for XML Schema as possible target technology is the main contribution of this paper.

A UML profile for XML Schema must fulfill several requirements. In particular, we are looking for a semantically equivalent representation of an XML schema in UML supporting a bijective mapping between both representations. A solution to this problem has to address the whole range of XML Schema concepts, such that any XML schema can be expressed in UML. Another requirement is to support round-trip engineering, i.e., transformation from XML

N. Koch, P. Fraternali, and M. Wirsing (Eds.): ICWE 2004, LNCS 3140, pp. 440–444, 2004.
© Springer-Verlag Berlin Heidelberg 2004

Schema to UML and back again without loss of schema information. Furthermore, a solution should maximize understandability of semantic concepts by users knowledgeable of UML but not XML Schema. Semantic equivalence is even more important when the UML models are to be used for application code generation, as it will happen in a model-driven development process.

This paper compares five main approaches for representing XML Schema in UML. The features of the approaches are compared based on a comprehensive set of transformation patterns fulfilling the above identified requirements. The patterns have been extracted from a previous effort to define a UML profile ([1]). In the next section, an overview of existing approaches is given, followed by the comparison results and a description of the transformation patterns in the final section.

2   Overview of Approaches

Existing work on representing XML Schema in UML has emerged from approaches to platform specific modeling in UML and transforming these models to XML Schema, with the recognized need for UML extensions to specify XML Schema peculiarities. [2] is the first approach of this kind to modeling XML schemas using UML. Although based on a predecessor to XML Schema, it introduces UML extensions addressing modelling of elements and attributes, model groups, and enumerations that can also be found in following approaches.

The approach by Carlson ([3]) describes an approach based on XMI rules for transforming UML to XML Schema. [3] also defines a UML profile which addresses most XML Schema concepts, except of simple content complex types, global elements and attributes, and identity constraints. Regarding semantic equivalence, the profile has some weaknesses in its representation of model groups, i.e., sequence, choice, and all. Based on the profile defined in [3], a two-way transformation between XML Schema and UML has been implemented in the commercially available tool "hypermodel"[1].

In [10], Provost has addressed some of the weaknesses of [3], addressing representation of enumerations and other restriction constraints, and of list and union type constructors, although the latter doesn't conform to UML.

Eckstein's approach ([5], in german, based on [4]) also defines a profile similar to that in [3], with some enhancements regarding simple types and notations.

Goodchild et al (in [8]) point out the importance of separating the conceptual schema, i.e., the platform independent model, from the logical schema, i.e., the platform specific model, a separation that is not considered in the other approaches. In [8], the logical schema is a direct, one-to-one representation of the XML schema in terms of a UML profile. The profile[2] covers almost all concepts of XML Schema, but several of its representations are not UML conform.

---

[1] http://xmlmodeling.com/hyperModel/

[2] A complete description can be found at
   http://titanium.dstc.edu.au/papers/xml-schema-profile.pdf

Our approach (in [1]) follows [8] in that it also aim at a one-to-one representation of XML schemas in an UML profile. The approach builds on the existing UML profiles for XML Schema, with some improvements and extensions.

Related work on mapping conceptual models expressed in UML or EER to XML Schema or DTD, has also identified various options for transforming conceptual-level concepts to XML Schema concepts [3,4,6,7,10]. Most of these transformations are, however, not unambiguously applicable in the reverse direction and would thus only be useful in an interactive transformation process, requiring a user's knowledge of the XML schema to be transformed to UML. Therefore, these approaches are not evaluated in this paper, although some of their results have influenced the design of the transformation patterns.

3 Comparison

A comparison of the features of each approach is provided in Table 1, organized along the various transformation patterns as described below. As can be seen, most of the approaches fail to fulfill the requirement of supporting all XML Schema concepts. Furthermore, some approaches represent XML Schema concepts in UML in a way supporting syntactic transformation but failing to provide semantic equivalence. [1] provides a solution satisfying the requirements, with the main improvements being solutions to represent model groups (MG) as well as global elements (EG, EW) and global attributes (AG, AW) in a way more compliant to UML semantics, to represent identity constraints (KY), and to represent simple types in a more concise, UML like way (ST3-4). For technical details on the differences of the approaches it is referred to [1].

Table 1. Comparison of UML profiles by transformation patterns

		CT		ST				EL							MG		KY			GE			
	SC	1	2	1	2	3	4	1	2	EG	EW	AL	AG	AW	1	2	1	2	GA	1	2	AN	NO
[3]	+	+		/	−			−	+		−	+			+								
[10]		+	+	+	−			+	+			+			−								
[5]			−	−	−			+	+		−	+		/	+								−
[8]	+	+	−	/	−			+	+	/	−	+			+		−	−	+			−	
[1]	+	+	+	+	+	+	+	+	+	+	+	+	+	+	+	+	+	+	+	+	+	+	+

Legend: + ... good support   / ... violation of UML semantics
                − ... incomplete support   *space* ... not supported

3.1 Transformation Patterns

Three design goals have guided the design of transformation patterns. First, it must be possible to represent any XML schema in UML, i.e., there must be a representation for each relevant XML Schema concept, in order to *facilitate round-trip engineering* without loss of schema information. Second, a representation of an XML schema has to be such that if the profile specific stereotypes are omitted, the result should - to the extent possible - convey the same meaning, in order to *facilitate understanding by non-XML Schema experts* and to support interoperability with tools not aware of the profile. This goal is also in line with the capability of UML stereotypes, which can only extend but not modify the semantics of UML concepts. Finally, the number of *UML constructs* necessary to represent a certain XML schema should be *minimal*, to improve readability. This goal can be achieved in some situations where UML concepts are more expressive than XML Schema concepts, allowing to represent certain patterns of XML Schema concepts using only one UML concept.

The transformation patterns are organized along the major XML Schema concepts, i.e., schema, complex types, simple types, elements, attributes, model groups (i.e., complex content), identity constraints, group definitions, annotations, and notations. A more detailed description of the transformation patterns can be found in [1].

SC   Represent every schema document as a stereotyped package.

CT1   Represent every global complex type as a stereotyped class.

CT2   Represent every local complex type as a stereotyped class nested into its containing class.

ST1   Represent every simple type that includes an enumeration constraint as a stereotyped enumeration.

ST2   Represent every simple type that does not include an enumeration constraint as a stereotyped primitive datatype.

ST3   Simplification of ST1/2: Merge the representation of a local simple type that is the type of an UML attribute with that attribute.

ST4   Simplification of ST1/2: Merge the representation of a list or union type defined local to a restriction type with the representation of the latter.

EL1   Represent a local element as a stereotyped association role of an association connecting the element's containing model group with the element's type.

EL2   Represent a local element as a stereotyped attribute of the class representing the containing model group if the element's type is a simple type.

EG   Represent every global element like a local element declaration with an additional stereotyped class. Represent its usage by generalizations to that class.

EW   Represent every element wildcard as a multiple classification constraint, indicating that occurrences can be instances of global elements as well.

AL   Represent every local attribute as a stereotyped attribute of the class representing the containing complex type or group.

AG   Represent every global attribute like a local attribute with an additional stereotyped class. Represent its usage by generalizations to that class.

AW   Represent every attribute wildcard as a multiple classification constraint, indicating that occurrences can be instances of global attributes as well.

MG1 Represent a model group as a stereotyped class where the stereotype depends on the group's compositor. Represent its usage by a composition.

MG2 Represent the grammar expressed by a model group tree as a constraint, using a textual notation which covers hierarchical structuring and ordering.

KY1 Represent a key constraint as a constraint attached to the class containing the representation of the element that is the key's scope.

KY2 Represent a key constraint whose selector does not contain union and wildcard steps as a constraint attached to the class selected by the selector.

GA   Represent every attribute group as an abstract stereotyped class with the attributes represented by AL. Represent its usage by generalizations.

GE1 Represent an element group as a stereotyped class with the elements represented by EL1 and/or EL2. Represent its model group and usage by MG1.

GE2 Represent an element group as an abstract stereotyped class with the elements represented by EL1 and/or EL2. Represent its model group by MG2 and its usage by generalizations.

AN   Represent every annotation as a set of stereotyped comments.

NO   Represent every notation declaration as a stereotyped literal in a stereotyped enumeration.

References

1. M. Bernauer, G. Kappel, and G. Kramler. A UML Profile for XML Schema. Technical Report,
   http://www.big.tuwien.ac.at/research/publications/2003/1303.pdf, 2003.

2. G. Booch, M. Christerson, M. Fuchs, and J. Koistinen. UML for XML Schema Mapping Specification. Rational White Paper, December 1999.

3. D. Carlson. *Modeling XML Applications with UML*. Addison-Wesley, 2001.

4. R. Conrad, D. Scheffner, and J. C. Freytag. XML Conceptual Modeling Using UML. In *19th International Conference on Conceptual Modeling (ER), Salt Lake City, Utah, USA*, volume 1920 of *Springer LNCS*, pages 558–571, 2000.

5. R. Eckstein and S. Eckstein. *XML und Datenmodellierung*. dpunkt.verlag, 2004.

6. R. Elmasri, Y. Wu, B. Hojabri, C. Li, and J. Fu. Conceptual Modeling for Customized XML Schemas. In *21st International Conference on Conceptual Modeling (ER), Tampere, Finland*, volume 2503 of *Springer LNCS*, pages 429–443. Springer, 2002.

7. T. Krumbein and T. Kudrass. Rule-Based Generation of XML Schemas from UML Class Diagrams. In *In Proceedings of the XML Days at Berlin, Workshop on Web Databases (WebDB)*, pages 213–227, 2003.

8. A. Goodchild N. Routledge, L. Bird. UML and XML Schema. In *13th Australian Database Conference (ADC2002)*, pages 157–166. ACS, 2002.

9. OMG. MDA Guide Version 1.0.1. OMG Document omg/2003-06-01,
   http://www.omg.org/docs/omg/03-06-01.pdf, 2003.

10. W. Provost. UML For W3C XML Schema Design.
   http://www.xml.com/lpt/a/2002/08/07/wxs_uml.html, August 2002.

Screen Readers Cannot See

Ontology Based Semantic Annotation for Visually Impaired Web Travellers

Yeliz Yesilada, Simon Harper, Carole Goble, and Robert Stevens

Information Management Group
Department of Computer Science
University of Manchester
Manchester M13 9PL, UK
yesilady@cs.man.ac.uk

Abstract. Travelling upon the Web is difficult for visually impaired users since the Web pages are designed for visual interaction [6]. Visually impaired users usually use screen readers[1] to access the Web in audio. However, unlike sighted users, screen readers cannot see the implicit structural and navigational knowledge encoded within the visual presentation of Web pages. Therefore, in a visually impaired user's environment, objects that support travel are missing or inaccessible. Our approach to remedy this is to annotate pages with an ontology, the Travel Ontology, that aims to encapsulate rich structural and navigational knowledge about these objects. We use *Semantic Web* technologies to make such knowledge explicit and computationally accessible. Our semi-automated tool, *Dante* identifies travel objects on Web pages, annotates them appropriately with the Travel Ontology and uses this to transform the pages to enhance the travel support. Thus *Dante* uses the Travel Ontology to enhance the travel experience of visually impaired users. This paper introduces the Travel Ontology, the annotation pipeline used in the annotation part of *Dante* and some transformation scenarios to illustrate how the annotations are used to guide the transformation of Web pages.

1 Introduction

This paper introduces a semi-automated tool, *Dante*, for the support of travel and mobility for visually impaired Web users. The paper first presents an ontology, the Travel Ontology, and the annotation pipeline facilitated within *Dante*, and then discusses how the Travel Ontology is used to transform pages to enhance the travel experience of visually impaired Web users.

The visual navigational objects that support easy movement around Web pages, or *mobility*, are not appropriate and accessible to visually impaired Web users. These objects are crucial to confident, easy and accurate navigation, which we call *travel* [6]. In order to support mobility, these objects and their roles need to be identified, explicitly specified and presented in a way to fulfil their intended roles. The idea behind *Dante* is to analyse Web pages to extract such objects and annotate them with terms from the Travel

---

[1] Screen readers are special applications that vocalise the onscreen data. Pages are typically read from the top left to the bottom right, line by line, one word at a time [6].

N. Koch, P. Fraternali, and M. Wirsing (Eds.): ICWE 2004, LNCS 3140, pp. 445–458, 2004.

Ontology that aims to encapsulate extensive knowledge about these objects. The Travel Ontology consists of several parts aiming to capture knowledge about how these objects are *presented* (their structural properties) and *used* (their role in supporting mobility) in a typical journey. These annotations, which are a way of associating extensive knowledge to these objects, can then guide the transformation of Web pages to enhance travel and mobility. For the annotation, we use *Semantic Web* technologies. However, unlike other examples[2], we are not annotating a Web page to convey the meaning, but rather to support mobility and convey information about the page itself. The architecture of *Dante*[3] is depicted in Figure 1 and its aim can be summarised as follows:

1. Identifying and extracting objects that support travel, travel objects, from the page;
2. Discovering their roles and structural properties;
3. Annotating the extracted objects by using the Travel Ontology;
4. Transforming the page with respect to these annotations.

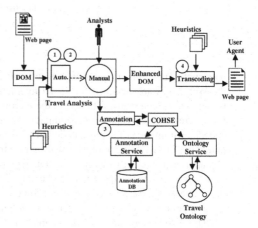

Fig. 1. The basic architecture of *Dante*.

In *Dante* (see Figure 1), the Travel Ontology is used as a controlled vocabulary to guide the transformation of Web pages. The COHSE[4] annotator is used to annotate pages with this ontology, the annotations are stored externally and accessed by the transformation component. The annotation process is encoded in a flexible annotation pipeline and the different parts of the ontology play an important role in this pipeline.

The rest of the paper is organised as follows: Section2 presents the motivation for our work. Section 3 explains the model of travel that is the foundation of *Dante* [17] and introduces the different parts of the ontology. Section 4 discusses how these different parts are used in *Dante*. Then, some example scenarios are explained in Section 5 that demonstrate how the annotated pages are used in the page transformation. Section 6 describes and discusses some related works. Finally, Section 7 provides a summary and offers some discussion.

---

[2] See http://annotation.semanticweb.org.

[3] [17] presents the travel analysis framework which is the foundation for *Dante*.

[4] Conceptual Open Hypermedia Service (COHSE) (http://cohse.semanticweb.org).

2   Motivation

Visually impaired people usually access Web pages either by using screen readers [9] or specialist browsers [3]. If the Web pages are properly designed and laid out in a linear fashion, these assistive technologies work satisfactorily. Some screen readers access the HTML source code rather than solely reading the *screen*, which enables them to provide better support. However, not many pages are properly designed; the focus is usually on the visual presentation which makes audio interaction almost impossible. Furthermore, chunking the page into several parts and presenting it in a nonlinear fashion is becoming popular which makes the provided functionalities of these assistive technologies insufficient. Moreover the popular Web sites prove that the available guidelines for designers in creating accessible pages [1] are rarely followed.

The home page of the Mozilla Foundation can be used to illustrate the problem (see Fig. 3 part labelled as A). The page is visually laid out into two columns with the main content in the right column. Since most screen readers render pages based on following tags in the HTML code, visually impaired users have to *read* the entire left column in order to access the right column. The page is quite long and therefore it takes an unacceptable length of time to read the whole page. Accessibility, and in particular *mobility*, is not only about the provision of alternative text for images, but also about how easy it is for a traveller to complete a successful journey. For example, if the user wants to directly access the "Documentation" part of the page, the only way is to read almost the entire page (see Fig. 3 part labelled as A). Therefore, the whole journey experience becomes frustrating and unsatisfactory. Further problems also exist when trying to gain an overview of the page[5].

As a summary, screen readers cannot see and understand the structural semantics implicitly encoded in the page so the mobility support is limited and fragile. Therefore, we need to make the implicit structural and navigational knowledge explicit and accessible to screen readers. The next section presents the Travel Ontology that aims to encode such knowledge.

3   The Travel Ontology

The Travel Ontology serves two purposes: (1) a representation of a shared conceptualisation of knowledge about the mobility of visually impaired people and structures widely supported by Web pages; (2) a controlled, shared vocabulary that can be communicated across applications. In the context of our tool, the ontology will be used as the controlled vocabulary to drive page transformations. Fundamentally, the ontology encodes three groups of concepts which will be presented in the following sections and which in summary hold information about:

- *Mobility* concepts: encapsulate the knowledge about the travel objects from real world mobility studies (how these objects are *used*). Objects can have a journey role which depends on the context of the journey being undertaken and can also have one or more environmental roles (Sect. 3.1);

---

[5] Please refer to [16] for detailed information.

– *Authoring* concepts: hold information about including hypermedia concepts and vocabularies used in previous work on transcoding and content management systems–encapsulate information about how the objects are *structured* and *presented* in Web pages (Sect. 3.2);

– The *context* of a journey: a Web journey can take place in different contexts [6] and concepts in this group provide contextual knowledge about a journey such as the purpose of the journey being undertaken (Sect. 3.3).

Table 1. The higher level concepts, their documentations and the number of the concepts in the each part of the Travel Ontology.

Part of the Ontology	Concept	Documentation and Example Children	No. of Children
Mobility Semantics:	EnvironmentalRole	Environmental features (elements) that are used or needed by travellers to complete a successful journey (e.g., WayPoint, TravelAssistant, etc.).	16
	JourneyRole	The role of an object in a particular context (e.g., Obstacle, Cue, OutOfView, etc.).	7
Authoring Semantics:	Atom	A coherent object that cannot be decomposed (e.g., Link, Headline, Caption, Footnote, Logo, etc.).	43
	Chunk	Several objects grouped together to form a coherent unit (e.g., Header, Footer, Section, Abstract, LinkMenu, SiteMap, etc.).	42
	Node	A composition of atom(s) and chunk(s) to form a meaningful group (meant to represent a Web page).	0
	Collection	A collection of nodes (meant to represent a Web site).	0
Context Semantics:	Purpose	Intention of either the user (e.g., Browsing, Scanning, etc.) or the object (e.g, AidsNavigation, AidsOrientation, etc.)	14

Due to the space limitations we cannot explain all of the concepts in the ontology[6]. However Table 1 provides an overview by presenting higher level concepts and the number of their children. A description of early work on the ontology can also be found in [16]. The ontology has been created using OilEd[7] and OWL[8].

3.1 Mobility Semantics

There has been extensive work undertaken in the mobility of visually impaired people in the physical world, which can be transferred to the Web world. In order to transfer and adapt real world metaphors to the Web world, *a model of travel* is introduced [6] and

---

[6] For the complete ontology, please refer to
http://augmented.man.ac.uk/ontologies/TravelOntology.owl.

[7] See http://oiled.man.ac.uk/.

[8] See http://www.w3.org/TR/owl-ref/.

extended in [17]. In order to complete a successful journey, travellers use or may need to use *travel objects*. These objects are mainly grouped into three broad categories:

Way points: These are points within a journey at which a decision may be made that directly facilitates the onward journey. Way points are also further classified and an example is "Decision point" which is the point in the journey where a traveller has to from different possible paths (e.g., link menu).

Orientation points: Knowledge about orientation suggests that a person needs information about location, distance and direction in order to be oriented in a journey and the objects that provide such information are orientation points (e.g., logo).

Travel assistants: Sighted or visually impaired travellers experience problems in orienting themselves from time to time in both familiar and unfamiliar environments where they use different strategies to re-orientate themselves. The objects that they use in these strategies are grouped as travel assistants [17] (e.g., site map).

Fundamentally, a traveller navigates and orientates by consulting, detecting and identifying these travel objects. Consultation, detection and identification are accomplished through the mobility instruments of in-journey guidance, previews, probes and feedbacks. These components form the model of travel [6].

Based on the model of travel, this part of the ontology holds information about the *travel objects*. Objects might have a specific role in an environment as explained above (travel objects) and based on the context, they might have another journey role. Therefore, beside the travel objects we also have concepts that are about the journey role of the objects. An object can be either *obstacle* or *cue* depending on the context of the journey being undertaken. An *obstacle* is an object that directly or indirectly obstructs the progress of a traveller to a specific destination and a *cue* is an object that orientates and encourages onward navigation [8]. The journey role is context dependent, for example a graphic site map could be a cue to a sighted user but it could be an obstacle to a visually impaired user.

Real world mobility studies also suggest that visually impaired people travel a journey in a different way to sighted people, using a number of different cues. For example, visually impaired people use simple information more frequently than complex information [6]. Knowledge of these differences and how visually impaired people travel provide a context for their travel on the Web and this part of the ontology aims to capture this knowledge. The encoded information in the ontology then could be used to provide better support for the provision of mobility.

3.2 Authoring Semantics

Authoring concepts hold information about the hypermedia concepts, vocabularies used in previous work on transcoding and content management systems. In this case, we do not consider the role(s) of the objects in the travel framework but we are more interested in how the objects are presented in the Web landscape. The Web landscape is defined as the combination of the page and the agent (e.g, browser and assistive technologies such as screen readers). These concepts are more to do with the specific structures that can be used to define the overall structure of a page including for example, sections, summaries, abstracts, footers, etc. These constructs are usually implicit in the visual

Table 2. Example travel objects extracted from the home page of the Mozilla Foundation and some examples of mapping authoring concepts to mobility concepts. The table should be read in conjunction with Fig. 3 part labelled as A. Please refer to [17] for further information about the mobility concepts.

No	Authoring Concepts	Documentation	is a kind of...	Some Inferred Mobility Concepts
1	Header	Is printed at the top of a page and can include a company logo, the page title, a link menu and etc.	Chunk	Way Edge
2	Logo	An emblem or a device used to identify the page or a site.	SpecialGraphic	Reference Point
3,21	LinkMenu	A list of links meant to represent a menu.	NavigationalList	Decision& Navigation Point
4	SearchEngine	Consists of an edit box and a button.	Chunk	Information Point
5	Label	An identifying marker attached to an object.	Atom	Identification Point
6	Footnote	A note attached to a part of a page.	Atom	WayPoint
7, 8, 11, 16	Section	A self-contained part of a page.	Chunk	Way Edge
8, 9, 12, 17	Heading	Indicates what the part of the page below is about.	Atom	Identification Point
13	Headline	Is the highlighted heading which identifies the most important part.	Heading	Identification Point
15	Chunk	Several objects grouped together to form a coherent unit.	AuthoringConcept	Way Point
18	NavigationalList	A list of links.	List	Decision Point
19	Footer	Is printed at the bottom of a page and can include copyright information, a list of links and etc.	Chunk	Way Edge
20	Copyright	Is a note about the copyright and is positioned at the bottom of a page.	Footnote	Way Point

presentation of the page, however since they are not explicitly encoded in the underlying source code (e.g., HTML), they are inaccessible in any other form of interaction (e.g., audio interaction through screen readers). The aim here is to define a vocabulary that is already widely used between the designers but not formally explained and defined, that is to say we try to make the domain knowledge explicit. This part of the ontology could be considered as an extension to HTML– aims to provide a rich set of concepts that can be used to describe the overall structure of the pages so that they will be accessible in any from of interaction.

The home page of the Mozilla Foundation can be used to explain some particular concepts in this part of the ontology. Figure 3 (part labelled as A) shows some annotations that has been done by using authoring concepts and Table 2 provides documentation and hierarchical information about these concepts.

3.3 Contextual Semantics

The concepts in this part of the ontology aim to encode contextual information about a typical journey. They particularly address the purpose; this could range from the travellers' purpose (information seeking, surveying, orientation, navigation, browsing, scanning, etc.) to the travel object's intended purpose which is in fact the designer's purpose. One of the possible roles that this part of the ontology could fulfill would be to obtain enough knowledge about the traveller's purpose and to transform pages accordingly. For example, if the traveller wants to scan a page, we could try to provide an overview of the page or if he (she) wants to orientate himself (herself) in the environment (wants to learn where he (she) is in the environment) we could provide objects that support orientational information such as a title, logo, etc. Travel objects can also play different roles in different contexts, for example, for a visually impaired user, a graphic is an obstacle in the context of information searching but a cue in the context of orientation.

The main problem with this contextual information is that it is difficult to obtain. Typically, the traveller's purpose is not explicitly specified (or well-defined) and also the traveller can engage in many different purposes as they travel through the environment.

4 The Annotation Accumulation

This section explains how different parts of the ontology, particularly authoring and mobility concepts, are facilitated in *Dante*. We use a pipeline approach to maintain flexibility in the basket of possible annotation formats. The pipeline (see Fig. 2):

1. Receives inputs from many disparate sources and in many different forms (RDF[9], DC[10], RSS[11], etc.) including manual annotations done by using annotation tools such as COHSE.
2. Harmonizes these inputs into a canonical form based on a uniform ontological framework.
3. Recruits ontological annotations manually, semi and fully-automatically.
4. Translates between annotation vocabularies associated with authoring concepts and with mobility concepts in order to provide extensive knowledge about their roles in the travel framework.
5. Better realises – and simplifies – the complex transcoding activity associated with our final goal based on these now expansive annotations.

Figure 2 shows the annotation flow and relates the flow to the architecture of *Dante* which is illustrated in Fig. 1 (See Fig. 1 for the parts labelled as 3 and 4 on Fig. 2). Annotations can be received in different formats and translated into a canonical form, which we propose to use authoring concepts as explained in Sect. 3.2. Authoring concepts mainly provide information about how these objects are *presented* and *structured*. After we acquire authoring concepts, we use a set of rules[12] to translate authoring concepts to

---

[9] See http://www.w3.org/RDF/.
[10] See http://dublincore.org/.
[11] See http://blogs.law.harvard.edu/tech/rss.
[12] See the next page for an horn clause representation of an example mapping rule.

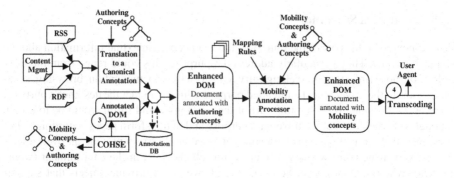

Fig. 2. The annotation pipeline (see Fig. 1 for the parts labelled as 3 and 4).

mobility concepts in order to accumulate enough knowledge about how these objects are *used* in a typical journey. We can of course bypass the translations by using COHSE [5] and our authoring, or mobility concepts to directly annotate the page.

The COHSE annotator uses XPointer[13] expressions to identify the region of the document and annotations are stored in an annotation service [5]. We have used the browser plug-in[14] version of the COHSE annotator to annotate Web pages. Although there are a number of available annotation tools including MnM and OntoAnnotate[15], we have preferred to use COHSE because of its compatibility with Mozilla which is also our annotation delivery environment. The prototype transformation part of *Dante* is implemented as a plug-in to Mozilla, and using both plug-ins can create a single environment for authoring and publishing the annotations. In addition, the browser can take care of malformed HTML documents. By using a plug-in approach, the transformer, as well as the annotator can access the DOM object built by the browser and can base the transformations and annotations on that.

After annotating pages with authoring concepts, we use a set of heuristic mapping rules and the underlying HTML source code in combination with the ontology to create an enhanced DOM annotated with both authoring and mobility concepts. The mapping rules are encoded in JESS[16] which is implemented as a Java servlet. We use the internal DOM tree of Mozilla to obtain the properties of annotated authoring concepts and send these to JESS in order to infer the mobility concepts based on the mapping rules. In more recent work, we believe by evolving the ontology to extend the existing properties of concepts, we will be able to better exploit the reasoning mechanism of OWL to infer the relationship between these two ontologies. After we acquire the mobility concepts, we extend the internal DOM tree by using both annotated authoring and inferred mobility concepts. This new DOM is now in a suitable format for transcoding and the usually complex process of transcoding is dramatically simplified. Table 2 shows some sample

---

[13] See http://www.w3.org/TR/xptr/.

[14] It also has a proxy server version.

[15] See http://annotation.semanticweb.org/tools for the list of annotation tools.

[16] See http://herzberg.ca.sandia.gov/jess/.

mappings based on Fig. 3 (part labelled as A) and the following horn clause represents an example mapping rule:

$$NavigationalList$$
$$\downarrow$$
$$NavigationalList \rightarrow DecisionPoint \wedge NavigationPoint$$
$$TextLink \rightarrow NavigationPoint \wedge TravelMemory$$
$$NavigationalList \wedge TextLink \rightarrow DecisionPoint \wedge NavigationPoint \wedge TravelMemory$$
$$\downarrow$$
$$DecisionPoint \wedge NavigationPoint \wedge TravelMemory \qquad (1)$$

This rule mainly applies to the objects that are annotated as a "NavigationalList" and all the links in the list are text. We confirm that the links are text and not images by checking the HTML source code (DOM tree). Therefore by using the provided annotations, the underlying source code and a set of rules, we can accumulate extensive knowledge about the role, structure and usage of the objects.

5   Using the Travel Ontology

We return to the home page of the Mozilla Foundation to demonstrate the implementations of some transformation heuristics based on our annotations (see Fig. 3). This page is used as an example since it is a typical corporation site and provides good demonstration of some of the issues concerning the mobility support provided by the page. Figure 3 (see part labelled as A) and Table 2 shows the annotations. The page is originally annotated with the authoring concepts (see Sect. 3.2), then the mobility concepts are inferred automatically from these annotations and the underlying source code[17]. The annotations are used to provide several techniques for enhancing provided mobility support. Essentially, the heuristics and transformations that we explain here are all simple but have high impact on the provided mobility support of the page and are good enough to illustrate how the annotations can drive the transformation of the pages.

Providing the Overview of the Page

We use the annotated headings[18] (identification points[19]) to provide a kind of table of contents (TOC) (see Fig. 3 part labelled as B). The TOC could be considered as a way of providing the *bird's eye view* (overview) of the page. The annotated chunks, sections and headings represent the fragments in the page. We add links from TOC to headings (identification points) and also back to the TOC to logically fragment the page. Based on the headings (identification points) and sections (way edges[20]) in the page, we logically fragment the page and allow user to have the preview of these logical fragments. These logical fragments aim to represent the implicit chunks within

---

[17] See the previous page (Sect. 4) for an horn clause representation of an example mapping rule.
[18] This type style indicates the concepts in the Travel Ontology.
[19] (A mobility concept) They identify an object, a place or a person in an environment [17].
[20] (A mobility concept) They are environmental elements that are linear (continuous) and act as boundaries between two areas [17].

the page. This is a technique to improve the intra (*within* the page) mobility support, but once we improve this, the inter (*between* the pages) and collection wide mobility supports (within the site) will also be improved.

We can also physically fragment the page by creating separate pages based on the chunks in the page and allow the user to move from TOC to these pages and back. These two approaches have pros and cons. For example, in the logical fragmentation, the user can continue to read the next chunk without returning back to the TOC. However, the number of links in the page (from/ to TOC) might be too many and difficult for the user to manage. The extra added links can increase the cognitive demand.

Fragmentation of the Web page is important for good mobility for visually impaired users. Physical or logical fragmentation divides the environment into more manageable and easy to travel units. Moreover, it makes the environment more regular, increases the information flow and supports granularity and consequently satisfies some of the mobility principles [6].

Enabling Movement to the Focus of the Page

Skip links are popular for enhancing the navigation, and thus the mobility support provided by the page for visually impaired users. They are mainly used at the top of the page to provide a link to the main content, so that the user does not have to *read* the unnecessary information and is mainly for avoiding repetitions. Therefore, we have a set of heuristics concerning the addition of skip links and particularly deciding upon their targets. The following two heuristics are examples for deciding upon a target for a skip link: (1) if an object is annotated as a headline then we could infer that the section after that is the most important part, therefore we provide a skip link to that object (see Fig. 3 part labelled as C); (2) if there is a decision point[21] closer to the top of the page, then we add a skip link at the top of the page pointing the first element just after the decision point. We have also assigned priorities to heuristics with the same purpose, in this case the first heuristic have higher priority than the second one. These heuristics are derived by analysing a number of pages and observing common patterns.

Structuring List of Links

The Mozilla home page is semantically organized into chunks, but there is no mechanism for visually impaired users to access those chunks randomly or glance through the chunks. Sighted users can change their focus easily and access the chunks randomly. Some screen readers provide a function for accessing the list of links in the page. It allows users to scan the page rather than reading the entire page. However this technique requires links to have proper labels so that they make sense when they are read out of context, but unfortunately many links are context dependent. For instance, in the home page of the Mozilla, there are links labelled as "More..." and many links repeated as "Windows", "Linux" which provide links to different versions of a specific product, but if they are not read together with the product heading, it is almost impossible to understand where these links point to.

---

[21] See Sect. 3.1 for the definition.

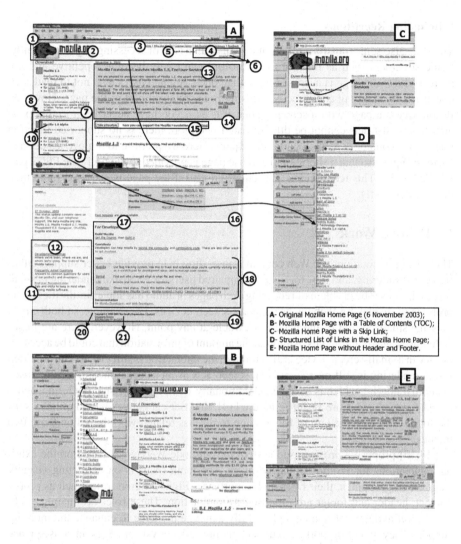

Fig. 3. The home page of the Mozilla Foundation with Transformations (06 November 2003). The part labelled as A should be read in conjunction with Table 2.

These are crucial techniques (e.g., providing a list of links and a list of headings) for the mobility of the user, but very much dependent on proper HTML design and tagging. These techniques can actually be improved by having the structural knowledge. For example, we can improve the provided list of links by putting links in a context but still keeping it short and concise for getting the overview. We propose to use the parts that are annotated as sections and chunks and by using the headings (identification points) in these parts, in order to provide a structure and context to links. This can be considered as grouping links (organizing) which is well-known to aid scanning and memorability of the links [14]. Figure 3 (see Part labelled as D) shows how we use annotations to structure the list of links in the Mozilla home page.

Eliminating Repetitions

There are also some transformations that are useful in case of accessing pages frequently. Some structures such as headers and footers can easily become repetitive and not quite useful if the page is accessed more than once. Sighted users tend not to read such constructs by skipping and directly focusing to the relevant part of the page. However, if you access a page with a screen reader, it is as if you have never been to that page and these constructs cannot be differentiated, therefore there is no supported function that allows you not *read* such parts of the page. Here we propose to remove header and footer in a page so that a shorter and concise page is provided to the user (see Fig. 2 part labelled as E). This technique is particularly useful if the page is accessed more than once or frequently.

6   Related Work

The goal of annotations for Web content transcoding is to provide better support either for audio rendering, and thus for visually impaired users, or for visual rendering in small screen devices. The problem of rendering Web pages in audio has some similarities to the problem of displaying Web pages on small-screen devices. For example, in both cases, only the small portion of the page is viewable at any point. However, there are major differences and requirements. Although the amount of information that could be accessed at once in a small-screen device is also limited, the interaction is still visual. The provided visual rendering is still *persistent* [13], screen acts as an external memory, as opposed to audio rendering which is *transient*. Additionally, compared to visual rendering, audio is less focused and more *serial* in nature [14], the user cannot easily and quickly shift the focus. It is then the aim of this section to discuss related work based on these two themes.

[4,15] propose a proxy-based system to transcode Web pages based on the external annotations for *visually impaired users*. The main focus is on extracting visually fragmented groupings, their roles and importance. Eight different roles such as proper content, header and footer are proposed for annotation. These roles are mainly at abstract level and are not rich enough to fully annotate the page to enhance the mobility support. They do not support deep understanding and analysis of pages, in consequence the supported transcoding is constrained by these proposed roles.

For *small-screen devices*, [11] proposes a system to transcode an HTML document by fragmenting it into several documents. The transcoding is based on an external annotation framework. Since the focus is the small-screen devices, physical and performance constraints of the devices need to be considered, such as screen size, memory size, and connection bandwidth. However, these are not the main requirements of the users accessing Web pages in audio and there are differences as explained above.

Another approach for content adaptation is page *clipping* [12]. The approach is annotating pages with elements such as keep (content should be preserved) and remove, and then at content delivery, filter the page based on these annotations. This approach is also used for converting HTML to VoiceXML [10]. This is simple and could be an efficient approach, however, our main goal is to identify the roles of the objects in a page and transform accordingly, rather than doing some kind of filtering.

7   Summary and Discussion

We have first introduced the Travel Ontology[22]. that aims to encapsulate the knowledge from real world mobility studies, previous work on transcoding and information about hypermedia concepts. Then, we have described a possible annotation and transformation approach based on this ontology. In particular, an annotation pipeline is introduced which is the core of this approach. The annotation pipeline is used to annotate Web pages by using different parts of the ontology. Some annotation and transformation scenarios are also explained to illustrate the application and usage of this pipeline.

The annotation pipeline is promising and in this paper we demonstrate that once the annotations are acquired, even the simple transformations can have high impact on the mobility of the user. The future work and the issues concerning the pipeline has two fold: annotation acquisition and the page transformation, and here we discuss some of the issues and future work based on these two folds.

Concerning transformations, we are currently investigating the creation of transformation heuristics and mapping rules based on the type and functionality of the site. [2] proposes eight categories of sites (what a site is and not what is it about) based on their functionalities and we are working on analysing a number of Web sites from each category and detect common structural patterns within and between the categories. This study will provide us a well-defined set of heuristics for different types of sites.

The transformation process has also raised several issues concerning the usage of XPointer and external annotations. Since we want to apply a number of transformation heuristics, applying one after the other could change the DOM tree and invalidate the existing XPointers in the annotation store. Therefore, in the current prototype, before the transformation process, we have included an intermediate stage to transform the external annotations to internal annotations by using the internal DOM tree of the browser. In this way, we are not actually modifying the original document and this intermediate stage is hidden from the user. This can be considered a partial solution because we still have the problem of dynamically changing pages. Some Web pages change their content and layout almost every day, therefore, even though the annotations are created and stored, they could be easily invalidated. Therefore, we envision incorporating the annotations and the Travel Ontology either with the content management systems or within the designing process. However, the annotations and the created prototype can be considered as a *proof of concept*; our aim is to demonstrate that the annotations and transformations can improve the mobility of visually impaired Web users.

Another possible solution to overcome the dynamically generated pages problem is to annotate pages automatically. Since the authoring concepts could be considered as an extension to structures supported by HTML, the translation rules that we have for mapping authoring concepts to mobility concepts could be extended to address HTML elements. This approach is important for automating the annotation process which could be done in two levels: first obtaining the properties of the travel objects based on the HTML structural elements and then based on the authoring concepts we can infer the mobility concepts. Therefore, we would have an automated process of annotating pages.

---

[22] For the complete ontology, please refer to
http://augmented.man.ac.uk/ontologies/TravelOntology.owl.

Our main goal is to improve the mobility support for visually impaired Web users and using the proposed Travel Ontology and also the annotation pipeline lead us to achieve our goal. The work presented here is still continuing and there is still some work to be done, in particular an evaluation of the annotation accumulation process.

Acknowledgments. Yeliz Yesilada gratefully acknowledges the scholarships awarded her by ORS and the Department of Computer Science of the University of Manchester.

References

1. Web content accessibility guidelines 1.0, 1999.
   http://www.w3.org/TR/1999/WAI-WEBCONTENT/.
2. E. Amitay, D. Carmel, A. Darlow, R. Lempel, and A. Soffer. The connectivity sonar: detecting site functionality by structural patterns. In *Proceedings of the fourteenth ACM conference on Hypertext and hypermedia*, pages 38–47, 2003.
3. C. Asakawa and T. Itoh. User interface of a home page reader. In *Proceedings of the Third International ACM Conference on Assistive Technologies*, pages 149–156, 1998.
4. C. Asakawa and H. Takagi. Annotation-based transcoding for nonvisual web access. In *Proceedings of the Fourth International ACM Conference on Assistive Technologies*, pages 172–179, 2000.
5. C. Goble, S. Bechhofer, L. Carr, D. D. Roure, and W. Hall. Conceptual open hypermedia = the semantic web? The Second International Workshop on the Semantic Web, 2001.
6. C. Goble, S. Harper, and R. Stevens. The travails of visually impaired web travellers. In *Proceedings of the Eleventh ACM on Hypertext and Hypermedia*, pages 1–10, 2000.
7. S. Harper. *Web Mobility for Visually Impaired Surfers*. PhD thesis, The University of Manchester, 2001.
8. S. Harper, R. Stevens, and C. Goble. Web mobility guidelines for visually impaired surfers. *Journal of Research and Practice in Information Technology Special Issue on HCI*, 33(2), July 2001.
9. Henter-Joyce, Inc. *Jaws.* http://www.hj.com.
10. N. Hopson. Websphere transcoding publisher: Html-to-voicexml transcoder, 2002. IBM developerWorks, http://www7b.boulder.ibm.com/.
11. M. Hori, G. Kondoh, and K. Ono. Annotation-based web content transcoding. In *Proceedings of the Ninth International World Wide Web Conference*, pages 197–211, 2000.
12. M. Hori, K. Ono, T. Koyanagi, and M. Abe1. Annotation by transformation for the automatic generation. In *Pervasive 2002*, pages 267–281, 2002.
13. J. Nielsen. Voice interfaces: Assessing the potential. Alertbox, January 2003.
14. I. Pitt and A. Edwards. *Design of Speech-Based Devices - a Practical Guide*. Springer, 2003.
15. H. Takagi and C. Asakawa. Transcoding proxy for nonvisual web access. In *Proceedings of the Fourth International ACM Conference on Assistive Technologies*, pages 164–171, 2000.
16. Y. Yesilada, S. Harper, C. Goble, and R. Stevens. Ontology based semantic annotation for enhancing mobility support for visually impaired web users. In *K-CAP 2003 Workshop on Knowledge Markup and Semantic Annotation*, 2003.
17. Y. Yesilada, R. Stevens, and C. Goble. A foundation for tool based mobility support for visually impaired web users. In *Proceedings of the Twelfth International Conference on World Wide Web*, pages 422–430, 2003.

Engineering the Presentation Layer of Adaptable Web Information Systems

Zoltán Fiala[1], Flavius Frasincar[2], Michael Hinz[1],
Geert-Jan Houben[2], Peter Barna[2], and Klaus Meissner[1]

[1] Technische Universität Dresden
Mommsenstr. 13, D-01062, Dresden, Germany
{zoltan.fiala,mh5,kmeiss}@inf.tu-dresden.de
[2] Technische Universiteit Eindhoven
PO Box 513, NL-5600 MB, Eindhoven, The Netherlands
{flaviusf,houben,pbarna}@win.tue.nl

Abstract. Engineering adaptable Web Information Systems (WIS) requires systematic design models and specification frameworks. A complete model-driven methodology like Hera distinguishes between the conceptual, navigational, and presentational aspects of WIS design and identifies different adaptation "hot-spots" in each design step. This paper concentrates on adaptation in the presentation layer and combines the modeling power of Hera with the versatile presentation capabilities of the AMACONT project. After discussing different aspects of presentation layer adaptation, the layout manager mechanism of AMACONT for describing the adaptable layout of ubiquitous Web presentations is introduced. Then the RDFS-based Hera schema for presentation models is presented, allowing to assign AMACONT layout descriptors to Hera slices. According to this formalization, Hera application model instances are automatically transformed to a component-based AMACONT implementation that can be adjusted to different end devices and output formats. The XML-based transformation process is explained in detail, and the resulting methodology is exemplified by a prototype application.

1 Introduction

Engineering *personalized* Web Information Systems (WIS) is a complex process that has to be based on disciplined, systematic methodologies. Among these we distinguish the model-based methodologies due to the numerous benefits they offer: easy system analysis, modular decomposition, adaptation "hot-spots", flexibility, maintainability etc. By identifying crucial phases of Web development, such an approach helps designers and programmers to proceed in a structured way.

Hera [1] is a model-driven design methodology and specification framework focusing on the development of personalized WIS. Based on the principle of separation of concerns it distinguishes three design steps: *conceptual design, navigational design,* and *presentation design.* At each design step different aspects

N. Koch, P. Fraternali, and M. Wirsing (Eds.): ICWE 2004, LNCS 3140, pp. 459–472, 2004.

of adaptation can be specified in terms of formal models [2]. In order to make the semantics of models explicit, Hera uses RDF(S) [3,4]. RDFS inheritance mechanism proved to be useful for reusing different design artifacts [2]. However, previously Hera's presentation model has not been formalized, nor was adaptation at the presentation level implemented in the Hera tools.

The AMACONT project [5] recently introduced a *component-based XML document format*. It enables to compose personalized ubiquitous Web presentations from reusable document components encapsulating adaptive content, behavior, and layout. A special focus of AMACONT lies on the presentation layer of adaptive Web applications. It allows to describe the layout of adaptable Web components in a device independent way. Furthermore, a document generator for adjusting those components to different formats and devices has been developed.

Taking advantage of the analogies between Hera's *slices* and AMACONT's *components*, this paper aims at combining the modeling power of Hera with the presentation capabilities provided by AMACONT. The AMACONT concept of abstract *layout managers* is adopted for the presentation model of Hera, and its RDFS-based formalization is provided. According to this formalization of the presentation model, Hera specifications can now be automatically transformed to AMACONT's adaptable Web components.

The paper is structured as follows. After addressing related work and different aspects of presentation level adaptation in Section 2, a short overview of the model-driven Hera specification framework is given in Section 3. Section 4 explains the layout manager mechanism of AMACONT in detail. Finally, Section 5 introduces the formalized Hera presentation model schema and depicts the overall data transformation and presentation generation process. As a proof of concept the proposed methodology was implemented for an art museum WIS. To help the reader grasp the different models, graphical excerpts are provided for the different RDFS model representations.

2   Presentation Layer Adaptation

2.1   Presentation Design

Recently, different approaches for modeling hypermedia or Web applications have emerged. Among the most significant contributions besides Hera we mention the Object Oriented Hypermedia Design Model (OOHDM [6]), the Web Modeling Language (WebML [7]), the UML-based Web Engineering approach (UWE [8]), Object-Oriented Web-Solutions Modelling (OOWS [9]), and the Object-Oriented Hypermedia Method (OO-H [10]). Even though utilizing different formalisms and notations, all these methodologies are similar in distinguishing among (1) the *conceptual* design of the application domain, (2) the *navigational* design defining the (abstract navigational) structure of the hypermedia presentation, and (3) the *presentation* design specifying the rendering of navigation objects (layout).

Presentation design aims at declaring the "look-and-feel" of a Web application independent from its implementation. For this reason, some WIS methodologies use explicit models allowing to compose the layout of Web presentations from abstract user interface elements (also called *abstract data views* in OOHDM or *user interface views* in UWE). On the other hand, methods like WebML do not include a specific model for expressing presentation at the conceptual level and hide the presentation in application specific XSLT stylesheets. The drawback of the latter approach is that system maintenance becomes difficult.

As a significant approach for the automatic generation of Web-based multimedia presentations we mention the Cuypers engine [11]. Its presentation design uses Prolog rules declaring qualitative and quantitative constraints on the spatial and temporal arrangement of presentation elements. Though being very flexible, the lack of an explicit model makes it difficult to predict (or enforce) how the presentation should look like in the end of the generation process. Recently, Cuypers was enhanced by a multimedia formatting vocabulary for explicitly specifying the visual layout of multimedia presentations. Similar to the well-proven layout management of TEX, it allows to adjust presentation elements according to a top-to-bottom (`vbox`) or a left-to-right (`hbox`) order. Still, more difficult arrangements (like the layout managers `GridLayout`, `BorderLayout`, or `OverlayLayout` from the Java AWT libraries) are not supported, yet.

In recent years, different XML-compliant user interface descriptions languages, like UIML and XIML have emerged [12]. However, besides abstract layout specification they also aim at modeling other UI aspects, such as domain objects, user tasks, or dialogs. In Human-Computer Interaction research user interface design has often not been integrated with the earlier stages in WIS design. Similar to the Cuypers approach, constraint-based techniques for dynamically adjusting abstract XML presentation descriptions to the displays of mobile devices are discussed in [13].

2.2   Adaptation in Presentation Design

As *personalization* and *adaptation* become prominent issues of WIS design, we claim that it is inevitable to include adaptation aspects in presentation design. Still, whereas adaptation has been extensively considered in conceptual and navigational design [2,7], adaptation in the presentation layer has not yet been a central issue of WIS methodologies. Nevertheless, in order to support users' different layout preferences and client devices, different adaptation aspects have to be specified in presentation design.

- Firstly, it is important to adjust *media instances* to varying technical system parameters provided by different network environments and client devices, such as bandwidth, display resolution, or color depth. In order to consider such differences, variants of selected media items have to be provided with different quality.
- A further adaptation target is the corporate design (the "look-and-feel") of the Web presentation. As an example, in an online shop it is common to provide different design variants according to different user properties (age, education, interests, visual impairments etc.) but also according to

external parameters (seasons, events, anniversaries etc.). Depending on these aspects, design elements such as background colors, fonts (size, color, type), or buttons can be varied.

– Finally, the *spatial* and *temporal* adjustment of layout elements is also an important personalization issue. Depending on the screen size, the supported document formats, and the interaction techniques provided by different client devices, the presentation components should be displayed accordingly. We mention 3 mechanisms for display adaptation: (1) *Reorganization*: In this case the arrangement of media elements on a Web page is adapted. Whereas for example the tabular arrangement of layout components may look good on conventional desktops, it could cause a lot of undesirable horizontal scrolling when being browsed on handhelds with limited display size. (2) *Exclusion*: Information being unsuitable for a particular browser (e.g. a picture gallery for a monochrome cellphone) or design elements without a semantic meaning (e.g. company logos in an online shop) can be excluded from presentations on devices with small displays or low bandwidth connections. (3) *Separation*: As an alternative to exclusion, it can be advantageous to put certain content pieces onto separate pages and automatically create hyperlinks to those pages. This mechanism is very useful to keep the structure of Web pages while providing a lot of information easily understandable on handhelds.

The mentioned examples represent static adaptation (also called *adaptability*), i.e. an adaptation that does not consider the user's browsing behavior. However, in some cases it is meaningful to consider dynamic adaptation (*adaptivity*), i.e. adaptation according to parameters that may change while the hypermedia presentation is being browsed. As possible scenarios (in presentation design) we mention the dynamic reorganization of presentation elements on a Web page when the user resizes her browser window or the delivery of alternative media instances when the available bandwidth for a mobile user is decreasing.

3   The Hera Methodology

A typical scenario in a WIS is that in response to a user query the system (semi-) automatically generates a hypermedia presentation. The generated hypermedia presentation needs to be tailored to the device characteristics and to the user preferences. Hera [1] is an example of a model-driven methodology for designing these aspects in a WIS. It proposes a sequence of steps that the WIS designer needs to follow: the conceptual design defining the data schema, the application design specifying the navigation through the data, and the presentation design describing the rendering of the data. During this entire process, possible adaptation aspects are included in the associated models [2]. This section concentrates on two of these models: the conceptual model and the application model. The presentation model (its extended definition) will be described in Section 5, after introducing the adaptive layout managers of AMACONT.

The *Conceptual Model* (CM) defines the schema of the data available in the WIS. It is composed of a hierarchy of concepts and concept relationships.

Concepts have associated attributes that refer to media items. Figure 1 gives an excerpt of the CM for our running example. Concepts are depicted in dark ovals and contain light ovals which stand for concept attributes. In the specification of relationship cardinalities the 'Set' construct is used on the side of the concept that can have more than one instance associated to one instance of the other concept.

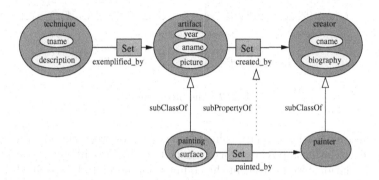

Fig. 1. The conceptual model

The media types associated to the concept attributes are described in the *Media Model* (MM), a submodel of CM. MM is a hierarchical model composed of media types. The most primitive media types are: Text, Image, Audio, and Video. Figure 2 shows an excerpt of the MM for our running example. Media types are depicted in dark rectangles.

Adaptation in the CM is based on the *conditional inclusion* of elements. Arbitrary complex conditions referencing (ranges of) data describing the device capabilities and user preferences can be used. As we do specify these conditions as XSLT conditions their expressive power is equivalent to the expressive power of XSLT conditions. This information is stored in a *user profile* containing attribute-value pairs according to a CC/PP [14] vocabulary. The light rectangles in Figure 2 depict two adaptation conditions considering screen size constraints. One condition requires that a long text for the technique description and a large image for the artifact pictures is used for PCs. The other condition stipulates that a short text for the technique description and a small image for the artifact pictures is used for PDAs. Remember that the selection of content variants with different quality is an important means of device adaptation.

The *Application Model* (AM) specifies the navigational aspects of the application. It is based on the notion of a *slice* which is a meaningful grouping of concept attributes that need to be shown together in the hypermedia presentation. A slice can be viewed as a presentation attribute associated to a concept. In this way the AM is an extension of the CM that provides a view over the CM.

The AM is composed of a hierarchy of slices and *slice relationships*. There are two kinds of slice relationships: compositional relationships (aggregation between

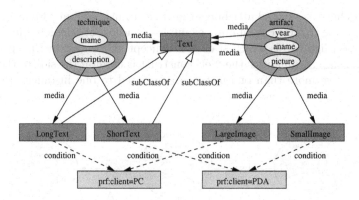

Fig. 2. The media model

slices) and navigational relationships (navigation between slices). If a compositional slice relationship relates slices associated with two different concepts, then the CM relationship involved in the composition needs to be specified. Figure 3 shows an excerpt of the AM for our running example. Slices are depicted (as their name suggests) by pizza-slice shapes. Hierarchical relationships between slices are omitted here due to lack of space (we refer the reader to [2] for details on this matter). In complete analogy to the CM, adaptation issues in the AM can be defined by attaching *appearance conditions* to slices.

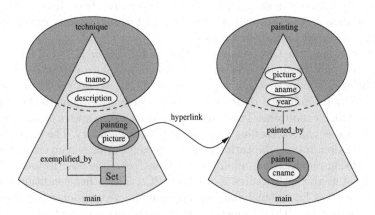

Fig. 3. The application model

4   AMACONT's Component-Based Document Model

The component-based document format of AMACONT [5] aims at building personalized ubiquitous Web applications by aggregating and linking *configurable document components.* These components are instances of an XML grammar representing adaptable content on different abstraction levels, i.e. layers in AMA-CONT (see Figure 4). *Media components* encapsulate concrete media assets by describing them with technical metadata. *Content units* group media components by declaring their layout in a device-independent way. Finally, *document components* define a hierarchy out of content units to fulfill a specific semantic role. The *hyperlink view* for defining typed links is spanned over all component layers. For a detailed introduction to the document model the reader is referred to [5].

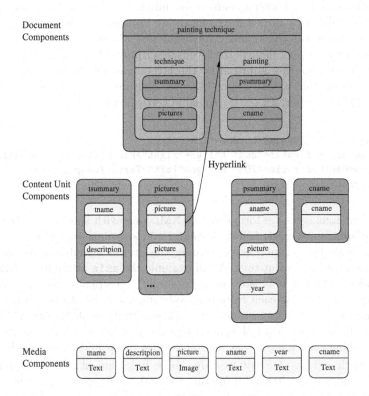

Fig. 4. The document model

In order to describe the *presentation* of component-based Web documents, AMACONT allows to attach XML-based layout descriptions [5] to components. Inspired by the layout manager mechanism of the Java language (AWT, Swing) and the abstract user interface representations of UIML or XIML [12], they describe a client-independent layout allowing to abstract from the exact resolution of the browser's display[1]. Furthermore, they also enable to declare simple

---

[1] In contrast to UIML or XIML, AMACONT offers a light-weight solution that focuses only on the rendering of components and not on other aspects like tasks, domain objects, or dialogs, that can be effectively dealt with in the CM or AM.

presentation layer adaptation rules. Note that layout managers of a given component only describe the presentation of its immediate subcomponents which encapsulate their own layout information in a standard component-based way.

Currently four layout managers are defined. BoxLayout lays out multiple components either vertically or horizontally. BorderLayout arranges components to fit in five regions: north, south, east, west, and center. It was chosen because it strongly resembles the structure of many Web pages consisting of a header, an optional footer, a main area and one or two sidebars. OverlayLayout allows to present components on top of each other. Finally, GridLayout enables to lay out components in a grid with a configurable number of columns and rows. Though it can be realized by nested BoxLayouts, we implemented it separately because WISs often present dynamically retrieved sets of data in a tabular way. The following code snippet depicts the layout description of a content unit containing two media components adjusted by the layout manager BoxLayout. An image (aligned right) and a text object (aligned left) are arranged above each other, taking 30 and 70 percent of the available vertical space.

```
<BoxLayout axis="yAxis" border="1">
   <ComponentRef ratio="30%" halign="right">Picture1</ComponentRef>
   <ComponentRef ratio="70%" halign="left">Text1</ComponentRef>
</BoxLayout>
```

Layout managers are formalized as XML tags with specific attributes. Two kinds of attributes exist: *layout attributes* and *subcomponent attributes*. Layout attributes declare properties concerning the overall layout and are defined in the corresponding layout tags. As an example the axis attribute of BoxLayout determines whether it is laid out horizontally or vertically. Subcomponent attributes describe how each referenced subcomponent has to be arranged in its surrounding layout. For instance, the halign attribute of Picture1 declares it to be right-justified. Table 1 summarizes the possible attributes of BoxLayout by describing their names, role, usage (required or optional) and possible values.

Even though most attributes are device independent, we also allowed two platform-dependent attributes in order to consider the specific card-based structure of WML presentations. The optional attribute wml_visible determines whether in a WML presentation the given subcomponent should be shown on the same card. If not, it is put onto a separate card that is accessible by an automatically generated hyperlink, the text of which is defined in wml_description. Note that this kind of content separation (see Section 2) provides scalability by fragmenting the presentation according to the very small displays of WAP-capable mobile phones.

The rendering of media objects is done at run time by XSLT stylesheets transforming components with abstract layout properties to specific output formats, such as XHTML, cHTML, and WML.

Table 1. BoxLayout attributes

Layout Attributes	Meaning	Usage	Values
axis	Orientation of the BoxLayout	req.	xAxis|yAxis
space	Space between subcomponents	opt.	int
width	Width of the whole layout	opt.	string
height	Height of the whole layout	opt.	string
border	Width of border between subcomponents	opt.	int
Subcomponent Attributes	**Meaning**	**Usage**	**Values**
halign	Horizontal alignment of subcomponents	opt.	left|center|right
valign	Vertical alignment of subcomponents	opt.	top|center|bottom
ratio	Space taken by subcomponent	opt.	percentage
wml_visible	Should be shown on same WML card?	opt.	boolean
wml_desc	Link description for WML	opt.	string

5 Putting It All Together

There are several analogies between *instances* of a Hera application model and *components* in AMACONT. Both represent meaningful presentation units bearing also some semantic role (e.g. painting or painting technique) and are recursive structures enabling an arbitrary depth of hierarchy. Moreover, both top-level slices and top-level document components correspond to pages to be presented on the user's display and may contain adaptation issues according to device profiles and user profile parameters. However, in contrast to application model instances AMACONT components also contain adaptive layout information. Note that layout in Hera is specified in the presentation model (hence, the extensions we made to the definition of this Hera model).

Taking advantage of these analogies and the fact that both Hera and AMA-CONT rest upon XML, our aim was to combine the modeling power of Hera and the versatile presentation capabilities of AMACONT. Therefore, the concept of adaptive layout managers was transferred to the Hera *Presentation Model* (PM). As in AMACONT, they can be assigned to Hera slices in order to declare the arrangement of their subslices in an implementation-independent way. Furthermore, the PM schema allowing to declare such assignments was formalized in RDFS. This formalization enables the *automatic mapping* of high-level Hera AM and PM specifications to AMACONT's implementation units, i.e. components.

5.1 PM Schema

The RDFS-based Hera presentation model supports two mechanisms: the definition of layout managers and their assignment to AM slices. Based on our running example, the following code snippet from a Presentation Model demonstrates how a layout manager can be assigned to a slice. The graphical form of this PM is shown in Figure 5.

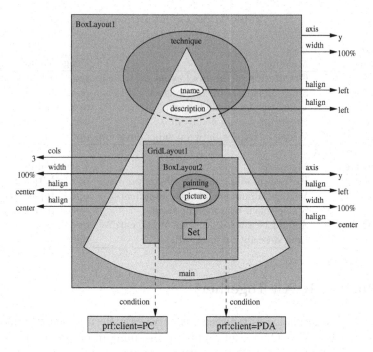

Fig. 5. A PM example

```
<Slice rdf:about="#Slice.technique.main">
    <layout rdf:resource="#BoxLayout1"/>
</Slice>
```

This assignment rule implies to visualize the slice `Slice.technique.main` according to the layout manager `BoxLayout1`. The following example shows how `BoxLayout1` is specified in detail.

```
<BoxLayout rdf:id="BoxLayout1">
   <axis>y</axis>
   <width>100%</width>
   <slice-ref rdf:resource="Slice.technique.tname"
           pres:halign="left"/>
   <slice-ref rdf:resource="Slice.technique.description"
           pres:halign="left"/>
   <access-element-ref rdf:resource="SetOfLinks_1"
           pres:halign="center"/>
</BoxLayout>
```

Attributes for components of AMACONT's layout manager (Section 4) have been adopted to describe the spatial adjustment of subslices. Both attributes describing the overall layout and attributes specifying the arrangement of each referenced subslice (`slice-ref`) or access element (`access-element-ref`) can be defined. Still, the layout manager of a slice only specifies how its immediate subslices are to be rendered. For the access element `SetOfLinks_1` the layout specification might look like this:

```
<Access-element rdf:about="#SetOfLinks_1">
 <layout rdf:resource="#GridLayout1"
         pres:condition="pres:client='PC'"/>
 <layout rdf:resource="#BoxLayout2"
         pres:condition="pres:client='PDA'"/>
</Access-element>
```

Note the attribute `pres:condition` that allows to declare simple *adaptation conditions* that reference parameters from the user/device profile. Whereas for example the paintings exemplifying the presented painting technique are arranged on a PC in a tabular way (GridLayout1), the small screen size of PDAs requires adjusting them below each other (BoxLayout2).

In contrast to AMACONT's layout managers (defined at instance level), Hera layout assignments have to be specified at *schema level*. Due to the dynamic nature of WIS applications, this means that the number of items in an access element is not known at design time. In such cases one should use either a `BoxLayout` with an undefined number of cells or a `GridLayout` so that only one of its dimensions (`columns` or `rows`) is predeclared. The missing dimensions are automatically computed at run time.

5.2   The Data Transformation Process

Figure 6 gives an overview of the data transformation process. It is composed of four transformation steps that are described in detail in the rest of this section.

In the first step, based on the attribute values from the user/platform profile, the conditions included in the different models are evaluated. Elements having a condition evaluated to false are removed from their corresponding models. As a result, an adapted conceptual model, an adapted application model, and an adapted presentation model are obtained. Note that this adaptation is done at the schema level. The rest of the transformation steps will be performed at the instance level (or data level).

The input data to the transformation pipeline is the conceptual model instance. The gathering of this data in response to a user query is outside the scope of this paper, see [1]. In the second step the conceptual model instance is used to populate the application model. The resulting application model instance represents the presentation navigational structure.

The third step aims at *mapping* AM instances to adaptable AMACONT components, and is realized by two transformations substeps. In the first substep slice composition references are resolved (*unfolding*) and AM instances with hierarchical slice structures (slices containing subslices) are created. In the second substep the unfolded AM instances are automatically *transformed* to hierarchical AMACONT component structures. First, top-level slices are mapped to top-level document components. Then, subslices and their attributes are recursively mapped to subcomponents according to the following rules:

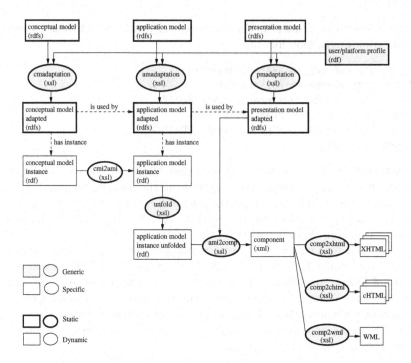

Fig. 6. The data transformation process

1. Concept attributes are mapped to media components. `Integer` and `String` attributes are assigned to text components, media attributes to corresponding media components (image, audio, video etc.).
2. Slices containing concept attributes from a single concept are mapped to single document components containing a content unit that aggregates the corresponding media components.
3. Slices referring to concept attributes and subslices from different concepts are mapped to composite document components containing child document components for each aggregated subslice. For those subslices this mapping process has to be performed recursively.

The *layout attributes* of the created AMACONT components are *configured* according to the PM schema. Beginning at top-level document components and visiting their subcomponents recursively, the appropriate AMACONT layout descriptors are added to the meta-information section of each component's header. Since the layout manager attributes of the Hera PM rest upon the layout concepts of AMACONT, this mapping is a straightforward process. Yet, for access elements (containing a variable number of subslices depending on a dynamic query) the concrete dimensions of `BoxLayout` or `GridLayout` have to be recalculated for each particular user request.

In the last (fourth) step the components are transformed to the corresponding output format. For instance, a `BoxLayout` in XHTML is realized by means of a table (and its specific attributes) with either one column or one row. However, not all layout managers can be visualized properly on all devices. As an example, since PDAs or WAP phones have very small displays, a horizontal BoxLayout is automatically converted to a vertical arrangement of subcomponents on those devices. Similarly, in the case of OverlayLayout only the upper component is presented on handhelds. Figure 7 shows two possible outputs of our running example, one for a PC (XHTML) and another for a PDA (cHTML).

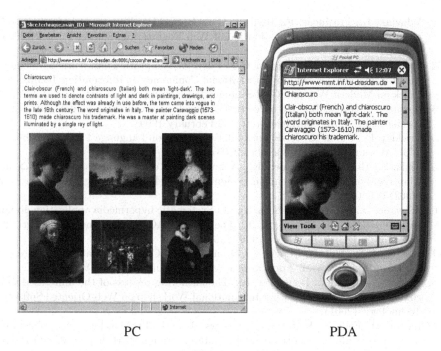

PC   PDA

Fig. 7. Desktop/PDA presentation

6   Conclusion and Future Work

In this work we have illustrated the role of presentation layer adaptation in WIS design. We have demonstrated how the Hera specification framework (and its implementation tools) can be complemented with the flexible implementation layer provided by the AMACONT project. Thus these high-level specifications can be mapped to components to be published in different output formats. It has resulted in an integrated framework (and tool set) that combines the capabilities of Hera at the conceptual and navigation levels with those of AMACONT at the presentation level.

A major focus in ongoing work concentrates on the dynamic coupling of Hera and AMACONT. The static presentation involved in adaptable Web presentations has to be enhanced by feedback mechanisms that allow to dynamically react to user's browsing behavior. For this, interactions have to be captured in the generated presentation and sent to the application layer, so that new application model instances can be created and passed back to the presentation layer (engine). With this extension we will also be able to deal with dynamic adaptation (adaptivity) in the joint system.

References

1. Vdovjak, R., Frasincar, F., Houben, G.J., Barna, P.: Engineering semantic web information systems in hera. Journal of Web Engineering, Rinton Press **2** (2003) 003–026
2. Frasincar, F., Barna, P., Houben, G.J., Fiala, Z.: Adaptation and reuse in designing web information systems. In: International Conference on Information Technology, Track on Modern Web and Grid Systems, IEEE Computer Society (2004) 387–391
3. Lassila, O., Swick, R.: Resource description framework (rdf) model and syntax specification. W3C Working Draft. (22 February 1999)
4. Brickley, D., Guha, R.: RDF Vocabulary Description Language 1.0: RDF Schema. W3C Working Draft. (10 October 2003)
5. Fiala, Z., Hinz, M., Meissner, K., Wehner, F.: A component-based approach for adaptive dynamic web documents. Journal of Web Engineering, Rinton Press **2** (2003) 058–073
6. Schwabe, D., Rossi, G., Barbosa, S.D.J.: Systematic hypermedia application design with OOHDM. In: Hypertext '96, The Seventh ACM Conference on Hypertext, Washington DC, 1996, ACM (1996) 116–128
7. Ceri, S., Fraternali, P., Bongio, A., Brambilla, M., Comai, S., Matera, M.: Designing Data-Intensive Web Applications. Morgan Kaufmann (2003)
8. Koch, N., Kraus, A., Hennicker, R.: The authoring process of the uml-based web engineering approach. In: First International Workshop on Web-Oriented Software Technology. (2001)
9. Pastor, O., Fons, J., Pelechano, V.: Oows: A method to develop web applications from web-oriented conceptual models. In: International Workshop on Web Oriented Software Technology (IWWOST). (2003) 65–70
10. Gomez, J., Cachero, C. In: OO-H Method: extending UML to model web interfaces. Idea Group Publishing (2003) 144–173
11. van Ossenbruggen, J., Geurts, J., Cornelissen, F., Hardman, L., Rutledge, L.: Towards second and third generation web-based multimedia. In: WWW10, The Tenth International Conference on the World Wide Web, Hong Kong, ACM (2001) 479–488
12. Souchon, N., Vanderdonckt, J.: A review of xml-compliant user interface description languages. In: Conference on Design, Specification, and Verification of Interactive Systems. Volume 2844 of Lecture Notes in Computer Science., Springer (2003) 377–391
13. Eisenstein, J., Vanderdonckt, J., Puerta, A.: Applying model-based techniques to the development of uis for mobile computers. In: 6th International Conference on Intelligent User Interfaces, ACM (2001) 69–76
14. Klyne, G., Reynolds, F., Woodrow, C., Ohto, H., Hjelm, J., Butler, M., Tran, L.: Composite Capability/Preference Profiles (CC/PP): Structure and Vocabularies. W3C Working Draft. (2003)

A Notation and Framework for Dialog Flow Control in Web Applications

Matthias Book and Volker Gruhn

Chair of Applied Telematics / e-Business,* Department of Computer Science
University of Leipzig, Klostergasse 3, 04109 Leipzig, Germany
{book, gruhn}@ebus.informatik.uni-leipzig.de

Abstract. The usability of web applications today often suffers from
the page-based medium's lack of intrinsic support for hierarchical dialog sequences mirroring the parent-child relationships between dialog
boxes in window-based user interfaces. For multi-channel applications,
an additional challenge lies in reconciling the device-independent business logic with the device-specific interaction patterns necessitated by
different clients' input/output capabilities. We therefore present a graphical Dialog Flow Notation that allows the specification of nestable dialog
sequences for different presentation channels. These specifications serve
as input for a Dialog Control Framework that controls the dialog flows
of complex web applications.

1 Introduction

Web engineers are faced with two major challenges today: The first is the difference between page-based and window-based user interface (UI) paradigms:
In window-based applications, any window can spawn "child windows", and
the completion of a dialog in a child window returns the user to the dialog in
the parent window. Users can rely on this predictable behavior that reinforces
their conceptual model and thus increases applications' usability [14]. In web
applications, however, only simple linear and branched dialog sequences can be
implemented with basic session state management techniques, while hierarchical
dialog sequences require more complex dialog control logic. Secondly, if an application shall be accessed through a variety of devices, their different input/output
(I/O) capabilities affect how users work with an application: A dialog that may
be completed in a single step on a desktop browser may have to be broken up into
multiple interaction steps on a mobile device. Yet, the server-side business logic
should remain independent of such client-side specifics [3,8]. This obviously calls
for a separation of presentation and business logic – however, that is not as trivial
as it sounds since the dialog control logic tends to get mixed up with the other
tiers. To address the issues of nestable dialogs and device-dependent interaction patterns, we introduce a Dialog Flow Notation that allows the specification
of complex dialog flows (section 2), and present a Dialog Control Framework
that provides the corresponding dialog control logic for black-box reuse in any
application (section 3).

---

* The Chair of Applied Telematics / e-Business is endowed by Deutsche Telekom AG.

N. Koch, P. Fraternali, and M. Wirsing (Eds.): ICWE 2004, LNCS 3140, pp. 473–477, 2004.
© Springer-Verlag Berlin Heidelberg 2004

2   The Dialog Flow Notation

The Dialog Flow Notation (DFN) specifies the sequence of UI pages and process-ing steps in an application, and the data exchanged between them. It models the dialog flow as a transition network called a **dialog graph**. The notation refers to the transitions as **events** and to the states as **dialog elements**. These ele-ments are further divided into hypertext pages (symbolized by dog-eared sheets and referred to by the more generic term **masks** in the DFN) and business logic operations (symbolized by circles and called **actions** here). Every dialog element can generate and receive multiple events. Which element will receive an event depends both on the event and the generating element (e.g., an event *e* may be received by action *1* if it was generated by mask *A*, but be received by action *2* if generated by mask *B*). Events can carry parameters containing form input submitted through a mask or data produced by the business logic to facilitate communication between elements. They are not bound to HTTP requests or responses, but can also link two actions or two masks. The DFN also provides **dialog modules** (symbolized by boxes with rounded corners) which encapsulate dialog graphs and enable the specification of nested dialog structures. When a module receives an event from the exterior dialog graph that it is embedded in, traversal of its interior dialog graph starts with the **initial event**. When the interior dialog graph terminates, it generates a **terminal event** that is prop-agated to the super-module and continues the traversal of the exterior dialog graph (Fig. 1). For more complex dialog structures, the DFN offers a number of additional event and element types [2] that we will not discuss here in detail.

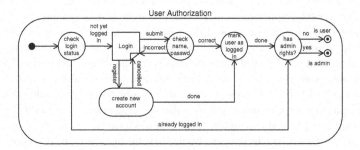

Fig. 1. Example: Dialog graph of *User Authorization* module

To cater to the different interaction patters required for different client de-vices, the DFN allows the specification of dialog flows for different presentation channels in multiple versions of a module and distinguishing them with **chan-nel labels** (Fig. 2). While the channels employ different dialog masks according to those devices' I/O capabilities, they use the same actions for processing the user's input, as indicated by the shading. This enables developers to reuse the device-independent business logic on multiple channels.

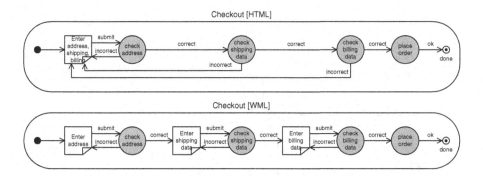

Fig. 2. Example: Dialog graphs of *Checkout* module on HTML and WML channel

3   The Dialog Control Framework

Web applications are usually designed according to the Model-View-Controller (MVC) paradigm [13], which suggests the separation of UI, business logic and control logic. The Dialog Control Framework (DCF) features a very strict implementation of the MVC pattern, completely separating not only the business logic and UI, but also the dialog flow specification and dialog control logic. As the coarse architecture (Fig. 3) shows, the action objects contain only calls to the business logic. The generic dialog control logic is contained in the **dialog controller** that receives events coming in through **channel servlets** on each presentation channel. It looks up the receivers of these events in the **dialog flow model** – a collection of objects representing dialog elements that hold references to each other to mirror the dialog flow, built upon initialization of the framework by parsing an XML-based representation of the graphical dialog flow specification. Depending on the receiver that the controller retrieved from the model for an event, it may call an action, forward the request to a mask, nest or terminate modules. The latter operations are performed on **module stacks**.

Due to the strict separation of tiers, device-independent applications can be built with minimal redundancy: Only the dialog masks and the dialog flow specifications need to be specified for the different presentation channels, while the business logic is implemented device-independently only once and the dialog control logic is provided by the framework. Since the dialog controller is aware of the whole dialog flow specified for each channel, it can manage complex dialog constructs such as nesting modules that would be hard to realize if the dialog control logic was distributed over all action objects.

4   Related Work

Most tools offering dialog control implementation support for web applications follow the MVC design pattern to facilitate easier dialog control. The Apache Jakarta Project's Struts framework [1] is the most popular solution today, however, it forces developers to combine business logic and dialog control logic in the

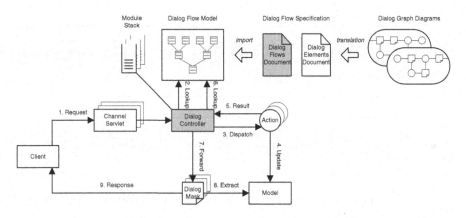

Fig. 3. Coarse architecture of the Dialog Control Framework

action objects, which renders the dialog control implementation cumbersome and inflexible. While the concept of an application-independent "screen flow manager" that determines the next view is described in the Java BluePrints [16], no framework seems to exist yet that employs this pattern to implement complex dialog constructs such as the arbitrarily nestable modules and device-specific dialog flows offered by the DCF. The World Wide Web Consortium's XForms initiative [5] is mostly concerned with the specification of widgets on pages and does not support nestable dialog modules.

Notations for the specification of web-based UIs mostly focus on data-intensive information systems, but not interaction-intensive applications [6]: Development processes such as RMM [11] and OOHDM [15], modeling notations and languages such as HDM-lite (used by the Autoweb tool [7]), and WebML [4] support the generation of web pages out of a large, structured data basis or provide dynamic views on database content, but do not allow the specification of highly interactive features with modular, nested dialog structures.

While the concept of modeling dialog systems as state-based systems is not new [9] and generic notations for this already exist (e.g. Statecharts [10]), we chose not to use any generic notation because expressing the particularities of web-based dialog flows (e.g. different dialog elements, modules and events) in those would be cumbersome in practice. Also, we wanted to provide the DFN with constructive instead of mere descriptive power, enabling developers to use complex dialog constructs intuitively without having to spell out their details in a generic notation.

5   Conclusions

The pragmatic approach advocated above notwithstanding, we are currently working on the definition of formal semantics that will enable us to reason about the specifications produced with the DFN (in addition to the operational semantics already defined by the DCF implementation). This can be achieved by showing that all DFN constructs can also be expressed by means of a more generic formalism, even if that would not be suitable for practical use.

While related methodologies tend to derive the web-based UI more or less directly from an established data model, the DFN does not make any assumptions about the underlying data model, but exclusively describes the users' interaction with the system. Thus, it should support a dialog-driven development process that emphasizes the ISO dialog principles of suitability for the task and conformity with user expectations [12] from the start.

References

1. Apache Jakarta Project. Struts. http://jakarta.apache.org/struts/
2. Book, M., Gruhn, V.: A Dialog Control Framework for Hypertext-based Applications. Proc. 3rd Intl Conf. on Quality Software (QSIC 2003), IEEE Press, 170–177
3. Butler, M., Giannetti, F., Gimson, R., et al.: Device Independence and the Web. IEEE Computing **6**, 5 (2002), 81–86
4. Ceri, S., Fraternali, P., Bongio, A.: Web Modeling Language (WebML): A Modeling Language for Designing Web Sites. Computer Networks **33** (2000), 137–157
5. Dubinko, M., Klotz, L.L., Merrick, R., et al.: XForms 1.0, W3C Recommendation (2003). http://www.w3.org/TR/2003/REC-xforms-20031014/
6. Fraternali, P.: Tools and Approaches for Developing Data-Intensive Web Applications: A Survey. ACM Computing Surveys **31**, 3 (1999), 227–263
7. Fraternali, P., Paolini, P.: Model-Driven Development of Web Applications: The Autoweb System. ACM Trans. on Information Systems **28**, 4 (2000), 323–382
8. Gaedke, M., Beigl, M., Gellersen, H.-W., et al.: Web Content Delivery to Heterogeneous Mobile Platforms. Advances in Database Technologies, LNCS 1552 (1998)
9. Green, M.: A Survey of Three Dialogue Models. ACM Trans. on Graphics **5**, 3 (1986), 244–275
10. Harel, D.: Statecharts: A visual formalism for complex systems. Science of Computer Programming **8**, 3 (1987), 231–274
11. Isakowitz, T., Stohr, E. A., Balasubramanian, P.: RMM: a methodology for structured hypermedia design. Comm. ACM **38**, 8 (1995), 34–44
12. International Organization for Standardization: Ergonomic requirements for office work with visual display terminals (VDTs) – Part 10: Dialogue principles. ISO 9241-10 (1996)
13. Krasner, G.E.: A Cookbook for using the Model-View-Controller User Interface Paradigm in Smalltalk. Journ. of Object-Oriented Programming **1**, 3 (1988), 26–49
14. Rice, J., Farquhar, A., Piernot, P., et al.: Using the web instead of a window system. Proc. CHI '96, 103–110. ACM Press (1996)
15. Schwabe, D., Rossi, G.: The object-oriented hypermedia design model. Comm. ACM **38**, 8 (1995), 45–46
16. Singh, I., Stearns, B., Johnson, M., et al.: Designing Enterprise Applications with the J2EE Platform, 2nd Edition. Addison-Wesley (2002)

A Framework for the Internationalization of Data-Intensive Web Applications

Alberto Belussi and Roberto Posenato

Dipartimento di Informatica - Università degli Studi di Verona
Ca' Vignal, Strada le Grazie, 15
37134 Verona, Italy
{alberto.belussi, roberto.posenato}@univr.it

Abstract. The globalization process makes it necessary to provide information in different languages in order to enlarge the audience of the information presented through the web. Therefore, it is often required to extend the web system for handling information in more than one language. This process is called internationalization of a system. An important requirement of this process is that it should be applied without a strong reorganization of the web application that implements the web site. We propose a general framework for the internationalization of data-intensive web applications based on the MVC-2 paradigm and a relational database system. This framework has been applied succesfully at the University of Verona (Italy) for the internationalization of the web sites of all departments and all faculties.

1 Introduction

In the last few years the globalization process has influenced the activities of any kind of organization around the world. One effect of this process concerns the production of information in more than one language. In general we call the adaption of an application to support a multilingual environment *internationalization of an application*, while the process of adaption of an application for a specific region or language, by adding local-specific components and translating text, is called *localization of an application*.

The internationalization of a web application can be a hard task, in particular if the application architecture does not conform to a standard schema, like the Model View Control (MVC) paradigm, or does not separate at least the logic and the presentation in different modules.

In this paper we propose a general framework for the internationalization of data-intensive web applications [6,5] based on the MVC-2 paradigm [1] and one or more relational database systems. This framework can also be applied to existing web applications with a low impact on code restructuring as shown by the experience at the University of Verona.

Previous works on data-intensive web applications regards mainly the definition of a design methodology and the implementation of case tools [7,5,4,6]. Many other papers in the human-computer interaction area face the general problem

N. Koch, P. Fraternali, and M. Wirsing (Eds.): ICWE 2004, LNCS 3140, pp. 478–482, 2004.

of internationalization and localization of data presentation in web sites, considering in particular aspects like symbols or color perception in different cultures, format conventions (i.e., date presentation), etc. [2]. To our knowledge, only in [8] a general approach for the internationalization of a web application including database schema extension is presented. In our approach, we extend the solution proposed in [8] by adding a general mechanism for queries specification and query results handling.

The paper is organized as follows. First, the problem of internationalization of a web application is described. Next, the proposed framework is presented by describing in details its components.

2   Problem Definition and Proposed Solution

In this paper with the term "web application" we refer to any software application that is accessible using a web browser. The internationalization of web applications regards *the implementation of a mechanism that is able to produce, for each page the web application generates (master page), a set of pages with the same content but each one in a different language (translated pages)*. This problem can have different solutions with respect to the architecture of the web application and the level of update between the master pages and the translated ones that we intend to maintain.

According to the architecture, different solutions of the internationalization problem can be applied. In particular, in *Static Web Applications* the replication of the static HTML files with the translation of their content in the languages of interest is the widely used solution; of course, the maintenance of the consistency between the different replications can become a time consuming work [3]. In *Data-Intensive Web Applications* the replication is still a chance but it requires to generate one or more copies of the whole system. An alternative solution is to make the application *language independent*. This can be achieved by a revision of the whole application consisting of the following three steps: (1) *Database extension*: the database has to be extended in order to store the translations of data that are subject to change with respect to the language; (2) *Queries rewriting*: the queries have to be rewritten to take into account the new tables containing data translations; (3) *Static text translation*: the static text inside script files (like JSP, ASP, etc.) has to be replaced by a call to a procedure that computes the right translation according to the required language.

We propose a framework for making a data-intensive web application language independent. In particular, the framework can be applied to applications adopting the MVC-2 paradigm [1] in order to obtain the following results: (1) it should make the application language independent in the sense that the application should work with a certain set of foreign languages and this set can be extended without requiring any code modification; (2) it should allow one to extend the set of attributes subject to translations without requiring any code modification; (3) it should require the minimal database extension, but, at the same time, the minimal effort in query rewriting and the minimal performance worsening in query processing.

Hereby we describe in details the proposed frameworks considering: database extension, queries rewriting and internationalization of state objects.

2.1   Database Extension and Queries Rewriting

A data-intensive web application interacts with one or more database servers, which provide dynamically the data to be published. This approach always guarantees web pages with up to date content. The internationalization process requires an extension of the database schema in order to store the translations of the information stored in the database.

We suggest the following general approach to extend the database schema, by supposing to adopt the Entity-Relationship model for the conceptual database design and a relational system for the database implementation:

1. For each entity type E with attributes $\{A_1, \ldots, A_n\}$ having some attributes $\{A_{i_1}, \ldots, A_{i_m}\}$ subject to translation, we specify a new entity type E_{trans}, weak entity of E, with the following attributes $\{language, A_{i_1}, \ldots, A_{i_m}\}$. This implies the creation of a new table $E_{\text{trans}}(\underline{K_E, language}, A_{i_1}, \ldots, A_{i_m})$ where K_E is the set of attributes representing the primary key of E.
2. For each relationship type R among entity types $\{E_1, \ldots, E_n\}$ with attributes $\{A_1, \ldots, A_n\}$ having some attributes $\{A_{i_1}, \ldots, A_{i_m}\}$ subject to translation, we replace R with a new entity type E_R, weak entity of $\{E_1, \ldots, E_n\}$, with the attributes $\{A_1, \ldots, A_n\}$ and we add a second entity type E_R_{trans}, weak entity of E_R, with the following attributes $\{language, A_{i_1}, \ldots, A_{i_m}\}$. This implies the creation of a new table $R_{\text{trans}}(\underline{K_R, language}, A_{i_1}, \ldots, A_{i_m})$ where K_R is the set of attributes representing the primary key of table R).

Regarding database schema extension other solutions could possibly be considered as discussed in [3]. After database extension, a query rewriting is necessary in order to include the translated attributes in the result of each query. The properties of this rewriting technique are the following ones: (1) it preserves the result cardinality that the query had before the internationalization; (2) it uses only two languages L_1 and L_2 as query parameters (these two languages are obtained by applying a custom rule to the preference languages list coming from the HTTP request, see [3] for details); (3) it extends each query result schema by applying the following rule: for each attribute A subject to translation, we replace A with three attributes $L0\text{-}A$, $L1\text{-}A$ and $L2\text{-}A$, containing its values in L_0 (master language) and its translations in L_1 and L_2 respectively.

Given a generic query, SELECT $E_1.A_1, \ldots, E_k.A_n$ FROM $E_1, \ldots, E_m$ WHERE C, suppose that the table E_1 has a translation table $E_{1\ trans}(\underline{K, language}, A_1)$, then the query must be rewritten as follows:

SELECT $E_1.A_1$ AS $"L0\text{-}A_1''$, $L1.A_1$ AS $"L1\text{-}A_1''$, $L2.A_1$ AS $"L2\text{-}A_1''$, $\ldots, E_k.A_n$
FROM E_1 LEFT JOIN $E_{1\ trans}$ AS $L1$ ON $E_1.K = L1.K$
            LEFT JOIN $E_{1\ trans}$ AS $L2$ ON $E_1.K = L2.K, \ldots, E_m$
WHERE C AND $L1.language =?$ AND $L2.language =?$

Notice that, after the rewriting process, the resulting query contains some parameters, represented as "?", which stand for the requested language L_1 and the alternative language L_2 respectively.

This rewriting technique can be trivially extended to the general case in which table $E_{1\,trans}$ contains more than one attribute and there are other tables E_i having a corresponding translation table $E_{i\,trans}$. Moreover, given a query containing m tables with attributes subject to translation, the number of outer joins that have to be added to the query is equal to $2m$.

2.2   Internationalization of State Objects

In a MVC-2 data-intensive web application, state objects represent both the request from the browser and the data (often given by tuples of queries results) needed to build the response. Given the goal of applying language independent extensions, the more suitable way to do the task is to insert, for each object property A subject to translation, a new property A-lang that will contain the language code of the value stored in A. In this way a state object can store values in any language with a minimal impact on its type restructuring.

Given a tuple t of a query result Q, having translated values stored in the same tuple, a state object O is created and is populated by applying the following approach: (1) for each attribute A of Q subject to translation choose one translated value in t according to a custom rule; (2) put the chosen value in the corresponding property A_i of O and its language-code into property A_i-lang; (3) finally, put the other values belonging to attributes not subject to translation in the corresponding properties of O.

Therefore, each state objects constructor having a query result tuple as parameter, have to be modified according to the new proposed approach. Nevertheless, this process can be avoided if all constructors based on query result tuple are replaced with a single meta-method *Populate*. Method *Populate* works as follow: given a state object, a query result tuple, the requested language L_1 and one ore more alternative languages, it fills the state object with tuple values according to L_1 and the alternative languages. *Populate* can be implement under the following conditions: (1) the query result is written as described in Section 2.1; (2) the state object representing a tuple of a query result Q contains at least as many properties as the attributes of Q where each property has the same name of the corresponding attribute of Q and contains a property for the language-code A_i-lang for each property A_i subject to translation; (3) the programming language provides introspection mechanism for the state object and for the query result object as Java language provides with Reflection/Introspection mechanism. The pseudo-code of *populate* is shown in [3].

3   The Experience at University of Verona

The proposed approach has been applied for the internationalization of the web sites of the faculties and departments of the University of Verona (UNIVR). The UNIVR web system is organized as follows: (1) a portal site composed of static HTML files; (2) 8 faculties sites, each generated by a data-intensive web application (Faculty On Line - FOL); (3) 24 departments sites, each generated by a data-intensive web application (Department On Line - DOL). Both FOL and DOL are developed according to the MVC-2 paradigm using Servlets and JavaServer Pages technology; all the data come from one database containing the information about the teaching and research activities of the whole University. We have applied the proposed framework for the internationalization of FOL and DOL during 2003 and now the faculties and departments sites can show pages in four foreign languages (English, French, German and Spanish) and Italian. The impact of the internationalization process of the UNIVR web system can be summarized as follows: the database schema, that contained 275 tables, now contains 340 tables and the Java classes of FOL (DOL) contain 117 SQL queries as before the internationalization and they contain about 5% code lines more.

4 Conclusions

In this paper we have illustrated a framework for the internationalization of a data-intensive web application. The proposed solution has been studied for an application based on the MVC-2 paradigm and interacting with a relational database system. The framework was successfully applied for the internationalization of the web sites of University of Verona.

References

1. D. Alur, J. Cruspi, and D. Malks. *Core J2EE Patterns: Best Practices and Design Strategies*. Prentice Hall, 2001.
2. N. Aykin. Internationalization and Localization of the Web Sites. In Hans-Jörg Bullinger and Jürgen Ziegler, editors, *Proceedings of HCI International '99*, pages 1218–1222, Munich, Germany, August 22–26 1999.
3. Alberto Belussi and Roberto Posenato. Internationalizing Data-Intensive Web Applications. Technical Report DI 16/2004, Dip. di Informatica-Università di Verona, 2004.
4. S. Ceri, P. Fraternali, A. Bongio, S. Butti, R. Acerbis, M. Tagliasacchi, G. Toffetti, C. Conserva, R. Elli, F. Ciapessoni, and C. Greppi. Architectural Issues and Solutions in the Development of Data-Intensive Web Applications. In *Proc. 1st Biennial Conf. on Innovative Data Systems Research*, Asilomar, CA, USA, January 5–8 2003.
5. S. Ceri, P. Fraternali, and S. Paraboschi. Design Principles for Data-Intensive Web Sites. *SIGMOD Record*, 28(1):84–89, 1999.
6. P. Fraternali. Tools and Approaches for Developing Data-Intensive Web Applications: A Survey. *ACM Computing Surveys*, 31(3):227–263, 1999.
7. P. Merialdo, P. Atzeni, and G. Mecca. Design and Development of Data-Intensive Web Sites: The Anareus Approach. *ACM Transactions on Internet Technology*, 3(1):49–92, February 2003.
8. Inderjeet Singh, Beth Stearns, Mark Johnson, and the Enterprise Team. *Design Enterprise Applications with the J2EE^{TM} Platform*. Addison-Wesley Publishing Company, second edition, 2002.

Using Web Services to Build Context-Aware Applications in Ubiquitous Computing

Gerhard Austaller, Jussi Kangasharju, and Max Mühlhäuser

Telecooperation Group
Department of Computer Science
Darmstadt University of Technology
64289 Darmstadt, Germany,
{gerhard,jussi,max}@tk.informatik.tu-darmstadt.de

Abstract. Ubiquitous and mobile web applications are typically very autonomous in nature, because they rely on additional information about the user's context. In this paper we present a general context model for including context information into ubiquitous and mobile web applications. Our model is based on layers, which cover the path from context sources to the application level, including all intermediate filtering and context fusion. As an example, we present a context-aware calendar application built according to our context model.

1 Introduction

The credo of ubiquitous computing is that hardware and software in everyday life should "disappear", and be as autonomous as possible. This requirement has large effects on the system design. Autonomy can be achieved through the use of additional information about the user's context. Our definition of context information follows that of Dey [1] and Schmidt [2], in that any relevant information about the user's situation can be considered to be context. In addition to this, we also consider as context information sources which are not in the user's immediate vicinity, but contain information that is relevant to the user at that time.

In this paper, we develop a general model for including context information into mobile and ubiquitous applications. Our model has several layers, from the context sources to the application, which perform all the tasks of context filtering and fusion, so that the application only receives the relevant information about the user's context.

As an example application of our model, we implement a context-aware calendar which keeps track of a user's appointments and reminds her when she should leave for her next appointment; this reminder naturally depends on where the user is, where the next appointment is, etc. In order to be able to exploit as many existing sources of context, we have decided to built our calendar using web services.

Hence, the contribution of this paper is two-fold. First, we present our general context model for building context-aware applications and services. Second, we present an implementation of our context model using a web services architecture.

This paper is organized as follows. Section 2 presents the context layers we propose and section 3 discusses the implementation of the context-aware calendar. We review related work in Section 4. Finally, Section 5 concludes the paper.

N. Koch, P. Fraternali, and M. Wirsing (Eds.): ICWE 2004, LNCS 3140, pp. 483–487, 2004.
© Springer-Verlag Berlin Heidelberg 2004

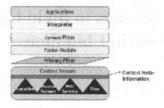

Fig. 1. Context Stack

2   Context Model

This section describes to conceptual model of our context stack. By introducing several layers of abstraction between the actual context source and the application, we allow programmers to use context information in their applications in an easy and straightforward manner. Such layered structures are widely used in programming (e.g., graphics libraries, TCP/IP network stack), but have only recently been considered by researchers in context aware computing [1]. Figure 1 shows the layers in our general context model. The rest of this section discusses the details of each layer.

Context Sensors

The lowest layer is the *Context Sensors* layer. This layer contains all the context sources which are of interest to us. Regardless of the name, we do not limit ourselves to actual physical sensors as context sources, such as temperature, light intensity, or noise level sensors. Context information such as calendar appointments or timetables are typically considered higher-level context information; however, we include them in this layer as well.

This layer feeds context information to the rest of the stack. It is responsible for expressing the context information in a suitable format and also adds metadata (e.g., a timestamp) to the information. This metadata is passed up along the stack so that the higher layers can decide whether that piece of information is still relevant.

Primary Filter

The next layer is the *Primary Filter* layer. Its main purpose is to protect the stack from being flooded by information. When context information is continuosly delivered from a source (e.g., a temperature reading), the application may be interested in only a few values every now and then. This is especially important for context sources which deliver their information by pushing it, instead of the application pulling it.

Fusion Module

The role of the *Fusion Module* is to fusion the context delivered through the Primary Filter. This fusioning can either make the context information easier to access (for the higher layers) or to get a higher-level representation of the raw context information. Some abstracting functionality is also included in the next higher layer, the Context Filter (see below).

An example of how the Fusion Module can provide easier access to context information is a positioning system. Consider a badge-based positioning system which is able to locate users at the granularity of a room. The Fusion Module can collect information from all sensors in all rooms and present a view to the higher layers which allows querying users. In this case, the Fusion Module only facilitates access to context information and does not change any information.

Context Filter

The role of the Context Filter is similar to the Primary Filter in that it filters information coming from the Fusion Module. However, the Context Filter acts on a higher level and is therefore able to perform "intelligent" filtering. For example, a positioning system may send periodic events indicating which user is in which room. The Context Filter takes these events and is able to generate higher-order events from them, such as "person X entered room Y".

Interpreter

The Context Filter only handles context of one kind while the Interpreter can deal with different sources of different kinds of context. This is important for higher-level reasoning and implying events which cannot be measured. An example is a meeting taking place in a room. In this case, there are many people in the room, the noise level indicates people speaking, and the lights are turned on. None of the individual context "readings" alone is sufficient to infer a meeting taking place, but put together, the Interpreter can deliver us this result.

Application

At the top of the stack are the applications using context. There are many possibilities to use context in applications. Context awareness is an enabling technology for new kinds of applications. It helps increase autonomy of applications, including adaption of behaviour and user interface.

3 Implementation of a Context-Aware Calendar

Our goal in implementing the context-aware calendar was to validate our context model, test the usability of such a calendar in everyday life, and to evaluate the suitability of web services for ubiquitous applications. Web services provide an open architecture where all service providers can freely compete. We believe this gives them a significant advantage over intergrated solutions where one provider is responsible for providing all services, with no major incentive to innovate. Good examples of the successes of open architectures are the Internet and the Web, as well as the iMode-service from NTT DoCoMo (as compared to the European WAP services, which represent more the integrated model).

Overview of the Calendar Application

The Coordinator is the core of the context-aware calendar. It runs the algorithms for service discovery, planning the notifications, and sending notifications. Planning is done by gathering information from several sources, the appointments database, a public transport timetable, and a positioning system. When the user should leave for her next appointment, the coordinator sends a notification to the user as a text message.

Appointments

The source for the actual calendar appointments was the Microsoft Exchange server for our group. The rather limited reminder possibilities offered by the Exchange server are replaced by our context-aware calendar. (The limited reminders in Exchange were

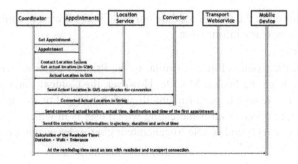

Fig. 2. Coordinator and its functionality.

actually a strong motivating factor for us choosing to implement a calendar as an example of our context model.)

Public Transport Timetable

We wrote a Java wrapper for accessing the information from the public transport timetables. The wrapper realizes a web service for querying any kind of timetables by separating the web service specific code from the HTML parser. Our wrapper presents an interface, specified in a WSDL document, which allows queries for getting from place A to place B. The interface returns the means of transport to take, how and where to change, and the total time of traveling.

Positioning System

For determining the current location of the user, we use the "O2 Handy Finder" provided by the operator O_2 The "Handy Finder" website returns a map as an image on which the user's location is plotted. The website also returns the coordinates as text in an HTTP-header. The coordinates express the longitude and latitude of the base station under which the user's mobile phone is currently located.

Coordinator

The core of the context aware calendar is the coordinator. The coordinator discovers the feasible services, coordinates the message exchange, and implements the planning algorithm. The coordinator is illustrated in Figure 2. The planning algorithm is at the heart of the coordinator. This algorithm is responsible for keeping the context information up-to-date and deciding when to send out the notification to the user.

Notification to the User

We use the standard text messaging (SMS) of GSM mobile phones for sending notifications to the user. The main advantages of SMS are two-fold. First, mobile phones are ubiquitous, hence most users already possess a device for receiving the notifications. Second, SMS is a push-based technology which is required of a notification service. Feedback from the phone back to the calendar is part of our future work.

4   Related Work

There has been lot of work in the area of context-aware computing. First applications include the phone forwarding application built on top of the Active Badge Location

System [4] and the GUIDE project [3]. With the upcoming mobility of devices, work such as [7] explored the efficient distribution of notifications to clients. Dey [1] introduced the separation of concerns and reusage in the design process of context aware systems. Later models include [2] and [8]. Recent work has studied automatic building of context models [9] or predicting context [10].

In contrast to the previous work, our context model explicitly formalizes the different layers between the context sources and the application. Formalizing the context model in layers gives us the advantage that we can use existing modules for each layer and plug in the appropriate modules or layers on-demand. Furthermore, our layered model, based on ubiquitous services, is very scalable, and can handle a large number of context sources, filter, and context consumers (applications) concurrently.

5   Conclusion

In this paper we presented a general context model for including context information into ubiquitous and mobile web applications. Our model contains 5 layers: context sensors, primary filter, fusion module, context filter, and interpreter. As an example, we presented a context-aware calendar application built according to our context model. We have built our calendar using web services, in order to take advantage of the many context sources on the Web, and because it makes our application open and easily extensible. We also discussed the usefulness of web services in ubiquitous and mobile web applications.

References

1. Dey, A.K.: Providing Architectural Support for Building Context-Aware Applications. PhD thesis, Georgia Institute of Technology (2000)
2. Schmidt, A., Gellersen, H.W.: Modell, Architektur und Plattform für Informationssysteme mit Kontextbezug. Informatik Forschung und Entwicklung **16** (2001)
3. Davies, N., Mitchell, K., Cheverst, K., Blair, G.: Developing a context sensitive tourist guide. In: First Workshop on Human Computer Interaction for Mobile Devices. (1998)
4. Want, R., Hopper, A., Falcão, V., Gibbons, J.: The Active Badge Location System. ACM Transactions on Information Systems **10** (1992) 91–102
5. Carzaniga, A., Rosenblum, D.S., Wolf, A.L.: Achieving scalability and expressiveness in an internet-scale event notification service. In: ACM Symposium on Principles of Distributed Computing, Portland, OR (2000)
6. Kügler, D., Vogt, H.: Marking: A privacy protecting approach against blackmailing. In: Public Key Cryptography PKC 2001, Cheju Island, Korea (2001)
7. Schilit, W.N.: A System Architecture for Context-Aware Mobile Computing. PhD thesis, Columbia University, New York, NY, US (1995)
8. Großmann, M., Leonhardi, A., Mitschang, B., Rothermel, K.: A world model for location-aware systems. Informatik **8** (2001) 22–25
9. Takada, T., Kurihara, S., Hirotsu, T., Sugawara, T.: Proximity mining: Finding proximity using sensor data history. In: IEEE Workshop on Mobile Computing Systems and Applications, Monterey, CA (2003)
10. Petzold, J., Bagci, F., Trumler, W., Ungerer, T.: The state predictor method for context prediction. In: UbiComp 2003: Adjunct Proceedings. (2003)

Model-Checking of Safety and Security Aspects in Web Service Flows

Shin Nakajima

National Institute of Informatics
and
PRESTO, Japan Science and Technology Agency
nkjm@nii.ac.jp

Abstract. Web service flow is essentially a description of a distributed collaboration system, in which more than one Web service providers participate. The flow should have safety properties such as deadlock freedom and application specific progress properties. At the same time, the flow should satisfy some security properties since it is executed in an open network environment. This paper introduces an idea of a lattice-based security label into BPEL, a Web flow description language being standardized, in order to detect potential insecure information leakage. It further discusses that both the safety and security aspects can be analyzed in a single framework using the model-checking verification techniques.

Keywords: Web Service Flow, Information Flow, Lattice-based Security Label, Model-Checking

1 Introduction

Web service is widely accepted as a new technology in business network environment in which each participant acts as a service provider [4]. And as a robust framework to compose lots of the service, Web service flow description languages are proposed [3][11][17] to express that Web service providers are combined to show collaborative behavior. Since the flow is executed in an open network environment such as the Internet, both safety and security are the two aspects of particular interest in the Web service framework.

Safety requires that the Web service flow, as a distributed collaboration description, is logically and functionally correct. The flow should be free from deadlock and satisfy some application specific progress properties [12]. And the model-checking verification techniques are shown successful for the automatic analysis of the safety aspect of Web service flows [8][13][14][15].

Security is one of the major concerns in the Web service framework. It needs some high-level security policy given as a non-functional property [1] and refers to various things depending on which layer in the Web service technology stack we are considering [4]. WS-Security deals with the secure end-to-end communication of the SOAP messaging, and WS-Authorization is proposed to be a standard

N. Koch, P. Fraternali, and M. Wirsing (Eds.): ICWE 2004, LNCS 3140, pp. 488–501, 2004.

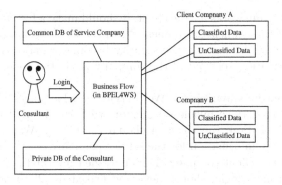

Fig. 1. Out-sourcing Web Service

service for the access control. Another important area regarding to security is the non-interference, which requires that information having different security levels does not interfere with each other. It is concerned with a problem of the information flow control to prevent the potential information leakage.

The problem of the information flow control has been a primary interest in the computer security. High-level access control policies and their enforcement have been proposed [1]. Especially, a lattice-based control model [7] provides a basis for various high-level access control policies including the information flow control [16].

Since the Web service framework is gaining a wide acceptance as a key infrastructure in the networked information systems, high-level security policy of the non-interference will become an important issue. For example, a Web-based service company, getting a contract of *out-sourcing* service from a client, implements its business logic in terms of Web service flows and accesses to classified documents in the client company. The business logic description is required to show that the classified information is never leaked at all. It is desirable to have a method to formally analyze whether the Web service flow is secure in view of the non-interference.

This paper proposes to use the model-checking verification technique [5] to analyze Web service flow descriptions in view of both safety and security. A main contribution of the paper is to show that BPEL [3] descriptions, with a small extension using the lattice-based security label [7], can be analyzed in terms of the non-interference.

2   Security Concerns in Web Service

2.1   Information Leakage in Web Service Flows

Figure 1 shows an example Web service scenario motivating our work. The service company gets a kind of *out-sourcing* contract from the client company A, and does some tasks previously done in the company A internally. In order that the service company works for the client, it should make a free access to classified documents as well as unclassified ones. When the whole scenario is implemented in the Web service framework, the security becomes a major concern since the classified information goes out of the company A via the open network such as the Internet.

The service company may use Web service flow languages such as BPEL [3] to implement its service business logic. In order for the BPEL description to access the information, the client A should establish a Web service server to provide necessary information for the service company.

In view of the client company A, its classified information, manipulated by the BPEL business logic, should never be leaked at all to, for example, the company B. The client company A may require the service company to show a formal certification that the confidentiality is satisfied. The classified information never interferes with less confidential data while the BPEL description works on the information.

Since Web service has its basis on the Internet, security is one of the major concerns in the technology standardization [4]. WS-Security deals with the secure end-to-end communication of the SOAP messaging service. It employs cryptography to make messages encrypted and to provide means for the sender signature. A. Gordon et al [9] employs the spi calculus for the verification of the security aspect of combining multiple communication protocols, each being implemented on top of SOAP. WS-Authorization is proposed to be a standard service for the access control of the Web service. The proposal includes a method for describing access control policies. It, however, does not deal with the non-interference problem arising from multiple accesses. In summary, the problem of controlling information leakage in the Web service flow has not been discussed in details so far in the Web service framework.

2.2 BPEL

As a standard language for describing Web service flows that compose more than one Web services, BPEL4WS (Business Process Execution Language for Web Service), or BPEL for short, was proposed. BPEL v1.0 was made public in July 2002 as a new language to supersede both WSFL [11] and XLANG [17]. And BPEL v1.1 [3] is considered in this paper.

BPEL is a behavioral extension of WSDL (Web Service Description Language) [2]. WSDL is basically an interface description language for Web service providers, which contains information enough for the clients to access. The client invokes a Web service provider using WSDL. The invocation is *one-shot*, which means that WSDL does not describe global states of the provider.

On the other hand, BPEL is a language for expressing behavioral compositions of Web service providers. It can express *a causal relationship* between multiple invocations by means of control and data flow links. BPEL employs a distributed concurrent computation model with variables. This paper mostly concerns with the distributed concurrent language aspect of BPEL.

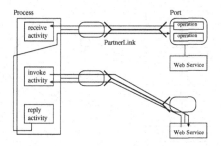

Fig. 2. Example Primary Entities in BPEL

Figure 2 illustrates some of primary language elements in BPEL. A main construct of the Web service flow is `Process`, which is a net-based concurrent description connecting more than one `Activity`'s with control links. Some of the primitive `Activity`'s, in turn, is a place that sends/receives messages to/from external Web service providers. Each Web service provider can be seen as a `Port` instance of a particular `Port Type`, which has appropriate WSDL description as its sub-elements. And `Partner Link` specifies which `Activity` is linked to a particular Web service provider of the `Port`.

BPEL provides a variety of primitive `Activity`'s. Some of them are shown in the example in Figure 2. The `receive` activity waits for invocation requests from the outside, the `invoke` activity initiates an execution request on the Web service provider and receives result values, and the `reply` returns some value to the original outside initiator as the result of the computation of the `Process`.

In addition to the above primitive `Activity`'s, BPEL provides an `assign` activity for accessing variables. It also has other activities concerning to implement control flows such as `sequence` (sequential executions), `switch` (branch on conditions), `while` (repetitions), and `flow` (concurrency). The `flow` activity corresponds to a flow graph that can represent concurrency. The flow graph consists of the `Activity`'s as nodes and `Link`'s as edges representing control links.

Last, BPEL introduces a lexical context with `scope` activity. The lexical context defines an effective scope of variables and various handlers such as exception. Further, `scope` activity can have a `serializable` attribute, which specifies multiple concurrent accesses to the variables inside the scope are serialized.

3   Lattice-Based Access Control

3.1   Basic Model

The problem of the information flow control is a primary interest in the computer security. The access control deals with the problem of deciding whether a particular user (Principal) can have an access to a particular resource (Target). Namely, each access can be checked in an individual manner. We can say, for example, that a principal P1 is permitted to have a read access to a target T1 while its write access to T2 is inhibited.

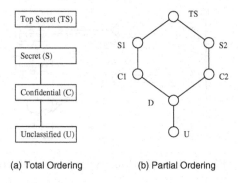

(a) Total Ordering   (b) Partial Ordering

Fig. 3. Lattice of Security Labels

The above basic access control alone, however, is not able to exclude invalid data-flows arising from a series of read and write accesses. In some cases, each individual access is permitted, but a resultant net data-flow potentially violates some global requirement. This is a problem of the information flow control [1].

Here is a simple example scenario regarding to the information flow control. A principal P1 writes to a target T2 the data read from another target T1. Further, another principal P2 reads from T2 and writes to T3. We assume here that all the four individual accesses are permitted, and also that we have a high-level security policy saying that T1 and T3 should be of non-interference with each other. The policy means, in particular, that the data originally stored in T1 should not be flowed into T3. However, a series of the accesses results in a global data-flow from T1 to T3 since each access is allowed.

In order to remedy the situation, a lattice-based approach to the information flow control has been proposed [7]. The idea is that we assign security labels to the principal as well as the target, and define a partial ordering between the labels. The label of the principal is called Security Clearance, and Security Classification for the case of the target.

The ordering $\succ$ reflects the intension of how one is more important than the other in view of the secrecy. We can write as below to represent that a security label SL_i is more secure than SL_j.

$$SL_i \succ SL_j$$

We assume that the set of security labels is finite and the ordering $\succ$ forms a finite lattice [6]. Figure 3 illustrates two example lattice of security labels. Figure 3 (a) is a simple case where four labels are arranged in a total order. Top Secret is more secure than Secret (TS $\succ$ S). Figure 3 (b) illustrates another example in which security labels form a lattice with partial orderings. C1 and C2 are more secure than D (C1 $\succ$ D $\wedge$ C2 $\succ$ D), but they are incomparable with each other. TS is a maximal of C1 and C2.

Further, we introduce a constraint relationship *dominates* defined as

$$SL_i \text{ dominates } SL_j \stackrel{\wedge}{=} SL_i \stackrel{*}{\succ} SL_j$$

For example, a document with a security classification of *secret* (S) dominates *unclassified* (U) documents. A senior member having a *secret* (S) security clearance can have a right access to both *secret* (S) and *unclassified* (U) documents. But a junior staff member with a *unclassified* (U) security clearance can only read *unclassified* (U) documents.

With the lattice-based approach, we can solve the example problematic situation mentioned above. Below L(X) refers to the security label attached to X, where X refers to either a principal or a target. First, we assume that the high-level security policy requires

not (L(T3) dominates L(T1)) .

If all the four accesses are allowed, we have the following four constraints satisfied.

L(P1) dominates L(T1)   ... [A1]
L(T2) dominates L(P1)   ... [A2]
L(P2) dominates L(T2)   ... [A3]
L(T3) dominates L(P2)   ... [A4]

By means of the transitivity of the dominates relationship, the four relations results in

L(T3) dominates L(T1),

which is in contradiction with the required security policy, and thus the access violation can be detected.

3.2 Declassification

The lattice-based method is a promising approach for the information flow control. However, the basic model in Section 3.1 is not practical. Its idea is basically to allow information flow only from low to high, which can exclude invalid flows resulting in a leakage of secure information.

This, however, causes a problematic situation. Once a principal with the highest security clearance reads some data, the data cannot be accessed or written to a target resource with a lower security classification. The information is swallowed into a *black-hole*. The lattice-based control method can be a basis for the confidentiality, but not adequate in view of the availability.

As a remedy for the availability problem, the idea of declassification is proposed [1]. In short, the basic lattice-based model employs the static security label only. On the other hand, the declassification model uses the security labels determined dynamically at runtime in checking the dominates relationships.

The following example considers a case where a principal P1 reads data from a target T1 and then writes it to another target T3. We further assume that the following three constraint relationships are satisfied.

L(P1) dominates L(T1)   ... [B1]
L(P1) dominates L(T3)   ... [B2]
L(T3) dominates L(T1)   ... [B3]

In particular the third relationship ([B3]) indicates that the security classification of T3 is higher than that of T1. Although [B3] shows that the flow from T1 to T3 is possible, the flow is not allowed according to the basic model. The reason comes in order.

The first relationship ([B1]) allows P1 reading data from T1. When P1 writes the data to T3, the second one ([B2]) is checked, which specifies that P1 is not allowed to write data to T3. Therefore, the flow from T1 to T3 is inhibited.

The declassification model relaxes the strict application of the static security labels in checking constraints. The model introduces a notion of DCL (DeClassified Label). We assume here that a trusted principal writes data to a target with a security classification that the principal dominates. The basic model disallows the write because the principal is more secure than the target. In the new model, we choose an appropriate DCL value from the underlying lattice, and use it in place of the label of the principal so that the write access is allowed. The value of DCL is the one dominating the target that the principal has a read access, and at the same time the one that the written target dominates.

For example, in the above case, we introduce the following three relationships in order to decide the value of DCL.

L(P1) dominates DCL   ... [C1]
DCL dominates L(T1)   ... [C2]
L(T3) dominates DCL   ... [C3]

The first relationship ([C1]) ensures that DCL is lower than P1, which is a basic global constraint on DCL. The second one ([C2]) shows that the flow from T1 to DCL is allowed, which is in accordance with the condition on P1 and T1 ([B1]). And the last one ([C3]) allows the flow from DCL to T3, which together with [C2], results in a global flow from T1 to T3 as requested. If the appropriate DCL does exist, then we can use the value in place of the security clearance of the principal for the checking process.

3.3   Global Analysis

According to the lattice-based access control model, each constraint rule is obtained at each execution point. In the first example in Section 3.1, the rule ([B1]) is obtained at the point where the principal P1 has a read access to the target T1. However, in order to check whether the information flow is possible or not, all the rules along (potential) execution paths should be collected. It is because the net information flow is possible only if all the rules along the execution path are satisfied. Therefore, a global flow analysis is needed for collecting rules.

The global flow analysis method is basically a data-flow analysis algorithm. For the case of the basic lattice-based model in Section 3.1, the label value of the security clearance of a principal moves downward as *a data token* in execution paths. And when an execution path reaches a point where the principal has either a read or write access to a target, the label value is checked against the *dominates* relationship at the point. The analysis should be done not for a single execution path, but for all the potential execution paths.

The analysis method becomes complicated when we employ the declassification model. As seen in Section 3.2, we have to show that an appropriate DCL value exists in the underlying lattice structure, which requires to solve a set of *dominates* constraint relationships. It, however, the method can be simplified.

Our simplified method is a minor variant of the above analysis for the basic model. As the label value flowing downward, we use an *initial* guess of DCL instead of the value of the principal. And at each execution point accessing a target TA, the value is updated as a *maximal* of its security label and the old DCL value. The initial value of DCL is set to be L(T0) which is the security classification label of the target T0, while T0 is what the principal has a read access firstly in the execution path.

For an illustration of the method, we use here a simple example. The scenario consists of a series of accesses, a read to T1, a read to T2, and a write to T3. We have three relationships [D1] to [D3] for the accesses. And we assume [D4] between the two targets, T1 and T2, that accept read accesses from the principal.

DCL_1 dominates L(T1)   ... [D1]
DCL_2 dominates L(T2)   ... [D2]
L(T3) dominates DCL_2 ... [D3]
L(T1) dominates L(T2)   ... [D4]

At the first read access ([D1]), DCL_1 is set to L(T1). At the second, our method sets DCL_2 to be a maximal of DCL_1 and L(T2), actually a maximal of L(T1) and L(T2). And in this example DCL_2 becomes L(T1) because of the rule [D4].

On the contrary, if we override DCL_2 at [D2] to be L(T2), we cannot detect a potential security violation in a case where the following relationships are also assumed.

L(T3) dominates L(T2)   ... [D5]
L(T1) dominates L(T3)   ... [D6]

Because of the rule [D6], the net flow is not secure. However, the rule [D3] allows such a flow because of the rule [D5] in the case where DCL_2 is L(T2).

In concluding this section, we have to point out that devising a precise analysis method needs the semantics of the language we are considering. In this paper, we have to consider BPEL semantics in details.

4   BPEL with Security Label

This section discusses how we introduce the notion of the security label into BPEL. Our information flow control method uses the lattice-based approach with the declassification.

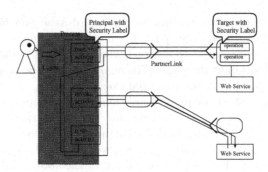

Fig. 4. BPEL with Security Label

We consider here an extension to BPEL. The extension includes (a) introducing the principal with security clearance, and (b) identifying `Port` with the target having security classification. Figure 4 schematically shows how we attach the security label information to the BPEL language elements.

First, we consider how to introduce the idea of principal to BPEL descriptions. Generally a principal represents a client user of the system, and its security clearance level is assigned in the authentication process of *login*. However, since more than one ways to implement the login process are possible, we cannot a priori decide how the security clearance is obtained. Therefore, we only introduce a new reserved variable `Principal`, and use the `assign` activity to set the value.

```
<assign>
  <copy>
    <from variable='...' part='...' />
    <to variable='Principal' property='Security Clearance' />
  </copy>
</assign>
```

`Principal` is a single-assignment variable, and read-only throughout the process execution afterward.

Second, we identify a Web service provider with a target having security classification. The Web service provider can be considered as a persistent data storage. BPEL allows to exchange information with the outside by means of messages through the `Link` to/from the `Port` (see Figure 4). And thus we identify `Port` with the target.

An alternative approach is to regard variables appeared in `assign` activity as the target because a variable is a place-holder for values. However, since the variables in `assign` activity are confined in the enclosing scope, the value is forgotten once the execution control is exited from the scope without any significant side-effects. We have not taken this approach.

Next, we need some XML representation for expressing the high-level security policy requirements using the dominates relationship. Each requirement would be either positive or negative. The whole security policy is a collection of such constraint relationships.

```
<securityPolicy name='orderingServicePolicy'>
  <admit>
    <dominates high='T2' low='T1' />
  </admit>
  <inhibit>
    <dominates high='T3' low='T1' />
  </inhibit>
</securityPolicy>
```

Last, the security lattice is defined in terms of a collection of successor ($\succ$) relationships. Below is a partial definition of the example lattice in Figure 3 (b).

```
<lattice name='systemB'>
  <succ high='TS' low='S1' />
  <succ high='TS' low='S2' />
  <succ high='S1' low='C1' />
  ...
</lattice>
```

5   Model-Checking of Extended BPEL

5.1   Overview

We propose to use the model-checking verification technique [5] to analyze our extended BPEL descriptions from the viewpoint of the lattice-based information flow control. It extends the work on model-checking WSFL descriptions for the analysis of the safety aspect [13] to include the security labels.

As seen in Section 3.3, the analysis basically needs to explore all the potential execution paths of a given extended BPEL description. We have to devise an analysis method that is faithful to the operational semantics of BPEL, which has concurrency as its core language primitives. Since global flow analysis of concurrent systems becomes complicated, we will not implement an algorithm from scratch, but devise a way of using an off-the-shelf model-checker for the analysis. It is because the model-checking technique has been successful for the verification and analysis of concurrent systems.

We use SPIN model-checker [10] for the analysis engine. It is because SPIN is a quite engineered tool that can handle a large state space efficiently. SPIN also provides various language primitives that are useful for the verification and analysis of practical software. In Section 5.2 we will consider how we encode BPEL language primitives in Promela, the input specification language of SPIN. At the same time, we will discuss why SPIN is useful for our purpose, namely as a prototyping engine for the analysis of the information flow control.

Roughly a BPEL process description is translated into a Promela process. However, it is not enough just to have a Promela process for the BPEL to be

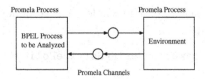

Fig. 5. Closed System

analyzed. The environment that communicate with the current BPEL, namely all the service providers that have interaction with the BPEL, should be explicitly represented. Figure 5 illustrates the situation where the environment is also modeled as a Promela process to have a *closed* system. And the communication is done by sending and receiving messages via Promela channels.

5.2   Encoding BPEL in Promela

As explained in Section 2.2, BPEL has a variety of language constructs to represent various activities. What to do is to give semantics to each activity in view of the security label analysis.

First we consider how to encode the control aspect of BPEL descriptions since the control flow becomes a basis for constructing the state space to be explored. Since each activity has different semantics in regard to establishing control flows, the control activity should be considered individually.

The `sequence` activity (sequential execution) is implemented by a Promela sequencing separator (`;`), and the `switch` (branch on conditions) turns out to be a Promela conditional statement (`if ... fi`). The `while` (repetition) is encoded with a Promela repetition statement (`do ... od`) with an appropriate loop condition checking as below.

```
do
   :: (<condition>) -> ...
   :: else -> break
od
```

Second, the `assign` activity is used for dealing with variable accesses. It establishes the flow `from` to `to` variables, and becomes a basis for constructing data-flows. The translation to Promela is mostly straight forward because we can use Promela variables.

Third, the `flow` activity, among others, provides concurrency in the activity execution in a single process description. The idea comes from the net-oriented concurrent language of WSFL [11]. Figure 6 illustrates an example `flow` activity. The example `flow` activity itself is enclosed in the top level `sequence`, which specifies a sequencing of three activities, `receive`, `flow`, and `reply`. The dotted line is meant to represent sequential execution in the diagram. The `flow` has three concurrently executing `sequence`'s, each having multiple primitive activities. The diagram also shows two solid curves, one from `invoke` to `invoke`

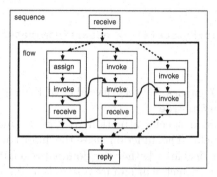

Fig. 6. Flow Activity Example

and another from `receive` to `invoke`. The curves add further control flows to synchronize execution of concurrently executing activities.

As discussed elsewhere on the model-checking of WSFL [13][14], we use Promela process to represent activities executing concurrently. In the example shown in Figure 6, we have three Promela processes as a translation of the `flow` activity with three enclosing `sequence`'s. Further, we use Promela variable to implement the synchronization in accordance with the semantics of the superimposed control flow shown as the solid curves in the diagram. We also deal with the DPE (dead-path elimination) feature relating to the concurrent `flow` activity. How we encode the DPE in Promela is reported in the previous work [14].

Last, the primitive activity (`invoke`, `receive`, or `reply`) is the point of the interaction with the target. In which direction the information is flowing, namely read or write, is our main concern.

For example, an `invoke` activity establishes an out-going information flow (write) to an external Web service whose `PortType` is `shippingService`.

```
<invoke partnerLink='customer'
        portType='shippingServicePT'
        operation='shippingNotice'
        inputVariable='shipNotice'>
```

And, in view of the security labels, a dominates relationship should satisfy in order to make the flow possible:

L(shippingServicePT/shippingNotice) dominates L(Principal).

Since the above `invoke` activity allows a flow from the current BPEL process, the channel send communication carries the security label of Principal.

```
cout!ShippingNotice(Principal);
```

Then the environment Promela process, playing a role of `shippingService`, receives the message and checks if the dominates relationships hold.

```
do
  :: cin?ShippingNotice(X) -> assert(dominates(self,X))
  ...
od
```

where the variable X carries the security label of Principal, and self refers to that of the shippingService.

It should be paid a special attention to how we implement the function dominates in Promela. The function uses the information equivalent to the given lattice. And it decides whether the dominates relationship holds between two input parameters, which will require a search in the lattice structure. Note that the function dominates is purely functional, having no-side effects.

If, in a simple-minded, we encode the function dominates in Promela directly, it will involve a lot of data-centric computation leading to a large state-space exploration, which is less efficient. Our approach is to implement the function dominates in C language by making use of the SPIN feature of the embedded C code [10]. From Promela descriptions, dominates is treated as a primitive function not increasing the size of the state space to be explored in the model-checking process.

6   Discussion and Conclusion

We have proposed to use the model-checking verification technique to analyze BPEL descriptions in view of both safety and security. In particular, our main interest in the security aspect is non-interference. Our proposal includes a small extension to the current BPEL language specification as well as the introduction of the lattice-based security label.

Although the security label used in the examples in this paper is simple, it is possible to encode other security policy for a variety of purposes. Actually R. Sandhu [16] discusses that various high-level security policies can be represented by means of the lattice-based control model.

Some literatures mention to use model-checkers in the analysis of the Web service flows. H.Foster et al [8] uses the LTSA model checker for the analysis of safety property of BPEL. S.Nakajima [13][14] uses the SPIN model-checker for the safety analysis of WSFL. S.Narayanan et al [15] uses a Petri Net formalism to provide decision procedures for the analysis of the Web service written in DAML. All these work concerns with the safety properties only. Using the model-checker in the analysis of the security property in the Web service flow is new.

Although the idea of the lattice-based approach to the information flow control is not new [1][7][16], the integration with the Web service technology, BPEL in particular, is new. Since it needs a fine-grained control and data flow analysis of BPEL descriptions, the analysis of the non-interference is a problem quite dependent on the BPEL semantics. It is tightly coupled with the Web service flow language specification. We cannot have a separate service component for such a purpose although the Web service framework currently seeks for independent components for various domains such as WS-Authorization or WS-Security [4].

Last, up to the time of writing this paper, we cover a core part of BPEL language only. BPEL is a large language that has many interesting features such as compensation, fault, and event handlers. To cover these features is left for future work.

References

1. M.A. Bishop. *Computer Security: Art and Science*. Addison-Wesley 2003.
2. E. Christensen, F. Curbera, G. Meredith, and S. Weerawarana. Web Service Description Language (WSDL). W3C Web Site, 2001.
3. F. Curbera, Y. Goland, J. Klein, F. Leymann, D. Roller, S. Thatte, and S. Weerawarana. Business Process Execution Language for Web Services. Version 1.1, May 2003.
4. F. Curbera, R. Khalaf, N. Mukhi, S. Tai, and S. Weerawarana. The Next Step in Web Services. *Comm. ACM*, Vol. 46, No. 10, pages 29–34, October 2003.
5. E. Clarke, O. Grumberg, and D. Peled. *Model Checking*. The MIT Press, 1999.
6. B. Davey and H. Priestley. *Introduction to Lattices and Order (2ed.)*. Cambridge, 2002.
7. D.E. Denning. A Lattice Model of Secure Information Flow. *Comm. ACM*, Vol.19, No.5, pages 236–243, May 1976.
8. H. Foster, S. Uchitel, J. Magee, and J. Kramer. Model-based Verification of Web Service Compositions. In *Proc. ASE 2003*, September 2003.
9. A. Gordon, K. Bhargavan, and C. Fournet. A Semantics for Web Services Authentication. In *Proc. POPL 2004*, pages 198–209, January 2004.
10. G.J. Holzmann. *The SPIN Model Checker*. Addison-Wesley 2004.
11. F. Leymann. Web Services Flow Language (WSFL 1.0). IBM Corporation, May 2001.
12. S. Nakajima. On Verifying Web Service Flows. In *Proc. SAINT 2002 Workshop*, pages 223–224, January 2002.
13. S. Nakajima. Verification of Web Service Flows with Model-Checking Techniques. In *Proc. Cyber World 2002*, pages 378–385, IEEE, November 2002.
14. S. Nakajima. Model-Checking of Web Service Flow (in Japanese). In *Trans. IPS Japan*, Vol.44, No.3, pages 942–952, March 2003. A concise version presented at OOPSLA 2002 Workshop on Object-Oriented Web Service, November 2002.
15. S. Narayanan and S.A. McIlraith. Simulation, Verification and Automated Composition of Web Services. In *Proc. WWW-11*, 2002.
16. R. Sandhu. Lattice-Based Access Control Models. IEEE Computer, Vol.26, No.11, pages 9–19, November 1993.
17. S. Thatte. XLANG – Web Services for Business Process Design. Microsoft Corporation, May 2001.

Reliable and Adaptable Security Engineering for Database-Web Services

Martin Wimmer[1], Daniela Eberhardt[2], Pia Ehrnlechner[2], and Alfons Kemper[1]

[1] Technische Universität München, 85748 Garching b. München, Germany
[2] Universität Passau, 94032 Passau, Germany
{wimmerma,kemper}@in.tum.de, {eberhard,ehrnlech}@db.fmi.uni-passau.de

Abstract. The situation in engineering security for Web services that access databases is as follows: On the one hand, specifications like WS-Security are concerned with the security management for Web services, while on the other hand there exist well established mechanisms for access control in the area of commercial database systems. In handling security for services that rely on database systems, two extreme approaches can currently be observed: The more database-centric one, where the access control decisions are left to the DBMS, and the service-centric authorization approach. The service-centric approach requires a Web service to run under control of the database system provider as operations like queries and updates have to be executed with comprehensive privileges. Authorization has to be enforced by the service itself. In case access control policies of a service are defined independently with regard to the database policies, authorization mismatches are likely to be induced.

In our new approach we bridge this gap between DBMS authorization and access control of Web services by supporting reliable and adaptable access control engineering. The policies of the DBMS constitute the basis for the authorization of Web services. These are therefore automatically extracted before they are refined by additional conditions. As a final step, it must be verified that service policies do not grant more permissions than database policies do, thus ensuring reliable service execution.

1 Introduction

The concept of Web services has attracted the interest of the research as well as the commercial sector. Web services (also called *services* or *e-services*) are autonomous software components that are uniquely identified by a URI and can be invoked by use of standard Internet protocols. Security and privacy issues are always in the center of concern of any distributed system. This is even more intensified when service execution and aggregation are done dynamically. Secure message exchange at the transport layer can be assured by the use of protocols like SSL and TSL, while message confidentiality and integrity are addressed by SAML [1] and WS-Security [2]. These specifications focus on the exchange of security credentials for authentication and authorization in the area of e-services. Most Web service development tools like .Net or JWSDP[1] support substantial

---

[1] Java Web Services Developer Pack

N. Koch, P. Fraternali, and M. Wirsing (Eds.): ICWE 2004, LNCS 3140, pp. 502–515, 2004.
© Springer-Verlag Berlin Heidelberg 2004

security functionality and allow the realization of sophisticated access control concepts for e-services.

When engineering Web services that depend on databases, which applies to the majority of business applications, the access control mechanisms of the underlying DBMS have to be taken into consideration, too. In this area, common authorization standards are discretionary access control (DAC), mandatory access control (MAC) [3] and role based access control (RBAC) [4,5]. Two extreme approaches regarding the access control of Web services that interface with databases can currently be observed. On the one hand, there exists a database-centric approach where the complete access monitoring is left to the database system. On the other hand, authorization can be enforced on the side of the service. This service-centric approach requires a service to run under control of the database system provider as operations like queries and updates have to be executed with comprehensive privileges. The common practice lies in-between these two extreme approaches. Consequently, two access control systems have to be taken into consideration, one for the service and one for the database. In case the two are administered independently, severe authorization mismatches are likely to occur.

Our approach addresses this topic and provides solutions for the reliable definition of service policies. Obviously the service policy depends on the permissions granted to the DBMS account that is used by the Web service to establish connections to the database. As depicted in Fig. 1, the authorization settings that are applicable in the database context are extracted automatically. The preprocessed policy is subsequently refined by the service developer, insofar, as further constraints are added. Apart from the modification of database policies, service policies can also be generated semi-automatically based on service specifications. In both cases, in order to guarantee reliable service execution, it must be ensured that the final Web service policy is a valid refinement of the database policy, in terms of being less permissive.

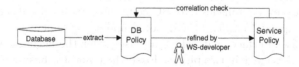

Fig. 1. Workflow of service policy definition.

Today it is common practice that database dependent Web applications have over-privileged or even total access to the DBMS. In case of attackers gaining control over the Web service, e.g., by infiltrating the computer on which the service is running, privacy and security threats arise. Concerning this, we present practical solutions for reducing the security risks for databases.

The remainder of this paper is structured as follows: In Sect. 2 we discuss security requirements of Web services that access databases. The basic techniques of our approach, which we integrated in our prototype Web service platform ServiceGlobe, are presented in Sect. 3. In Sect. 4 we describe how to design access control for Database-Web services and additionally elaborate on the dynamic exchange of policies. Finally, Sect. 5 presents some related work, prior to a conclusion and a brief discussion of future work in Sect. 6.

2   Considering Access Control of Database-Web Services

In this section we describe the shortcomings that arise when e-service policies and database policies are defined in an uncorrelated manner. We illustrate these regarding an example of a hospital administration scenario. As depicted in Fig. 2 we use a simplified model of a hospital data set, assuming that patients and physicians are uniquely identified by their names.

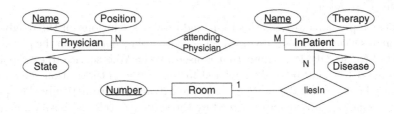

Fig. 2. Entity-Relationship diagram of a simplified hospital application.

As use case we consider a portal for physicians that allows them to modify the therapy of patients. The implementation might be realized as illustrated in Fig. 3. A quite elementary e-service named *Hospital-WS* is created, which, behind the scenes, establishes a JDBC-connection to the database *Hospital-DB*. By invoking *updateTherapy()* the denoted update statement is executed.

The service interfaces with the database under the account of *db_user*. Authorization takes place in two phases: First, the requestor has to be authorized to invoke *updateTherapy()* depending on the service policy. Second, the execution of the aforementioned query under the account of *db_user* has to be allowed. Several shortcomings can be observed if the two authorization policies deviate:

– Obviously, the access control of the service depends on the authorization settings of the DBMS. The service can at most provide functionality that is also supported by the database. If this condition is not satisfied, a successful authorization on part of the service is no guarantee for effective service execution as the DBMS can still deny access on certain resources. Ensuring this relationship thus states a precondition for reliable service execution.

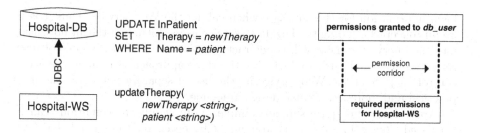

Fig. 3. Illustration of the portal realization and the associated access control.

– In order to avoid administration overhead, connections to databases are oftentimes established under over-privileged accounts. As illustrated in Fig. 3
db_user is granted more privileges than needed to perform *updateTherapy()*
of the *Hospital-WS* service. This constitutes an avoidable safety risk.
In the case of attackers gaining control over the service by exploiting flaws
of the system, they – in the worst case – will also be able to execute any
command *db_user* is privileged to execute. As a consequence severe inconsistencies and privacy violations may arise. Our intention is to reduce these
risks by providing access to the resource only through a tailored permission
corridor as illustrated in the right part of Fig. 3.

Considering the service method *updateTherapy()*, a plain verification whether
access to the database will be allowed is not sufficient. Physicians shall only be
granted access to the information concerning patients of whom they are the
attending physicians. Access to any other medical record has to be denied. This
check can be performed in one of the following ways.

User related views: Security on the level of data sets or single columns can
be attained by views that are related to database users. Assuming that the
column *physicianName* of *attendingPhysician* contains user identifiers of the
database system the following view represents a restricted copy of *InPatient*.

```
CREATE VIEW InPatientView AS
SELECT * FROM InPatient p
WHERE EXISTS (SELECT * FROM attendingPhysician
   WHERE  patientName = p.Name AND physicianName = USER)
```

Authorization by query: Obviously, the authorization check can also be included in the original query by joining *InPatient* and *attendingPhysician*.
External policy: New policy languages like XACML allow the expression of
fine-grained conditions. So, another solution would be to formulate the constraint as part of a self-contained Web service policy.

User related views constitute a well suited authorization mechanism. One
disadvantage is that clients require database accounts and have to supply their

login information for the database when calling the Web service. Thus it is no useful concept for hiding the DBMS to service users. Including the authorization into the query statement will counteract the software design principle of separating security and business logic. So, the third approach of refining the access control on part of the Web service by the use of separate policies is the most practical and moreover flexible design guideline.

Apart from this quite simple example, more significant conditions can be expressed. Regarding our scenario it might be necessary to demand that first-year residents should not be allowed to change the therapy of patients, though they might be the corresponding attending physicians. Changing the therapy requires a chief physician to agree to the resident's decisions. Such constraints can not be expressed with common access control techniques of databases, because authorization in this case depends on complex context information and security credentials of several subjects have to be evaluated.

3   Policy Management

We integrated the required authorization functionality in our Web service platform ServiceGlobe. Before we present details of how policies are generated and compared, we give a brief introduction to the eXtensible Access Control Markup Language (XACML) which we use as policy language.

3.1   Short Introduction to XACML

XACML [6] is based on XML and is consequently well applicable as policy language in Web service environments: Existing parser technologies can be utilized and basic language constructs are well known to the community thus increasing acceptability.

XACML provides a request/response mechanism to support communications. A typical scenario for employing XACML is depicted in Fig. 4: A distinguished Web service operates as Policy Enforcement Point, PEP. A PEP has to ensure that requestors are authorized to execute the demanded operation and to access the requested resources. Therefore the incoming SOAP-request has to be transformed into an appropriate XACML-request. This is done by the Context Handler. The XACML-request document is passed to the Policy Decision Point, PDP. The PDP evaluates the request against applicable policies that are supplied by a Policy Administration Point (PAP). The result is sent back to the Web service that either aborts the execution and returns an error message or executes as demanded.

A `Policy` consists of a `Target`, a set of `Rules` and optional `Obligations` that specify the access conditions. `Rules` contain most of the logic of a `Policy`. A single `Rule` is set up by a `Target`, an optional `Condition` and an `Effect` that will be either `Permit` or `Deny`. The way several rules are combined in a `Policy` is specified by its rule combining algorithm that, among others, can be `deny-overrides` or `permit-overrides`. While the first one states that `Deny` is

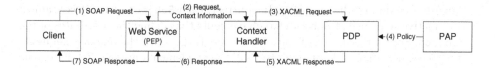

Fig. 4. Control flow of the authorization process

returned in case any rule evaluates to `Deny`, the second will return `Permit` in the analogous situation[2]. In case a processing error occurs `Indeterminate` is returned. A `Policy` evaluates to `NotApplicable` if none of its `Rules` applies. XACML defines further combining algorithms and allows the definition of new ones.

If the authorization decision depends on further constraints these are coded by the optional `Condition` of a `Rule` that either evaluates to `True`, `False` or `Indeterminate`. `Conditions` can be quite complex, i.e., any arbitrary Boolean function can be expressed. The refinement of a `Rule` takes place by imposing further constraints on its `Target`, thus restricting the `Rule`'s applicability.

The `Target` of a `Policy` or `Rule` is composed of a set of `Subjects`, a set of `Resources` and a set of `Action` elements. The Target thus constitutes the actor, the module to be accessed and the operation to be performed. In case any of the mentioned elements are not explicitly determined, `AnySubject`, `AnyResource` and `AnyAction` are used.

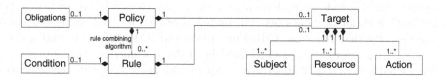

Fig. 5. XACML components (adapted from [6])

In order to use XACML for policy enforcement the SOAP request must be transformed into an XACML `Request`. A `Request` is composed of one or many `Subject` elements that represent the initiator of a `Request`, e.g., identities of humans or other e-services. Required elements of a `Request` are its `Resource` and `Action` that specify the resource for which access is requested and the way access shall be performed. A `Request` is evaluated against applicable `Policy` definitions and `Rules`, whose `Target` matches with the `Request`. The set of `Subjects` of a

---

[2] The respective combining algorithm either prioritizes permissions or prohibitions. In the following we use `permit-overrides` due to the assembly of database policies that consist of privileges. Consequently, an evaluation to `NotApplicable` states that access is denied.

`Target` is evaluated disjunctively. In contrast, each `Subject` element contains a conjunctive sequence of `SubjectMatch` elements that define the attributes of the `Subject`. So, for the match of the subject of a Target with the one of a `Request`, it is necessary that at least one of the `Subject` elements applies, while for the match of one `Subject` element it is necessary that all associated attributes match with the `Request`. Analogous considerations apply to `Resources` and `Actions`. The way `Targets` are evaluated are significant for Def. 1 in Sect. 3.3.

In the following we equate terms like policy or subject with the corresponding XACML terms, i.e., `Policy` or `Subject`.

3.2 Web Service Platform ServiceGlobe

We integrated the functionality for access control management in our prototype ServiceGlobe. ServiceGlobe [7] is a lightweight, distributed and extensible e-service platform. It is completely implemented in Java and based on standards like XML, SOAP, WSDL, and UDDI. ServiceGlobe specific services are mobile code. They can be loaded from code repositories and executed on so-called *service hosts*. These are standard Internet servers additionally running a ServiceGlobe runtime engine.

Two security issues arise in the given situation. On the one hand, security for service hosts has to be ensured: Because possibly unknown Web services are loaded, the execution of erroneous or even malicious code must be monitored. Security for service hosts is based on the Java security architecture, i.e., the Java sand-box mechanism, as described in [8].

On the other hand, communication between services and clients must be secure which includes confidential message exchange as well as authentication and authorization of requestors. The exchange of security credentials is based on WS-Security that relies on XML-Encryption and XML-Signature and specifies how security information is embedded in SOAP-documents. Authentication of service requestors constitutes the pre-requisite for the subsequent access control.

3.3 Authorization Functionality

The access control functionality described in the following paragraphs has been implemented in Java and was integrated into the ServiceGlobe platform. An Oracle 9i installation was used as relational DBMS for examining the correlation of database and e-service authorization concepts.

Generation of policies, requests and user profiles. As we focus on Web services that interact with databases, service operations are related to SQL-commands. Instead of writing policy and request documents from scratch, a preprocessing of SQL statements allows the preparation of these XACML constructs. In particular, the referenced tables or columns form resources while operations like update or select constitute actions. Thus targets of policies and rules as well as requests can be formulated. In general, the generated documents need to be refined by the service developer. This means that the access rules are redesigned more restrictively by additional conditions. For example, the subject identity that specifies to whom the policies apply cannot be automatically extracted from SQL-commands and has to be added by the service developer.

As motivated in Sect. 2, accessing the database via the account of a highly privileged user shall be avoided due to security considerations. Again, the required privileges are extracted from the SQL-statement and scripts for database user profiles are generated. These profiles are designed to establish exactly the authorization corridor needed for the particular service.

Extraction of database policies. The extraction of the access rules of the underlying DBMS depends on the specific database system. Taking an Oracle DBMS as an example, privileges are stored in data dictionary views like *user_tab_privs*. Policies of the following three categories are generated:

Role assignment policies: Commonly, databases support role based access control. This type of policy is used to assign roles to users or, in order to support hierarchical RBAC, to senior roles. This refers to [5] as senior roles acquire the permissions of their junior roles. Following the recommendation of [9], policies are generated consisting of rules, whose target is composed as follows: The actual role constitutes the resource, while the subject is either a user or a senior role. The target's action is of an *enable*-state. See [5,9] for further issues on separation of duty that is beyond the scope of this paper.

Permission policies: A *permission policy* defines a privilege that can be granted to users and/or roles. The target of a *permission policy* is not specified in order to enable its assignment to arbitrary roles and users. That means that the elements of the target are `AnySubject`, `AnyResource` and `AnyAction`. Each policy contains one rule that represents the privilege to execute a certain operation on a resource, e.g., update on a table.

Base policies: A policy of this category assigns permissions to users or roles. This is done by defining the policy target with the respective user or role identity as subject. The granted privileges are expressed by referencing the appropriate *permission policies*. These policies are included by the use of `PolicyIdReference` elements of the XACML specification.

3.4   Partial Order for Policies

The refinement of access rules demands a way to compare policies in order to determine whether one policy is more restrictive than another one. An informal definition of *more restrictive* is that fewer permissions are granted to fewer subjects under harder constraints. Before we define a partial order for policies, the following preceding considerations regarding the comparisons of targets and rules have to be made.

Definition 1. *Partial order for targets*
Let T_1 and T_2 be targets, with $T_1.sub$, $T_2.sub$ denoting the associated sets of

subjects, $T_1.res$, $T_2.res$ the sets of resources and $T_1.act$, $T_2.act$ the sets of actions. A target T_1 is subordinate or equal to a target T_2, $T_1 \sqsubseteq T_2$, if and only if

$$(\forall s_1 \in T_1.sub : \exists s_2 \in T_2.sub : s_1 \sqsupseteq s_2) \wedge \tag{1.1}$$

$$(\forall r_1 \in T_1.res : \exists r_2 \in T_2.res : r_1 \sqsubseteq r_2) \wedge \tag{1.2}$$

$$(\forall a_1 \in T_1.act : \exists a_2 \in T_2.act : a_1 \sqsubseteq a_2) \tag{1.3}$$

The relation $a \sqsubseteq b$ with a and b both being either subjects, resources or actions denotes that a *is subordinate or equal to b regarding the authorization context*. This means that less privileges are associated with a than with b. A Target is said to be subordinate to another target if it applies to less subjects, resources as well as actions. Nevertheless, Def. 1 demands more than a common subset relation: According to (1.2) (respectively (1.3)), for every element r_1 of $T_1.res$ ($a_1 \in T_1.act$) an element r_2 of $T_2.res$ ($a_2 \in T_2.act$) must exist with r_1 being included in r_2 (a_1 being a sub-action of a_2). The opposite applies to subjects: (1.1) states that for a requestor it must be harder to fulfill s_1 than s_2, thus s_1 being of higher order in the sense of authorization than s_2.

	Target T_1		**Target T_2**
subjects	{chief-physician}	$\sqsupseteq$	{physician}
resources	{InPatient.Therapy}	$\sqsubseteq$	{InPatient}
actions	{select}	$\sqsubseteq$	{update, select}

Fig. 6. Example of a target comparison: T_1 is subordinate to T_2.

Let's assume that physicians are granted the permissions to execute update and select on the table *InPatient*. The appropriate target T_2 is depicted in Fig. 6. T_1 constitutes a subordinate version of T_2 because of the following reasons: First of all, T_1 applies to chief physicians. In the meaning of RBAC, chief-physician constitutes a senior role of physician. As senior roles acquire the permissions of their junior roles, the subject of T_2 is subordinate to the subject of T_1. Second, T_1 applies to a restricted resource, as the column *Therapy* is only an extract of the complete table *InPatient*. Third, the set of operations is reduced to select.

A rule R consists of a target ($R.tgt$), an optional condition ($R.cnd$) and its effect ($R.efc$) that can be either `Permit` or `Deny`. Def. 2 defines a partial order for rules.

Definition 2. *Partial order for rules*
A rule R_1 is equal to or more restrictive than a rule R_2, $R_1 \sqsubseteq R_2$, if

$$((R_1.efc = R_2.efc = Permit) \wedge (R_1.tgt \sqsubseteq R_2.tgt) \wedge$$
$$(R_1.cnd \sqsubseteq R_2.cnd)) \vee \tag{2.1}$$

$$((R_1.efc = R_2.efc = Deny) \wedge (R_2.tgt \sqsubseteq R_1.tgt) \wedge$$
$$(R_2.cnd \sqsubseteq R_1.cnd)) \tag{2.2}$$

(2.1) denotes the case that both rules express permissions. The target of the more restrictive rule has to be more specific and the condition of the rule must be retained or even strengthened. As a consequence R_1 denotes a restricted privilege compared to R_2. Analogously (2.2) states that R_1 constitutes a more general prohibition and therefore is also more restrictive than R_2. According to this, the relationship of rule sets can be defined as follows:

Definition 3. *Partial order for rule sets*
A set of rules RS_1 is equal to or more restrictive than a set of rules RS_2, $RS_1 \sqsubseteq RS_2$, if and only if

$$(\forall R_1 \in RS_1 : R_1.efc = Permit \Rightarrow \exists R_2 \in RS_2 : R_1 \sqsubseteq R_2) \wedge \qquad (3.1)$$

$$(\forall R_2 \in RS_2 : R_2.efc = Deny \Rightarrow \exists R_1 \in RS_1 : R_1 \sqsubseteq R_2) \qquad (3.2)$$

Please note that $\sqsubseteq$ refers to access rights granted. Thus (3.1) states that privileges are restricted while (3.2) constitutes an expansion of prohibitions.

With Def. 4 we provide a partial order for policies. As commercial database systems commonly do not support the declaration of prohibitions, we use the following restrained definition:

Definition 4. *Partial order for (permissive) policies*
Let P_1 and P_2 be policies with the rule combining algorithm of P_1 as well as of P_2 being permit-overrides and the effect of any rule of P_2 being Permit. P_1 is equal to or more restrictive than P_2, in short $P_1 \sqsubseteq P_2$, if the target T_1 of P_1 is equal to or subordinate to the target T_2 of P_2, and its set of rules is equal to or more restrictive than the set of rules of P_2.

Def. 4 does not exclude that P_1 contains prohibitions in contrast to policy P_2. A comparison of the semantics of two policies is undecidable in the general case because of the expressiveness of rule conditions. As the access control rules of database systems are not restricted by additional conditions, policy comparison is eased and computable.

4   Engineering Adaptable Access Control Policies

The reliable definition of service policies can take place in two ways. One approach is to extract and adapt database policies. An alternative is to generate the service policies based on the predefined service functionality.

Adapting database policies. This approach is practical for administering the access control of already implemented Web services. In this case the service functionality as well as the database interaction are already given. As depicted in Fig. 1, the access control rules that apply to the user, whose account is employed to establish the connection to the database, are extracted. These constitute the maximum set of privileges that can be granted to the Web service users. The privileges are stored in *permission policy* sets as presented in Sect. 3. The Web

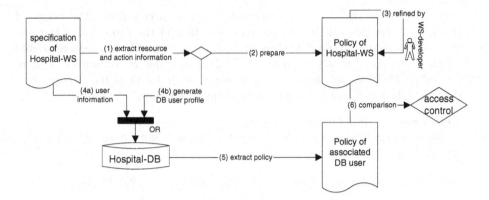

Fig. 7. Policy development process

service developer is able to select the *permission policies* that are applicable for the service operation. The rights can be further adapted and restricted by additional conditions. Finally, by the definition of *base policies*, these possibly modified privileges are assigned to user profiles of the Web service domain. In order to guarantee that the service policies are supported by the database, they are compared to the extracted database policies according to Def. 4.

Defining policies – starting from the service's point of view. Reliable Web service development starts with the specification of the desired functionality. As the service interacts with one or more underlying databases, service operations are related to SQL-statements. Thus, it is recommended to generate the service policy based on the specification (steps (1) and (2) of Fig. 7). Similar to the previous approach, the service developer can restrict the service policy by additional conditions (step (3)): Considering our Web service portal for physicians, the constraint of granting only attending physicians access to their patients' medical records can be formulated.

The extraction of the database policy is illustrated in the lower part of Fig. 7. This policy depends on the database account that is used to run interactions with the DBMS. Step (4a) represents the case that information about an already existing profile is provided by the service specification document, while step (4b) outlines that a new profile is generated that is appropriate for the service functionality. In step (5) the access rights of the respective profile are extracted and converted into XACML policies.

In the general case the Web service provides its own user management that differs from the one of the database. This is reasonable as the DBMS shall not be visible to service users. Consequently, in order to enable comparison of service policies and database policies (step (6)), service users have to be associated with database accounts. This can be achieved by the use of policies that are similar to the *role assignment policies* presented in the previous section.

Multiple policies and exchange of policies. Web service environments are highly dynamic, especially when services constitute mobile code that can be executed on arbitrary hosts as in the case of ServiceGlobe. In order to show how the presented techniques can be utilized for a flexible authorization design, we focus on a new use case for our hospital scenario. We assume that an e-service named *Management-WS* for administrative officers exists, which is used to inquire and change information about physicians as well as the allocation of beds. As illustrated in Fig. 8 the *Employee Policy* regulates the access for hospital employees on the side of the Web service. Connection to the DBMS is established under the account of *db_user1*. Assuming that an emergency situation arises, designated experts need to gather information about human resources and free capacities from institutions like police and fire departments, aid organizations and hospitals, in order to manage the catastrophic event. In the normal case, access for persons of foreign domains will be denied. By temporarily adding an appropriate policy that is tailored to the requirements of *Emergency coordinators*, access can be granted as long as the emergency situation persists and be revoked afterwards. In Fig. 8 an additional switch of the database connection is shown. This approach is advisable when the required access rights for the database vary in both situations.

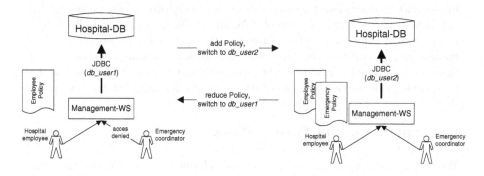

Fig. 8. Dynamic exchange of policies.

Thus, instead of developing partially redundant services for different situations, existing ones can be reused. Obviously this approach is scalable and flexible because the ports of services can be independently adapted to different situations by the dynamic exchange of policies.

5   Related Work

Several research platforms that are concerned with the access control management of distributed systems have been presented, among the first ones *Policy-Maker* and *KeyNote* [10]. Some more recent approaches deal with the security management of Web service applications, e.g., [11] shows how to define XACML policies for service interfaces and [12] presents an RBAC policy framework for Web services. Typically, it is entirely up to the service developer to define the access policies for services. To the best of our knowledge there does not exist any security system that focusses as much on the relationship between service policies and the access control of underlying resources – especially databases – like our approach.

Web service platforms and development toolkits like Bea WebLogic, IBM WebSphere or the freely available JWSDP employ Java 2 security technology, which enables the realization of sophisticated authentication and authorization for most Web applications. Nevertheless business and security logic are oftentimes admixed. In our approach, authorization and service implementation are decoupled, thus easing the maintenance of applications.

Data Grids, as representatives of distributed systems, provide the infrastructure for sharing resources in wide area networks, involving numerous data providers as well as consumers. The Community Authorization Service (CAS) approach [13] enables resource administrators to delegate the authorization management to the community. [14] describes an approach for fine-grained authorization for single resources. As the new grid platform Open Grid Service Architecture (OGSA) introduces Web service techniques into the Grid area, mechanisms for security management for e-services are also employed in the Grid context. In [14] it is mentioned that the use of XACML would be a practical alternative to the previously employed policy language. But resource administrators have to ensure on their own that the deployed access policy conforms with the authorization of the underlying resource. Our approach addresses this issue for databases by verifying that service policies constitute valid refinements of database policies.

6   Conclusion and Future Work

We have described our approach of a more reliable and adaptable engineering of access control for database dependent Web services: Service developers are assisted by the preparation of policy and request documents. Considering this, one approach is to extract the authorization settings of the underlying databases and use them as a basis for a subsequent definition of service policies. As an alternative access control of services can be designed based on service specifications. By verifying that the access control of a service constitutes a valid refinement of the corresponding database policies, service deployment is getting more reliable. In this way, access control is relocated to the Web application and adapted to the requirements of the Web service, which thus operates as a gatekeeper for the database as, by blocking unauthorized access at an early stage, denial of service attacks on the underlying database can be prevented. In contrast to database systems, services can be replicated more easily. Additionally, security for underlying databases is improved by adequate user profiles that are generated automatically with regard to service requirements. Thus security and privacy threats in case of service infiltrations are reduced.

A further significant aspect is the separation of security and business logic. Because of the application logic not being mixed with the security functionality, concise software design is enabled and code adaptations in case of policy changes are avoided. Web services are designed for application to application communication. Thus, the dynamic creation of service coalitions has to be considered. Further research topics include the delegation of rights and roles across administrative domains.

References

1. E. Maler, P. Mishra, and R. Philpott, "Assertions and Protocol for the OASIS Security Assertion Markup Language (SAML) v1.1," specification, OASIS, Sept. 2003.
2. B. Atkinson, G. Della-Libera, S. Hada, M. Hondo, and P. H.-B. et. al., "Web Services Security (WS-Security)," specification, IBM, Microsoft Corp., VeriSign Inc., April 2002.
3. S. Castano, M. G. Fugini, G. Martella, and P. Samarati, *Database Security.* ACM Press, Reading, MA, USA: Addison-Wesley, 1995.
4. R. Sandhu, D. Ferraiolo, and R. Kuhn, "The NIST Model for Role-based Access Control: Towards a unified standard," *proceedings of the 5th ACM Workshop on Role-Based Access Control*, pp. 47–64, July 2000.
5. D. F. Ferraiolo, R. Sandhu, S. Gavrila, D. R. Kuhn, and R. Chandramouli, "Proposed NIST Standard for Role-Rased Access Control," *ACM Trans. Inf. Syst. Secur.*, vol. 4, no. 3, pp. 224–274, 2001.
6. S. Godik and T. Moses, "eXtensible Access Control Markup Language (XACML)," specification, OASIS, February 2003.
7. M. Keidl, S. Seltzsam, K. Stocker, and A. Kemper, "ServiceGlobe: Distributing E-Services across the Internet (Demonstration)," in *Proc. of the Conf. on Very Large Data Bases (VLDB)*, pp. 1047–1050, 2002.
8. S. Seltzsam, S. Börzsönyi, and A. Kemper, "Security for Distributed E-Service Composition," in *Proc. of the 2nd Intl. Workshop on Technologies for E-Services (TES)*, vol. 2193 of *Lecture Notes in Computer Science (LNCS)*, pp. 147–162, 2001.
9. A. Anderson, "XACML RBAC Profile," working draft, OASIS, June 2003.
10. M. Blaze, J. Feigenbaum, and A. D. Keromytis, "The Role of Trust Management in Distributed Systems Security," in *Secure Internet Programming*, pp. 185–210, 1999.
11. T. Moses, "XACML profile for web-services," working draft, OASIS, September 2003.
12. R. Bhatti, J. B. D. Joshi, E. Bertino, and A. Ghafoor, "Access Control in Dynamic XML-based Web-Services with X-RBAC," 2002.
13. V. Welch, F. Siebenlist, I. Foster, J. Bresnahan, K. Czajkowski, J. Gawor, C. Kesselman, S. Meder, L. Pearlman, and S. Tuecke, "Security for Grid Services," tech. rep., Globus Alliance, June 2003.
14. K. Keahey, V. Welch, S. Lang, B. Liu, and S. Meder, "Fine-Grain Authorization Policies in the GRID: Design and Implementation," tech. rep., 1st International Workshop on Middleware for Grid Computing, 2003.

Supporting Secure Deployment of Portal Components

Martin Gaedke, Johannes Meinecke, and Martin Nussbaumer

University of Karlsruhe, Institute of Telematics,
IT-Management and Web Engineering Research Group,
Engesserstr. 4, 76128 Karlsruhe, Germany
{gaedke,meinecke,nussbaumer}@tm.uni-karlsruhe.de

Abstract. With the growth of the World Wide Web, it has become more and more important to find implementation models tailored especially for Web applications. Unlike traditional applications, Web portals are required to be constantly up to date and are therefore often subject to changes at runtime. Consequently Web application frameworks have been developed that allow the construction and manipulation of Web pages consisting of pre-built components as an alternative to re-programming. The capability of such systems rises with the number of available components. Hence it is advisable to facilitate their deployment and exchange with a supporting architecture. The achieved increased use of third party components also results in higher risks for the provider of the portal. Especially the resource access by the contained code poses a potential threat and lowers the acceptance for foreign components. This paper proposes a robust architecture for the installation, administration and exchange of portal components and addresses the need for protection against malicious code.

1 Introduction

During the past years the World Wide Web has changed noticeably and is nowadays quickly moving forward towards a platform for distributed applications and services. Individual Web pages are typically aggregated to Web portals. Many elements of these portals are not specific to a single site and should therefore be subject to reuse. Component-Based Software Engineering (CBSE) [1] offers an answer to that problem by delegating functionality to separately exchangeable software artifacts. Consequently, CBSE strategies have been adopted for the development and evolution of Web applications [2], which is commonly denoted by the term *Component-Based Web Engineering* (CBWE).

Another concept for distributing Web application functionality is the use of Web services. In contrast to components that are hosted at the owner's realm, using a Web service hosted by third party requires trust. In other words, functionality is provided by granting access to the service instead of deploying it. This raises concerns regarding matters of trust and security. A big software company, for example, will not be convinced to manage their accountancy with the help of a Web service, possibly provided by a direct competitor. It will be less reluctant to buy a component from the same vendor and use it on one of their own servers, allowing it to keep control of the sensitive accounting data.

N. Koch, P. Fraternali, and M. Wirsing (Eds.): ICWE 2004, LNCS 3140, pp. 516–520, 2004.
© Springer-Verlag Berlin Heidelberg 2004

Another aspect of Web portals is the required degree of flexibility. The information and functionality they offer has to be adapted quite frequently [3], these changes should be made as simple as possible. The WebComposition approach forms a solid foundation by focusing on configuring solutions instead of re-programming. An implementation of that approach, the WebComposition Service Linking System (WSLS) [4], has been developed. It provides a framework and supporting runtime system to assemble Web sites by using and configuring components.

In order to improve the degree of reuse, the components have to be transported between component-exchanging portals. This paper focuses on issues concerning the secure deployment, exchange and management of components for Web portals. We will investigate the current state of the art of according technologies and present an approach to deal with a selection of unsolved problems.

2 State of the Art

The application of CBSE concepts to the development of Web portals is not a new idea and has already been adopted by a range of systems:

A traditional strategy relies on the usage of software development environments like Microsoft Visual Studio .NET or the Sun ONE Application Framework. Graphical tools allow the construction of Web pages from components, with the possibility of integrating new components into the environment. The resulting applications have to be compiled and deployed on a Web server. After that, the formerly independent parts cannot be distinguished anymore, nor is it possible to insert new components or adjust existing ones without returning to the development phase.

Other solutions can be achieved by a second approach: resorting to component-based portal frameworks like Microsoft SharePoint Services [5] and PHP-Nuke [6]. Comparably to content management systems, these portals enable administrators to edit their pages by using Web interfaces to insert and adjust interactive page components. In addition to a set of supplied components, the integration of independently developed software artifacts is supported. In many cases, the process of installing the new component files is not covered by a Web interface. Its complexity hinders widespread use of foreign components.

Another strategy for extendable portals is pursued by the use of Web Services. The *Web Services for Remote Portlets* (WSRP) [7] among others builds on this strategy by exporting reusable functionality including markup code generation into distant Web services. This makes the component installation process obsolete but poses other problems, as already mentioned.

The last regarded approach is the support for propagating components by publishing them with component repositories. Most corresponding systems focus on offering efficient means for searching the pool of components. A repository especially intended for CBWE is introduced in [2]. In this case, searching is supported by supplying extendable ways of representing and categorizing the contained components with arbitrary metadata. The technical retrieval in combination with the installation of a component into a portal is, however, left outside the concept.

3   Aspects of Deploying Components for Web Applications

Given the state of the art, we designed a new architecture integrating component deployment with the exchange supported by a component repository. Special attention was paid to the reuse of third-party components with regard to protection against malicious code. Another investigated aspect not presented here due to limited space concerned the integration of licensing mechanisms.

In the context of Component-Based Web Engineering, we relate the term *exchange* to the complete course of events necessary for a component deployed on one Web portal to be transported and installed on another. We chose a distributed approach with the subjects of exchange stationed at the portal servers and a central directory serving as a registry for information about their properties and locations. Thus, this concept allows for applying the same infrastructure for the deployment of components as used for Web service discovery and integration.

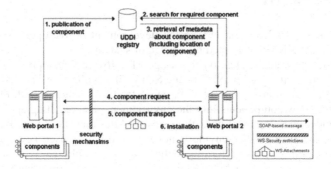

Fig. 1. Component Exchange Process

Figure 1 shows the individual steps of a component exchange between two portals. All activities are covered by supporting software, meaning that steps like contacting the UDDI registry are transparent for the portal administrators. To supplement the limited features of SOAP, some of the SOAP-based protocols of the Web Service Enhancements (WSE) [8] are used for the realization of the component request and transport. For example, the WS-Attachement protocol [9] allows sending large binary data sets (the component files) attached to the XML-encoded SOAP message. Also, WS-Security [10] provides the means for integrating security mechanisms into the inter-portal communication.

A problem still largely unsolved by the state of the art is the security risk that comes with the deployment of third-party portal components. Usually distributed in binary form, without additional mechanisms there is no way of monitoring or controlling their accesses on resources and data potentially worth of protection. Therefore, we integrated the concept of a robust code environment within the overall architecture.

Figure 2 contains an overview of a concept for a robust code environment. As a basic rule, code producers are to digitally sign their components. This prevents other parties from unnoticeably tampering with the binary code. It also helps to uniquely identify the authors to determine the set of rights issued to the component. During the installation process an early security check is performed. Among other aspects, the contained metadata is reviewed with respect to any statements about the behavior of the component. These could for example include declarations of resources the component needs to access, allowing the prevention of destabilizing problems at runtime. From the security perspective, this alone does not sufficiently protect the server, as the authors cannot be relied on correctly declaring all accesses. Therefore, additional security control at runtime restricts the installed code in its resource usage. Both mechanisms during installation and runtime are controlled by a flexible security policy differentiating between several levels of trust towards the component authors.

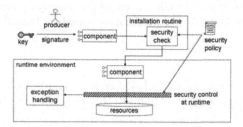

Fig. 2. Protection Mechanism against Foreign Code

4 Pretoria System

The Pretoria System implements the necessary support for the presented concepts. As the underlying technological platform for the component administration software and the component model, the Microsoft .NET Framework was chosen. Being a new member of the WebComposition approach, the Pretoria Administration Suite provides a secure infrastructure for component exchange. The screenshot in figure 3 shows a typical view of a component and some of its metadata. It allows administrators to install new components, manage existing ones and participate in the exchange process. The software is available for download at
http://mw.tm.uni-karlsruhe.de/projects/pretoria.

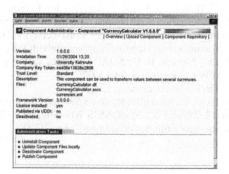

Fig. 3. View of an Installed Component within the Pretoria Administration Suite

5 Conclusion and Future Work

In this paper, we discussed the deployment of components into Web portals and the support for their propagation through repositories. The evaluation of the state of the art raises the need for a system combining the exchange with the deployment process. Also the use of foreign code calls for additional resource protection. The problem can be solved with a distributed architecture making use of Web service technologies.

Plans for the future are to transform the presented architecture to other platforms like EJB or SharePoint, as it is independent of the underlying component model. Further plans are to integrate license mechanisms based on Digital Rights Management (DRM)

Acknowledgement. This material is based on research for the Mobile University (M-University) project supported by Microsoft Research Ltd and Microsoft Deutschland GmbH.

References

1. Heineman, G. T., Councill, W. T.: Component-Based Software Engineering - Putting the Pieces Together. Addison-Wesley, Boston (2001)
2. Gaedke, M., Rehse, J.: Supporting Compositional Reuse in Component-Based Web Engineering. In Proceedings of the ACM Symposium on Applied Computing, ACM Press, (2000) 101-106
3. Koch, N., Rossi, G.: Patterns for Adaptive Web Applications. In 7th European Conference on Pattern Languages of Programs, Germany (2002)
4. Gaedke, M., Nussbaumer, M.: The WebComposition Service Linking System (WSLS) project site. Germany (2002): http://mw.tm.uni-karlsruhe.de/projects/wsls/ (2/2004)
5. Microsoft: Microsoft SharePoint Products and Technologies – Web Site, USA (2004): http://www.microsoft.com/sharepoint/ (2/2004)
6. PHPNuke: PHPNuke Advanced Content Management System – Web Site (2004). http://phpnuke.org/ (2/2004)
7. Kropp, A., Leue, C., Thompson, R.: Web Services for Remote Portlets Specification – Web Site, USA (2004): http://www.oasis-open.org/committees/wsrp/ (2/2004)
8. Powell, M.: Programming with Web Services Enhancements 2.0. MSDN, USA (2003): http://msdn.microsoft.com/webservices/building/wse/default.aspx (2/2004)
9. Barton, J. J., Thatte, S., Nielsen, H. F.: SOAP Messages with Attachments, W3C Note 11 December 2000, WWW Consortium, USA (2000), http://www.w3.org/TR/SOAP-attachments (2/2004)
10. Kaler, C., Hallam-Baker, P., Monzillo, R.: Web Services Security: SOAP Message Security. Working Draft 17, 27 August 2003, OASIS Web Site, USA (2003): http://www.oasis-open.org/committees/documents.php (2/2004)

A System for Interactive Authorization for Business Processes for Web Services*

Hristo Koshutanski and Fabio Massacci

Dip. di Informatica e Telecomunicazioni - Univ. di Trento
via Sommarive 14 - 38050 Povo di Trento (ITALY)
{hristo, massacci}@dit.unitn.it

Abstract. Business Processes for Web Services are the new paradigm for virtual organization. In such cross organizational partnerships no business partner may guess a priori what kind of credentials will be sent by clients nor the clients may know a priori the needed credentials for the successful completion of a business process. This requires an interaction between server and clients.

We propose a framework for managing the authorization interactions for business processes and a BPEL4WS based implementation using Collaxa server. Our model is based on interaction between servers and clients and exchange of requests for supplying or declining missing credentials.

Keywords: Web Services, Business Processes For Web Services, Credential-Based Systems, Interactive Authorizations.

1 Introduction

Business Processes (BPs) for Web Services (WS) is the new buzzword for e-commerce integration. BPs allow for a lightweight integration of business partners' services and the establishment of virtual enterprises on the Web. To support this process a number of standards have emerged: SOAP and WSDL for basic functionalities, BPEL4WS and ebXML for complex business processes.

Business Processes are distributed among different partners and all communications are channeled by the invocation of web services by the client. The major difference with traditional access control is that each "task" of the workflow is offered as a web service that can be activated by anyone and thus credentials must be used to enforce access control.

In this paper we discuss our system for reasoning about access control for BPs for WS. The basic intuition is that partners, offering web services in a BP, do not know a priori what credentials clients may need to present nor clients know exactly which services they want, as the BP may take different paths. So, we need an interactive process in which the client starts a business process and

---

* This work is partially funded by the IST programme of the EU Commission FET under the IST-2001-37004 WASP project and by the FIRB programme of MIUR under the RBNE0195K5 ASTRO Project and RBAU01P5SS Project.

N. Koch, P. Fraternali, and M. Wirsing (Eds.): ICWE 2004, LNCS 3140, pp. 521–525, 2004.

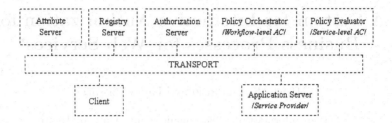

Fig. 1. System Architecture

the partners evaluate client's current credentials to determine whether they are sufficient or something is missing. Then they get back to the client which may decline some requested credential and a new path must be sought.

We need to find a way for WS partners to find a solution assuming they only know their policies. Further, it does not make sense for a BP to ask all potentially useful credentials (too demanding and privacy intruding for clients) nor such option is practical, considering that WS partners may prefer to ask for some credentials directly to clients rather than making them publicity available.

We have given a semantics to the framework using Datalog, as customary in many approaches to workflow and trust management [1,2,3,4,5]. This allow us to ground the intuitive question: "How does a WS partner determine the credentials needed for granting a request?" into a formally defined procedure.

We have implemented the framework using BPEL4WS server and a front-end to an abduction/deduction engine.

Notice that we are solving a different problem than trust negotiation [5] where both client and server already know what they want and use a sophisticated protocol to disclose each others' credentials to build trust. Trust negotiation could well be applied on top of this framework.

2   System Architecture

In this section we sketch the architecture of the system. We refer to [6] for additional information on the rationale behind the architecture. At the time of writing we have done an initial prototype including the main entities of the system, given below. Figure 1 shows a view of the architecture.

PolicyEvaluator   takes endpoint decisions on access control. Each partner is represented by a PolicyEvaluator. It encapsulates the partner's specific authorization policy, and presents it as a service using WSDL.

PolicyOrchestrator   is responsible for the workflow level authorization. It decides which partners are involved and according to some orchestration security policies combines the corresponding PolicyEvaluators in a form of a business process executable by the AuthorizationServer.

AuthorizationServer *locates* and *manages* all needed PolicyEvaluators and returns an appropriate result to the ApplicationServer. Also, it is responsible for managing all *interactions* with the Client.

An authorization example of the message flow in our architecture is the following: after an ApplicationServer has been asked for a Web Service by the Client, it requests the AuthorizationServer to confirm whether the Client has enough access rights for that service or not. Then the AuthorizationServer, having client's current credentials and the service request, calls the PolicyOrchestrator for a policy composition process indicating what should be done for taking a decision. Once getting the policy process the AuthorizationServer executes it, communicates with all partners involved and manages their interaction with the Client. When the final decision is taken (grant/deny) the AuthorizationServer informs the ApplicationServer.

3   The Framework

In our framework each partner has a *security policy for access control* $\mathcal{P}_\mathcal{A}$ and a *security policy for disclosure control* $\mathcal{P}_\mathcal{D}$. $\mathcal{P}_\mathcal{A}$ is used for making decision about usage of all web services offered by a partner while $\mathcal{P}_\mathcal{D}$ is used to decide the credentials whose need can be potentially disclosed to the client.

To execute a service of the fragment of BP, under the control the partner, the user will submit a set of *presented credentials* $\mathcal{C}_\mathcal{P}$, a set of *declined credentials* $\mathcal{C}_\mathcal{N}$ and a *service request* r. We assume that $\mathcal{C}_\mathcal{P}$ and $\mathcal{C}_\mathcal{N}$ are disjoint.

The formal model is described at length in [7], in Figure 2 we show the summary of the algorithm.

We use the symbol $P \models L$, where P is a policy and L is either a credential or a request to specify that L is a logical consequence of a policy P. P is *consistent* $(P \not\models \perp)$ if there is a model for P. Abduction solution (step 3b of algorithm in Fig. 2) over a policy P, a set of predicates H with defined p.o. over subsets of H and a ground literal L is a set of ground atoms E such that: (i) $E \subseteq H$; (ii) $P \cup E \models L$; (iii) $P \cup E \not\models \perp$; (iv) any set $E' \prec E$ does not satisfy all conditions above; Traditional p.o.s are subset containment or set cardinality.

The use of declined credentials is essential to avoid loops in the process and to guarantee the success of interaction in presence of disjunctive information. For example suppose we have alternatives in the partner's policy (e.g., "present either a VISA or a Mastercard or an American Express card"). An arbitrary alternative can be selected by the abduction algorithm and on the next interaction step (if the client has declined the credential) the abduction algorithm is informed that the previous solution was not accepted. The process can continue until all credentials have been declined (and access is denied) or a solution is found (and access is granted). Additional details on the formal model can be found in [7].

1. extract from the client's input the set of presented credentials $C_\mathcal{P}$ and the set of declined credentials $C_\mathcal{N}$
2. verify that the request is a logical consequence of the credentials, namely $\mathcal{P}_\mathcal{A} \cup C_\mathcal{P} \models r$
3. if the check succeeds then access is granted, otherwise
   a) compute the set of *disclosable and not declined credentials* as
      $C_\mathcal{D} = \{c \mid c \text{ credential that } \mathcal{P}_\mathcal{D} \cup C_\mathcal{P} \models c\} \setminus C_\mathcal{N}$
   b) use abduction to find a minimal set of missing credentials $C_\mathcal{M} \subseteq C_\mathcal{D}$
      such that both $\mathcal{P}_\mathcal{A} \cup C_\mathcal{P} \cup C_\mathcal{M} \models r$ and $\mathcal{P}_\mathcal{A} \cup C_\mathcal{P} \cup C_\mathcal{M} \not\models \bot$
   c) if no such set exists then $\bot$ is sent back to the user, otherwise
   d) communicate $C_\mathcal{M}$ back to the client and iterate the process.

Fig. 2. Interactive Access Control for Stateless WS

4   Implementation

For our implementation, Collaxa[1] is used as a main BPEL manager (on the AuthorizationServer side) for executing and managing all policy composition processes returned by the PolicyOrchestrator and for the implementation of the AuthorizationServer itself. Some of Collaxa's main characteristics:

– it supports many WS standards as BPEL4WS, WSDL, SOAP, etc;
– it interoperates with platforms as BEA's WebLogic and Microsoft .NET;
– it is easy to integrate Java modules (classes) within a BPEL process;
– deploying a process on Collaxa is actually compiling it down to Java code that is internally executed by the JVM when invoked.

The AuthorizationServer itself is a BPEL process deployed under Collaxa that internally deploys the policy process returned by the PolicyOrchestrator as an internal web service and internally executes it. The advantage is that if the AuthorizationServer is requested to get an access decision for a service that has already been asked for it and there is no change in the workflow policy then the AuthorizationServer *does not* deploy the service's policy process again but just (internally) executes it. In that way we speed up the access decision time by *JIT compilation of authorization processes*.

PolicyOrchestrator in the current prototype is just a mapping between a service resource and its workflow policy process. We assume that the process is already created by some GUI (e.g., could be used any BPEL visual tool generator) and is available to the orchestrator.

PolicyEvaluator is a Java module that acts as a wrapper for the DLV system[2] (a disjunctive datalog system with negations and constraints) and implements our interactive algorithm for stateless WS (Fig. 2). For deductive computations we use the disjunctive datalog front-end (the default one) while for abductive computations, the diagnosis front-end.

---

[1] Collaxa BPEL Server (v2.0 rc3) – www.collaxa.com
[2] DLV System (r. 2003-05-16) – www.dlvsystem.com

5   Future and Ongoing Work

There are a number of issues that are currently the subject of research to improve the usability of our system. Following are the key points in our future and ongoing work.

The current system processes credentials at an high level: defines what can be inferred and what is missing from a partner's access policy and a user's set of credentials. There is the need of a suitable platform for the actual distributed management of credentials at lower levels (namely actual cryptographic verification of credentials). We decided to use PERMIS infrastructure [8] because it incorporates and deals entirely with X.509 Identity and Attribute Certificates. It allows for creating, allocating, storing and validating such certificates. Since PERMIS conforms to well-defined standards we can easily interoperate with the other entities (partners) in a BP.

Next step in the framework is to use algorithms for credentials' chain discovery as in [9]. Then, once a client collects all credentials and supplies them back to the service provider, it can be used, as a preprocessing step (before running the access control procedure), for tracking all credentials provided by him.

Since we are at an initial stage of our prototype, we have only run limited experiments. Substantial large scale experiments are yet to be worked out to determine the running performance of the algorithm. Cassandra, a role based policy language, and its policies for the UK's EHR could be a good candidate for a benchmark [10].

References

1. Li, N., Mitchell, J.C., Winsborough, W.H.:   Design of a role-based trust-management framework. In: Proc. of IEEE SS&P. (2002)
2. Kang, M.H., Park, J.S., Froscher, J.N.:   Access control mechanisms for inter-organizational workflow. In: Proc. of ACM SACMAT. (2001) 66–74
3. Bertino, E., et al.: The specification and enforcement of authorization constraints in workflow management systems. ACM TISSEC **2** (1999) 65–104
4. Atluri, V., Chun, S.A., Mazzoleni, P.: A Chinese wall security model for decentralized workflow systems. In: Proc. of ACM CCS. (2001) 48–57
5. Yu, T., Winslett, M., Seamons, K.E.: Supporting structured credentials and sensitive policies through interoperable strategies for automated trust negotiation. ACM TISSEC **6** (2003) 1–42
6. Koshutanski, H., Massacci, F.: An access control framework for business processes for Web services. In: Proc. of ACM Workshop on XML Security. (2003)
7. Koshutanski, H., Massacci, F.: Interactive access control for Web Services. In: the 19th IFIP Information Security Conference (SEC). (2004) (to appear).
8. Chadwick, D.W., Otenko, A.: The PERMIS X.509 role-based privilege management infrastructure. In: the 7th ACM SACMAT. (2002) 135–140
9. Li, N., Winsborough, W.H., Mitchell, J.C.: Distributed credential chain discovery in trust management. Journal of Computer Security **11** (2003) 35–86
10. Becker, M.Y., Sewell, P.: Cassandra: Flexible trust management, applied to electronic health records. In: Proceedings of the 17th IEEE Computer Security Foundations Workshop (CSFW). (2004) (to appear).

Web Engineering Curriculum: A Case Study of an Evolving Framework

Yogesh Deshpande

University of Western Sydney
Locked Bag 1797, Penrith South DC
NSW 1797, Australia
y.deshpande@uws.edu.au

Abstract. In their comprehensive review of computing disciplines, the Joint (ACM and IEEE-CS) Task Force on Computing Curricula identified a group of subjects as Net-centric, to be taught at under-graduate level. Web Engineering was still in its infancy at the time. We started a Web Engineering specialization at master's level in 1999 and have recently reviewed it comprehensively. Based on our experience in teaching different aspects of Web development at both under-graduate and graduate levels, this paper proposes a framework to design curricula for Web Engineering that can evolve in tandem with the evolution of the Web. The framework helps to dovetail the knowledge areas in a coherent manner avoiding a smorgasbord approach to curriculum design.

1 Introduction

The need for disciplined approaches and new methods and tools for development has been well recognised by Web site and application developers and expert commentators [2, 4, 10-12]. Originating from Document Engineering [13] and Web Site Engineering [10] Web Engineering continues to develop as a specific area of work, as attested to by workshops, special tracks and international conferences, along with two new journals [8, 9]. Web Engineering arose out of widespread and genuine concerns about how Web sites and applications were, and are, being developed. They led to a working definition of Web Engineering as "the application of systematic, disciplined and quantifiable approaches to development, operation and maintenance of Web-based applications" [3].

The phenomenal growth of the Web created a matching demand in courses that taught Web site and application development. Commercial training institutions were the first to offer courses in Web technologies and at the height of the dot com boom numbered in tens of thousands across the world. Universities were generally uninterested in offering such short training courses but dealt with the new technologies by initiating or modifying undergraduate courses in specific areas, such as programming, networking, human-computer interaction and so on. At a more generic level, the ACM and IEEE-CS, in their most recent review of computing curricula [1], published in 2001, identified net-centric computing as one of the 14 areas to represent the body of knowledge for computer science. The development of Web Engineering has been too recent for an explicit mention as a body of knowledge.

N. Koch, P. Fraternali, and M. Wirsing (Eds.): ICWE 2004, LNCS 3140, pp. 526–530, 2004.

The first Workshop on Web Engineering at WWW7 devoted half a session to the discussion of appropriate graduate curriculum. As a result, at the University of Western Sydney (UWS), we offered Web Engineering as a specialization at master's level in 1999. Elsewhere, Greenspun has described how he and his colleagues taught Web development at MIT without dealing with curriculum design at a more general level. Whitehead [14] has specifically addressed the formulation and issues of Web Engineering curriculum at graduate level by identifying the relevant knowledge areas.

The master's course in Web Engineering at UWS has just undergone a full review. Since Web Engineering was not covered by the Task Force, we did not have a specific and relevant framework for us to work with. However, their recommendations have been useful in the exercise as also the references cited above.

During our deliberations, it became clear that the identification of knowledge areas may turn out to be too specific and time-bound. Web Engineering is still young. The constituent body of work is rapidly building up and, like the Web itself, will continue to evolve. The teaching of Web Engineering, therefore, requires a blend of currently established body of work and ongoing research. Graduate students in Web Engineering have to be prepared for a level of enquiry bordering on research work and experiments with emerging technologies. Designing an appropriate curriculum for Web Engineering thus involves more than identifying knowledge areas.

Consequently, we had to construct a framework for the Web Engineering curricula which would be flexible enough to accommodate both the existing and evolving knowledge areas. This short paper broadens the framework and develops the underlying principles, to facilitate further discussions by specifically addressing the curricular issues. It does not cover details of our implementation and revisions. Section 2 describes and briefly discusses the initial framework and aims and objectives of the course. Section 3 presents the revised framework. Section 4 concludes the paper with recommendations for further work and discussions.

2 Initial Framework for Web Engineering Curriculum

One way to arrive at a curriculum would be to answer the following, sequential questions.

1. What are the aims of Web Engineering?
2. What are the activities comprising Web Engineering?
3. What are the knowledge areas that will facilitate the activities?
4. How can these knowledge areas be combined to build a curriculum?

These are broad questions that do not consider specific, pedagogical and institutional concerns, in the same way that the Task Force left the responsibility of tailoring degree courses to individual institutions. The four questions, in their logical order, are predicated on a relatively stable field of study. They assume that a field of study such as Web Engineering 'exists' and that there are 'activities' in this field that people agree upon. It is then a question of identifying the knowledge areas relevant to these activities in order to build a curriculum.

However, Web Engineering did not evolve so logically nor has its evolution stopped. The limited role of activities in defining a curriculum in this context becomes obvious as the early concerns with Document Engineering and Web Site Engineering were overtaken by the growing complexity of Web development and the experiences of Web developers and researchers during that time. Figure 1 from [3], encapsulates those concerns in six rising levels of complexity.

6. Web Project Planning and Management
5. Web-based System
4. Web Site Construction
3. Web Site Design
2. Web Page Design
1. Web Page Construction

Fig. 1. Levels of complexity of Web development [11]

We first started teaching Web development at the undergraduate level, in 1997. Initially, the subjects built up the students' skills and knowledge to level 4, viz. Web Site Construction, appropriate for the undergraduates. However, such a focus does not fully address a whole gamut of issues, such as life-long learning (i.e. developing capabilities to master new technologies and developments) or to discharge their social, legal, ethical and professional responsibilities that come to the fore more forcefully when dealing with the Web than is the case with normal software development. Consequently, we decided to offer a specialization in Web Engineering at the master's level to tackle two additional questions:

5. How much of the complexity, technical and non-technical, should be addressed directly by the curriculum and indirectly through student projects?
6. How can future developments be accommodated in building a curriculum?

The specialization in Web Engineering was structured according to Figure 1, enrolled computing graduates, and addressed the six questions in its delivery through case studies, active discussions, assignments and feedback on students' projects.

2.1 Aims and Objectives of a Course in Web Engineering

Based on the previous discussion, we started the master's course with the aims to:
1. provide graduates with a critical appreciation of IT/IS methodologies, the Web technologies, innovation, and their roles within an organisation;
2. enable graduates to build Web applications using multimedia and hypermedia based upon sound methodologies in project management and people management;
3. prepare graduates to fulfil their social, legal, ethical and professional obligations through case studies and on-going analysis of current developments;
4. develop graduates' expertise in new technologies used in intranets, extranets and the Internet;
5. enable graduates to administer Web and application servers and manage content and information;
6. provide a global business and IT perspective to the graduates.

3 Revised Framework for Web Engineering Curriculum

Figure 1, over time, proved to be too specific (e.g. in its attention to page construction and design). The students also started to acquire some of these skills at undergraduate levels. Hence, we began the review by revising Figure 1 to Figure 2.

4. Project Management
3. Web Applications
2. Web sites
1. Internet Technologies

Fig. 2. A Framework for Web Engineering Curriculum

The revised model facilitated further analysis of where each relevant technology, protocol and standard fits in, what issues (social, ethical, legal and others) need to be addressed at each layer and how to understand and manage each layer in curricular terms. However, neither figure properly accommodates the recent arrivals of Web Services, Mobile Computing and component-based application development. These are more advanced topics with a degree of complexity and the interdependence not found in the early Web applications. Hence, we extended the model as in Figure 3.

Project Management		
Web Services	Mobile Computing	... (advanced apps)
Web Applications (incl Server Management)		
Web sites	Non-Web site Internet (component-based applications)	
Internet Technologies		

Fig. 3. A Revised Framework for Web Engineering

Figure 3 is an abstraction (and a superset of Figure 2) that allows for identification and development of other layers and sub-layers. The model combines the treatment of knowledge areas and complexities associated with Web developmental activities, and consciously attempts to address the issues of future developments as they may affect the curricula. The Web Engineering curriculum can now be formulated as part core and part optional or elective to suit local conditions.

4 Recommendations for Future Work

This short paper has presented a framework for a Web Engineering curriculum and its evolution. The major advantage of the framework is that it separates out levels of complexity in the activities that constitute Web Engineering, making it flexible and adaptable to the changing circumstances. It also clarifies the place of relevant knowledge areas. It then becomes possible to think of 'flavours' of curriculum to suit the local, institutional conditions, strengths and weaknesses, pedagogical issues and research strengths. Examples of these variations can be cited in terms of student demographics and expectations, demand for more 'topical' courses, local industry participation through project work, available expertise, and research trends. Furthermore, 'the proof of the pudding' means that all these courses must be rigorously evaluated from the students' and employers' points of view and the actual outcomes. These issues will be the subject of another paper.

Finally, it needs to be acknowledged that this framework has not taken on board what might be regarded as 'information systems', i.e. more sociological and/or management, point of view. More work is needed to identify and analyse these issues and then solve the concomitant problems.

Acknowledgments. The author would like to thank all the members of the School of IT and other colleagues who participated in the development of this framework.

References

1. CC01 (2001) The Joint Task Force on Computing Curricula, IEEE Computer Society and Association for Computing Machinery, *Computing Curricula 2001*, vols 1 and 2, Ironman Draft, February 2001, http://www.acm.org/
2. Cutter Consortium, *Research Briefs*, 7 Nov 2000
3. Deshpande, Y., Murugesan, S., Ginige, A. Hansen, S., Schwabe, D., Gaedke, M. and White, B. (2002) Web Engineering, *Journal of Web Engineering*, vol 1, no. 1, 3-17
4. Glass, R. (2001) Who's Right in the Web Development Debate?, *Cutter IT Journal*, vol 14, no. 7, pp 6-10
5. *IEEE Multimedia*, Special issues on Web Engineering, vol 8, nos 1 and 2, Jan-Mar 2001 and Apr-Jun 2001
6. *International Journal of Web Engineering and Technologies (IJWET)* http://www.inderscience.com/ijwet/
7. *Journal of Web Engineering*, Rinton Press, http://www.rintonpress.com/journals/jwe
8. Murugesan, S., Deshpande, Y., Hansen, S. and Ginige, A. (1999) Web Engineering: A New Discipline for Development of Web-based Systems, *Proceedings of the First ICSE Workshop on Web Engineering*, International Conference on Software Engineering, Los Angeles, May 1999. http://aeims.uws.edu.au/WebEhome/ICSE99-WebE-Proc/San.doc (shortly to be restored)
9. Murugesan, S. and Deshpande, Y. (2001) *Web Engineering*, Lecture Notes in Computer Science- Hot Topics, vol 2016, Springer Verlag, 2001
10. Powell, T.A. (1998) *Web Site Engineering*, Prentice-Hall, Upper Saddle River, NJ
11. Pressman, R.S. (1998) Can Internet-Based Applications Be Engineered? *IEEE Software*, September/October 1998
12. Pressman, R.S. (2001) Web Engineering: An Adult's Guide to Developing Internet-Based Applications, *Cutter IT Journal*, vol 14, no. 7, pp 2-5
13. White, B. (1996) Web Document Engineering, SLAC-PUB-7150, May 1996, http://www.slac.stanford.edu/pubs/slacpubs/7000/slac-pub-7150.html (based on a tutorial presented at the World Wide Web Conference WWW5, Paris, 1995)
14. Whitehead, J. (2002) A Proposed Curriculum for a Masters in Web Engineering, *JWE*, vol 1, no. 1

Behaviour Recovery and Complicated Pattern Definition in Web Usage Mining

Long Wang and Christoph Meinel

Computer Department, Trier University,
54286 Trier, Germany
{wang, meinel@}ti.uni-trier.de

Abstract. Data mining includes four steps: data preparation, pattern mining, and pattern analysis and pattern application. But in web environment, the user activities become much more complex because of the complex web structure. So user behaviours recovery and pattern definition play more important roles in web mining than other applications. In this paper, we gave a new view on behaviour recovery and complicated pattern definition. We used several methods to recover different user behaviours, such as simple behaviour, sequence visiting, tree structure behaviour, acyclic routing behaviour and cyclic routing behaviour. Based on various recovered behaviours, we raised how to define complicated usage patterns. These usage patterns include constraint association rules, constraint sequential patterns, deepest access paths, shortest access paths, tree structure accessing patterns, parallel visiting patterns, circle visiting patterns and so on. We also gave some experiment results about these complicated access patterns which reveal some interesting usage behaviours.

1 Introduction

Web usage mining is an application of data mining methods in web field. Traditional data mining methods include association rules, sequential patterns, clustering, classifications [1] and other methods combining with machine learning methods such as Naïve Byes, Neural net and Markov model. The steps for data mining include data preparation, pattern mining, and pattern analysis and pattern application [2]. Web usage mining aims to find the hidden usage patterns from web usage data, and in web environment, these usage data are mostly recorded as web server logs.

However, it is acknowledged that the web application is totally different from other traditional data mining application, such as "Goods Basket" model. We can interpret this problem from two aspects:

1) *Weak Relations between user and site*:
   Visitors could access the web site at any time from any place and even without any clear idea about what they want from the web. On the other hand, it is not easy for the site to discriminate different users. WWW brings great freedom and convenience for users and sites, and great varieties among them as well. So the relation between supply and demand becomes weak and vague.

N. Koch, P. Fraternali, and M. Wirsing (Eds.): ICWE 2004, LNCS 3140, pp. 531–543, 2004.
© Springer-Verlag Berlin Heidelberg 2004

2) *Complicated behaviours*:

Hyperlink and back tracking are the two important characters in web environment, which make user's activities more complicated. For the same visited contents, different users can access them with different patterns. Also, the user's behaviours are recorded as visiting sequence in web logs, which can not exactly reflect the user's real behaviours and web site structures.

In web environment, user behaviours are hidden in usage data, so access patterns are various and different from other applications.

In this paper, we give a new view on web usage mining. We prefer on recovering user's activities from usage data and defining new usage patterns from recovered behaviours. The task of behaviour recovery aims to recover user's activities from these URL sequences. The user's complicated activities through the site, such as back tracking and circle visiting, are recorded as URL sequences in web logs. We give several methods to recover different behaviours. They are simple behaviour (single item and sequence access), tree structure behaviour, acyclic routing and cyclic routing behaviour. The choice of proper recovery methods depends on what kind of usage patterns we want to mine in the succeeding step. Based on these recovered behaviours, we extend the definition for web usage mining. Besides the traditional usage patterns, we also raised Constraint Association Rules, Constraint Sequential Patterns, Tree Structure Accessing Patterns, Parallel Visiting Patterns and Circle Visiting Patterns.

The rest of this paper is organized as follows. In section 2, we review the work related with the problem we consider here. In section 3 we describe the formal definitions of behaviours recovery and complicated pattern definition. Section 4 concerns on the five recovery methods, we give a real example of how to recover user's navigational behaviours. Section 5 is a detailed explanation of how to define complicated usage patterns from user's recovered behaviours. In section 6, we give some experiment results that describe the recovered behaviours and complicated usage patterns. Section 7 is a short conclusion.

2 Related Works

The four general steps for data mining don't give clear tasks for behaviour recovery and usage pattern definitions. Behaviour recovery should be included in data preparation, and pattern definitions are made before pattern mining. So these two steps should exist between data preparation and pattern mining.

The tasks of data preparation in web usage mining include:

- Collection of usage data for web visitors: Most usage data are often recorded as kinds of web server logs. In E-Commerce and other services that need user registration, usage data are recorded as other file format.
- User identification: it is easy to identify different users in E-Commerce and other registration situation, though it can not be

avoided that some private personal registration information is misused by hackers. But for common web sites, it seems not easy to identify different users. In this situation, user can freely visit the web site. User's IP, Cookies and other limited client information, such as agent and version of OS and browsers, can be used for user identification. In this step, the usage data for different users are separately collected.

- Session construction: after user identification, different sessions for the same user should be reconstructed from this user's usage data collected in the second step. A session is a visit performed by a user from the time she enters the web site till she leaves [3]. Two time constraints are needed for this reconstruction, one is that the duration for any session can not exceed a defined threshold; the other is that the time gap between any two continuously accessed pages can not exceed another defined threshold.

- Behaviour recovery: reconstructed sessions are not enough to depict the varieties of user navigation behaviours in web usage mining. In most cases, any kinds of usage behaviours are only recorded as a URL sequence in sessions. The revisiting and back tracking result in the complexity of user navigation, so the task of recovery aims to rebuild the real user behaviour from the linear URLs in sessions. We will give a detailed explanation in section 4.

Pattern mining aims to mine the defined patterns from the usage data collected in the step of data preparation. The already existing patterns include association rules (or frequent item set), sequential patterns, the most forward access patterns [4], tree structure access patterns [5], clustering and classification. These patterns are originally mined from the sessions, while not from the recovered behaviours; also the desired patterns are defined even before the data preparation, while not after the behaviour recovery, so it is inevitable that these patterns can not exactly depict the usage behaviours. In [6] a query mechanism is raised that can query the user behaviours. This mechanism allows the input of freely defined access patterns, and then it queries these patterns from reorganized usage data. But this query mechanism can not depict complicated patterns such as tree structure access patterns and cyclic routing patterns. And also the storage reorganization for usage data requires much memory space.

3 Problem Statements

In web usage mining, time set, users set and web pages set are the three key entities, which are defined as a T, U and P. A session is a visit performed by a user from the time when she enters the web site to the time she leaves. A session is a page sequence ordered by timestamp in usage data record and is defined as $s = <p_1, p_2 \dots p_m>$ ($p_i \in P$, $1 \leq i \leq m$), and these pages can form another page set $s' = \{p'_1, p'_2 \dots p'_k\}$, ($p'_i \in s$, $p'_i \Leftrightarrow p'_j$, $1 \leq i,j \leq k$). User behaviour is recovered from the session for this user and defined as $b = (s', R)$, where R is the relations among s' and all user behaviours bs form a behaviour set named B.

An access pattern is some pages organized in an explainable way that some users accessed at some time, and it is mined from recovered user behaviours. "Explainable way" means that access pattern can give a reasonable and meaningful interpretation, either from web site semantics or web structure, or even from time factor and geographic factor. Access pattern is defined as $A = (B', M)$, where B' is mined from B and have the same format as B and M is the meaningful interpretation for B'.

The goal of behaviour recovery is to recover the user behaviour b from the right session s, because user behaviours are hidden in sessions. The goal of access pattern definition is to define the required pattern we want to mine from the recovered behaviours.

4 Behaviours Recovery

As explained in the former sections, sessions reconstructed from usage data record only the accessed pages sequence ordered by timestamp, but not reveal the real activities for these pages. It is user behaviours that record user's interest and real activities through the web site. From the point of site structure, a web site is a directed graph, and in this graph, the vertex is a page and the directed edge is a hyperlink between two pages. From the point of site semantics, a web site is a knowledge web characterized with concept hierarchy. So user behaviours reveal not only the required content during his visiting, but also some of site structure and concept hierarchies, and also reveal the activities on these structures and hierarchies characterized with revisiting, back tracking and book marking. So user behaviour recovery is necessary for usage understanding.

On the other hand, all the user behaviours are latent in sessions, so different recovering methods can construct different behaviours. The strategy for proper recovering method is correlated with what kind of access patterns we want to mine in the next step. From simple to complex, we show here some strategies of behaviour recovery. We illustrate this problem from a real session collected from our server logs (www.telematik-institut.org). We reconstruct the sessions based on the strategy explained in section 2. This session is listed as following:

$$s = <0, 292, 300, 304, 350, 326, 512, 510, 513, 512, 515, 513, 292, 319, 350, 517, 286 >$$

In this session, the pages are labelled with IDs. For simplicity, in the later sections, we replace all the pages with their corresponding IDs if there is not extra explanation. In this session, this user raised 17 page/times access requirements. 0 and 286 were accessed separately as entrance and exit pages. Besides the entrance and exit pages, there are two groups of pages, one group is (300, 304, 326, 510, 513, 319, 517, 515) which were accessed only once, and the other group is (292, 350, 512) which were accessed more than once. Now we will explain several strategies for recovering different user behaviours.

4.1 Simple Behaviours Recovery

This strategy is the simplest one and overlooks all the repeated pages in a session. It includes two kinds of behaviours.

The first is that user behaviours are represented with only those unique accessed pages, which is the simplest recovery strategy. So simple user behaviours can be recovered from this session as:

$$s' = \{0, 292, 300, 304, 350, 326, 512, 510, 513, 515, 319, 517, 286\}.$$

The second method is that user behaviours are represented with those unique accessed pages and also the access sequence among these pages. For those pages accessed more than once, we concern only the first happening. Based on this thinking, user behaviours for this session can be recovered as:

$$<0 - 292 - 300 - 304 - 350 - 326 - 512 - 510 - 513 - 515 - 319 - 517 - 286>$$

From the user behaviours recovered by the first method, association rules and frequent item sets can be mined in further step. Sequential patterns can be mined from the user behaviours recovered by the second method.

4.2 Tree Structure Behaviours Recovery

The simple recovery strategies listed above play great importance in data mining. While in web usage mining, revisiting and back tracking are the two important characters in user behaviours, which take place as the form that some pages were accessed more than once during a session. Those pages accessed more than once led to different access directions, which formed behaviours like tree structure. Tree structure behaviours not only depicted the visiting patterns, but also revealed some conceptual hierarchy on site semantics.

In the tree structure behaviour, each different page happens only once. To recover access tree t from session s, we used a page set named P to store the unique pages that already exist in t, and we also used a pointer pr pointing to the last recovered node during recovering in t. The recovery strategy is:

1) Set t = **NULL**;
2) Read the first entrance page in s as the tree root r, let pr pointing to r and insert this page to P;
3) Read new page from s and judge if the same page exist in P;
    i) Exist in P:
        4) Find this already existing node n in t and set pr point to this node,
        5) Go to step 3.
    ii) Not exist in P:
        4) Insert this new page to P,
        5) Create a new node and insert this new node as a new child for pr,
        6) Let pr point to this new node,
        7) Go to step 3.

The tree structure behaviours for the above session can be recovered with our strategy as the following figure:

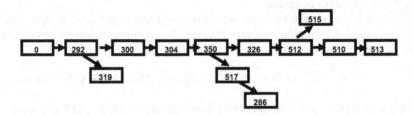

Fig. 1. Tree Structure behaviour

Tree structure behaviours can help to mine those access patterns with tree structure and also help to mine most forward sequential patterns or deepest access path.

4.3 A Cyclic Routing Behaviours Recovery

A web site is a complex directed graph, and further we can take one visiting for a user as a routing process to find interesting contents. Even for the same page contents, different users could access them with different routing methods, which revealed personal difference in visiting custom and understanding.

"Acyclic routing behaviour" means that during one visiting (session), there existed at least two different pages between which there were at least two different access paths. This behaviour indicts that user can access the same destined content from the same start content but via different paths. With acyclic routing behaviours, we can further query the shortest path and most popular path between two pages.

The final recovered behaviour is like a lattice structure defined as *l*, and we also used *P* to store unique pages in *l*, and *pr* pointing to the last recovered node during recovering in *l*. We used the following strategy to rebuild the acyclic routing in a session.

1) Set *l* = **NULL**;
2) Read the first entrance page in **s** as the top node *t*, led *pr* pointing to *t* and insert this page to *P*;
3) Read new page from **s** and judge if the same page exist in *P*;
  i) Exist in *P*:
    4) Find this same existing node **n** in *l* and judge the relation between **n** and *pr*,
      a) **n** can be backward tracked from *pr*
        5) Set *pr* point to **n**,
        6) Go to step 3.
      b) **n** can be forward tracked from *pr*
        5) Build new edge directed from *pr* to **n**, if there is not directed edge from *pr* to **n**.
        6) Set *pr* point to **n**,
        7) Go to step 3.

        c) *n* can not be tracked from *pr* in a single direction
          5) Build new edge directed from *pr* to *n*,
          6) Set *pr* point to *n*,
          7) Go to step 3.
  ii) Not exist in *P*:
        4) Insert this new page to *P*,
        5) Create a new node and insert this new node as a new child for *pr*,
        6) Let *pr* point to this new node,
        7) Go to step 3.

Based on the above strategy, we can recover acyclic routing behaviour from the same example. The following figure displays the final result.

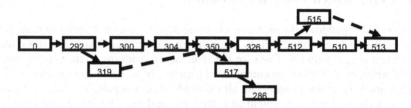

Fig. 2. Acyclic routing behaviour

4.4 Cyclic Routing Behaviours Recovery

Besides recovering acyclic routing behaviours, we also tried to recover cyclic routing behaviours. The premise for recovering tree structure, acyclic routing and cyclic routing behaviours is the happenings of revisiting and back tracking during one session. Revisiting and back tracking are two special characters in web usage mining, which can be seldom recorded in super markets. The revisiting happened sometimes due to the site structure. Currently most sites have complex structure and even frame-based structure, so this phenomenon happens more popularly. The repeated pages usually play great importance in usage navigation, web structure and web semantics.

We have made a statistic for revisiting and back tracking on two web sites, one is www.telematik-institut.org and the other is www.tele-task.de. The former is frame-based, while the latter is free designed. Even after filtering those adjacent repeat pages, we found that in 12% and 4% of sessions there exist revisiting or back tracking phenomenon.

The strategy for recovering cyclic routing behaviour is similar with but more complicated than recovering acyclic routing, because this strategy builds backward links for repeat pages, and tracking among pages needs complex structures. The following figure shows cyclic routing behaviours recovered from the same example.

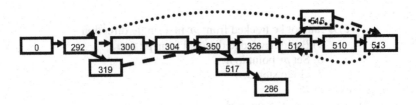

Fig. 3. Cyclic routing behavior

Different recovery strategies can yield different user behaviors, so the choice of proper strategy depends on what kind of patterns we want to mine in the next step.

5 Complicated Pattern Definitions

The tasks of pattern definition aim to define access patterns wanted to mine from recovered user behaviours. Within one visit for a user, there may exist more than one different access patterns. Even for the same access patterns, there may be more than one explanation. Due to the complicated structure of web site and varieties in user behaviours, it is hardly to numerate all the kinds of access patterns. Access patterns are the reflection of the site content and structures and must be interpreted by them. For the same page set but with different user behaviours, we can get different access patterns. Concrete pattern definition is necessary to understand user visiting tendency and interest. Besides to define the traditional patterns, we pay more attentions on how to define some new complicated patterns, which depict the user real visiting interest more exactly.

5.1 Traditional Pattern Definition

Similar to the other data mining applications, there are some already known usage patterns, such as association rules, frequent item sets, sequential patterns, clustering and classifiers [1]. We here concern on the patterns that related with association rules and sequential patterns.

Association rules and frequent item sets aims to find those co-occurred pages in sessions by a number of users. In this case, the user access patterns can be represented by these co-visited pages. Further investigating these co-visited pages, there may be content or structural relations among them.

Sequential pattern is an extension of association rules and frequent item sets. It cares not only the co-occurred pages in sessions, but also the visiting sequence among them.

It is very clear that repeated pages could not exist in these two kinds of patterns, and all the repeat pages are removed in behaviour recovery.

5.2 New Pattern Definition

Access pattern in web environment can be much more complicated than other pattern mining. The traditional patterns listed above are not enough to depict the user behaviours in web environment, but they are the basic patterns to define more complicated patterns. Before defining access patterns, we must make an investigation about single user behaviours through the site, which is the task in behaviour recovery. As explained in former sections, time, user and pages are the three key factors in user behaviours and in access pattern definition as well, and also, the complicated site structures give us heuristics to define some more complicated patterns. From simple to complicated, we defined the new patterns as followings.

5.2.1 Constraint Association Rules

The difference between association rules and constraint association rules is that the latter aims to mine association rules with specified constraints defined before mining process. The constraints can be defined from the structure of user behaviour. Here we give some constraint association rules we used.

Frequent entrance pages and frequent exit pages: these two kinds of patterns are the simplest to understand user behaviour. We can find how the user was induced to begin his visit and why he left the site.

Frequent entrance pages with specified exit pages and frequent exit pages with specified entrance pages: these two kinds of patterns are to find the binary relations between entrance pages and exit page. The most favourite pairs can interpret the relations between entrance and exit.

Frequent pages that led to different access pages: not only from the point of site structure, but also from the factors that affect user behaviours, the pages that led to different access paths are very important to understand the accessing varieties from the same pages. Such pages are repeated pages, and it is due to the happening of the revisiting and back tracking during one session. From the semantics level, the contents of such pages should have multi-concept attributes; from the site structure, many different pages may be linked to such pages.

5.2.2 Constraint Sequential Patterns

Just like constraint association rules, constraint sequential patterns can help to understand those sequential patterns with constraints defined from site structure or user behaviour. We used the following patterns:

Frequent sequence with specified start page or end page: sequence patterns defined in section 5.1 have not any constraints before mining. With these constraint patterns here, we can find the most popular paths after or before defined pages, and these paths can show the different importance in deciding different access patterns.

Frequent sequence with or without hyperlinks: not all the continuously accessed pages in a session are connected with hyperlinks, and there are surely also some continuous pages without any hyperlinks. The use of bookmark by local browser, scripts, search query and some interactive forms can produce some unlinked pages in a session. The site holder should strengthen those favourite sequences with hyperlinks, but those unlinked sequences are the most desired contents that the corresponding users wanted.

Deepest access path after one page: in this case, all the user behaviours are recovered as a tree structure and every branch in this tree can be looked as an access path for this user. This kind of patterns are the longest branches after one page in this tree, and they are not only one of the most favourite paths for some visitors, but also can give visitors as much information as possible.

5.2.3 Frequent Tree Structure Access Patterns

The deepest access path list above has already related with tree structure patterns, because its definition is based on the recovered tree structure behaviours, but it takes a form of page sequence and reveals some linear relations among pages.

Tree structure pattern displays the detailed repeated pages and their diverse access paths. The most favourite tree access patterns are the most popular parts in web structure, or maybe display more reasonable organization for desired contents.

5.2.4 More Complicated Access Patterns

More complicated access patterns are the patterns with directed and undirected graph structure, and they are complicated routing within the site to find proper contents or just for navigations. Such access patterns are more exactly close to the users' real activities through the web sites.

Tree structure pattern ignores all the repeated pages in session, though the construction for this tree depends on those repeated pages as listed in section 4.2. This means that from the final constructed tree, we do not know the previous pages for the repeated pages.

More complicated accessing pattern concerns on such revisit and back tracking information. In our work, we focus on two kinds of patterns, one is *parallel visiting patterns* and the other is *circle visiting patterns*.

Parallel visiting patterns show the different access paths between one couple of start page and end page. We can further find the shortest paths between any two pages. This kind of pattern can be mined from recovered acyclic routing behaviours.

Circle visiting patterns aim to explain the frequent back tracking paths in sessions. Back tracking can happen because of site structure as frame-based site or because of some reminding information about previous pages when user accessed succeeding pages. They can be mined from those recovered cyclic routing behaviours.

6 Experimental Results

Two kinds of server logs are used in our experiments. One is collected from www.telematik-institut.org and the other is from www.tele-task.de. The time durations are over 5 moth and 14 months respectively. The general differences between these two sites and their logs are in the following table:

Table 1. Difference between TI and TT

	telematik-institut(TI)	tele-task(TT)
Site Scale	Middle	Small
Design Style	Frame based	Free designed
Pages	11988	1785
Users	27626	14854
Sessions	62570	29013

Firstly we calculate the session length for these two sites, and figure 4 shows the distribution of sessions by length. We can find a similar distribution by length for these two sites. An average session has 3~4 pages.

We think that different pages could play different roles for the user behaviour reconstruction: some pages are always visited as entrance pages for sessions, some pages are much easier to be exit pages, and other pages are as middle or navigation pages. The distribution by different roles can give us more about web structure and usage information

Let S be the set of all sessions and $|S|$ be the number of sessions in S. For a single page p, we set **Sum(p)** be the accessed number in S, and **Sum(p)** can be larger than $|S|$ because of revisiting in sessions. We denote by **E(p)** the number of sessions that accessed p as entrance page, **M(p)** the number of sessions that accessed p as middle page and **X(p)** the number as exit page. To evaluate the performance of these roles for a page p, we defined four properties:

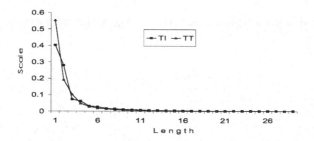

Fig. 4. Distribution of sessions by length

1) outer entrance support:

$$oe\text{-}support(\boldsymbol{p}) = \frac{E(p)}{|S|}$$

2) inner entrance support:

$$ie\text{-}support(\boldsymbol{p}) = \frac{E(p)}{E(p) + M(p) + X(p)}$$

3) outer exit support:

$$ox\text{-}support(\boldsymbol{p}) = \frac{X(p)}{|S|}$$

4) inner exit support:

$$ix\text{-}support(\boldsymbol{p}) = \frac{X(p)}{E(p) + M(p) + X(p)}$$

The general statistics about entrance and exit pages for two sites are shown in the next table:

Table 2. Entrance and exit page for TI and TT

	Telematik-institut(TI)	tele-task(TT)
Total pages	11988	1785
Entrance pages	6072	215
Exit pages	5295	225

The distribution for pages by these properties is shown in the next four figures:

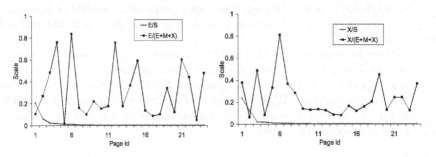

Fig. 5. Measures for entrance page (TI)   **Fig. 6.** Measures for exit page (TI)

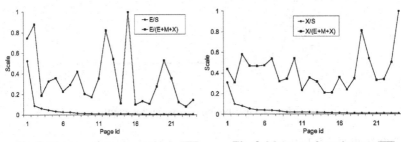

Fig. 7. Measures for entrance page (TT)   **Fig. 8.** Measures for exit page (TT)

From these four figures, we found that some pages are always accessed with entrance pages with their *ie-support* near to 1, and some pages are always exit pages with their *ix-support* near to 1. There are also some entrance pages with their *oe-support* near to or even larger than *ie-support* (*in* Fig 5 *and* 6), so do some exit pages, which happened due to the repeat visiting in sessions.

We also found that the distribution of entrance and exit pages revealed the web structure. For TT site, the homepage is the most important entrance page, because this site is dedicated to a project and homepage has the major content. But TI site is greatly different from TT site, because it owns two language versions and diverse information, and many users entered this site by search engine. But we find some similar usage tendency on these two sites if the homepages are ignored: exit page is better to discriminate different group of users than entrance page. The next two figures are made based on most frequent 24 entrance and exit pages. Exit page has a higher average scale than entrance page, as shown 2.1% vs. 1.6% for TI and 2.6% vs. 1.8% for TT.

7   Conclusions

In this paper, we tried a new view on web usage mining. We focused on user behaviour recovery and access pattern definition, because they are the basis for further pat-

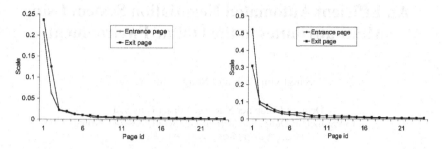

Fig. 9. Entrance vs. Exit (TI)   **Fig. 10.** Entrance vs. Exit (TT)

tern mining and require more concerning. Behaviour recovery enhances the tasks in data preparation, and new defined access patterns help to understand the diversities among users and also the complicated web structures. The new defined access patterns are good extension and combination of traditional patterns.

But for usage mining, pattern mining is the core. In the future, we will try to use different mining methods to mine our defined patterns. We have already developed some pattern mining methods, which can give us 11 basic patterns. These basic patterns can be used to further get incremental usage information.

References

1. J. Srivastava, R. Cooley, M. Deshpande and P. Tan: Web Usage Mining: Discovery and Application of Usage Patterns from Web Data, ACM SIGKDD, (2000)
2. R. Cooley, B. Mobasher and J. Srivastava: Data Preparation for Mining World Wide Web browsing Patterns, Knowledge and Information System, Vol.1, No.1, pp.5-32, (1999)
3. M. Spiliopoulou, B. Mobasher, B. Berendt and M. Nakagawa: A Framework for the Evaluation of Session Reconstruction Heuristics in Web Usage Analysis, INFORMS Journal on Computing, 15, 171-190
4. Ming-Syan Chen, Jong Soo Park and etc.: Data Mining for Path Traversal Patterns in a Web Environment. Proceedings of the 16th International Conference on Distributed Computing Systems (1996)
5. Mohammed J. Zaki: Efficiently Mining Frequent Trees in a Forest. In SIGKDD'02 (2002)
6. Bettina Berendt, Myra Spiliopoulou: Analysis of navigation behaviour in web sites integrating multiple information systems. The VLDB Journal, (2000)

An Efficient Automated Negotiation System Using Multi-attributes in the Online Environment

Sanghyun Park and Sung-Bong Yang

Dept. of Computer Science, Yonsei University
134 Shinchon-Dong, Seodaemun-Gu, Seoul, 120-749, Korea
{psh,yang}@cs.yonsei.ac.kr

Abstract. In this paper we propose an efficient negotiation agent system that guarantees the reciprocity of the attendants in a bilateral negotiation on the e-commerce. The proposed negotiation agent system exploits incremental learning based on artificial neural networks to generate counter-offers and is trained by the previous offers that have been rejected by the other party. During a negotiation, the software agents on behalf of the buyer and the seller negotiate each other by considering the multi-attributes of a product. The experimental results show that the proposed negotiation system achieves better agreements than other negotiation agent systems that can be operable under the realistic and practical environment. Furthermore, the proposed system carries out negotiations about twenty times faster than other negotiation systems on the average.

1 Introduction

Software agents have been playing an important role in e-commerce. Nowadays, agent mediated negotiation has received considerable attention in the field of automated trading [1,2]. However, they have not been developed sufficiently at the level of robust systems applicable to commercial web sites for e-commerce considering the importance of software agents that carry out negotiations on behalf of buyers or sellers. Such underdevelopment is due to the facts that the attributes, which may influence the buyer's behavior, cannot be defined precisely and that the success of a negotiation is dependent not only on the price but on certain abstract factors such as diverse inclination of buyers or sellers.

The Persuader system in the work of Sycara [3] utilizes the concepts of argumentation. In this system, mediation has been modeled by considering an iterative negotiation, multiple issues and multiple agents. However, a negotiation, as defined in the Persuader system, is a mutual selection of outcome and precludes any intervention by outside parties [4]. The persuasion mechanisms operate on the beliefs of agents with the aim of changing one or both parties' beliefs. Therefore, the Persuader system has no concern about the fact that it is not necessary for the agents to have similar beliefs at the end of the negotiation.

Kasbah [5] has proposed some negotiation strategies involved in negotiations for the real world applications. In Kasbah, however, a negotiation is carried out over an only single attribute such as price and the agents could not adopt any negotiation

N. Koch, P. Fraternali, and M. Wirsing (Eds.): ICWE 2004, LNCS 3140, pp. 544–557, 2004.

strategy for themselves. The number of strategies that are delegated to the agents is limited to only three and even their selections are not autonomous.

Negotiation agent architecture for structured interactions in the real world environment has been proposed by Faratin et al. [4]. Several negotiation systems have been implemented with the architecture in the paper of Faratin et al. [4,6]. These negotiation systems are capable of dealing with multiple attributes in a bilateral negotiation and of reaching an agreement through interactions between the agents. Among the various strategies for negotiations, the strategies based on the personal information of the other party could guarantee high profits for both participants in a negotiation [6]. However, under the environment of the online and real-time negotiations with unspecific persons, it is unrealistic that an agreement has been reached under the assumption that a negotiation is carried out with the personal information of the other party. Furthermore, the negotiation systems operating without the information of the other party cannot guarantee the profits for reciprocity.

Other negotiation systems considering interactions between agents have been studied by Fatima et al. [1] and Faratin et al. [7] In theses studies, time constraint was considered as an additional attribute. For adaptive agent based negotiation, Oliver [8] showed that agents could learn strategies using a genetic algorithm-based learning technique and Oprea [9] proposed a negotiation system that used a feed forward artificial neural network as the learning ability of a negotiation model in the context of agent-based e-commerce. These studies have shown satisfying results on negotiation under long-term deadlines; however, their systems require longer time interval to obtain better deals.

In this paper, we propose a negotiation agent system based on the incremental learning method. The aim of the proposed system is to increase the efficiency of negotiation in terms of both the execution time and the profits of the participants for reciprocity. The proposed system guarantees to obtain agreements within reasonable time. Note that time is not an issue of a contract. The proposed negotiation agent system has been implemented using interactions among the agents as in the Faratin's systems [4,6].

For the experiment, the negotiation agent systems considering interactions between the buyer and the seller agents [4,6] have also been implemented and experimented with the various datasets to compare with the proposed negotiation system. The experimental results show that the average relative error of the proposed negotiation agent system with respect to the negotiation system under *ideal* assumptions that one party knows the personal negotiation information about the other party, is within only about 2% and that the proposed system achieves better agreements than other negotiation agent systems that can be operable under the realistic and practical environment with unspecific persons. Furthermore, the proposed system carries out negotiations about twenty times on average faster than other negotiation systems implemented in this paper.

The remainder of the paper is organized as follows. Section 2 defines a trading model in which a negotiation carries on. Section 3 describes various negotiation systems including the proposed negotiation agent system. Section 4 provides the experimental results that compare the proposed system with the previous negotiation agent systems. Finally, the conclusions are made in Section 5.

2 The Negotiation Agent Model

2.1 The Multi-attribute Utility Theory

In this paper, the multi-attribute utility theory (MAUT) [10,11] is applied to evaluate the profits of buyers and sellers considering multi-attributes of the merchandise. Therefore, each attribute of the merchandise has a weight indicating the relative preference to each of other attributes.

The utility function in MAUT can be expressed in terms of the weights of the attributes and the values of the evaluation function at *the offer values* of the attributes, where the offer value of an attribute is the value of the attribute in a contract. Therefore, a contract that consists of the offer values of all the attributes can be regarded as a "proposal" in the real negotiations. The value of the utility function can be denoted as the profit of either a buyer or a seller. The utility function $V^k(X)$ can be expressed as follows.

$$V^k(X) = \sum_{i=1}^{n} \left(w_{j_i}^k \cdot v_{j_i}^k (x[j_i]) \right), \quad \sum_{1 \le i \le n} w_{j_i}^k = 1, \quad 0 \le v_{j_i}^k \le 1 \tag{1}$$

where k indicates either a buyer or a seller agent, $J = \{j_1, j_2, \dots, j_n\}$ is the set of attributes j_i $(1 \le i \le n)$, $X = \{x[j_1], x[j_2], \dots, x[j_n]\}$ is a contract composed of the values of all the attributes, $x[j_i]$ is the *offer value* of attribute j_i, $w_{j_i}^k$ is the weight of attribute j_i for agent k, and finally $v_{j_i}^k (x[j_i])$ is the evaluation function for $x[j_i]$ for agent k.

2.2 The Evaluation Function

The evaluation function for an attribute can be expressed in terms of *the request value* and *the allowable value* of the attribute, where the request value of the attribute is the maximum value for the attribute that an agent wants to acquire from the other party in the negotiation and the allowable value of the attribute is the maximum value for the attribute to which an agent concedes during the negotiation. The evaluation function can be written as follows.

$$v_{j_i}^q(x[j_i]) = \frac{x[j_i] - allowable \ \ value}{request \ \ value - allowable \ \ value}, \quad 0 \le v_{j_i}^q \le 1 \tag{2}$$

If the offer value, $x[j_i]$, is out of the range from the allowable value to the request value, the value of the evaluation function is set to zero or one depending on $v_{j_i}^q$. That is, if $v_{j_i}^q < 0$, it is set to zero, and if $v_{j_i}^q > 1$, it is set to one. Let the set of values $\left\{ v_{j_1}^q(x[j_1]), v_{j_2}^q(x[j_2]), \dots, v_{j_n}^q(x[j_n]) \right\}$ be a *normalized value set*. The following equation obtained from Equation (2) computes the *offer value* $x[j_1]$ of attribute j_i.

$$x[j_i] = \left(1 - v_{j_i}^q(x[j_i])\right) \times \left(allowable \quad value\right) + v_{j_i}^q(x[j_i]) \times \left(request \quad value\right) \qquad (3)$$

Therefore, from Equation (3) we can obtain an offer from its corresponding normalized value set.

2.3 The Trading Model

In the trading model adopted in this paper, we deal only with bilateral negotiations, because a multilateral negotiation is an extension of a bilateral one. We also concern mainly with finding a faster and better agreement in a bilateral negotiation. By the better agreement we mean the agreement for reciprocity; the profit is not partial to one over the other participant and rather the agreement guarantees as much profits as possible for both participants.

Although various commodities can be traded in a negotiation agent system, in this paper, we have chosen used cars for trading, because used cars could reflect various propensities to consume. In the trading model, the buyer wants to purchase a used car from the seller who deals various types of used cars. Although there may be several cars with the same model, a negotiation can still be carried on, because each car has different values on attributes in general.

The attributes of a used car for a negotiation are set to its price, the mileage and the warranty of the car. In the trading model, we assume that the buyer wants to purchase a specific car that the seller has presented. The seller has his or her own values on the attributes such as the request values, the allowable values and the weights. The buyer has also such negotiation information. The agent representing a party has all the negotiation information that the party has. However, the agent for one party does not know any negotiation information about the other party except the information regarding a contract.

The input datasets for bilateral negotiations in this paper are prepared so that each attribute could reflect all possible variations. Tables 1 and 2 show sample datasets for the buyer and the seller, respectively.

Table 1. A sample dataset for the buyer

Attributes	Request values	Allowable values	Weights
Price (Dollars)	2,000	5,500	0.5
Mileage (Miles)	5,000	100,000	0.3
Warranty (Months)	24	12	0.2

Table 2. A sample dataset for the seller

Attributes	Request values	Allowable values	Weights
Price (Dollars)	6,000	3,000	0.5
Mileage (Miles)	40,000	10,000	0.2
Warranty (Months)	6	18	0.3

Table 1 shows that the buyer wants to purchase a car with $2,000. The buyer may make a concession to the seller by $5,500 if the seller proposes a contract that is more profitable to the buyer in the mileage or the warranty than the previous contract. Furthermore, the buyer wants a car with 5,000 miles and may also make a concession to the seller by 100,000 miles if better offers in other attributes are proposed. The warranty is requested for 24 months from the buyer and also allowed up to 12 months according to the values of the other attributes. The weights of the attributes shown in Table 1 indicate that the buyer conceives the price as the most important factor in purchasing a car, the mileage as the next and the warranty as the least significant factor. Table 2 shows the negotiation information for the seller and can be explained similarly.

2.4 The Negotiation Process

A negotiation with multi-attributes involves various contracts with the same value of utility, so called the *iso-value curve* [12]. Each agent proposes a contract or provides counter-offers that lie on the iso-value curve with respect to the combinations of the values of attributes. The generation of a contract has a significant effect on the negotiation efficiency such as the profits of the attendants in the negotiation and the execution time of the negotiation. In the negotiation systems in the work of Faratin et al. [6], a contract, which seems to be the closest to the opponent's last offer among the contracts on the iso-value curve, is proposed to the other party. In this case, the negotiation efficiency can be very high when the agent of one party knows the negotiation information of the other such as the opponent's weight for each attribute. However, since the negotiation information of one party cannot be exposed to the other party in a practical commercial transaction, it is not easy to find a contract that is the closest to the opponent's last offer. Fig.1 shows an overview of the process of a negotiation for the negotiation systems implemented in this paper [4].

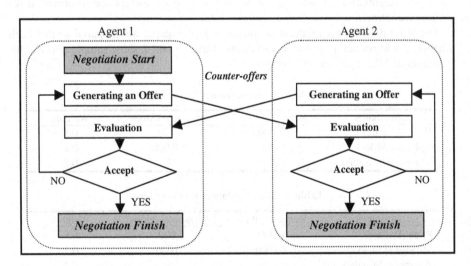

Fig. 1. The process of a negotiation in the agent systems

One agent as a participant in a bilateral negotiation offers a contract (an offer) to the other agent, and then the agent who receives the offer may accept it or generates a counter-offer as another contract. The utility functions for the profits of both participants are evaluated as described in the previous section.

3   The Negotiation Agent Systems

The trade-off mechanism is a kind of deliberative mechanism [4], and has been suggested to implement the transactions of the two agents participated in a bilateral negotiation. The trade-off mechanism enables an agreement to be reached through the transactions of agents and is capable of reflecting a practical environment for negotiations. However, since the previous negotiation systems based on the trade-off mechanism have never considered the execution time for a negotiation, they cannot handle negotiations well in the online environment and may not perform multi-lateral negotiations efficiently in the online environment as well.

3.1   The Trade-Off Mechanism

A *trade-off* can be defined informally as the mechanism in which one party lowers its values on some attributes and demands more on other attributes at the same time. Therefore, a trade-off is a search for a contract that is equally valuable to the previously offered contract, but that may benefit the other party.

Let X be an offer from agent q to the other party, and Y be a subsequent offer from the other party to agent q. A trade-off for agent q with respect to Y can be defined as follows

$$tradeoff_q(X,Y) = Z \qquad (4)$$

where q is either the buyer agent or the seller agent, Z is the contract that satisfies $V^k(Z) = V^k(X)$ and is assumed to be the offer that is the most similar to Y.

When the similarity between two offers is evaluated with the information of the other party such as the weights under the assumption that an agent is acquainted with the information about the other party, an agreement can be found under the guarantee of high profits of the participants in a negotiation [6]. However, the similarity must be evaluated under a practical condition that one participant in a negotiation is not aware of the other party's information. Therefore, the similarity based on the Euclidean distance is used for evaluation in order to implement the negotiation systems considering interactions between the buyer and the seller agents [4, 6, 12]. In the process of a negotiation, a value of the utility function is reduced by a predetermined amount, if a deadlock during the negotiation occurs due to keeping up the values of the utility function [6].

3.2 The Negotiation System Based on Incremental Learning

3.2.1 An Artificial Neural Network

In this paper, the effects of the learning agents are investigated with focusing on the reciprocity and on the execution time in a negotiation system. An online learning method such as the incremental learning method, therefore, is more appropriate for a negotiation agent system in the e-commerce than an offline learning method such as the batch learning, considering the environment of the online and real-time negotiations with unspecific persons [13]. The negotiation agent system proposed in this paper is designed to conduct a negotiation by using the incremental learning method in generating a contract, in contrast to the negotiation systems with trade-off mechanisms based on the similarity [4, 6]. Fig. 2 illustrates the structure of an artificial neural network for a trading model proposed in this paper. This model can be applicable to a general trading model by creating the same number of nodes in each input and output layer as that of attributes. The input and the output layers have three nodes each, since we consider three attributes for a product in the proposed system. Each node corresponds to an attribute of a product. The sigmoidal function is established as the activation functions of both the hidden layer and the output layer [14].

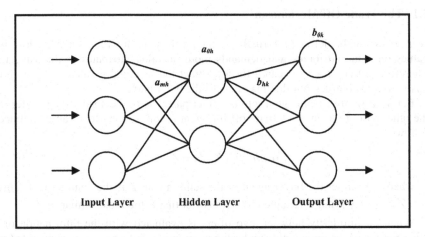

Fig. 2. The structure of an artificial neural network for the proposed negotiation system

3.2.2 The Learning Process

The negotiation agent system proposed in this paper follows the negotiation protocol illustrated in Fig. 1. Incremental learning process is employed in order to generate counter-offers. The learning process consists of two processes; *the initial learning process* and *the run-time learning process*. Fig. 3 shows the proposed negotiation procedures to which these two learning processes for *generating an offer* are added. The initial learning process initializes an artificial neural network through repetitive learning. The run-time learning process simultaneously generates a contract (a counter-offer) and carries out learning with the artificial neural network based on the initial learning process.

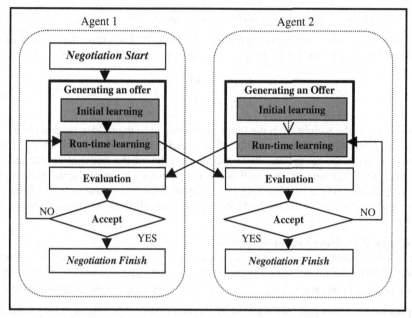

Fig. 3. Two learning processes for generating an offer in the proposed negotiation agent system

3.2.3 The Initial Learning Process

In the initial learning process, the input layer node m has the value of $v^q_{j_m}$ ($m = 1, 2, \ldots, n$) which is the evaluation value of the initial offer from the other party. The target of the output layer node k is $v^q_{j_k}$ ($k = 1, 2, \ldots, n$) which is the evaluation value of an offer that is very close to the first contract proposed from the other party. The offer is chosen out of offers on the *iso value curve*. Therefore, each node in the input and output layers has a value between zero and one. The criterion of the similarity in the initial learning process is based on the distance between a pair of contracts. The run-time learning process, however, is not dependent on the similarity.

In Fig. 2 the error terms δ_k and δ_h in the output and the hidden layers can be expressed as follows, respectively.

1) The error term δ_k of the output layer node k can be written as

$$\delta_k = o_k(1 - o_k)(t_k - o_k) \quad (k = 1, 2, \ldots, n) \tag{5}$$

2) The error term δ_h of the hidden layer node h can be written as

$$\delta_h = o_h(1 - o_h) \sum_{k \in outputs} b_{hk}\delta_k \quad (h = 1, 2, \ldots, n\text{-}1 \text{ and } k = 1, 2, \ldots, n) \tag{6}$$

where o_k and t_k are the output and target values of the output layer node k, respectively, o_h is the output values of hidden layer node h, and b_{hk} is the weight from the hidden layer node h to the output layer node k.

The weight w_{xy} from node x to node y can be updated by $w_{xy} \leftarrow w_{xy} + \eta \delta_y p_{xy}$ (η = the learning rate, p_{xy} = the input from node x to node y). Therefore, the weights of the artificial neural network for the proposed system are updated as follows.

$$\begin{cases} a_{mh} \leftarrow a_{mh} + \eta \delta_h p_{mh} \\ b_{hk} \leftarrow b_{hk} + \eta \delta_k p_{hk} \end{cases} \qquad (7)$$

where a_{mh} is the weight from the input layer node m to the hidden layer node h.

In the beginning, all the weights of the artificial neural network in the initial learning process are set to zero. Note that the weights of the artificial neural network after the initial learning process will become non-zeroes because the weights are updated repeatedly. The initial learning process establishes the *initial weights* of the artificial neural network for the run-time learning process through repetitive learning.

3.2.4 The Run-Time Learning Process

The run-time learning process generates a contract and carries out a learning process on the artificial neural network after the initial learning process. In this process the input layer node m has the value of $v_{j_m}^q$ ($m=1,2, \dots , n$) which is the evaluation value of the previous contract that was rejected by the other party. The output value of the artificial neural network is converted to the *offer value* for each attribute j_k ($k =1,2, ..., n$) by Equation (3), and these *offer values* for the entire attributes constitute a counter-offer for the other party.

For example, when agent 1 rejects a contract {$200, 20,000km, 18mos.} offered by agent 2, the contract are converted to the normalized value set {0.766, 0.684, 0.612}, which was computed with Equation (2). This normalized value set is then fed into the neural network of agent 2. Assume that the output of the neural network is {0.728, 0.691, 0.545}. Then this output is now converted to {$210, 19,000km, 15mos.} with Equation (3) as a counter-offer, and the weights of the network are updated with the backpropagation of the neural network by Equation (7).

The utility of the target is preserved as the current utility of the iso-value curve. If an agreement cannot be reached until a certain number of rounds in a negotiation, the utility is decreased with a predetermined rate. If the agreement cannot be reached within 100 rounds in a negotiation, the utility is decreased with 0.01 and carries out the negotiation. In the run-time learning process, the number of iterations for learning is increased monotonically as the number of rounds in the negotiation is increased. In the experiment, the learning rate is set to 0.01 during the negotiation process.

The proposed negotiation system utilizes the incremental learning method to generate counter-offers and is trained by the previous offer that has been rejected by the other party. Therefore, under the realistic and practical environment of negotiations, the incremental learning agent system is able to perform negotiations more rapidly and to guarantee more profits of the participants compared with the negotiation systems based on the similarity and the trade-off mechanism [6].

4 The Experimental Results

4.1 The Input Datasets

The proposed negotiation system is compared with the negotiation systems using the trade-off mechanism in [6]. The seller's negotiation data are generated randomly within the range from Min to Max values in Table 3. The weights of the price and the mileage for a seller are chosen randomly within the ranges of the preferences in Table 3, respectively. The weight of the warranty is determined with the equation in the table entry after the weights of the price and the mileage have been chosen. Two hundred sellers are created for the experiments.

The buyer's negotiation data are generated according to Tables 4 and 5. In these tables, Pmax, Mmax, and Wmin are the request values of the price, the mileage, and the warranty for a seller created in Table 3, respectively. Similarly, Pmin, Mmin, and Wmax are the allowable values of the price, the mileage, and warranty for a seller created from Table 3, respectively. In Tables 4 and 5, α is introduced to indicate how much the negotiation range of an attribute for one party intersects with that of the same attribute of the other party. By a negotiation range we mean the range from a request value to an allowable value of an attribute for a party. α is chosen randomly within the range of α in Tables 4 or 5 to create the buyer's request and allowable values for each attribute. We create one hundred buyers from Table 4 and another one hundred buyers are created with Table 5. A buyer created from Table 4 is likely to have negotiation ranges that are less similar to those of a seller, while the negotiation ranges of a buyer created from Table 5 are more similar to those of a seller. We call the buyer data created from Table 4 the Negotiation Dataset I and the buyers data from Table 5 the Negotiation Dataset II.

Table 3. The constructions of seller's negotiation data

Attribute	Request values [Min, Max]	Allowable values [Min, Max]	The range of preference
Price (Dollars)	[5000, 10000]	[1500, 3000]	[0.4, 0.6]
Mileage (Miles)	[30000, 100000]	[10000, 20000]	[0.2, 0.4]
Warranty (Months)	[6, 12]	[14, 36]	1 − {**the weight of price + the weight of mileage**}

Table 4. The Negotiation Dataset I

Attribute	Request value	Allowable value	The range of α
Price (Dollars)	Pmin+(Pmax–Pmin)·α	Pmax+(Pmax-Pmin)·α	[-0.4, 0.1]
Mileage (Miles)	Mmin+(Mmax-Mmin)·α	Mmax+(Mmax-Mmin)·α	[-0.4, 0.1]
Warranty (Months)	Wmax+(Wmax-Wmin)·α	Wmin+(Wmax-Wmin)·α	[-0.1, 0.4]

Table 5. The Negotiation Dataset II

Attribute	Request value	Allowable value	The range of α
Price (Dollars)	Pmin+(Pmax-Pmin)·α	Pmax+(Pmax-Pmin)·α	[-0.25, 0.1]
Mileage (Miles)	Mmin+(Mmax–Mmin)·α	Mmax+(Mmax-Mmin)·α	[-0.25, 0.1]
Warranty (Months)	Wmax+(Wmax-Wmin)·α	Wmin+(Wmax-Wmin)·α	[-0.1, 0.25]

4.2 The Experiment Environment

The Negotiation Datasets I and II include various inclinations of buyers and sellers. The experiments are carried out on these datasets to compare the performance of the proposed negotiation agent system with those of other negotiation systems based on the trade-off mechanism. At each agreement for all the negotiation systems, the difference between the profits of the buyer and the seller in a bilateral negotiation has never exceeded 0.03. Therefore, the performance of a negotiation agent system can be determined with the summation of the profits of both the buyer and the seller.

In order to compare the incremental learning system proposed in this paper (Incremental Learning System, *ILS*), three negotiation agent systems proposed by Faratin el al. [6] have also been implemented. The first system is the negotiation agent system using the similarity based on the information of the other party (Similarity-Information System, *SIS*). The second one is the negotiation agent system using the similarity based on the distance between contracts, without using the information of the other party (Similarity-Distance System, *SDS*). The last system is the negotiation agent system generating offers randomly, without considering the other party (Random System, *RS*). Note that, among these negotiation agent systems, SIS is more advantageous in utility than other systems, because SIS operates under the assumption that the agent of one party knows the personal information of the other party such as the weights of attributes.

4.3 The Experimental Results

Fig. 4 shows the average bilateral profits for the negotiation systems on the Negotiation Datasets I and II. The average bilateral profits indicate the summation of the buyer's and the seller's profits. As shown in this figure, SIS obviously achieves the best agreements for reciprocity, because SIS operates under the assumption that the personal information of one party such as the weights of the attributes is available to the other party in a negotiation. The figure also shows that ILS produces better agreements for reciprocity than other negotiation agent systems in the practical environment.

Fig. 5 shows the average relative errors of ILS, SDS and RS with respect to SIS on the Negotiation Datasets I and II. For these two datasets, the average relative errors of ILS are 2.17% and 1.84%, which are lower than those of SDS, respectively. Observethat ILS provides better agreements on the Negotiation Dataset II than on the Negotiation Dataset I, since the negotiation range of a buyer created from the Negotia-

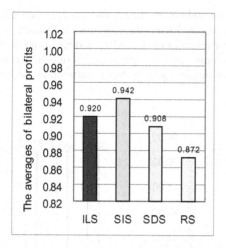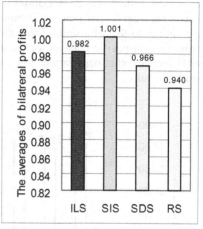

Fig. 4. The average bilateral profits for the negotiation systems on the Negotiation Dataset I (left) and Dataset II (right)

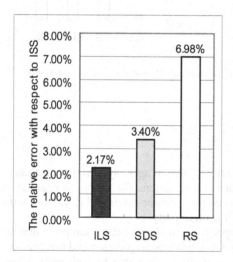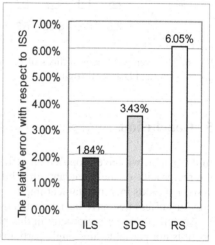

Fig. 5. The average relative errors of ILS, SDS and RS to SIS on the Negotiation Dataset I (left) and Dataset II (right)

tion Dataset II is more similar to those of a seller. Considering both datasets, ILS is superior to SDS in bilateral negotiations. Fig.4 also shows that RS has higher relative errors than other negotiation systems for both datasets.

Fig. 6 shows the average execution times for the negotiation agent systems on the datasets. For the Negotiation Dataset I, the average execution time of ILS is 1.7 seconds; ILS is at least twenty times faster than others. For the Negotiation Dataset II, the average execution time of ILS is 1.1 seconds; ILS is at least twenty seven times faster than other systems. The execution times for the Negotiation Dataset I are longer than those for the Negotiation Dataset II throughout all the negotiation agent systems, because the negotiation range of a buyer created from the Negotiation Dataset II is more similar to that of a seller. From the viewpoint of the online and real-time negotiation with unspecific persons for the e-commerce, ILS performs more efficient negotiations than other negotiation systems considering both the execution time and negotiation results.

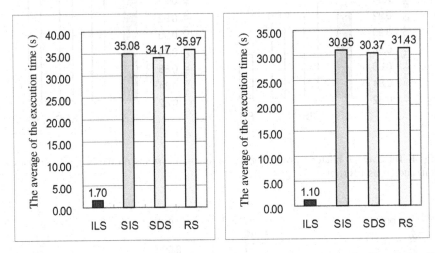

Fig. 6. The average execution times of the negotiation agent systems on the Negotiation Datasets I (left) and Dataset II (right)

5   Conclusions

In this paper, we have proposed an efficient negotiation agent system that guarantees the reciprocity of the attendants in a bilateral negotiation. The proposed negotiation system exploits incremental learning in generating counter-offers and is trained by the previous offers that have been rejected by the other party.

An agreement for reciprocity in this paper is reached under the assumption that the profit is not partial to any single participant in a bilateral negotiation and that the contract of the agreement guarantees as much profits as possible to both participants. Therefore, since the difference between the profits of the buyer and the seller is maintained under a predetermined threshold, a negotiation system can be evaluated by the sum of the profits of both the buyer and the seller.

We have implemented three negotiation agent systems based on the work from Faratin et al. (2000) to compare the performance of the proposed negotiation agent system. The experimental results show that under the realistic and practical environment of negotiations the proposed system is more efficient in negotiations than others in terms of both the profits for reciprocity and the execution time. The improvement in the incremental learning method and the expansion to multilateral negotiations are left as future researches.

References

1. Jennings, N. R., Faratin, P., Lomuscio, A. R., Parsons, S., Sierra, C., Wooldridge, M.: Automated negotiation: prospects, methods and challenges. Int. J. of Group Decision and Negotiation, Vol. 10, Issue 2. (2002) 199-215
2. Fatima, S. S., Wooldridge, M., Jennings, N. R.: Multi-Issue Negotiation Under Time Constraints. Proc. of 1st Int. Joint Conf. on Autonomous Agents and Multi-Agent Systems, July 15-19, Bologna, Italy (2002) 143-150
3. Sycara, K.: Multi-Agent Compromise via Negotiation. Distributed Artificial Intelligence, Vol. 2. (1989) 119-139
4. Faratin, P., Sierra, C., Jennings, N. R., Buckle, P.: Designing Responsive and Deliberative Automated Negotiators. Proc. AAAI Workshop on Negotiation: Settling Conflicts and Identifying Opportunities, Orlando, USA (1999) 12-18
5. Chavez, A., Maes, P.: Kasbah: An Agent Marketplace for Buying and Selling Goods. Proc. 1st Int. Conf. on the Practical Application of Intelligent Agents and Multi-Agent Technology, London, UK (1996)
6. Faratin, P., Sierra, C., Jennings, N. R.: Using Similarity Criteria to Make Negotiation Trade-offs. Proc. 4th Int. Conf. on Multi-Agent Systems, Boston, USA (2000) 119-126
7. Faratin, P., Sierra, C., Jennings, N. R.: Negotiation Decision Functions for autonomous agents. Int. J. of Robotics and Autonomous Systems, Vol. 24, Issue 3-4. (1998) 159-182
8. Oliver, J.,: A Machine Learning Approach to Automated Negotiation and Prospects for Electronic Commerce. Journal of Management Information Systems, Winter 1996/1997
9. Oprea, M.,: An Adaptive Negotiation Model for Agent-Based Electronic Commerce. Studies in Informatics and Control, Vol. 11, No. 3 (2002)
10. Barbuceanu, M., Lo, W.: A Multi-Attribute Utility Theoretic Negotiation Architecture for Electronic Commerce. Proc. 4th Int. Conf. on Autonomous Agents, Barcelona, Catalonia, Spain (2000)
11. Keeney, R. L., Raiffa, H.: Decisions with Multiple Objectives. Cambridge University Press (1993)
12. Raiffa, H.: The Art and Science of Negotiation. Harvard University Press (1982)
13. Soo, V., Hung, C.: On-Line Incremental Learning in Bilateral Multi-Issue Negotiation. Proc. 1st Int. Joint Conf. on Autonomous Agents and Multi-Agent Systems, Bologna, Italy (2002)
14. Smith, M.: Neural Networks for Statistical Modeling. International Thomson Computer Press (1996)

Local Nonnegative Matrix Factorization for Mining Typical User Session Profile[*]

Jixiang Jiang[1], Baowen Xu[1,2**], Jianjiang Lu[1,2,3], and Hongji Yang[4]

[1] Department of Computer Science and Engineering, Southeast University,
Nanjing, 210096, China
[2] Jiangsu Institute of Software Quality, Nanjing, 210096, China
[3] PLA University of Science and Technology, Nanjing 210007, China
[4] School of Computing, De Montfort University, Leicester, LE1 9BH, England

Abstract. Understanding the evolving user session profile is key to maintaining service performance levels. Clustering techniques have been used to automatically discover typical user profiles from Web access logs. But it is a challenging problem that many clustering algorithms yield poor results because the session vectors are usually high dimensional and sparse. Although standard non-negative matrix factorization (SNMF) can be used in reducing the dimensionality of the session-URL matrix, the clustering results is not precise, because the basis vectors SNMF gets are not orthogonal and usually redundancy. In this paper, we apply local nonnegative matrix factorization (LNMF), which get basis vectors as orthogonal as possible, to reduce the dimensionality of the session-URL matrix. The experiment results show that LNMF performs better than SNMF for mining typical user session profile.

1 Introduction

Many web servers keep a access log of their users. Analysis of these logs can provide information on how to restructure a Web site for better performance[1]. Recently, new techniques[2] have been proposed to automatically discover "typical user session profiles", which are temporally compact sequences of Web accesses users often visit.

In the context of discovering Web user profiles based on clustering, a vector space model is used to represent the user sessions by assigning each vector attribute to a given URL on the Web site. However, in the case of Web sessions, the user sessions form extremely high dimensional and sparse data matrices. The key problem lies in the fact that many clustering algorithms yield poor results because of the high dimensionality[3]. To solve this problem, one method is applying standard non-negative matrix factorization (SNMF) method, often called NMF[5], to reduce the dimensionality of the session-URL matrix as presented in [4]

---

[*] This work was supported in part by the NSFC (60373066, 60303024), National Grand Fundamental Research 973 Program of China (2002CB312000), National Research Foundation for the Doctoral Program of Higher Education of China.]

** Corresponding author: Baowen Xu, Department of Computer Science and Engineering, Southeast University, Nanjing, 210096, China. Email: bwxu@seu.edu.cn

N. Koch, P. Fraternali, and M. Wirsing (Eds.): ICWE 2004, LNCS 3140, pp. 558–562, 2004.

Though the approach in[4] is effective, there are still some problems remained, among which a major one is that the SNMF do not require the base vectors be orthogonal. This may cause information redundancy and weaken the precision of results. In this paper, we apply local nonnegative matrix factorization (LNMF)[6], which get basis vectors as orthogonal as possible, to reduce the dimension of the session-URL matrix. Also, we propose a metric to measure the clustering results. The experimental results show that the LNMF performs better than SNMF in mining typical user session profiles.

2   Mining Typical User Session Profiles

Now, we describe all the steps of mining typical user session profiles: first cluster the URL-session vectors. Then measure the clustering results and find the best one. Third summarize typical user session profile from the best clustering result.

2.1   Clustering the URL-Session Vectors

First, like the steps in [4], we can get user sessions from server access logs, and form a URL-session matrix. Here, a user session is defined as accesses from the same IP address, such that the duration of elapsed time between two consecutive accesses in the session is within a prespecified threshold. Each URL in the site is assigned a unique number $i \in \{1,2,...,m\}$, where m is the total number of valid URLs. Thus, the jth user session is encoded as a m dimensional vector $x_j=(x_{1j}, x_{2j}..., x_{mj})^T$, where $x_{ij}=1$ if i^{th} URL is accessed during the jth session, otherwise $x_{ij}=0$. All the n user session vectors form a non-negative session-URL matrix $X = (x_{ij})_{m \times n}$.

Second, we apply LNMF to reduce the dimensionality of the session-URL matrix $X = (x_{ij})_{m \times n}$. LNMF finds non-negative matrices $U=(u_{ij})_{m \times r}$ and $V = (v_{ij})_{r \times n}$ such that $X \approx UV$. Each column in X is called primary vector, and its corresponding column in V is called projecting vector.

Third, we use the spherical k-means algorithm[4] to cluster the vectors in V. There are four steps: i) normalize all vectors v_j to a unit vector which is still denoted as v_j. ii) apply spherical k-means algorithm to cluster these vectors into k partitions $\{\pi_j\}_{j=1}^k$, where each $\pi_j (1 \le j \le k)$ denotes a cluster. iii) count the number of vectors each cluster $\pi_j (1 \le j \le k)$ contains, and discard the clusters whose number of vectors are less than q. Then we get the clustering result $\{\pi_j\}_{j=1}^{\tilde{k}}$, where $\tilde{k}(\tilde{k} \le k)$ denotes the number of left clusters. vi) repeat ii) and iii) several times, and select the best clustering result according to their relative distance, which is defined in session 2.2

2.2   Measuring the Clustering Results

Here we present a metric to measure the "compactness" and "distinctness" of the clusters. It is the ratio of the "average intercluster distance" to the "average intracluster distance". The formal definition of these concepts are given below:

Definition 1. Suppose the primary vector of the ith and j^{th} sessions are x_i and x_j respectively, then the distance between the two sessions are defined as:

$$S(i,j)=1-\frac{x_i^T x_j}{\|x_i\|\cdot\|x_j\|} \tag{1}$$

Definition 2. Given a clustering result $P=\{\pi_j\}_{j=1}^{\tilde{k}}$, its intracluster pair set $D_1(P)$ and its intercluster pair set $D_2(P)$ are defined as:

$$D_1(P)=\{(i_1,i_2)\,|\,v_{i_1},v_{i_2}\in\pi_n,i_1<i_2,n=1..\tilde{k}\} \tag{2}$$

$$D_2(P)=\{(i_1,i_2)\,|\,v_{i_1}\in\pi_n,v_{i_2}\in\pi_m,i_1<i_2,n,m=1..\tilde{k},n\neq m\} \tag{3}$$

Suppose i and j ($i<j$) are two session numbers. "$(i,j)\in D_1$" means the ith and the jth session are in the same cluster. "$(i,j)\in D_2$" means they are in different clusters.

Definition 3. Given a clustering result $P=\{\pi_j\}_{j=1}^{\tilde{k}}$, let $D_1(P)$ and $D_2(P)$ denote its intracluster pair set and intercluster pair set respectively, and n_1, n_2 denotes the number of pairs in $D_1(P)$ and $D_2(P)$, then the average intracluster distance $L_1(P)$ and the average intercluster distance $L_2(P)$ are defined as follows, where $S(i_1,i_2)$ denote the distance between the ith and j^{th} session:

$$L_1(P)=\frac{\sum\limits_{(i_1,i_2)\in D_1(P)} S(i_1,i_2)}{n_1} \tag{4}$$

$$L_2(P)=\frac{\sum\limits_{(i_1,i_2)\in D_2(P)} S(i_1,i_2)}{n_2} \tag{5}$$

Definition 4. The metric relative distance $RD(P)$ is as follows:

$$RD(P)=L_1(P)/L_2(P) \tag{6}$$

Clusters in a clustering results with low relative distance are tight, compact and well-separated from others, and can be seen better than the ones with high relative distance.

2.3 Summarizing Typical User Session Profile

Suppose we got the best clustering result, which contain k clusters $\{\pi_j\}_{j=1}^{k}$, here we present a method to summarize typical user session profile from each cluster.

Let $\pi_i=\{v_1^i,v_2^i,\cdots,v_l^i\}$, be the ith cluster, where $v_j^i=(v_{1j}^i,v_{2j}^i,...,v_{rj}^i)^T$, whose corresponding primary vector is $x_j^i=(x_{1j}^i,x_{2j}^i,...,x_{mj}^i)^T$. We use the primary vectors to construct a m dimensional vector $P_i=(P_{1i},P_{2i},...,P_{mi})^T$ as follows:

$$P_i = \frac{1}{l}\sum_{j=1}^{l} \frac{x_j^i}{\|x_j^i\|} \qquad (7)$$

Generally the components of P_i represent the probability of access of each URL during the profile, where P_{ki} measure the significance of the kth URL to the profile.

Table 1. Clustering results(SNMF)   **Table 2.** Clustering results(SNMF)

r	10	20	30	40	50
n	17	18	14	13	11
RD	0.483	0.394	0.289	0.381	0.277
r	60	70	80	90	100
n	12	10	9	9	9
RD	0.297	0.292	0.238	0.193	0.247
r	110	120	130	140	150
n	11	7	10	5	10
RD	0.135	0.109	0.107	0.149	0.127

r	10	20	30	40	50
n	20	17	15	11	11
RD	0.500	0.393	0.170	0.124	0.095
r	60	70	80	90	100
n	9	6	8	8	6
RD	0.066	0.046	0.062	0.073	0.047
r	110	120	130	140	150
n	7	7	9	8	8
RD	0.046	0.049	0.057	0.065	0.055

Table 3. Typical User Session Profile

1	0.686-/music/machines/Analogue-Heaven 0.686-/machines/Analogue-Heaven 0.026-/music/machines/Analogue-Heaven/email.html
2	0.964-/music/machines/Analogue-Heaven
3	0.670-/music/machines 0.670-/machines 0.049-/music/machines/guide 0.019-/machines/manufacturers 0.018-/music/machines/manufacturers/Moog/Modular
4	0.964-/music/machines
5	0.643-/machines/categories/midi-cv-sync/midi 0.288-/music/machines/categories/midi-cv-sync/midi/midi-history 0.232-/music/machines/categories/midi-cv-sync/midi/midi-specs 0.192-/music/machines/categories/midi-cv-sync/midi
6	0.964- /music/machines 0.901-/music/machines/samples.html 0.067-/music/machines/manufacturers/ARP/Odyssey/samples 0.026-/music/machines/manufacturers/Roland/SH-synths/samples 0.025-/music/machines/manufacturers/Roland/JX/samples 0.025-/music/machines/manufacturers/Roland/TR-606/samples 0.025-/music/machines/links
7	0.688-/machines 0.688-/music/machines 0.025-/music/machines/samples.html 0.021-/music/machines/features

3   Experimental Results

In our experiments, we use the log data during a period of 1/1/98 to 6/1/98 downloaded from http://www.cs.washington.edu/research/adaptive. First, we set the maximum elapse time of a session to 45 minutes and totally get 449 valid URLs and 7577 sessions from the logs, for these URLs and sessions, we get the session-URL matrix X. Then we apply the SNMF and LNMF respectively to reduce the high dimension of the session-URL matrix X. Third, for each projecting matrix V, we set $k=400$ and $q=100$ and get the all clustering results, listed in table 1 and 2. At last we compare these clustering results, and mine typical user session profiles from the best one, which are listed in table 3.

Table 1 and Table 2 show the cluster numbers n and the relative distance RD of the clustering results based on SNMF and LNMF with different projecting vector dimension r. From the tables, we can see that value of n fluctuate wildly in table 1, while in table 2 numbers is more stable. Also the relative distance is much smaller in table 2 than in table 1, this means that the clustering results in table 2 is more precise. The reason of the difference may be that the SNMF makes the basis matrix U generated more randomly and cause information redundancy. So that the clustering results based on SNMF fluctuate wildly and have less precision. While the LNMF adds more additional constrains on the basis vectors and solves these problems. From this, we get the conclusion that the cluster method based on LNMF is more suitable in mining typical session profile.

4   Conclusions

In this paper, LNMF is proposed instead of SNMF in the field of mining typical user session profiles. The experimental results show that the method based on LNMF performs better than the method based on SNMF. In the future we will take more consideration into the impact of other constraints in this field.

References

1. Cooley, R., Mobasher, B., Srivastava, J.: Web mining: Information and Pattern discovery on the World Wide Web. Proceeding. of International Conference on Tools with Artificial Intelligence, Newport beach, USA (1997) 558-567
2. Nasraoui, O., Frigui, H., Krishnapuram, R.: Extracting Web User Profiles Using Relational Competitive Fuzzy Clustering. Internatiol Journal on Artifical Intelligence Tools, 9(4) (2000) 509-526
3. Hanm, J., Kamber., M.: Data Mining: Concepts and Techniques. Morgan Kaufmann Publishers (2000)
4. Lu, J.J., Xu, B.W., Yang, H.J.: Matrix dimensionality reduction for mining Web access logs. Proceeding of IEEE/WIC International Conference on Web Intelligence, Halifax, CA (2003) 405-408
5. Lee, D.D., Seung, H.S.: Learning the parts of objects by non-negative matrix factorization. Nature 401 (1999) 788-791
6. Li, S.Z., Hou, X.W., Zhang, H.J.: Learning spatially localized parts-based representation. Proceeding of the CVPR'01 Conference, Hawaii, USA (2001) 207-212

An Architecture for Personalized Systems Based on Web Mining Agents

María N. Moreno*, Francisco J. García, and M. José Polo

Dept. Informática y Automática. University of Salamanca. Salamanca. Spain
mmg@usal.es*

Abstract. The development of the present web systems is becoming a complex activity due to the need to integrate the last technologies in order to make more efficient and competitive applications. Endowing systems with personalized recommendation procedures contributes to achieve these objectives. In this paper, a web mining method for personalization is proposed. It uses the information already available from other users to discover patterns that are used later for making recommendations. The work deals with the problem of introducing new information items and new users who do not have a profile. We propose an architectural design of intelligent data mining agents for the system implementation.

1 Introduction

The task of finding products or services for Internet users is becoming more tedious every time. The numerous web sites existing nowadays make available more information than a user can manage. On the other hand, the quick growth of the electronic business activities has contributed to increase the market competition. A way for improving the competitiveness of traditional trade companies is to take advantage of business intelligence strategies supported by techniques like data mining. In the e-commerce environment these procedures can also be applied but they have been extended to deal with problems of the web systems. Personalized recommender systems provide users with intelligent mechanisms to search products to purchase. This is a way to avoid the problem of *information overload* due to the great quantity of information accessible through the Web [1].

The quality of the recommendations for the users has an important effect on the clients' retention. Users refuse poor recommender systems which can cause two types of error: *false negatives*, which are products that are not recommended, though the customer would like them, and *false positives*, which are products that are recommended, though the customer does not like them [2]. The most serious errors are false positives, because these errors will cause negative reactions in the customers and thus they won't probably visit the site again. The use of procedures to find customers characteristics that increase the probability of buying recommended products can help to avoid these problems. Data mining techniques and intelligent agents play an important role in the development of efficient personalized recommender systems. In this work, we present a recommendation methodology based on web mining that uses diverse information as user's attributes, rating and

N. Koch, P. Fraternali, and M. Wirsing (Eds.): ICWE 2004, LNCS 3140, pp. 563–567, 2004.
© Springer-Verlag Berlin Heidelberg 2004

usage data. The core of the methodology is an algorithm that generates and refines association rules used for making personalized recommendations. Our proposal should provide recommender systems with more relevant patterns that minimize the recommendation errors. The architecture suggested for these systems is constituted by intelligent agents; one of them is in charge of doing data mining tasks.

2 Related Work

The two main recommendation methods are: collaborative filtering and a content-based approach [4]. The first technique is one of the most successful methods and it was based initially on nearest neighbor algorithms. These algorithms predict product preferences for a user, based on the opinions of other users. The opinions can be obtained explicitly from the users as a rating score or by using some implicit measures from purchase records as timing logs [12]. In the content based approach text documents are recommended by comparing between their contents and user profiles. The main shortcoming of this approach in the e-commerce application domain, is the lack of mechanisms to manage web objects such as motion pictures, images, music, etc. Collaborative filtering also has limitations in the e-commerce environment. Rating schemes can only be applied to homogeneous domain information. Besides, sparsity and scalability are serious weaknesses which would lead to poor recommendations [2]. Sparsity is caused by the fact that the number of ratings needed for prediction is greater than the number of the ratings obtained. The reason for this is that collaborative filtering usually requires user explicit expression of personal preferences for products. Performance problems in searching for neighbors is also a limitation. The computation time grows linearly with both the number of customers and the number of products in the site. Another obstacle is the first-rater problem that takes place when new products are introduced [3].

There are two approaches for collaborative filtering, *memory-based* (*user-based*) and *model-based* (*item-based*) algorithms. **Memory-based** algorithms, also known as *nearest-neighbor* methods, were the earliest used [11]. They treat all user items by means of statistical techniques in order to find users with similar preferences (*neighbors*). The advantage of these algorithms is the quick incorporation of the most recent information, although the search for neighbors in large databases is slow [13].

Data mining technologies have also been applied to recommender systems. **Model-based** collaborative filtering algorithms use these methods in the development of a model of user ratings. This approach was introduced to reduce the sparsity problem and to get better recommender systems. Some examples of these methods are the Bayesian network analysis [13], the latent class model [1], rule-based approaches [4], decision tree induction combined with association rules [2], horting [14]. Web mining methods build models based mainly on users' behaviour more than in subjective valuations (ratings). This is the main advantage of this approach that allows avoiding the problems associated with traditional collaborative filtering techniques [6].

3 Recommendation Methodology

In this section, a methodology for personalized recommendations is presented. It uses information about consumer preferences and user attributes.

The first step of the methodology is the selection of the best rated products. A list of products ordered from most to less popular is generated. The aim of this step is to reduce the number of association rules generated and to obtain rules applicable to a wide range of customers. The selected records are the inputs for the second step in which the association rules are generated. The rules relate product attributes with user attributes and preferences, in this way it is possible to identify products that will be of interest to a given customer with a specific profile. The initial rules are refined in order to obtain strong patterns that avoid the false positive recommendations. The association rules are also a solution to the problem of the introduction of new users. When a new customer uses the system his profile is obtained and recommendations for him are generated according his profile. In the third step, the recommendations are made. The recommendations are based on the patterns obtained, which relate user attributes with product attributes. For new and old users the system recommends products with characteristics adapted to their profile. The rules enable to recommend new products whose characteristics agree with the preferences of the users. New products with new characteristics are always recommended. This is the way to deal with the first-rater problem. The process is iterative and uses the new information about products and users to feedback the system. New association models are built when the system has a significant quantity of new information. The architectural design of the system is shown in figure 1. It contains three main agents:

- Data mining agent builds the recommendation models. It is in charge of generating and refining association rules. It uses the information provided by the data management agent periodically.
- Recommendation agent receives the requests from the users, takes their preference profile and uses the data mining models to make personalized recommendations.
- Data management agent collects and manages the storage of the information about new user preferences and new products. It is connected with the

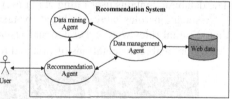

Fig. 1. Simplified architecture of the recommender system

data mining agent to provide the data that are used periodically in the generation of new models.

4 Association Analysis

Methods for rule discovery are widely used in many domains. They have been adopted to target marketing or personalized e-commerce recommendation service.

We use the concept of unexpectedness [9] for refining association rules. The refinement of association rules provides recommender systems with more confident rules and serves to solve conflicts between rules. In an earlier work [7] we have used several visualization techniques and data mining methods to build and validate models for software size prediction. We found that the best attributes for classification give good results in the refinement of associations rules in the area of projects management. The presented recommender procedure follows the approach of using these attributes in a rules' refinement algorithm wich works with web usage data. In classification problems, the *label* attribute is the target of the prediction process. The attributes used are the best in discriminating the different values of the label attribute. They are obtained by computing the entropy of the attribute [8].

The refinement procedure starts with a set of rules which relate items. Then we search for unexpected patterns that could help us to increase the confidence or to solve ambiguities or inconsistencies between these rules. The refinement process fits into a generic iterative strategy [10]. Each iteration consists of three steps: 1) generation of unexpected patterns for a belief, 2) selection of a subset of unexpected patterns that will be used to refine the belief, and 3) refining the belief using selected patterns and the best attributes for classification. The process ends when no more unexpected patterns can be generated. We have instantiated this generic strategy and created a specific refinement process [8]. The principal feature of our approach is the gradual generation of the unexpected patterns. We take advantage of knowledge of good attributes for classification and use them progressively, beginning with the best. This simplifies the selection of patterns and the refinement process.

5 Experimental Data Treatment

The experimental study was carried out using data from MovieLens recommender system developed by. the GroupLens Research Project at the University of Minnesota The database contains user rating about movies that belong to 18 different genres.

Association rules were produced by taking the records with a rate value greater than 2.Initial rules were generated and visualized by using *Mineset* [5]. Figures 2 and 3 are graphical representations of first and refined rules respectively (LHS → RHS).

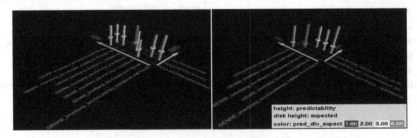

Fig. 2. Initial rules   **Fig. 3.** Refined rules

Initial rules represented in the figure 2 are rules that relate "Genre-Time Stamp" with the user's occupation. Time stamp is the time that the user spent in a product. Refined rules (figure 3) use the attribute "age" combined with "occupation" RHS. Good rules are those with high values of pred_div_expect (predictability/expected predictability). The graphs show that these values increase in the refined rules.

6 Conclusions

The personalized recommendation engines contribute to improve the service to the clients and the competitiveness. In this paper, a methodology for recommendation based on an algorithm for refining association rules proposed. The methodology deals with the case of making recommendations for new users. It provides systems with more relevant patterns, which lead to more effective recommendations. Rules obtained from the refinement procedure have higher values of confidence. This means that the recommendations are more accurate and the number of false positive recommendations is reduced.

References

1. Cheung, K.W., Kwok, J.T., Law, M.H. and Tsui, K.C.: Mining customer product ratings for personalized marketing. Decision Support Systems, 35 (2003) 231-243.
2. Cho, H.C., Kim, J.K., Kim, S.H.: A personalized recommender system based on web usage mining and decision tree induction. Expert Systems with App. 23 (2002), 329-342.
3. Konstant, J. Miller, B., Maltz, D., Herlocker, J. Gordon, L. and Riedl, J.: GroupLens: Applying collaborative filtering to usenet news. Comm. of the ACM, 40 (1997), 77-87,.
4. Lee, CH., Kim, Y.H., Rhee, P.K.: Web personalization expert with combining collaborative filtering and association rule mining technique. Expert Systems with Applications 21 (2001), 131-137.
5. Mineset user's guide, v. 007-3214-004, 5/98. Silicon Graphics (1998).
6. Mobasher, B., Cooley, R. and Srivastava, J.: Automatic personalization based on web usage mining, Communications of the ACM, 43 (8) (2000), 142-151.
7. Moreno, M.N., Miguel, L.A., García, F.J., Polo, M.J.: Data mining approaches for early software size estimation. Proc. 3rd ACIS International Conference On Software Engineering, Artificial Intelligence, Networking and Parallel/Distributed Computing (SNPD'02), 361-368, Madrid, Spain (2002).
8. Moreno, M.N., Miguel, L.A., García, F.J., Polo, M.J.: Building knowledge discovery-driven models for decision support in project management. Dec.Support Syst. (in press).
9. Padmanabhan, B., Tuzhilin, A.: Knowledge refinement based on the discovery of unexpected patterns in data mining. Decision Support Systems 27 (1999) 303– 318.
10. Padmanabhan, B., Tuzhilin, A.: Unexpectedness as a measure of interestingness in knowledge discovery. Decision Support Systems 33 (2002) 309– 321.
11. Resnick, P., Iacovou, N., Suchack, M., Bergstrom, P. and Riedl, J.: Grouplens: An open architecture for collaborative filtering of netnews. Proc. of ACM CSW'94 Conference on Computer.Supported Cooperative Work, 175-186, (1994).
12. Sarwar, B., Karypis, G., Konstan, J., Riedl, J.: Item-based collaborative filtering recommendation algorithm. Proc. of the tenth Int. WWW Conference (2001), 285-295.
13. Schafer, J.B., Konstant, J.A. and Riedl, J.: E-commerce recommendation applications. Data Mining and Knowledge Discovery, 5 (2001), 115-153.
14. Wolf, J., Aggarwal, C. Wu, K.L. and Yu, P.: Horting hatches an egg. A new graph-theoretic approach to collaborative filtering. Proc. of ACM SIGKDD International Conference on Knowledge Discovery and Data Mining, San Diego, C.A., (1999).

WISE: A Web-Based Intelligent Sensor Explorer Framework for Publishing, Browsing, and Analyzing Sensor Data over the Internet

Kien A. Hua, Rui Peng, and Georgiana L. Hamza-Lup

School of Computer Science, University of Central Florida
Orlando, FL 32816, U.S.A
{kienhua, rpeng, ghamza}@cs.ucf.edu

Abstract. In this paper, we present WISE, an Internet-scale framework for publishing, browsing, and analyzing real-time sensor data. This environment enables providers to advertise their sensors on the Internet, and unsolicited users to locate desired sensors through a scalable peer-to-peer search facility. A specialized browser allows a user to remotely control the incoming data streams which activate corresponding plug-ins, such as a visualization module, to present the data in an intelligible way. Therefore, WISE also facilitates sharing of sensor data analysis tools in the form of software plug-ins.

1 Introduction

Nowadays pervasive sensing systems ranging from short-range wireless ad hoc sensor networks to more powerful capture devices are becoming a reality. As more and more sensor-based services become part of our daily life, they call for new technologies that enable publishing, searching, and browsing sensor data on the Internet. Consider the following scenario. A stream monitoring sensor network is deployed in a brook by a group of geographers. The sensors measure water temperatures, turbidity and precipitation, and periodically send back the data to an Internet-connected computer. These data arrive as a stream and are published on the Internet by the geographers. Independently, a biologist, studying the life zone in the same brook, searches for the information on the Internet. Within a few seconds, she learns about the data published by the geographers, and starts to browse and analyze the data stream on her own computer. As another example, a government might want to stimulate economy by publishing real-time traffic data, collected through sensing devices along expressways. Availability of such information would encourage development of many new commercial products such as a more intelligent GPS system that can reroute a trip when recognizing slow traffic ahead. In order to enable such kind of services on sensor data, we propose in this paper a new framework, called WISE (*Web-based Intelligent Sensor Explorer*), for sensor information sharing over the Internet. We envision an all-new Internet where innumerable sensing systems, deployed by numerous publishers, exposing different data which can be shared freely

N. Koch, P. Fraternali, and M. Wirsing (Eds.): ICWE 2004, LNCS 3140, pp. 568–572, 2004.

with a wide variety of unsolicited users, much like the way web pages are publicly shared today.

Recently there has been a growing interest on sensor data management with research activities focusing mainly on either: (1) dealing with packet routing and power conservation issues in sensor networks [3], or (2) managing the sensor networks at the application layer as a distributed database [2, 5, 7]. These techniques view the entire sensor network logically as a distributed database sharing the same schema. These schemes, though effective in their defined problem scales (i.e., tailored to supporting a given data provider to serve a predefined group of users), will not work well in the new sensor data sharing environment that we envision in this paper. The proposed WISE framework is NOT a sensor database management system. We summarize some of the differences between the current state-of-the-art and the proposed environment in Table 1.

Table 1. Differences between Sensor Database Management Systems and WISE

	Sensor Database Management Systems	Proposed WISE
Number of Data Providers	One	Numerous
Data Users	Targeted users	Unsolicited users
Schema Design	Homogeneous	Heterogeneous
Data Usage	to support specific applications	Ad hoc browsing of data sources through a browser

2 WISE Framework

We revisit the scenario of the geographers to illustrate how this framework facilitates this application. To publish the data, a *Sensor Data Description Advertisement* (**SDDA**) is created on a *Sensor Data Server* (**SDS**) to hold the meta-data, and publish them into the Internet. At the same time, the sensor proxy [4] collects intermittent data from sensors in the brook, packages incoming sensor data into tuples and forwards them to the SDS. When a biologist looking for related sensors enters search criteria into a local *Sensor Data Browser* (**SDB**), this software uses a distributed search facility to look for relevant SDDAs. As the browser displays a list of relevant SDDAs on the screen, the biologist identifies the desired sensor and clicks on it. In response, the browser establishes a session with the SDS using a *Sensor Stream Control Protocol* (**SSCP**), gets the real-time stream using a *Sensor Stream Transport Protocol* (**SSTP**), and directs the data to the Visualizer for display. The various components are described in the following subsections.

2.1 Canonical SDDA Format

Each SDDA is an XML document for advertising a sensor service consisting of a collection of related sensors. A sample SDDA is given in Fig. 1.

```
<?xml version="1.0" encoding="UTF-8" ?>
<!-- edited with XMLSPY v2004 rel. 3 U (http://www.xmlspy.com) by Rui Peng (University of Central Florida)
<SDDA xmlns:xsi="http://www.w3.org/2001/XMLSchema-instance" xsi:noNamespaceSchemaLocation="C:\Rui\www2004
    \figures\SDDA.xsd">
    <ServiceName>Great Book Monitoring</ServiceName>
    <ServiceDescription>Monitors the water temperature, turbidity and precipitation in the Great Brook</ServiceDescription>
  - <Sensor>
      <SensorName>Great Brook</SensorName>
      <SensorDescription>Monitors the water temperature, turbidity and precipitation in the Great Brook</SensorDescription>
      <ServerIP>132.170.1.40</ServerIP>
      <ServerPort>3721</ServerPort>
      <SensorID>gbrook</SensorID>
      <Protocol>SSCP</Protocol>
    - <StreamFormat>
      - <DataField>
          <FieldName>Temperature</FieldName>
          <FieldType>byte</FieldType>
          <FieldLength>1</FieldLength>
          <Unit>Fahrenheit</Unit>
          <FieldDescription>Water temperature</FieldDescription>
        </DataField>
      - <DataField>
          <FieldName>Turbidity</FieldName>
          <FieldType>decimal</FieldType>
          <FieldLength>4</FieldLength>
          <Unit>NTU</Unit>
          <FieldDescription>Water turbidity</FieldDescription>
        </DataField>
      - <DataField>
          <FieldName>Precipitation</FieldName>
          <FieldType>decimal</FieldType>
          <FieldLength>4</FieldLength>
          <Unit>Inch</Unit>
          <FieldDescription>Precipitation depth</FieldDescription>
        </DataField>
      - <DataField>
          <FieldName>Time</FieldName>
          <FieldType>time</FieldType>
          <FieldLength>4</FieldLength>
          <Unit>ms</Unit>
          <FieldDescription>Time when the data is sampled at the sensor</FieldDescription>
        </DataField>
      </StreamFormat>
    </Sensor>
</SDDA>
```

Fig. 1. A sample SDDA

2.2 Sensor Data Server (SDS) and Sensor Data Browser (SDB)

The SDS is responsible for managing incoming data from sensor proxies and delivering the data to SDBs. It has three major components, namely the *Publish Manager,* the *Stream Manager,* and the *Session Manager.* The *Publish Manager* accepts registrations from sensor proxies and publishes the corresponding SDDAs into the Internet. The *Stream Manager* manages buffers for incoming data, and directs them to either local applications, or remote SDBs, or both. The *Server Session Manager* accepts client requests and control messages using SSCP and delivers the stream to clients using SSTP. A client uses two separate channels to interact with the server, one for control messages, and one for data. The control channel is bi-directional, but the data channel only goes in one direction.

The SDB consists of two components, the *Client Session Manager* and a simple *Visualizer* module. The *Client Session Manager* has three major functionalities. First, it is responsible for accepting user search criteria and discovering SDDAs on the Internet. Second, it connects to SDS's and establishes a client session for each incoming stream. A client session also has two channels, control channel and data channel. Third, it directs data to the *Visualizer* module for presentation to the user. The *Visualizer* is responsible for displaying the incoming data stream on the screen.

2.3 Communication Protocols

Two application-layer communication protocols are used in WISE framework, namely SSCP and SSTP. The SSCP is used for control message exchange on the control channel between an SDS and an SDB. As an analogy, the SSCP acts as a network remote control providing a set of useful methods for a client to control the "playback" of the sensor stream. SSCP does not deliver the stream itself, but rather uses SSTP for real-time data transmission. The control methods are as follows.

- **PREPARE.** Request the SDS to allocate resources for a sensor stream and prepare for the data delivery.
- **START.** Request the SDS to start the data transmission through the data channel. This operation can also be used to resume data transmission after a pause operation.
- **PAUSE.** Temporarily stop the stream transmission without releasing server resources. Any data transmitted during the pause period are lost.
- **STOP.** Notify the SDS to stop the data transmission and free server resources.

Before sending a data frame, the SDS wraps it with an SSTP header. The *sequence number* in the header increments by one for each SSTP packet and is used by the SDB to detect packet loss and ensure in-order delivery.

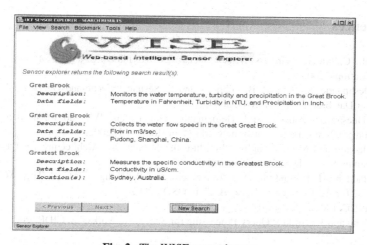

Fig. 2. The WISE sensor browser

2.4 Search Mechanism

Although WISE can be configured to work with any search engine as long as it recognizes the sensor metadata, we opt for a peer-to-peer search mechanism to avoid bottleneck and achieve better scalability. Peers in WISE use a *distributed hash table*

(**DHT**) function to facilitate index storage and access. When an SDS publishes an SDDA, it is cached by a nearby service peer, and its index is pushed to the network according to the hash function. When an SDB searches for an SDDA, the SDB issues a query to a nearby service peer, which calculates the DHT function and finds the peer that contains the index for the SDDA. The SDB then gets the index from that peer and finds the target SDDA. Interested readers are referred to [6] for a detailed discussion of this search technique.

3 Prototype

We have developed a WISE prototype using the design and techniques presented in the last section. The current version has a simple user interface with a basic set of functionalities. A screen shot of the SDB is shown in Fig. 2. The user can enter a set of keywords as the search criteria. After the results are brought up by the browser, the user can select a service by clicking on its name. This will activate the Visualizer which allows the user to choose from a number of different visualization methods.

The current prototype is intended as a proof of concept. Future research will provide a more complete browser with functionalities such as the plug-in capability. We also need to do a more in-depth evaluation of the effectiveness and scalability of the search mechanism.

References

1. E. H. Callaway, Wireless Sensor Networks: Architecture and Protocols, Auerbach Publications, 2003.
2. A. Deshpande, S. Nath, P. B. Gibbons and S. Seshan, "Cache-and-Query for Wide Area Sensor Databases," in SIGMOD, 2003.
3. D. Ganesan, D. Estrin, and J. Heidemann, "Dimensions: Why do we need a new data handling architecture for sensor networks?" in HotNets-1, 2002.
4. S. Madden and M. J. Franklin, "Fjording the Stream: An Architecture for Queries over Streaming Sensor Data," in ICDE, 2002.
5. S. Madden, M. J. Franklin, J. M. Hellerstein, and W. Hong, "TAG: A Tiny AGgregation Service for Ad-Hoc Sensor Networks," in OSDI, 2002.
6. Project JXTA, http://www.jxta.org.
7. Y. Yang and J. Gehrke, "Query Processing for Sensor Networks," in CIDR, 2003.

Semantic Information Generation from Classification and Information Extraction

Tércio de Morais Sampaio Silva[1], Frederico Luiz Gonçalves de Freitas[2],
Rafael Cobra Teske[1], and Guilherme Bittencourt[1]

[1] Universidade Federal de Santa Catarina - Florianópolis - SC - Brasil
{tercio|cobra|gb}@das.ufsc.br
[2] Universidade Federal de Alagoas - Maceió - AL - Brasil
fred.freitas@mail.tci.ufal.br

1 Introduction

This paper presents MASTERWeb, a multi-agent system for classification and information extraction from Web pages. The multi-agent approach allows that agents, specialized in the different page classes of a cluster, share common information through a cooperation process. The goal of the system is to provide the user with information that is less noisy and more focused in his interests. To represent the domain knowledge, the system uses ontologies and frames [4]. The extraction module explores implicit structures of the page class to extract the information efficiently. It consists of an expert system in which the knowledge is stored using ontologies. MASTERWeb is a cognitive multi-agent system for integrated manipulation of information where each agent has the responsibility for the classification of the page contents inside a knowledge domain [2]. The MASTERWeb system is based on the principle that some page classes may be interrelated, for instance, instances of the page class "scientific events" may contain information or links to "researchers" page class through the attribute "chairman of the event".

The web pages are treated according to two views: content view and functional view. The content view allows to discriminate page classes through particular characteristics, such as keywords and structural similarity. Moreover, the content view allows to collect all pages that potentially belong to the processed class, guaranteeing the covering of the domain. These pages are collected through search engines such as Google, Yahoo and Altavista, using predefined keywords. The functional view allows to discriminate web pages according to their role in the linking between pages and in the presentation and storage of relevant data. The possible roles for a page class are: (i) content-pages; (ii) auxiliary-pages; (iii) content-page lists; (iv) Recommendations (content-pages that belong to another class and may be used in the cooperation process among the agents); and (v) garbage-pages.

There are two kinds of knowledge in the MASTERWeb system: operational knowledge and declarative knowledge. The operational knowledge is represented by production rules that determine how each agent should behave inside the multi-agent society and during the page treatment. On the other hand, ontologies are used to represent the declarative knowledge about the syntactic and semantic structure of the information.

N. Koch, P. Fraternali, and M. Wirsing (Eds.): ICWE 2004, LNCS 3140, pp. 573–574, 2004.
© Springer-Verlag Berlin Heidelberg 2004

2   Case Study and Results

The proposed multi-agent architecture was used to extract information from pages in the domain of scientific events. The knowledge about the information to be extracted was included as instances of the adequate classes of the science ontology. In the development of ontologies, the Protégé-2000 [5] tool was employed. The inference engine used in the system is Jess (Java Expert System Shell) [3]. The use of the JessTab plug-in [1] allowed the manipulation of the ontologies developed in the Protégé-2000 system by the Jess rules.

The system performance was evaluated by experiments. A corpus composed by 148 web pages about scientific events, such as workshops and conferences was used. The system tried to extract information about: event location, deadline, and subject area. Table 1 shows the results. The system effectiveness is computed as percentage of information correctly extracted.

Table 1. Results

Event Place	Deadline	Subject Areas	Total
74.07%	71.43%	61.4%	67,06%

3   Conclusion and Future Work

We presented MASTERWeb, a multiagent system to classify and extract information from Web pages in a specific domain. Presently, we are developing more extraction rules and making more extensive tests with the system, directly using the Web as page source. We are also studying the application of machine learning techniques in order to improve the knowledge acquisition process.

Future work includes application of the system in different domains, such as the traveling and tourism, e-government and e-education. We also intend to apply the system as a support to build a tool able to automatically create Web pages with semantic tags in XML using the simple HTML versions of the pages as input, in the framework of the Semantic Web.

References

1. Henrik Eriksson. Jesstab plugin for protégé. Dept. of Computer and Information Science, Linköping University. http://www.ida.liu.se/ her/JessTab, 2000.
2. Frederico Freitas and G. Bittencourt. An ontology-based architecture for cooperative information agents. In *Proceedings of International Joint Conferences on Artificial Intelligence 2003 – IJICAI'03*, Alacapuco, Mexico, August 2003.
3. Ernest J. Friedman-Hill. *Jess, The Rule Engine for the Java Platform*. Sandia National Laboratories, Livermore, CA, distributed computing systems edition, September 2003.
4. Marvin Minsky. A framework for representing knowledge. In *Psicology of Computer Vision*, pages 211–281. McGraw-Hill, 1975.
5. N. F. Noy, R. Fergerson, and M. Musen. The knowledge model of protege-2000: Combining interoperability and flexibility, 2000.

A Study on the Secure Business Web Service Based on ebXML

Dongil Shin[1], Dongkyoo Shin[1*], Baek-Ho Sung[1], and Jun-Hong Song[2]

[1]Department of Computer Science and Engineering, Sejong University
98, Kunja-Dong, Kwangjin-Ku, Seoul 143-747, Korea
{dshin, shindk, guardia}@gce.sejong.ac.kr
[2]Industrial Bank of Korea (IBK), 50, 2-ga Ulchi-ro, Chung-gu, Seoul, Korea
lovelysong@ibk.co.kr

Abstract. While there is tremendous e-business value in the ebXML (Electronic Business using eXtensible Markup Language), security remains an unsolved problem and one of the largest barriers to adoption. XML Security technologies that have been emerging recently have extensibility and flexibility that is suitable for security implementation such as encryption, digital signature, access control and authentication. In this paper, we propose secure business Web Service models based on ebXML that allow trading partners to securely exchange XML based business transactions by employing XML security technologies.

1 Introduction

XML Security technologies emerging recently have extensibility and flexibility suitable for security implementation such as encryption, digital signature, access control and authentication. They are recommended to be used in ebXML security implementations. XML security technologies such as XML digital signatures [2] and SAML (Security Assertion Markup Language) [4] can be exploited to solve this problem. XML Encryption [1] is also recommended to solve the loss of confidentiality problem. Also, XKMS (XML Key Management Specification) [3] is recommended by the ebXML security team for key management as a substitute for PKI. In this paper, we propose secure business Web Service models based on ebXML that allow trading partners to securely exchange XML based business transactions by employing XML security technologies.

2 Secure Business Web Services Model Based on ebXML

We propose two ebXML business scenarios ensuring the trust relationship within the real trading partners. The first scenario performs a user authentication and updates the CPP in the repository. The procedure for the first scenario is presented in the form of

---

* Correspondence author

N. Koch, P. Fraternali, and M. Wirsing (Eds.): ICWE 2004, LNCS 3140, pp. 575–576, 2004.
© Springer-Verlag Berlin Heidelberg 2004

a sequence diagram in Figure 1, where each box in the diagram denotes a Web Service or an application program. The second scenario performs business transactions within the trading partners, where security requirements are satisfied by applying security modules to implement business processes, as shown in Figure 2. In these scenarios, each XML security is constructed as a Web Service, which follows the Web Services standards proposed by the W3C and OASIS [1,2,3,4].

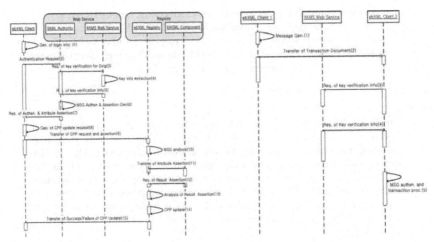

Fig. 1. Sequence Diagram – Senario 1   **Fig. 2.** Sequence Diagram – Senario 2

3 Design and Implementation of the Test Software

We constructed a test software, which focuses on security for registry/repository and messaging, and then targets system performance for the two business scenarios under a secure and reliable environment. XML Signature and XML Encryption are applied to the business transactions in the MSH (Message Service Handler) of ebXML client applications, registry, XKMS and SAML Web Services. We tested two scenarios by analyzing the messages in each step from Figure 1 and 2.

References

1. Imamura T., Dillaway B., Simon E.: XML Encryption Syntax and Processing, W3C Recommendation (2002), http://www.w3.org/TR/2002/REC-xmlenc-core-20021210/
2. Bartel M., Boyer J., Fox B., LaMacchia B. and Simon E.: XML Signature Syntax and Processing, W3C Recommendation (2002), http://www.w3.org/TR/xmldsig-core/
3. Ford W., Baker H., Fox B., Dillaway B., LaMacchia B., Epstein J. and Lapp J.: XML Key Management Specification (XKMS) Version 2.0, W3C Working Draft (2003), http://www.w3.org/TR/2003/WD-xkms2-20030418/
4. Maler E., Mishra P., Philpott R.: Assertions and Protocol for the OASIS Security Assertion Markup Language (SAML) V1.1, OASIS Committee Specification (2003) http://www.oasis-open.org/committees/download.php/3406/oasis-sstc-saml-core-1.1.pdf

Website Modeling and Website Generation

Bernhard Thalheim[1], Klaus-Dieter Schewe[2], Irina Romalis[3],
Thomas Raak[1,3], and Gunar Fiedler[1]

[1] University Kiel, Institute of Computer Science, Olshausenstrasse 40, 24098 Kiel,
Germany
[2] Massey University, Private Bag 11 222, Palmerston North, New Zealand,
[3] Cottbus University of Technology, Computer Science Insitute, PostBox 101344,
03013 Cottbus, Germany

Website Specification

Websites become more often based on data warehouse architectures. Our group uses the website modeling language SiteLang [TD01]. This language has reached a maturity that allows simple application and goes far beyond what other approaches can handle: It is powerful, consistent, has a well-developed theory fundament [Tha00a,Tha00b], does not allow to create confusing specifications, uses a powerful methodology [ST00,Tha03] applied in three dozen projects, and has a playout and layout specification supporting database-backed generation of websites.

Application in Projects Resulting in Installation of Large or Huge Websites

The approach presented in this paper is based on the experience the Cottbus Information Services team gained during successful development of 36 large or huge websites (partially with more than 15.000 pages), e.g., 17 large municipality websites (*information and community sites*), 5 *service sites*, 2 large *learning sites*, 4 *group and community sites*, 1 *e-government sites*, 1 huge *B2B site*, and 1 cable-net backed, set-top-box based TV-internet platform.

Automatic Generation, Orchestration, and Maintenance of Websites

The SiteLang specification can be developed by an editor that has been developed for support of our website projects and is applied for generation of websites. The storyboard editor uses a four window representation representing **scenarios, dialogs and dialog steps, database and content base,** and **story properties**. The website developer uses the editor backed by a database that contains the website structure and functionality. The editor supports integration of content obtained from other content systems and databases. This information is used for automatic generation of the website whenever content, structuring, and functionality are changed. Website developers do no longer develop XML document hills. Instead, the XML documents are generated by the system.

N. Koch, P. Fraternali, and M. Wirsing (Eds.): ICWE 2004, LNCS 3140, pp. 577–578, 2004.

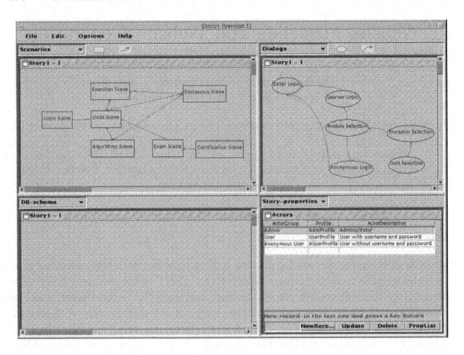

Fig. 1. A Screeenshot from the Storyboard Editor

References

[ST00]   K.-D. Schewe and B. Thalheim. Tutorial Notes. ER 2000, 2000.

[TD01]   B. Thalheim and A. Düsterhöft. Sitelang: Conceptual modeling of internet sites. In *Proc. ER'01, LNCS 2224, Springer*, pages 179–192, 2001.

[Tha00a] B. Thalheim. *Entity-relationship modeling – Foundations of database technology*. Springer, Berlin, 2000. See also http://www.informatik.tu-cottbus.de/∼thalheim/HERM.htm.

[Tha00b] B. Thalheim. Readings in fundamentals of interaction in information systems. Reprint, BTU-Cottbus, accessible through http://www.informatik.tu-cottbus.de/∼thalheim, Collection of papers by C. Binder, W. Clauß, A. Düsterhöft, T. Feyer, T. Gutacker, B. Heinze, J. Lewerenz, M. Roll, B. Schewe, K.-D. Schewe, K. Seelig, S. Srinivasa, B. Thalheim, 2000.

[Tha03]   B. Thalheim. Co-design of structuring, funtionality, distribution, and interactivity of large information systems. Coumputer Science Reports 15/03, Cottbus University of Technology, Computer Science Institute, 2003.

Improving Web Sites by Automatic Source Code Analysis and Modifications

Krzysztof Ciebiera and Piotr Sankowski

Warsaw University, Warszawa 02-097 ul. Banacha 2, Poland,
{ciebiera,sank}@mimuw.edu.pl
http://www.mimuw.edu.pl

1 Introduction

We propose an automatic tool for analysis and transformation of PHP programs which may be used in many different situations including:

- layer (presentation, logic, database) separation,
- authorization verification,
- security audits,
- performance improvements.

Our tool is based on system of rules which describe possible transformations and calculations, but as opposed to most of existing refactoring tools we use very intuitive method of applying rules based on program flow. In our opinion this approach is more convenient to learn and to use by ordinary developers.

2 System Overview

System works in following steps:

1. A set of PHP files is parsed and the code trees are build.
2. Parser reads code transformation rules from configuration files.
3. Rules are applied to code tree in one or many passes.
4. Resulting HTML is normalized and searched for common parts.
5. Finals results are written to files.

3 Sample Applications

3.1 Layer Separation

In most of Web programs it is possible to separate at least three layers:

- presentation,
- logic,
- database operations.

N. Koch, P. Fraternali, and M. Wirsing (Eds.): ICWE 2004, LNCS 3140, pp. 579–580, 2004.

Transformation is performed in two phases. First we find all functions which are responsible for presentation by checking if they can call echo or print directly or by calling other function. Those functions are modified to return generated output together with their original results. Such functions have attribute Function Prints set. In second phase we only go through main program and split it into appropriate layers. There are different set of rules for statements generating output and not generating it.

An example of simple if statement transformation is shown below:

```
singlecontextrule(1
| if ($1) {$*2 exists{tor{name{'Echo'},
  name{'Print'},tisset{'Function Prints'}
  }}}
|template "{if (\$\$3)}", $*2 ,
  template "{/if}"
| $$3 = $1; if ($$3) {$*2}
);
singlecontextrule(9
| if ($1) {$*2}
|
| if ($1) {$*2}
);
```

The first rule fits only those if statements which call either echo or print or any function which has Function Prints attribute set. After fitting the rule two if statements are outputted, one goes into PHP code and another into Smarty template. Also new variable $3 is created which will be evaluated only once and then its value will be used in both PHP code and Smarty template. The second rule as it has higher priority will be executed otherwise.

Using Topic Maps in an E-learning Context

Marie-Hélène Abel, Dominique Lenne, Claude Moulin, and Ahcene Benayache

UMR CNRS 6599, BP 20529
60205 Compiègne cedex, France
+33 (0)3 44 23 49 50
{Marie-Helene.Abel, Dominique.Lenne, Claude.Moulin, Ahcene.Benayache}@utc.fr

Abstract. E-learning leads to evolutions in the way of designing a course. Diffused through the web, the course content cannot be the pure transcription of a face to face course content. A course unit can be seen as an organization in which different actors are involved. These actors produce documents, information and knowledge that they often share. Within the MEMORAe[1] project [1] we design an ontology-based document-driven memory which we think as being particularly adapted to an e-learning situation. We precise the choice of the Topic Maps formalism that we use for knowledge representation.

1 A Learning Organizational Memory

A course unit is based on knowledge and competencies it should provide, on actors (learners, instructors, trainers, course designers, administrators, etc.) and on resources of different types (definitions, exercises with or without solution, case studies, etc.), and different forms (reports, books, web sites, etc.). In this sense, a course is an organization. A common approach to tackle the knowledge management problem in an organization consists in designing an organizational memory [2]. In order to share information in an organization, actors have to use a common terminology, especially when they are geographically distant. A given word or expression must have the same meaning for everyone. It is one of the reasons why organizational memories are often based on ontologies.

The learning organizational memory we propose aims at facilitating knowledge organization and management for a given course or training, and at clarifying competencies it allows to acquire.

2 The Choice of the Topic Maps Formalism

We have to consider two levels for modeling the memory and building ontologies: the first one is generic; the other one is specific and is relative to a particular training program. These two levels are both used for document and resource indexing and for

---

[1] The MEMORAE project is supported by STEF, a research pole of the Picardie region.

N. Koch, P. Fraternali, and M. Wirsing (Eds.): ICWE 2004, LNCS 3140, pp. 581–582, 2004.

helping to navigate between the knowledge elements of the memory that serve to index the documents.

The modeling of a training memory contains three elements: two ontological parts and the way to index documents on them. The modeling must at least allow three operations: (1) The reunion of two ontologies: the generic one and the application one; (2) The substitution of an application ontology by another one coming from another domain; (3) The attachment of document indexing on the reunion of two ontologies.

The choice of the formalism(s) for representing the memory is very decisive. It must go beyond the hybrid aspect of the modeling (ontology and indexing), favor the interoperability between various tools that have to deal with the memory (edition, updater, consultation, navigation, etc.).

The Topic Maps formalism (TM) [3] is useful to define and manipulate the information attached to resources. That provides a logical organization to a large quantity of resources keeping them accessible and facilitating the navigation between them.

Overall, we chose the TM formalism because it keeps a semantic level close enough to the model of our memory. With an ontology oriented point of view, this formalism allows to envisage the important following characteristics:

– It is possible to consider some topics as generic concepts and other as concept instances;
– It is possible to consider associations, scopes and occurrences as roles between concept topics;
– Associations have no limitation in their member number;
– The occurrence relation allows to directly attach resources to concepts (the same resource can appear in several occurrence relations and be accessible from more than one concept);
– Relations (associations, occurrence) and concept labels can be defined inside scopes. This allows to simply implementing annotations (or points de view in the memory).

To definitely adopt this formalism, we verified it was possible to simply add ontological missing features and mainly the relation superclass-subclass for building hierarchies of concepts.

References

1. Abel M.-H., Lenne D., Cissé O., "E-Learning and Organizational Memory", Proceedings of IC-AI'02, Las Vegas, June 2002.
2. Rabarijaona A., Dieng R., Corby O., Ouaddari R., Building a XML-based Corporate Memory, IEEE Intelligent Systems, Special Issue on Knowledge Management and Internet, p. 56-64, May-June 2000.
3. IEC, "International Organization for Standardization (ISO)", International Electronical Commission (IEC), Topic Map, International Standard ISO/IEC 13250, 19 April 1999.

A Component-Based WebGIS Geo-Union

Yingwei Luo, Xiaolin Wang, and Zhuoqun Xu

Dept. of Computer Science and Technology, Peking University, Beijing, P.R.China, 100871
lyw@pku.edu.cn

Abstract. A component-based WebGIS system Geo-Union is introduced, including its architecture, functional partition and web application mode.

1 Introduction

Assigning functions in reason and improving performance are two key issues for
making WebGIS more practicable [1]. So based on analyzing modeling technique of
component-based WebGIS, we construct a practicable, multi-level WebGIS system.

2 A Component-Based WebGIS: Geo-Union

Geo-Union has a four-level architecture: application layer, component layer, service
layer and storage layer, where service layer has different units to provide both client
services and server services. Figure1 shows the architecture [2].

(1) Storage layer is the ground of Geo-Union. Storage layer is responsible for storage and management of both spatial data and non-spatial data based on ORDB. (2)
Service layer is in charge of spatial data access and process, which can be divided
into another two parts: Geo-Union client provides data access and process services to
component layer, and Geo-Union server provides data access and process services to
Geo-Union client through interacting with storage layer. Geo-Union server can manage different spatial data resources, and also can reply to different spatial data requests from different clients. (3) Component layer provides a rich set of services
(components) to develop domain-oriented GIS applications for further developers.
Component layer provides interface of GIS functions to users, but the implementation
details are completed in service layer. (4) Application layer is to exploit application
systems for different domains by assembling and integrating Geo-Union components.

Most of functions are implemented in service layer. Geo-Union server side is just
to provide spatial data access. But Geo-Union client supports to develop domain-
oriented applications. In order to provide flexible developing mode, around map
visualization objects, we designed another six types of objects: spatial data access
objects, map edit objects, spatial analysis objects, mouse tool objects, utility objects

N. Koch, P. Fraternali, and M. Wirsing (Eds.): ICWE 2004, LNCS 3140, pp. 583–584, 2004.

and AppTool. Figure 2 shows the architecture of service layer, the roles of different objects and their relationships [2]. Figure 3 shows the Web application mode.

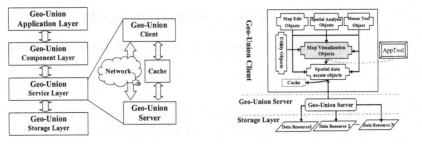

Fig. 1. Geo-Union Architecture   **Fig. 2.** Functional Partition of Service Layer

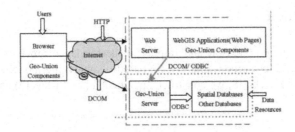

Fig. 3. Web Application of Geo-Union

3   Conclusion

Geo-Union has finished a preliminary component-based model for distributed WebGIS, and has got into use in many fields with sound effects.

Acknowledgements. This work is supported by the National Research Foundation for the Doctoral Program of Higher Education of China (20020001015); the National Grand Fundamental Research 973 Program of China (2002CB312000); the National Science Foundation of China (60203002); the National High Technology Development 863 Program (2002AA135330); the Beijing Science Foundation (4012007).

References

1. Li Bin: A Component Perspective on Geographic Information Services, Cartography and Geographic Information Science, 27(1): 75-86(2001).
2. Dept. of Computer Science and Technology, Peking University: Operation and Component Guide for Geo-Union Enterprise (in Chinese), Technology Material, http://gis.pku.edu.cn.

Engineering a Semantic Web for Pathology

Robert Tolksdorf[1] and Elena Paslaru Bontas[2]

Freie Universität Berlin
Institut für Informatik, AG Netzbasierte Informationssysteme
Takustr. 9, D-14195 Berlin Germany
research@robert-tolksdorf.de, http://www.robert-tolksdorf.de
paslaru@inf.fu-berlin.de

1 Introduction

By using telepathology approaches like virtual microscopy, pathologists analyze high quality digitised histological images on a display screen instead of conventional glass slides at the common microscope. Currently, most of the applications in this domain restrict their retrieval capabilities to automatical picture analysis, ignoring corresponding medical reports or patient records. Therefore, they have the essential drawback that they operate exclusively on structural or syntactical image parameters such as color, texture and basic geometrical forms while ignoring the real content and the actual meaning of the pictures. Medical reports, as textual representations of the pictural represented *content* of the slides, capture *implicitly* the actual semantics of what the picture graphically represent, for example "a tumor" in contrast to "a red blob" or "a colocated set of red pixels". The meaning of the textual content (and of the digital slides), can be extracted and represented *explictly* by means of ontology-driven text processing algorithms. In this paper we propose a *semantic* retrieval system for the domain of lung pathology, which correlates both text and image information and offers advanced content-based retrieval services for diagnosis, differential diagnosis and teaching tasks. At the core of the system is a Semantic Web based knowledge base, gathering ontological domain knowledge, rules describing key processes in pathology and an archive of concrete medical reports. The usage of *Semantic Web* standards and medicine thesauri facilitates the realization of a distributed infrastructure for knowledge share and exchange. In the remaining of the paper we introduce the main features of the retrieval system we are building, with a focus on the construction of the knowledge base for lung pathology and summarize planned future work.

2 Building a Semantic Web for Pathology

The project "Semantic Web for Pathology"[1] aims to realize a Semantic Web-based text and picture retrieval system for the pathology domain. We foresee

---

[1] The project is funded by the Deutsche Forschungsgemeinschaft, as a cooperation among the Charité Institute of Pathology, the Institute for Computer Science at the FU Berlin and the Department of Linguistics at the University of Potsdam, Germany.

several valuable uses of the planned system in routine pathology. First, it may be used as an assistent tool for diagnosis tasks. Since knowledge is made explicit, it supports new query capabilities for diagnosis tasks. Second, advanced retrieval capabilities may be used for educational purposes by teaching personnel and students. Currently, enormous amounts of knowledge are lost by being stored in data bases, which are behaving as real data sinks. They can and should be used for teaching, e.g. for case-based medical education. Third, quality assurance and checking of diagnosis decisions can be effectuated more efficiently because the system uses axioms and rules to automatically check consistency and validity. Finally, explicit knowledge can be exchanged with external parties like other hospitals. The representation within the system is already the transfer format for information. Semantic Web technologies are by design open for the integration of knowledge that is relative to different ontologies and rules.

At the core of the retrieval system is a domain knowledge base formalized with Semantic Web technologies. It puts together available medical knowledge sources from UMLS [2], generic ontologies, rules and medical reports and adapt this information to the requirements of our concrete application domain "lung pathology". The knowledge base/ontology coordinates the text processing and information extraction procedures. The case report archive in textual form is analyzed using ontology-based text processing algorithms and annotated with concepts from the ontology. Besides, new implicit knowledge from these texts is extracted and integrated in the ontology. As main input for the medical knowledge base we use UMLS, as the more complex medical thesaurus currently available. UMLS as in the actual release contains over 1,5 million concepts from over 100 medical libraries and is permanently growing. Nevertheless, UMLS libraries, though containing a huge amount of concepts or termini have seldom been developed for machine processing, but rather as controlled vocabularies and taxonomies for specific tasks in medicine. From a strict Semantic Web point of view they proved to be deficiently designed and incomplete. Therefore, the first step in generating an ontology based on the UMLS thesaurus was to specify a methodology to overcome these drawbacks. Further on, due to the huge amount of information within UMLS we had to identify the relevant UMLS libraries or concepts and integrate additional information, which is not covered by UMLS by now, but has proved to be relevant for our application domain.

We have generated a core domain ontology in OWL based on the original UMLS knowledge base. We leave additional details about the modelling primitives and the identification of application-relevant UMLS concepts to another paper. After an automatic discovery of the (logical) inconsistencies of the modell, the next step will be the manual adaptation of the OWL ontology in order to correct these errors and to include pathology-specific knowledge, like the concrete structure of case reports and frequently-used concepts from texts not supported by UMLS, contained in a lexicon generated by the lexical analysis of the corpus.

---

[2] http://umls.nlm.nih.gov

Enhancing Decoupling in Portlet Implementation

Salvador Trujillo, Iñaki Paz, and Oscar Díaz

University of the Basque Country, San Sebastian (Spain)
{struji,jibparei,oscar}@si.ehu.es

1 Introduction

A Portlet is a Web component that processes requests and generates dynamic content. Portlet consumers (e.g. a portal) use Portlets as pluggable user interface components. Typically, a Portlet is rendered as a window in the portal, the Portlet being a main building block for portal construction. The recent delivery of standards, namely, *Web Services for Remote Portlets*[1] and *Java Specification Request* 168[2] promise to bring interoperability to the Portlet realm. Nothing is said about how the Portlet should be implemented. However, Portlet implementation could be quite an issue. Presentation and even the navigation logic could need to change not only for maintenance reasons, but also to cater for the idiosyncrasies of distinct Portals. Therefore, variability, and thus decoupling, is a main issue in Portlet development. In contrast to servlet techniques (i.e. modularisation), a single Portlet needs to implement (1) **control** code to determine which action is being requested, (2) what **action** needs to occur, (3) what **state** to leave the Portlet in, and (4) what **view** (fragment) to render back to the user. Without appropriate decoupling patterns, this code can mix up different concerns, making the separate evolution of each concern a real maintenance problem. This work[3] revises distinct approaches that gradually achieve higher levels of decoupling.

2 Decoupling

The Action from the State. Cleaner Portlet code can be obtained by using the state pattern as proposed in [1]. A Portlet is modeled as a state machine where a state is defined for each Portlet fragment, and arrows are labelled with the actions that achieve the transition between fragments. A state has an associated view which in turn, embeds the potential set of actions. Unfortunately, the control-flow is hard-coded in both actions and fragments. This pattern facilitates the introduction of states but offers no help to weave the new states into the flow of the existing states.

The Action from the View. A step forward is the use of the Model-View-Controller paradigm, an evolution of the former where the control logic is decoupled in a new element, the *controller*. No information about the Views is introduced in the action but

---

[1] WSRP standardizes the interface between the Portlet consumer and the producer.

[2] JSR168 standardizes the interface between the Portlet container and the Portlet itself in Java.

[3] This work was partially supported by the Spanish Science and Technology Ministry (MCYT) under contract TIC2002-01442. Salvador Trujillo enjoys a doctoral grant for the MCYT.

N. Koch, P. Fraternali, and M. Wirsing (Eds.): ICWE 2004, LNCS 3140, pp. 587–588, 2004.

rather on the controller definition. Moreover, the flow is described as a set of *Front-end* rules: the antecedent expresses a predicate over the result of an action (i.e. *success* or *error*) whereas the consequent states the next fragment to be rendered (e.g. *flight-Search.jsp*). As an example, this approach is followed by the eXo Portlet Framework (http://www.exoplatform.org). However, the coupling between the view and the action still exists. The view contains the distinct actions the End-user can execute through it, but still a direct mapping from the views to the actions exists. Indeed, the action-view dependence is only moved to the controller, and still exists. No real independence between the Actions and the Views exists.

The View from the Action. For Portlets to become real components, Portlet implementation should be engineered to cope with the changes and variations the Portlet needs to cope with during its life time. That is, the Portlet should be built in such a way that the impact and cost of performing changes will be minimal. To attain this goal, we propose to decouple also the view form the action. In addition to *Front-end* rules, we introduce *Back-end* rules that dictate the actions to be executed based on the interaction achieved through the previous view. The controller comprises both *Front-end* and *Back-end* rules, which describe the whole flow, and neither action nor view contain a reference to each other, clarifying the development and reducing the impact of a change.

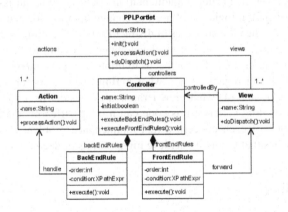

In brief, as with any other component, Portlets need to be engineered for variability. This work describes distinct approaches that gradually achieve higher levels of decoupling, and hence, enhance Portlet variability. This effort is part of a wider endeavour in attempting to apply a product-line approach to Portlet implementation.

Reference

1. T. Hanis, S. Thomas, and C. Gerken. Applying the State Pattern to Websphere Portal Portlets, 2002.
   http://www-106.ibm.com/developerworks/websphere/library/techarticles/0212_hanis/hanis1.html.

A Metadata Model for the Design and Deployment of Document Management Systems

Federica Paganelli[1], Omar Abou Khaled[2], Maria Chiara Pettenati[1], and
Dino Giuli[1]

[1] University of Florence, Department of Electronics and Telecommunications
via S. Marta 3, Florence, 50100, Italy
{paganelli, pettenati}@achille.det.unifi.it
giuli@det.unifi.it
[2] University of Applied Sciences of Western Switzerland,
Department of Computer Sciences
Boulevard de Perolles 80, Fribourg, 1700, Switzerland
omar.aboukhaled@eif.ch

Abstract. This work aims to address the issues of unstructured document management, by proposing a set of metadata: the DMSML (Document Management and Sharing Markup Language). DMSML represents a set of document properties, which are relevant to document management and render business and organizational information explicit, in a way which promotes reuse, interoperability and integration with heterogeneous systems.

A huge amount of organizational information is formalized in unstructured documents. Due to their intrinsic characteristics, management of unstructured documents presents critical issues: difficult information search and retrieval, poor interoperability among information systems, poor reuse of content, as well as of business information, related to the context of use of documents in organizations (i.e. business processes and organizational schema).

The objective of this work is to address these issues, by proposing a Metadata Model, called DMSML (Document Management and Sharing Markup Language). DMSML represents a set of document properties, which are relevant to document management and render business and organizational information explicit, in a way which promotes reuse, user-driven extensibility and interoperability with heterogeneous systems.

In order to cope with the issues of document indexing, search and retrieval, and reuse of documented and business information, the process of metadata specification has been focused on the selection a set of labels representing content- as well as context-related properties of documents. Content properties relate to what the document contains or is about, thus providing to users and applications useful hints to help document search and retrieval and improve the reuse of documented information. Context-related metadata express the "by whom,

N. Koch, P. Fraternali, and M. Wirsing (Eds.): ICWE 2004, LNCS 3140, pp. 589–590, 2004.

where, how, under which constraints and for which purpose" a document is being accessed, transmitted and modified. In this way, business information related to the practices of use of documents is made explicit, promoting formalization, exchange and reuse of this valuable information.

In DMSML we represent these two dimensions of unstructured document properties, by distinguishing three main parts, or modules:

- The *Descriptive Information Model*, i.e. the set of properties, which describes and identifies the document (e.g. title, author, date and subject).
- The *Collaboration Model*, which formalizes how the organizational resources are structured (the organizational model) and how access to information resources is regulated (the access right policy), on the basis of the organizational roles or responsibilities of individuals.
- The *Process Model*, which specifies the lifecycle of the document. The document lifecycle usually consists of the following stages: creation, review, publication, access, archive and deletion. A specific lifecycle may not implement all these stages, or implement others.

The DMSML specification is based on a three-layered model, promoting human understanding of the metadata specification (*Conceptual Layer*), logical data modeling (*Logical Layer*), and machine-understanding and interoperability with other applications (XML Schema-based *Physical Layer*).

DMSML supports the conception of a completely declarative approach for the design and automatic deployment of Document Management Systems. The use and proper adaptation of DMSML enable to configure a DMS according to the specific requirements of an organization, providing specific methods and mechanisms to exploit the business knowledge detained by the end users, and leveraging on the compliance with technical and business metadata standards.

A DMSML Framework prototype has been developed, which provides the user with automated support for the adaptation and use of the metadata set and the deployment and operation of a Document Management System. It consists of three parts: a DMS Configurator, which is a graphical interface for the creation of DMSML instance documents, representing the requirements of an organization, a DMS Engine, which automatically deploys a Document Management System, properly configured according to the specifications encoded in the DMSML instance, and a DMS Web Application, providing basic Document Management features. The description of the information resources and the policies for the proper management of these resources (i.e. document lifecycles, access policies, etc.) are encoded in the DMSML instance. The operation of the DMS Web Application (e.g. upload of new documents and creation of new folders) is mapped into proper updating of the DMSML instance.

Some testing activities in real application scenarios are planned in the research progress. Possible scenarios to test the approach are envisaged within two application domains: the management of legal documents (with the support of the Institute for Legal Documentation, http://www.ittig.cnr.it/) and the lifecycle of scientific grey literature in a research institution (with the CERN Library, http://library.cern.ch/).

MSC-Based Formalism for Automated Web Navigation

Vicente Luque Centeno, Carlos Delgado Kloos, Luis Sánchez Fernández, and
Norberto Fernández García

Departamento de Ingeniería Telemática
Universidad Carlos III de Madrid,
Avda. Universidad, 30, E-28911 Leganés, Madrid, Spain

Abstract. This article presents an approach to model navigation tasks
on the Deep Web [3] with a well known Software Engineering formalism,
namely Message Sequence Charts [2] standard from the ITU, in combination with W3C XPath [4] expressions. This modelling can be used to
build Wrapper Agents [1] that might automate Web navigation for the
user.

1 MSC-Based Formalism

Web navigation may be expressed in terms of MSC [2] components. Both Web
clients and Web servers may be represented by **MSC instances** (vertical lines).
HTTP requests and answers may be represented by **MSC messages** (horizontal
arrows) communicating MSC instances. Vertical axis is also considered as a time
axis (top levels are executed before bottom levels).

However, Web navigation not only consists of a single HTTP transaction.
Navigation through the Deep Web [3] requires several links to be followed and
several forms to be properly filled in. This requires considering the document's
internal structure as well. W3C XPath expressions can be used to properly choose
which links should be followed next or how should forms be filled in. **MSC
actions** (rectangles) might be used for embedding XPath-based data extraction
rules as well as other user-defined routines. Figure 1 shows two instances: a Web
client and a Web server. After the Web client executes some procedure A(), it
submits a filled-in form to the server by an HTTP POST request. Once the
Web server receives that request, the corresponding procedure B() is executed
(maybe a CGI program or a servlet) to handle that request and an answer page
is returned back to the client. Only when the Web client receives the answer
message, it starts executing the C() procedure.

Some decisions have to be made during navigation, just as a user behind a
browser would do. For instance, it is common that a Web link has to be followed
only if some condition occurs, perhaps following other link otherwise. **MSC's
inline expressions** may represent these alternative and repetitive behaviours.
Just as repetitive or alternative navigation behaviours may be internally structured, also MSC inline expressions may nest.

N. Koch, P. Fraternali, and M. Wirsing (Eds.): ICWE 2004, LNCS 3140, pp. 591–592, 2004.

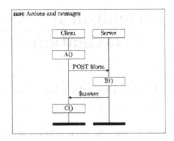

Fig. 1. Instances, messages and actions

Modularized components or parameterized navigation procedures may also be expressed with **MSC references** (curved corner rectangles). Figure 2 shows both an example of a reference to a sub MSC named Identif and its definition. MSC references allow the definition of complex MSC in terms of smaller parts.

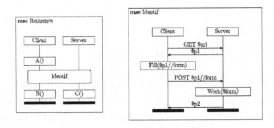

Fig. 2. MSC reference

Acknowledgements. The work reported in this paper has been partially funded by the project Infoflex *TIC2003-07208* of the Spanish Ministry of Science and Research.

References

1. V. L. Centeno, L. S. Fernandez, C. D. Kloos, P. T. Breuer, and F. P. Martin. Building wrapper agents for the deep web. In *Third International Conference on Web Engineering ICWE 2003, Lecture Notes in Computer Science LNCS 2722, Ed. Springer*, pages 58–67, Oviedo, Spain, July 2003.
2. ITU-T. Recommendation z.120: Message sequence chart (msc). In *Formal description techniques (FDT)*, Geneva, Switzerland, 1997.
3. M. P. Singh. Deep web structure. *Internet Computing*, 6(5):4–5, Sept.-Oct. 2002.
4. W3C. Xml path language (xpath) 2.0. *W3C Working Draft 02 May 2003*, 2003.

A Procedure for Development and Execution of Process-Based Composite Web Services

Dimka Karastoyanova and Alejandro Buchmann

Technische Universität Darmstadt
Department of Computer Science
Hochschulstrasse 10, 64289
Darmstadt, Germany
dimka@gkec.tu-darmstadt.de
buchmann@informatik.tu-darmstadt.de

Abstract. The paper proposes a methodology for development and execution of Web service compositions. It uses a common process meta-model and accommodates approaches for code and functionality reuse applying templates, and dynamic selection and invocation of participating WSs at run time.

1 Introduction

Web service (WS) technology targets the integration of applications across organizational boundaries and over the Web. It is not yet a mature middleware technology. There is no standard methodology to guide the creation and execution of WS-based compositions, called WS-flows, and to accommodate approaches addressing process development automation, flexibility and adaptability. In this paper we introduce the main steps of such a methodology, based on WS-flows life cycle [3].

2 Procedure for Development and Execution of WS-flows

To meet the requirements on the design of WS-flows we propose a simple procedure, presented in Fig. 1. Each phase prescribes an approach addressing different aspects of a process definition [3]. During the *process template modeling and assembly phase* templates are modeled using the constructs of a common meta-model and are assembled with additional business logic to produce abstract process definitions. Templates are units of code and functionality reuse. The resulting process definitions avoid specifying any references to WS instances, and in a more complex approach avoid references to WSs portTypes. *Process definition generation* phase is used to transform the templates created in the previous phase into executable process definitions using meta-programming applications like code generators, or XML transformations. Real flexibility of the WS-flows can be achieved if the commitment to a specific process definition language is deferred to the latest possible transformation.

N. Koch, P. Fraternali, and M. Wirsing (Eds.): ICWE 2004, LNCS 3140, pp. 593–594, 2004.
© Springer-Verlag Berlin Heidelberg 2004

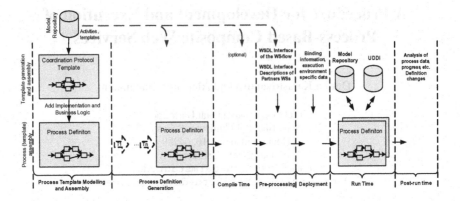

Fig. 1. Procedure for development and execution of WS-flows.

The *compile time* and *pre-processing time* are optional phases but in some cases they might be necessary depending on the targeted definition language. Upon *deployment* the WS-flow definition is enriched with execution environment specific data, and with details about the participating WSs (e.g. BPEL4WS [2]). During *execution time* process instances are created and executed. The use of a common process model enables dynamic selection of WSs, based on their QoS characteristics, and WS invocation at run time. A more flexible solution advocates the use of reflective activities to allow changes to be made in the process definition at run time (Fig. 1). The information gathered during run time can later be used in the *post-run time* phase to analyze the process progress and logic and change it accordingly.

3 Conclusion

We introduce a procedure for development and execution of WS-flows. It is based on the use of a common process model. During the build time phases a WS-flow definition is modeled and generated from templates. The procedure relies strongly on enabling process definition reuse and technology leverage; it reduces manual work and shortens development time. Automating the procedure is instrumental for its success and depends on the existence of appropriate tools for template modeling and transformation. The methodology can be used to create process definitions in multiple languages, e.g., BPEL [2] and BPML [1]. It facilitates the development of flexible WS-flows by providing means to allow dynamic selection and invocation of WSs during process execution.

References

1.   Arkin, A. et al., *"Business Process Modeling Language"*, BPMI.org, 2002.
2.   Curbera, F. et al., *"Business Process Execution Language for Web Services 1.0"*, 2002.
3.   Karastoyanova, D., A Methodology for Development of Web Service-based Business Processes, In *Proceedings of AWESOS 2004*, April 2004.

Towards Integrating Autonomously Created Knowledge Descriptions for the Semantic Web

Christian Mönch and Sari Hakkarainen

NTNU, Trondheim, Norway
{moench,sari}@idi.ntnu.no

1 Creating Knowledge Representations for the Semantic Web

In order for the Semantic Web to succeed, it has to be created in a decentralized way, analogous to the Web. In our model, the Semantic Web is composed by a number of individual entities. Every entity is an artifact, created by a creator. An entity contains a knowledge representation that contains knowledge about its associated resources. The creation of the knowledge representation is part of the creation of the entity. The knowledge representation is instantiated as an internal representation that is not visible to the outside, except for the creator of the entity.

Entities communicate by exchanging symbols. Symbols may be single words or more complex structures, e. g. RDF documents. Associated with each entity are two functions that allow to map between symbols and the internal representation of the knowledge:

1.) The *interpretation* function maps a symbol to the internal representation of the entity in a given time.

2.) The *expression* function maps a subset of the internal representation of an entity to symbols.

The interpretation and expression functions are depending on the structure and the state of the entities, i. e. on the internal representation. The interpretation function is parameterized by the background knowledge represented in an entity. The expression function is dependent of the symbols the creator chose for the represented knowledge, which is defined by the entity.

1.1 The Problem of Heterogeneous Knowledge Representations

Without continuous mutual agreement on different aspects of the knowledge representation heterogeneous knowledge representations will be created (cf. [1]). The reason is that the creator of an entity has to:

1.) select the part of their knowledge that should be represented in the entity, and

2.) select the granularity of the knowledge as well as the embedding of the knowledge into supporting structures.

The large number of individual decisions makes it very likely that different creators will create different entities and therefore differences in the expression and interpretation function, that are parameterized by the knowledge represented in the entity. As a result, different entities may map a given symbol on different concepts and/or identical symbols on different concepts.

N. Koch, P. Fraternali, and M. Wirsing (Eds.): ICWE 2004, LNCS 3140, pp. 595–596, 2004.
© Springer-Verlag Berlin Heidelberg 2004

Since continuous mutual agreement on different aspects of the knowledge representation would be a conceptually centralized process, it can not be afforded and heterogeneous knowledge representations will emerge. In order for two entities to incorporate each others knowledge, the heterogeneity between them has to be resolved.

2   On Demand Resolution of Heterogeneity

If we want to allow the autonomous creation of knowledge representations —and that seems to be the only feasible way to create the Semantic Web— we need a strategy to cope with heterogeneity of knowledge descriptions. Our solution to an automated resolution is inspired by the mechanisms of discrepancy-resolution between persons. Individual persons acquire their knowledge in isolation. We can not decide whether our knowledge is identical —or compatible— because there is no cross-introspection. However, communication is used to detect and resolve differing interpretations of symbols. Individuals exchange symbols which they usually interpret in a compatible way, because they share a large amount of knowledge. But they may at some point of the communication experience a semantic mismatch and redirect their communication to disambiguate their interpretation of the exchanged symbols. In order to do so, the semantic mismatch has to be detected and quantified.

The heterogeneity makes it impossible to compare symbols directly in order to detect a semantic mismatch. Our solution is based on a, possibly repeated, verification step. Let us assume, entity B interprets a symbol S_A that was uttered by entity A. In order to verify its interpretation, entity B asks entity A for the validity of its interpretation. To do so, it utters its interpretation of symbol S_A as the symbol S_B. This is then send to entity A, together with a symbol $S_{context}$ that describes the context of symbol S_B. Entity A interprets S_B using $S_{context}$, and calculates a distance value that tells entity B how accurate its interpretation of symbol S_A was.

The communication between the entities has to be grounded, i. e. based on symbols whose interpretation is by convention bound to one concept. In order to avoid a rigorous centralized definition process, we propose to use a large set of not exactly defined, but commonly understood symbols, e. g. WordNet. Of course there will be individual differences in the interpretation of the symbols. But these differences will be limited to individual subsets of the symbols. If we compare interpretations of a sufficiently large set of symbols, we will find a large number of compatible interpretations.

Measuring distances between parts of knowledge representations is difficult and not yet solved problem. Approaches for ontology comparison [2] might be applicable to this problem.

References

1. Mönch, C., Hakkarainen, S.: A Communication Based Approach to Integrate Decentraly Created Knowledge Descriptions. In: Proceedings of the WWW 12. (2003)
2. Mädche, A., Staab, S.: Measuring similarity between ontologies. In: Proceedings Of the EKAW-2002, Madrid, Spain, October 1-4, 2002. LNCS, Springer (2002)

XWebProcess: Agile Software Development for Web Applications

Américo Sampaio[1], Alexandre Vasconcelos[1], and Pedro R. Falcone Sampaio[2]

[1] Centro de informática, Universidade Federal de Pernambuco
Recife, Pernambuco – Brazil
{atfs,amlv}@cin.ufpe.br
[2] Computation Department, University of Manchester Institute of Science and Technology
United Kingdom
{p.sampaio}@co.umist.ac.uk

Abstract. Accelerating application development and reducing time to market is a highly valuable feature of a software process. For web-based applications, in particular, project development efforts often need to comply with severe time constraints imposed by the strategic business importance of the web. In this paper we describe XWebProcess, an agile process for web-based application development. XWebProcess is grounded on the principles underlying Extreme Programming and is aimed at building high quality web applications in a time effective way. XWebProcess' agility has been compared to XP via an experimental setting which shows its superiority in supporting web development dimensions such as requirements gathering, user navigation design, and software testing, while retaining the agile property of Extreme Programming.

1   XWebProcess

Some core elements of web application engineering that XWebProcess addresses are:
- Non-functional requirements such as concurrency, load balancing, security and distribution, which play an important role in the operation of web applications. The number of concurrent users can be substantial and appropriate software and hardware infrastructure may also be necessary.
- Different kinds of clients accessing the system via distinct browsers and protocols. Therefore it is important to identify different OS and hardware architectures underlying the system.
- Navigation and presentation aspects. In web applications, user interfaces often contain graphics, animations, links and text requiring attractive UI designs and simple navigability.

XWebProcess seeks to combine the key elements of Extreme Programming with process structures tailored to tackle the characteristics and factors of web engineering identified above, therefore providing an efficient and effective approach to the construction of web applications.

N. Koch, P. Fraternali, and M. Wirsing (Eds.): ICWE 2004, LNCS 3140, pp. 597–598, 2004.

The main reasons for leveraging Extreme Programming as the base software process are:

- XP is an agile process that is showing positive results in many software development projects. A recent survey presents some important quantitative data about a large number of XP projects built by different software companies worldwide. The projects varied in size, kind of application and application domain. Almost all XP projects finished on time and on budget and, among them, 28% represented web projects.
- Recent contributions acknowledge the value of XP for web application development while recognizing the need for adaptations in the XP process to better suit the web application problem landscape.
- The wide availability of literature and project case studies simplifying the task of best practice identification.

The creation of XWebProcess can be summarized in four key steps. First, the must have features of a web engineering process were identified (e.g. disciplines, activities, artifacts, roles, etc.). Second, XP was modeled using OMG´s software process engineering metamodel (SPEM) to obtain a better abstraction for representing the process and also to help its adaptation towards web application development. Third, adaptations of XP´s elements and the inclusion of novel elements (disciplines) were performed to tailor the method to a web engineering framework. Finally, the process elements of XWebProcess were detailed and specified using SPEM.

XWebProcess is described in two views using SPEM to facilitate process construction. The use of SPEM enables an abstract description of the software process core elements (artifacts, roles, activities, etc.) and the description of how they relate to each other. The SPEM notation also helps to illustrate the adaptations and tailorings performed over XP to target web application development. SPEM was chosen due to its OMG standard status for software process modeling and due to the extensive endorsement provided by software companies such as IBM, Rational Software and Unisys.

The first view of the process model uses UML´s activity diagram with the discipline stereotype defined in SPEM as shown in. This model helps to understand how the process behaves through time (dynamic view). The second view of the process details each discipline of the process using UML´s class diagram alongside with SPEM stereotypes to represent common software process elements such as roles, activities and artifacts and the relationship among them.

It is important to mention that XWebProcess is a general web development process that does not depend on any specific technology, method, tool or technique. For instance, the process can be supported either with .NET or J2EE platforms. It also works with OOHDM or OOWS that are design methods for web applications. What is important to consider is if the specific method, tool or technology will have a negative impact on the agility of the process.

Automating Standards-Based Courseware Development Using UML

Andreas Papasalouros[1], Symeon Retalis[2], and Nikolaos Papaspyrou[1]

[1] National Technical University of Athens, 9 Heroon Polytechniou, 157 80 Zografou, Greece
{andpapas,nickie}@softlab.ntua.gr
[2] University of Piraeus, 80 Karaoli & Dimitriou, 185 34 Piraeus, Greece
retal@unipi.gr

Abstract. In this paper we discuss the automatic construction of web-based courseware applications from XML descriptions of appropriate UML models. The created applications conform to a related Learning Technology Standard for learning material interchange, namely the IMS Content Packaging standard.

1 Introduction

In this paper we demonstrate the automatic generation of courseware applications based on proper UML models. These models have been defined as a UML profile. A design model of a courseware application consists of three views or submodels:

- An *Activity Model*, which depicts the abstract solution of the learning problem under consideration in terms of activities that the learner is engaged in and resources, that is, physical, binary entities that are incorporated into the application, such as images or java applets.
- A *Navigation Model*, which describes the hypertext structure of the application by defining nodes and links and their mapping to the elements of the Activity Model.
- A *Presentation Model* which defines the user interface of the application in the form of templates for web pages.

This generation is based on specific technologies and specifications, such as the XML Metadata Interchange (XMI) [3] and XSL Transformations [4]. Furthermore, the produced courseware conforms to the IMS Content Packaging (CP) Specification [1] for defining interchangeable bundles of learning content.

2 The Transformation

The method for the automatic courseware generation is briefly described here. First, a designer creates a model for the application under development using

N. Koch, P. Fraternali, and M. Wirsing (Eds.): ICWE 2004, LNCS 3140, pp. 599–600, 2004.
© Springer-Verlag Berlin Heidelberg 2004

a general purpose UML tool. This model follows the structure presented in the previous section and provides an abstract representation of the content, structure and presentation of the application. The UML tool is used to provide an XML serialization of the model in XMI format. A number of UML tools are available with this capability. The designer also provides the *resources* which are physical files that will be incorporated into the application.

The courseware generation is carried out by a tool which we have developed. This tool is based on XSL Transformations and consists of a number of XSL files, called by a small Java application. The input to this tool, for a particular application, consists of an XMI description and associated resources. All the Activity, Navigation and Presentation Models are contained into the XMI description. The tool transforms the structural description of the Navigation Model into HTML code, incorporating the resources of the Activity Model and applying the templates of the Presentation Model.

The tool generates the code of the Courseware Application. This consists of a set of HTML pages. The tool also generates an XML description of the structure of the courseware that is called a *manifest file* [1]. The HTML Pages together with the manifest description constitute a bundle of learning material that conforms to the IMS Content Packaging Learning Technology standard. This bundle is reusable and portable. It can be easily deployed into proper web-based systems which conform to the same standard and be presented to learners.

3   Future Work

We are extending this approach for standards-based courseware generation in the direction of conditional sequencing of learning content, as it is specified in the IMS Simple Sequencing Specification [2]. Sequencing refers to the automatic selection of different activities for delivering to individual learners according to their history of interaction with the learning material, i.e. their performance in on-line tests. We are also developing a specialized tool for authoring of courseware UML models, that is expected to be more usable for model authors than general purpose UML tools.

References

1. IMS: IMS Content Packaging Version 1.1.3, http://www.imsproject.org (2003)
2. IMS: IMS Simple Sequencing Version 1.0, http://www.imsproject.org (2003)
3. OMG: The Unified Modeling Language v.1.5, http://www.omg.org/uml (2003)
4. W3C: XSL Transformations Version 1.0, http://www.w3.org/TR/xslt (1999)

WING: A Web Probing, Visualization, and Performance Analysis Service

Leszek Borzemski and Ziemowit Nowak

Wroclaw University of Technology
Wybrzeze Wyspianskiego 27
50-370 Wroclaw, Poland
{leszek.borzemski; ziemowit.nowak}@pwr.wroc.pl

Abstract. An open network service Wing has been developed for the purpose of Web probing, visualization and performance analysis from the user perspective. Wing downloads target page to the service location and returns to the user a page showing HTTP timeline chart and both detailed and aggregated information about web page downloading. Contrary to other systems that use their own Web clients developed for particular visualization tools only, Wing supports real-life studies as it uses a real Web browser. Wing employs all features of HTTP/1.1 and can process scripts so we can automate the usage of the service and apply it to the advanced Internet measurements.

1 Introduction

Along with the development of computer networks, network protocol visualization tools have been designed. They are used for better understanding of computer network. Nowadays the most important visualization challenge is HTTP protocol, and especially Web page downloading. Both end-users and site administrators are anxious to get knowledge about the downloading using different browsers. We present Wing, a network service for Web probing, visualization and performance analysis from the user perspective.

2 Web Page Measurement and Visualization

Passive and active measurement techniques can be used for visualization of Web transactions. Most of them are active probing projects that are based on the target Web page measurement employing a special measuring tool. Unfortunately, to the authors' knowledge available such network services use their own Web browsing methods. Using specially developed browsers does not ensure that we get adequate results. Probably the MyKeynote [2] is the most advanced benchmarking service that measures Web site's performance and its availability from a word-wide network of measurement agents. Unfortunately, the MyKenote client uses HTTP/1.0 protocol that is not common in the Internet now. Leading browsers, such as MS Internet Explorer,

N. Koch, P. Fraternali, and M. Wirsing (Eds.): ICWE 2004, LNCS 3140, pp. 601–602, 2004.

use more advanced HTTP/1.1 protocol. Since the browsers download Web pages in different ways giving different results, it appears necessary to develop tools supporting real-life studies.

3 Wing Service

The Wing (Web ping) Internet service has been developed for the purpose of Web probing, visualization and performance analysis from the user perspective. Our service gathers, stores in a database and visualizes data about the real Web browser's activity. Today's implementation is done for MS IE but our service can monitor activity of any browser. It employs all features of HTTP/1.1 and can process scripts so we can automate the usage of the service and apply it to the advanced Internet measurements.

Wing is activated by a remote user request sent to Wing controller targeting URL to be tested. As the service is invoked, the Wing controller calls a local Web client that issues GET request to target URL as well as GET requests for all objects that are embedded in a target page. Wing monitors and time-stamps all browser's activities, determines the end of web page downloading and preprocesses gathered data into the format convenient for further analysis, as well as for visualization. Data is stored in a database server. Wing returns to the remote user a web page visualizing how the target Web page has been loaded locally. The return page shows HTTP timeline chart and both detailed and aggregated information about web page downloading.

Wing supports IP, TCP, UDP, DNS and HTTP protocols, logging a dozen parameters of HTTP transactions and TCP connections, thus facilitating a much deeper analysis. For example, we used it in the research on the estimation of the HTTP throughput and TCP Round-Trip Time (RTT) on Internet link between a Web browser and World-Wide Web server [1]. Wing estimated the RTT based on the measurements of time spacing between the SYN packet sent by the client and the SYN-ACK packet received by the client.

4 Conclusions

Our free network service has the ability to allow visualization of the real-life Web browsers including MS IE and Linux based solutions. It can periodically gather data for further off-line analysis, not only for the ad hoc visualization needs. Thus we can monitor target Web page downloading behavior over demanded period of time.

References

1. Borzemski L., Nowak Z.: Estimation of HTTP throughput and TCP Round-Trip Times, Proceedings of 10th Polish Teletraffic Symposium, IEEE Chapter, Cracow (2003) 335-352
2. http://www.mykeynote.com

Preparing for Service-Oriented Computing: A Composite Design Pattern for Stubless Web Service Invocation

Paul A. Buhler[1], Christopher Starr[1], William H. Schroder[1], and José M. Vidal[2]

[1] College of Charleston, Dept. of Computer Science,
66 George Street, Charleston, SC 29424, USA
{buhlerp, starrc, schroderw}@cofc.edu
[2] University of South Carolina, Computer Science and Engineering
Columbia, SC 29208, USA
vidal@sc.edu

Abstract. The ability to dynamically bind to Web services at runtime is becoming increasingly important as the era of Service-Oriented Computing (SOC) emerges. With SOC selection and invocation of Web service partners will occur in software at run-time, rather than by software developers at design and compile time. Unfortunately, the marketplace has yet to yield a predominate applications programming interface for the invocation of Web services. This results in software that is deeply ingrained with vendor-specific calls, which is problematic because Web service technology is changing at a rapid pace. In order to leverage the latest developments, code often needs to be heavily refactored to account for changing invocation interfaces. This paper explores the mitigation of this problem through the application of software design patterns.

1 Introduction

Web services will be the foundational technology that will underpin future distributed, Internet-based computing systems as the worlds of Service-Oriented Computing (SOC), Multiagent Systems (MAS), and Business Process Management (BPM) converge. Software toolkits, which build on open standards such as HTTP, SOAP, WSDL and UDDI, allow developers to compose web services into robust business applications by harnessing the power standards. Unfortunately, the marketplace has yet to yield a predominate toolkit represented by a standard Applications Programming Interface (API) for dynamic, fully stubless invocation of Web services.

The lack of a standard API results in software that is deeply ingrained with vendor-specific API's. However, because Web service technology is changing at a rapid pace with new tools and techniques frequently becoming available, code often needs to be significantly refactored to account for changing interfaces. To compensate for this problem, we have used software engineering principles and software design patterns to create a composite pattern, which insulates Web service client code from the peculiarities of any specific vendor interface. This framework approach enhances code

N. Koch, P. Fraternali, and M. Wirsing (Eds.): ICWE 2004, LNCS 3140, pp. 603–604, 2004.

stability while providing the flexibility to experiment with various approaches to the dynamic invocation of Web services.

Just as Web services are components intended to be composed, there is a growing realization that design patterns can be composed or aggregated into larger units. As early as 1997, it was shown that composite patterns could possess a set of characteristics that exceeded those of the individual contributing patterns [4]. The notion that patterns and pattern compositions can be used as premier design components for design creation, changes the design approach by introducing larger-grained design components. This approach is used in the Pattern-Oriented Analysis and Design (POAD) technique [5]. The pattern concept has been applied with coarser granularity at the architectural level as architectural patterns [1] and the application domain level as framework patterns [3].

To isolate the application interface from its implementation, a Composite Pattern for Web service Invocation was constructed using a composition of design patterns. To achieve the desired level of flexibility and extensibility for the framework, the overall class structure of the design is provided by the Bridge pattern. The decoupling avoids a permanent binding between an abstraction and its implementation allowing the implementation to be selected or switched at runtime. Additional flexibility can be derived by introducing the Factory Method pattern. The Factory Method is a creational design pattern, which defers the instantiation of a product to subclasses localized external to the client application [2]. The pattern has applicability when the client cannot anticipate the class of objects it needs until runtime.

The composition of the Factory Method and the Bridge provide a combination of design assets which decouples clients from the concrete implementations, enabling the choice of implementation to be made based upon some runtime condition. The resulting composite pattern of the Bridge and Factory Method patterns provides an agile software design for the decoupling of the invocation services that are found and bound at run-time.

References

[1]   Buschmann, F. *Pattern-oriented software architecture : a system of patterns*. Wiley, Chichester ; New York, 1996.

[2]   Gamma, E. *Design patterns : elements of reusable object-oriented software*. Addison-Wesley, Reading, Mass., 1995.

[3]   Johnson, R.E. Documenting frameworks using patterns. In *Proceedings of the Conference on Object-Oriented Programming Systems, Languages, and Applications (OOPSLA)*, ACM Press, 63-70, 1992.

[4]   Riehle, D. Composite Design Patterns. In *Proceedgins of the Conference on Object-Oriented Programming, Systems, Languages, and Applications (OOPSLA)*, ACM Press, 218-228, 1997.

[5]   Yacoub, S.M. and Ammar, H.H. *Pattern oriented analysis and design : composing patterns to design software systems*. Addison-Wesley, Boston, MA, 2004.

An Architectural Model to Promote User Awareness on the Web

Claudio O. Gutiérrez[1], Luis A. Guerrero[2], and César A. Collazos[3]

[1]Departament of Computer, Universidad de Magallanes, Avenida Bulnes 01855
Punta Arenas, Chile
cjoelg@ona.fi.umag.cl
[2]Departament of Computer Science, Universidad de Chile, Blanco Encalada 2120
Santiago, Chile
luguerre@dcc.uchile.cl
[3]Departament of Compute Science, Universidad del Cauca, Campus Tulcan
Popayan, Colombia
ccollazo@unicauca.edu.co

Abstract. Every day more people use the Web as a tool to collaborate and to do work group. Nevertheless, as collaborative tool, the Web does not have one of the most important features of this kind of tools: a user awareness system. User awareness gives the possibility to receive feedback about people that could be interested in the same concern and give the possibility to share knowledge about the sources or Web pages that they consider relevant.

1 Introduction

The main focus of this paper is to propose a new architectural model on the Web to promote user awareness. The primary goal of this model is to offer the necessary mechanisms to the final users of the Web in order to give them the possibility of establish communication and collaboration with their couples. Similar situations happen in some virtual environments (see for example [1]). These awareness mechanisms are based on the delivery of historical information of those who have visited the same Web sites. The information provided by the system contains data surrendered by people that visited these places. These data assure the possibility to establish further communication with people that already visited those places. This information is compound basically for data such as name, e-mail, comments and interests, to mention the most relevant. Our architecture is implemented in Java and one of the main advantages is that we do not alter the current operation of the Web.

Most of the technology used to present information tipically focus on the use of direct audio and video connection as an aid to collaboration among remotely located people. The technologies to promote the use of the audio and the video generally require of high-speed dedicated connections. However most of the people that have used the Web have different connection types, with different access speeds and where in general the connections are not stable. The collaboration that takes place is basically asynchronous and the people have a few opportunities to meet with another. Moreover the browsers are mainly tools focused to lend services to a single user,

N. Koch, P. Fraternali, and M. Wirsing (Eds.): ICWE 2004, LNCS 3140, pp. 605–606, 2004.
© Springer-Verlag Berlin Heidelberg 2004

which even increases the invisibility of them. On the other hand, we could notice the Web as a big share workspace where a lot of people is dedicated to reading activities where shared objects are in the same site. In these context the activities of other people could be an important factor respect to the interest that causes a site or a specific Web page. In other words, we are giving importance to one of the entities most important of the Web: the final users. The model we propose provides a kind of awareness where the final users receives feedback about people that are interested in the same topic.

2   Architecture of the Proposed Model for User Awareness

Our main objective is to provide Web users with awareness about other users. The interaction among our model components is over TCP/IP communication protocol.

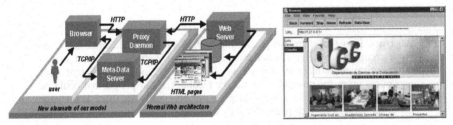

Fig. 1. (a) The Model Architecture;   (b) The Browser Interface

Figure 1a shows our model design, which maintains the components and the current operation of the Web architecture. However our proposal points to extend this architecture, adding components that provide user's awarenes in the Web. The advantage of this schema is that the model does not modify the components neither the operation of the conventional architecture of the Web. The figure 1b depicts our sample browser. This one is composed of three main panels: the left hand side shows the names of people that are already registered in the system and had visited this page recently. The right side shows the current Web page the user is browsing, and on the top level there is a normal toolbar that support standard functions of the conventional Web browsers.

Reference

[1] Shapiro, E. Virtual Places - A Foundation for Human Interaction. Proceedings of WWW2, the 2nd International World Wide Web Conference, Chicago, IL. May 1994.

UML Profile for OWL

Dragan Djurić, Dragan Gašević, Vladan Devedžić, and Violeta Damjanović

FON – School of Business Administration, University of Belgrade, POB 52, Jove Ilića 154,
11000 Belgrade, Serbia and Montenegro
dragandj@mail.ru, gasevic@yahoo.com,
devedzic@galeb.etf.bg.ac.yu, vdamjanovic@posted.co.yu
http://goodoldai.org.yu

Abstract. The paper presents Ontology UML Profile (OUP) that is based on
OWL and a metamodel – Ontology Definition Metamodel. OUP is defined in
the context of the MDA four-layer architecture and current the OMG's effort
for ontology development. The proposed UML profile enables usage of the
well-known UML notation in ontology development more extensively.

1 Ontology UML Profile: An Overview

The Semantic Web and its XML-based languages are the main directions of the future
Web development. Domain ontologies are the most important part of the Semantic
Web applications. In order to overcome the gap between software engineering
practitioners and AI techniques, there are a few proposals for UML usage in ontology
development [1]. But, UML itself does not satisfy needs for representation of
ontology concepts that are borrowed from description logics, and that are included in
Semantic Web ontology languages (e.g. RDF, RDF Schema, OWL, etc.). The OMG's
Model Driven Architecture (MDA) concept has the ability to create (using
metamodeling) a family of languages that are defined in the similar way like the UML
is. Currently, there is a RFP (Request for Proposal) within OMG that tries to define a
suitable language for modeling Semantic Web ontology languages in the context of
MDA [2. According to this RFP we give our proposal of such architecture, which
consists of: Ontology Definition Metamodel (ODM) and Ontology UML Profile
(OUP) [3]. ODM is a metamodel defined using Meta-Object Facility (MOF), and is
based on the Web Ontology Language (OWL).

OUP enables graphical editing of ontologies using UML diagrams as well as other
benefits of using mature UML CASE tools. OUP is based on the basic UML
constructs (model elements) that are customized and extended with new semantics by
using four *UML extension mechanisms* defined in the UML Specification:
stereotypes, tag definitions, tagged values, and constraints. *Stereotypes* enable
defining virtual subclasses of UML metaclasses, assigning them additional semantics.
OUP support the following OWL concepts: classes, individuals, properties, and
statements. Since OUP supports ontology statements we can model ontology
instances using OUP. We shortly illustrate the OUP's class concept. Class is one of
the most fundamental concepts in ODM and Ontology UML Profile. In ODM,
Ontology Class has several concrete species, according to the class description:

N. Koch, P. Fraternali, and M. Wirsing (Eds.): ICWE 2004, LNCS 3140, pp. 607–608, 2004.

Class, Enumeration, Union, Intersection, Complement, Restriction and AllDifferent. These constructs in the Ontology UML Profile are all inherited from the UML concept that is most similar to them, UML Class. But, we must explicitly specify that they are not the same as UML Class, which we can do using UML stereotypes. An example of Classes modeled in Ontology UML Profile is shown in Figure 1. We implemented the XSLT that transforms the OUP ontologies into OWL [4]. We tested this solution on the well-known Wine ontology. We used OUP to develop two ontologies: the Petri net ontology and the ontology of philosophers and saints.

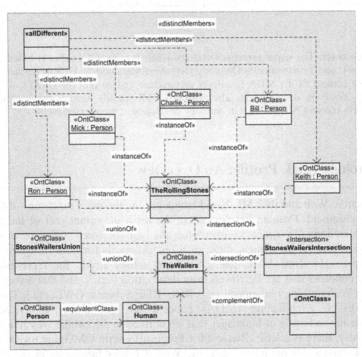

Fig. 1. Class Diagram showing relations between Ontology Classes and Individuals in the Ontology UML Profile

References

1. Cranefield, S.: Networked Knowledge Representation and Exchange using UML and RDF, Journal of Digital information, Vol. 1, No.8, http://jodi.ecs.soton.ac.uk (2001)
2. Ontology Definition Metamodel Request for Proposal, OMG Document: ad/2003-03-40, http://www.omg.org/cgi-bin/doc?ad/2003-03-40 (2003)
3. Djurić, D. et al: Ontology Modeling and MDA, Journal on Object Technology, Vol. 4, No. 1 (2005) forthcoming
4. Gašević, D. et al: Converting UML to OWL ontologies, In Proceedings of the 13th International World Wide Web Conference, NY, USA (2004) forthcoming

Building and Operating an E-business Platform – Technical Challenges and Other Pitfalls

Peter Zoller

BMW AG
Sapporobogen 6-8
80788 München
peter.zoller@bmw.de

Abstract. This short paper describes the challenges faced and experiences gathered during build-up and first year of operation of the BMW Group b2b-platform. It is divided into three sections: first a brief outline on the project and the main difficulties during system implementation is given. Afterwards challenges and experiences concerning operation of the platform are presented. The paper ends with conclusions.

1 Project Details and Difficulties During Implementation

In December 2000 the BMW management board decided to implement an e-business-platform in order to meet the future challenges of electronic business. After evaluating tools and products for the central services and components, in June 2002 the build-up of the b2b-platform started.

The core components of the platform are a portal frontend providing role-based navigation, an authentication and authorization service (EAM, **E**nterprise **A**ccess **M**anagement), an LDAP-based user and role store (LAAS) and a web based interface for delegated user management. The designated user group comprised about 8000 partner users from roughly 2000 companies, mainly located in Europe. The rollout of the B2B-Portal was planned for the beginning of 2003.

Although using a standard web architecture and limiting both portal functionality and supported client systems in order to minimize technical risks, several technical challenges had to be faced:

- The EAM had an LDAP interface and could smoothly be integrated with LAAS, but performance of the whole system was bad in the beginning because of different optimization strategies of the two components.
- The configuration of the web servers containing the EAM plugin proved to be error-prone and extremely sensitive against changes of the server configuration (even against changes in the operating system)

2 System Operation – Good Performance and High Availability Are Not Enough

Since June 2003 the BMW b2b-platform (partner portal) is available under https://b2b.bmw.com. On workdays we currently have about 2000 user sessions (logins), the average login in the central components takes about 350 ms and building

N. Koch, P. Fraternali, and M. Wirsing (Eds.): ICWE 2004, LNCS 3140, pp. 609–610, 2004.

up the personalized portal page takes about 2-3 seconds for the initial access. Availability within the first 6 months has exceeded 99.8%, the system runs very stable. Meanwhile about 12.000 external and more than 17.000 internal users have access to the b2b-platform.

Nevertheless we have been confronted with some serious problems:

- Browser problems: even though we have restricted the set of supported browsers and avoided the use of applets and Java script as far as possible, browser problems caused the majority of helpdesk calls. The reasons were either real browser bugs, misconfigurations on client side (JDK, cookies, caching) or seldom html/java script coding errors in the applications.
- Time-consuming and expensive user support: end user error reports are often unexact ("portal doesn't work", "portal is slow") and do not distinguish between browser, internet-connection, portal and applications. Since the platform is a rather complex system and one important component (the user's browser) is not within our reach, support and debugging is very difficult and time consuming.
- Integrating applications into a central platform is a complex process. A variety of departments is involved and since the number of applications grew rapidly (currently more than 35 have already been integrated), additional resources and improved integration-processes were needed.
- Configuration management is very costly: a valid system configuration consists of numerous configuration files and database/LDAP entries. Migrating a new configuration (e.g. after integrating a new application) from test environment to integration environment and afterwards to production environment requires a lot of manual configuration since many commercial products don't support configuration propagation out of the box. Some vendors even don't offer any interfaces at all. Some technical features of the platform are not used because efficient maintenance would not be possible.

3 Conclusions

The launch of the new BMW partner portal in June 2003 has been very successful, especially considering the tight time schedule of the project. The key to success was the use of standards and the strong restriction of functionality that was implemented. Although availability and performance of the system are very good, operating the platform provided the major challenges of this project:

- End user support is costly especially if the audience is as heterogeneous as typically in b2b-platforms. The reasons are technically insufficient error reports on the one hand and an infrastructure that is very complex to debug on the other hand.
- Configuration Management of complex infrastructures is not supported sufficiently by tools and standards.
- Developing efficient processes for the technical integration of applications into the platform considering organizational structures is an essential task.
- The use of standards usually guarantees a general technical compatibility of components but leaves enough room for individual usage and optimization strategies. This might result in an absolutely unacceptable performance of the platform, although the standard is obeyed and the interfaces are optimized by each component.

Model-Driven Web Development with VisualWADE[1]

Jaime Gómez

Web Engineering Group. DLSI. Universidad de Alicante 03690 Alicante SPAIN
jgomez@dlsi.ua.es

Abstract. VisualWADE[2] is a model-driven web development environment for web applications that includes model-based code generation techniques. This paper describes the capabilities of that environment and how Web applications can be generated in an automated way.

1 Description

The focus of this work is the presentation of the tool VisualWADE, a CASE (Computer-Aided Software Engineering) tool to develop Web applications. VisualWADE provides an operational environment that supports the methodological aspects of the OO-H Web design method [1]. The goal of this tool is to simplify the design and implementation of Web-based information [4][5]. This is addressed from an object-oriented perspective by means of enhanced conceptual models. With VisualWADE, a Web application is modeled by three major design dimensions; Structure describes the organization of the information managed by the application in terms of the pieces of content that constitute its information domain and their semantic relationships. Navigation is concerned with the facilities for accessing information ands for moving across the application content. Finally, Presentation affects the way in which the application content and navigation commands are presented to the user.

At conceptual level, applications are described by means of high level primitives which specify the structural, navigational and presentational views making an abstraction from any implementation issue. Those primitives are expressed with the UML [3] notation. Structural modeling primitives describe the types of objects that constitute the information domain and their semantic relationships. An standard UML class diagram is used to model that structural view. Derivations can also be expressed in that structural modeling to enrich the system specification. VisualWADE provides an extended OCL-like language [2] to specify formulas for derived attributes. This language can be viewed as an action language [3] for Web applications and provides a powerful mechanism to support code-generation capabilities in the environment.

Navigation modeling primitives express the access paths to objects of the information domain and the available inter- and intra-object navigation facilities, again without committing to any specific technique for implementing access and navigation. The designer specifies a navigation view of the system by means of a UML profile. This profile has been defined on the top of the main navigation primitives provided

---

[1] This paper has been partially supported by the Spain Ministry of Science and Technology, project number TIC2001-3530-C02-02.

[2] VisualWADE can be reached at http://www.visualwade.com

N. Koch, P. Fraternali, and M. Wirsing (Eds.): ICWE 2004, LNCS 3140, pp. 611–612, 2004.

by the OO-H method and following the UML 2.0 specification (these primitives are `collections, navigational classes, navigational targets` and a taxonomy of `links`). The OCL-like language is also used in navigation models to specify preconditions (navigation constraints in origin) and filters (navigation constraints in destination). A set of well-known visualization patterns can be applied over navigational models to refine the way the user navigates through the system. Some of them are `indexes, guided tour, indexed guided tour` and `show all`. The designer can also specify the activation of services in the navigation modeling. These services are a set of predefined methods provided by the environment. They correspond to the classical CRUD operations used in the development of data-intensive applications. Other works in this area like WebRatio [4] have shown how a wide variety of Web applications can be modeled with this set of predefined operations.

Presentation modeling aims at representing the visual elements of the application interfaces in a way that abstracts from the particular language and device used in the delivery. In VisualWADE, starting from a navigation model, a default presentation that fullfills that specified navigation can be obtained applying model transformation rules. As a result a set of abstract pages (expressed in XML) are generated. The independent specification of presentation, separate from structure and navigation, is particularly relevant in Web context, because the final rendering of the interface depends on the browser and display device and thus there may be the necessity to map the same abstract presentation scheme to different designs and implementations. This is the reason why the VisualWADE presentation model includes web-enabled hypermedia authoring capabilities. In fact, this model can be viewed as a kind of authoring tool (i.e. Frontpage or Dreamweaver) were the designer renders the final look and feel of the application using WYSIWYG techniques. Also, animation (prototyping) capabilities are provided in that model. In this way, the designer can navigate through the links and abstract pages generated to test the navigation model. When a presentation model has been refined a model compiler generates the final target in the desired implementation environment. Three deliverables are generated. These are the dynamic pages that constitute the Web user interface, the middleware navigation pages that constitute the navigation engine and the database script. Currently, we provide well-tested model compilers for php/mySQL, php/Oracle, php/SQLserver technologies.

References

1. J. Gómez, C. Cachero. OO-H method: Extending UML to Model Web Interfaces. Information Modeling for Internet Applications. Pages. 50-72. Idea Group. 2002.
2. J. Warmer, A. Kleppe. The Object Constraint Language: Getting Your Models Ready for MDA. Addison-Wesley, 2003.
3. S. Mellor, M. Balcer. Executable UML: a Foundation for Model-Driven Architecture. Addison-Wesley, 2003.
4. WebRatio. http://www.webratio.com/
5. A. Knapp, N. Koch, F. Moser and G. Zhang. ArgoUWE: A CASE Tool for Web Applications. In EMSISE03 held in conjunction with OOIS03, 14 pages, September 2003

WebRatio, an Innovative Technology for Web Application Development

Roberto Acerbis[1], Aldo Bongio[1], Stefano Butti[1], Stefano Ceri[2],
Fulvio Ciapessoni[1], Carlo Conserva[1], Piero Fraternali[2], and
Giovanni Toffetti Carughi[2]

[1] Dipartimento di Elettronica, Politecnico di Milano,
P.za L. Da Vinci 32, 20123 Milano, Italy
[2] WebRatio, P.le Gerbetto 6, 22100 Como, Italy

1   Introduction

WebRatio [5] is a software tool representative of a particular approach to the development of Web applications, called the "model-driven approach". It claims that more and more efforts should be spent on the application modeling, and reusable implementations should be automatically or semi-automatically produced from high-level models.

The distinguishing feature of WebRatio is the adoption of formal graphical languages for the specification of data intensive Web applications, and the semi-automatic generation of code from such specifications. Web applications are specified using the Entity-Relationship (ER) model for data requirements, and the Web Modelling Language (WebML) [2,4] for the functional requirements.

The supported ER model is quite conventional, with a few limitations that make the ER schema easier to map onto a standard relational schema; this standard schema is then used by the WebRatio implementation as either the schema of a newly designed database supporting the Web application, or as a reference for mapping to pre-existing data sources.

WebML is a visual language for expressing the hypertextual front-end of a data-intensive Web application, i.e., the interfaces presented to the users for content browsing and management. WebML includes primitives for modelling such aspects as:

1. The structuring of the application into different hypertexts (called site views) targeted to different user groups or access devices.
2. The hierarchical organization of a site view into areas.
3. The pages that constitute the actual application interface, the content units contained in each page, with their relationship to the elements of the data model (entities and relationship).
4. The operations and services that can be activated from the application pages.
5. The links that connect pages, content units, and operations to provide users with suitable interactions on the browsers (e.g., anchors, radio buttons, forms for data entry).
6. Session-level information and personalization aspects.

N. Koch, P. Fraternali, and M. Wirsing (Eds.): ICWE 2004, LNCS 3140, pp. 613–614, 2004.
© Springer-Verlag Berlin Heidelberg 2004

2   The WebRatio Editing Tool

The WebRatio editing tool focuses on five main aspects:

1. Data design: supports the design of the ER data schemas, with a graphical user interface for drawing and specifying the properties of entities, relationships, attributes, and generalization hierarchies.
2. Hypertext design: assists the design of site views, providing functions for drawing and specifying the properties of areas, pages, units, and links.
3. Data Mapping: permits declaring the set of data sources to which the conceptual data schema has to be mapped, and automatically translates ER diagrams and OCL expressions into relational databases and views.
4. Presentation design: offers functionality for defining the presentation style of the application, allowing the designer to create XSL style sheets and associate them with pages, and organize page layout, by arranging the relative position of content units in the page.
5. Code generation: automatically translates site views into running Web applications built on top of the J2EE, Struts, and .NET platforms.

WebRatio internally uses XML and XSL as the formats for encoding both the specifications and the code generators: XML is used for describing data and hypertext schemas, whereas XSL is used for generating the graphic properties and layout of the page templates, for validity checking, and for automatic project documentation. The extensive use of XML and XSL facilitates custom extensions, which apply both to the WebML language, which can be extended with user-defined units and operations, and to the tool functions, which can be enriched with custom consistency checkers, documentation and code generators, and presentation rules.

3   Related Work

The development of Web sites with a model-driven approach has been addressed by two important research projects, namely Araneus [1] and Strudel [3].

References

1. Atzeni, P., Masci, A., Mecca, G., Merialdo, P., Sindoni, G.: The Araneus Web-Base Management System. Proc. Int. Conf. ACM-SIGMOD 1998, Seattle USA (June 1998) 544–546
2. Ceri, S., Fraternali, P., Matera, M.: Conceptual modeling of data-intensive Web applications. IEEE-Internet Computing 6(4) (July-August 2002) 20–30
3. Fernandez, M. F., Florescu, D., Kang, J., Levy, A. Y., Suciu D.: Overvew of Strudel - A Web-Site Management System. Networking and Information Systems 1(1) (1998), 115–140
4. WebML Web Site: http://www.webml.org
5. WebRatio Site Development Studio: http://www.webratio.com

Modeling the Structure of Web Applications
with ArgoUWE

Alexander Knapp, Nora Koch, and Gefei Zhang

Ludwig-Maximilians-Universität München
{knapp,kochn,zhangg}@pst.ifi.lmu.de

Abstract. The UWE methodology provides a systematic, UML-based approach for the development of Web applications. The CASE tool ArgoUWE supports the design phase of the UWE development process. It is implemented as a plugin module of the open source ArgoUML modeling tool. The construction process of Web applications is supported by incorporating the semi-automatic UWE development steps as well as the OCL well-formedness rules of the UWE metamodel.

The increasing complexity of Web applications requires mainly process and tool support. Such support is offered by the UWE ("UML-based Web Engineering" [3]) method and the ArgoUWE [2] CASE tool[1]. The main features of ArgoUWE are the support of visual modeling, UML compliance, and open source characteristic. The design of a Web application is performed according to the UML-based notations and the steps defined by the UWE method.

UWE is an UML-based, object-oriented, iterative, and incremental approach for the development of Web applications. In a single iteration, a use case model, a conceptual model, a navigational model, and a presentation model are built or refined. The use case model reflects the requirements on the Web application and the conceptual model comprises the entities the Web applications is based on. The navigational model builds on the conceptual model, presenting the navigation structure of the Web application between the different entities and offering means for accessing the entities through querying, menu selection, etc. The presentation model refines the navigational model by adding the layout. The presentation model complements the navigation model by giving the layout view. All these models of a Web application are supported by convenient UWE notations that are built on UML notations. The UWE process defines the development steps for building Web applications and, in particular, includes semi-automatic tasks for generating the navigational model from the conceptual model and the presentation model from the navigational model.

ArgoUWE supports the structural modeling tasks of UWE. On the one hand it offers tailored editors for the UWE notations used for conceptual, navigational, and presentation modeling of Web applications. On the other hand, ArgoUWE provides several semi-automatic model transformations that occur in the UWE process. As these model transformations are UWE-metamodel-based, both consistency between the different models and integrity of the overall Web application model with respect to UWE's OCL constraints are ensured by the tool. In particular, in a conceptual model classes can

---

[1] http://www.pst.ifi.lmu.de/projekte/argouwe

N. Koch, P. Fraternali, and M. Wirsing (Eds.): ICWE 2004, LNCS 3140, pp. 615–616, 2004.
© Springer-Verlag Berlin Heidelberg 2004

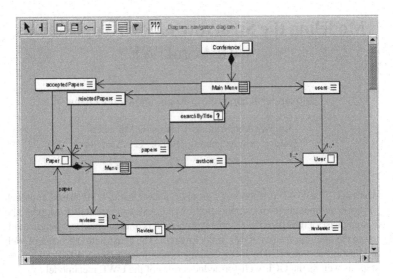

be marked for navigation and the annotated conceptual model can be turned into a navigational model by creating navigation classes and associations for marked conceptual classes. In the navigational model, ArgoUWE can add automatically access primitives, like queries and menus, between navigation classes that refine the navigational structure (see figure above). Finally, ArgoUWE can infer a presentation model from a navigation model automatically. Consistency of models is not enforced during modeling, but can be triggered any time by the user thus supporting and not constraining the developer in creating models. For a comparison with other tools we refer to [2].

ArgoUWE is implemented as a plugin into the open-source UML modeling tool ArgoUML [1]. ArgoUWE reuses the UML-metamodel-based modeling techniques of ArgoUML. The support of ArgoUML for UML's standard model interchange format XMI is put to use by an extension of XMI by the Web modeling profile of UWE. ArgoUML being an open-source tool with an active developer community, plugin developers have to face rapid version changes and a sometimes poor documentation. However, the interest of availability and the possibility to adapt ArgoUWE, which again is open-source, to user-specific needs outweigh these disadvantages.

ArgoUWE is part of the OpenUWE tool environment for model-driven generation of Web applications. ArgoUWE is used in design whereas UWEXML is employed for semi-automatic generation of Web applications from the design model.

References

1. http://www.argouml.org.
2. A. Knapp, N. Koch, F. Moser, and G. Zhang. ArgoUWE: A CASE Tool for Web Applications. In *Proc. 1st Int. Wsh. Engineering Methods to Support Information Systems Evolution (EMSISE'03)*, Genève, 2003. 14 pages.
3. N. Koch and A. Kraus. The Expressive Power of UML-based Web Engineering. In D. Schwabe, O. Pastor, G. Rossi, and L. Olsina, editors, *Proc. 2nd Int. Wsh. Web-Oriented Software Technology (IWWOST'02)*. CYTED, 2002.

WELKIN: Automatic Generation of Adaptive Hypermedia Sites with NLP Techniques[*]

Enrique Alfonseca, Diana Pérez, and Pilar Rodríguez

Computer Science Department, Universidad Autonoma de Madrid,
Carretera de Colmenar Viejo, km. 14,5,
28043 Madrid, Spain
{Enrique.Alfonseca, Diana.Perez, Pilar.Rodriguez}@ii.uam.es
http://www.ii.uam.es/~ealfon

Abstract. The demonstration shows the system WELKIN, a multilingual system that analyses one or several source texts with a cascade of linguistic-processing modules, including syntactic analyses, text identification and text classification techniques, in order to fill in a database of information about it. That information is later used to generate on-the-fly adaptive on-line information sites according to some user profiles.

1 Introduction

WELKIN[1] is an on-going project which started three years ago, whose aim is to build automatically adaptive on-line hypermedia sites from electronic texts using Natural Language Processing techniques [1,2]. It differs from previous approaches in that the knowledge base is generated automatically from source texts. Figure 1 shows the architecture of the system, which is divided into two steps: an off-line processing in which the texts are analysed and several internal databases are created, and an on-line processing step, in which the web pages are generated, when users access the system, in an adaptive way.

2 Offline Processing Step

During the **off-line** processing, the domain-specific texts provided by the user are analysed with some modules, which can be configured by the user. Currently, the following modules are available:

- Linguistic processing tools: tokenisation, sentence splitting, stemming, chunking, and a shallow dependency parser.
- Term extraction: the unknown domain-specific terms that have a high frequency of appearance in the documents are automatically considered relevant terms and collected.

---

[*] This work has been sponsored by CICYT, project number TIC2001-0685-C02-01.
[1] http://agamenon.ii.uam.es/welkin/

N. Koch, P. Fraternali, and M. Wirsing (Eds.): ICWE 2004, LNCS 3140, pp. 617–618, 2004.

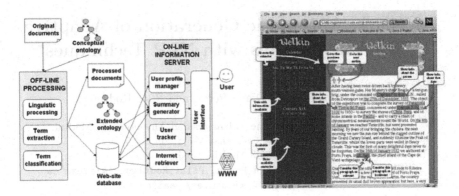

Fig. 1. *Left:* High-level architecture of WELKIN. *Right:* Screenshot.

- Special terminology identification: there are modules which are specialist for identifying dates and scientific names inside the texts.
- Finally, a module that classifies the unknown terms, automatically, inside a semantic network, so some meaning can be inferred from their position.

The cited modules are currently available for English and Spanish, so texts in both languages can be processed. The output of this step, apart from annotating the texts with the output of the modules, is also to build a database with all the information that could be extracted. This step is fully automatised, so the whole web site can be generated just by executing a script that indicates which modules to use.

3   Online Processing Step

After a brief description and show of the off-line step, the demonstration will centre on the on-line step, which involves the ways in which users can interact with the system. This includes the creation of their initial profiles, and the manners in which WELKIN adapts the contents according to them. The possibilities for adaptation include:

- An automatic summarisation of the generated pages, depending on the user's reading speed and available time.
- A selection of the contents inside each page, according to a profile of interests.
- An additional tool to guide a search on Internet for terms from the web site.

References

1. Alfonseca, E.: An Approach for Automatic Generation of Adaptive Hypermedia using Knowledge Discovery, Text Summarisation and other Natural Language Processing Techniques. Ph.D. thesis, Universidad Autónoma de Madrid (2003)
2. Alfonseca, E., Rodríguez, P.: Modelling users' interests and needs for an adaptive on-line information system. Volume 2702 of Lecture Notes in A.I. (2003) 76–80

Authoring and Dynamic Generation of Adaptive E-courses

Rosa M. Carro[1], Manuel Freire[1], Estefanía Martín[1], Alvaro Ortigosa[1],
Pedro Paredes[1], Pilar Rodríguez[1], and Johann Schlichter[2]

[1] Escuela Politécnica Superior, Universidad Autónoma de Madrid
28049 Madrid, Spain
{Rosa.Carro, Manuel.Freire, Estefania.Martin, Alvaro.Ortigosa,
Pedro.Paredes, Pilar.Rodriguez}@ii.uam.es
[2] Institute for Informatics, Technical University of Munich
85748 Munich, Germany
Schlichter@in.tum.de

Abstract. Adaptive hypermedia constitutes a pretty rich resource for developing web-based courses. With the aim of dynamically generating adaptive e-courses, we have developed the TANGOW system which, starting from the course components and their adaptation capabilities (specified independently and out of the adaptation engine), generates different courses for students with different profiles, supporting several adaptation strategies. An integral part of any adaptive hypermedia system is the set of authoring tools to specify the course components and their adaptation capabilities. Without adequate tool support, authors may feel that it is "not worth the effort" to add adaptation to their courses. However, the development of this type of tools is not an easy task. The main goal of our authoring and visualization tools is to provide a simple interface to create such courses. This demo would demonstrate i) the dynamic generation of tailored e-courses that include individual and collaborative activities and ii) the use of authoring tools for the creation of such courses.

1 The Delivery System

The current version of TANGOW [1][4] supports the adaptation, for each student, of:

- The presence/absence of topics and activities.
- The organization of topics, which leads to the course structure.
- The navigational guidance provided, which can be different through the course.
- The requirements to access a topic or to start accomplishing an activity, which can be different for different types of students.
- The multimedia contents used to generate the pages presented to the students. The most suitable version can be selected for each student at runtime.
- The collaboration workspaces to support collaboration activities among users, including the specific problem to be proposed to each group and the set of tools to support the collaboration, which can be chosen depending on the users' preferences and learning styles, among other criteria.

N. Koch, P. Fraternali, and M. Wirsing (Eds.): ICWE 2004, LNCS 3140, pp. 619–620, 2004.

Concerning the users' aspects taken into account during the adaptation process, the system can use any information considered as relevant by the course designer, who can specify it at the beginning of the course creation. Some aspects considered are:

- Personal features, such as age and language.
- Learning style: visual/textual, sequential/global, sensitive/intuitive, etc [3].
- Preferences: type of information desired (specific/general) or strategy (theory-examples-exercises, exercises-examples-theory), among others.
- Actions performed and scores got during the interaction with the course.

The way courses are generated at runtime according to the user profile and to the adaptation possibilities of each course[4] will be shown in the demonstration.

2 The Authoring Tools

In order to support the specification of the adaptation possibilities of a TANGOW-based course, we created a formalism based on the use of teaching tasks and teaching rules, which has been recently extended to support adaptation of collaboration activities [1]. We have developed authoring tools to help the course designers to specify each course and its adaptation possibilities [4].

Course builder tool. It covers the entire authoring process, including course design, creation and edition of course components (rules, tasks and hypermedia fragments) and the adaptation capabilities. It supports the simulation of the course for different student profiles, and course overview generation.

Graph-based course builder tool. It supports the generation and exploration of high-level course overviews. Courses are graph-based represented and can be visualized in different ways by using filtering and clustering utilities. This tool also allows the edition of the course components [2].

Cooperative workspace tool. It will facilitate the definition of the adaptive cooperative workspaces included in the latest version of the system.

References

1. Carro, R.M., Ortigosa, A., Martín, E., Schlichter, J.: Dynamic Generation of Adaptive Web-based Collaborative Courses. In: Decouchant, D. and Favela, J. (eds.): Groupware: Design, Implementation and Use. LNCS 2806. Springer-Verlag Berlin Heidelberg (2003) 191-198
2. Freire, M., Rodriguez, P.: A graph-based interface to complex hypermedia structure visualization. In: Proceedings of Advanced Visual Interfaces 2004. ACM-Press (2004) In Press
3. Paredes, P., Rodriguez, P.: Considering Sensing-Intuitive Dimension to Exposition-Exemplification in Adaptive Sequencing. In: De Bra, P., Brusilovsky, P. and Conejo, R. (eds.): Adaptive Hypermedia and Adaptive Web-Based Systems. LNCS 2347. Springer-Verlag, Berlin Heidelberg (2002) 556-559
4. TANGOW and related tools: http://tangow.ii.uam.es/opah

Author Index

Lecture Notes in Computer Science

For information about Vols. 1–3035

please contact your bookseller or Springer-Verlag

Vol. 3080: J. Desel, B. Pernici, M. Weske (Eds.), Business Process Management. X, 307 pages. 2004.

Vol. 3079: Z. Mammeri, P. Lorenz (Eds.), High Speed Networks and Multimedia Communications. XVIII, 1103 pages. 2004.

Vol. 3078: S. Cotin, D.N. Metaxas (Eds.), Medical Simulation. XVI, 296 pages. 2004.

Vol. 3077: F. Roli, J. Kittler, T. Windeatt (Eds.), Multiple Classifier Systems. XII, 386 pages. 2004.

Vol. 3076: D. Buell (Ed.), Algorithmic Number Theory. XI, 451 pages. 2004.

Vol. 3074: B. Kuijpers, P. Revesz (Eds.), Constraint Databases and Applications. XII, 181 pages. 2004.

Vol. 3073: H. Chen, R. Moore, D.D. Zeng, J. Leavitt (Eds.), Intelligence and Security Informatics. XV, 536 pages. 2004.

Vol. 3072: D. Zhang, A.K. Jain (Eds.), Biometric Authentication. XVII, 800 pages. 2004.

Vol. 3071: A. Omicini, P. Petta, J. Pitt (Eds.), Engineering Societies in the Agents World. XIII, 409 pages. 2004. (Subseries LNAI).

Vol. 3070: L. Rutkowski, J. Siekmann, R. Tadeusiewicz, L.A. Zadeh (Eds.), Artificial Intelligence and Soft Computing - ICAISC 2004. XXV, 1208 pages. 2004. (Subseries LNAI).

Vol. 3068: E. André, L. Dybkjær, W. Minker, P. Heisterkamp (Eds.), Affective Dialogue Systems. XII, 324 pages. 2004. (Subseries LNAI).

Vol. 3067: M. Dastani, J. Dix, A. El Fallah-Seghrouchni (Eds.), Programming Multi-Agent Systems. X, 221 pages. 2004. (Subseries LNAI).

Vol. 3066: S. Tsumoto, R. Słowiński, J. Komorowski, J.W. Grzymala-Busse (Eds.), Rough Sets and Current Trends in Computing. XX, 853 pages. 2004. (Subseries LNAI).

Vol. 3065: A. Lomuscio, D. Nute (Eds.), Deontic Logic in Computer Science. X, 275 pages. 2004. (Subseries LNAI).

Vol. 3064: D. Bienstock, G. Nemhauser (Eds.), Integer Programming and Combinatorial Optimization. XI, 445 pages. 2004.

Vol. 3063: A. Llamosí, A. Strohmeier (Eds.), Reliable Software Technologies - Ada-Europe 2004. XIII, 333 pages. 2004.

Vol. 3062: J.L. Pfaltz, M. Nagl, B. Böhlen (Eds.), Applications of Graph Transformations with Industrial Relevance. XV, 500 pages. 2004.

Vol. 3061: F.F. Ramos, H. Unger, V. Larios (Eds.), Advanced Distributed Systems. VIII, 285 pages. 2004.

Vol. 3060: A.Y. Tawfik, S.D. Goodwin (Eds.), Advances in Artificial Intelligence. XIII, 582 pages. 2004. (Subseries LNAI).

Vol. 3059: C.C. Ribeiro, S.L. Martins (Eds.), Experimental and Efficient Algorithms. X, 586 pages. 2004.

Vol. 3058: N. Sebe, M.S. Lew, T.S. Huang (Eds.), Computer Vision in Human-Computer Interaction. X, 233 pages. 2004.

Vol. 3057: B. Jayaraman (Ed.), Practical Aspects of Declarative Languages. VIII, 255 pages. 2004.

Vol. 3056: H. Dai, R. Srikant, C. Zhang (Eds.), Advances in Knowledge Discovery and Data Mining. XIX, 713 pages. 2004. (Subseries LNAI).

Vol. 3055: H. Christiansen, M.-S. Hacid, T. Andreasen, H.L. Larsen (Eds.), Flexible Query Answering Systems. X, 500 pages. 2004. (Subseries LNAI).

Vol. 3054: I. Crnkovic, J.A. Stafford, H.W. Schmidt, K. Wallnau (Eds.), Component-Based Software Engineering. XI, 311 pages. 2004.

Vol. 3053: C. Bussler, J. Davies, D. Fensel, R. Studer (Eds.), The Semantic Web: Research and Applications. XIII, 490 pages. 2004.

Vol. 3052: W. Zimmermann, B. Thalheim (Eds.), Abstract State Machines 2004. Advances in Theory and Practice. XII, 235 pages. 2004.

Vol. 3051: R. Berghammer, B. Möller, G. Struth (Eds.), Relational and Kleene-Algebraic Methods in Computer Science. X, 279 pages. 2004.

Vol. 3050: J. Domingo-Ferrer, V. Torra (Eds.), Privacy in Statistical Databases. IX, 367 pages. 2004.

Vol. 3049: M. Bruynooghe, K.-K. Lau (Eds.), Program Development in Computational Logic. VIII, 539 pages. 2004.

Vol. 3047: F. Oquendo, B. Warboys, R. Morrison (Eds.), Software Architecture. X, 279 pages. 2004.

Vol. 3046: A. Laganà, M.L. Gavrilova, V. Kumar, Y. Mun, C.K. Tan, O. Gervasi (Eds.), Computational Science and Its Applications – ICCSA 2004. LIII, 1016 pages. 2004.

Vol. 3045: A. Laganà, M.L. Gavrilova, V. Kumar, Y. Mun, C.K. Tan, O. Gervasi (Eds.), Computational Science and Its Applications – ICCSA 2004. LIII, 1040 pages. 2004.

Vol. 3044: A. Laganà, M.L. Gavrilova, V. Kumar, Y. Mun, C.K. Tan, O. Gervasi (Eds.), Computational Science and Its Applications – ICCSA 2004. LIII, 1140 pages. 2004.

Vol. 3043: A. Laganà, M.L. Gavrilova, V. Kumar, Y. Mun, C.K. Tan, O. Gervasi (Eds.), Computational Science and Its Applications – ICCSA 2004. LIII, 1180 pages. 2004.

Vol. 3042: N. Mitrou, K. Kontovasilis, G.N. Rouskas, I. Iliadis, L. Merakos (Eds.), NETWORKING 2004, Networking Technologies, Services, and Protocols; Performance of Computer and Communication Networks; Mobile and Wireless Communications. XXXIII, 1519 pages. 2004.

Vol. 3040: R. Conejo, M. Urretavizcaya, J.-L. Pérez-de-la-Cruz (Eds.), Current Topics in Artificial Intelligence. XIV, 689 pages. 2004. (Subseries LNAI).

Vol. 3039: M. Bubak, G.D.v. Albada, P.M. Sloot, J.J. Dongarra (Eds.), Computational Science - ICCS 2004. LXVI, 1271 pages. 2004.

Vol. 3038: M. Bubak, G.D.v. Albada, P.M. Sloot, J.J. Dongarra (Eds.), Computational Science - ICCS 2004. LXVI, 1311 pages. 2004.

Vol. 3037: M. Bubak, G.D.v. Albada, P.M. Sloot, J.J. Dongarra (Eds.), Computational Science - ICCS 2004. LXVI, 745 pages. 2004.

Vol. 3036: M. Bubak, G.D.v. Albada, P.M. Sloot, J.J. Dongarra (Eds.), Computational Science - ICCS 2004. LXVI, 713 pages. 2004.